Ordnance Surv

STREET ATLAS
West Kent

Contents

III   *Key to map symbols*

IV-V   *Key to map pages*

VI   *Administrative and post code boundaries*

1   *Street maps*

190   *Town plans of Ashford and Canterbury*

191   *Town plans of Dover and Folkestone*

192   *Index of hospitals, railway stations, schools, shopping centres, street names and universities*

GW00602820

PHILIP'S

First edition published 1989
Third edition published 1994
First colour edition published 1997
Reprinted in 1999 by

Ordnance Survey® and George Philip Ltd., a division of
Romsey Road   Octopus Publishing Group Ltd
Maybush   Michelin House
Southampton   81 Fulham Road
SO16 4GU   London SW3 6RB

ISBN 0-540-07366-0 (hardback)
ISBN 0-540-07376-9 (spiral)

To the best of the Publishers' knowledge, the information in this atlas
was correct at the time of going to press. No responsibility can be
accepted for any errors or their consequences.

The representation in this atlas of a road, track or path is no evidence
of the existence of a right of way.

**The mapping between pages 1 and 191 (inclusive) in this atlas is
derived from Ordnance Survey® OSCAR® and Land-Line® data,
and Landranger® mapping.**

Ordnance Survey, OSCAR, Land-Line and Landranger are registered
trade marks of Ordnance Survey, the national mapping agency of
Great Britain.

Printed and bound in Spain by Cayfosa

Motorway (with junction number)	**British Rail station**
Primary routes (dual carriageway and single)	**Docklands Light Railway station**
A roads (dual carriageway and single)	**Private railway station**
B roads (dual carriageway and single)	**Bus, coach station**
Minor through road (dual carriageway and single)	**Ambulance station**
Minor roads	**Coastguard station**
Roads under construction	**Fire station**
Railways	**Police station**
Tramway, miniature railway	**Casualty entrance to hospital**
Rural track, private road or narrow road in urban area	**Church, place of worship**
Gate or obstruction to traffic (restrictions may not apply at all times or to all vehicles)	**Hospital**
All paths, bridleways, byway open to all traffic, road used as a public path	**Information centre**
The representation in this atlas of a road, track or path is no evidence of the existence of a right of way	**Parking**
29 **130** **Adjoining page indicators**	**Post Office**
	West Kent College — **Important buildings, schools, colleges, universities and hospitals**
Leeds Castle **Non-Roman antiquity**	**County boundaries**
ROMAN FORT **Roman antiquity**	River Medway **Water name**

Acad	**Academy**	Mon	**Monument**
Cemy	**Cemetery**	Mus	**Museum**
C Ctr	**Civic Centre**	Obsy	**Observatory**
CH	**Club House**	Pal	**Royal Palace**
Coll	**College**	PH	**Public House**
Ex H	**Exhibition Hall**	Resr	**Reservoir**
Ind Est	**Industrial Estate**	Ret Pk	**Retail Park**
Inst	**Institute**	Sch	**School**
Ct	**Law Court**	Sh Ctr	**Shopping Centre**
L Ctr	**Leisure Centre**	Sta	**Station**
LC	**Level Crossing**	TH	**Town Hall/House**
Liby	**Library**	Trad Est	**Trading Estate**
Mkt	**Market**	Univ	**University**
Meml	**Memorial**	YH	**Youth Hostel**

Stream

River or canal (minor and major)

Water

Tidal water

Woods

Houses

■ The dark grey border on the inside edge of some pages indicates that the mapping does not continue onto the adjacent page

■ The small numbers around the edges of the maps identify the 1 kilometre National Grid lines

The scale of the maps is 5.52 cm to 1 km (3½ inches to 1 mile)

0	¼	½	¾	1 mile
0	250 m 500 m	750 m	1 Kilometre	

IV

Key to map pages

CITY OF LONDON
MARYLEBONE
WESTMINSTER
LAMBETH
WANDSWORTH
LEWISHAM
MITCHAM
CARSHALTON
CROYDON
SUTTON
WARLINGHAM
CATERHAM
REDHILL
REIGATE
HORLEY
London (Gatwick) Airport
CRAWLEY
EAST GRINSTEAD

DAGENHAM
UPMINSTER
Thamesmead
WOOLWICH
GREENWICH
ELTHAM
ERITH
SLADE GREEN
CRAYFORD
BEXLEY
DARTFORD
Stone
Swanscombe
NORTHFLEET
GRAVESEND
TILBURY
GRAYS
Chadwell St Mary
South Ockendon
Shorne
Cobham
Luddes

Due to open Mid 1997
Due to open Late 1998

River Thames

Mottingham
SIDCUP
CHISLEHURST
BROMLEY
BECKENHAM
St Paul's Cray
Swanley
Hextable
Darenth
Bean
Southfleet
Longfield
Istead Rise
Hartley
Horton Kirby
Farningham
ORPINGTON
Farnborough
Keston
Badgers Mount
West Kingsdown
Fawkham Green
New Ash Green
Stansted
Meopham
Culverstone Green
Downe
Cudham
Knockholt Pound
Shoreham
Otford
Kemsing
Wrotham
Ightham
Trottiscliffe
Addington
Borough Green
West Malling
Snod
Biggin Hill
Woldingham
Brasted
Westerham
Sundridge
SEVENOAKS
Plaxtol
Mereworth
West Peckham
Nettles
Ide Hill
Sevenoaks Weald
Underriver
Shipbourne
Hadlow
Crockham Hill
Hildenborough
East Peckham
Four Elms
Chiddingstone Causeway
Leigh
TONBRIDGE
Edenbridge
Lingfield
Marsh Green
Hever
Chiddingstone
Tudeley
Five Oak Green
Paddock Wood
Matfield
Smallfield
Newchapel
Dormansland
Penshurst
Markbeech
Bidborough
SOUTHBOROUGH
Pembury
Cowden
Fordcombe
Speldhurst
ROYAL TUNBRIDGE WELLS
Crawley Down
Turners Hill
Worth Abbey
Hartfield
Ashurst
Langton Green
Groombridge
Bells Yew Green
Frant
Lambe
Withyham
Eridge Green
Wadhurst
Sharpthorne
Wych Cross
Balcombe
CROWBOROUGH
Mark Cross
Tidebrook
Stone
Handcross
Staplefield
Danehill
Nutley
High Hurstwood
Mayfield
Witherenden Hill
Burwash
CUCKFIELD
HAYWARDS HEATH
Newick
Uckfield
Maresfield
Five Ashes
HEATHFIELD
Bolney
Framfield
Brightlin

Roads referenced: A13, A11, A40, A206, A207, A2, A3, A202, A205, A24, A23, A232, A2022, A233, A22, A25, A21, A224, A225, A20, A227, M25, M20, M26, M23, M26, A228, A264, A217, A26, A267, A272, A275, A265, A21

Map page references
1	2/3	4
5	6/7	8/9	10/11	12/13
22/23	24/25	26/27	28/29	30/
36/37	38/39	40/41	42/43	44/
50/51	52/53	54/55	56/57	58/
66/67	68/69	70/71	72/73
81	82/83	84/85	86/87	88/
96/97	98/99	100/101	102/103
112/113	114/115	116/117	118/119
128/129	130/131	132/133	134/135
144/145	146/147	148/149	150/151
160/161	162/163	164/165
174/175

Page Scale
30/ These pages are at 3½ inches to the mile

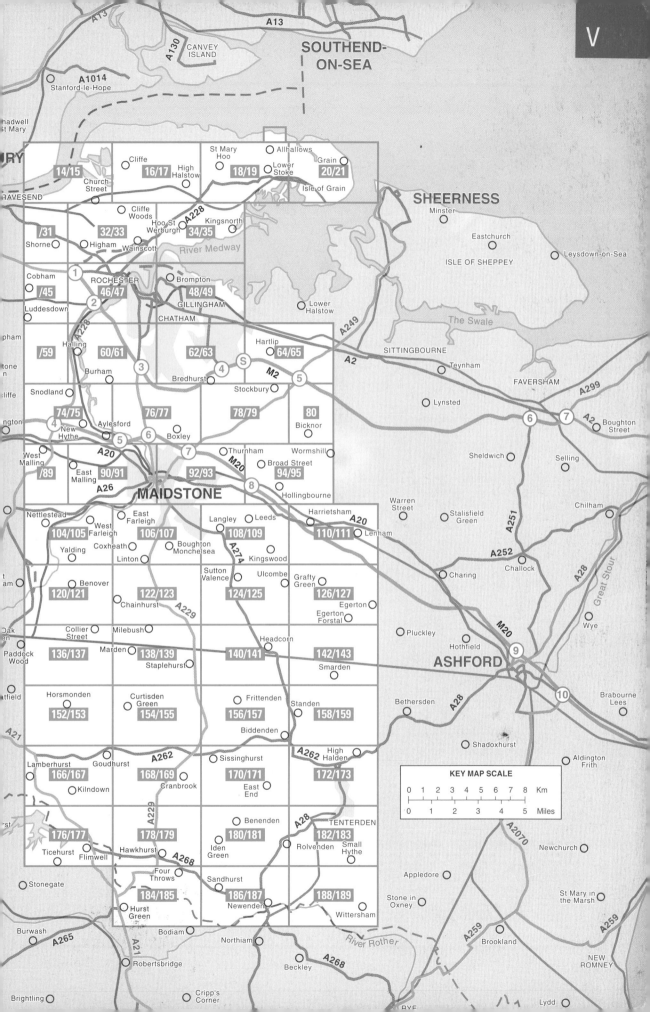

A3

A13

A13

A130

CANVEY ISLAND

SOUTHEND-ON-SEA

A1014
Stanford-le-Hope

adwell
t Mary

Cliffe

St Mary
Hoo

Allhallows

Grain

14/15

16/17

High
Halstow

18/19

Lower
Stoke

20/21

RY

RAVESEND

Church
Street

Isle of Grain

SHEERNESS

Minster

Cliffe
Woods

Hoo St
Werburgh

A228

Kingsnorth

Eastchurch

Leysdown-on-Sea

/31

32/33

34/35

Shorne

Higham

Wainscott

River Medway

ISLE OF SHEPPEY

Cobham

1

ROCHESTER

Brompton

The Swale

/45

46/47

48/49

Lower
Halstow

2

GILLINGHAM

Luddesdown

CHATHAM

A249

SITTINGBOURNE

A2

Teynham

FAVERSHAM

A299

pham

/59

Halling

60/61

Hartlip

64/65

62/63

S

tone
n

Burham

3

Bredhurst

4

M2

5

Stockbury

Lynsted

A2

Boughton
Street

ffe

Snodland

74/75

76/77

78/79

80

Bicknor

6

7

gton

4

New
Hythe

Aylesford

5

6

Boxley

7

Thurnham

Wormshill

Sheldwich

Selling

West
Malling

/89

East
Malling

90/91

A20

92/93

M20

8

Broad Street

94/95

A26

MAIDSTONE

Hollingbourne

Chilham

Warren
Street

Stalisfield
Green

A251

Nettlestead

West
Farleigh

East
Farleigh

Langley

Leeds

Harrietsham

A20

104/105

106/107

108/109

110/111

Lenham

A252

Charing

Challock

A28

Yalding

Coxheath

Linton

Boughton
Monchelsea

A274

Kingswood

Benover

Sutton
Valence

Ulcombe

Grafty
Green

Pluckley

M20

Wye

120/121

122/123

124/125

126/127

Chainhurst

A229

Egerton

Hothfield

9

Egerton
Forstal

Collier
Street

Milebush

Headcorn

ASHFORD

Oak
en

Paddock
Wood

Marden

138/139

140/141

142/143

136/137

Staplehurst

Smarden

10

field

A21

Horsmonden

Curtisden
Green

Frittenden

Standen

Brabourne
Lees

152/153

154/155

156/157

158/159

Bethersden

A28

Biddenden

Shadoxhurst

Lamberhurst

Goudhurst

A262

Sissinghurst

A262

High
Halden

Aldington
Frith

166/167

168/169

170/171

172/173

Kilndown

Cranbrook

East
End

A2070

Newchurch

A28

TENTERDEN

176/177

178/179

Benenden

180/181

182/183

Small
Hythe

St Mary in
the Marsh

Ticehurst

Flimwell

Hawkhurst

A268

Iden
Green

Rolvenden

Appledore

Four
Throws

Sandhurst

Stone in
Oxney

Stonegate

184/185

186/187

188/189

A259

NEW
ROMNEY

Hurst
Green

Newenden

Wittersham

Burwash

A265

A21

Bodiam

Northiam

River Rother

Brookland

A259

Robertsbridge

Beckley

A268

Brighting

Cripp's
Corner

RYE

Lydd

KEY MAP SCALE

0 1 2 3 4 5 6 7 8 Km

0 1 2 3 4 5 Miles

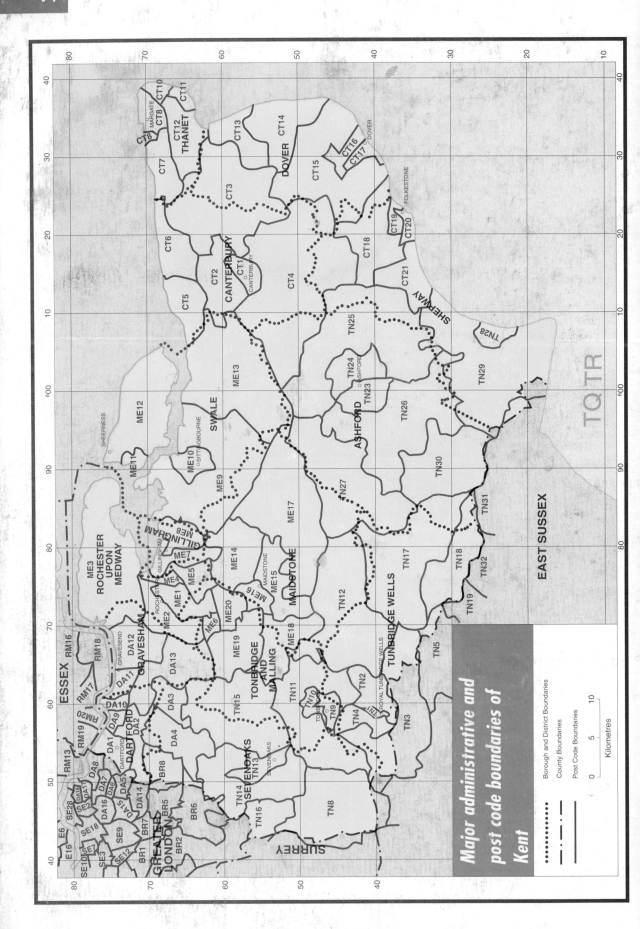

Major administrative and
post code boundaries of
Kent

Borough and District Boundaries

County Boundaries

Post Code Boundaries

Kilometres

0   5   10

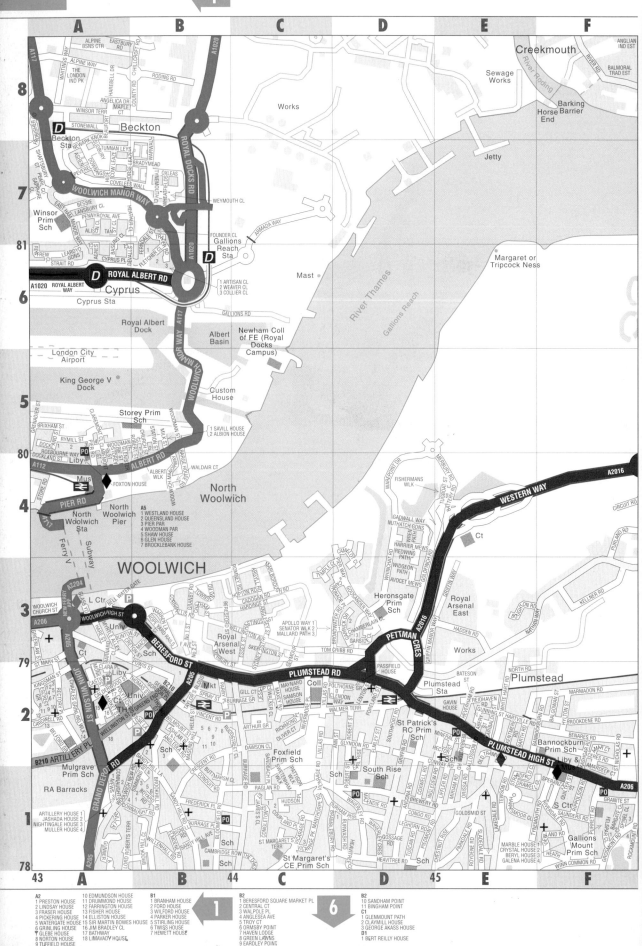

A2
1 PRESTON HOUSE
2 LINDSAY HOUSE
3 FRASER HOUSE
4 PICKERING HOUSE
5 WATERGATE HOUSE
6 GRINLING HOUSE
7 GLEBE HOUSE
8 NORTON HOUSE
9 TUFFIELD HOUSE
10 EDMUNDSON HOUSE
11 DRUMMOND HOUSE
12 FARRINGTON HOUSE
13 FISHER HOUSE
14 ELLISTON HOUSE
15 SIR MARTIN BOWES HOUSE
16 JIM BRADLEY CL
17 BATHWAY
18 LIMAVADY AV

B1
1 BRANHAM HOUSE
2 FORD HOUSE
3 WILFORD HOUSE
4 PARKER HOUSE
5 STIRLING HOUSE
6 TWISS HOUSE
7 HEWETT HOUSE

B2
1 BERESFORD SQUARE MARKET PL
2 CENTRAL CT
3 WALPOLE PL
4 ANGLESEA AVE
5 TROY CT
6 ORMSBY POINT
7 HAVEN LODGE
8 GREEN LAWNS
9 EARDLEY POINT

B2
10 SANDHAM POINT
11 BINGHAM POINT

C1
1 GLENMOUNT PATH
2 CLAYMILL HOUSE
3 GEORGE AKASS HOUSE

D1
1 BERT REILLY HOUSE

6

1

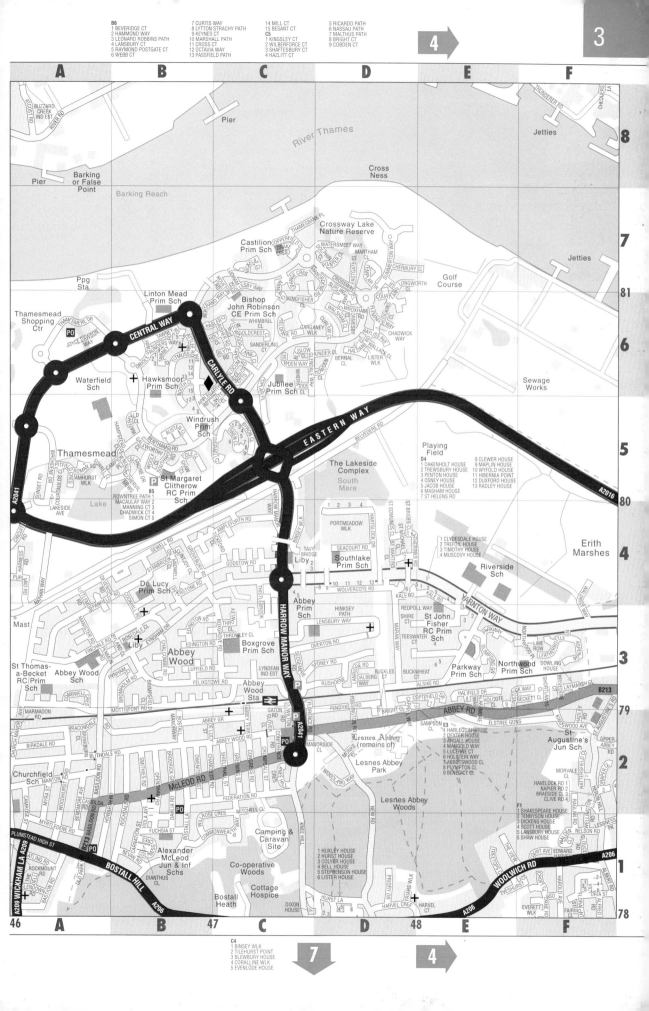

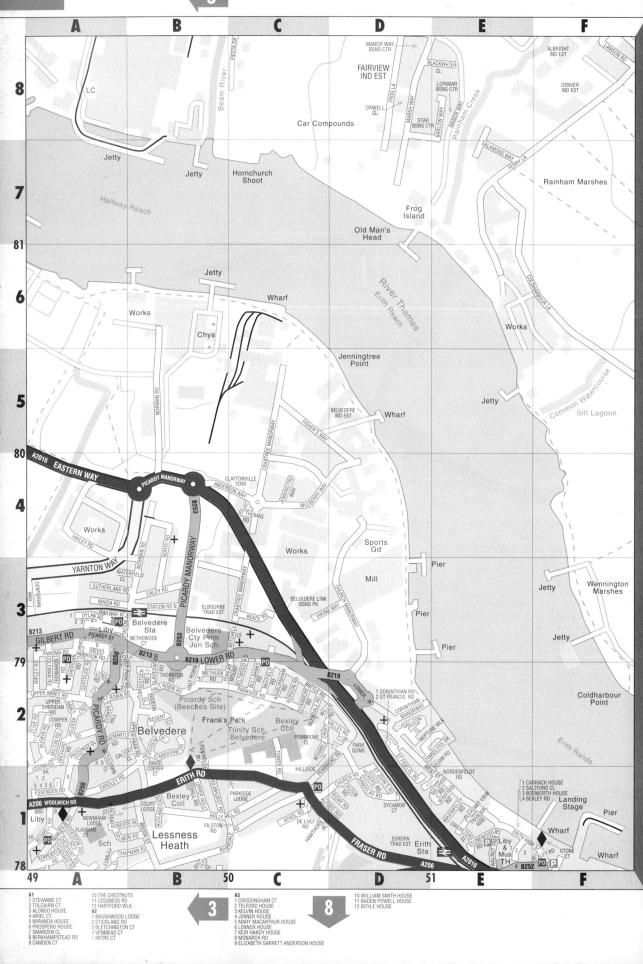

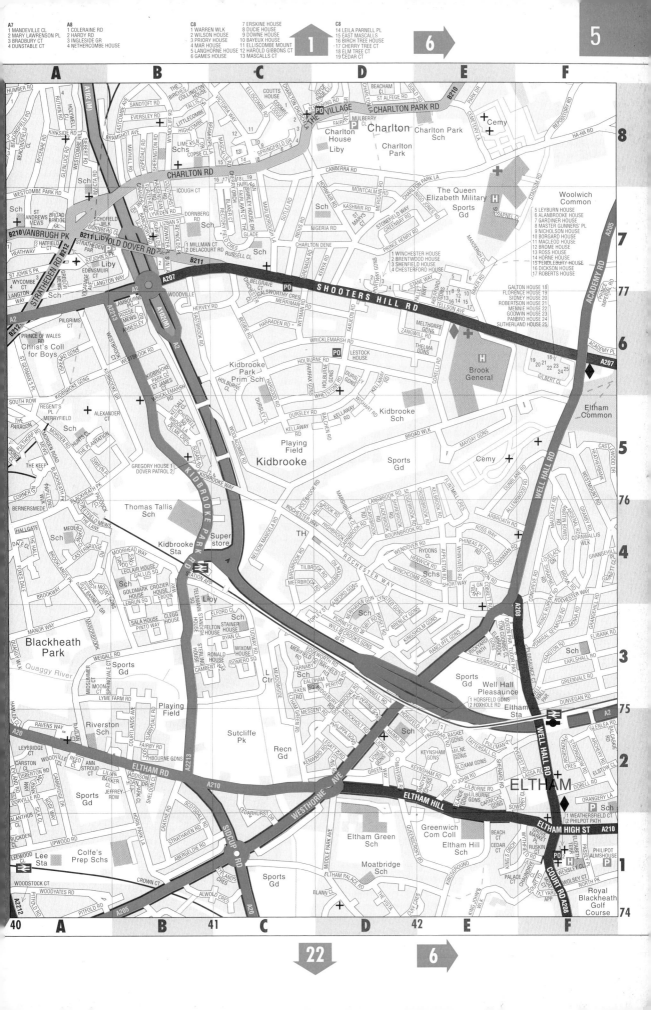

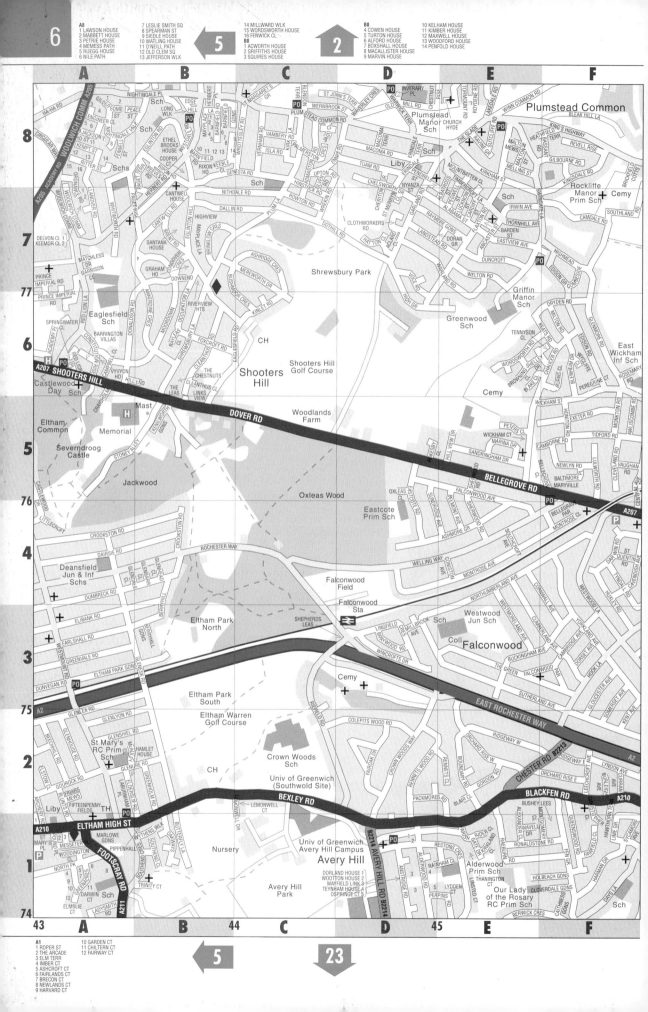

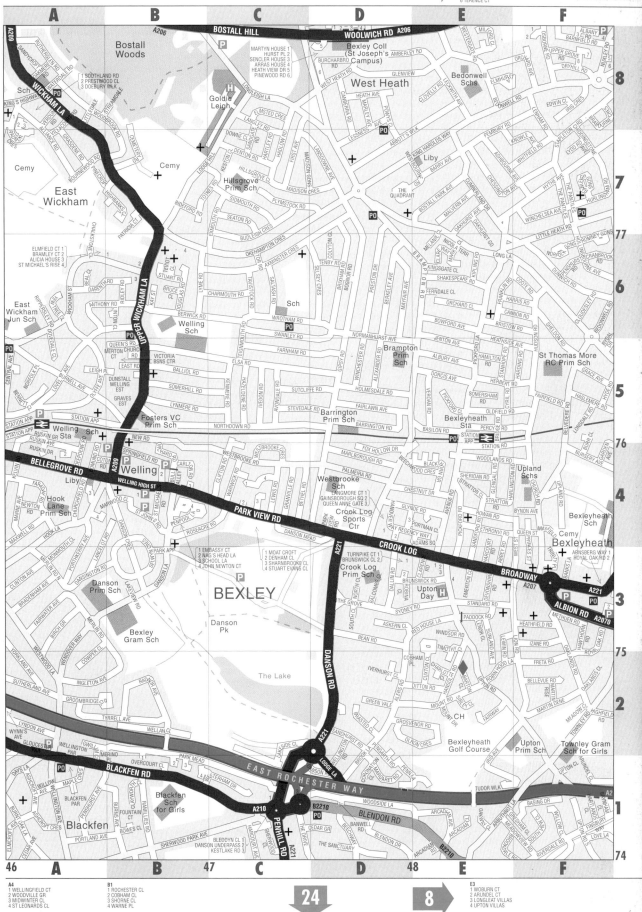

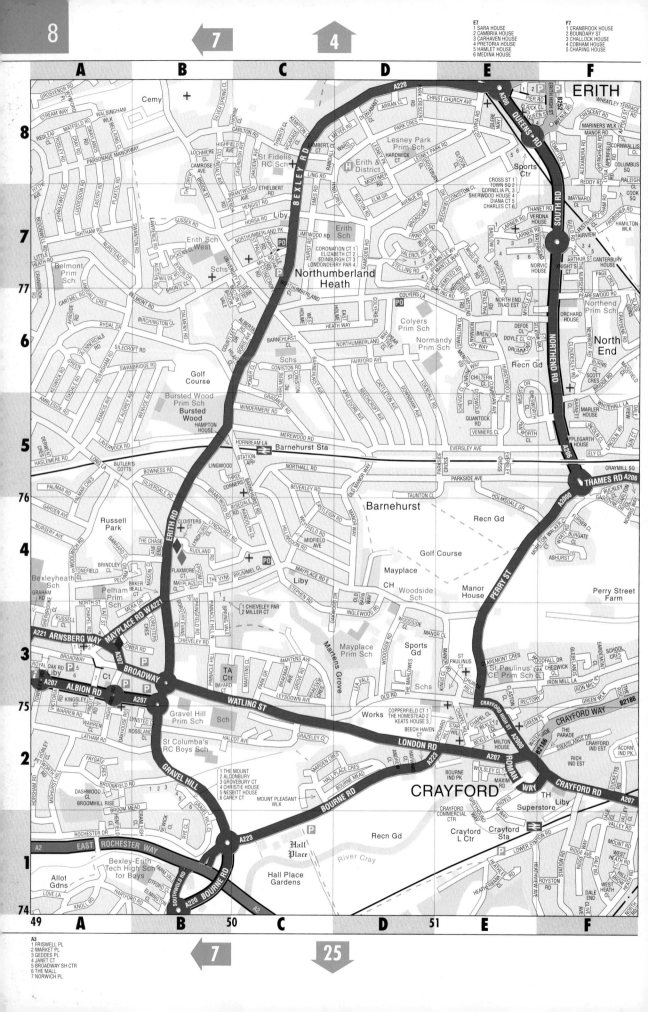

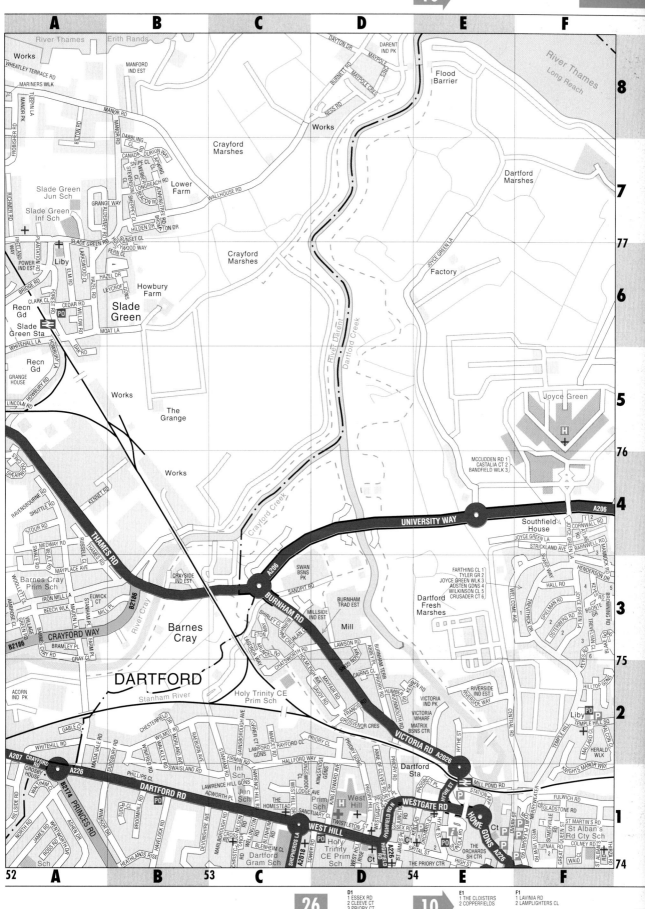

9

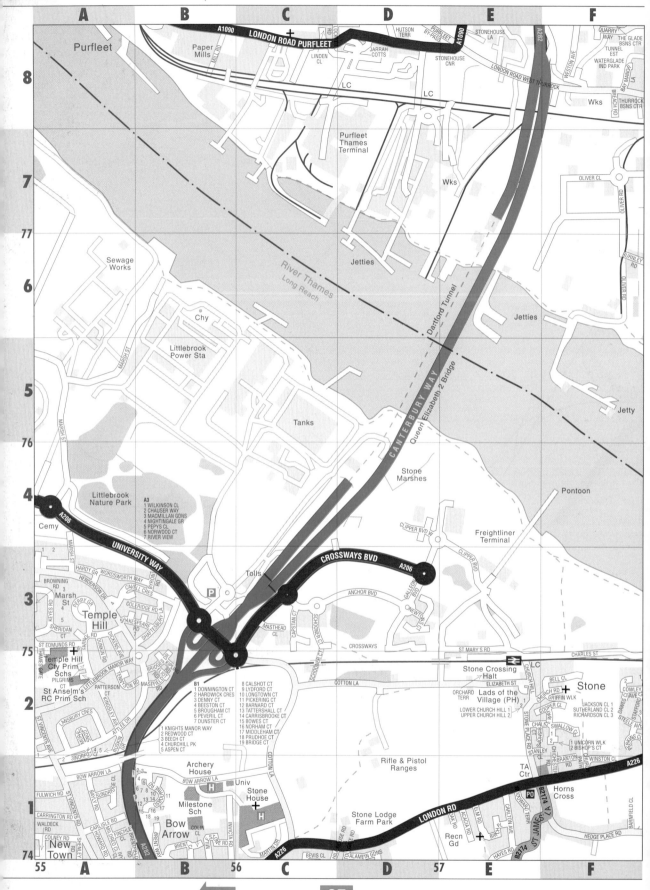

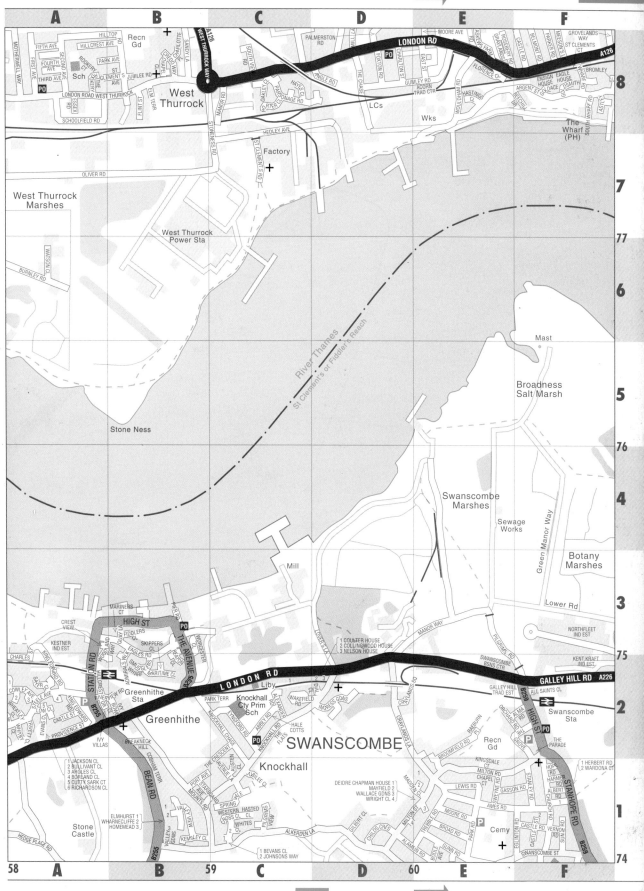

12

A   B   C   D   E   F

HILLTOP
MOTHERWELL WAY
FIFTH AVE
FOURTH AVE
SECOND AVE
FIRST AVE
HILLCREST AVE
Recn
Gd
ST THURROCK WAY
A126
WEST THURROCK WAY
PALMERSTON RD
LONDON RD A126
MOORE AVE
GROVELANDS WAY
ST CLEMENTS
CT
THIRD AVE
PARK AVE
SOUTH AVE
CHARLTON ST
FOXTON RD
ANGLE RD
EAST ST
ROCKBERY RD
GRANTLAND
ASPENS FARM
BELMONT RD
PARKER RD
NELSON RD
ENSIGN
HOUSE
EAGLE
HOUSE
BROMLEY
RD
PO
Sch
ROOKERY
THE
ST CLEMENT S AVE
JUBILEE RD
CHAPEL
CROFT WAY
SANDY LA
MANOR RD
HAYES CL
OAKLEY CL
THE CHASE
GUMLEY RD
FLORENCE CL
ACORN
TRAD CTR
WOULDHAM CL
HASTINGS CL
BEECHILL
ARGENT ST
D ACE
LA
OSMITH
WISARD RD
CASTLE RD
8
LONDON ROAD WEST THURROCK
ESSEX X
SCHOOLFIELD RD
ELM TERR
FLINT RD
STONENESS RD
PARSONAGE RD
ST CLEMENTS RD
West
Thurrock
LCs
Wks
BEECHILL
BRU
The
Wharf
(PH)
CASTLE

OLIVER RD
HEDLEY AVE
Factory

West Thurrock
Marshes

West Thurrock
Power Sta

BURNLEY RD
WATSON RD

Stone Ness

River Thames
St Clement's or Fiddler's Reach

Mast

Broadness
Salt Marsh

Swanscombe
Marshes

Sewage
Works

Green Manor Way

Botany
Marshes

Lower Rd

NORTHFLEET
IND EST

Mill

CREST
VIEW
MARINERS
CT
HIGH ST
PO
FIDDLERS
SKIPPERS CL
EAGLES CL
MERRD
KESTNER
IND EST
KING EDWARD RD
QUAY LA
SMAL GL
WOODLAND WAY
WORCESTER
MARITIME CL
THE AVENUE
PIER RD
BEAN RD
1 COULTER HOUSE
2 COLLINGWOOD HOUSE
3 NELSON HOUSE
LOVERS LA
PILGRIMS RD
MANOR WAY
SWANSCOMBE
BSNS CTR
KENT KRAFT
IND EST.
75

CHARLES
COWLEY RD
SALT RD
STATION RD
Greenhithe
Sta
B255
Greenhithe
LONDON RD
Liby
Knockhall
Cty Prim
Sch
PARK TERR
WAKEFIELD
RD
INGRESS GDNS
CRAYLANDS RD
GALLEY HILL RD A226
GALLEY HILL
TRAD EST
ALL SAINTS CL
B259
HIGH ST
Swanscombe
Sta
2

STEELE AVE
WHEATLY
WHITBY RD
LOW CL
CASTLE ST
EVANS CL
PROVIDENCE ST
IVY VILLAS
BREAKNECK
HILL
CORHAM TERR
KNOCKHALL CHASE
EVANSFORD RD
KNOCKHALL RD
ABBEY RD
ALEXANDER
HALE
COTTS
THE
FLATS
DIAL
CRAYLANDS LA
SWANSCOMBE
RASBURN
ORCHARD RD
ALMA
RD
GROVE
PO
THE
PARADE
1 HERBERT RD
2 WARDONA CT

1 JACKSON CL
2 BULLIVANT CL
3 ARGLES CL
4 BORLAND
5 CUTTY SARK CT
6 RICHARDSON CL
BEAN RD
PORT AVE
THE CRESCENT
STARBOARD
VALE
JUBILEE CL
MOUNT RD
Knockhall
SWANSCOMBE
DEIDRE CHAPMAN HOUSE 1
MAYFIELD 2
WALLACE GDNS 3
WRIGHT CL 4.
BROOMFIELD RD
Recn
Gd
MILTON RD
CHAPEL
CT
KINGSDALE
STANLEY RD
CHURCH RD
STANHOPE RD
B259
1

ELMHURST 1
WHARNECLIFFE 2
HOMEMEAD 3
VALLEY GDNS
KEMSLEY CL
WESTERN
VALLEY VIEW
HASTED
CROSS CL
WHITES
PILGRIMS
VIEW
SPRING
ALKERDEN LA
GILBERT CL
CHILDS CRCS
MADDEN
MILTON ST
MOORE RD
TREBLE RD
BROAD RD
ALAMEIN RD
GUNN RD
BOOTLE AVE
PARK RD
AMES RD
LEWIS RD
GASSON RD
WEYNE RD
PARK RD
Cemy
EGLINTON RD
VERNON RD
CASTLE RD
ALBERT RD
SWANSCOMBE ST
HARMER
RD

Stone
Castle
HEDGE PLACE RD
B255
1 BEVANS CL
2 JOHNSONS WAY

28   12

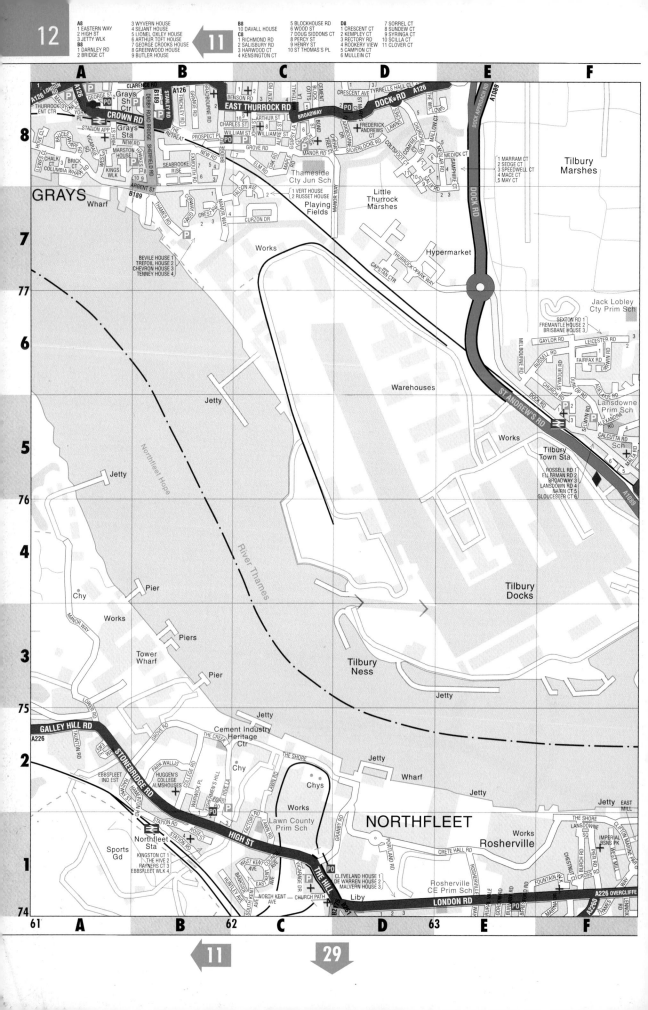

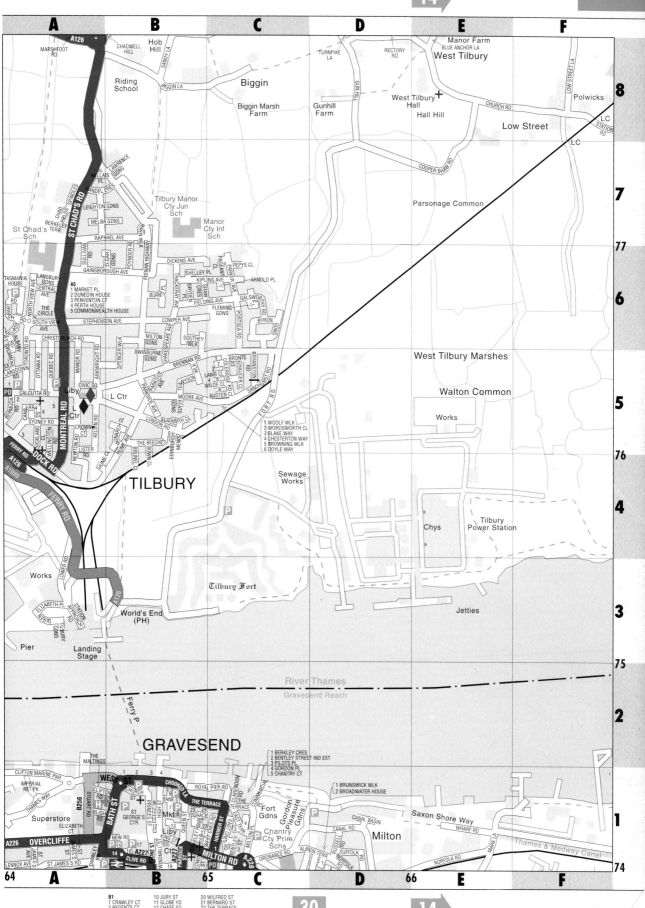

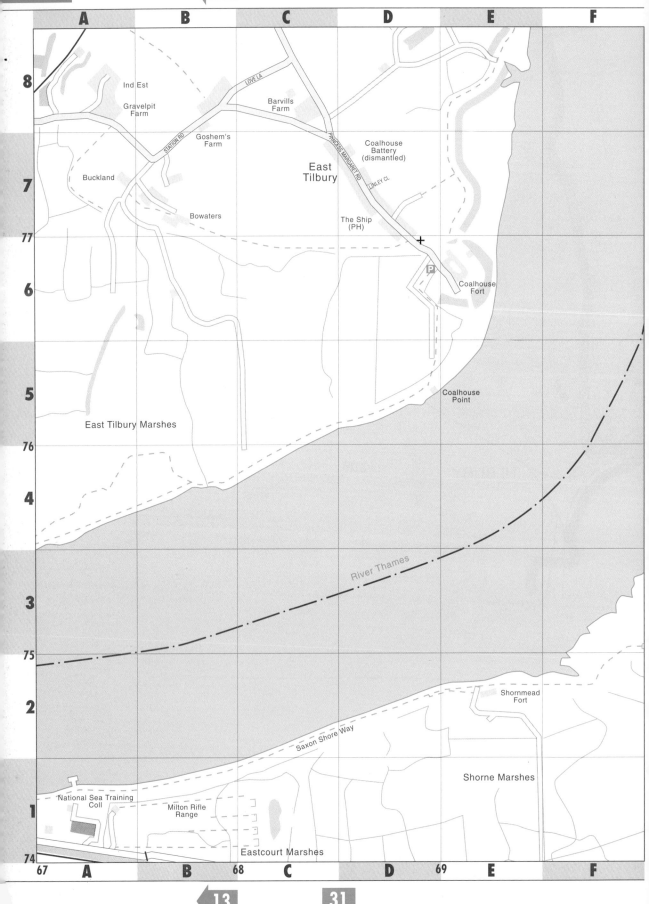

16

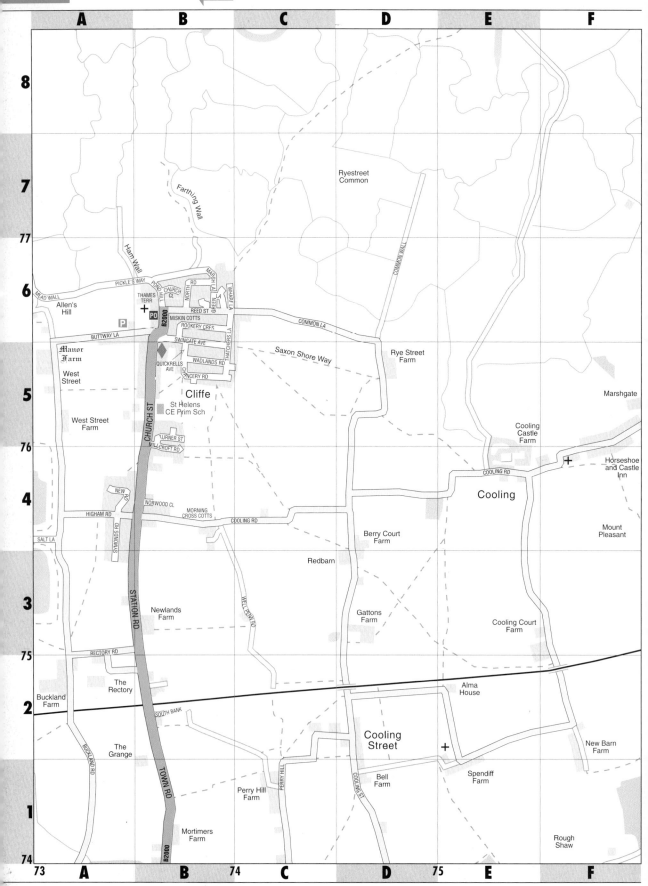

| A | B | C | D | E | F |

8

7

Ryestreet
Common

77

Farthing Wall

COMMON WALL

6

Ham Wall

PICKLE'S WAY

MEAD WALL

Allen's
Hill

THAMES TERR

CHURCH CL

POND HILL

NORTH

MARSH LA

CHURCH RD

REED ST

WHARF LA

GREEN

+

PO

B2000

MISKIN COTTS

ROOKERY CRES

COMMON LA

BUTTWAY LA

SWINGATE AVE

THATCHERS LA

Saxon Shore Way

Rye Street
Farm

Marshgate

Manor
Farm

QUICKRELLS AVE

WADLANDS RD

CHANCERY RD

West
Street

Cliffe

Cooling
Castle
Farm

5

St Helens
CE Prim Sch

West Street
Farm

CHURCH ST

TURNER ST

MILLCROFT RD

COOLING RD

+

Horseshoe
and Castle
Inn

76

NEW RD

NORWOOD CL

MORNING
CROSS COTTS

Cooling

4

HIGHAM RD

OLD SCHOOL RD

COOLING RD

Berry Court
Farm

Mount
Pleasant

SALT LA

Redbarn

STATION RD

Newlands
Farm

WELL PENN RD

Gattons
Farm

Cooling Court
Farm

3

75

RECTORY RD

The
Rectory

Alma
House

Buckland
Farm

SOUTH BANK

Cooling
Street

2

BUCKLAND RD

The
Grange

TOWN RD

PERRY HILL

COOLING ST

Bell
Farm

+

Spendiff
Farm

New Barn
Farm

Perry Hill
Farm

1

Mortimers
Farm

B2000

Rough
Shaw

74

A B C D E F

8
7
77
6
5
76
4
3
75
2
1
74

Cooling
Marshes

Old Sea Wall

Decoy Fleet

The Mean

Swigshole

Buckland
Marshes

Buckland Fleet

Decoy
Farm

Whalebone
Marshes

Masts

Saxon Shore Way

Northward Hill

DECOY HILL RD

Eastborough
Farm

Northward Hill
Nature Reserve

Clinchstreet
Farm

COOLING RD

Bromhey
Farm

Childs
Farm

Eastborough
Bungalow

Buckhole
Farm

MARSH CRES

NORTHWOOD AVE

THAMES AVE

LONGFIELD AVE

MEDWAY AVE

WILLOWBANK DR

LIPWELL HILL

BUCKHOLE FARM RD

HARRISON DR

EDEN RD

GOODWOOD CL

High
Halstow

High Halstow
Cty Prim Sch

THE STREET

Dalham
Farm

COOLING RD

FORGE LA
✝ PH

ST MARGARET'S
CT

HILL FARM
CL

PO

CHRISTMAS LA

LC

WYBOURNES LA

Wybournes
Farm

Ducks
Court

Lodge Hill
Wood

Wybornes
Wood

Solomon's
Farm

A228 RATCLIFFE HIGHWAY

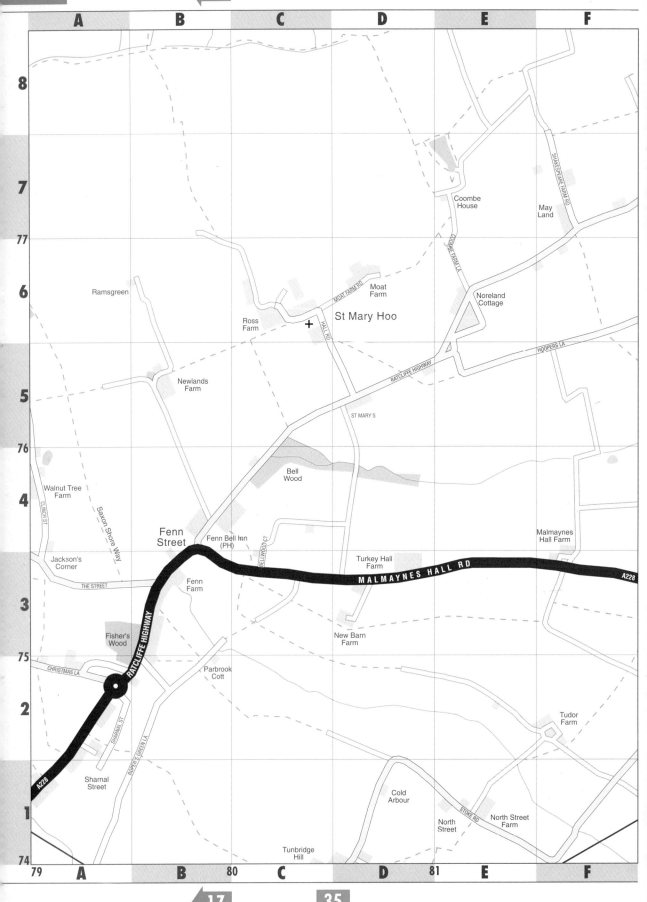

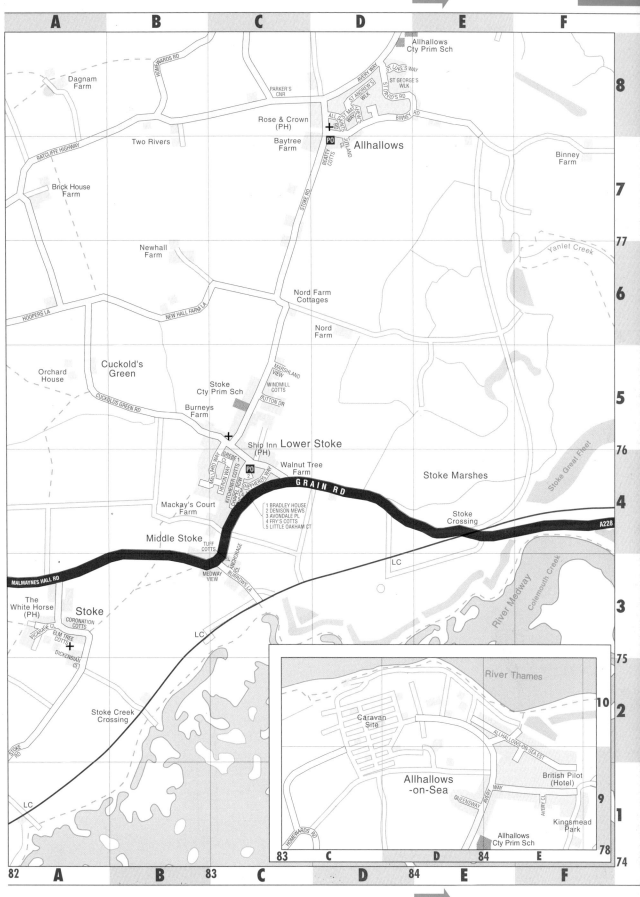

19

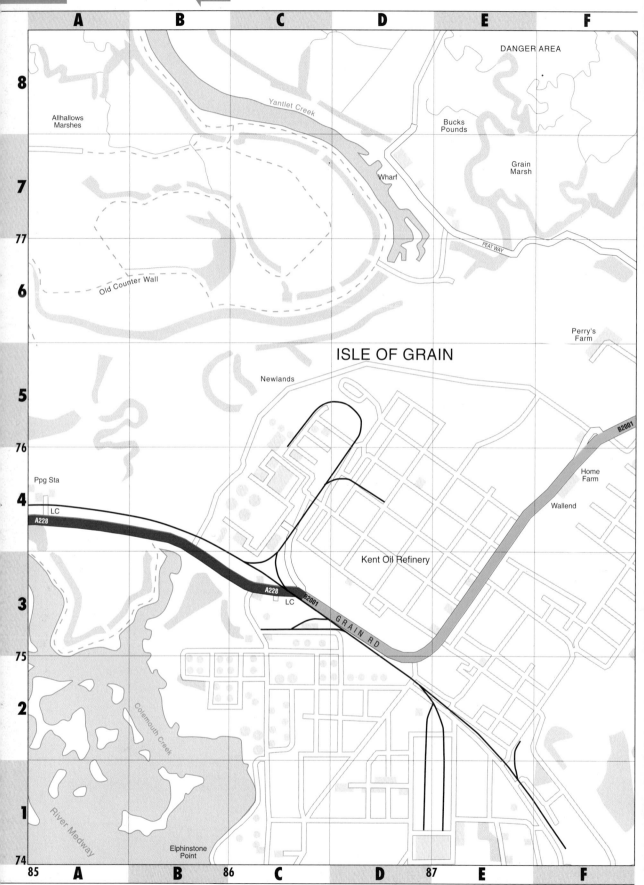

ISLE OF GRAIN

DANGER AREA

Allhallows Marshes

Yantlet Creek

Bucks Pounds

Grain Marsh

Wharf

PEAT WAY

Old Counter Wall

Perry's Farm

Newlands

B2001

Ppg Sta

LC

Home Farm

Wallend

A228

A228

LC

B2001

Kent Oil Refinery

GRAIN RD

Colemouth Creek

River Medway

Elphinstone Point

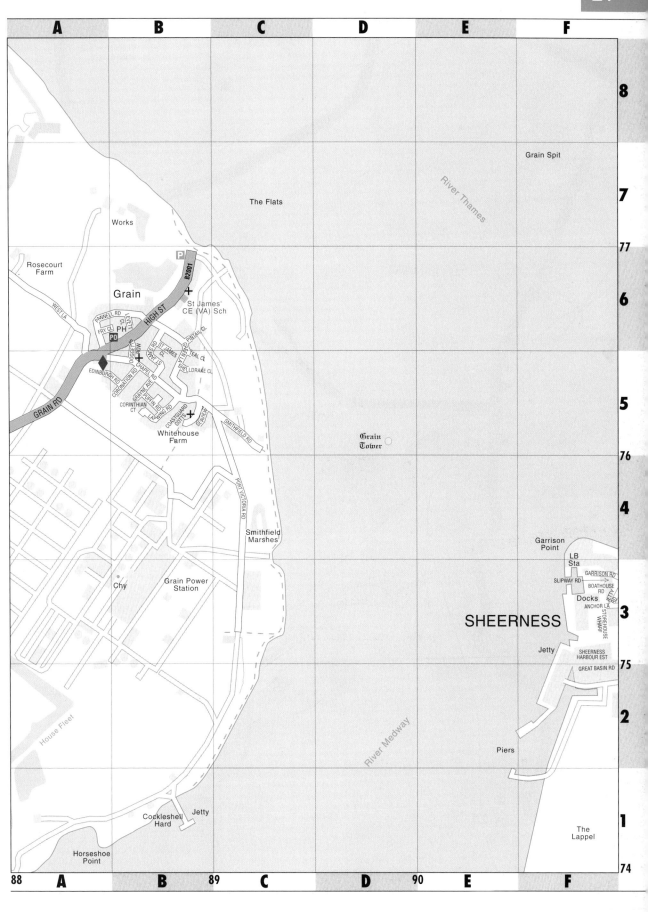

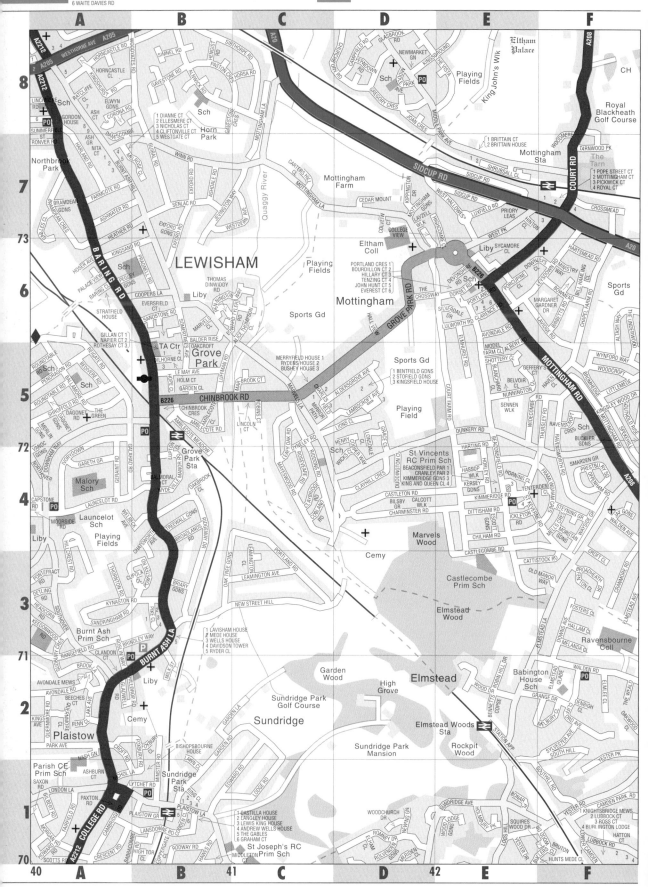

22

A8
1 WILDWOOD CL
2 ST MILDREDS RD
3 SWALLOW CT
4 HONEYSUCKLE CT
5 VENTURE CT
6 WAITE DAVIES RD
7 CHERITON CT
8 ASKHAM LODGE
9 SYON LODGE

5

Grid reference labels

A B C D E F

8 73 7 6 5 72 4 3 71 2 1 70

40 A 41 B C 41 D 42 E F

Map labels

LEWISHAM

Mottingham

Grove Park

Plaistow

Sundridge

Elmstead

Eltham Palace

Royal Blackheath Golf Course

Northbrook Park

Horn Park

Mottingham Farm

Mottingham Sta

The Tarn

Eltham Coll

Quaggy River

Playing Fields

Sports Gd

Playing Field

Marvels Wood

Cemy

Castlecombe Prim Sch

Elmstead Wood

Ravensbourne Coll

Castlecombe Prim Sch

Babington House Sch

Garden Wood

High Grove

Sundridge Park Golf Course

Sundridge Park Mansion

Rockpit Wood

Elmstead Woods Sta

Burnt Ash Prim Sch

Malory Sch

Launcelot Sch

Playing Fields

Parish CE Prim Sch

St Joseph's RC Prim Sch

Middleton

Grove Park Sta

Sundridge Park Sta

St Vincents RC Prim Sch

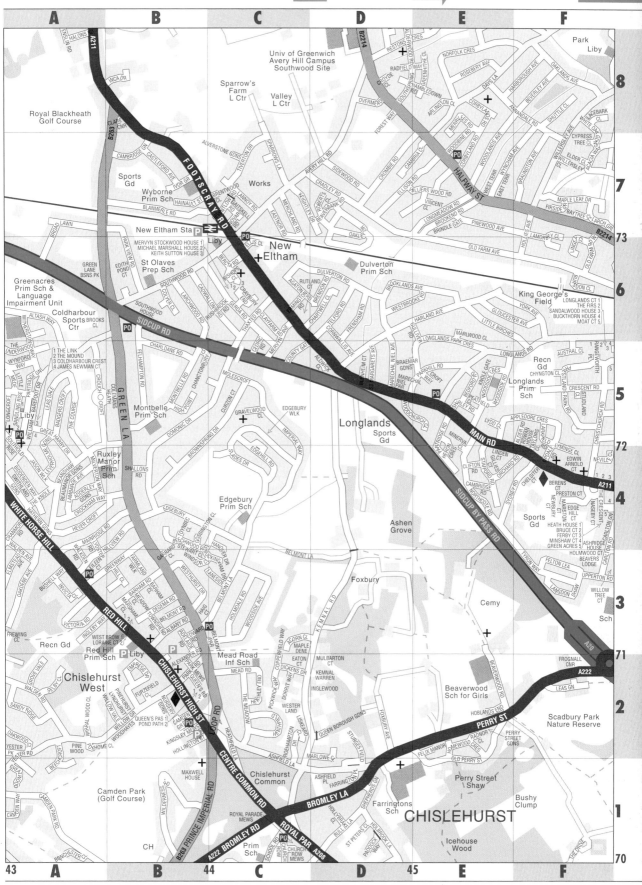

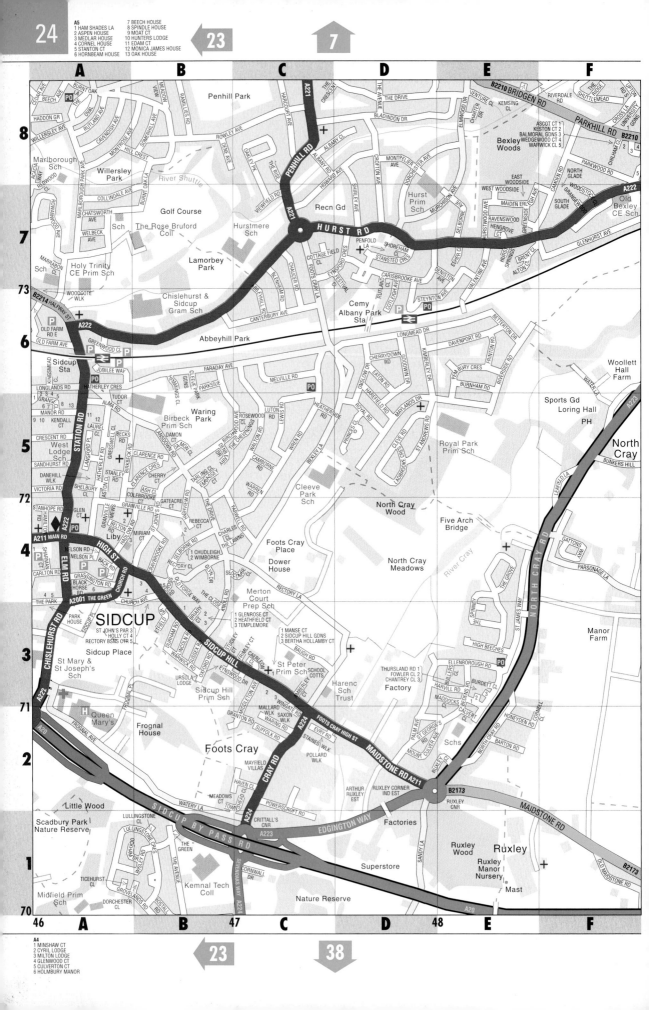

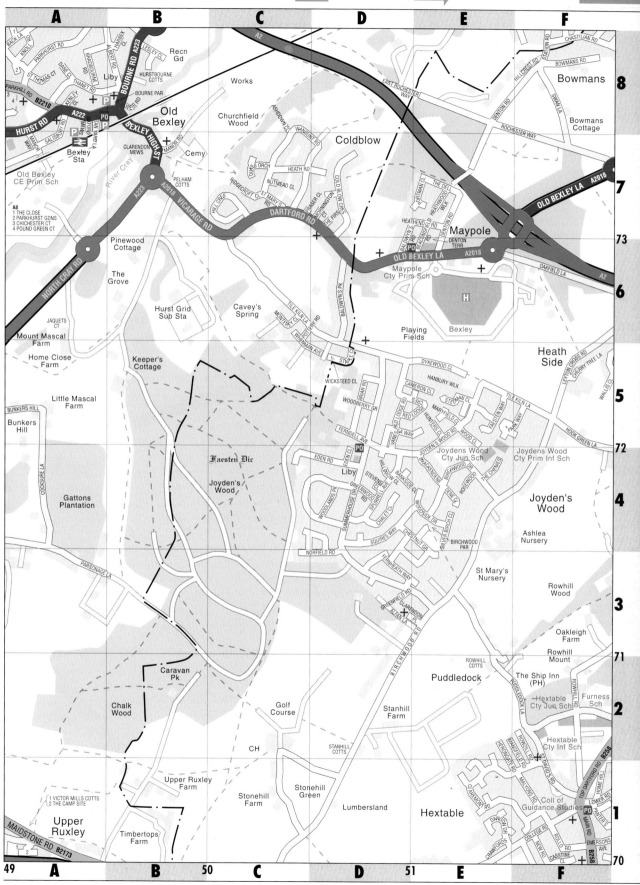

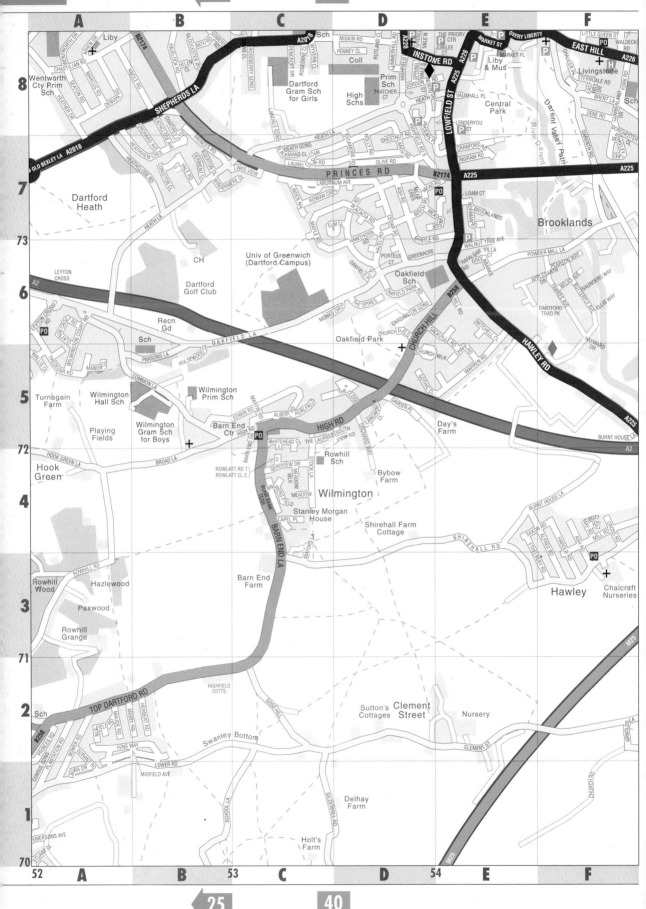

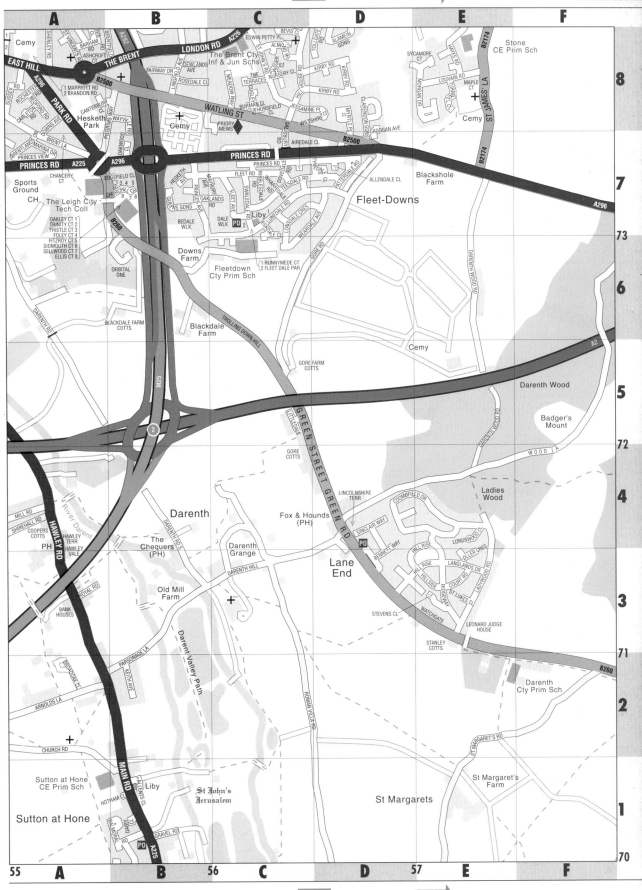

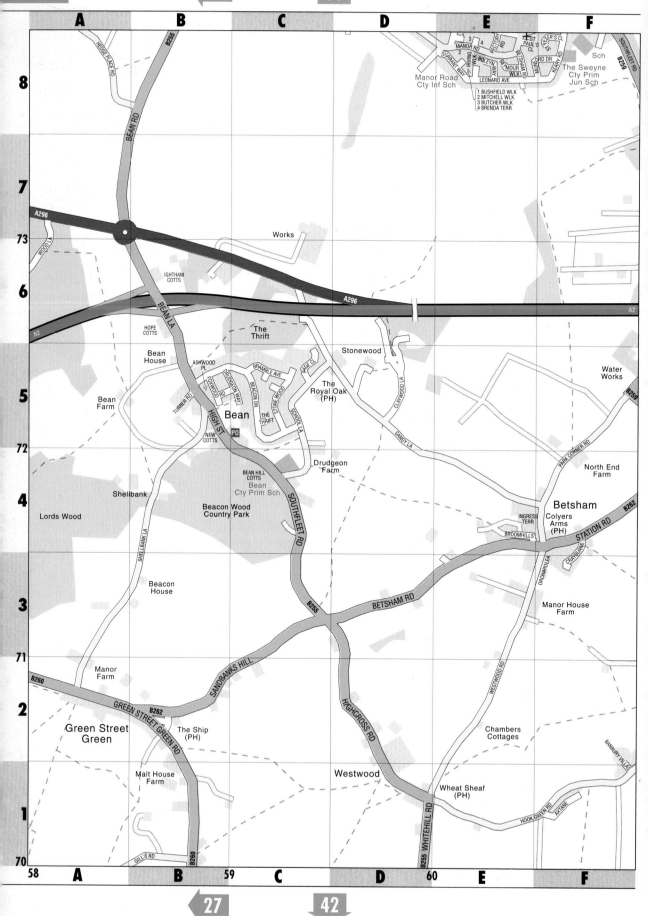

A B C D E F

8

7

73

6

58 A B 59 C D 60 E F

Manor Road
Cty Inf Sch

The Sweyne
Cty Prim
Jun Sch

1 BUSHFIELD WLK
2 MITCHELL WLK
3 BUTCHER WLK
4 BRENDA TERR

Sch

MANOR RD
RECTORY RD
ST PAUL'S CL
BEKER'S CL
KEARY RD
SOUTHFLEET RD
B259
BETSHAM RD
MINT RD DR
MOUR WLK
SEL WLK
BOLEYN WY
IRVING WLK
DURRANT WAY
LEONARD AVE

Works

A296

A2

HEDGE PLACE RD

BEAN RD
B255

WOOD LA

A296

A2

IGHTHAM COTTS

BEAN LA

HOPE COTTS

Bean
House

The
Thrift

Stonewood

Water
Works

B259

Bean
Farm

ASHWOOD PL

BRAMBLE AVE

PAGE CL

The
Royal Oak
(PH)

CLAYWOOD LA

TURNER RD

FOXWOOD RD
DRUDGEON WAY

BEACON DR

STONE WOOD

THE THRIFT

SCHOOL LA

Bean

PO

NEW
COTTS

HIGH ST

Drudgeon
Farm

SANDY LA

PARK CORNER RD

North End
Farm

72

BEAN HILL
COTTS

Bean
Cty Prim Sch

Betsham

Colyers
Arms
(PH)

B262

Shellbank

SHELLBANK LA

Beacon Wood
Country Park

SOUTHFLEET RD

INGRESS
TERR

BROOMHILLS

STATION RD

CRAYBURNE

ORCHARD LEA

Lords Wood

Manor House
Farm

4

Beacon
House

B255

Betsham RD

3

71

Manor
Farm

SANDBANKS HILL

HIGHCROSS RD

WESTWOOD RD

Chambers
Cottages

B260

GREEN STREET GREEN RD

B262

2

Green Street
Green

The Ship
(PH)

BANBURY VILLAS

Malt House
Farm

Westwood

Wheat Sheaf
(PH)

HOOK GREEN RD

AXTANE

1

GILL'S RD

B260

B255 WHITEHILL RD

70

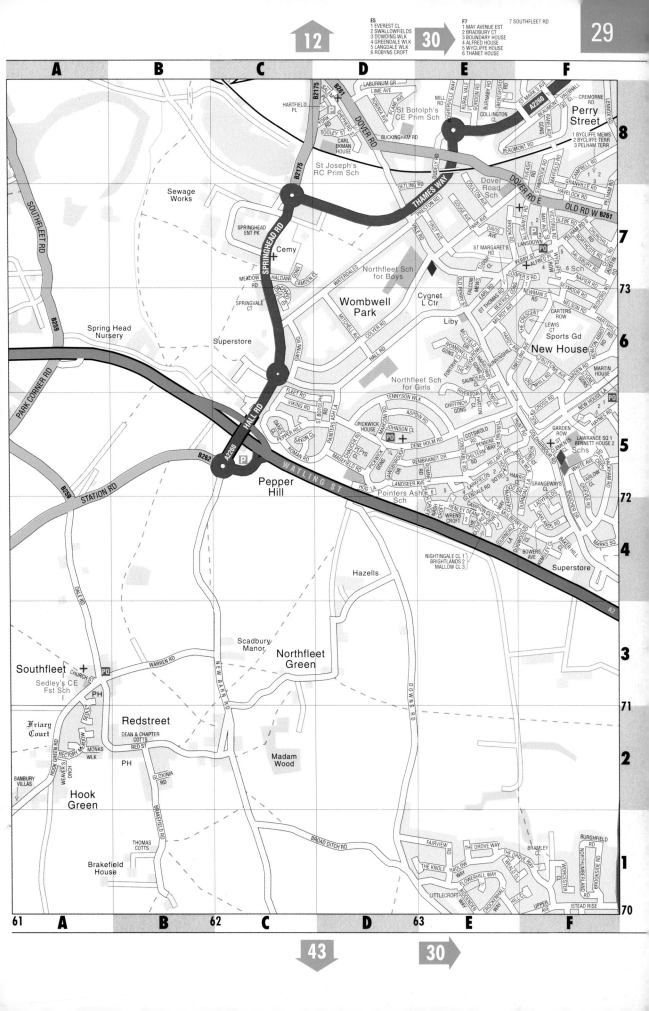

B8
1 CLAREMONT PL
2 LYDIA COTTS
3 VICTORIA AVE
4 WILLIAM HOUSE
5 PETER ST
6 HOME MEAD CL

← **29**

B8
7 HOMEMEAD
8 GRAVESHAM CT
9 PRESENTATION HOUSE
10 ST ANDREW'S RD
C8
1 WATERLOO ST

↑ **13**

C8
2 CHRIST CHURCH CRES
3 CHRIST CHURCH RD
4 ALBERT MURRY CL
D8
1 BRUNSWICK WLK
2 CANAL ROAD IND PK

Gravesend Gram Sch for Girls
TA Ctr
GRANGE HOUSE
Gravesend Gram Sch for Girls
Woodlands Pk
Cemy
Liby
New House La
St George's CE Sch
SHEARS GREEN CT
Mid Kent Golf Course

Windmill Hill
St Thomas's Almshouses
Convent Prep Sch
Holy Trinity CE Prim Sch
Gravesend Gram Sch for Boys
St John's RC Prim Sch
St John's RC Sch
Liby

MILTON RD
EAST MILTON RD
OLD RD W
OLD RD E
ROCHESTER RD
WROTHAM RD
WATLING ST

Denton Marshes
Denton
Westcourt Marshes
Caravan Pk
Sewage Works
North West Kent Coll of Tech
THE MALTINGS ENT CTR
Northcourt Cty Prim Sch
Westcourt Cty Prim Sch
Westcourt
Recn Gd
Raynehurst Cty Prim Sch
Thamesview Sch

Kings Farm
Whitehill Schs
Liby
Christian Fields
Kings Farm Cty Prim Sch
Southfields Sch
Ifield Sch
Sports Gd
Kings Farm Cty Prim Sch
Parrock Farm
Riverview Park
Riverview Cty Jun & Inf Schs
THE ALMA

Singlewell
Liby
Singlewell Cty Prim Sch
Winters Croft
Abbots Field
Ruffets Wood
The Glades
The Hollies
Watling St Hotel
Claylane Wood

Hotel

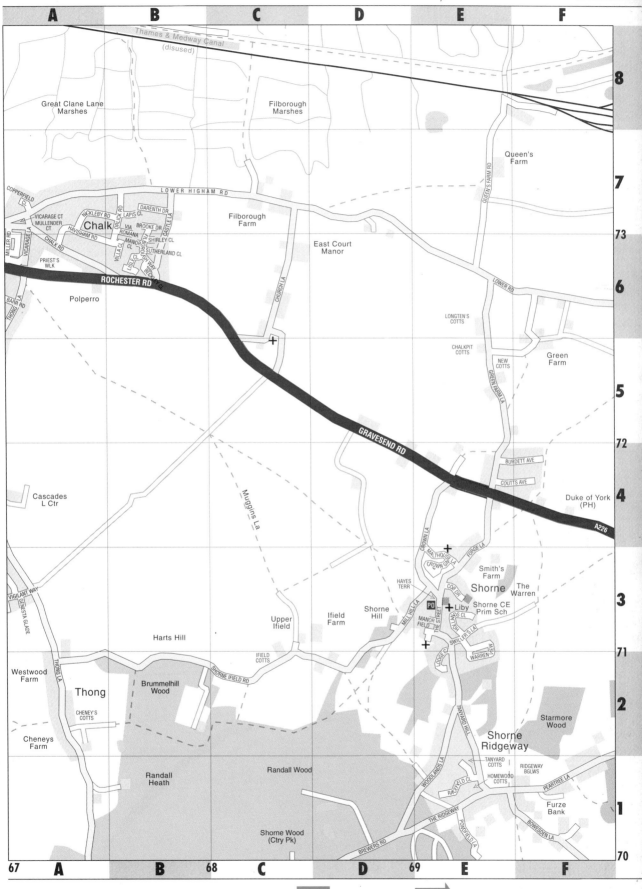

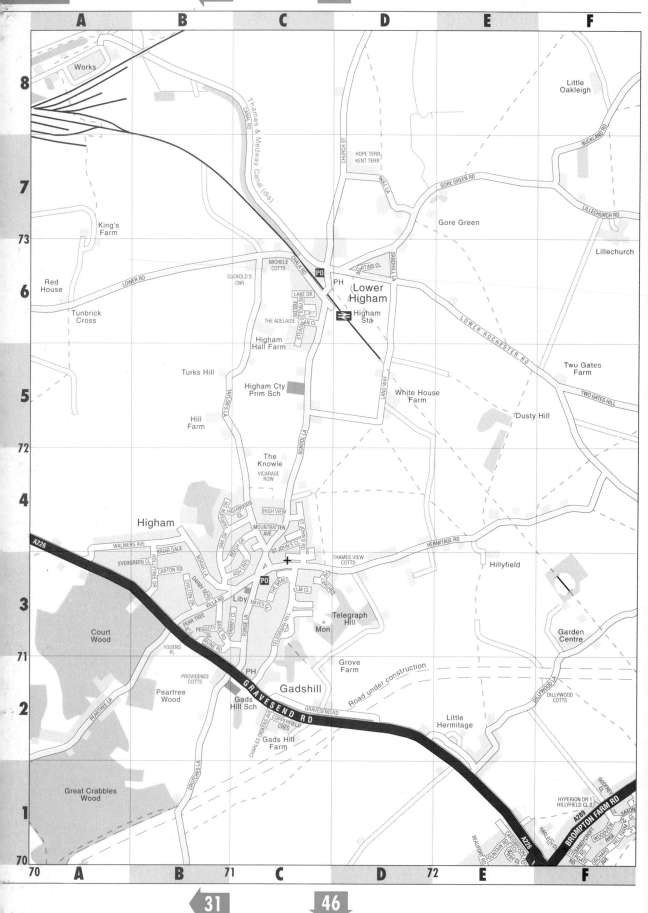

A B C D E F

8 Works

Little
Oakleigh

Thames & Medway Canal (dis)

CANAL RD

CHURCH ST

BUCKLAND RD

7 Hope Terr
Kent Terr

BULL LA

Gore Green Rd

LILLECHURCH RD

73 King's
Farm

Gore Green

SANDHILL LA

Lillechurch

6 Red
House

LOWER RD

MICHELE
COTTS

CUCKOLD'S
CNR

PO

PH

Lower
Higham

Higham Sta

MARTINS CL

LOWER ROCHESTER RD

Tunbrick
Cross

LAKE DR

THE ADELAIDE

REYNOLDS CL
STEADMAN CL
FIELDS

Two Gates
Farm

Higham
Hall Farm

Higham Cty
Prim Sch

LAND WAY

White House
Farm

TWO GATES HILL

5 Turks Hill

TAYLOR'S LA

SCHOOL LA

Dusty Hill

Hill
Farm

72 The
Knowle

VICARAGE
ROW

4 Higham

HIGHWOODS
CL

FAIRVIEW DR

OAK DR

BEECH GR

HIGH VIEW

MOUNTBATTEN
AVE

ST JOHN'S CL

Hermitage RD

Hillyfield

WALMERS AVE

BRIAR DALE

NORAH LA

ASH CRES

ST JOHN'S RD

THAMES VIEW
COTTS

EVERGREEN CL

HOLLYTREE DR

CARTON RD

DARBY GDNS

CHILTON DR

VILLA RD

PO

THE BRAES

CJM CL

THE ARCHES

3 Court
Wood

PEAR TREE
PL

PEGGOTY
CL

BRAE LA
SPURGEY CL
FORGE LA

IRVINE RD

Liby

HAYES CT

TELEGRAPH HILL

Mon

Telegraph
Hill

Garden
Centre

71 YOUENS
PL

PROVIDENCE
COTTS

PH

Grove
Farm

Road under construction

DILLYWOOD LA

DILLYWOOD
COTTS

A226

Peartree
Wood

2 PEARTREE LA

CRUTCHES LA

GRAVESEND RD

Gads
Hill Sch

CHARLES DICKENS AVE

COPPERFIELD
CRES

Gadshill

GRAVESEND RD

Little
Hermitage

Gads Hill
Farm

1 Great Crabbles
Wood

HYPERION DR 1
HILLYFIELD CL 2

GODFREY CL

A289

SAXON
RISE

HILL PARK CL

BROMPTON FARM RD

BEAUFORT RD

FOUNTAIN RD

CARISBROOKE RD

A226

HARLECH CL

EASTSANDYCROFT
WESTSANDYCROFT

WOODVIEW

EASTGATE
RD

ORCHARD
AVE

70

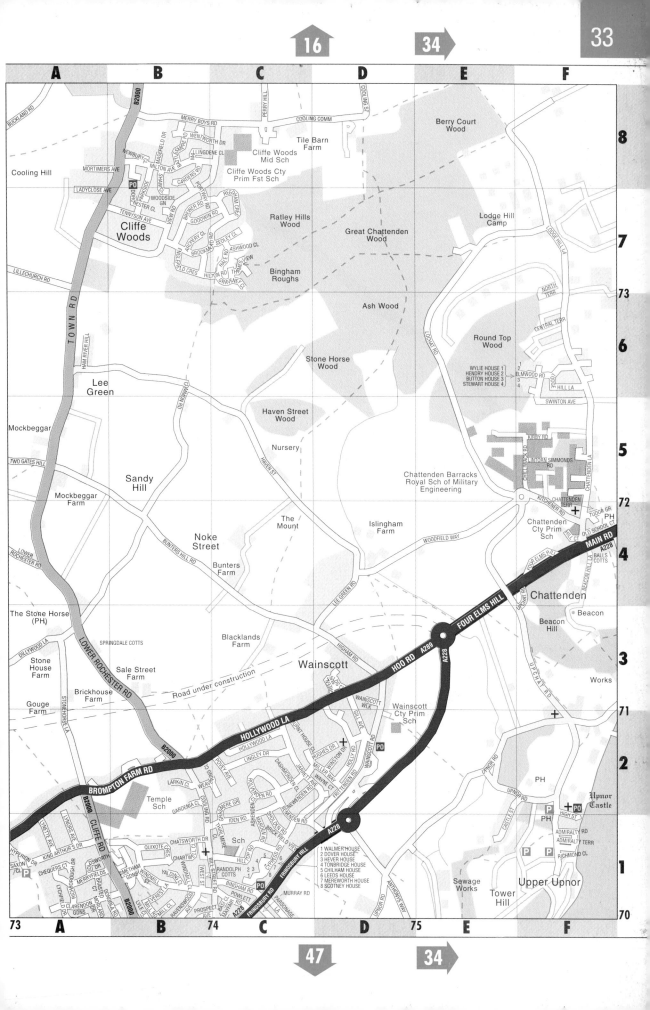

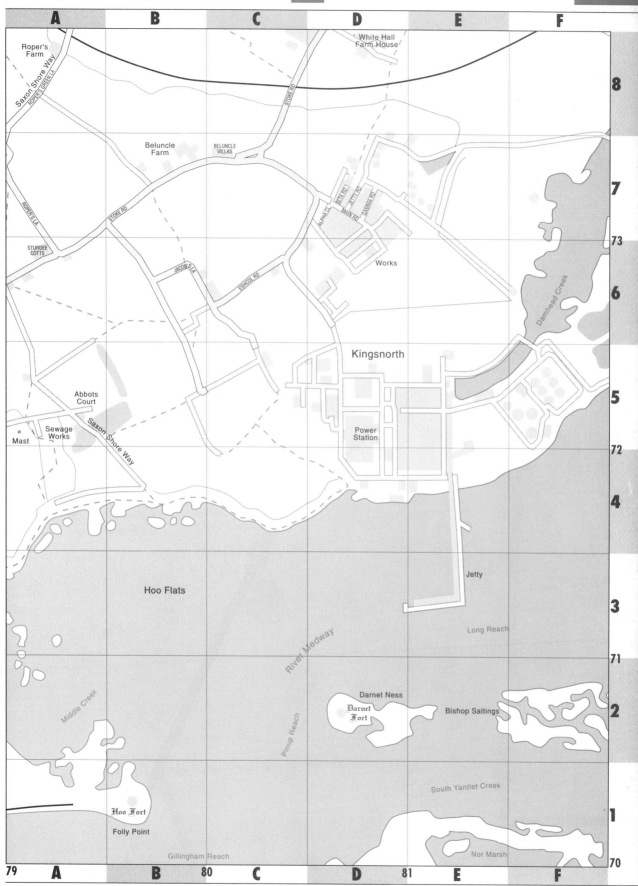

A B C D E F

8

7

73

6

5

72

4

3

71

2

1

70

White Hall
Farm House

Roper's
Farm

Saxon Shore Way

ROPER'S GREEN LA

Beluncle
Farm

BELUNCLE
VILLAS

STOKE RD

ROPER'S LA

Stoke RD

ALPHA CL

BETA RD

MAIN RD

JETTY RD

GAMMA RD

STURDEE
COTTS

JACOB'S LA

ESHCOL RD

Works

Kingsnorth

Damhead Creek

Abbots
Court

Saxon Shore Way

Sewage
Works

Mast

Power
Station

Jetty

Hoo Flats

River Medway

Long Reach

Pinup Reach

Middle Creek

Darnet Ness

Darnet
Fort

Bishop Saltings

South Yantlet Creek

Hoo Fort

Folly Point

Gillingham Reach

Nor Marsh

36

A5
1 MONTAGUE TERR
2 TAVISTOCK RD
3 CHATSWORTH HOUSE

A6
1 MARINA CL
2 CHEVENEY WLK
3 BROMLEY MANOR MANSIONS
4 THE MALL
5 WESTMORELAND PL

B8
1 HANSOM TERR
2 DAINTON CL
3 ST TIMOTHY'S MEWS
4 ANDRINGHAM LODGE
5 KENDALL LODGE
6 SUMMERFIELD

7 WINSTON CT
8 THE LAURELS

22

C7
1 WESTLAND LODGE
2 DAIRSIE CT
3 BEECHFIELD COTTS
4 THE OASIS
5 CROMARTY CT
6 SILVERSTONE CT

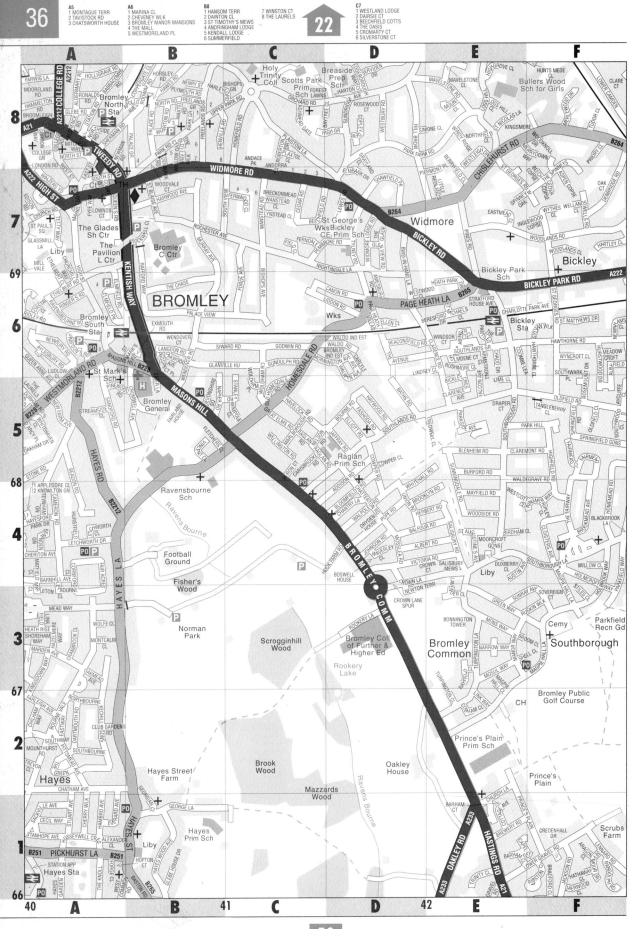

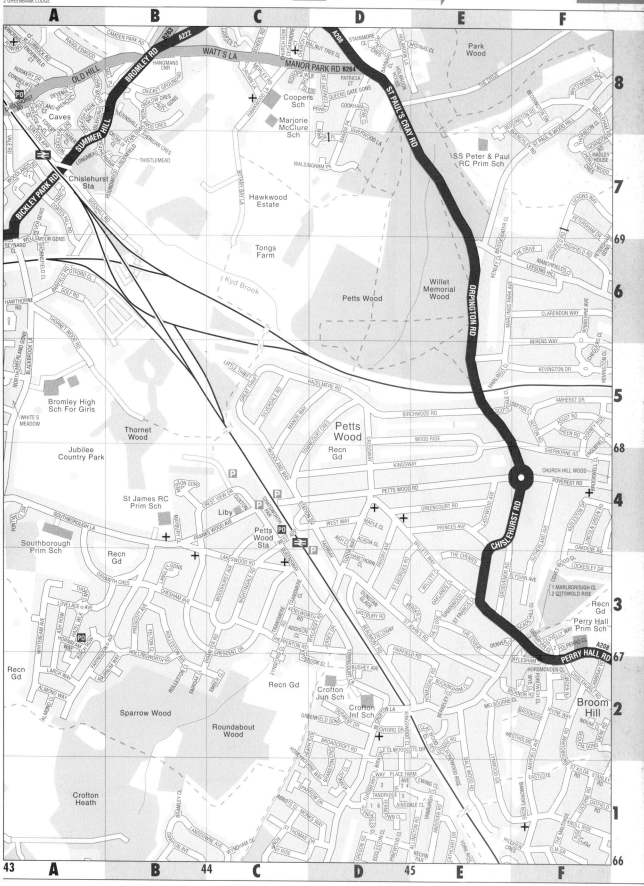

B6
1 SELWYN PL
2 LEIGH TERR
3 WOULDHAM TERR
← 37

C5
1 MOUNTFIELD WAY
2 HORTON TOWER
3 ELMSTONE TERR
4 TIDEBROOK CT
5 BELGRAVE CL
6 SANDWAY PATH
↑ 24

C5
7 HARBLEDOWN PL
8 BAPCHILD PL
9 ALKHAM TOWER

A B C D E F

B7
1 SWANSCOMBE HOUSE
2 HAVERSTOCK CT
3 ARRANDENE HOUSE
4 BROOMFIELD HOUSE
5 HEADLEY HOUSE
6 KENLEY HOUSE
7 LADYWELL HOUSE

Ski Ctr

A20

Home Farm Cotts

Ruxley Golf Course

Golf Ctr

CH

Cray Valley Golf Course

Barnfield Bank

CHAPMAN'S LA

Pauls Cray Hill Park

St Paul's Wood Hill

Grays Farm Production Village

Grays Farm Prim Sch

Bromley Valley Gymnastics Ctr Liby

Rectory Paddock Sch & Research Unit

Crayfields Ind Pk

1 RIVERSIDE CL
2 RIVER COTTS
3 GARDEN COTTS
4 THE CRAYS PAR

St Paul's Cray

Leesons Prim Sch

St Pauls Cray CE Prim Sch

Hockenden Wood

Murray Bsns Ctr

St Mary Cray Sta

Orpington Trad Est

Cemy

Market Meadow

Nugent Ind Pk

Nightingale Cnr

Chesterfield Cl

STAR LA

Sheepcote Farm

BLACKSMITHS LA

The Warren

Poverest Prim Sch

St Mary Cray

Kevington Prim Sch

Shawcroft Sch

C4
1 WOODCHURCH CT
2 RIVERSIDE CT
3 SPRING LODGE
4 HUNTON HOUSE
5 LUDDESDOWN HOUSE
6 BRENZETT HOUSE
7 COPPER BEECH CL
8 ROBERTS CL

CROCKENHILL RD

Kevingtown

B258

Recn Gd

St Mary Cray Prim Sch

Derry Downs

Griggs Cross

Recn Gd

Allot Gdns

Wendover Way

A208 PERRY HALL RD

A208

Walden Manor

1 SAMUEL PALMER CT
2 THE HERITAGE
3 SHANNON CT

Mus

Cemy

Liby

Recn Gd

Ramsden Prim Sch

East Hall Rd

COURT ROAD ORPINGTON BY-PASS

A224

Coll

The Walnuts

L Ctr

Ramsden

DENECOURT 1
CRUNDALE TOWER 2
QUILTER GDNS 3
ARUN CT 4

The Priory Sch

Griff's Wood

Lone Barn Farm

46 A 47 B C 48 D E F

← 37   52

D1
1 BREDGAR HOUSE
2 WITTERSHAM HOUSE
3 CHALLOCK HOUSE
4 HOLLINGBOURNE TOWER
5 THURNHAM HOUSE
6 PECKHAM HOUSE
7 STOCKBURY HOUSE
8 EASTLING HOUSE
9 NEWINGTON HOUSE

10 FAWKHAM HOUSE
11 HOUGHAM HOUSE
12 BEKESBOURNE TOWER
13 LENHAM HOUSE
14 LAMBERHURST CL
15 LODDEN CT
16 KENNETT CT
17 EDEN CT
18 CUCKMERE CT
19 DARENTH CT

20 MEDWAY CT
21 MEON CT
22 STOUR CT
23 RAVENSBOURNE CT
24 ROTHER CT
25 RYE FIELD
26 BOX TREE WLK

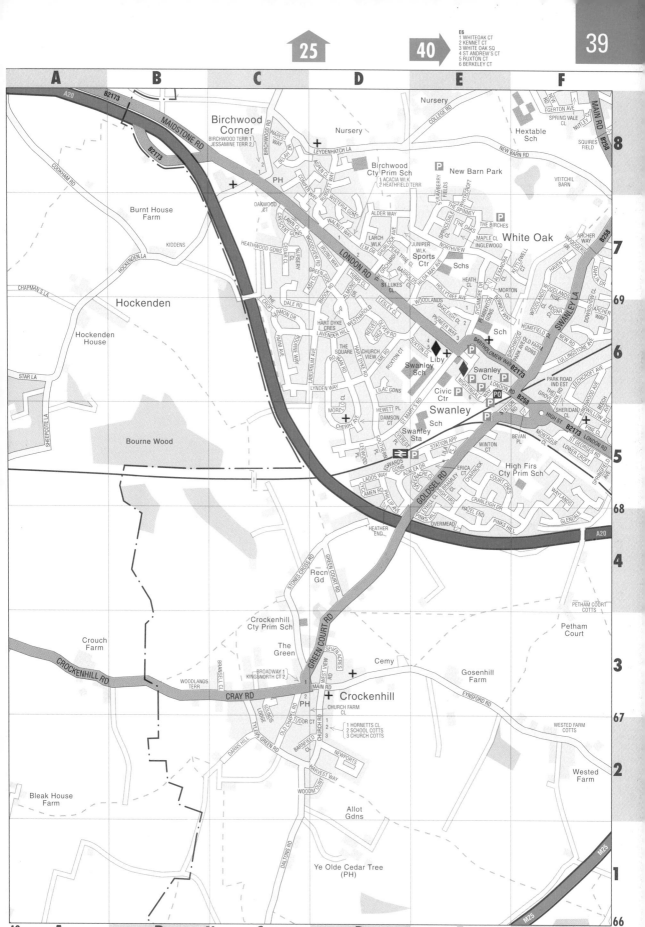

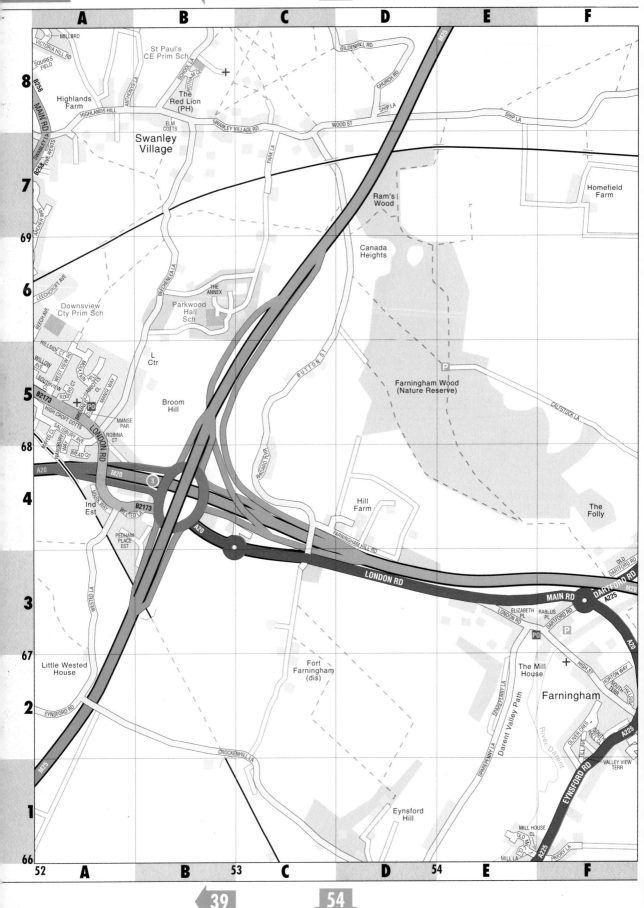

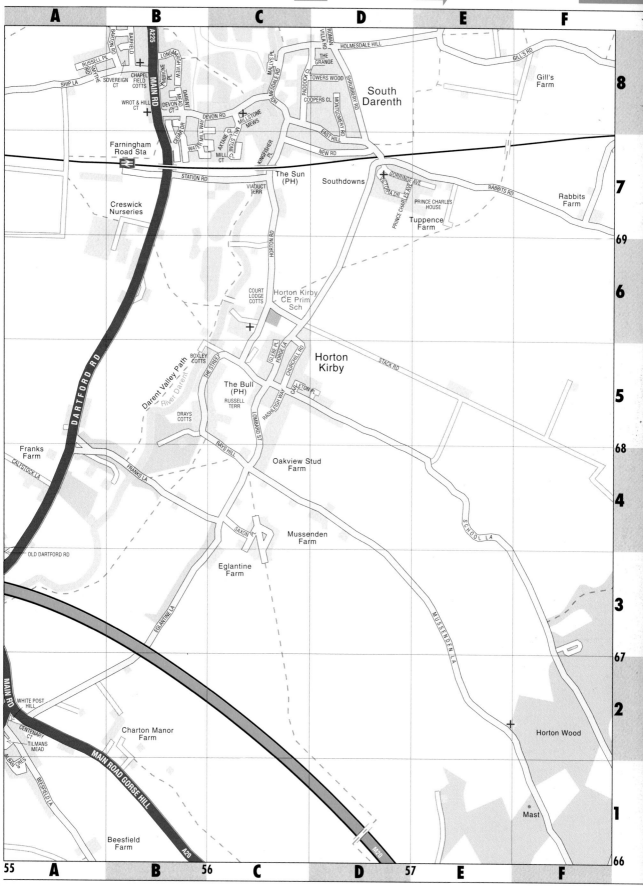

A B C D E F

8
7
69
6
5
68
4
3
67
2
1
66

South Darenth

Gill's Farm

Holmesdale Hill

The Grange
Towers Wood
Coopers Cl

Farningham Road Sta

The Sun (PH)

Southdowns

Rabbits Rd

Rabbits Farm

Creswick Nurseries

Station Rd

Viaduct Terr

Prince Charles House

Tuppence Farm

Gorringe Ave
Victoria Dr

Horton Rd

Court Lodge Cotts

Horton Kirby CE Prim Sch

Stack Rd

Darent Valley Path

River Darent

Boxley Cotts

Horton Kirby

Glebe Pl
Forge La
Churchill Rd

The Bull (PH)

Russell Terr

Rashleigh Way
Lombard St
Carleton Pl

Drays Cotts

Rays Hill

Oakview Stud Farm

Franks Farm

Franks La

Caltstock La

School La

Old Dartford Rd

Saxon

Mussenden Farm

Eglantine Farm

Eglantine La

Dartford Rd

Mussenden La

Main Rd

White Post Hill

Centenary Ct
Tilmans Mead

Albion Cres

Beesfield La

Charton Manor Farm

Horton Wood

Mast

Main Road Gorse Hill

A20

A20

Beesfield Farm

55 A B 56 C D 57 E F 66

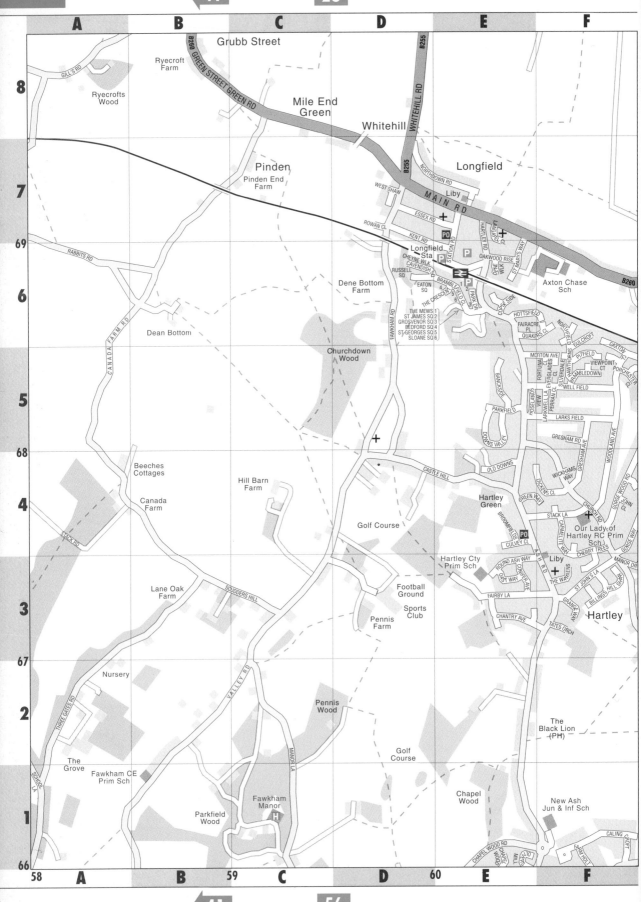

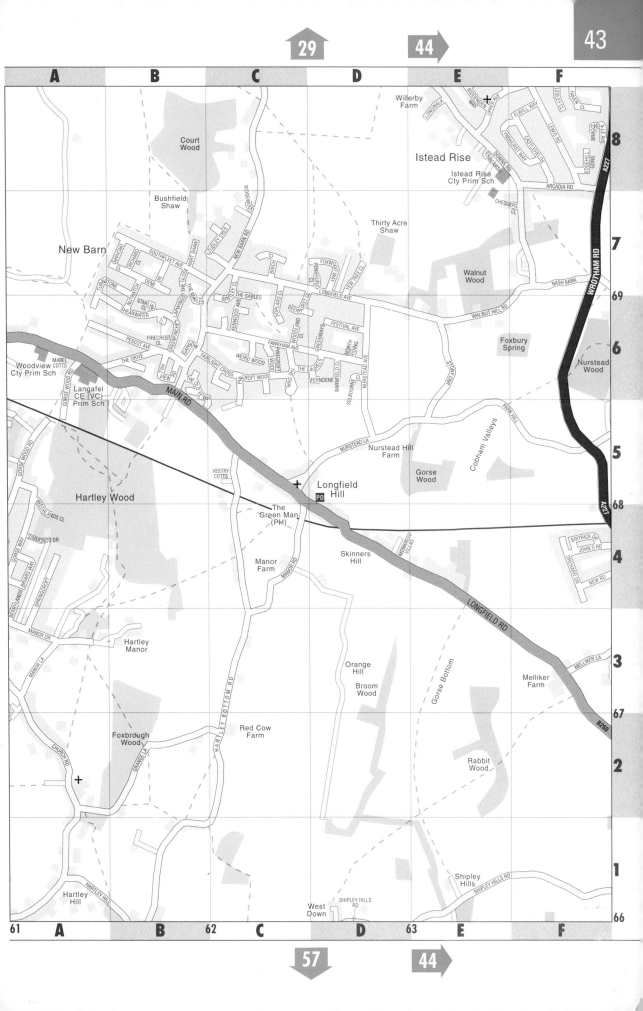

A B C D E F

8
7
69
6
5
68
4
67
3
2
1
66

Court
Wood

Bushfield
Shaw

New Barn

Willerby
Farm

Istead Rise

Istead Rise
Cty Prim Sch

ARCADIA RD

BIDDENDEN WAY
LONGWALK
UPPER AVE
ELWILL WAY
CASTLEFIELDS
LEWIS RD
LESLEY CL
HAZEL CL
EDGEHILL GDNS
2ND AVE
BRACON
1ST AVE
ROSEARTH
DOWNS RD
LYNDHURST WAY
CHEQUERS CL

WROTHAM RD
A227

Thirty Acre
Shaw

Walnut
Wood

NASH BANK

WALNUT HILL RD

Foxbury
Spring

Nurstead
Wood

STUDLEY CRESS
NEW BARN RD
RIDGEWAY
BIRCH
FOXWD
WAY
FIRST CL
PENSHURST
LONGFIELD AVE
YEW TREE CL
DEEN
The Gables
BRINDLEY CL
POPLARS CL
KENWOOD AVE
WOODLAND
GREENWAYS
FESTIVAL AVE
NORTH
RIDING
NURSTEAD AVE

Southfleet Ave
ORCHARD
DENE
HART SHAW
THE CLOSE
THE MAPLES
DR
LAPWINGS
GREENFINCHES
ORCHARD CL
TURNSTONE
NUTHATCH
STARLIG
CL
SHEARWATER
FIRECREST CL
PESCOT AVE
THE DRIVE
SPARROW
FAIRLIGHT CROSS
WEIRD WOOD
FAWKHAM AVE
PINECROFT
CROFT WOOD
THE OVAL
THE LAURELS
FERNDENE
BARNFIELD CL
SEL BOURNE
MAIN RD

New Barn

Woodview
Cty Prim Sch
MABEL
COTTS
GORSE WOOD RD
Langafel
CE (VC)
Prim Sch
FITH
VIEW
RD
THE OLD VICG WY

VESTRY
COTTS

Nurstead La
Nurstead Hill
Farm

NURSTEAD LA

Gorse
Wood

Cobham Valleys

PARK HILL

COBHAM RD

A227
A221

Longfield
Hill
PO

The
Green Man
(PH)

Skinners
Hill

MAGPIE
GREEN

Hartley Wood

BEECHLANDS CL
SIMMONDS DR
GORSE WOOD RD
GORSE WAY
BERRYLANDS
BRIARS WAY
SPRINGCROFT
MANOR DR
MANOR LA

Manor
Farm

MANOR RD

Hartley
Manor

HARTLEY BOTTOM RD

Orange
Hill

Broom
Wood

Gorse Bottom

Longfield Rd
LONGFIELD RD

Melliker
Farm

MELLIKER LA

BIRTRICK DR
ST JOHN'S RD
ORCHARD DR
NEW RD

B260

Foxbrough
Wood

CHURCH RD
GRANGE LA

Red Cow
Farm

Rabbit
Wood

Shipley
Hills

SHIPLEY HILLS RD

Hartley
Hill

HARTLEY HILL

West
Down

SHIPLEY HILLS
RD

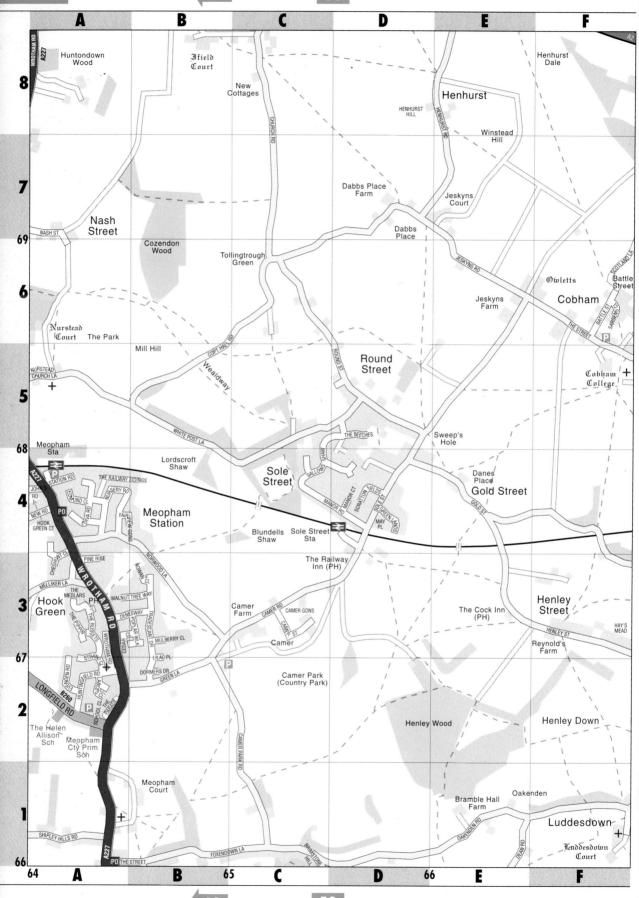

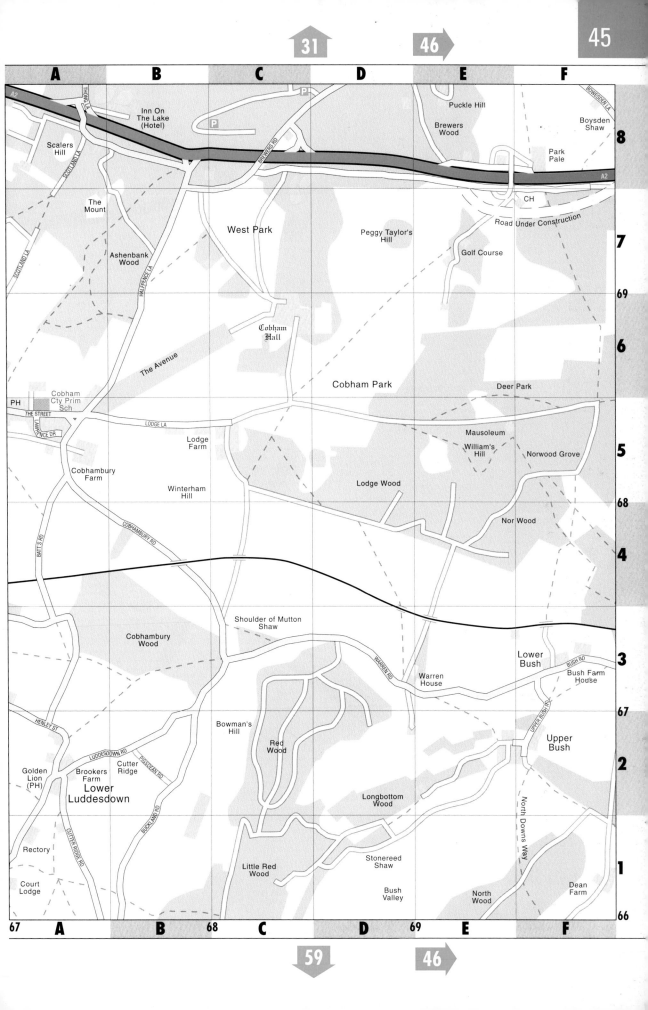

A   B   C   D   E   F

A2

Thong La

Inn On The Lake (Hotel)

Scalers Hill

Scotland La

The Mount

Ashenbank Wood

West Park

Halfpence La

Brewers Rd

P

P

Puckle Hill

Brewers Wood

Boysden Shaw

Bowsden La

Park Pale

A2

CH

Road Under Construction

8

Peggy Taylor's Hill

Golf Course

7

69

Scotland La

Cobham Hall

The Avenue

6

Cobham Park

Deer Park

PH

Cobham Cty Prim Sch

THE STREET

LAWRENCE DR

LODGE LA

Lodge Farm

Mausoleum

William's Hill

Norwood Grove

5

68

Cobhambury Farm

Winterham Hill

Lodge Wood

Nor Wood

BATT'S RD

COBHAMBURY RD

4

Shoulder of Mutton Shaw

Cobhambury Wood

WARREN RD

Warren House

Lower Bush

Bush Farm House

BUSH RD

3

67

HENLEY ST

Bowman's Hill

Red Wood

UPPER BUSH RD

Upper Bush

Golden Lion (PH)

LUDDESDOWN RD

Brookers Farm

Cutter Ridge

PIGSDEAN RD

Lower Luddesdown

BUCKLAND RD

Longbottom Wood

North Downs Way

2

CUTTER RIDGE RD

Rectory

Court Lodge

Little Red Wood

Stonereed Shaw

Bush Valley

North Wood

Dean Farm

1

66

67   A   B   68   C   D   69   E   F

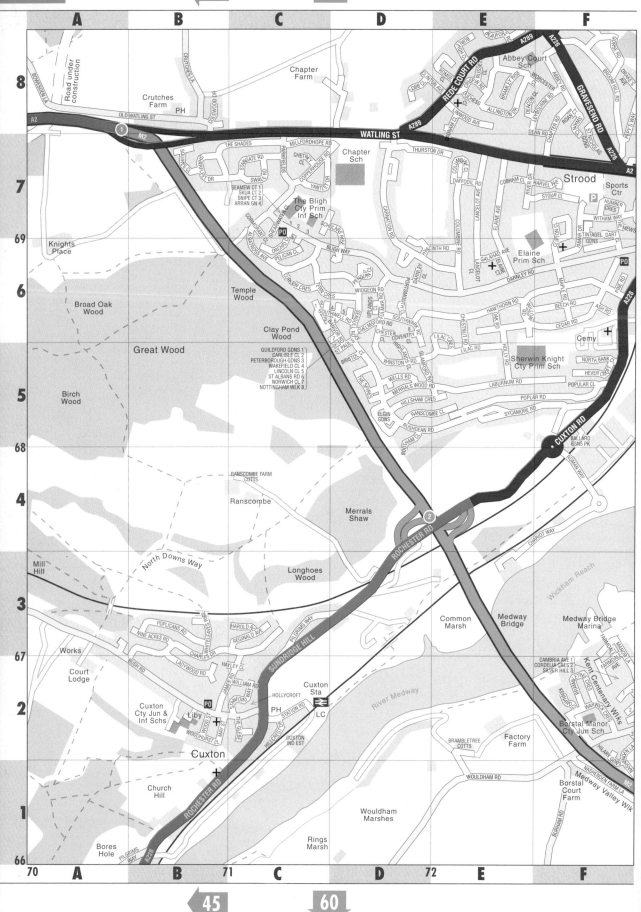

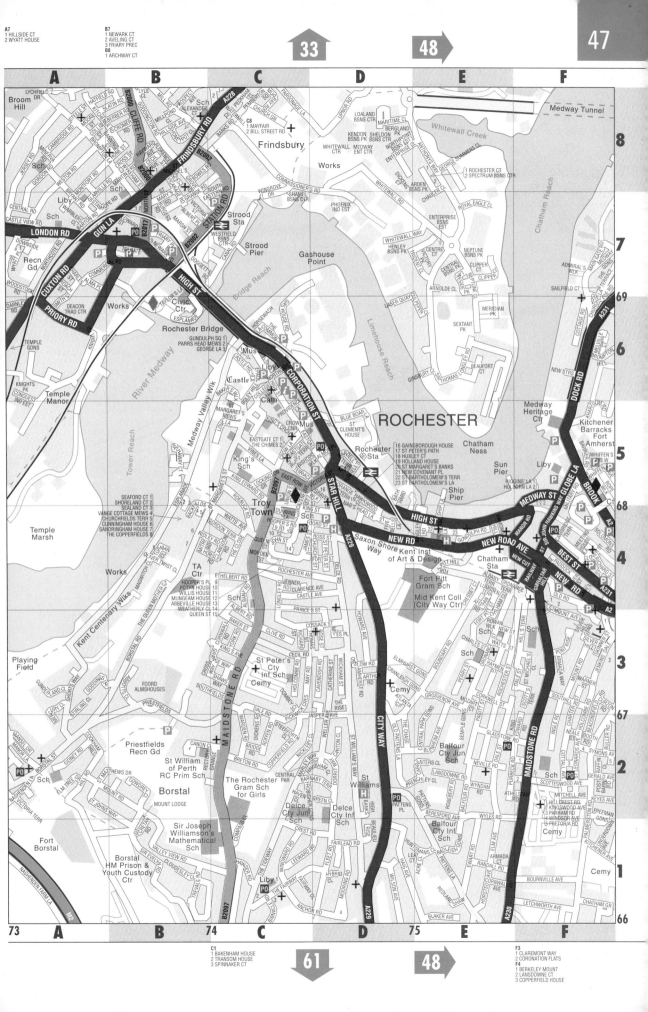

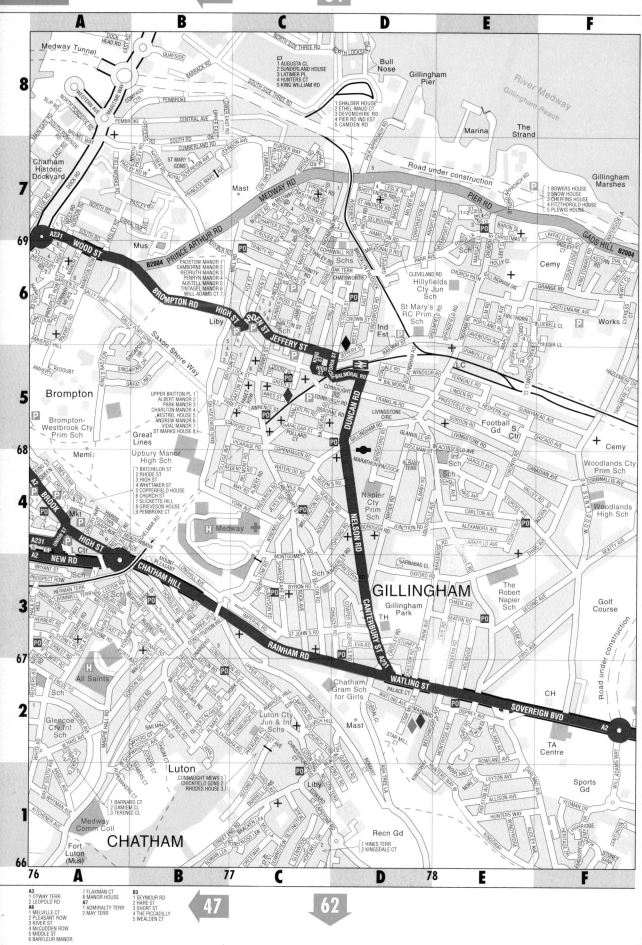

A3
1 OTWAY TERR
2 LEOPOLD RD
A6
1 MELVILLE CT
2 PLEASANT ROW
3 RIVER ST
4 McCUDDEN ROW
5 MIDDLE ST
6 BARFLEUR MANOR

7 FLAXMAN CT
8 MANOR HOUSE
A7
1 ADMIRALTY TERR
2 MAY TERR

B3
1 SEYMOUR RD
2 HARE ST
3 SHORT ST
4 THE PICCADILLY
5 WEALDEN CT

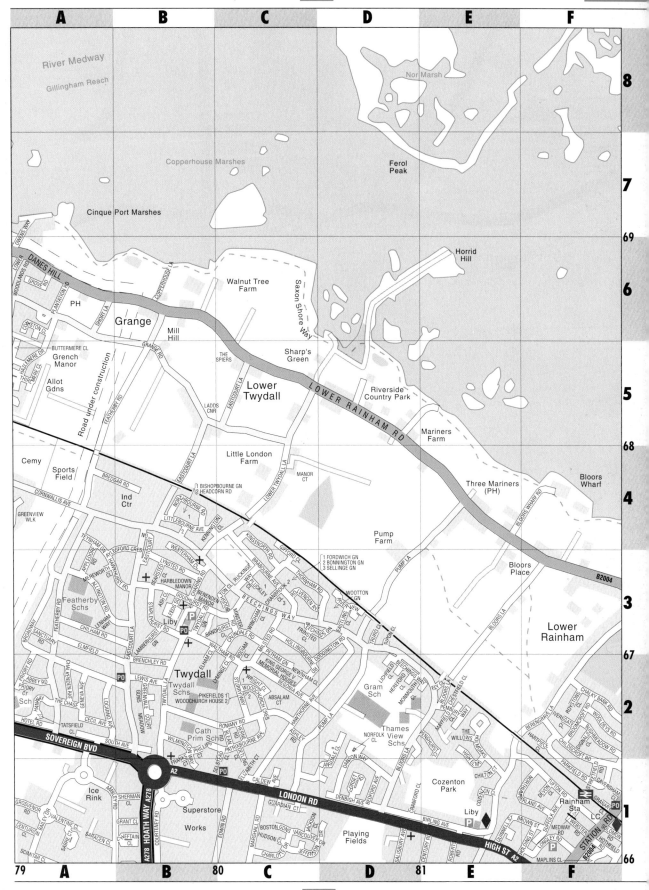

River Medway
Gillingham Reach

Nor Marsh

Copperhouse Marshes

Ferol Peak

Cinque Port Marshes

Horrid Hill

DANES HILL

LOWER DANES HILL

Walnut Tree Farm

Saxon Shore Way

PH

Grange

Mill Hill

GRANGE RD

THE SPIERS

Sharp's Green

Grench Manor

BUTTERMERE CL

Allot Gdns

Lower Twydall

LADDS CNR

Riverside Country Park

LOWER RAINHAM RD

Mariners Farm

Cemy

Sports Field

Little London Farm

MANOR CT

LOWER TWYDALL LA

Three Mariners (PH)

Bloors Wharf

BREDGAR RD

CORNWALLIS AVE

Ind Ctr

1 BISHOPBOURNE GN
2 HEADCORN RD

Pump Farm

BLOORS WHARF RD

GREENVIEW WLK

LITTLEBOURNE AVE

KINGSNORTH RD

PUMP LA

Bloors Place

B2004

Featherby Schs

WESTERHAM RD

1 FORDWICH GN
2 BONNINGTON GN
3 SELLINGE GN

Lower Rainham

HARBLEDOWN MANOR

BENENDEN MANOR

BEECHINGS WAY

WOOTTON GN

BLOORS LA

Liby

Twydall

TRURO CL

Twydall Schs

KING GEORGE V MEMORIAL HOUSES

Gram Sch

PIKEFIELDS
WOODCHURCH HOUSE

WOODCHURCH CRES

ABSALAM CT

HEREFORD

Cath Prim Sch

ROMANY RD

NORFOLK CL

Thames View Schs

The Willows

SOVEREIGN BVD

LONDON RD

HOATH WAY A278

A2

Ice Rink

Superstore Works

Cozenton Park

Liby

Rainham Sta

Playing Fields

HIGH ST A2

STATION RD

B2004

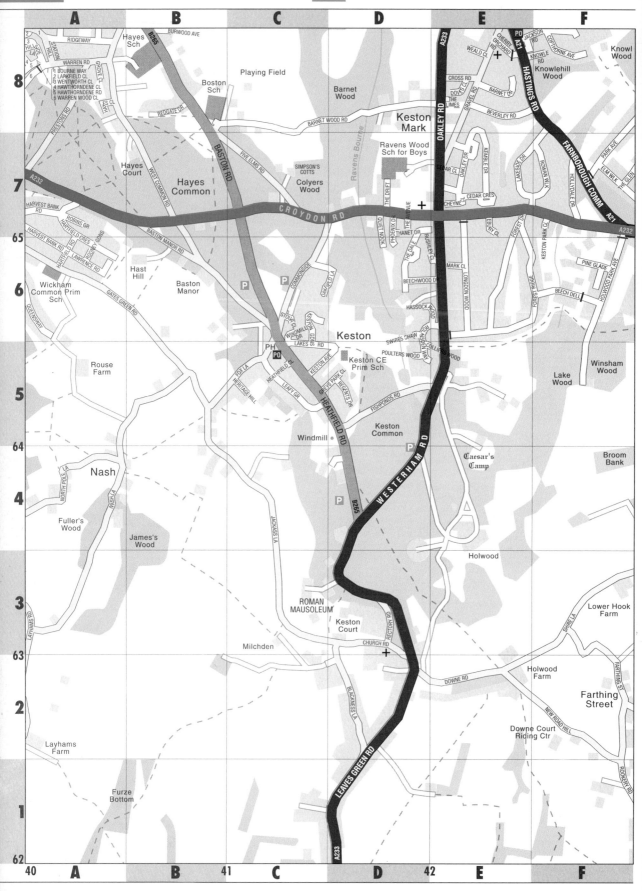

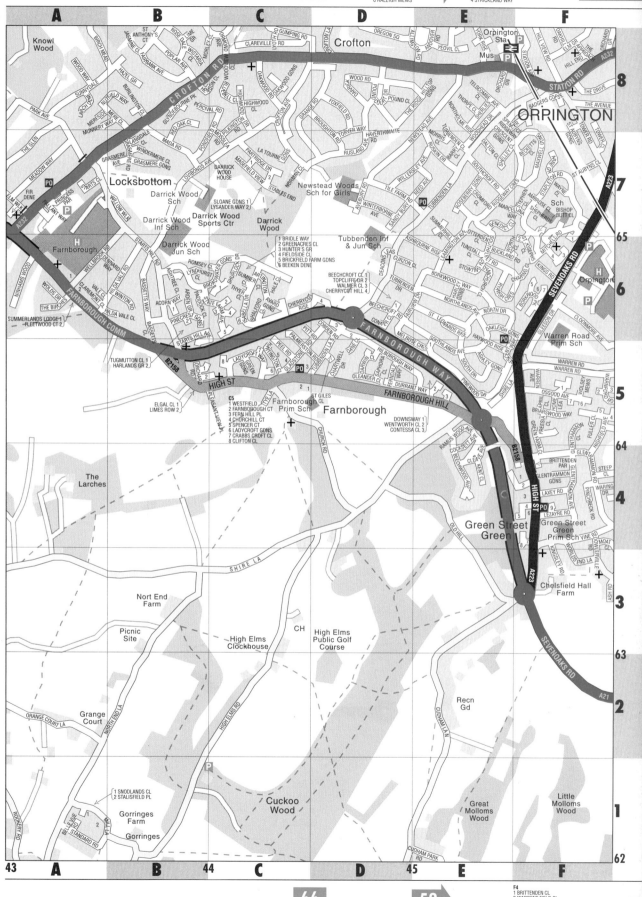

F5
1 OSGOOD GDNS
2 AMBERLEY CL
3 RAWLINGS CL
4 BEBLETS CL
5 FIR TREE CL
6 RALEIGH MEWS

F5
7 KING HENRY MEWS
F6
1 HEALY DR
2 MARSDEN WAY
3 TAYLOR CL
4 STRICKLAND WAY

5 DRYLAND AVE
6 ADCOT WLK
7 LICHDALE CL

F4
1 BRITTENDEN CL
2 WARDENS FIELD CL
3 WINNEPEG DR
4 SUPERIOR DR
5 HURON CL
6 MANITOBA GDNS
7 LYNNE CL
8 FLINT CL
9 BAKERS MEWS

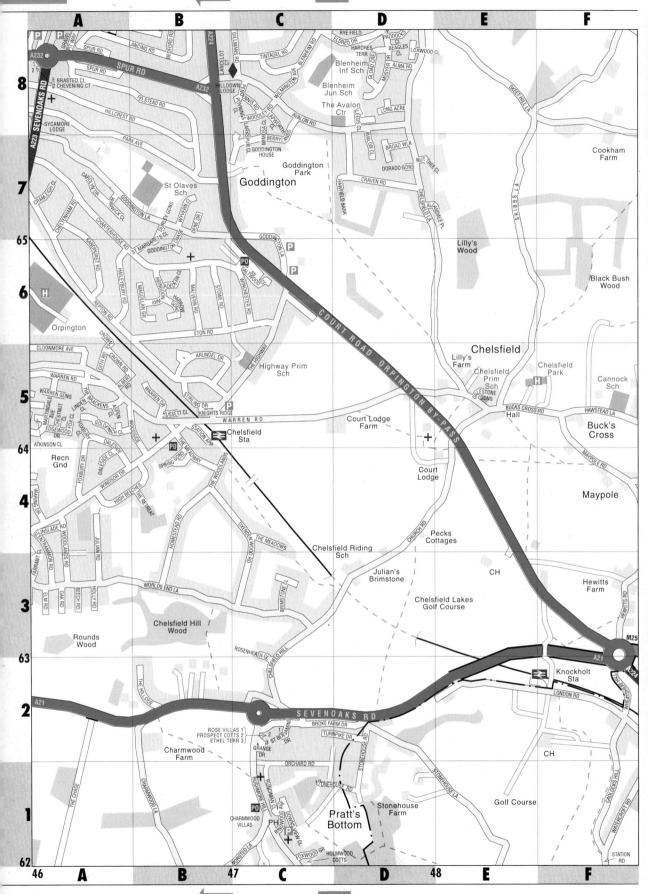

A   B   C   D   E   F

SPUR RD

1 BRASTED CL
2 CHEVENING CT

SYCAMORE LODGE

HILLCREST RD

PARK AVE

SPUR RD
SPUR RD

LANCING RD

BEDFORD RD

FELSTEAD RD

SEVENOAKS RD

A223

A232

A224

LANCELOT CL

GILLMANS RD

HILLDOWN LODGE

TINTAGEL RD

BLENHEIM RD

WILMINGTON AVE

RYE FIELD

ELDRED DR

HARDRES TERR

PADDOCKS

BEAGLES CL

LOXWOOD CL

Blenheim Inf Sch

ALMA RD

MOSTYN DR

GLOAD CRES

Blenheim Jun Sch

LONG ACRE

BROAD WLK

The Avalon Ctr

AVALON RD

LEEDS CL

AVALON CL

DORADO GDNS

NUT TREE CL

Goddington House

Goddington Park

Goddington

St Olaves Sch

CRANLEIGH CL

CAROLYN DR

CHETTENHAM RD

GODDINGTON LA

RENWICK CT

CHARTERHOUSE RD

ST MARGARETS CL

GODDINGTON CHASE

DURLEY GDNS

WYVERN CL

DENE DR

CRAVEN RD

SKIBBS LA

SKEET HILL LA

Cookham Farm

Black Bush Wood

Lilly's Wood

CHELSFIELD LA

ALDERDALE PL

HAWFIELD BANK

GODDINGTON LA

SALTWOOD

WINCHESTER RD

STONE RD

ETON RD

ABINGDON WAY

MAGDELAN GR

MALVERN RD

HARROW GDNS

REPTON RD

HAILEYBURY RD

SANDHURST RD

CLOONMORE AVE

Orpington

COURT ROAD ORPINGTON BY-PASS

Chelsfield

Lilly's Farm

Chelsfield Prim Sch

Chelsfield Park

Cannock Sch

CHELSTONE GDNS

BUCKS CROSS RD

Bucks Cross Hall

HAWSTEAD LA

Buck's Cross

MAYPOLE RD

Maypole

WARREN RD

WARREN GDNS

MARTINDALE AVE

CHESTNUT CL

EDGEWOOD DR

ATKINSON CL

LINDEN CL

THE BRACKENS

ASPEN CL

GOLY-NCH CL

FOXBURY

WOODSIDE

DALESIDE

EDITH RD

CROWN RD

ALBERT RD

CROWN DR

WARREN DR

RUSSETT CL

STIRLING DR

KNIGHTS RIDGE

ARUNDEL DR

THE HIGHWAY

Highway Prim Sch

Court Lodge Farm

Court Lodge

Recn Gnd

HARRISON RD

GLINSLADE RD

WOODLANDS RD

TRAMMON RD

FARRANT CL

ELM RD

OAK RD

HOLLY RD

BEECH RD

JULIAN RD

HIGH BEECHES

THE RETREAT

DALESIDE CL

FOXBURY DR

WINDSOR DR

SPRING GDNS

STATION APP

THE MEADWAY

THE WOODLANDS

Chelsfield Sta

HOMESTEAD RD

OXENDEN WOOD RD

THE MEADOWS

BRIMSTONE CL

Chelsfield Riding Sch

Julian's Brimstone

CHURCH RD

Pecks Cottages

CH

Chelsfield Lakes Golf Course

Hewitts Farm

HEWITTS RD

WORLDS END LA

Chelsfield Hill Wood

Rounds Wood

ROSENHEATH CL

CHELSFIELD HILL

M25

A21

A224

Knockholt Sta

LONDON RD

THE HILLSIDE

A21

SEVENOAKS RD

Charmwood Farm

CHARMWOOD LA

THE CHASE

ROSE VILLAS 1
PROSPECT COTTS 2
ETHEL TERR 3

ST BENJAMINS

GRANGE DR

Broke Farm Dr

TURNPIKE DR

ORCHARD RD

RUSHMORE HILL

RUSHMORE HILL

DOWNE VIEW CL

FUNCTMAN CL

STONEHOUSE RD

STONEHOUSE RD

STONEHOUSE LA

Stonehouse Farm

CH

Golf Course

Pratt's Bottom

Charmwood Villas

PH

FOXWOOD CL

NORSTED LA

HOLMWOOD COTTS

CAD LOCKS HILL

WATERCROFT RD

STATION RD

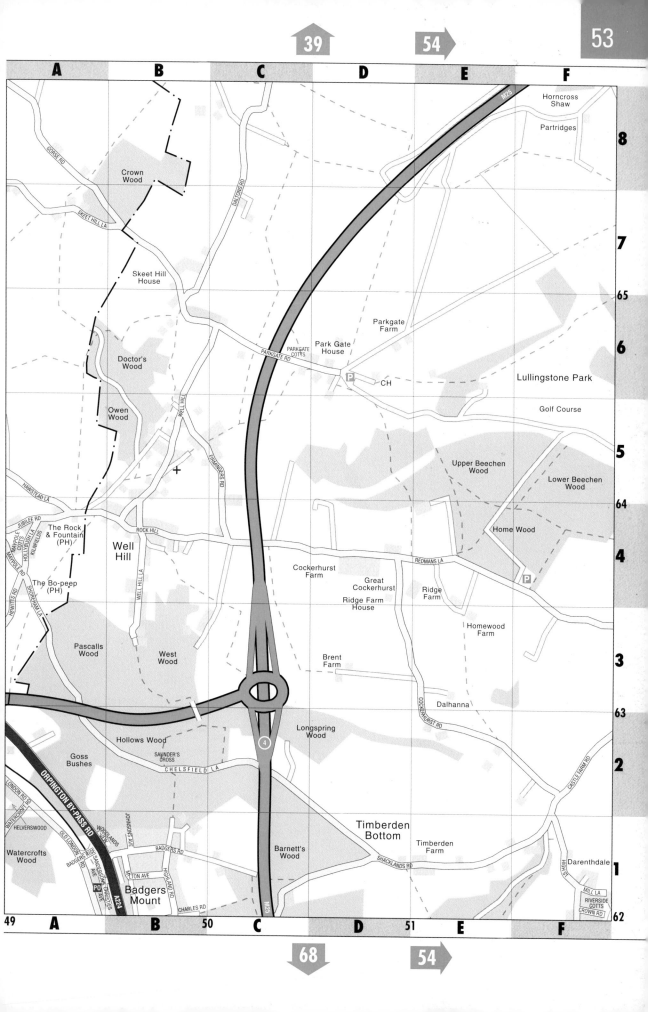

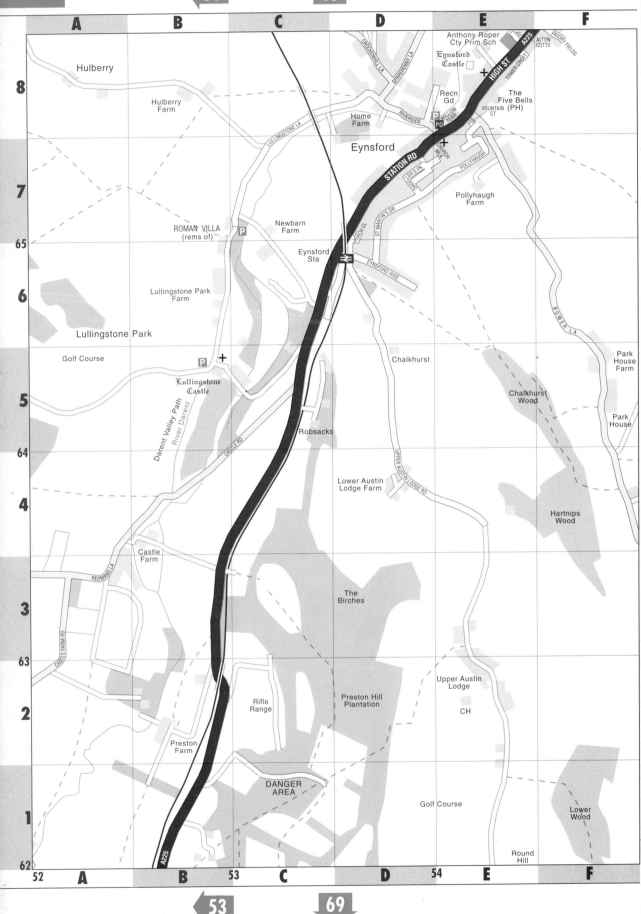

A B C D E F

BESSELS LA

Firpound
Shaw

DONKEY LA

A20

MAIN ROAD GORSE HILL

Alchin's
Wood

Lincoln
Kennels

8

Speedgate
Farm

MASSENDEN LA

GABRIEL SPRING RD

Gabrielspring
Wood

M20

GABRIEL SPRING ROAD (EAST)

Speed
Gate

THREE GATES RD

Olivers
Shaw

Gorse Hill
Farm

SCRATCHERS LA

7

65

M20

MAPLESCOMBE LA

COLIN CHAPMAN WAY

6

Hotel

Brands Hatch
Circuit

Lower Park
Wood

Kingsdown
Farm

Grove
Wood

5

Maplescombe

Adder Bank
Shaw

Maplescombe
Farm

SYMONDS
CL

GILLIES RD

NEAL RD

VIKING WK

64

Bower Park
Farm

BLUE CHALET
IND PK

MILLFIELD RD

KLPS CL

STACKLANDS
CL

SHERBOS

RNE CL

OAKLANDS
CL

LOVELACE
CL

HEVER AVE

REGE

NCY CL

4

HEVER RD

PO
P

WESTFIELD
COTTS

BOTSOM LA

MILKFIELD RD

FLORENCE FARM
MOBILE HOME PK

THE BRIARS

MULTON RD

WELLS CL

ASTOR

PENSHURST
RD

WHITEGATES
AVE

WOOD VIEW
CL

HEVER WOOD RD

Church
Wood

Hog
Wood

KNATTS VALLEY RD

Sidehilly
Wood

CLEARWAYS
BSNS EST

LONDON RD

MITCHEM CL

CHANCEL
CL

ROVING

3

RUSHETTS RD

KINGSFISHER

BAKERS

SOUTHFIELDS RD

WAYLAND RD

63

KINGSFIELD
CL

Liby

LET

ASH TREE DR

3

THE

BLACKTHORN

THE GRANGE

SPARROW CL

High Castle
Wood

The Gamecock
(PH)

WEST
KINGSDOWN
IND EST

2

KINGSFIELD RD

1

2

A20

MEADOW BANK CL 1
POUND BANK CL 2
BIRCHWAY 3

ASHEN GROVE RD

CHERRY TREE GR

East Hill

EAST HILL RD

KNATTS VALLEY RD

West Kingsdown

SCHOOL LA

1

Knatts Valley

THE GROVE

Caravan
Pk

Stacklands
Wood

62

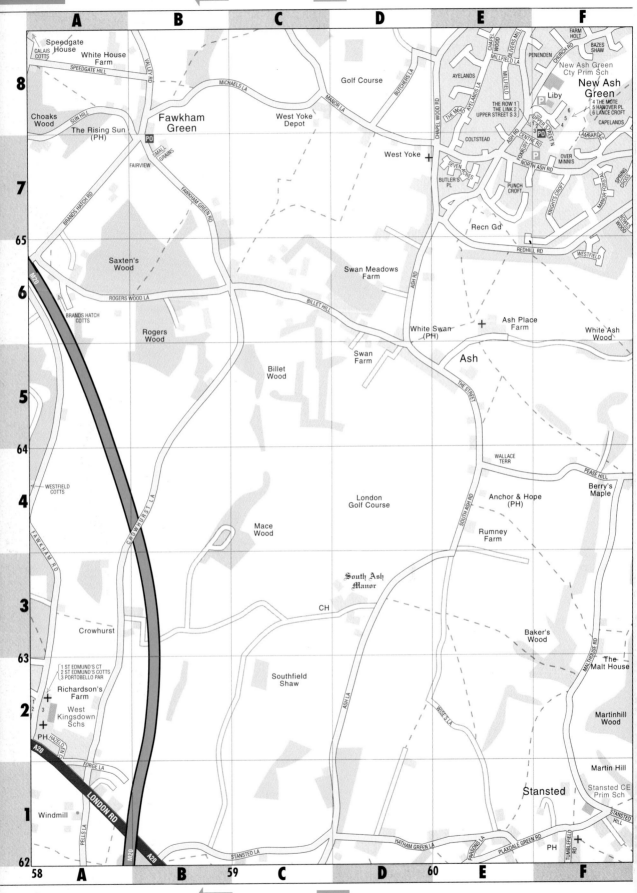

A   B   C   D   E   F

Speedgate
House
CALAIS
COTTS
White House
Farm
SPEEDGATE HILL
VALLEY RD
MICHAELS LA
Golf Course
BUTCHERS LA
CHAPEL WOOD RD
FARM
HOLT
PENENDEN
BAZES
SHAW
MILLFIELD LA
OLIVERS MILL
CHURCH RD
New Ash Green
Cty Prim Sch
AYELANDS
AYELANDS LA
MILLFIELD
New Ash
Green
8
Choaks
Wood
SUN HILL
The Rising Sun
(PH)
Fawkham
Green
West Yoke
Depot
MANOR LA
THE MEAD
Liby
THE ROW 1
THE LINK 2
UPPER STREET S 3
4 THE MOTE
5 HANOVER PL
6 LANCE CROFT
6
5
4
PO
FAIRVIEW
SMALL
GRAINS
West Yoke
COLTSTEAD
ASH RD
FOXBURY
CENTRE RD
UPPER S STREET N
3 PO
NORTH ASH RD
OVER
MINNIS
CAPELANDS
LAMBARDES
7
FAWKHAM GREEN RD
BRANDS HATCH RD
SEVEN
ACRES
BUTLER'S
PL
PUNCH
CROFT
KNIGHTS CROFT
TALISFER FORD RD
MANOR FORTH RD
SPRING
CROSS
BOW'S
WOOD
65
Saxten's
Wood
Recn Gd
REDHILL RD
WESTFIELD
6
M20
BRANDS HATCH
COTTS
ROGERS WOOD LA
Rogers
Wood
BILLET HILL
Swan Meadows
Farm
ASH RD
White Swan
(PH)
Ash Place
Farm
White Ash
Wood
Billet
Wood
Swan
Farm
Ash
THE STREET
5
64
WALLACE
TERR
PEASE HILL
Berry's
Maple
CROWHURST LA
4
WESTFIELD
COTTS
London
Golf Course
Anchor & Hope
(PH)
SOUTH ASH RD
Mace
Wood
Rumney
Farm
FAWKHAM RD
South Ash
Manor
CH
Baker's
Wood
MALTHOUSE RD
The
Malt House
3
Crowhurst
63
1 ST EDMUND'S CT
2 ST EDMUND'S COTTS
3 PORTOBELLO PAR
Southfield
Shaw
ASH LA
Martinhill
Wood
Richardson's
Farm
2 3
West
Kingsdown
Schs
WISS'S LA
2
PH
HAZELD
A20
Martin Hill
Stansted CE
Prim Sch
Martin Hill
Stansted
FORGE LA
LONDON RD
PELLS LA
M20
A20
STANSTED LA
HATHAM GREEN LA
PARSONS LA
PLAXDALE GREEN RD
TUMBLEFIELD RD
PH
STANSTED
HILL
Windmill
1
62

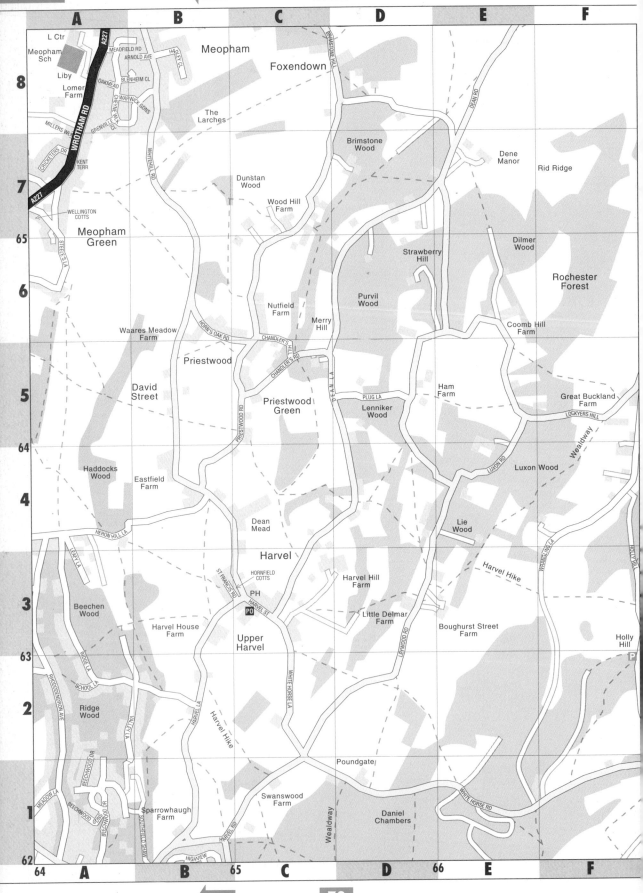

A   B   C   D   E   F

8

7

65

6

5

64

4

3

63

2

1

62

64   A   B   65   C   D   66   E   F

Meopham

Foxendown

L Ctr
Meopham
Sch
Liby
Lomer
Farm
MEADFIELD RD
ARNOLD AVE
ILKLEY CL
BLENHEIM CL
OAKMEAD
WARWICK GDNS
CHEYNE WLK
GRENVILLE CL
WROTHAM RD
A227
MILLERS WK
KENT TERR
CRICKETERS DR
A227
WELLINGTON COTTS
WHITEHILL RD

The Larches

Brimstone
Wood

Dunstan
Wood

Dene
Manor

Rid Ridge

Wood Hill
Farm

Meopham
Green

STEELE'S LA

Strawberry
Hill

Dilmer
Wood

Rochester
Forest

Waares Meadow
Farm

Nutfield
Farm

Purvil
Wood

Merry
Hill

Coomb Hill
Farm

Priestwood

HORN'S OAK RD

CHANDLER'S HILL

CHANDLER'S RD

DEAN LA

David
Street

Priestwood
Green

PLUG LA

Lenniker
Wood

Ham
Farm

Great Buckland
Farm

LOCKYERS HILL

PRIESTWOOD RD

Haddocks
Wood

Eastfield
Farm

LUXON RD

Luxon Wood

Wealdway

Dean
Mead

Lie
Wood

HERON HILL LA

LEAY LA

Harvel

St Francis Rd

HORNFIELD
COTTS

Harvel Hill
Farm

Harvel Hike

WRANGLING LA

HOLLY HILL

Beechen
Wood

HORSE LA

SCHOOL LA

Harvel House
Farm

HARVEL LA

HARVEL ST

PH

PO

Upper
Harvel

Little Delmar
Farm

LEYWOOD RD

Boughurst Street
Farm

Holly
Hill

P

Ridge
Wood

RHODODENDRON AVE

BEECHWOOD DR

VALLEY LA

MEADOW LA

BEECHWOOD

BEECHWOOD DR

SOUTHFIELD SHAW

Sparrowhaugh
Farm

HARVEL RD

HIGHVIEW

WHITE HORSE LA

Swanswood
Farm

Wealdway

Poundgate

Daniel
Chambers

WHITE HORSE RD

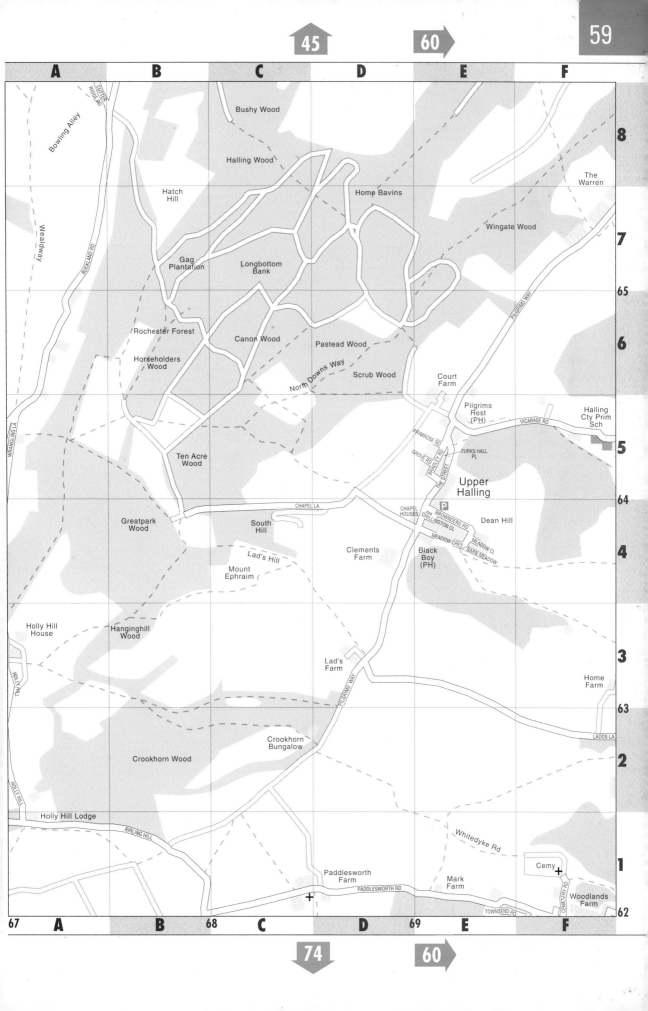

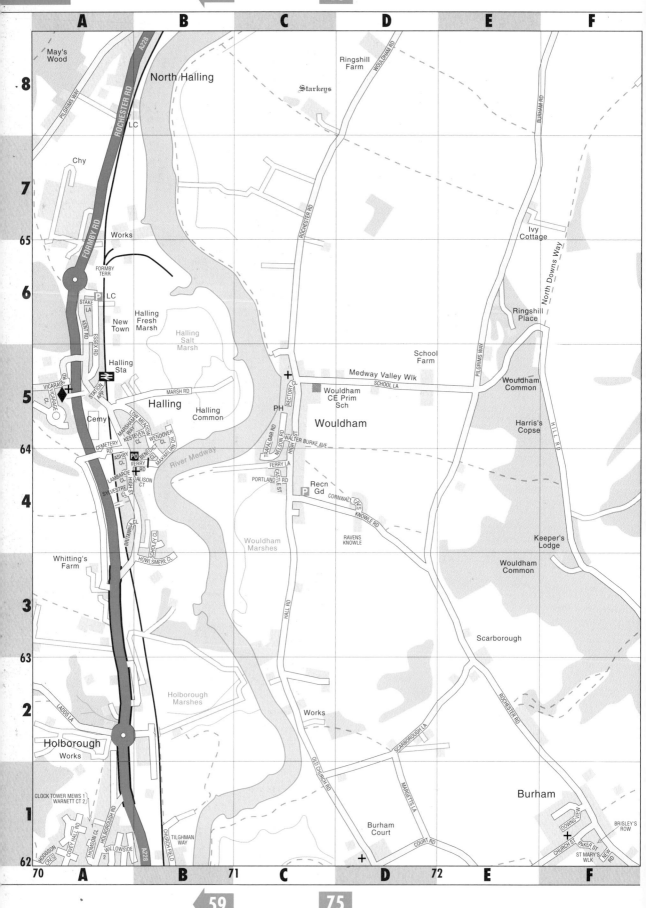

May's Wood

North Halling

Ringshill Farm

WOULDHAM RD

Starkeys

8

PILGRIMS WAY

ROCHESTER RD

A228

LC

Chy

BURHAM RD

7

Works

Ivy Cottage

65

North Downs Way

ROCHESTER RD

FORMBY TERR

6

P LC

STAKE LA

KENT RD

Ringshill Place

New Town

Halling Fresh Marsh

FORMBY RD

ESSEX RD

Halling Salt Marsh

PILGRIMS WAY

School Farm

Halling Sta

Medway Valley Wlk

SCHOOL LA

Wouldham Common

STATION APP

MARSH RD

VICARAGE RD

5

Halling

RECTORY CL

Wouldham CE Prim Sch

VICARAGE CL

Cemy

PH

Harris's Copse

CEMETERY RD

Halling Common

NELSON RD

Wouldham

HILL RD

LOW MEADOW

MARSHAM WAY

KESTEVEN CL

WENDOVER CL

64

ASHBY CL

BENEDICT CL

MAXIMILIAN RD

TRAFALGAR RD

HIGH ST

WALTER BURKE AVE

PO

FERRY RD

DALISON CT

River Medway

FERRY LA

LAMBARDE CL

SYLVESTRE CL

CASTLE ST

4

HIGH ST

PORTLAND RD

Recn Gd

P

CORNWALL GDNS

Keeper's Lodge

BRITANNIA CL

SCHOOL RD

Wouldham Marshes

KNOWLE RD

RAVENS KNOWLE

Wouldham Common

Whitting's Farm

HOWLSMERE CL

3

HALL RD

Scarborough

63

Holborough Marshes

ROCHESTER RD

2

Works

LADDS LA

Holborough

SCARBOROUGH LA

OLD CHURCH RD

Works

MARGETTS LA

Burham

DOWNS VIEW

CLOCK TOWER MEWS 1
WARNETT CT 2

HOLBOROUGH RD

BRISLEY'S ROW

1

BAKER ST

HODGSON CRES

COVEY HALL RD

THOMSON CL

WILLOWSIDE

A228

TILGHMAN WAY

CHURCH FIELD

Burham Court

COURT RD

CHURCH ST

ST MARY'S WLK

NEW RD

62

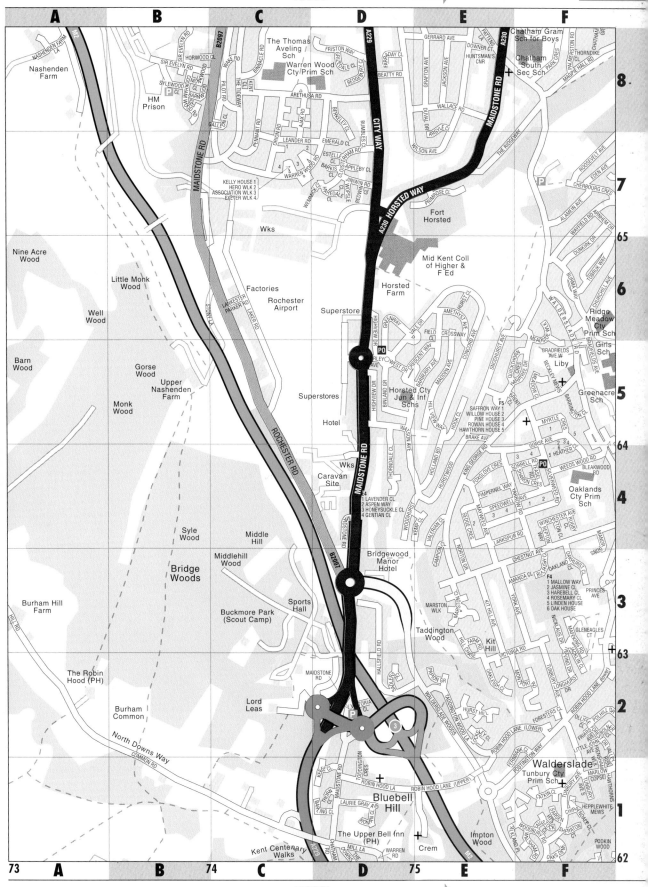

A B C D E F

Nashenden Farm

Nashenden Farm La

Nine Acre Wood

Well Wood

Barn Wood

Monk Wood

Little Monk Wood

Gorse Wood

Upper Nashenden Farm

Syle Wood

Middle Hill

Bridge Woods

Middlehill Wood

Buckmore Park (Scout Camp)

Burham Hill Farm

The Robin Hood (PH)

Burham Common

North Downs Way

COMMON RD

Kent Centenary Walks

HM Prison

SIR EVELYN RD

HORWOOD CL

PILOT RD

THE TIDEWAY

SYLEWOOD CL

GALLI CL

MAIDSTONE RD

LANKESTER PARKER RD

LAKER RD

STONEY LA

ROCHESTER RD

MAIDSTONE RD

B2097

B2097

The Thomas Aveling Sch

Warren Wood Cty Prim Sch

Rochester Airport

Factories

Wks

Superstores

Hotel

Wks

Caravan Site

Sports Hall

Lord Leas

WAKE RD

KENT

BINNACLE RD

FRISTON WAY

GRICGLE CL

BEDGEBURY CL

ARETHUSA RD

PENNANT RD

ORION RD

LEANDER RD

ALAX RD

BERKELEY CL

EMERALD CL

ESTELLE RD

WARREN WOOD RD

BARKIS CL

APPLEBY CL

WESTMOR CL

HAREDALE CL

WIPSLE

JINIWIN RD

BEDWIN RD

KELLY HOUSE 1
HERO WLK 2
ASSOCIATION WLK 3
EXETER WLK 4

A229

CITY WAY

A230 HORSTED WAY

FARDAY CL

FRIDAY CL

BEATTY RD

BUMBLES CL

PRIMROSE CL

GERRARD AVE

GRAFTON AVE

JACKSON AVE

WALLACE RD

DIVAL RD

ARGYLE CL

WILSON AVE

DOWNER CL

HUNTSMAN'S CNR

PATTENS

MAIDSTONE RD

A230

Chatham Gram Sch for Boys

Chatham South Sec Sch

THE RIDGEWAY

Fort Horsted

Mid Kent Coll of Higher & F Ed

Horsted Farm

Superstore

Superstores

Horsted Cty Jun & Inf Schs

HIGHVIEW DR

BINLAND GR

WASON AVE

THORNDALE CL

WOODHURST

GREENWAY

WEST DR

VALE DR

FIELD

CROSSWAY

AMETHYST WAY

CRESCENT WAY

CONCORD AVE

BARBERRY CL

MADDEN AVE

TIL VIEW WAY

HOOK CL

HOLLAND RD

HURSTWOOD

KING GEORGE RD

FOXGLOVE CRES

PIMPERNEL WAY

SEDGE CRES

SPEEDWELL AVE

CAMPION CL

VALERIAN CL

MAYWEED AVE

LARKSPUR RD

WINCHESTER AVE

NORTON GR

KEMP CL

Bridgewood Manor Hotel

Taddington Wood

MARSTON WLK

Kit Hill

AMETHYST WAY

SMODHURST AVE

QUICKTHORN

MARPTREE DR

BECKLEY MEWS

MEADS

MYRTLE CRES

GORSE AVE

SORRELL CL

SILVERMEAD RD

TEASEL

SHARON CRES

CHESTNUT AVE

WALDERSLADE RD

BRADFIELDS AVE W

BRADFIELDS AVE

HEATHER CL

WEEDS WOOD RD

BLEAKWOOD RD

Liby

Oaklands Cty Prim Sch

Ridge Meadow Cty Prim Sch

Girls Sch

Greenacre Sch

EDEN AVE

CHERBOURG CRES

ROOSEVELT AVE

ALAMEIN AVE

WATFIELD RD

WINFIELD GR

DUNKIRK DR

TOBRUK WAY

BURMA WAY

CHURCHILL AVE

RIDGE WAY

BARRINGTON

RUGBY

OAKLAND DR

BLACKDALE CL

AMANDA CL

DARHURST CL

MANOR

SNODS

MALLOW WAY

JASMINE CL

HAREBELL CL

ROSEMARY CL

LINDEN HOUSE

OAK HOUSE

F4

F5

SAFFRON WAY 1
WILLOW HOUSE 2
PINE HOUSE 3
ROWAN HOUSE 4
HAWTHORN HOUSE 5

LAVENDER CL 1
ASPEN WAY 2
HONEYSUCKLE CL 3
GENTIAN CL 4

BRAKE AVE

FARM

REPTON

YARROW RD

YARROW AVE

MAGPIE HALL RD

PARK RD

THORNDIKE AVE

CHATHAM

PALMERSTON RD

KIT HILL AVE

YORK AVE

FARM HILL AVE

KIT HILL

FARM HILL

VICTORIA RD

GLENEAGLES CT

NICHOLAS DR

PRINCES AVE

OLLIFFE CL

POLHILL CL

AVEY

LITTLE JOHN AVE

DALEHAM CL

VALLEY

TUNBURY AVE

MARLOW COPSE

HEPPLEWHITE MEWS

Walderslade

Tunbury Cty Prim Sch

Bluebell Hill

MAIDSTONE RD

VICTORIA CRES

KEFE CL

TODDINGTON CRES

THORN CL

BARTING CL

LAURIE GRAY AVE

ROBIN HOOD LA

ROBIN HOOD LANE (LOWER)

ROBIN HOOD LANE (UPPER)

HALLSFIELD RD

SIDLEY RD

PAPION GR

OAKLEIGH CL

MONKTON

TUNBURY AVE

LONGHURST DR

HURST HILL

FOSTINGTON WAY

WALDERSCADE WOODS LA

FORESTERS CL

FRANKBANK CL

PADDINGTON WOOD LA

TRENOWETH

MAIDSTONE RD

The Upper Bell Inn (PH)

Crem

Impton Wood

WARREN RD

MILL LA

CHATHAM RD

A229

M2

Crem

PODKIN WOOD

CATKIN CL

WOODBURY RD

CHIP PANDAM

TUNBURY AVE

SHERATON

HAWTHORNS

8

7

65

6

5

64

4

63

3

2

62

1

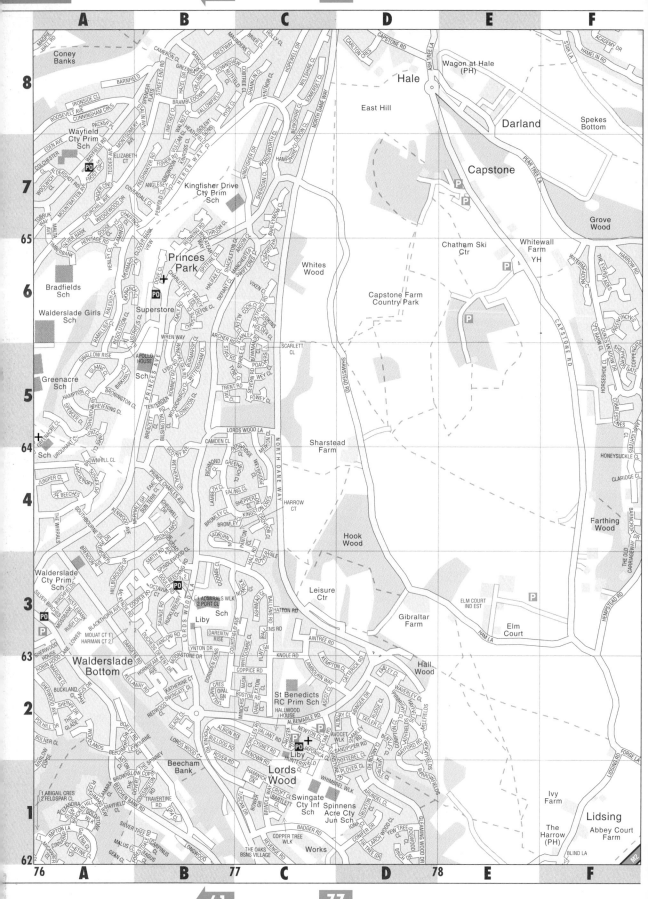

A B C D E F

8

Coney Banks

Hale

Wagon at Hale (PH)

East Hill

Darland

Spekes Bottom

7

Wayfield Cty Prim Sch

Capstone

Kingfisher Drive Cty Prim Sch

Grove Wood

65

Chatham Ski Ctr

Whitewall Farm YH

6

Bradfields Sch

Princes Park

Whites Wood

Capstone Farm Country Park

Walderslade Girls Sch

Superstore

5

Greenacre Sch

Apollo House Sch

Scarlett CL

Sharstead Farm

64

Sch

Honeysuckle CL

Claridge CL

4

Harrow Ct

Farthing Wood

Hook Wood

3

Walderslade Cty Prim Sch

Liby

Sch

Leisure Ctr

Gibraltar Farm

Elm Court Ind Est

Elm Court

63

Sherwood House

Walderslade Bottom

Hall Wood

2

St Benedicts RC Prim Sch

Hallwood House

Liby

Beecham Bank

Lords Wood

Ivy Farm

Lidsing

Abbey Court Farm

1

1 Abigail Cres 2 Feldspar CL

Swingate Cty Inf Sch

Spinnens Acre Cty Jun Sch

The Harrow (PH)

The Oaks Bsns Village

Works

Blind La

62

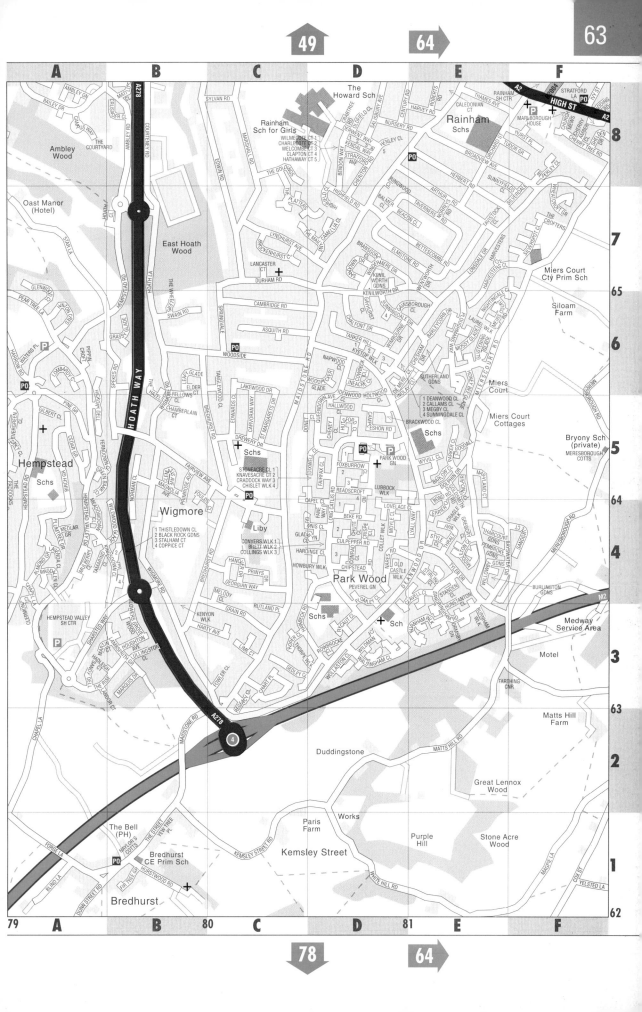

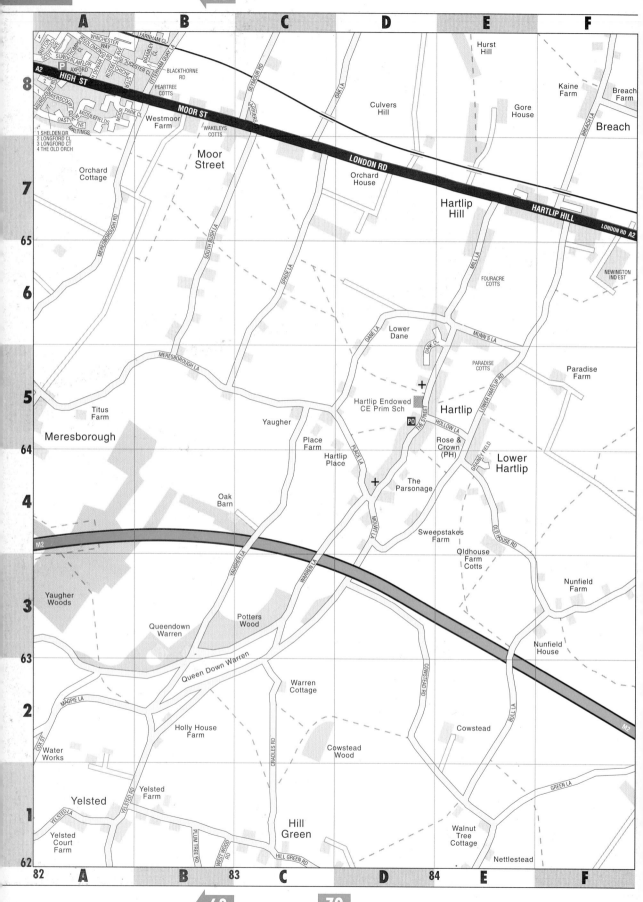

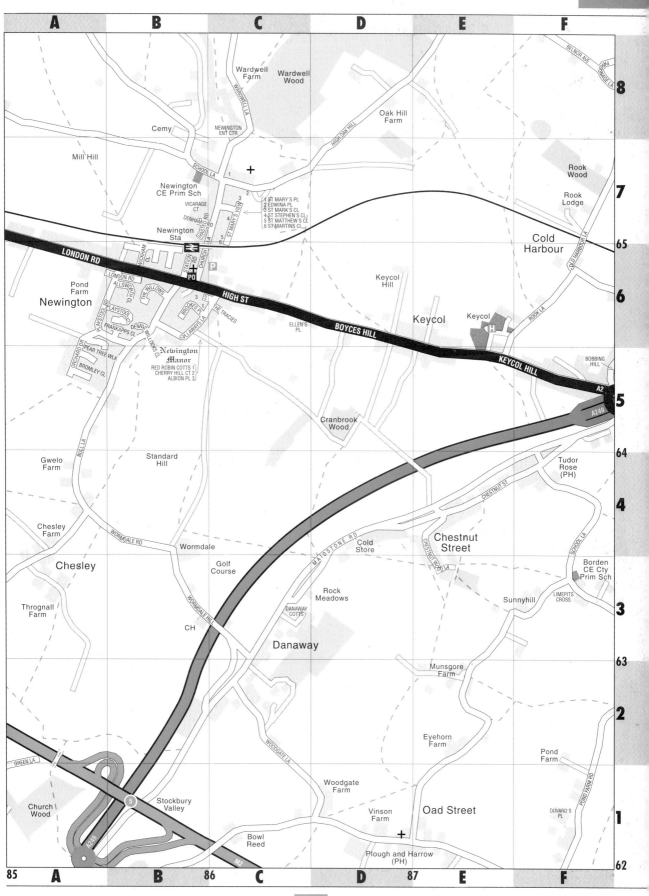

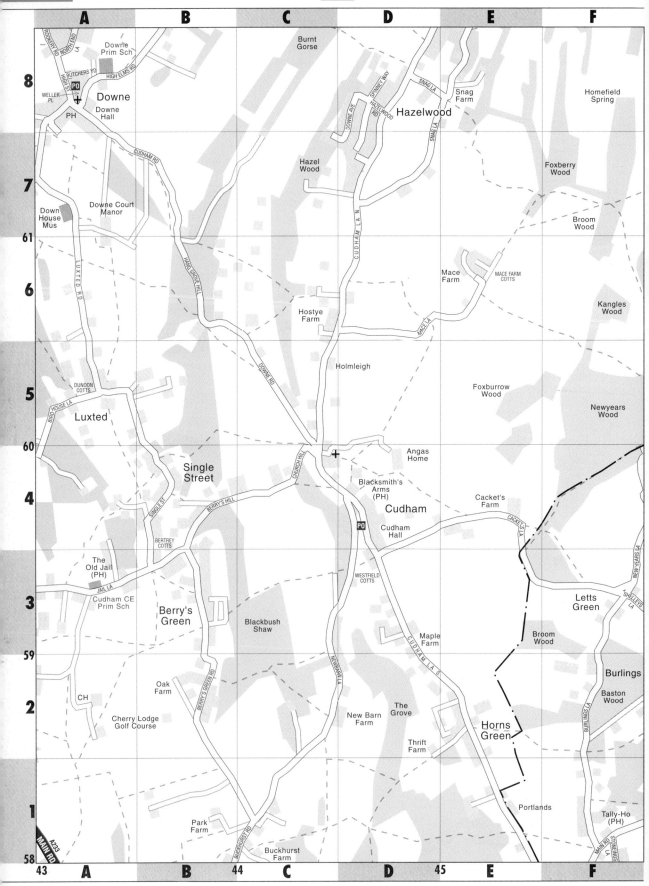

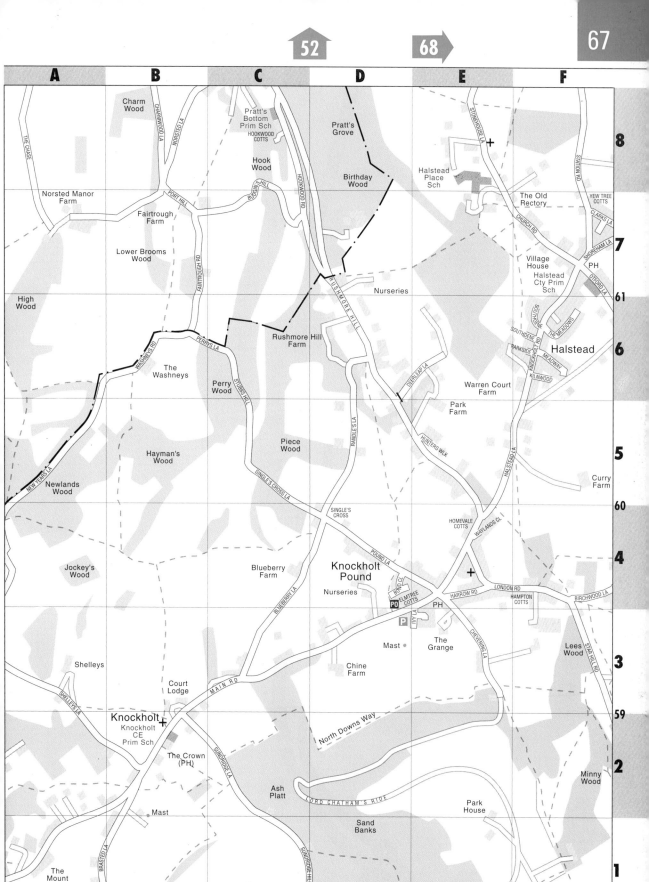

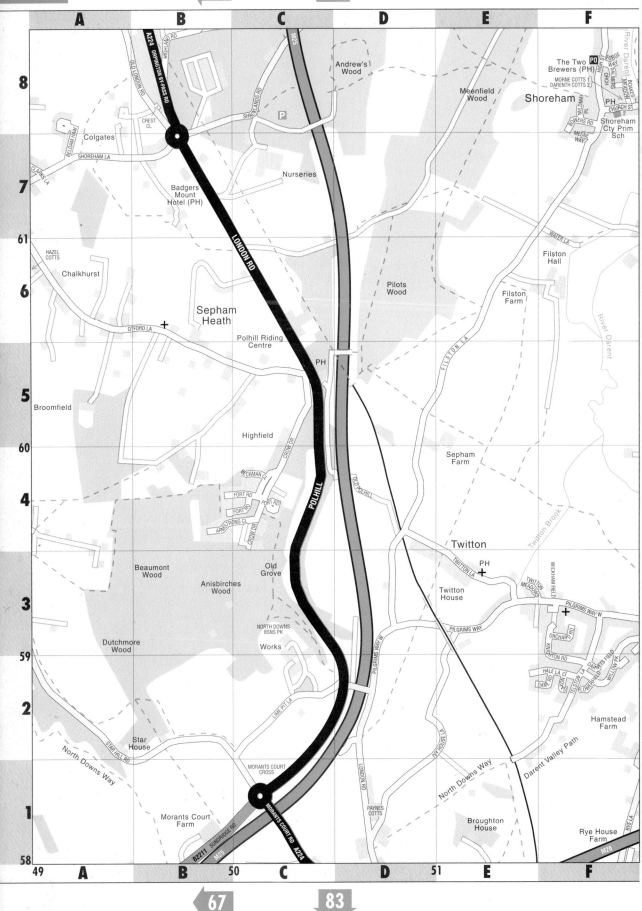

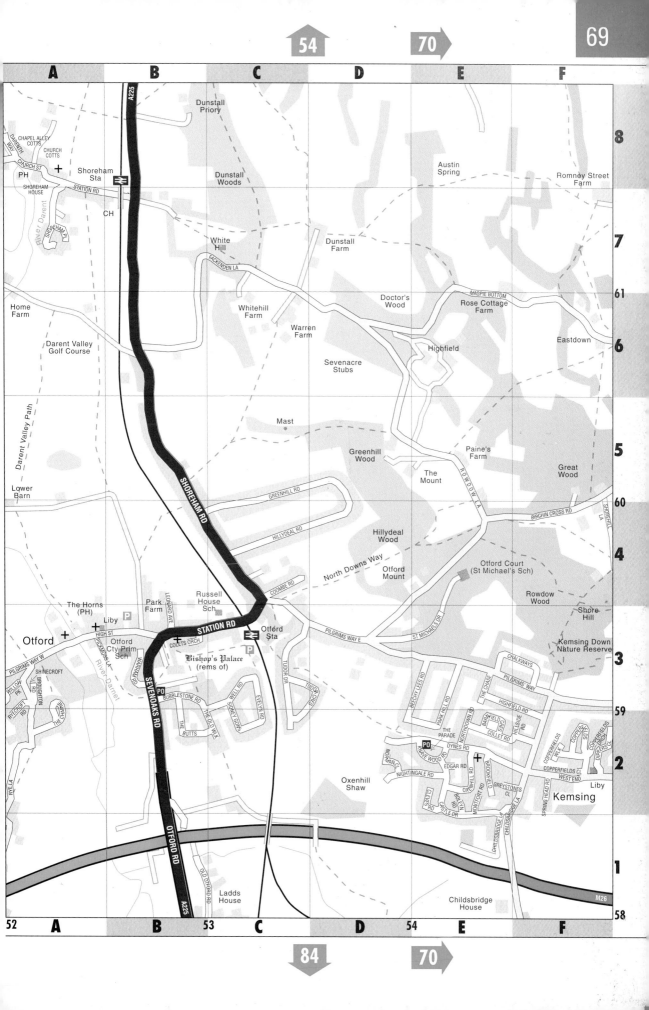

A B C D E F

8

7

61

6

5

60

4

3

59

2

1

58

Dunstall Priory

Dunstall Woods

CHAPEL ALLEY COTTS
DARENTH WAY
CHURCH COTTS
CHURCH ST
PH
SHOREHAM HOUSE
Shoreham Sta
STATION RD
CH
SHOREHAM PL
River Darent

White Hill

FACKENDEN LA

Dunstall Farm

Austin Spring

Romney Street Farm

Home Farm

Whitehill Farm

Warren Farm

Doctor's Wood

Rose Cottage Farm

MAGPIE BOTTOM

Eastdown

Darent Valley Golf Course

Sevenacre Stubs

Highfield

Darent Valley Path

SHOREHAM RD

Mast

Greenhill Wood

Paine's Farm

Great Wood

Lower Barn

GREENHILL RD

HILLYDEAL RD

The Mount

ROWDOW LA

Hillydeal Wood

BIRCHIN CROSS RD

SHOREHILL LA

North Downs Way

Otford Mount

Otford Court (St Michael's Sch)

Rowdow Wood

Shore Hill

COOMBE RD

The Horns (PH)
Park Farm
LEONARD AVE
Russell House Sch
STATION RD
Otford Sta
PILGRIMS WAY E
ST MICHAELS DR

Kemsing Down Nature Reserve

Otford
Liby
HIGH ST
Otford Cty Prim Sch
COLETS ORCH
Bishop's Palace (rems of)

PILGRIMS WAY W
SHINECROFT
WARHAM RD
SEVENOAKS RD
PO
BUBBLESTONE RD
WELL RD
SIDNEY GDNS
TUDOR DR
TUDOR CRES

CHALKWAYS
PILGRIMS WAY
BEECH LEES RD
PARK HILL RD
THE CHASE
BARFIELD
HIGHFIELD RD
HILLSIDE RD
COPPERFIELDS

WILLOW PK
RYECROFT RD
BROUGHTON RD
THE CHASE
RYE LA
THE BUTTS
THE OLD WLK

River Darent

THE PARADE
PO
KNAVE WOOD
DYNES RD
WORTHINGTON RD
COLLET RD

NIGHTINGALE RD
EDGAR RD
BROOKFIELD
GREYSTONES CL

COPPERFIELDS WY
COPPERFIELDS CL
WEST END
Liby

Kemsing

Oxenhill Shaw

OTFORD RD
OLD OTFORD RD
A225
Ladds House

OXENHILL RD
BOLEYN CL
CLELANDS RD
CASTLE DR
MOUNTFORT RD
CHITTISBRIDGE LA
CHILDSBRIDGE LA
SPRING HEAD RD

Childsbridge House

M26

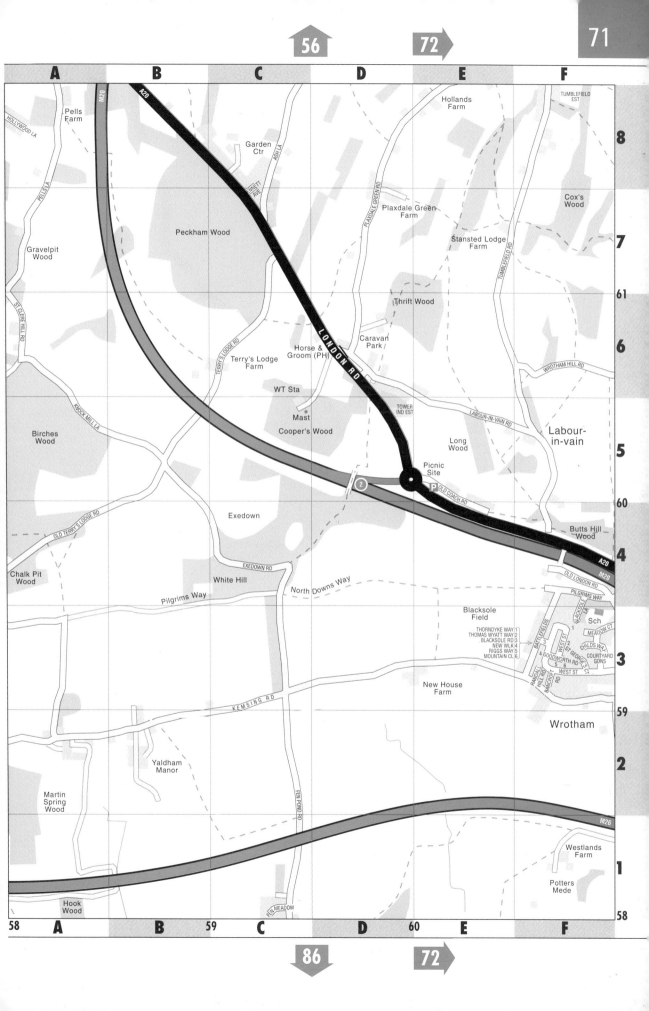

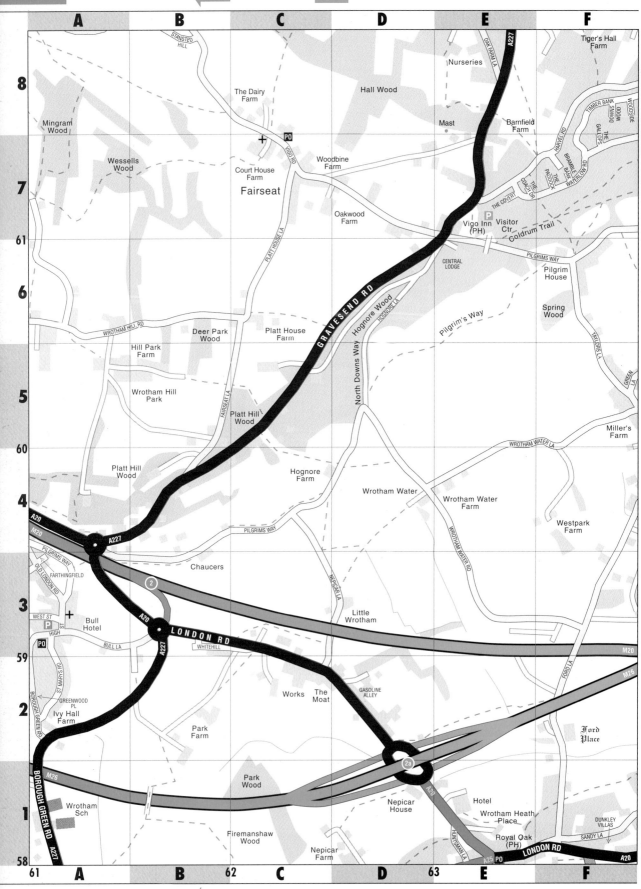

A   B   C   D   E   F

8

Tiger's Hall Farm

Nurseries

Mingram Wood

The Dairy Farm

Hall Wood

Mast

Barnfield Farm

TIMBER BANK

WOODSIDE

LOOM SHAW

THE GALLOPS

7

Wessells Wood

Court House Farm

Fairseat

Woodbine Farm

THE CONDUCTOR

BRAMBLE BANK

THE PADDOCK

WATERLOW

OLD

61

Oakwood Farm

Vigo Inn (PH)

Visitor Ctr

Coldrum Trail

PILGRIMS WAY

Pilgrim House

6

WROTHAM HILL RD

Deer Park Wood

Platt House Farm

GRAVESEND RD

Hognore Wood

HOGNORE LA

CENTRAL LODGE

Pilgrim's Way

PILGRIMS WAY

Spring Wood

TAYLORS LA

GREEN LA

Hill Park Farm

5

Wrotham Hill Park

FAIRSEAT LA

Platt House LA

Platt Hill Wood

North Downs Way

Miller's Farm

60

WROTHAM WATER LA

Platt Hill Wood

Hognore Farm

Wrotham Water

Wrotham Water Farm

Westpark Farm

4

A20

M20

A227

Chaucers

PILGRIMS WAY

WROTHAM WATER RD

3

PILGRIMS WAY

OLD LONDON RD

FARTHINGFIELD

A20

2

LONDON RD

A227

WHITEHILL

Little Wrotham

NEPICAR LA

M20

FORD LA

M26

WEST ST

HIGH ST

Bull Hotel

BULL LA

PO

59

Works

The Moat

GASOLINE ALLEY

ST MARYS RD

BOROUGH GREEN RD

GREENWOOD PL

Ivy Hall Farm

2

Park Farm

Park Wood

Nepicar House

2a

A20

Ford Place

Hotel

Wrotham Heath Place

DUNKLEY VILLAS

M26

BOROUGH GREEN RD

A227

Wrotham Sch

1

Firemanshaw Wood

Nepicar Farm

Royal Oak (PH)

HUNTSMAN LA

A25

PO

SANDY LA

LONDON RD

A20

58

61   A   B   62   C   D   63   E   F

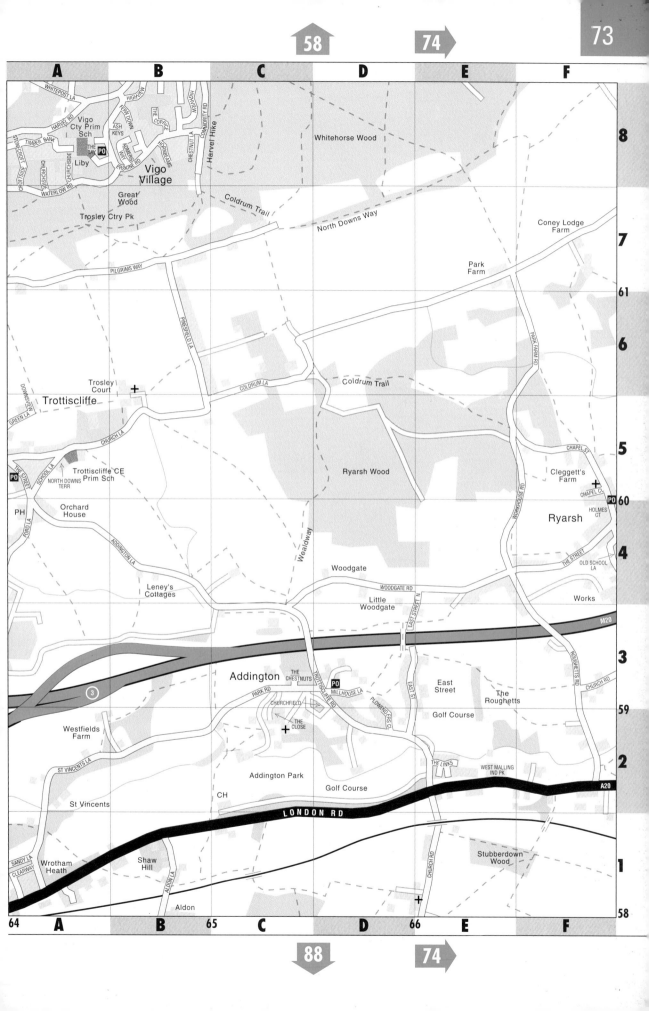

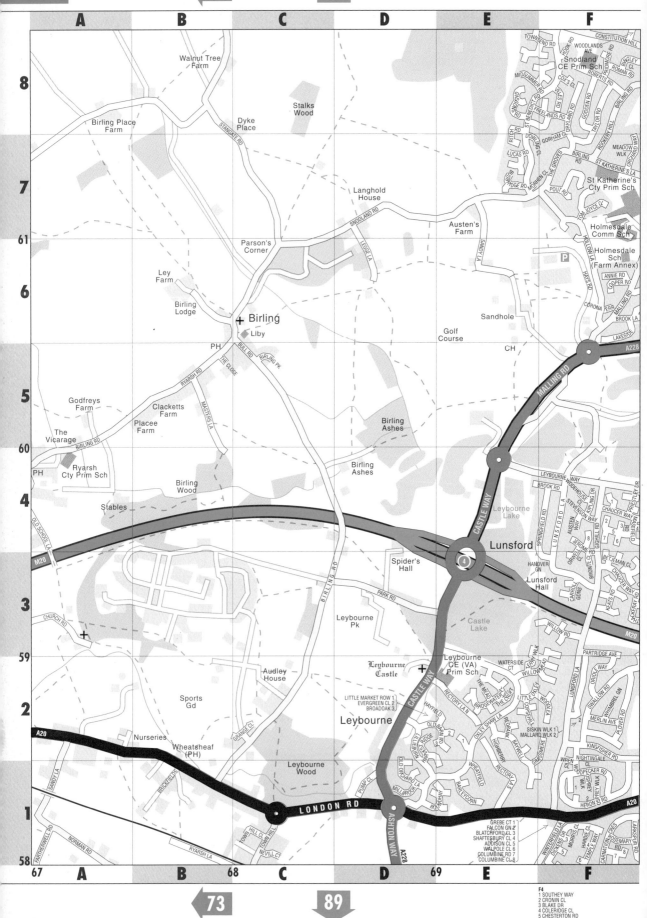

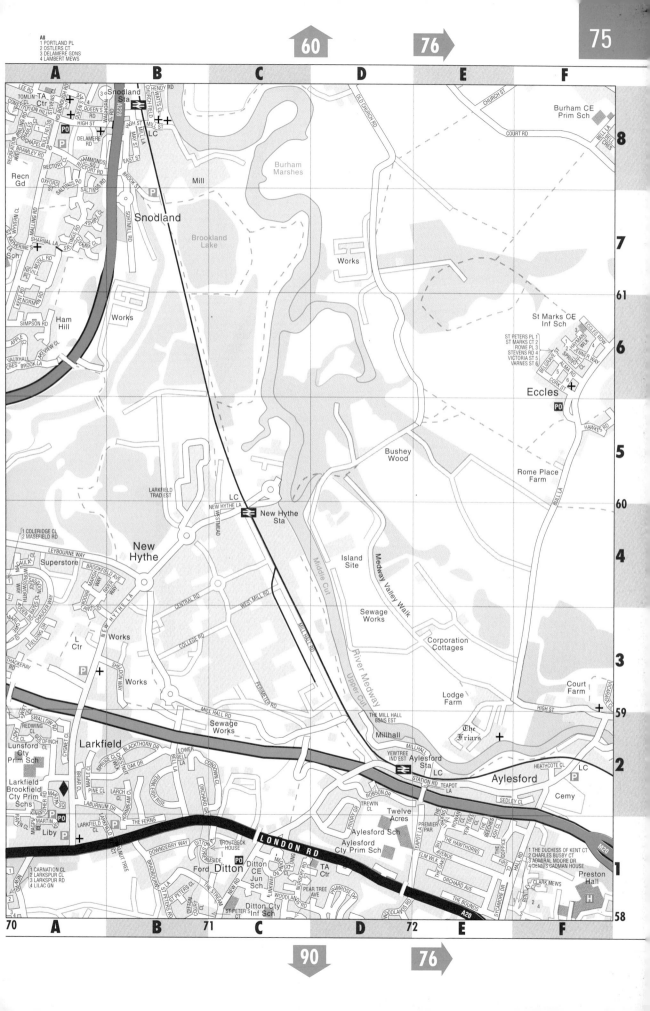

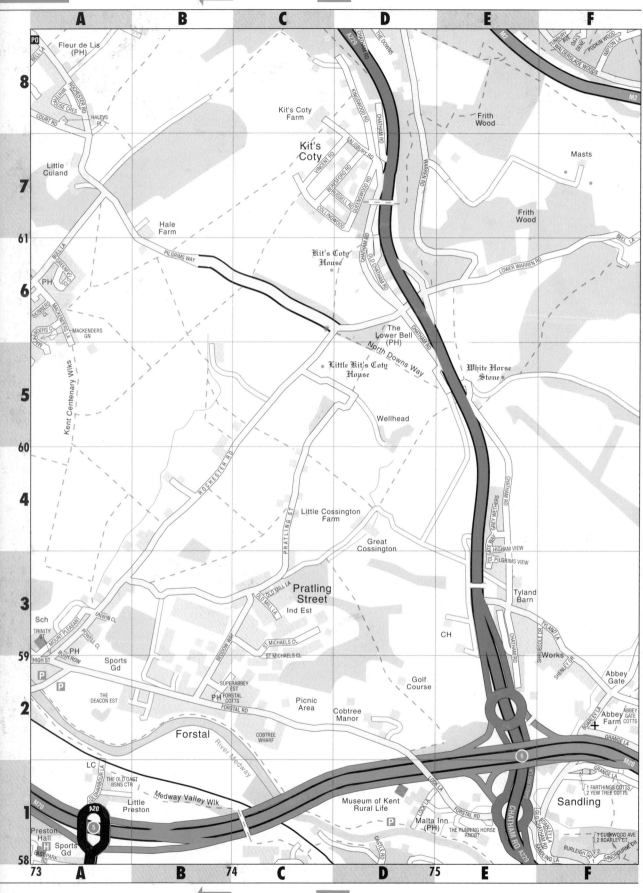

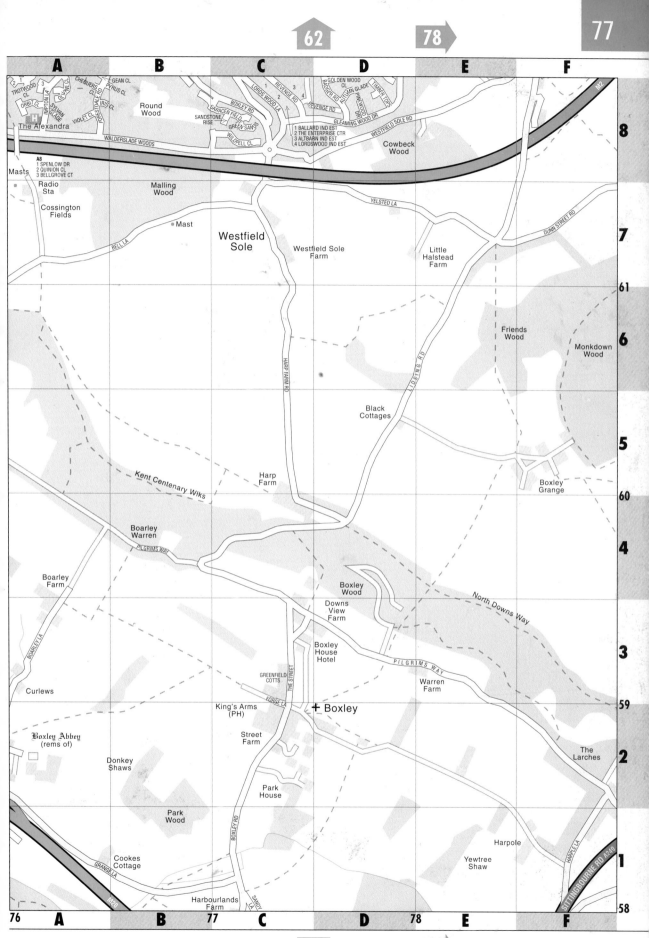

M2

Round
Wood

The Alexandra

A8
1 SPENLOW DR
2 QUINION CL
3 BELLGROVE CT

Masts

Radio
Sta

Cossington
Fields

Malling
Wood

Mast

Westfield
Sole

Westfield Sole
Farm

Little
Halstead
Farm

YELSTED LA

DUNN STREET RD

HARP FARM RD

LIDSING RD

Friends
Wood

Monkdown
Wood

Black
Cottages

Kent Centenary Wlks

Harp
Farm

Boxley
Grange

BELL LA

Boarley
Warren

PILGRIMS WAY

Boarley
Farm

BOARLEY LA

Curlews

Boxley
Wood

Downs
View Farm

North Downs Way

Boxley
House
Hotel

PILGRIMS WAY

Warren
Farm

GREENFIELD
COTTS

THE STREET

FORGE LA

King's Arms
(PH)

+ Boxley

Boxley Abbey
(rems of)

Street
Farm

Donkey
Shaws

The
Larches

Park
House

Park
Wood

BOXLEY RD

Harpole

Yewtree
Shaw

HARPLE LA

SITTINGBOURNE RD A249

M20

GRANGE LA

Cookes
Cottage

Harbourlands
Farm

SANDY LA

WALDERSLADE WOODS

TROTWOOD CL
ORBIT CL
IMPTON LA
SYLVAN
VILLAGE
ARTHSDALE RD
VIOLET CL
CHEQUERS CL
GEAN CL
PYRUS CL
IRIS CL
SANDSTONE
RISE
SARACEN FIELDS
GREEN SANDS
WILDFELL CL
BOXLEY RD
LORDS WOOD LA
REVENGE RD
REVENGE RD
GOLDEN WOOD
CL
BADGER RD
AUTUMN GLADE
PINEWOOD
DR
TIMBER TOPS
GLEAMING WOOD DR
WESTFIELD SOLE RD

1 BALLARD IND EST
2 THE ENTERPRISE CTR
3 ALTBARN IND EST
4 LORDSWOOD IND EST

Cowbeck
Wood

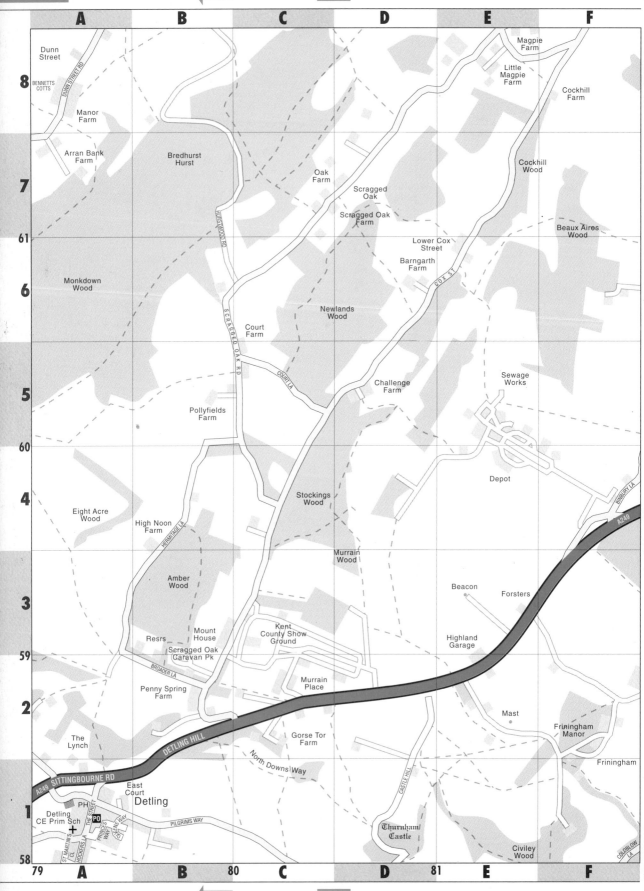

A B C D E F

8

7

61

6

5

60

4

3

59

2

1

58

Dunn
Street

BENNETTS
COTTS

DUNN STREET RD

Manor
Farm

Arran Bank
Farm

Monkdown
Wood

Eight Acre
Wood

High Noon
Farm

HERMITAGE LA

Amber
Wood

Resrs

Mount
House

Scragged Oak
Caravan Pk

BROADER LA

Penny Spring
Farm

The
Lynch

SITTINGBOURNE RD

A249

DETLING HILL

East
Court

Detling

PH

PD

ST MARTIN'S CL

HOCKERS LA

THE STREET

PRINCES WAY

DESERT WAY

Detling
CE Prim Sch

PILGRIMS WAY

Bredhurst
Hurst

HURSTWOOD RD

SCRAGGED OAK RD

Court
Farm

COURT LA

Pollyfields
Farm

North Downs Way

Kent
County Show
Ground

Murrain
Place

Gorse Tor
Farm

Oak
Farm

Scragged
Oak

Scragged Oak
Farm

Newlands
Wood

Stockings
Wood

Murrain
Wood

Challenge
Farm

Lower Cox
Street

Barngarth
Farm

COX ST

Beacon

Forsters

Highland
Garage

Mast

CASTLE HILL

Thurnham
Castle

Magpie
Farm

Little
Magpie
Farm

Cockhill
Wood

Beaux Aires
Wood

Cockhill
Farm

Sewage
Works

Depot

BINBURY LA

A249

Friningham
Manor

Friningham

Civiley
Wood

COLDBLOW LA

79 A 80 B C 81 D E F

A B C D E F

HILL GREEN RD
NORTHDOWN
BULL LA
CHURCH LA
Plum Tree Farm
PLUM TREE RD
PO PH
HARROW CT
SHRUB CT
Stockbury
Church Farm
HONEYCROCK HILL
AMES HILL
8

WEST WOOD RD
West Wood
Parsonage Farm
CHURCH HILL
A249
YELSTED RD
Four Oaks
Appsmoor Farm
South Street
Beaux Aires House
SOUTH STREET RD
Hillside Farm
7
61

Maple House
Hove Cottage
Steppes Hill Farm
Steps Hill Wood (Nature Reserve)
PH
SOUTH GREEN LA
Beaux Aires Farm
CHALKY RD
STEPS HILL RD
Squirrels Farm
Keepers Cottage
HAYES LA
6

Hall Wood
BIMBURY LA
Longreach Wood
Squirrel Wood
5

Bimbury Cottages
Ballingdane
60

RUMSTEAD LA
Rumsted Court
RUMSTEAD RD
Yetnor Farm
OLD FORGE LA
4

Longton Wood
SOUTH LEES LA
Old Forge Farm
3

Appsfield
Cam Hill Farm
59

Friningham Farm
Little Budds Farm
Long Wood
South Leas Farm
2

COLDBLOW LA
COLDHARBOUR LA
PONDS FARM RD
Pond Farm
Hucking
CHURCH RD
Wireless Transmitting Station
1

Coldblow
Stanhope Farm
SCRAGGED OAK RD
BROAD STREET HILL
PH
58

82 A B 83 C D 84 E F

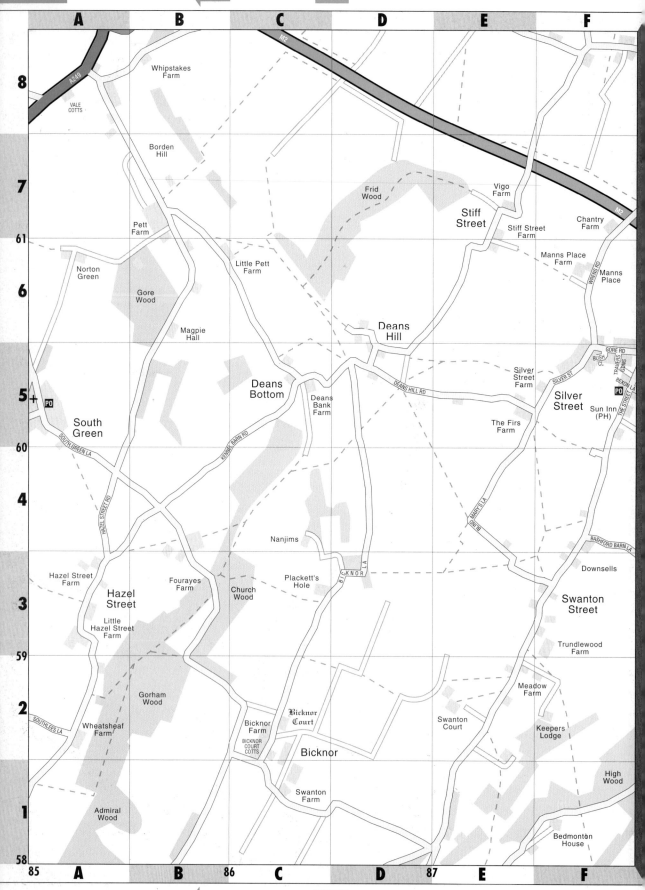

A   B   C   D   E   F

8

VALE
COTTS

Whipstakes
Farm

M2

Borden
Hill

7

Frid
Wood

Vigo
Farm

Stiff
Street

Chantry
Farm

Pett
Farm

Stiff Street
Farm

61

Manns Place
Farm

Manns
Place

Norton
Green

Little Pett
Farm

6

Gore
Wood

Deans
Hill

Magpie
Hall

Silver
Street
Farm

GORE RD
BUSH
CL

TRAVERS
GDNS

Silver
Street

BEXON LA

PO

Deans
Bottom

DEANS HILL RD

SILVER ST

5   +   PO

Deans
Bank
Farm

The Firs
Farm

Sun Inn
(PH)

South
Green

SOUTH GREEN LA

60

KENNEL BARN RD

4

HAZEL STREET RD

ST MARY'S LA

BICKNOR LA

BASHFORD BARN LA

Nanjims

Downsells

Hazel Street
Farm

Fourayes
Farm

Plackett's
Hole

3

Hazel
Street

Church
Wood

Swanton
Street

Little
Hazel Street
Farm

Trundlewood
Farm

59

Gorham
Wood

Meadow
Farm

2

SOUTHLEES LA

Wheatsheaf
Farm

Bicknor
Farm

Bicknor
Court

Swanton
Court

Keepers
Lodge

BICKNOR
COURT
COTTS

Bicknor

High
Wood

1

Admiral
Wood

Swanton
Farm

Bedmonton
House

58

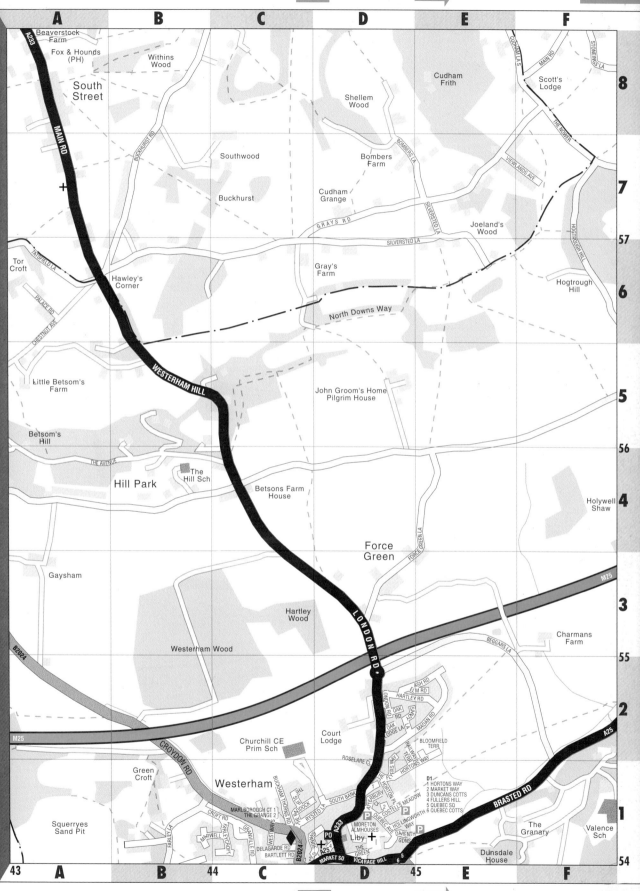

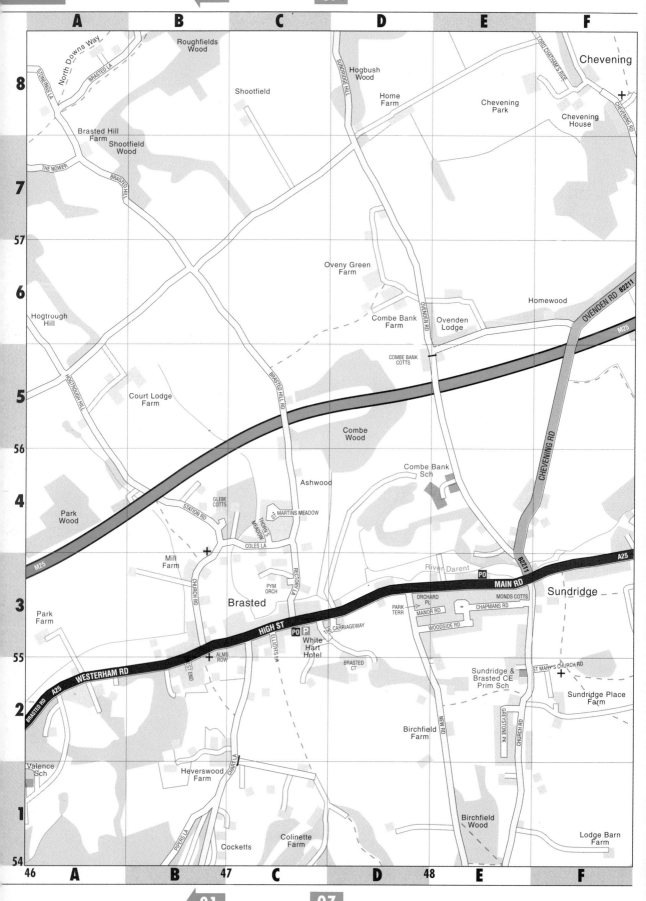

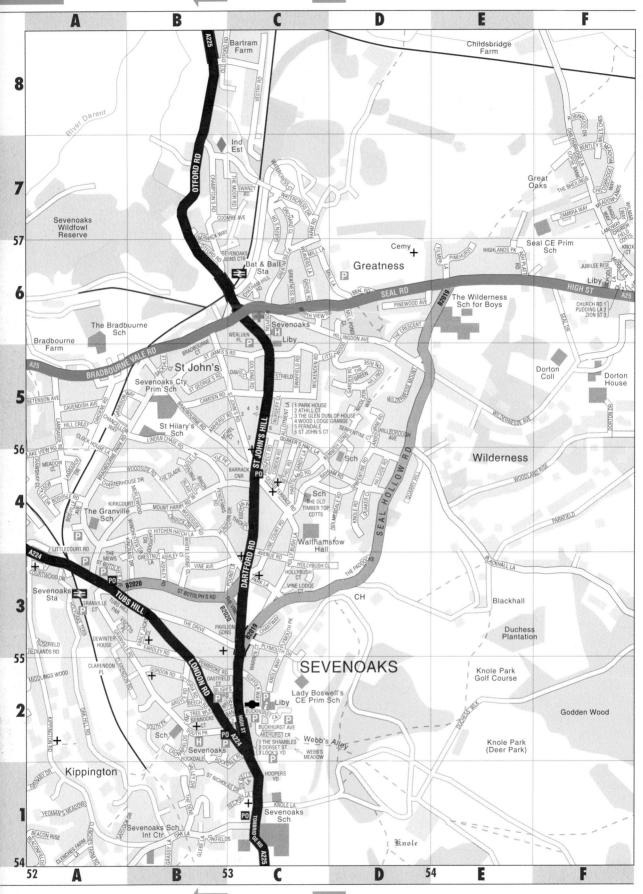

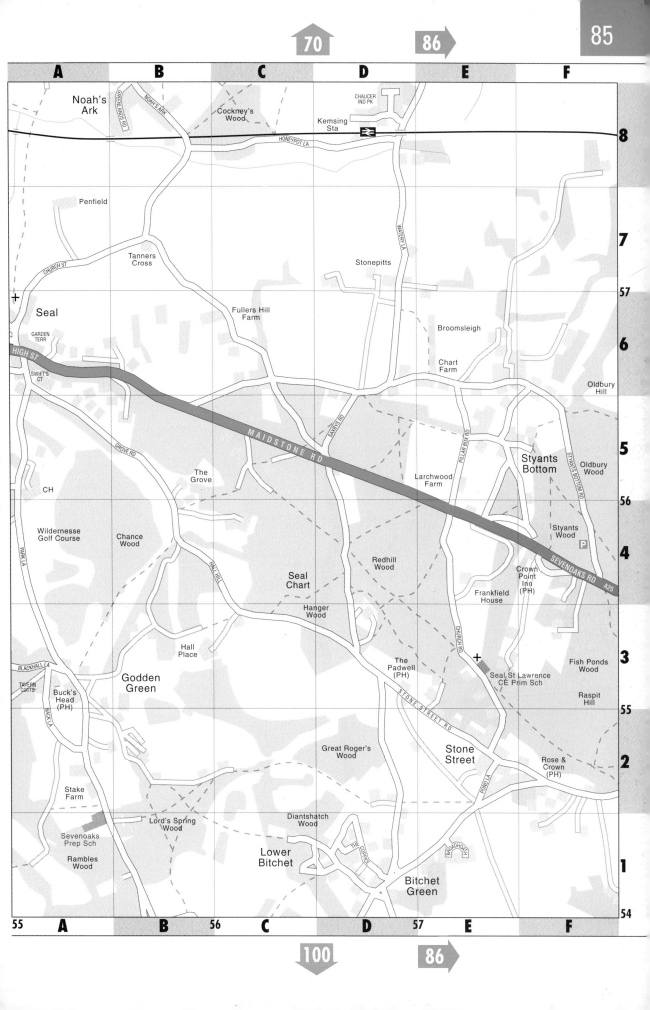

85 71

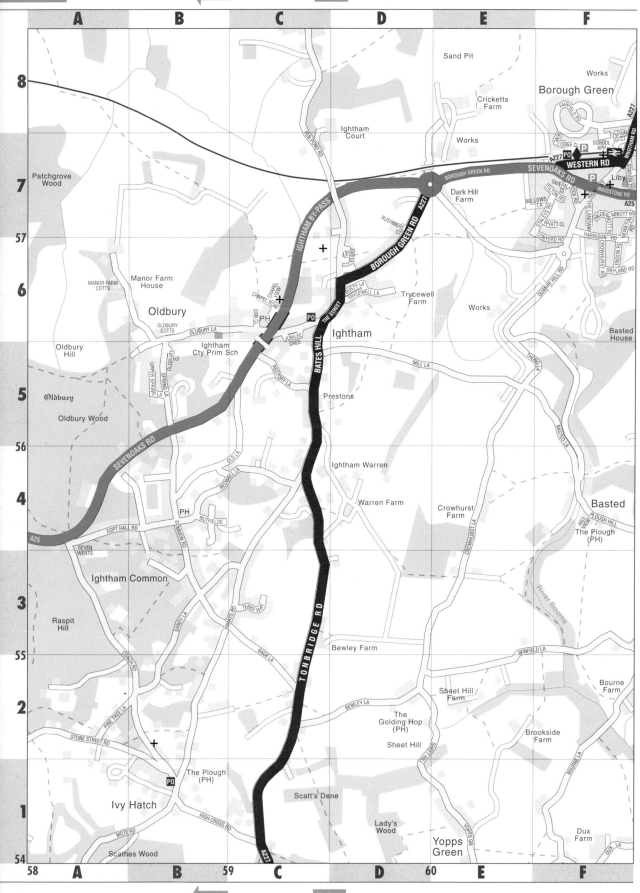

85 101

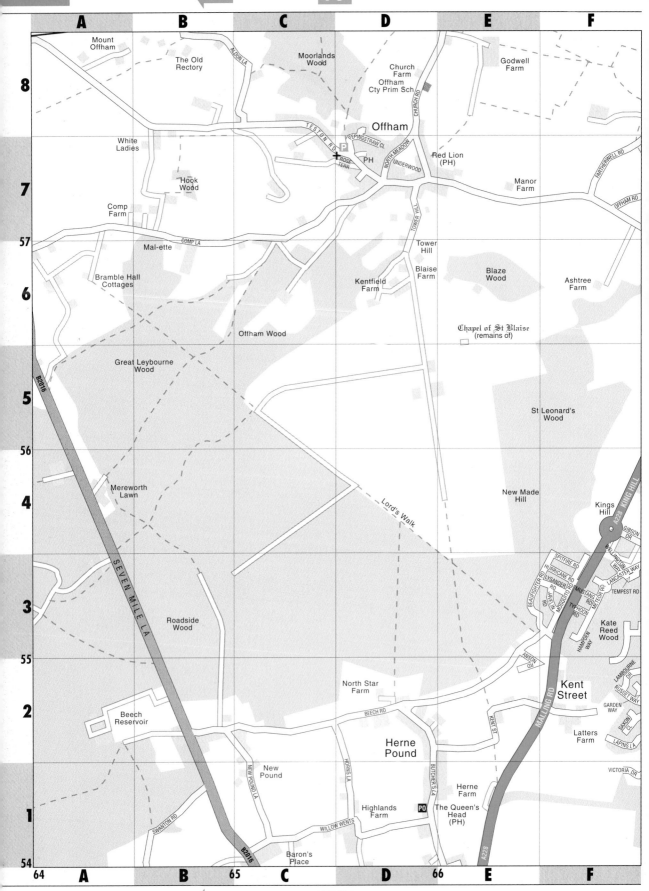

A B C D E F

8

Mount Offham
The Old Rectory
ALDON LA
Moorlands Wood
Church Farm
Offham Cty Prim Sch
Godwell Farm

Offham

7

White Ladies
TESTON RD
REPINGSTRAW CL
North Meadow
Underwood
Red Lion (PH)
FARTHERMELL RD
OFFHAM RD
Manor Farm

Hook Wood
P
ROSE TERR
PH

57

Comp Farm
COMP LA
Mal-ette

Tower Hill
Blaise Farm
Blaze Wood
Ashtree Farm

6

Bramble Hall Cottages
Kentfield Farm

Offham Wood

Chapel of St Blaise (remains of)

Great Leybourne Wood

5

B2016

St Leonard's Wood

56

Mereworth Lawn

4

Lord's Walk
New Made Hill
Kings Hill
A228 KING HILL

GIBSON DR
SPITFIRE RD
HURRICANE RD
LYSANDER RD
MUSTANG RD
METEOR RD
TYPHOON RD
WELLINGTON WAY
LANCASTER WAY
TEMPEST RD
Kate Reed Wood
BEAUFIGHTER RD
JAVELIN RD
MOSQUITO RD

3

Roadside Wood

55

ANSON RD
HAMPDEN WAY

Kent Street

North Star Farm

2

Beech Reservoir
BEECH RD
Herne Pound
KENT ST
MALLING RD
Latters Farm
LAMBOURNE DR
RUSSET WAY
GARDEN WAY
SAXON CL
LAPINS LA
VICTORIA DR

New Pound Lane
New Pound
HORNS LA
BUTCHER'S LA
Herne Farm
The Queen's Head (PH)

1

SWANTON RD
Highlands Farm
PO
WILLOW WENTS
A228

54

64 A B 65 C D 66 E F

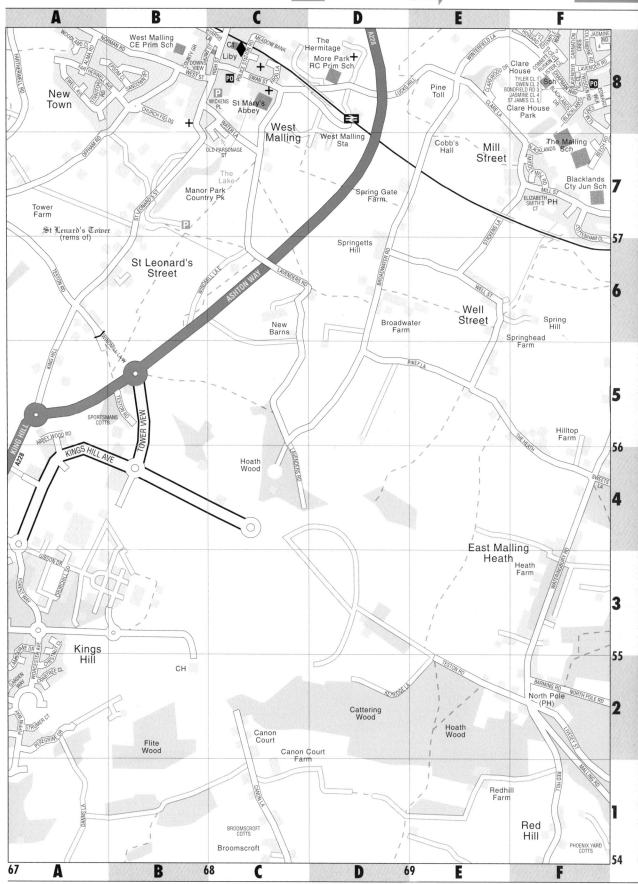

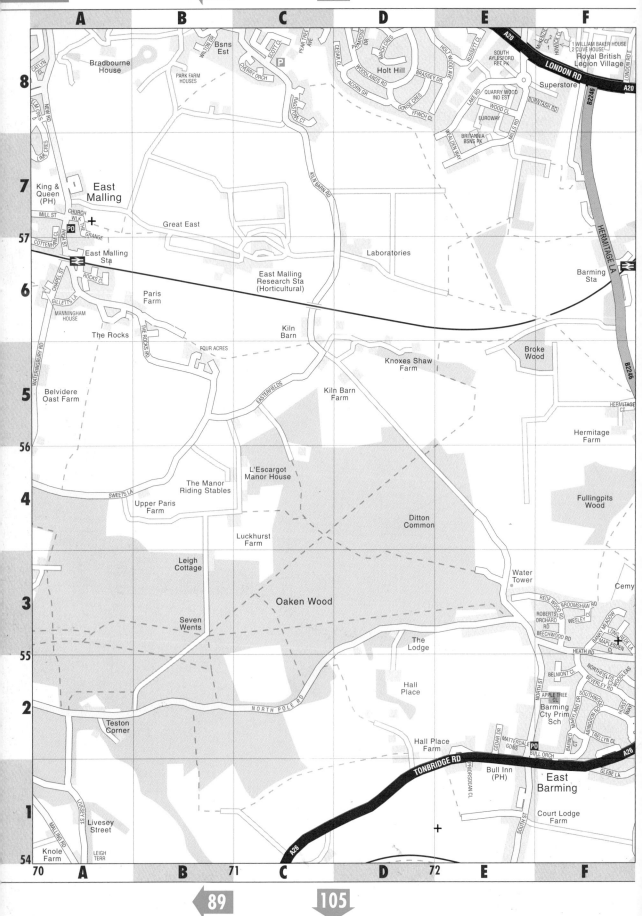

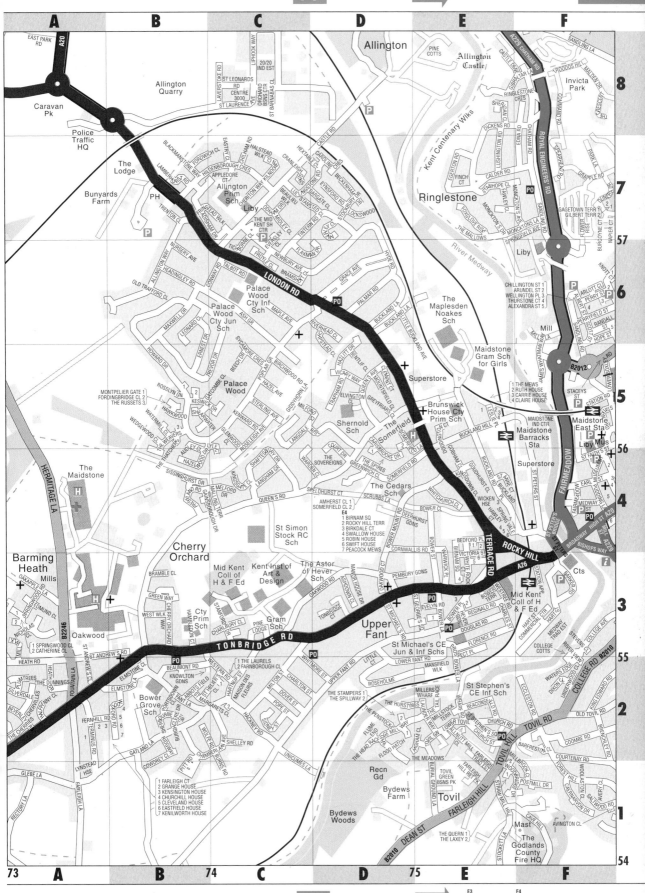

E3
1 NEWTON CL
2 ORCHARD PL
3 OLDCHURCH CT
4 RYECOURT CL
5 WHITE ROCK PL
6 VICTORIA CT

F4
1 HAVOCK LA
2 MARKET ST
3 MARKET COLONNADE
4 MARKET BLDGS
5 ROYAL STAR ARC
6 MIDDLE ROW

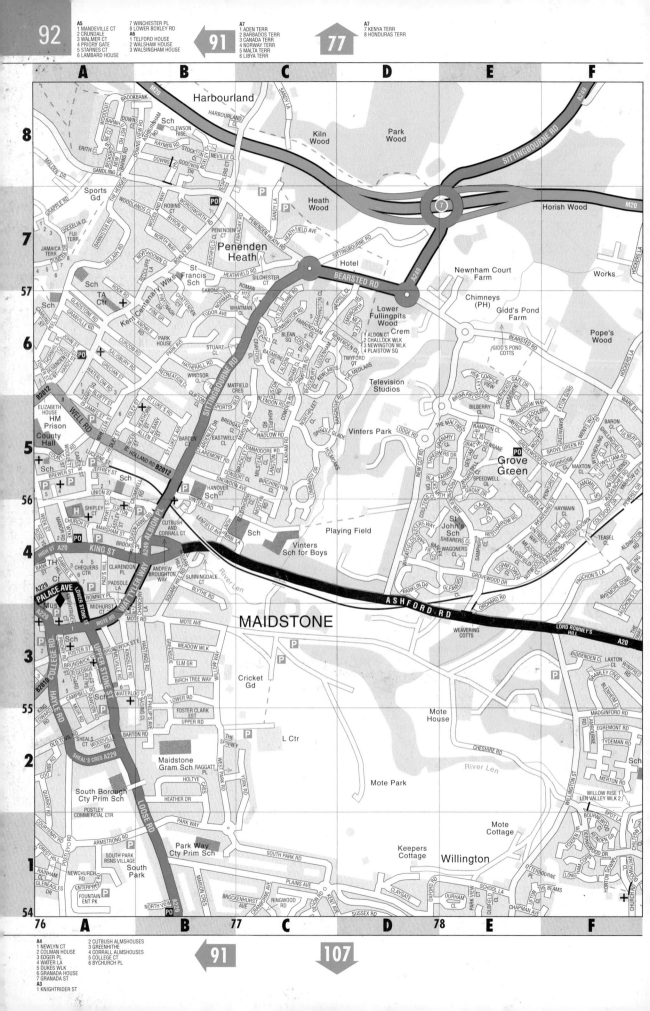

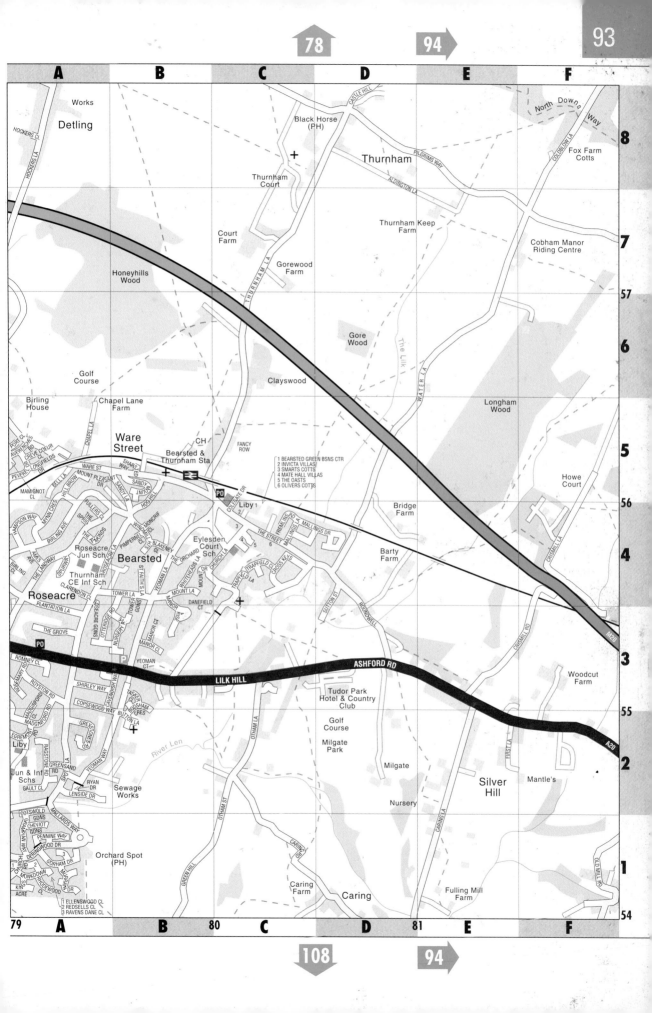

A B C D E F

8

7

57

6

5

56

4

3

55

2

1

54

82 A B 83 C D 84 E F

Coldharbour

Eastfield Farm

Hucking Hill House

Admiral House

SCRAGGED OAK RD

COLDHARBOUR LA

North Downs Way

Cat's Mount

Little Scragged Oak Farm

Scragged Oak

Smokes Wood

London Wood

Chitt's Wood

BROAD STREET HILL

Bolton's Wood

Whitehall

WHITEHALL RD

Broad Street Farm

Broad Street

PILGRIMS' WAY

North Downs Way

Ripple

Allington Farm

Little Allington

Snarkhurst Wood

Newlands Wood

Stricketts Garden

HOLLINGBOURNE HILL

BANK COTTS

Manor House

UPPER ST

PH

PILGRIMS' WAY

M20

Hollingbourne Sta

Little Snagbrook

Hollingbourne Cty Prim Sch

Hollingbourne

White Heath

MUSKET LA

A20

Eyhorne Farm

Eyhorne Street

PRO'S MEAD

CULPEPER CL

HADLEY GDNS

MUSKET LA

ATHELSTAN GW

BOURNESIDE TERR

EYHORNE ST

TILE

FIELDS

HASTED

Godfrey House

Oak Meadow Farm

GREENWAY COURT RD

Musketstone

Eyhorne Green

PH PO

OLD MILL RD

ASHFORD RD

ASHFORD RD

Target Cottage

Old Mill Farm

The Great Danes Hotel

B2163 PENFOLD HILL

Oakfield

A20

M20

Coombe Wood

HOSPITAL RD

HARPSWOOD

River Len

8

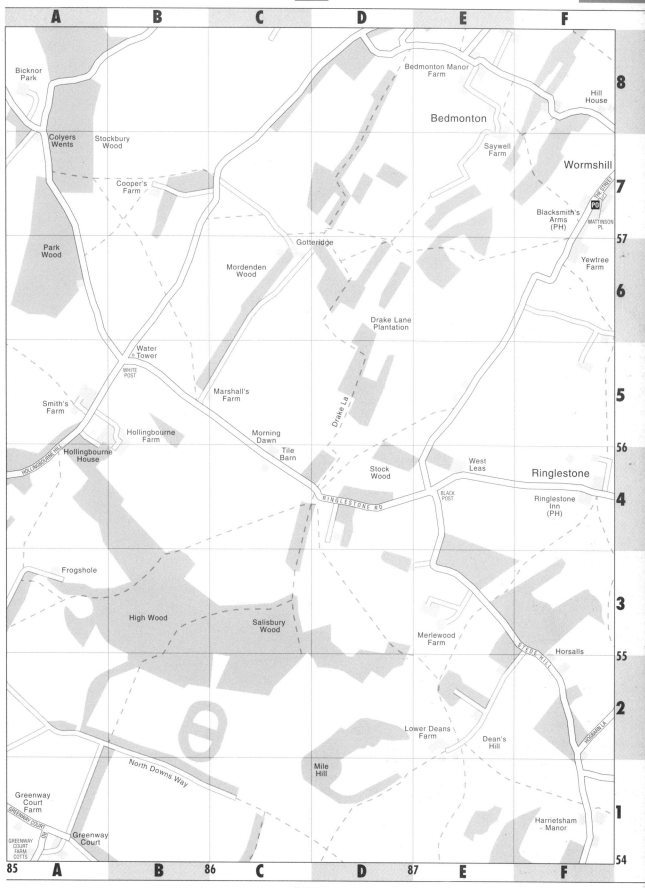

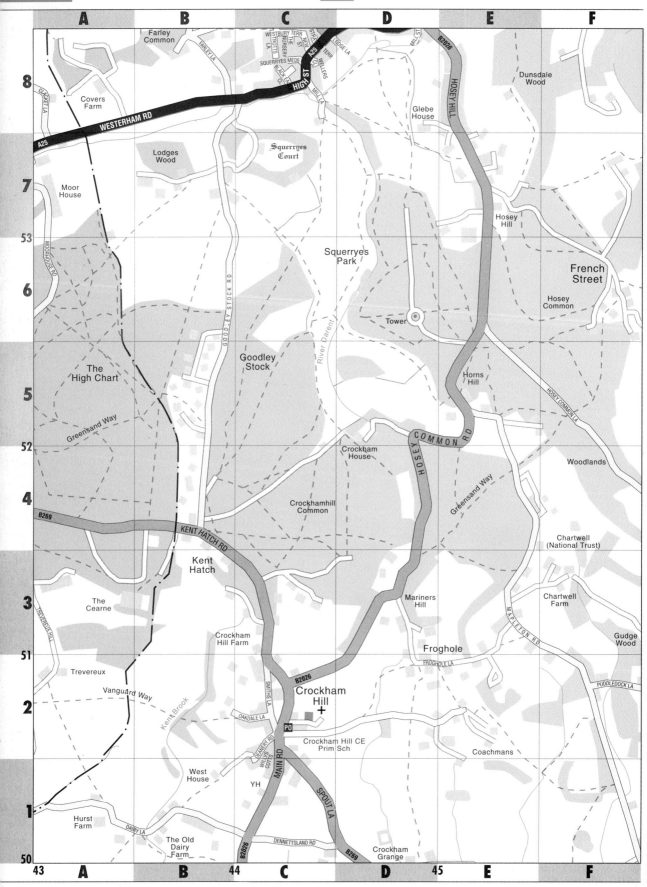

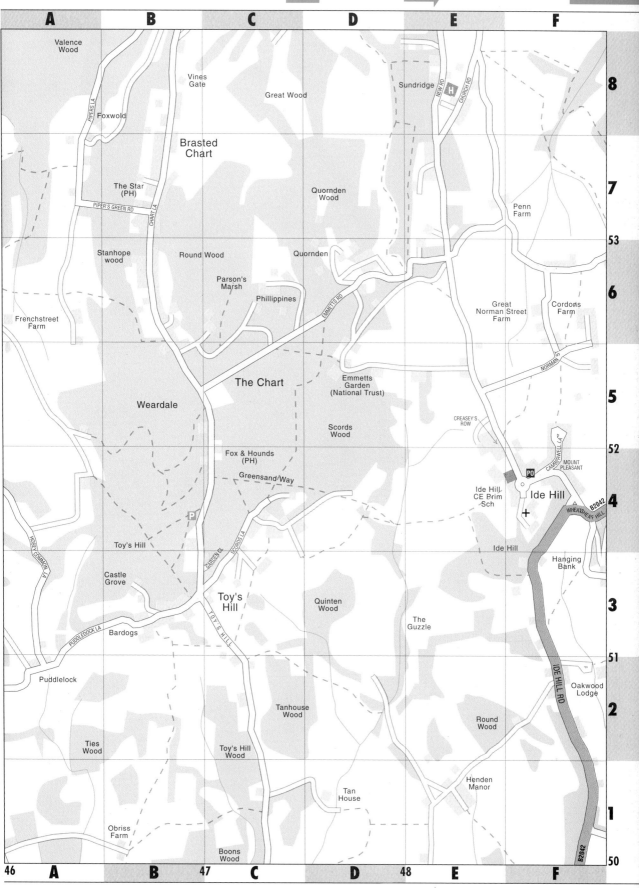

97

83

Greenlane Wood

B2042

Dibden

A21

DIBDEN LA.

Whitley

Mildridge Wood

Willow Wood

SEVENOAKS BY-PASS

Hawks Wood

BACK LA.

8

7

Mill Bank Wood

GOLDSMITH'S BOTTOM

53

Whitley Forest

Brook Place

6

Whitley Row

The Woodman (PH)

Apps Hollow

OAK LA.

Roundabout Wood

A21

Dust Wood

CHAPEL WLK.

Hyde's Forest

Pitfield Wood

GRACIOUS LANE'S END

WHITE HOUSE LA.

NIGHTINGALE LA.

THE PANTYLES

5

Goathurst Common

York's Hill

RYCROFT LA.

WHITE HOUSE RD.

52

Sheephill Wood

Bayley's Hill

Everlands

P

LADY AMHERST'S DR

Brockhill Wood

4

B2042

Stubbs Wood

Greensand Way

Hanging Bank

Yorkshill Farm

BAYLEY'S HILL

Wickhurst Manor

WICKHURST RD.

3

Boarhill

Harbour Hook

Hatchlands Farm

51

2

Bowzell Farm

BOWZELL RD.

1

Bowzell Wood

Scollops Farm

Old House Farm

50

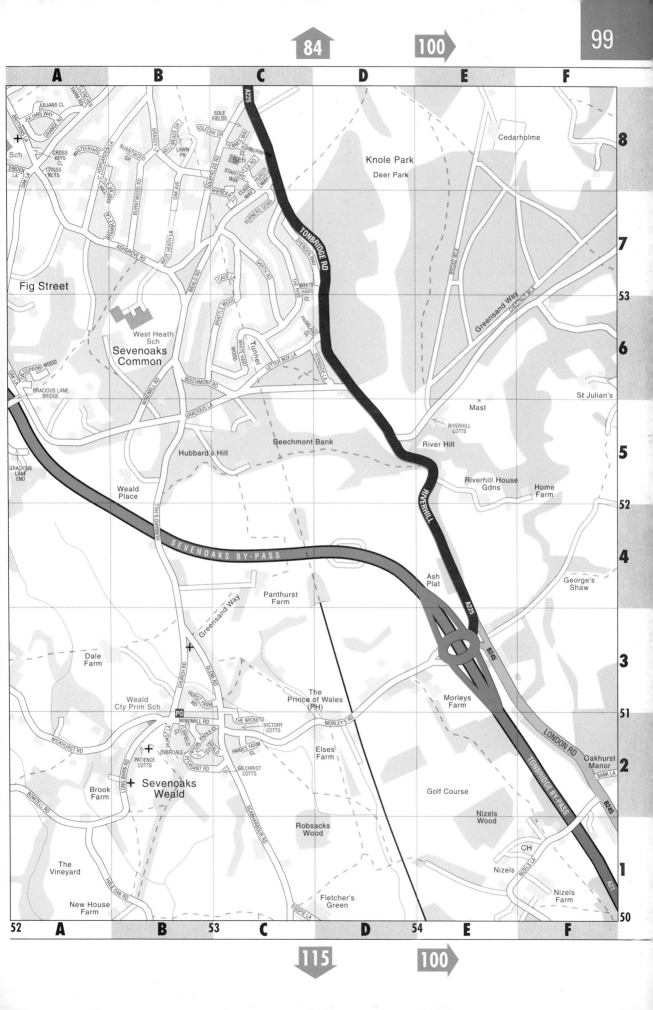

Julians Way
JULIANS CL
CLENCHES FARM RD
GRANGE RD
BRITTAINS LA
Sch
CROSS KEYS CL
DIBDEN LA
CROSS KEYS
WHITEFRIARS
HOPGARDEN LA
BURNTWOOD RD
GR
BURNTWOOD RD
LITTLE VG LING
HILL
BIRCHMEAD
MT E
ASHGROVE RD
WEST HEATH LA
OAK AVE
WEALD RD
GRASSY
WELLMEADE DR
LAWN PK
OAK LA
SOLEFIELDS RD
SOLEOAK DR
FIENNES WAY
SOLE FIELDS
SHENDEN CL
STAFFORD WAY
CLARE WAY
LEA RD
HURST WAY
ASHBURNHAM CL
A225

Fig Street

West Heath Sch
Sevenoaks Common
SHENDEN WAY
TONBRIDGE RD
TURNERS GDNS
GARTH RD
THE RISE
WHITE HART CL
CADE LA
BRATTLE WOOD
WHITE HART WOOD
Tunnel
PARK LANE CL
FERNSIDE LA
LETTER BOX LA

Knole Park
Deer Park

Cedarholme

BROAD WLK
CHESTNUT WLK
Greensand Way

53

7

8

6

Beechmont RD
Hubbard's Hill
Beechmont Bank
Mast
River Hill
St Julian's
RIVERHILL COTTS

5

Gracious Lane Bridge
GRACIOUS LA
GSPRING WOOD
OAK LA

GRACIOUS LANE END

Weald Place

RIVERHILL

Riverhill House Gdns

Home Farm

52

HUBBARD'S HILL

SEVENOAKS BY-PASS

Ash Plat

George's Shaw

A225

4

Greensand Way

Panthurst Farm

Dale Farm

Weald Cty Prim Sch
CHURCH RD
GLEBE RD
HURST FARM RD
PO
WINDMILL RD
ELMFIELD
KNOLE CL
INTON
WEALD
THE WICKETS
PAIGES FARM CL
VICTORY COTTS

The Prince of Wales (PH)

MORLEY'S RD

Morleys Farm

B245

51

3

WICKHURST RD
PATIENCE COTTS
OVERDALE
HURST LA
LONG BARN LA
PLEASANT RD
GILCHRIST COTTS
Sevenoaks Weald
Brook Farm
Elses Farm

Golf Course

Nizels Wood

LONDON RD
Oakhurst Manor
BANK LA
TONBRIDGE BY-PASS
B245

2

BOWZELL RD
HALE OAK RD
SCABHARBOUR RD
Robsacks Wood
CH
Nizels
NIZELS LA
Nizels Farm

The Vineyard
New House Farm
EGGPIE LA
Fletcher's Green

A21

1

50

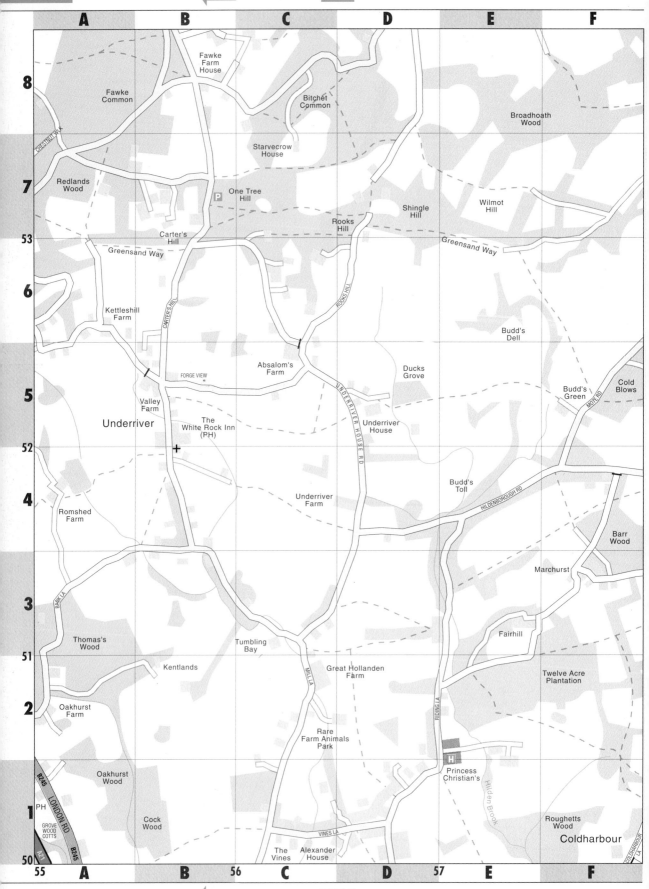

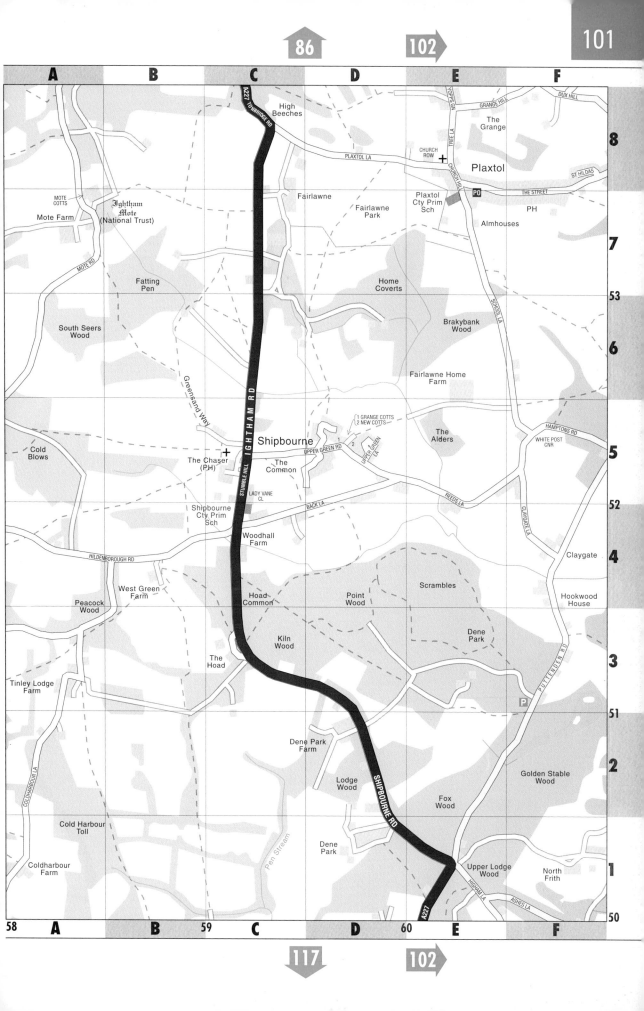

86
102
117
102

A227 TONBRIDGE RD

High Beeches

PLAXTOL LA

TREE LA

GRANGE HILL

DUX HILL

The Grange

CHURCH ROW

ST HILDAS

Plaxtol

CHURCH HILL

PO

THE STREET

Plaxtol Cty Prim Sch

PH

Fairlawne

Fairlawne Park

Almhouses

MOTE COTTS

Ightham Mote (National Trust)

Mote Farm

SCHOOL LA

Home Coverts

Brakybank Wood

MOTE RD

Fatting Pen

53

South Seers Wood

Fairlawne Home Farm

Greensand Way

IGHTHAM RD

HAMPTONS RD

WHITE POST CNR

Cold Blows

Shipbourne

The Chaser (PH)

1 GRANGE COTTS
2 NEW COTTS

1

UPPER GREEN RD

2

UPPER GREEN LA

The Alders

5

The Common

STUMBLE HILL

LADY VANE CL

REEDS LA

52

CLAYGATE LA

Shipbourne Cty Prim Sch

BACK LA

Woodhall Farm

Claygate

4

HILDENBOROUGH RD

Scrambles

Hookwood House

West Green Farm

Hoad Common

Point Wood

Dene Park

Peacock Wood

PUTTENDEN RD

Tinley Lodge Farm

Kiln Wood

The Hoad

3

COLDHARBOUR LA

Dene Park Farm

P

51

Golden Stable Wood

2

Cold Harbour Toll

Lodge Wood

Fox Wood

Pen Stream

Dene Park

Upper Lodge Wood

North Frith

1

Coldharbour Farm

SHIPBOURNE RD

HIGHAM LA

ASHES LA

A227

50

58   A   B   59   C   D   60   E   F

A B C D E F

8

DUX HILL
BOURNE VALE
THE STREET
BROOK LA
OLD SOAR RD

Quarry Wood

Plaxtol Spoute
COUNCIL HOUSES

Broadfield Farm

SPINNERS WENTS

THE NURST

7

LONG MILL LA
ALLENS LA

Allen's Farm

SWANTON RD

Wealdway

Peckham Hurst

53

Upper Farm

Rats Castle

Crooked Chimneys

ROUGHWAY LA

Mills

Roughway

Gover Hill

Gover Hill

BARTON COTTS

Dunk's Green

Adams Well

FORGE LA

6

DUNK'S GREEN RD

Greensand Way

Stickland's Wood

The Kentish Rifleman (PH)

The Artichoke Inn (PH)

PILLAR BOX LA

5

Puttenden Manor Farm

Fish Farm

Hamptons

PARK RD

Oxen Hoath

HAMPTONS RD

52

Hamptons Park

OXENHOATH RD

Vines Farm

MATTHEWS LA

4

River Bourne

Four Wents

Oxen Hoath Park

Park Farm

Oxenhoath Mill Farm

Pear Tree Farm

3

Clearhedges Wood

Frith Wood

Mount Pleasant

Cricketers Cottage Farm

51

CARPENTERS LA

The Common

COMMON RD

LONEWOOD WAY

A26

2

Stallion's Green

HIGH HOUSE LA

STEERS PL

PALMERS BROOK

Yewtree Wood

Hadlow

MAIDSTONE RD

CEMETERY LA

The Harrow (PH)

Cemy

North Frith Farm

Hope Farm

THE PADDOCK

MARSHALL GDNS

HOPE AVE

TWYFORD RD

GREAT ELMS

THE CHERRY ORCH

SMITHERS CL

Park Villas

1

MILL VIEW

THE FREEHOLD

P

TAUNTER RD

SCHOOL LA

BROOKFIELDS

CHESFIELD CL

WATER SLIPPE

50

61 A 62 B C 63 D E F

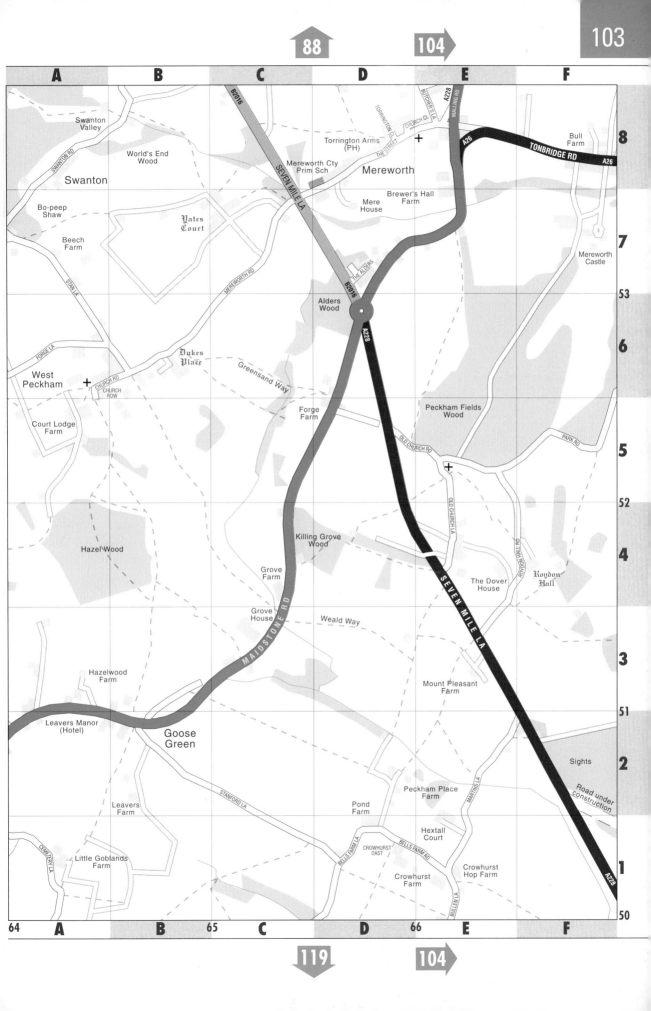

103
89

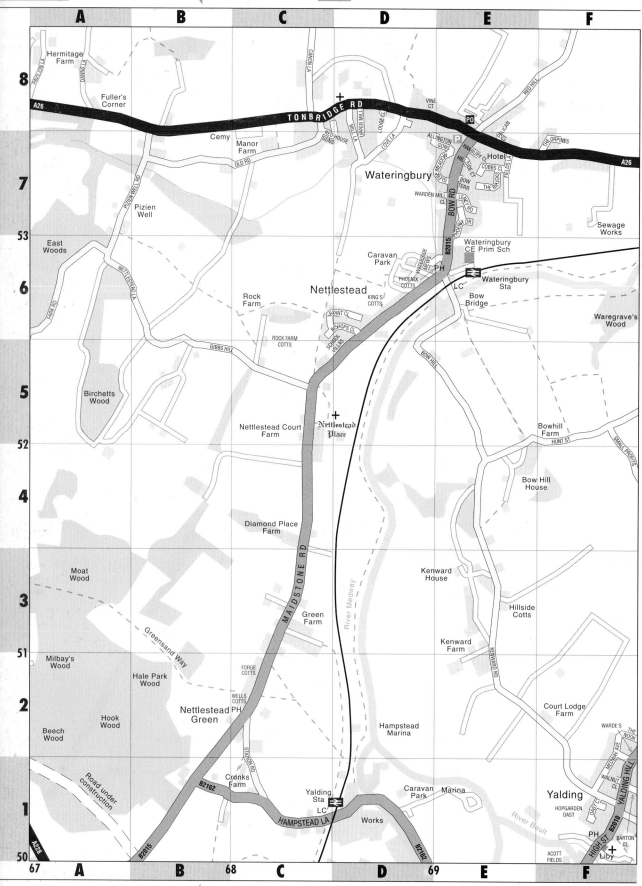

103
120

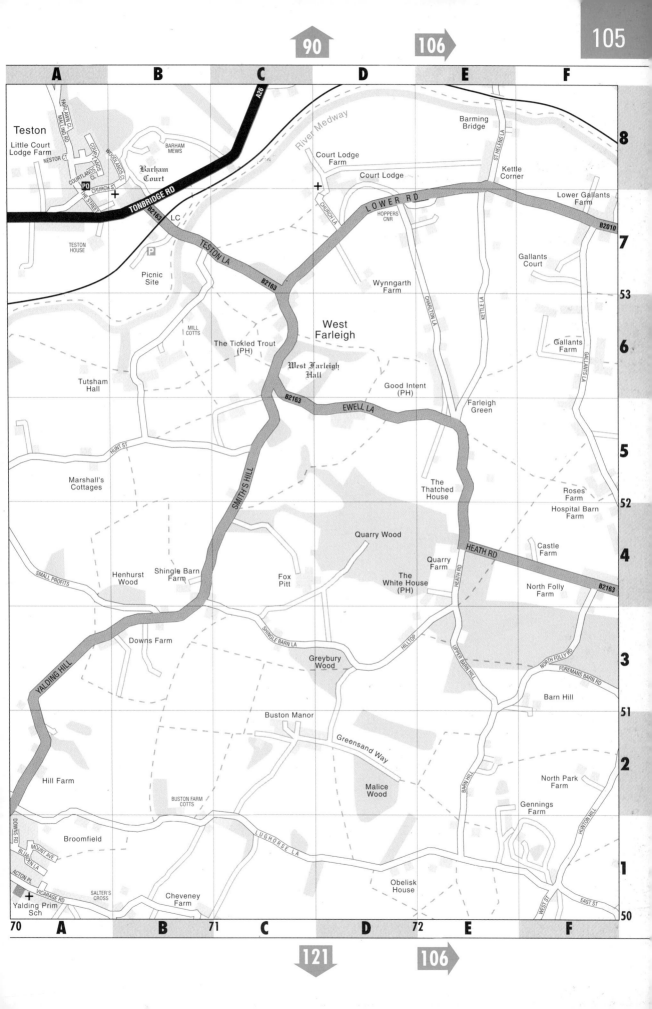

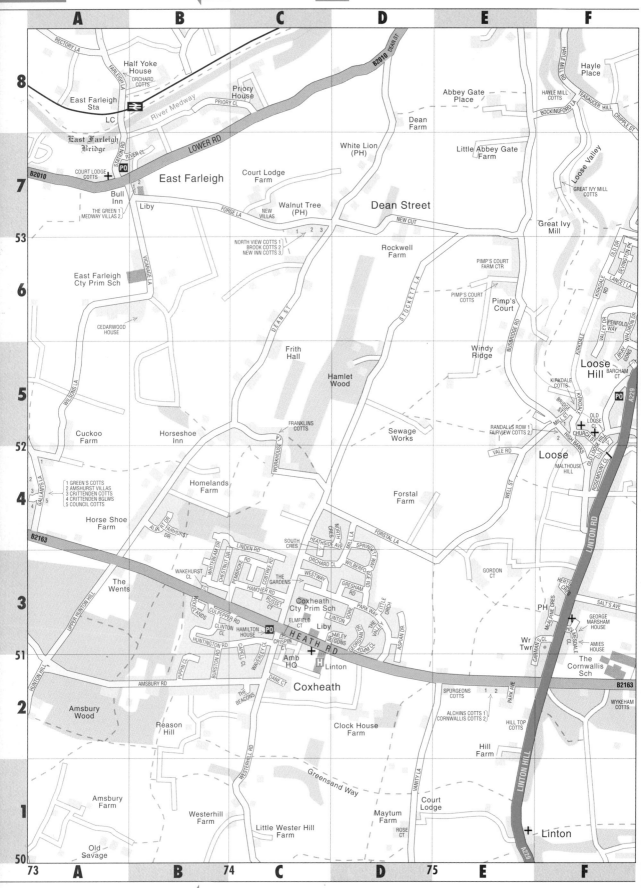

D7
1 ROCHESTER HOUSE
2 CANTERBURY HOUSE
3 CAMBRIDGE AVE
4 WINCHESTER HOUSE
5 SALISBURY HOUSE

D8
1 MEDWAY HOUSE
2 DARENTH HOUSE
3 THAMES HOUSE
4 STOUR HOUSE
5 ROTHER HOUSE

E7
1 SWALE HOUSE
2 TRENT HOUSE
3 SHROPSHIRE TERR
4 HUNTINGDON WLK
5 DERWENT HOUSE
6 INVERNESS HOUSE

7 GLASGOW HOUSE
8 ABERDEEN HOUSE
9 TEES HOUSE
10 TYNE HOUSE

E8
1 HARDWICK HOUSE
2 NEATH CT

3 CUCKMERE HOUSE
4 TAMAR HOUSE
5 HUMBER HOUSE
6 ORWELL HOUSE
7 WAVENEY HOUSE
8 WELLAND HOUSE

92

F5
1 CAPETOWN HOUSE
2 JOHANNESBURG HOUSE
3 HERON APARTMENTS
4 LIVINGSTONE WLK
5 NELSON HOUSE
6 BALMORAL HOUSE

108

F6
1 AINTREE HOUSE
2 ASCOT HOUSE
3 CHEPSTOW HOUSE
4 FOLKSTONE HOUSE
5 TITCHFIELD CL
6 FONTWELL CL

7 DONCASTER CL
8 HAVANT WLK
9 PLUMPTON WLK
10 FAREHAM WLK
11 DENSTEAD WLK
12 ANDOVER WLK
13 GROOMBRIDGE SQ

107

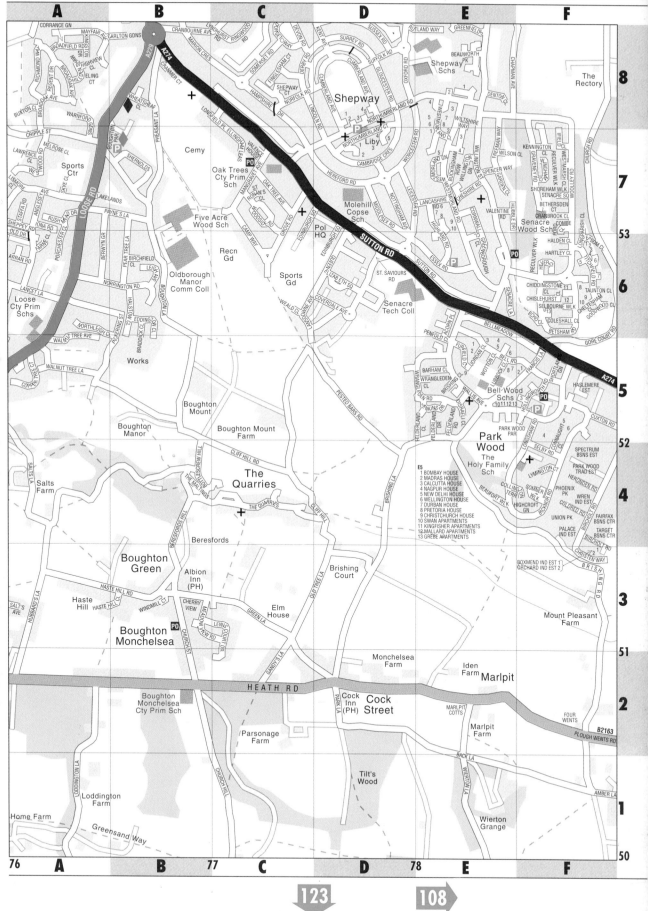

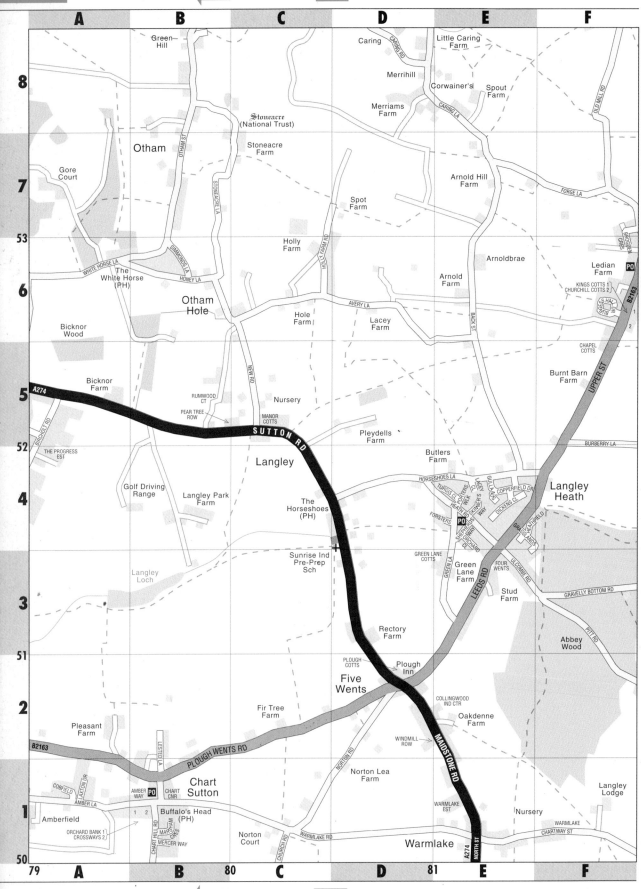

94
110

A B C D E F

8
7
53
6
5
52
4
3
51
2
1
50

Sewage Works

Leeds & Broomfield CE Prim Sch

Ashbank

ASHBANK COTTS

Battel Hall

Leeds

The George Inn (PH)

Abbey Farm

UPPER ST

FARMER CL

LOWER ST

WYKEHAM GR

GEORGE LA

PENFOLD HILL

B2163

P

Park Gate Inn (PH)

CH

Golf Course

Leeds Castle

A20

M20

ASHFORD RD

HOSPITAL RD

Warren Wood

Forge House

GREENWAY COURT RD

GREENWAY LA

A20

M20

Chegworth

The Great Water

River Len

Church Farm

Broomfield

Roses Farm

Chegworth Court

CHEGWORTH RD

Park Barn Farm

PARK BARN RD

BURBERRY LA

Scrub Wood

BROOMFIELD RD

Glebe Dene

King's Wood

Caravan Site

The Apiary

Works

Kingswood Farm

GRAVELLY BOTTOM RD

PITT RD

CROSS DR

Cherry Tree Farm

Kingswood

Kingswood Cty Prim Sch

CHARLESFORD AVE

WHITEHALL DR

ASHFORD DR

THORNE CROFT

ELDER CL

CHESTNUT DR

TALL TREES CL

LOVELL RD

THE WALDENS

BUSHY GR

WYCHLINGS

BELL WAY

THE WALK

CAYSER DR

WILDWOOD CL

HOLLY TREE CL

HEATHERWOOD

PH

PO

LENHAM RD

WATTELLA

Chartway Street

CHARTWAY ST

Church Farm

CHARLTON LA

WORKHOUSE RD

Street Farm

Manor Farm

MORRY LA

College Farm

ULCOMBE HILL

82 A 83 B C 84 D E F

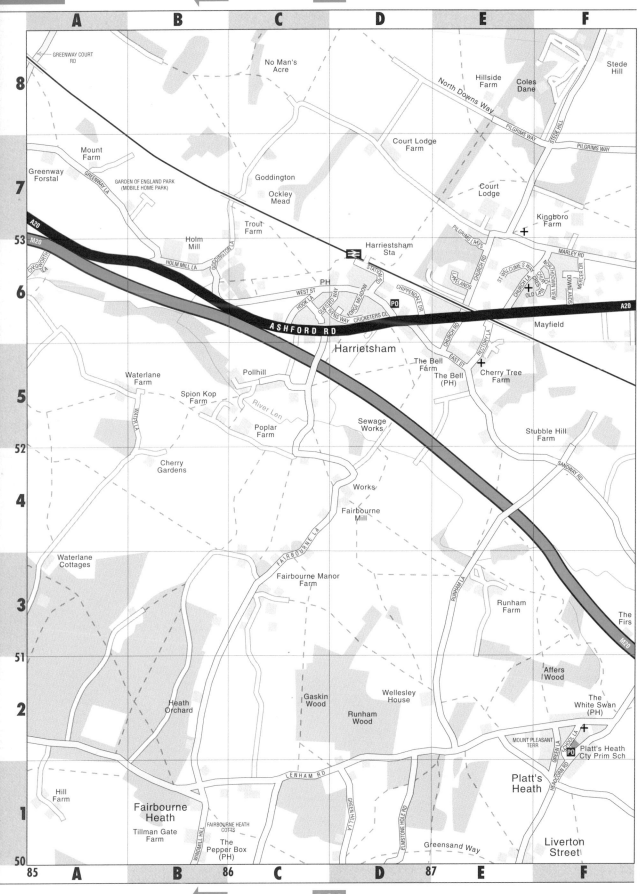

GREENWAY COURT RD

No Man's Acre

Hillside Farm   Coles Dane   Stede Hill

8

North Downs Way

PILGRIMS WAY   STEDE HILL

Mount Farm   Court Lodge Farm   PILGRIMS WAY

Greenway Forstal   GREENWAY LA   GARDEN OF ENGLAND PARK (MOBILE HOME PARK)   Goddington   Court Lodge   Kingboro Farm

7   Ockley Mead   +

HOLM MILL LA   Trout Farm   MARLEY RD

53   A20   Holm Mill   GODDINGTON LA   PILGRIMS WAY   CHURCH RD   ST WELCOME'S WAY   +   MERCER DR   DOWNSMEAD

M20   HOLM MILL LA   LAKELANDS   OLD LA N   CHURCH VIEW

CHEGWORTH LA   Harriestsham Sta   +

6   WEST ST   FORGE MEADOW   STATION RD   CHIPPENDALE DR   A20

HOOK LA   QUESTED WAY   OWENS WAY   CRICKETERS CL   PO   CHURCH RD   Mayfield

ASHFORD RD   EAST ST   RECTORY LA

Harrietsham   The Bell Farm   +   Cherry Tree Farm

Waterlane Farm   Pollhill   The Bell (PH)

5   Spion Kop Farm   CHURCH LA

WATRI LA   River Len   Sewage Works   Stubble Hill Farm

52   Cherry Gardens   Poplar Farm   SANDWAY RD

4   Works

Fairbourne Mill

Waterlane Cottages   FAIRBOURNE LA   RUNHAM LA   The Firs

3   Fairbourne Manor Farm   Runham Farm   M20

51   Affers Wood

2   Heath Orchard   Gaskin Wood   Wellesley House   The White Swan (PH)

Runham Wood   MOUNT PLEASANT TERR   +   GREEN RD   SCHOOL LA   PO   Platt's Heath Cty Prim Sch

LENHAM RD   Platt's Heath

Hill Farm   GREEN HILL LA   ELMSTONE HOLE RD

1   Fairbourne Heath   Liverton Street

Tillman Gate Farm   FAIRBOURNE HEATH COTTS   Greensand Way

WINDMILL HILL   The Pepper Box (PH)

50

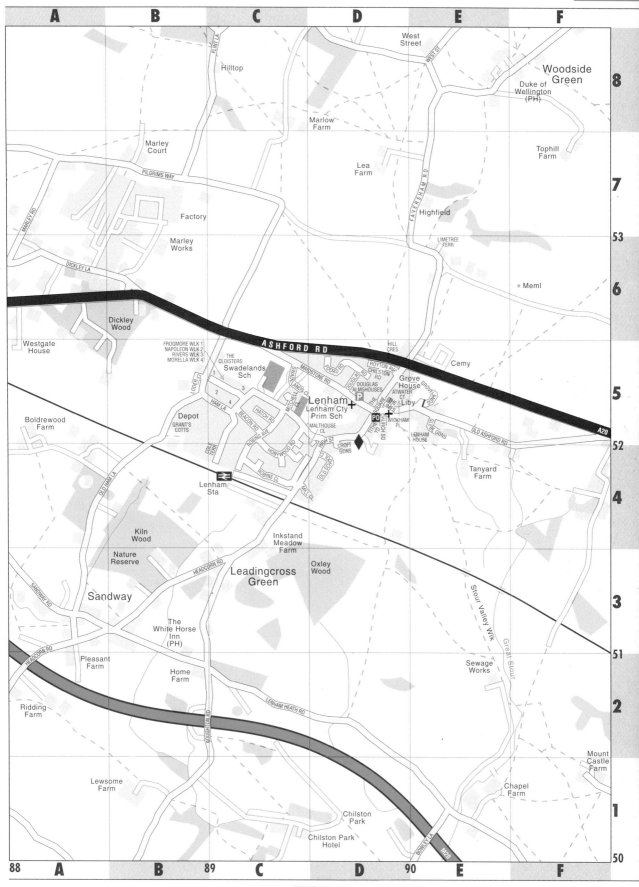

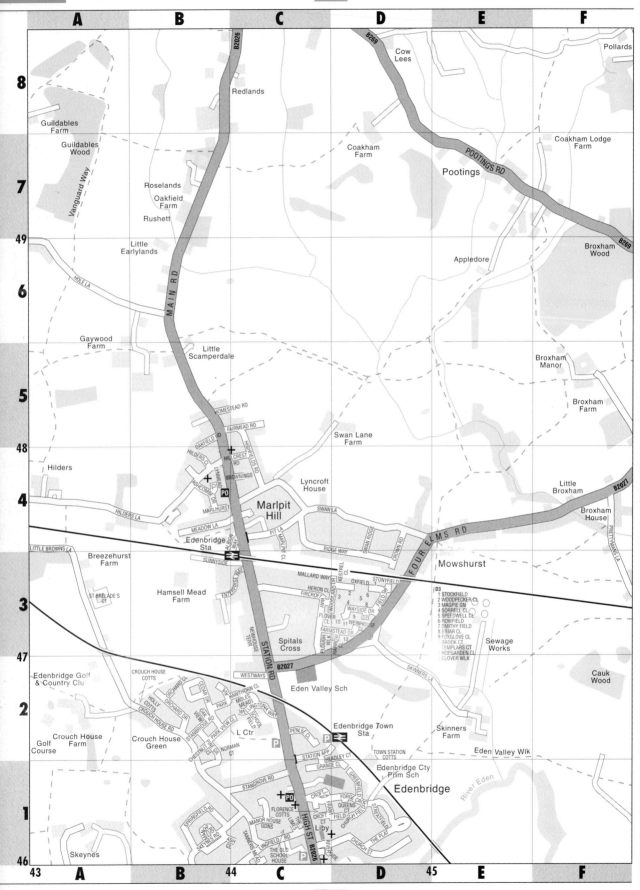

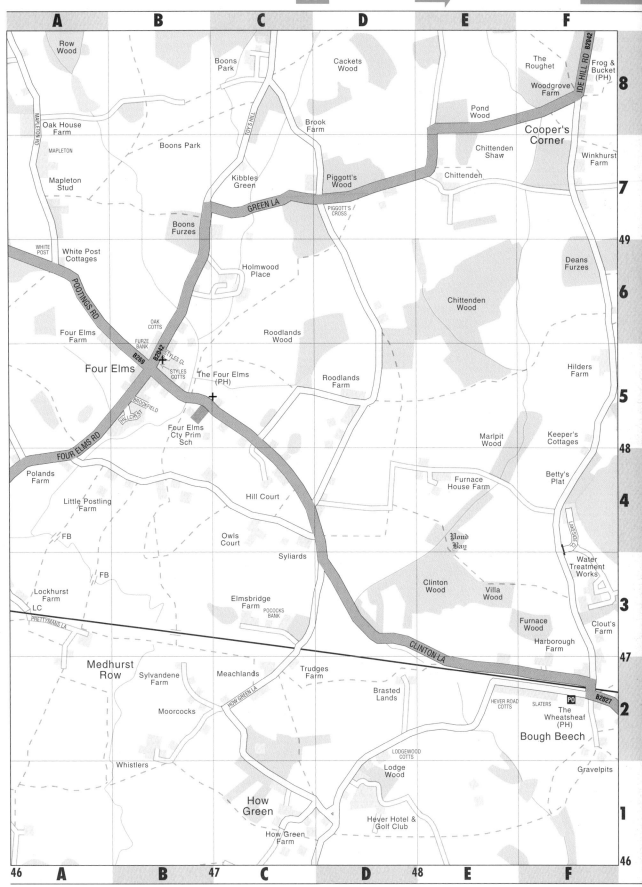

113
98

	A	B	C	D	E	F

8

Faulkners
Hill Farm

Bushes
Wood

Bushes
Plantation

Winkhurst
Green

Bushes
Farm

7

Nature
Reserve

Nature
Centre

49

Bore Place

Hale
Oak
Farm

Deans
Wood

Field
Trail

Sharp's
Place

6

Batfold
Wood

5

Bough Beech Resr

Kilnhouse
Farm

The Old
Forge

Little
Sidcup

Hale
Farm

Little
Hale

Bushy
Wood

48

Damper's
Wood

Brownings
Cottage

Hickens

Brownings
Farm

4

CH

Mountjoy
Farm

Polebrook
Farm

Birdfield
Plantation

Charcott
Farm

3

Cole's
Farm

Breeches
Wood

Waterlake

47

The
Horseshoes

Chiddingstone
Causeway

Camp
Hill

Waterlake
Cottage

Somerden

2

CHEQUERS HILL
COTTS THE CLOSE
B2027

Jessop's
Farm

Baldocks

DUKES MEADOW
CAMP HILL
CHAP'S CL
B2027

PO

Trad
Est

River Eden

Penshurst
Sta

STATION
HILL

Ppg
Sta

Chested
Farm

Beckett's
Farm

1

Mill
Farm

Chested

Sandhole

46

113
130

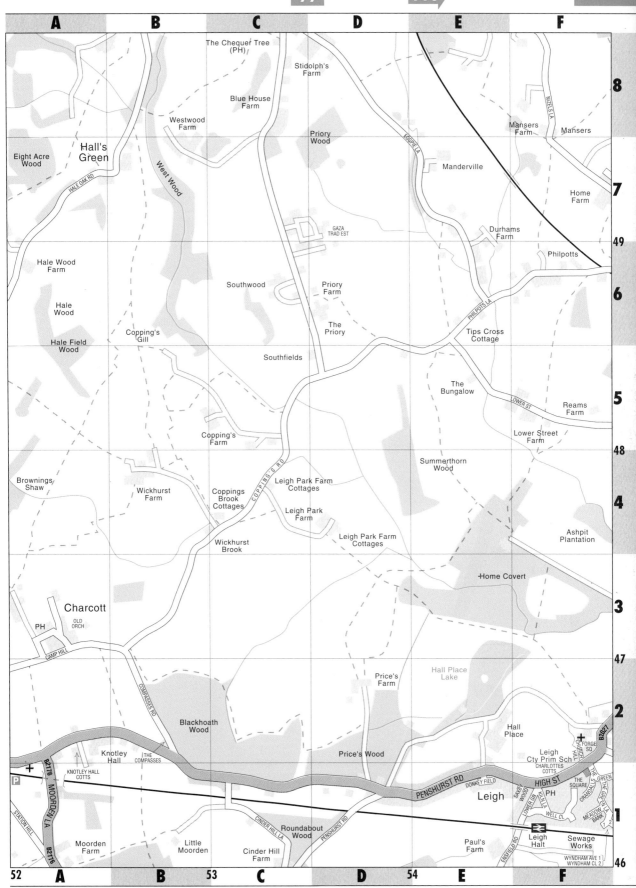

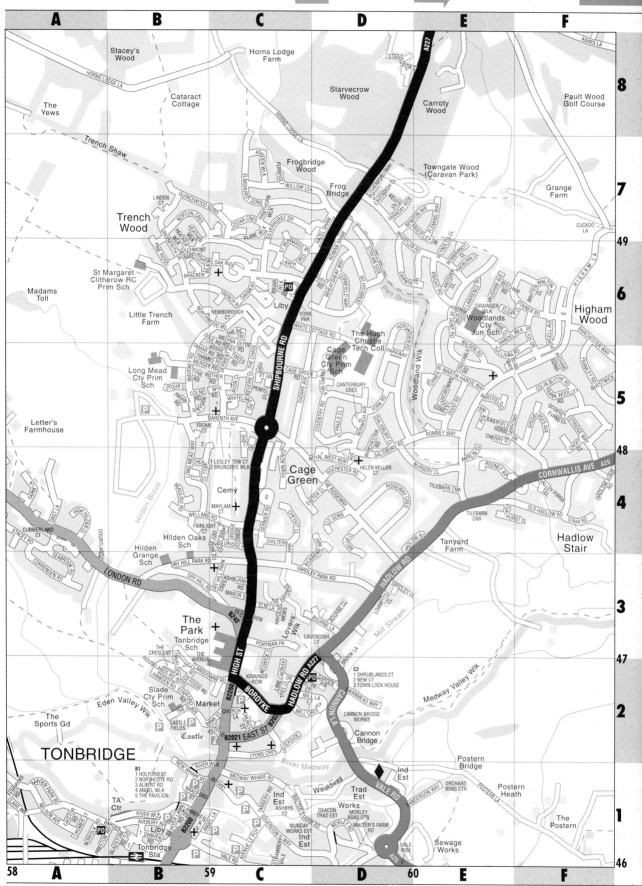

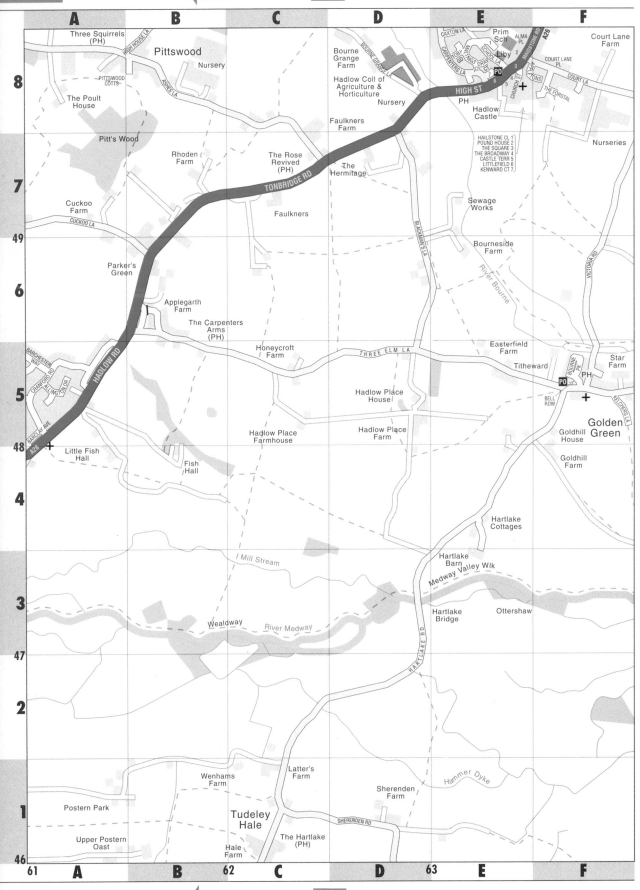

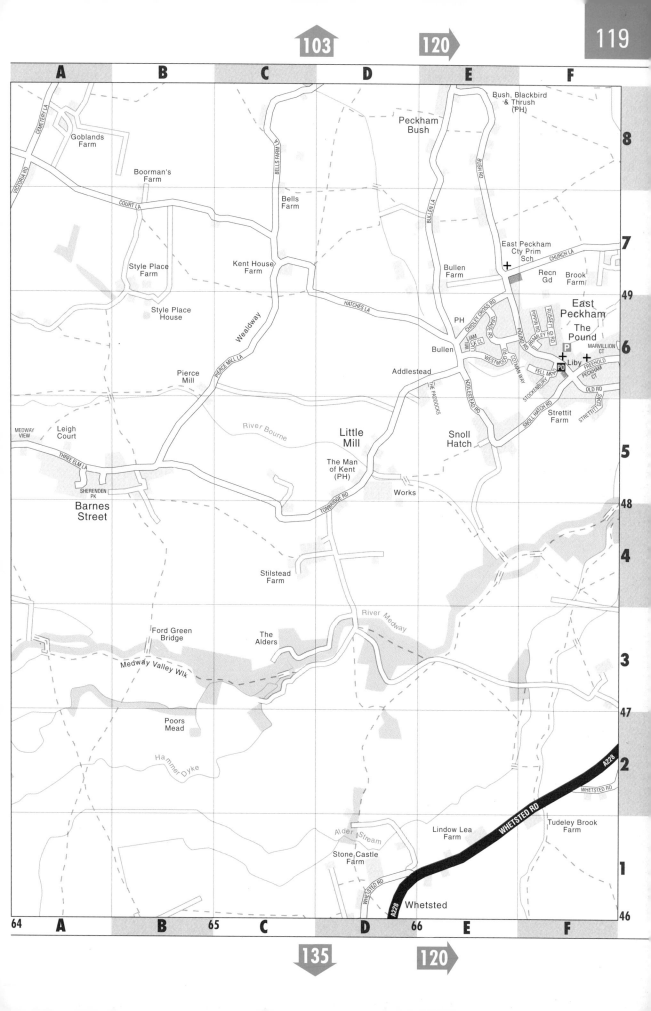

Bush, Blackbird & Thrush (PH)

Peckham Bush

Goblands Farm

Boorman's Farm

Bells Farm

Bells Farm La

CEMETERY LA

VICTORIA RD

COURT LA

Style Place Farm

Kent House Farm

Style Place House

BULLEN LA

BUSH RD

East Peckham Cty Prim Sch

CHURCH LA

Bullen Farm

Recn Gd

Brook Farm

East Peckham

The Pound

CHIDLEY CROSS RD

DRAGE RD

PIPPIN RD

BROMLEY RD

RUSSETT RD

WILLIAM CL

ROUND RD

MARVILLION CT

Weaidway

PIERCE MILL LA

PH

Bullen

WESTWOOD

COTMAN WAY

P
PO

Liby

FREEHOLD

PECKHAM CT

Hatches La

Addlestead

STOCKENBURY

FELL MEAD

Strettit Farm

OLD RD

Pierce Mill

THE PADDOCKS

ADDLESTEAD RD

SNOLL HATCH RD

STRETTIT RD

River Bourne

Little Mill

Snoll Hatch

MEDWAY VIEW

Leigh Court

THREE ELM LA

SHERENDEN PK

The Man of Kent (PH)

Works

Barnes Street

TONBRIDGE RD

Stilstead Farm

River Medway

Ford Green Bridge

The Alders

Medway Valley Wlk

Poors Mead

Hammer Dyke

Alder Stream

Stone Castle Farm

Lindow Lea Farm

WHETSTED RD

A228

Tudeley Brook Farm

WHETSTED RD

WHETSTED RD

A228

Whetsted

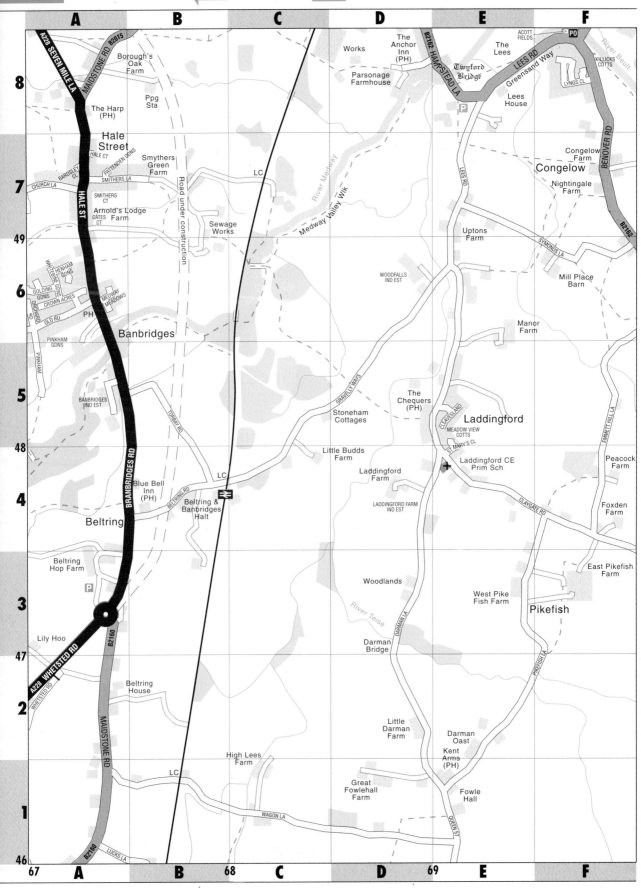

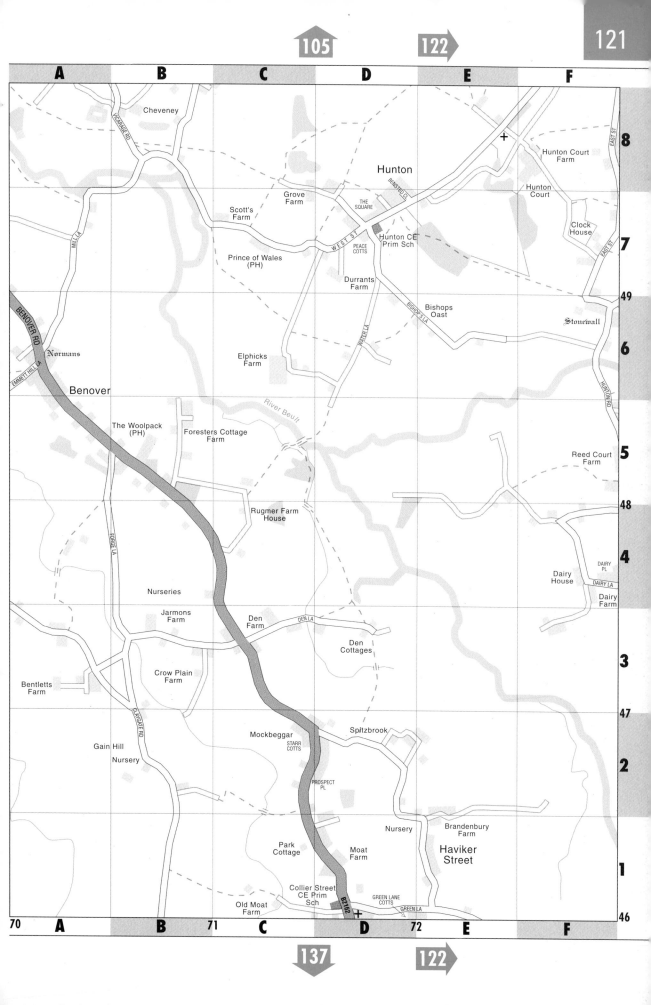

105
122
137
122

A B C D E F

Cheveney

VICARAGE RD

MILL LA

Hunton

Grove
Farm

THE
SQUARE

BENSTED CL

Hunton Court
Farm

Scott's
Farm

WEST ST

Hunton CE
Prim Sch

Hunton
Court

Prince of Wales
(PH)

PEACE
COTTS

Clock
House

EAST ST

EAST ST

Durrants
Farm

Bishops
Oast

BISHOPS LA

WATER LA

Stonewall

BENOVER RD

Normans

EMMETT HILL LA

Elphicks
Farm

HUNTON RD

Benover

River Beult

The Woolpack
(PH)

Foresters Cottage
Farm

Reed Court
Farm

FORGE LA

Rugmer Farm
House

Nurseries

Dairy
House

DAIRY
PL

DAIRY LA

Jarmons
Farm

Den
Farm

DEN LA

Dairy
Farm

Den
Cottages

Crow Plain
Farm

Bentletts
Farm

CLAYGATE RD

Spitzbrook

Mockbeggar

STARR
COTTS

Gain Hill
Nursery

Nursery

Brandenbury
Farm

PROSPECT
PL

Park
Cottage

Moat
Farm

Haviker
Street

Collier Street
CE Prim
Sch

B2162

GREEN LANE
COTTS

GREEN LA

Old Moat
Farm

70 71 72

49 6 7 8

48 4 5

47 2 3

46 1

105

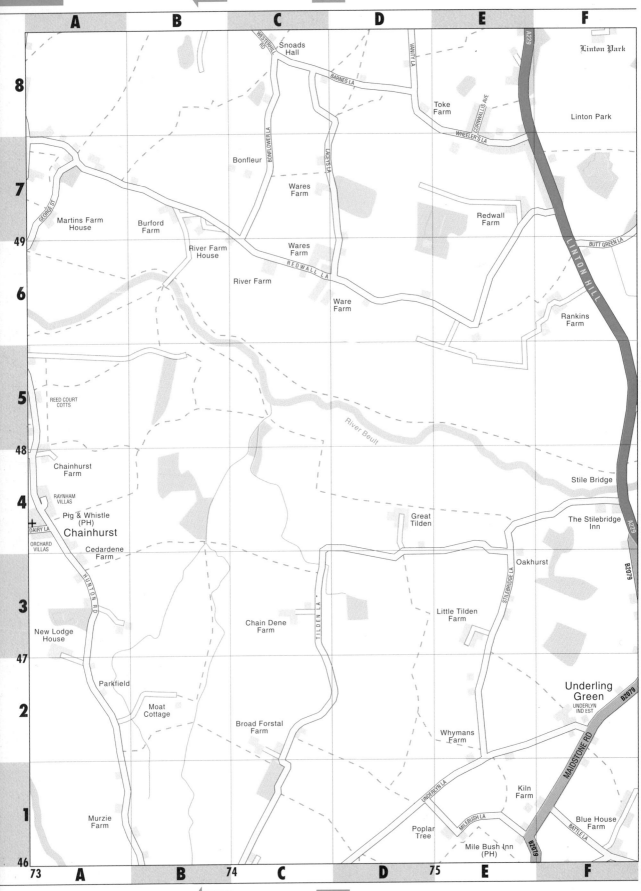

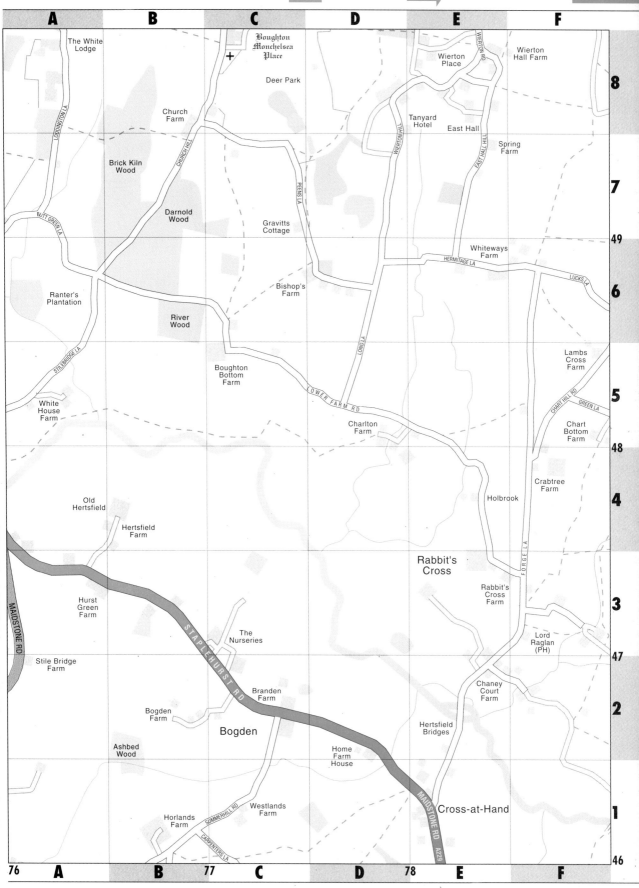

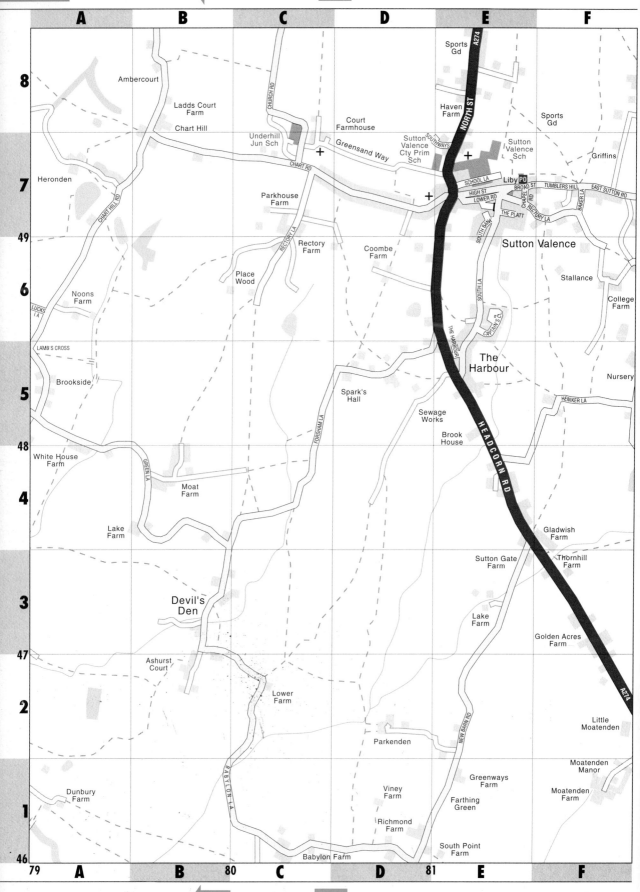

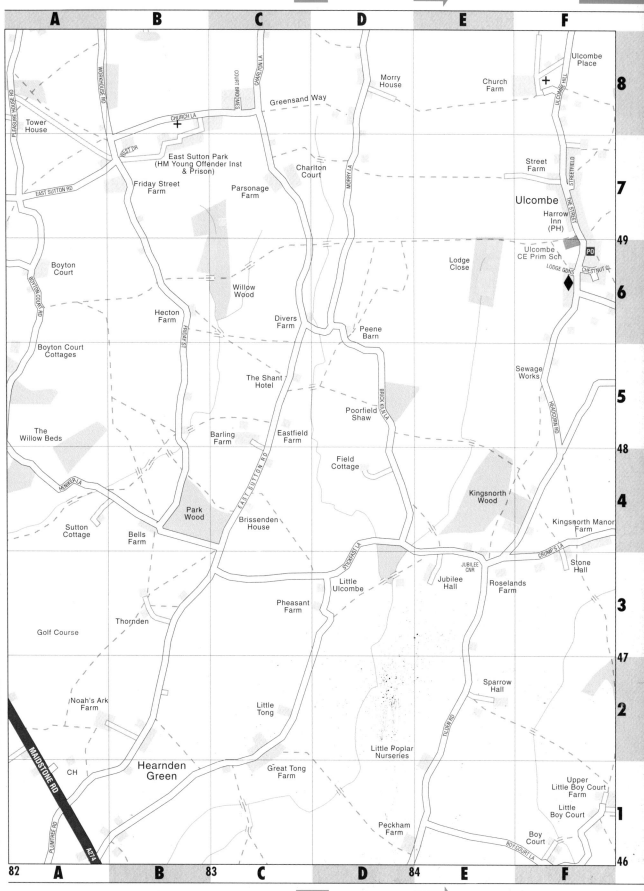

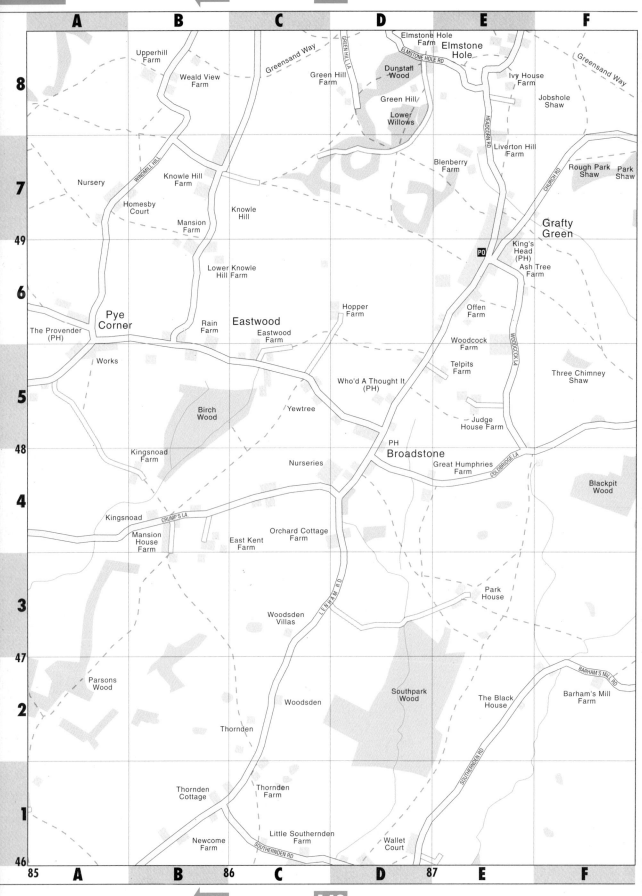

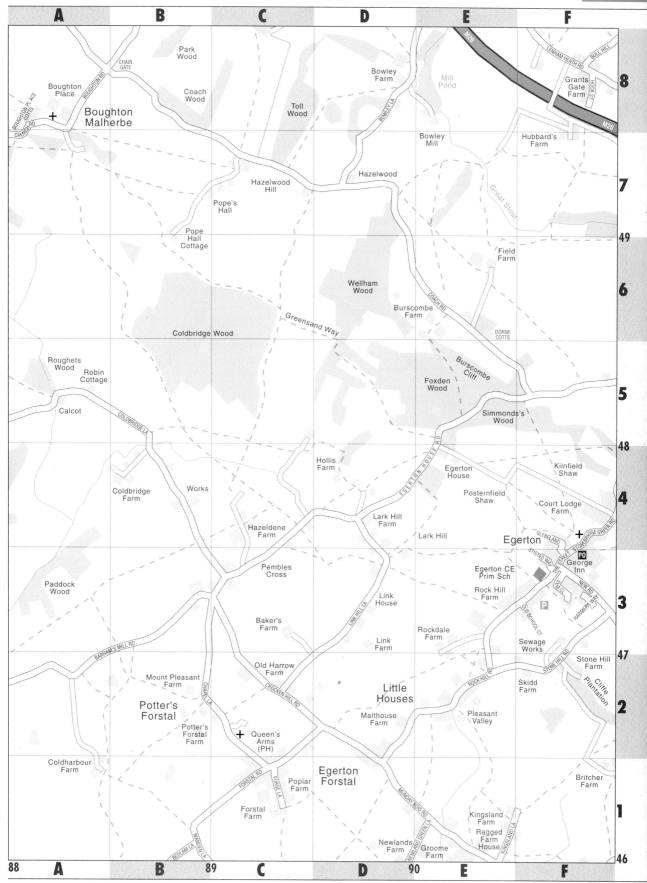

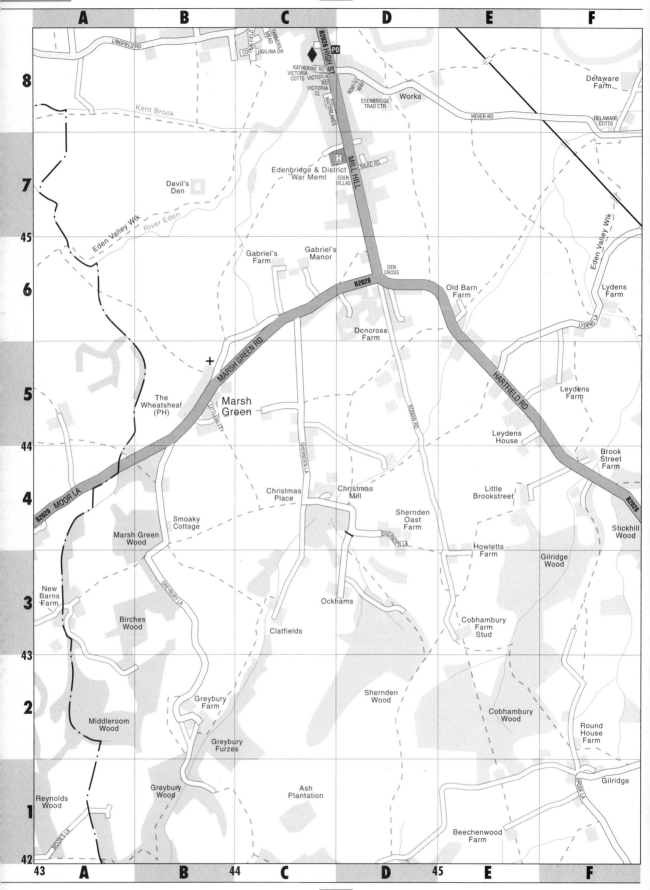

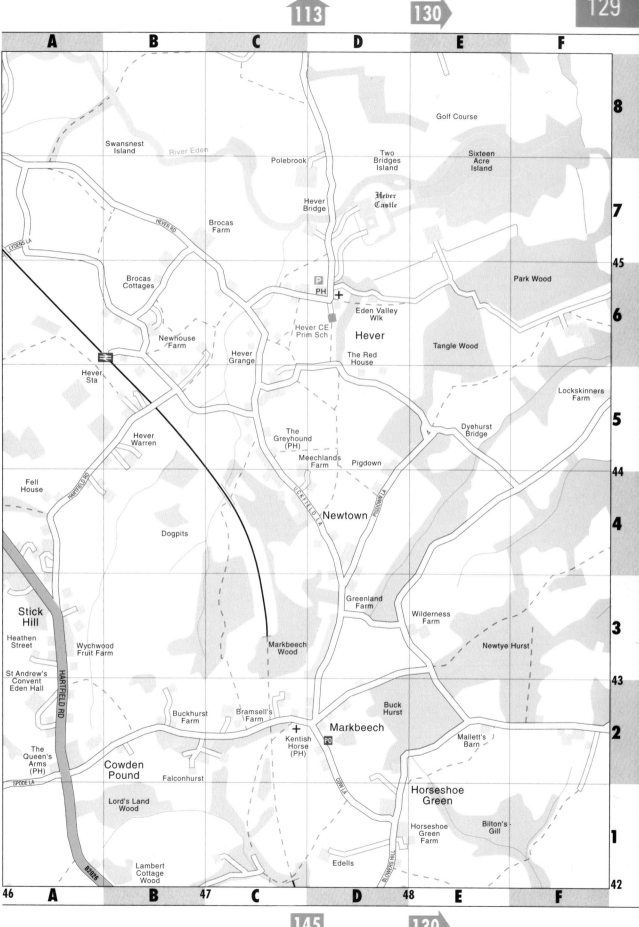

Golf Course

Swansnest
Island

River Eden

Two
Bridges
Island

Sixteen
Acre
Island

Polebrook

HEVER RD

Brocas
Farm

Hever
Bridge

Hever
Castle

Park Wood

Brocas
Cottages

P
PH

Eden Valley
Wlk

Hever

LYDENS LA

Newhouse
Farm

Hever CE
Prim Sch

Hever
Sta

Hever
Grange

Tangle Wood

The Red
House

Locskinners
Farm

Hever
Warren

The
Greyhound
(PH)

Dyehurst
Bridge

HARTFIELD RD

Meechlands
Farm

Pigdown

Fell
House

Dogpits

UCKFIELD LA

Newtown

PIGDOWN LA

Stick
Hill

Greenland
Farm

Wilderness
Farm

Heathen
Street

Wychwood
Fruit Farm

Markbeech
Wood

Newtye Hurst

St Andrew's
Convent
Eden Hall

Buckhurst
Farm

Bramsell's
Farm

Buck
Hurst

HARTFIELD RD

The
Queen's
Arms
(PH)

Cowden
Pound

Falconhurst

Kentish
Horse
(PH)

PO

Markbeech

Mallett's
Barn

SPODE LA

Horseshoe
Green

B2026

Lord's Land
Wood

COW LA

Horseshoe
Green
Farm

Bilton's
Gill

Lambert
Cottage
Wood

BLOWERS HILL

Edells

129 **114**

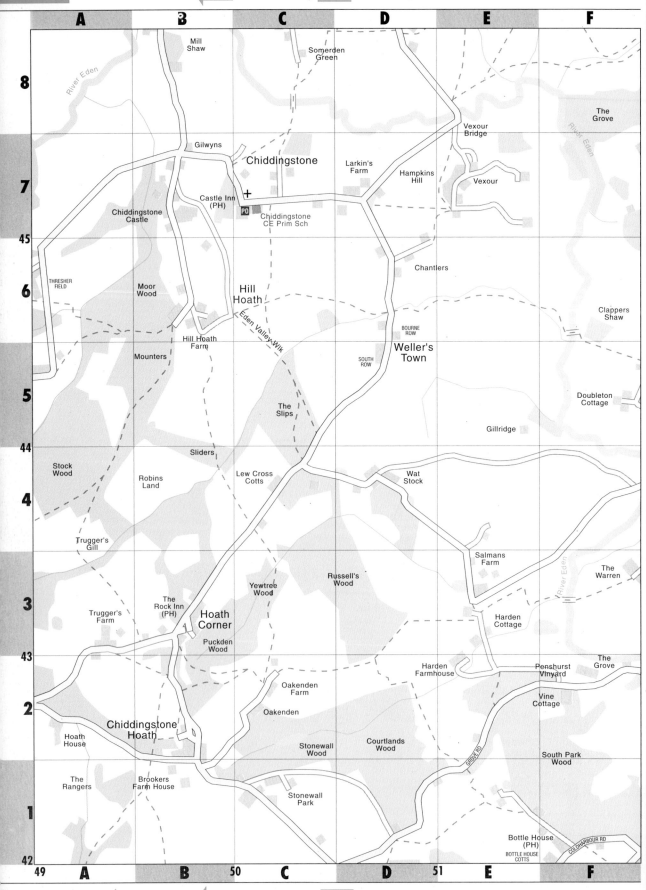

129 **146**

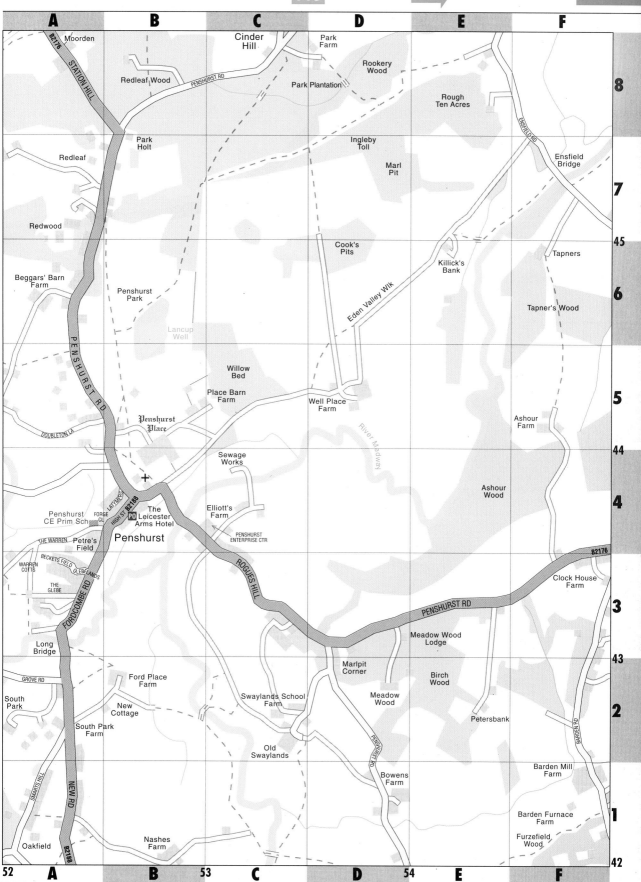

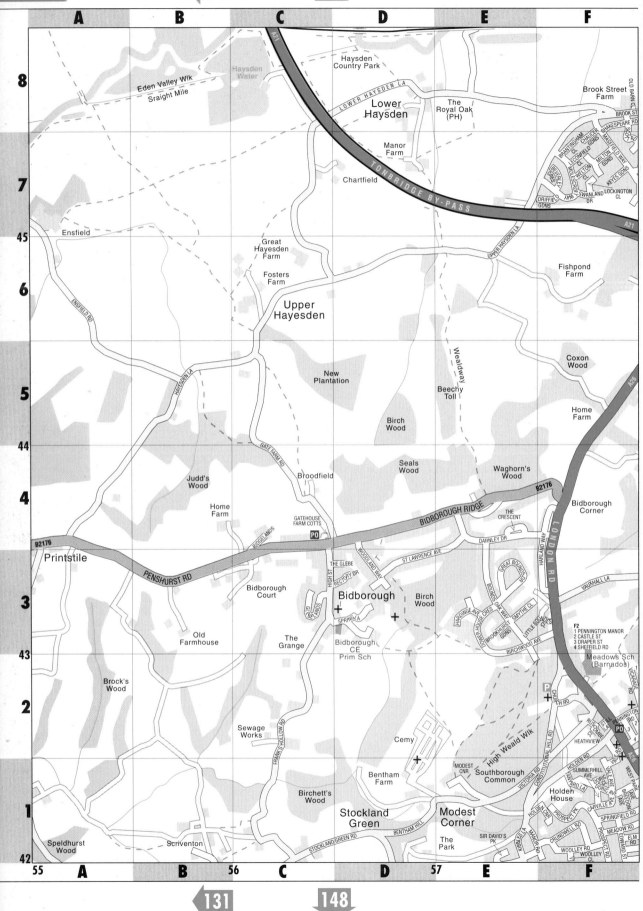

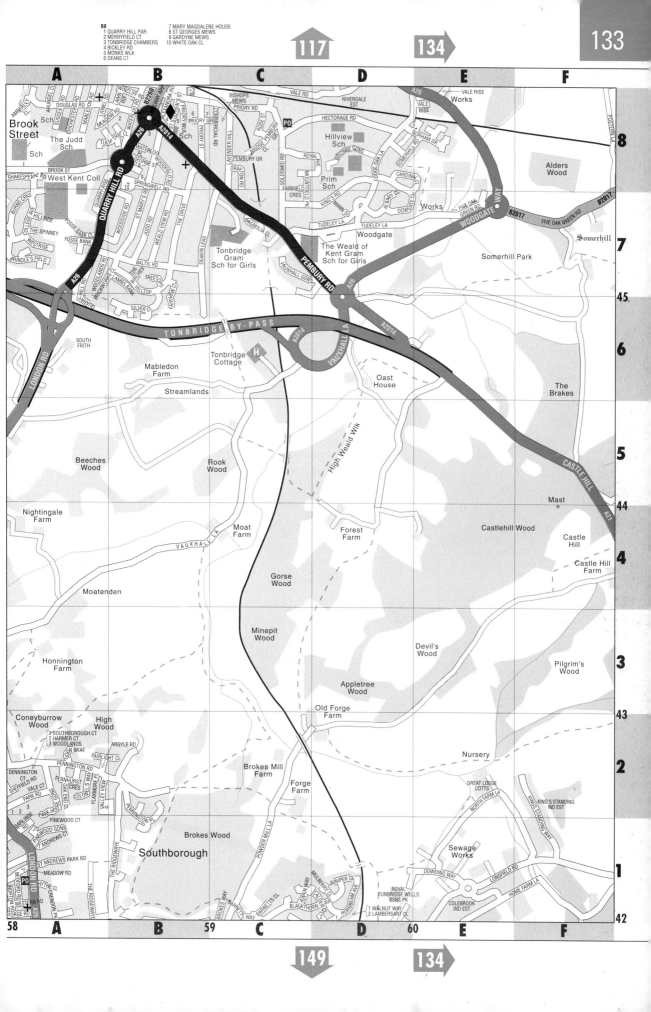

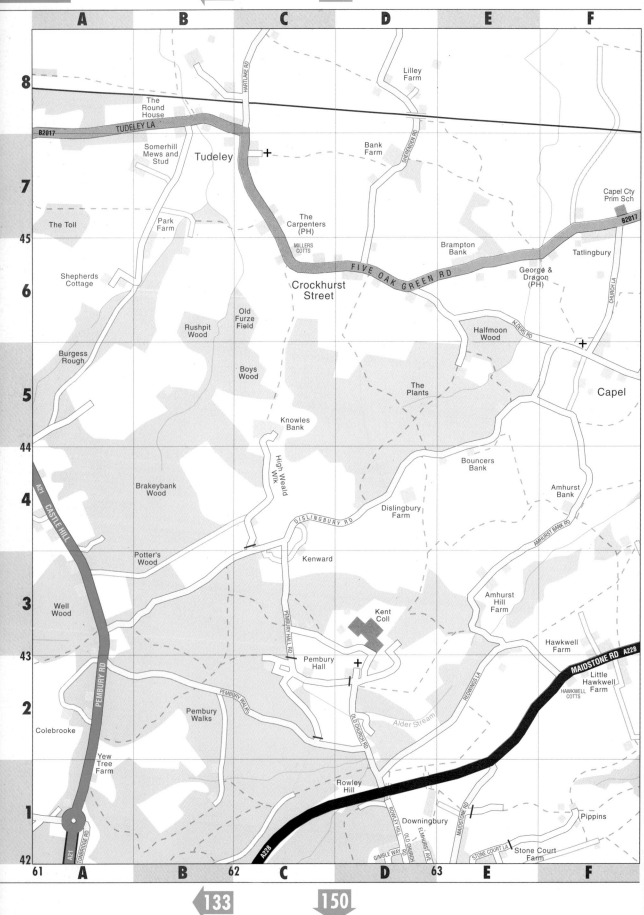

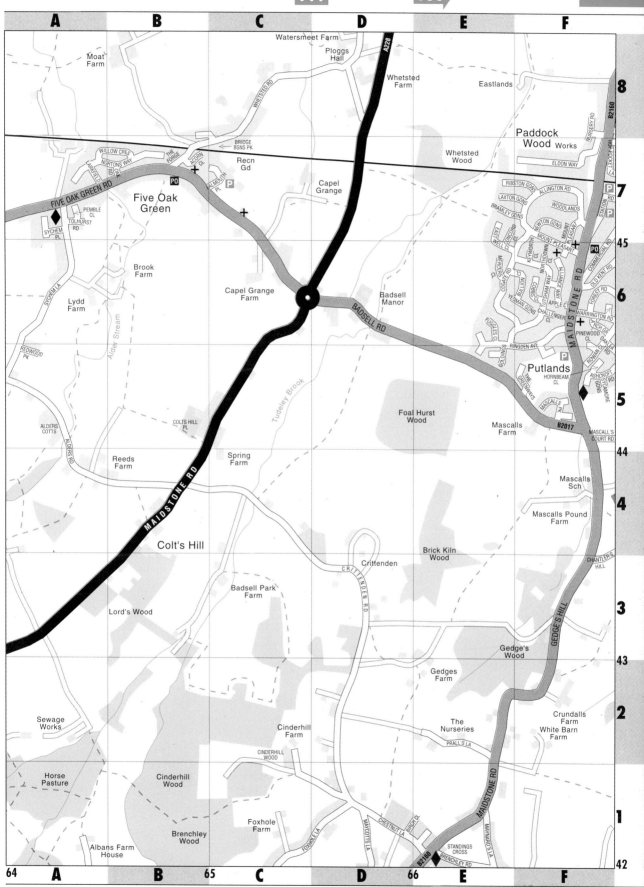

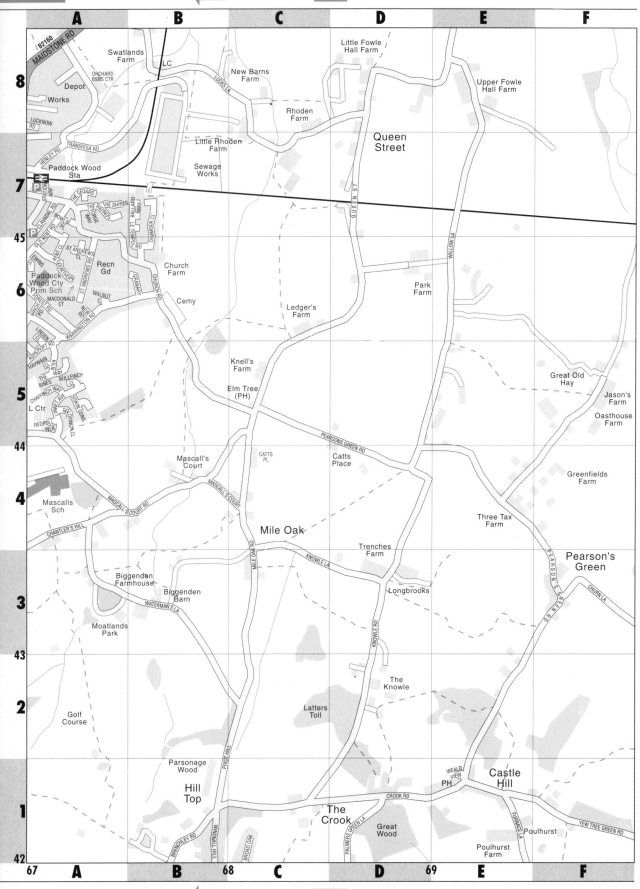

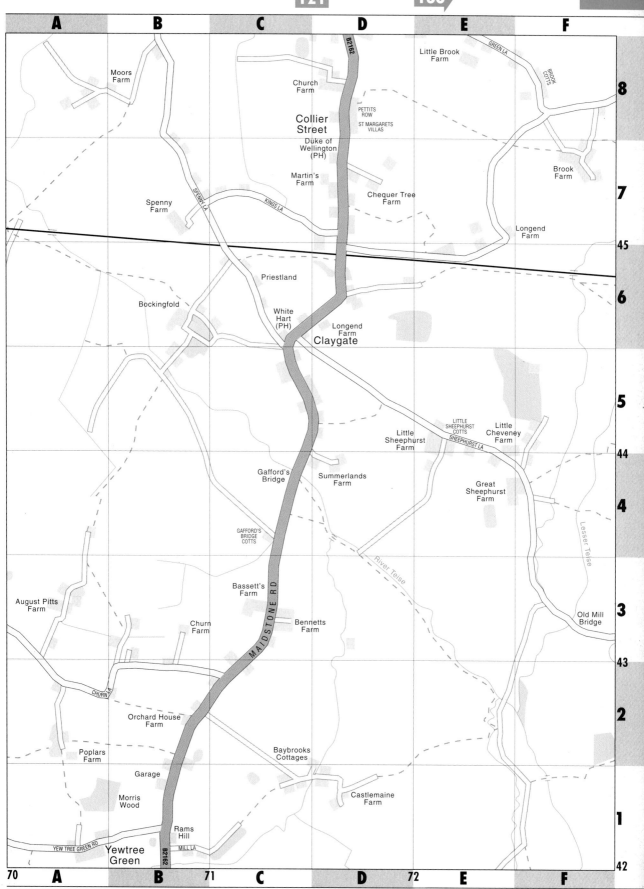

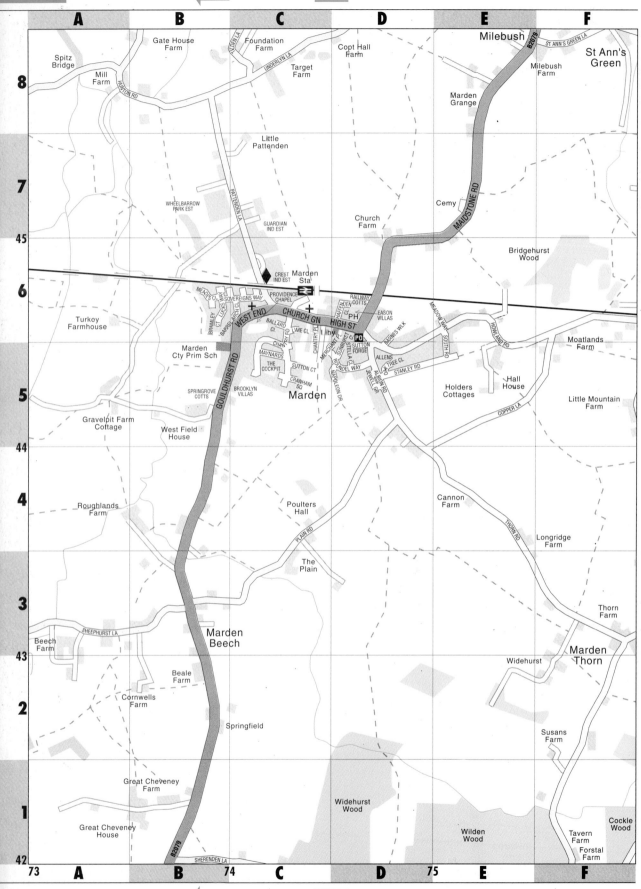

8

SUMMERHILL RD
BATTLE LA
Little Crew Den
Allingham Farm
Summer Hill
Sundridge Nurseries
MAIDSTONE RD A229
Sweetlands Farm

7

Manor Farm
Wanshurst Green
CARPENTERS LA
Newhaven Farm
Clapper Farm

45

6

Springfield Cottage
Overbridge Farm
CLAPPER LA
Duckhurst Farm
Abbotsleigh
Knowles Hill
Sewage Works

HOWLAND RD
NEWTOWN COTTS
GEORGE ST
Staplehurst Sta

5

LINDRIDGE LA
Mountain Farmhouse
Lindridge
MARDEN RD
Limekiln Farm
Fouracre
Works
PARKSTONE PK
DOUGLAS BLDGS
LODGE RD
STATION APP
STATION RD
HONEYCREST IND PK
MARKET GARTH
MOTUM
WINCH'S
CRES
PH ST
FISHERS RD
NEWTN
FISHERS CL
DR
Fisher's Farm

44

Baldwins Farm
Hen & Duckhurst Farm
WATKINS CL
CORNER FARM GRO
BROOKS CL
TOWN HILL
NORTH DOWNS
HURST CL
1 BENDEN CL
2 WEAVERS CL
3 KNOWLES WLK
HEADCORN RD

4

Great Pagehurst Farm
Staplehurst
STANSLEY GRN
OLIVER RD
POPE DR
BUTCHERS CL
REEVES CL
THATCHER RD
BATHURST CL
SURRENDEN RD
COWTHER CL
CHESTNUT
CORNWALLIS
ALEN SQ
CORNFORTH CL
POYNTELL RD
STAPLE CDR
SLANEY RD
MARIAN SQ

3

PAGEHURST RD
Little Pagehurst
Aydhurst Farm
BOWER WLK
BATHURST RD
GYBBON RISE
FLETCHER RD
OFFEN'S DR
USBORNE CL
Staplehurst Cty Prim Sch Liby
THE PARADE COTTS
LIME
HIGH ST
PO
CHAPEL LA
FIR TREE CL

The Wild Duck (PH)
Dourne Farm
VINE WK
BELL LA
JAGGARD WAY
MCI CL
KIRKMAN CT
SOUTH BANK

43

2

FRITTENDEN RD
HANMER WAY
SHERN WAY
CHURCH GN
CHURCH GN
HALLWARDS

The Laurels
Clarkes Farm
FIVE OAK LA
Henhurst Farm
PINNOCK LA
The Quarter
Iden Park

1

PRISTLING LA
Saynden Farm
GOUDHURST RD
Brattle Farm Mus
CRANBROOK RD A229
Ely Court
Gooseberry Wood

42

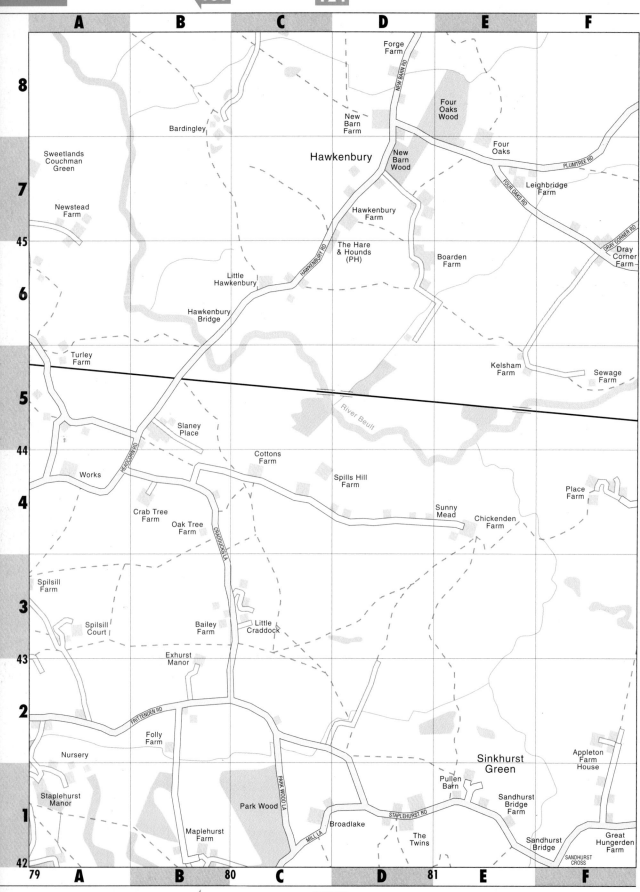

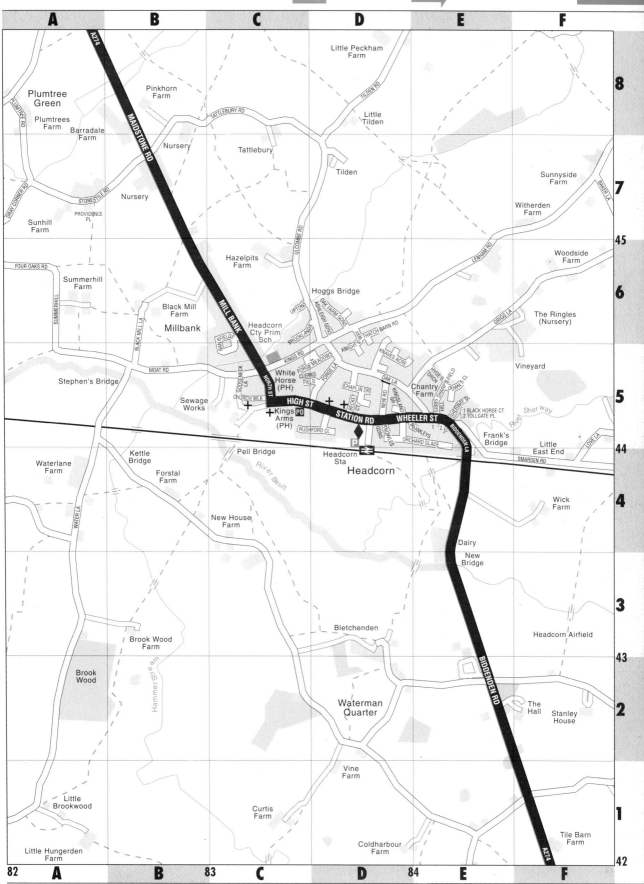

A · B · C · D · E · F

8
7
45
6
5
44
4
3
43
2
1
42

Plumtree Green
Plumtrees Farm
Barradale Farm
Pinkhorn Farm
Nursery
Little Peckham Farm
TATTLEBURY RD
Tattlebury
Little Tilden
TILDEN RD
Tilden
Sunnyside Farm
BAKER LA
Witherden Farm
Woodside Farm
TRAY CORNER RD
STONESTYLE RD
Nursery
Nursery
PROVIDENCE PL
Sunhill Farm
FOUR OAKS RD
Summerhill Farm
SUMMERHILL
Hazelpits Farm
ULCOMBE RD
Hoggs Bridge
UPTONS
Headcorn Cty Prim Sch
OAK FARM GDNS
ASHLEIGH GDNS
BROOKLANDS
KINGS RD
Knights Av
THATCH BARN RD
KNAVES ACRE
LEMHAM RD
GRIGG LA
The Ringles (Nursery)
Vineyard
Black Mill Farm
Millbank
BLACK MILL LA
MOAT RD
MILL BANK
BAKFIELD
GOOSENECK
CHURCH WLK
NORTH ST
Stephen's Bridge
Sewage Works
White Horse (PH)
FORGE MEADOWS
CLERKS FIELD
FORGE LA
CHAPLIN DR
BECKET CL
NEW RD
OAK LA
KINGSLAND GR
Chantry Farm
HYDE'S
ORCH
GIBBS HILL
SHARP'S FIELD
DOWL'S CL
SPEEDWAY CL
Vineyard
HIGH ST
Kings Arms (PH)
PO
STATION RD
RUSHFORD CL
WHEELER ST
KNOWLES
KNOWLES GDNS
ORCHARD GLADE
BRAMLEYS
1 · 2
1 BLACK HORSE CT
2 TOLLGATE PL
River Sher Way
Frank's Bridge
Little East End
BIDDENDEN LA
Waterlane Farm
WATER LA
Kettle Bridge
Forstal Farm
Pell Bridge
River Beult
P
Headcorn Sta
Headcorn
SMARDEN RD
Wick Farm
LOVE LA
New House Farm
Dairy
New Bridge
Brook Wood Farm
Hammer Stream
Brook Wood
Bletchenden
Headcorn Airfield
BIDDENDEN RD
Waterman Quarter
The Hall
Stanley House
Little Brookwood
Vine Farm
Curtis Farm
Coldharbour Farm
Tile Barn Farm
A274
Little Hungerden Farm

MAIDSTONE RD
A274

82 · A · B · 83 · C · D · 84 · E · F · 42

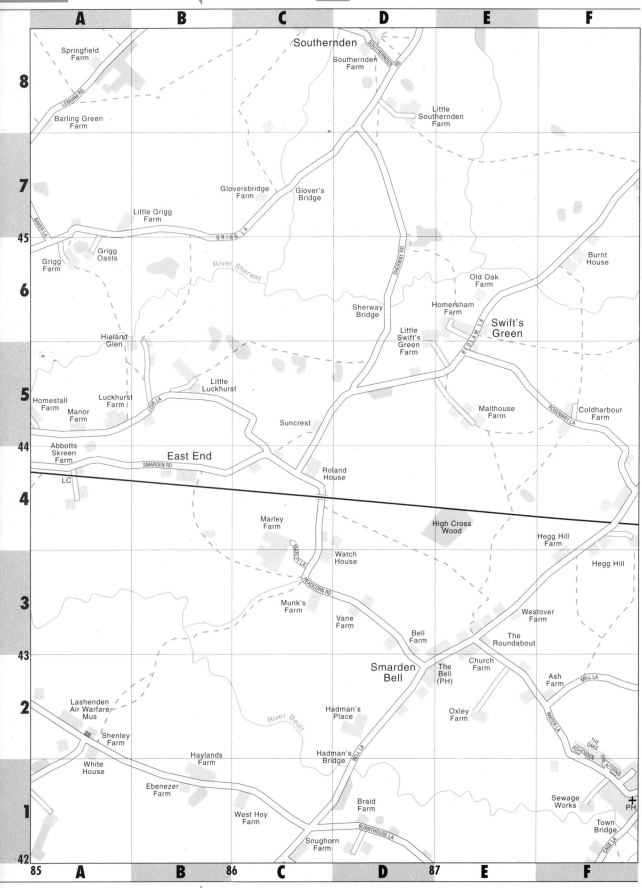

Southernden

Springfield Farm

Barling Green Farm

LENHAM RD

Southernden Farm

Little Southernden Farm

SOUTHERNDEN RD

8

Gloversbridge Farm

Glover's Bridge

7

Little Grigg Farm

GRIGG LA

45

BAKER LA

Grigg Oasts

Grigg Farm

River Sherway

SHERWAY RD

Old Oak Farm

Homersham Farm

Burnt House

6

Sherway Bridge

Little Swift's Green Farm

BEDLAM LA

Swift's Green

Hieland Glen

LOVE LA

Little Luckhurst

5

Homestall Farm

Manor Farm

Luckhurst Farm

Suncrest

Malthouse Farm

ROSEMARY LA

Coldharbour Farm

44

Abbotts Skreen Farm

SMARDEN RD

East End

Roland House

LC

High Cross Wood

Hegg Hill Farm

4

Marley Farm

MARLEY LA

Watch House

Hegg Hill

HEADCORN RD

3

Munk's Farm

Vane Farm

Bell Farm

Westover Farm

The Roundabout

43

Smarden Bell

The Bell (PH)

Church Farm

Ash Farm

MILL LA

Lashenden Air Warfare Mus

Hadman's Place

Oxley Farm

WATER LA

THE OAKS

2

Shenley Farm

River Beult

BELL LA

ASHENDEN

THE ACORNS

White House

Haylands Farm

Hadman's Bridge

Ebenezer Farm

Braid Farm

Sewage Works

PH

1

West Hoy Farm

Snughorn Farm

BURNTHOUSE LA

Town Bridge

CAGE LA

42

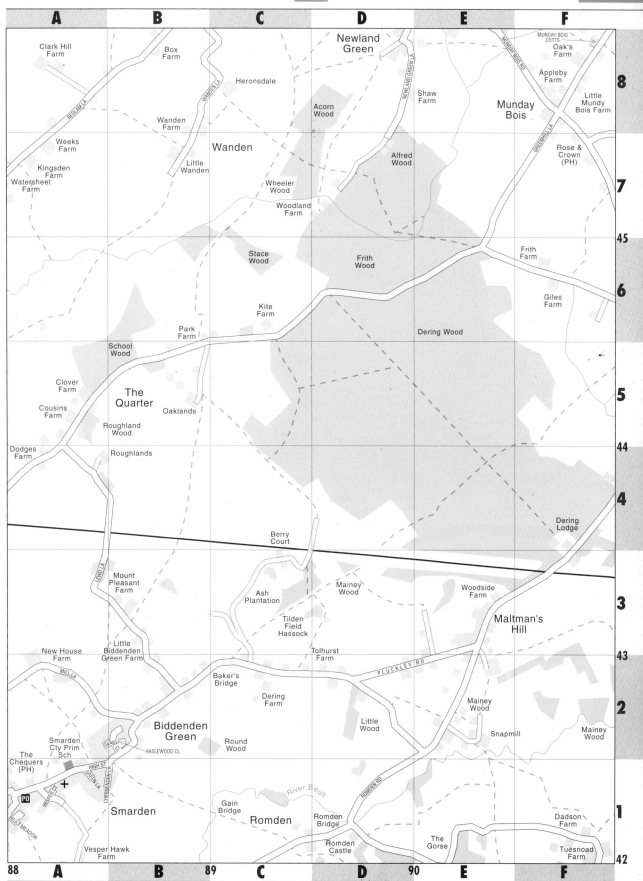

Clark Hill Farm

Box Farm

Heronsdale

Newland Green

Munday Bois Cotts

Oak's Farm

WANDEN LA

Wanden Farm

Acorn Wood

NEWLAND GREEN LA

Shaw Farm

MUNDAY BOIS RD

Appleby Farm

Munday Bois

Little Mundy Bois Farm

8

BEDLAM LA

Weeks Farm

Little Wanden

Wanden

Alfred Wood

GREENHILL LA

Rose & Crown (PH)

Kingsden Farm

Watersheet Farm

Wheeler Wood

Woodland Farm

7

45

Stace Wood

Frith Wood

Frith Farm

Giles Farm

6

Kite Farm

Park Farm

Dering Wood

School Wood

Clover Farm

The Quarter

Oaklands

5

Cousins Farm

Roughland Wood

44

Dodges Farm

Roughlands

4

Dering Lodge

Berry Court

LEWD LA

Mount Pleasant Farm

Ash Plantation

Mainey Wood

Woodside Farm

3

Tilden Field Hassock

Maltman's Hill

New House Farm

Little Biddenden Green Farm

Tolhurst Farm

PLUCKLEY RD

43

MILL LA

Baker's Bridge

Dering Farm

Mainey Wood

2

GLEBE

Smarden Cty Prim Sch

HASLEWOOD CL

Biddenden Green

Round Wood

Little Wood

Snapmill

Mainey Wood

The Chequers (PH)

HIGH ST

GREEN LA

CHESSENDEN LA

ROMDEN RD

River Beult

Gain Bridge

Romden

Romden Bridge

Dadson Farm

1

PO

VESPER CT

Smarden

The Gorse

BEULT MEADOW

Vesper Hawk Farm

Romden Castle

Tuesnoad Farm

42

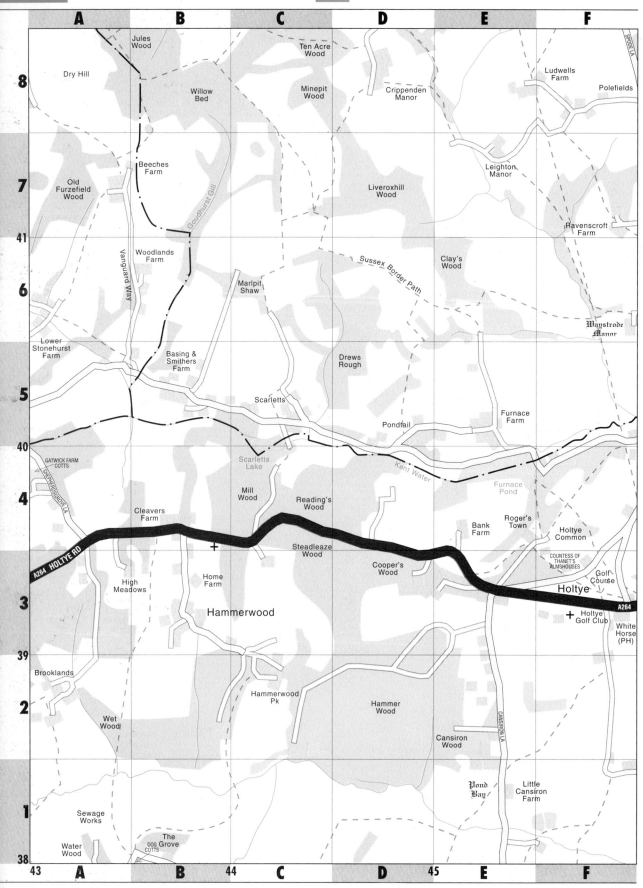

A B C D E F

8 Dry Hill Jules Wood Willow Bed Ten Acre Wood Minepit Wood Crippenden Manor Ludwells Farm Polefields

SPODE LA

7 Old Furzefield Wood Beeches Farm Liveroxhill Wood Leighton Manor Ravenscroft Farm

41 Goudhurst Gill

6 Woodlands Farm Marlpit Shaw Sussex Border Path Clay's Wood Waystrode Manor

Vanguard Way

Lower Stonehurst Farm Basing & Smithers Farm Drews Rough

5 Scarletts Scarletts Pondtail Furnace Farm

40 Gatwick Farm Cotts Scarletts Lake Kent Water Furnace Pond

SHEPHERDSGROVE LA

4 Cleavers Farm Mill Wood Reading's Wood Bank Farm Roger's Town Holtye Common

COUNTESS OF THANET'S ALMSHOUSES

A264 HOLTYE RD High Meadows Home Farm Steadleaze Wood Cooper's Wood Golf Course

Holtye

3 Hammerwood Holtye Golf Club A264 White Horse (PH)

39 Brooklands

2 Wet Wood Hammerwood Pk Hammer Wood CANSIRON LA Cansiron Wood Little Cansiron Farm

Pond Bay

1 Sewage Works The Grove DOG COTTS

38 Water Wood

43 A B 44 C D 45 E F

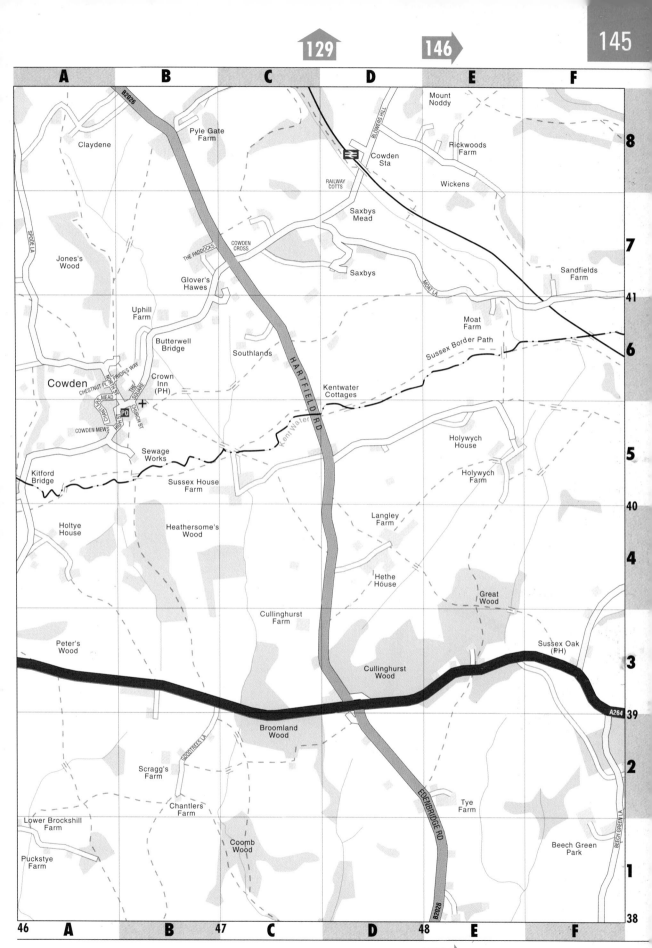

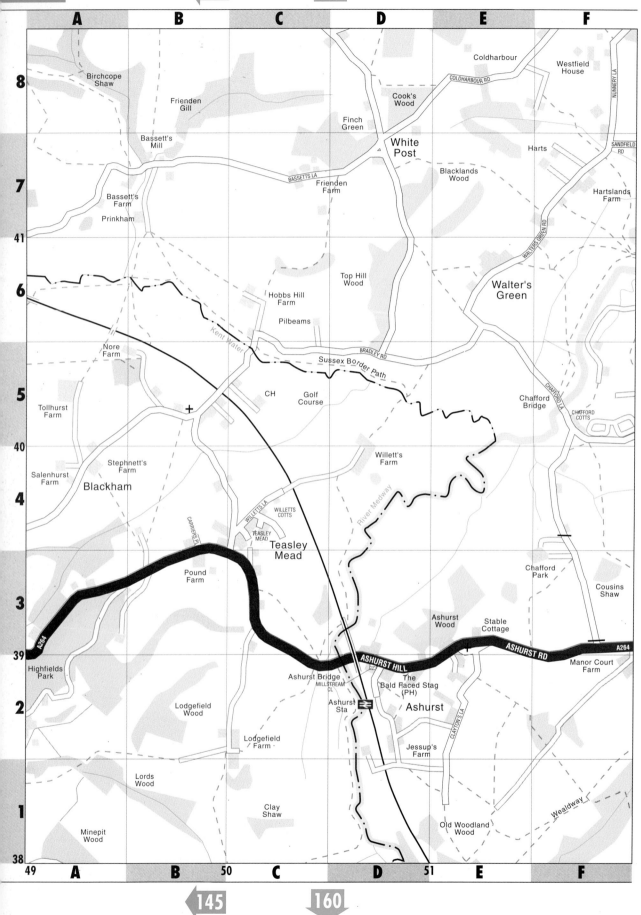

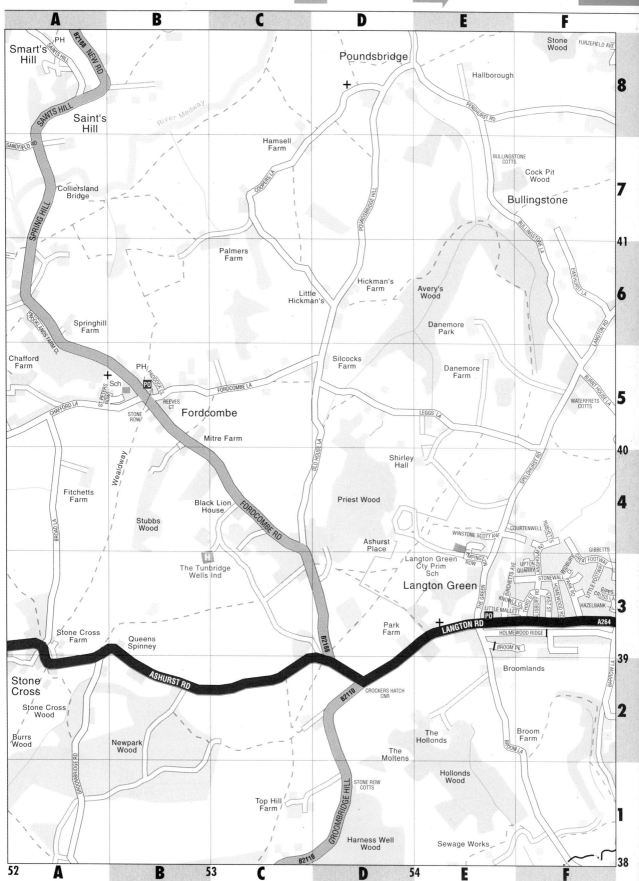

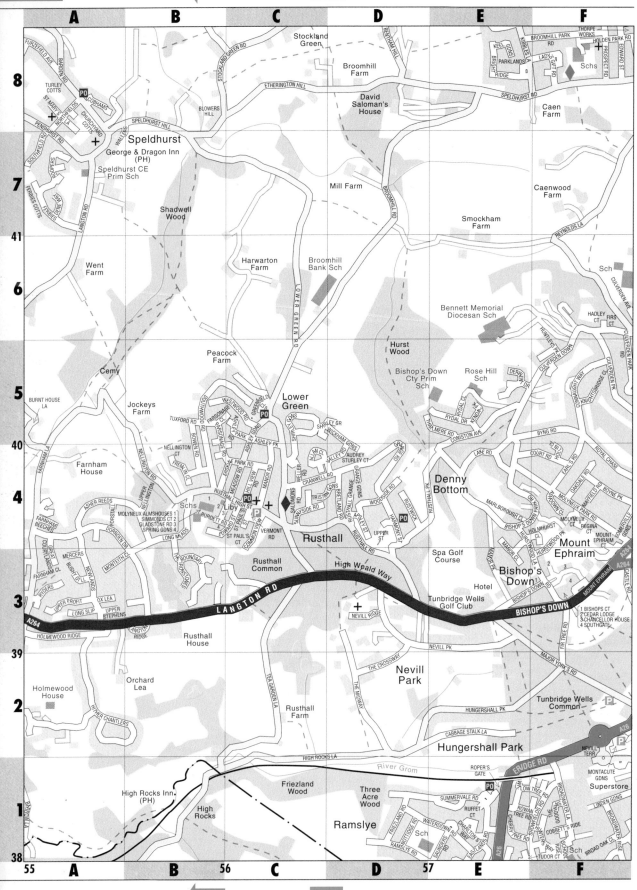

147 132

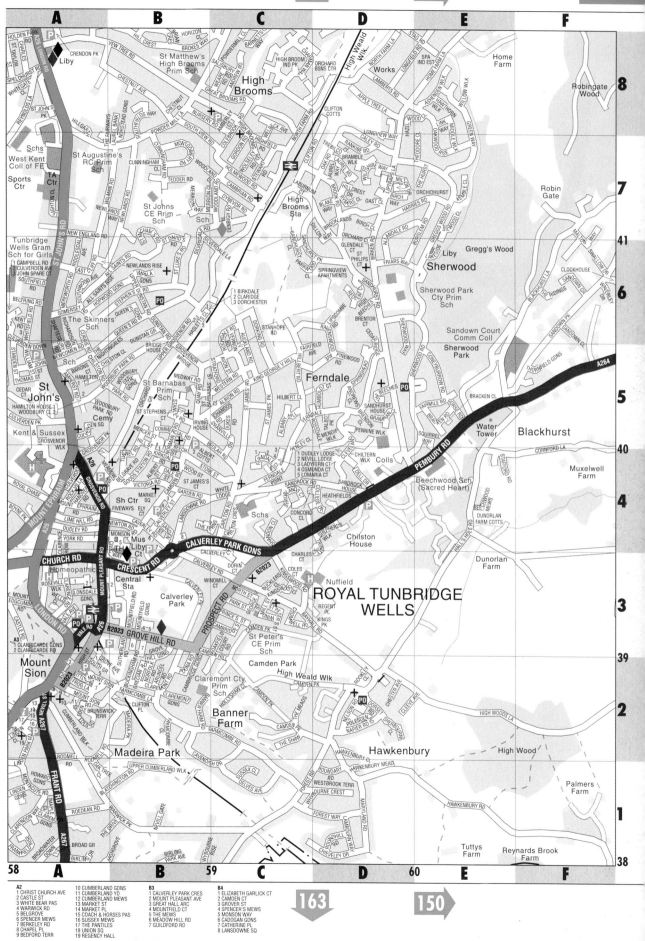

A2
1 CHRIST CHURCH AVE
2 CASTLE ST
3 WHITE BEAR PAS
4 WARWICK RD
5 BELGROVE
6 SPENCER MEWS
7 BERKELEY RD
8 CHAPEL PL
9 BEDFORD TERR
10 CUMBERLAND GDNS
11 CUMBERLAND YD
12 CUMBERLAND MEWS
13 MARKET ST
14 MARKET PL
15 COACH & HORSES PAS
16 SUSSEX MEWS
17 THE PANTILES
18 UNION SQ
19 REGENCY HALL

B3
1 CALVERLEY PARK CRES
2 MOUNT PLEASANT AVE
3 GREAT HALL ARC
4 MOUNTFIELD CT
5 THE MEWS
6 MEADOW HILL RD
7 GUILDFORD RD

B4
1 ELIZABETH GARLICK CT
2 CAMDEN CT
3 GROVER ST
4 SPENCER'S MEWS
5 MONSON WAY
6 CADOGAN GDNS
7 CATHERINE PL
8 LANSDOWNE SQ

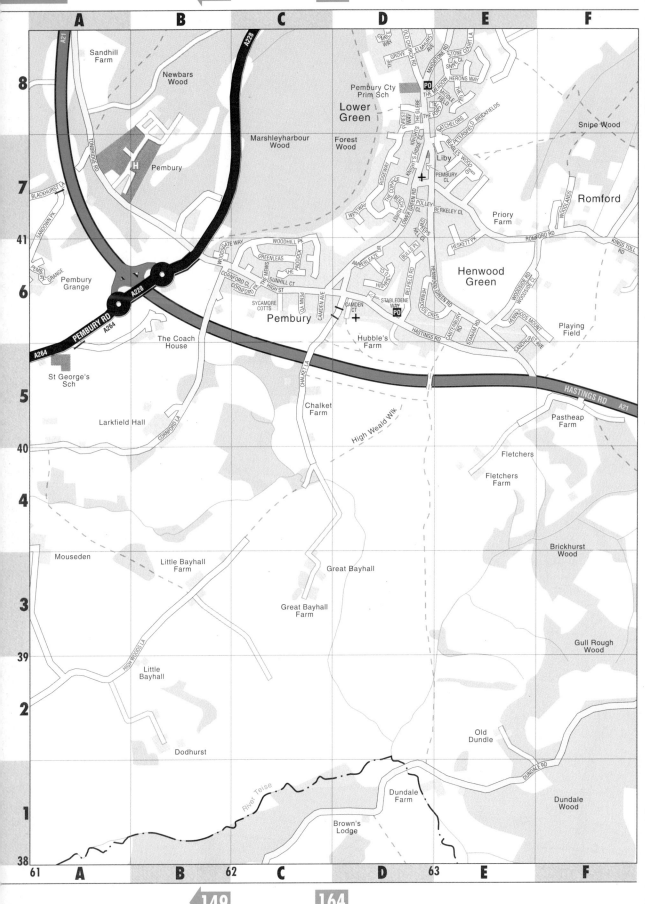

149
134
149
164

A   B   C   D   E   F

8

7

41

6

5

40

4

3

39

2

1

38

61   A   B   62   C   D   63   E   F

Sandhill Farm
Newbars Wood
Marshleyharbour Wood
Forest Wood
Lower Green
Pembury Cty Prim Sch
Snipe Wood
Romford
Pembury
Liby
Priory Farm
Pembury Grange
Henwood Green
Blackhurst La
Pembury Rd
A228
A264
The Coach House
Playing Field
St George's Sch
Hastings Rd
A21
Larkfield Hall
Chalket Farm
High Weald Wlk
Pastheap Farm
Fletchers
Fletchers Farm
Mouseden
Little Bayhall Farm
Great Bayhall
Brickhurst Wood
Great Bayhall Farm
Gull Rough Wood
Little Bayhall
Old Dundle
Dodhurst
River Teise
Dundale Farm
Dundale Wood
Brown's Lodge
Hubble's Farm

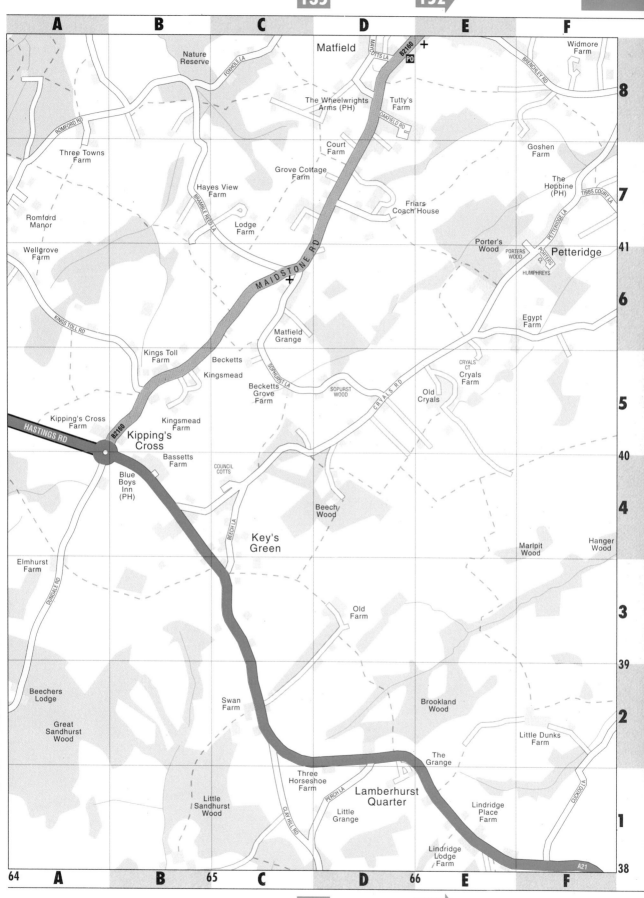

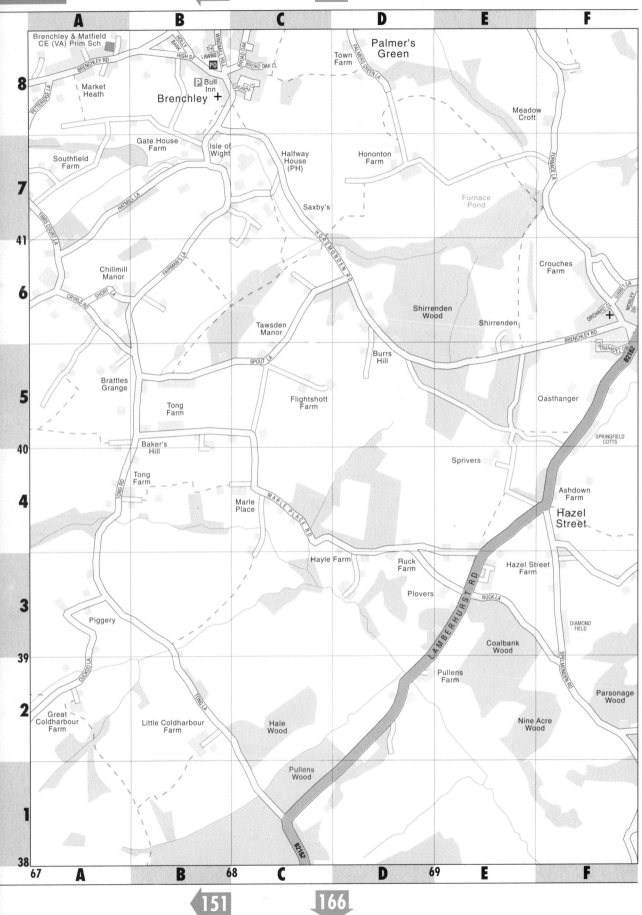

151 136

A B C D E F

8
7
41
6
5
40
4
3
39
2
1
38

Brenchley & Matfield CE (VA) Prim Sch

Market Heath

Southfield Farm

PETTERIDGE LA

BRENCHLEY RD

HATMILL LA

TIBBS COURT LA

Gate House Farm

HOLLY BANK
HIGH ST
WINDMILL HILL
THE LAWNS
PO
BROAD OAK
BROAD OAK CL
CHURCH CL

Bull Inn
Brenchley

Isle of Wight

Halfway House (PH)

Saxby's

Palmer's Green

Town Farm

PALMERS GREEN LA

Hononton Farm

Meadow Croft

FURNACE LA

Furnace Pond

Crouches Farm

GIBBET LA
MORLEY DR
ORCHARD CL
FROMMDEZ DR
B2162

Chillmill Manor

CRYALS RD
SHORT LA
FAIRMAN'S LA

Tawsden Manor

HORSMONDEN RD

Shirrenden Wood

Shirrenden

BRENCHLEY RD

Oasthanger

SPRINGFIELD COTTS

Brattles Grange

Tong Farm

SPOUT LA

Flightshott Farm

Burrs Hill

Sprivers

Ashdown Farm

Hazel Street

Baker's Hill

TONG RD

Tong Farm

Marle Place

MARLE PLACE RD

Hayle Farm

Ruck Farm

Plovers

LAMBERHURST RD

RUCK LA

Hazel Street Farm

DIAMOND FIELD

SPELMONDEN RD

Piggery

CUCKOO LA

TONG LA

Coalbank Wood

Pullens Farm

Parsonage Wood

Great Coldharbour Farm

Little Coldharbour Farm

Hale Wood

Nine Acre Wood

Pullens Wood

B2162

67 A B 68 C D 69 E F

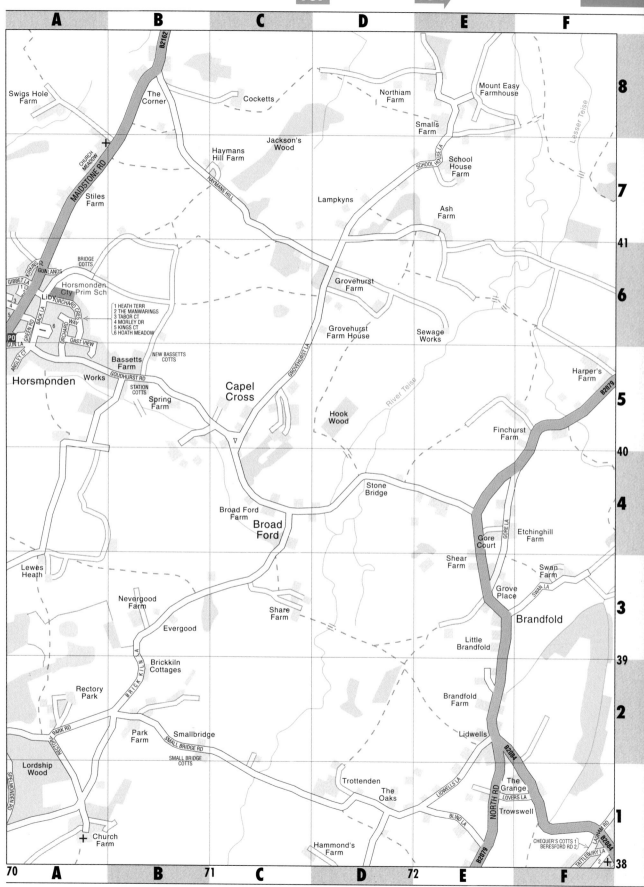

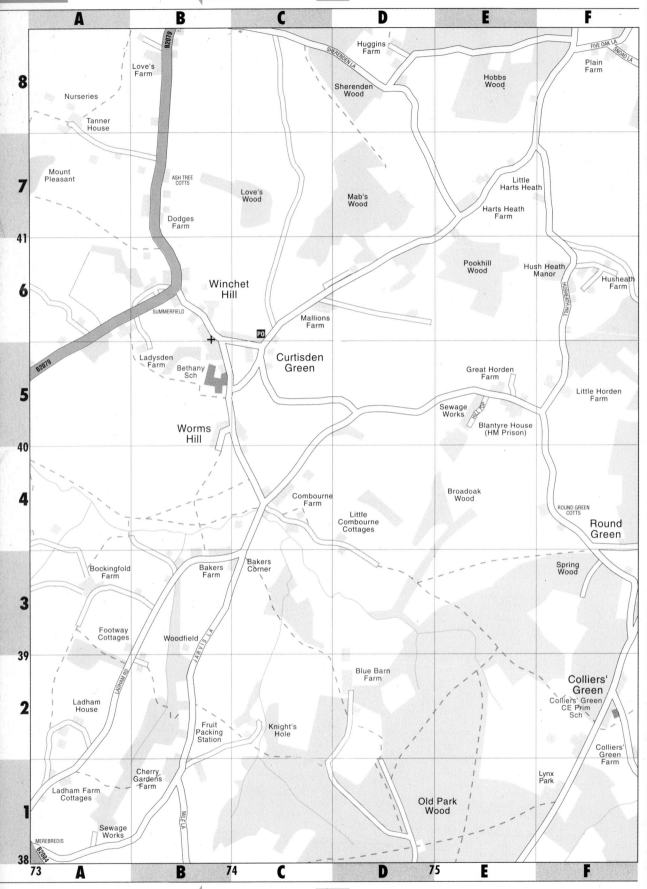

	A	B	C	D	E	F

8

Love's Farm

B2079

Nurseries

Tanner House

Huggins Farm

FIVE OAK LA · SNOAD LA

Plain Farm

SHERENDEN LA

Sherenden Wood

Hobbs Wood

7

Mount Pleasant

ASH TREE COTTS

Love's Wood

Mab's Wood

Little Harts Heath

Harts Heath Farm

Dodges Farm

41

Pookhill Wood

Hush Heath Manor

Husheath Farm

HUSHEATH HILL

6

Winchet Hill

SUMMERFIELD

Mallions Farm

PO

5

B2079

Ladysden Farm

Bethany Sch

Curtisden Green

Great Horden Farm

Little Horden Farm

Sewage Works

HILL LA

Blantyre House (HM Prison)

Worms Hill

40

4

Combourne Farm

Little Combourne Cottages

Broadoak Wood

ROUND GREEN COTTS

Round Green

3

Bockingfold Farm

Bakers Farm

Bakers Corner

Spring Wood

Footway Cottages

Woodfield

JARVIS LA

39

LADHAM RD

Blue Barn Farm

Colliers' Green

Ladham House

Colliers' Green CE Prim Sch

2

Fruit Packing Station

Knight's Hole

Colliers' Green Farm

Cherry Gardens Farm

Lynx Park

MILE LA

Old Park Wood

1

Ladham Farm Cottages

Sewage Works

MEREBREDIS

B2084

38

73	A		B	74	C		D	75	E		F

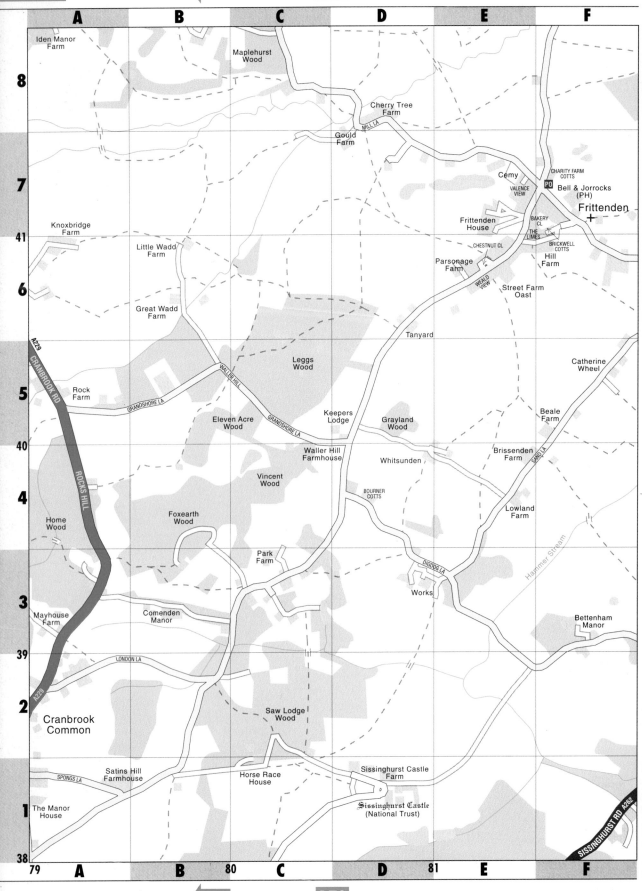

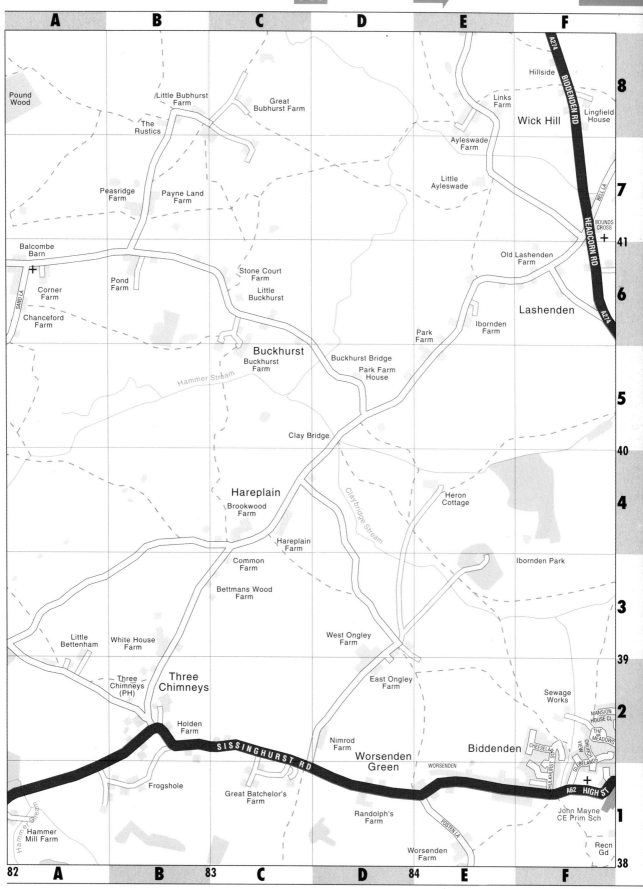

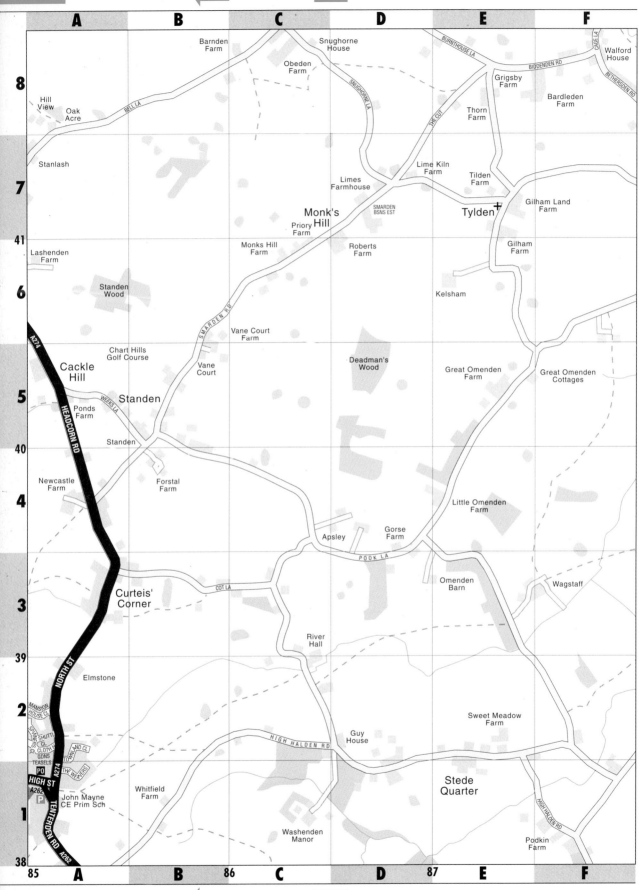

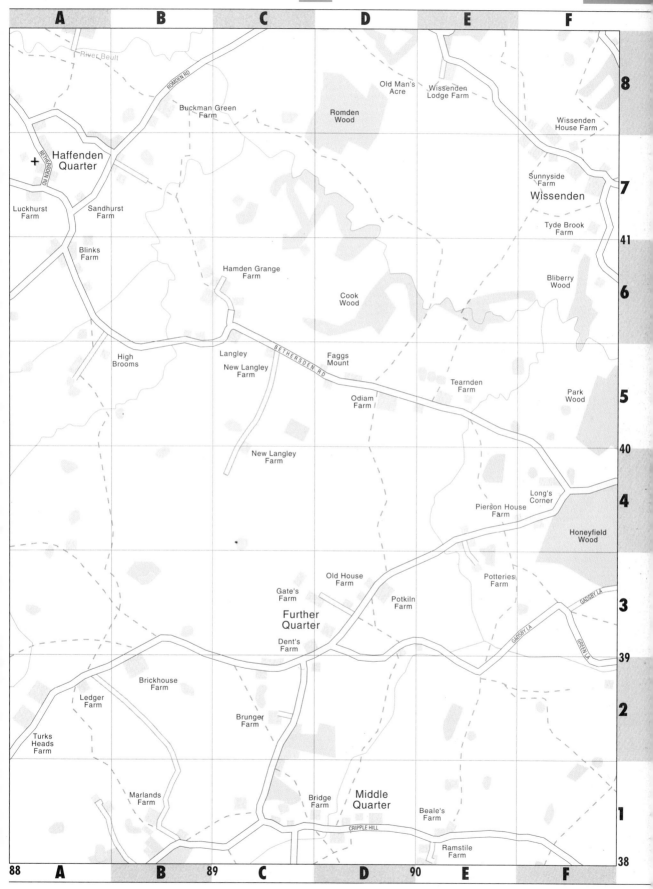

A   B   C   D   E   F

8

Old Man's Acre
Wissenden Lodge Farm
Romden Wood
Wissenden House Farm

Haffenden Quarter
+

Buckman Green Farm

River Beult
ROMDEN RD

Sunnyside Farm

Wissenden

7

Luckhurst Farm
Sandhurst Farm
BETHERSDEN RD

Tyde Brook Farm

41

Blinks Farm

Hamden Grange Farm

Cook Wood

Bliberry Wood

6

High Brooms

Langley
New Langley Farm
BETHERSDEN RD

Faggs Mount

Odiam Farm

Tearnden Farm

Park Wood

5

New Langley Farm

40

Long's Corner

4

Pierson House Farm

Honeyfield Wood

Old House Farm

Potteries Farm

Gate's Farm

Further Quarter

Potkiln Farm

GADSBY LA

3

Dent's Farm

GADSBY LA

GREEN LA

39

Brickhouse Farm

Ledger Farm

Brunger Farm

2

Turks Heads Farm

Marlands Farm

Bridge Farm

Middle Quarter

Beale's Farm

1

CRIPPLE HILL

Ramstile Farm

38

88   A   B   89   C   D   90   E   F

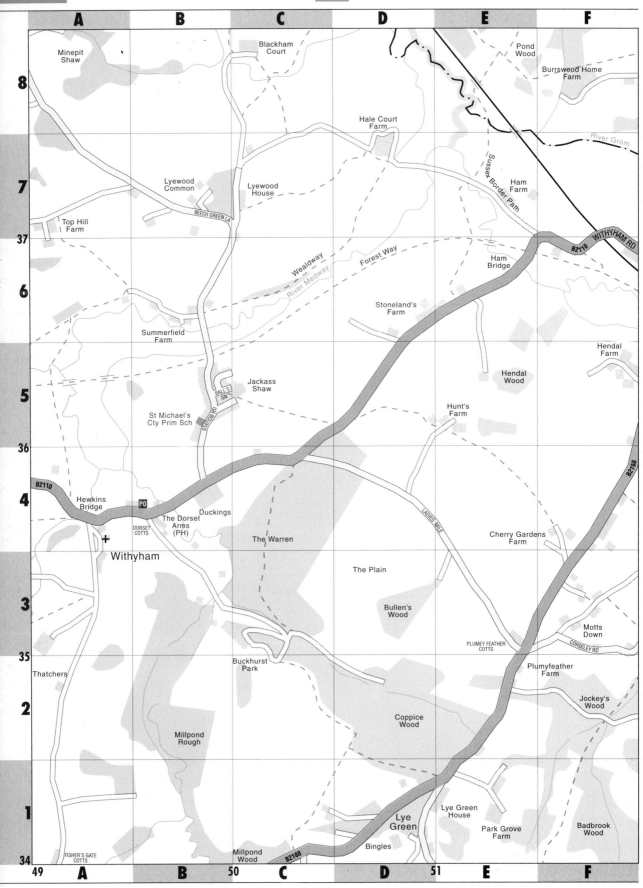

A B C D E F

8

Minepit Shaw

Blackham Court

Pond Wood

Burrswood Home Farm

River Grom

Hale Court Farm

7

Lyewood Common

Lyewood House

Ham Farm

Sussex Border Path

37

Top Hill Farm

BEECH GREEN LA

WITHYHAM RD

B2110

Wealdway

Forest Way

Ham Bridge

6

River Medway

Summerfield Farm

Stoneland's Farm

Hendal Farm

Hendal Wood

5

Jackass Shaw

BALL'S GN

STATION RD

St Michael's Cty Prim Sch

Hunt's Farm

36

B2188

4

B2110

Hewkins Bridge

PO

Duckings

The Dorset Arms (PH)

DORSET COTTS

The Warren

LADIES MILE

Cherry Gardens Farm

Withyham

The Plain

Bullen's Wood

Motts Down

3

35

Thatchers

Buckhurst Park

PLUMEY FEATHER COTTS

CORSELEY RD

Plumyfeather Farm

Jockey's Wood

2

Millpond Rough

Coppice Wood

1

Lye Green

Lye Green House

Park Grove Farm

Badbrook Wood

Millpond Wood

Bingles

FISHER'S GATE COTTS

B2188

34

49 A B 50 C D 51 E F

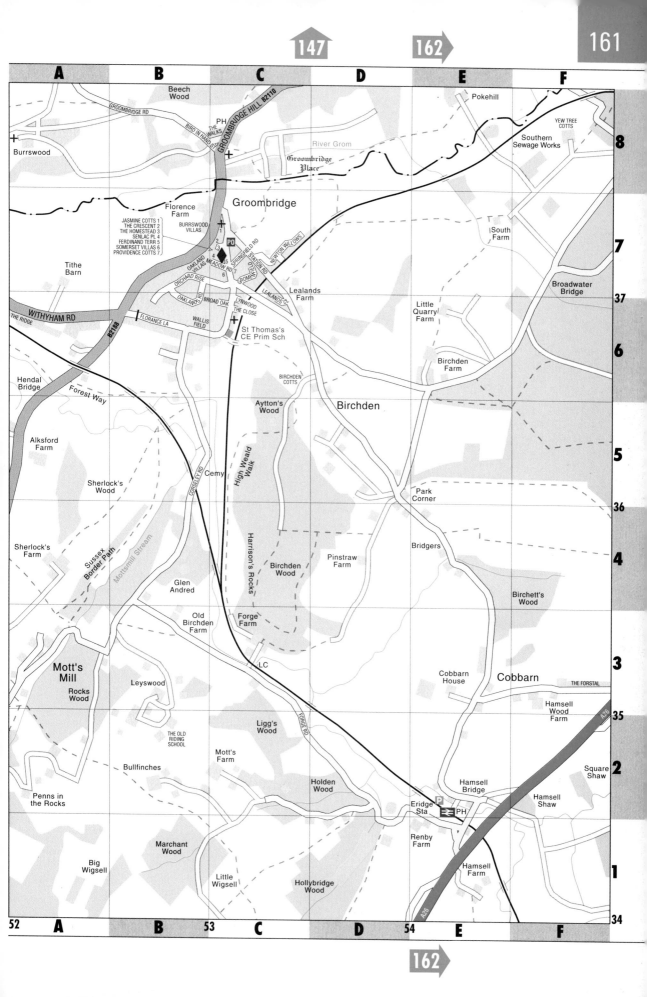

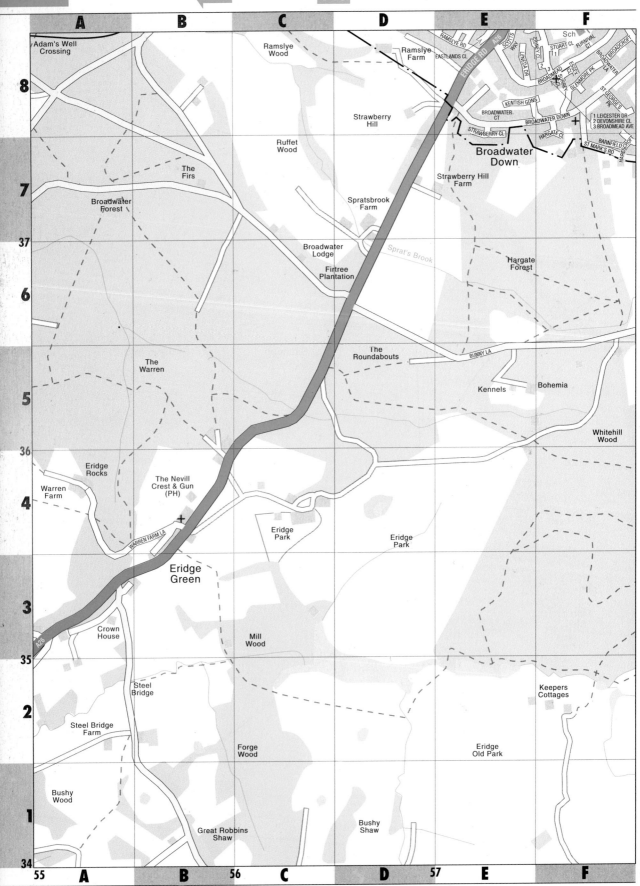

A B C D E F

8

7

37

6

5

36

4

3

35

2

1

34

55 A B 56 C D 57 E F

Adam's Well Crossing

Ramslye Wood

Ramslye Farm

RAMSLYE RD
EASTLANDS CL
A26
SCOTTS WN
STANLEY CL
LANEDA DR
STUART CL
FURNIVAL CT
BROADCROFT
1
2
3
Z
Sch
BROADMEAD
Z
GLENMORE PK
BERRY
ST GEORGE'S PK
ST MARK'S RD
HAREDEANS
HARGATE CL
BARNFIELDSCROFT
1 LEICESTER DR
2 DEVONSHIRE CL
3 BROADMEAD AVE

Strawberry Hill

Ruffet Wood

BROADWATER DOWN
BROADWATER CT
KENTISH GDNS
STRAWBERRY CL

Broadwater Down

The Firs

Broadwater Forest

Strawberry Hill Farm

Spratsbrook Farm

Sprat's Brook

Broadwater Lodge

Firtree Plantation

Hargate Forest

The Warren

The Roundabouts

BUNNY LA

Kennels

Bohemia

Whitehill Wood

Eridge Rocks

The Nevill Crest & Gun (PH)

Warren Farm

WARREN FARM LA

Eridge Park

Eridge Park

Eridge Green

A26

Crown House

Mill Wood

Steel Bridge

Keepers Cottages

Steel Bridge Farm

Forge Wood

Eridge Old Park

Bushy Wood

Great Robbins Shaw

Bushy Shaw

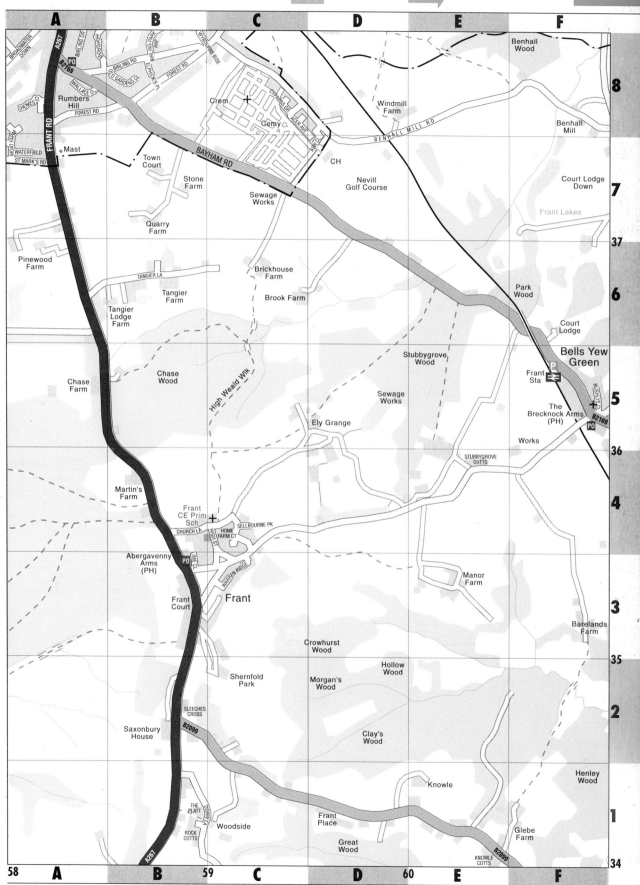

163 150

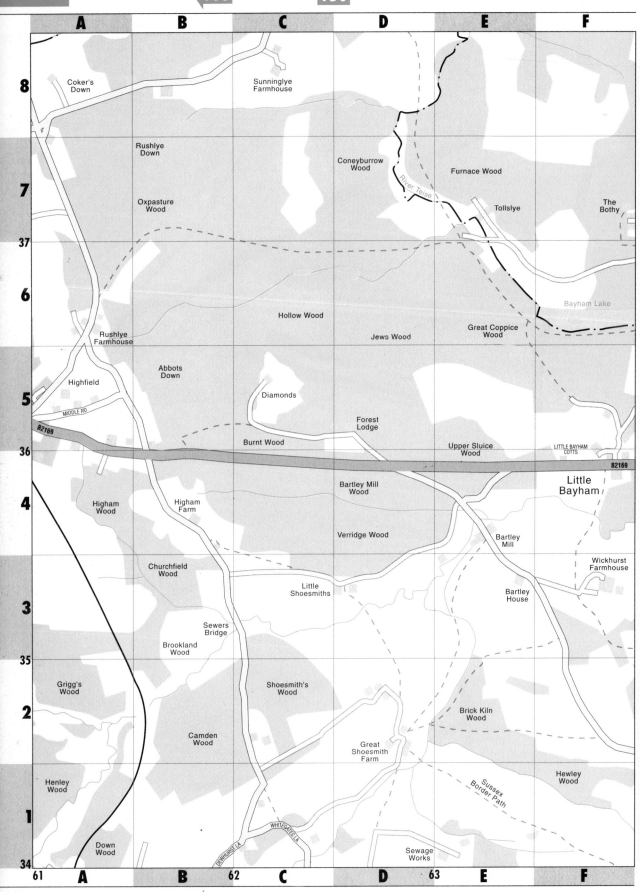

163 174

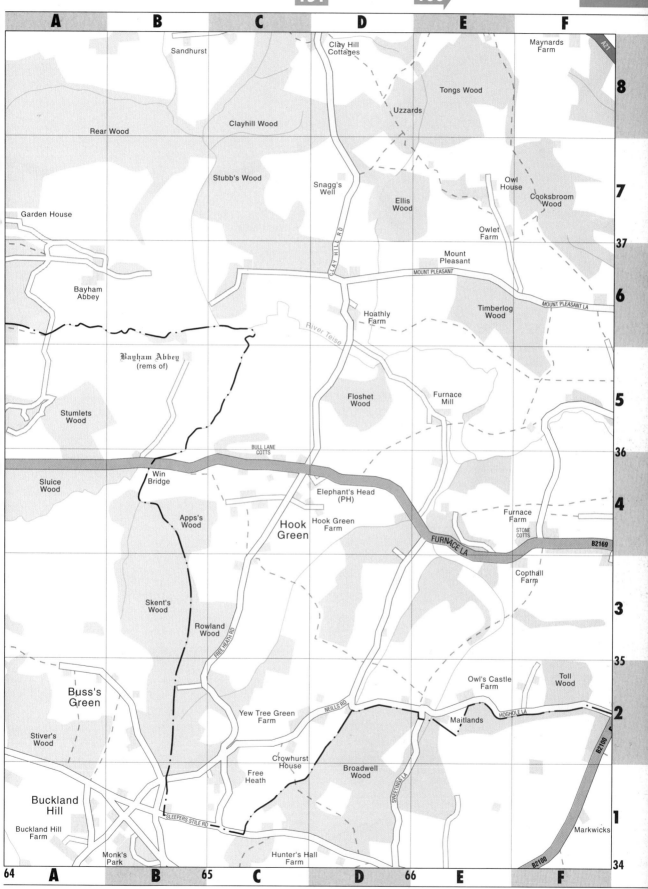

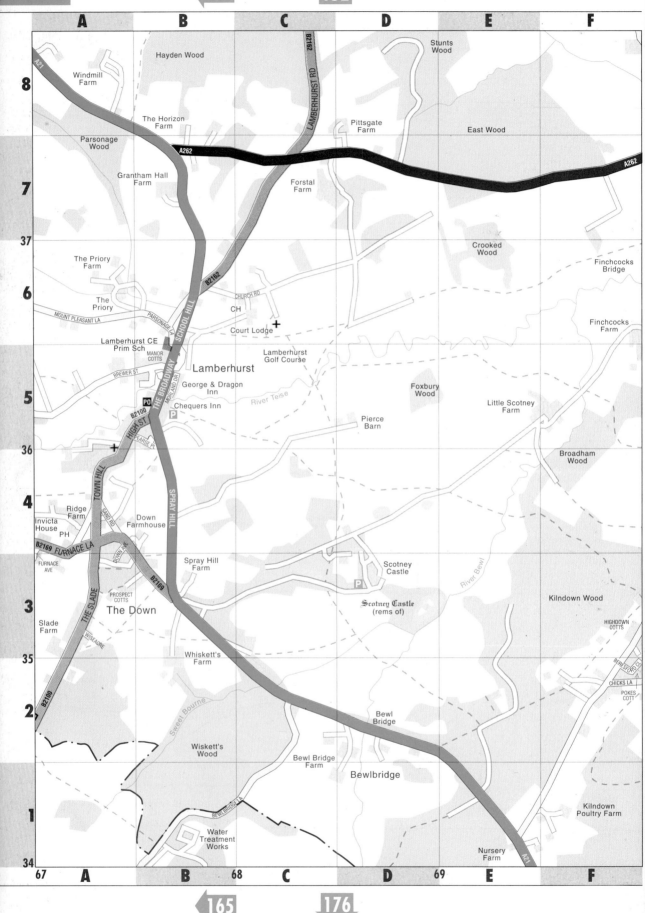

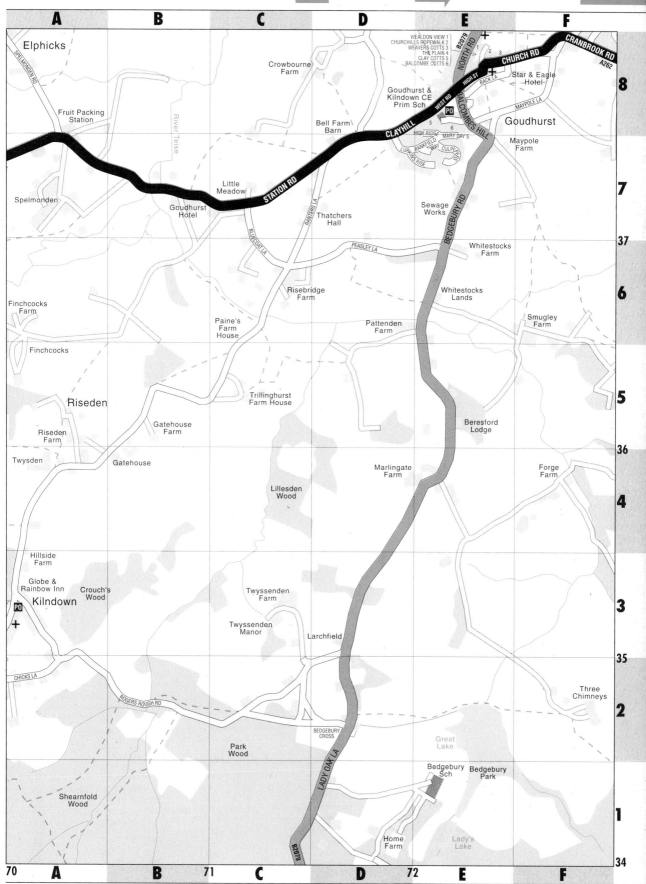

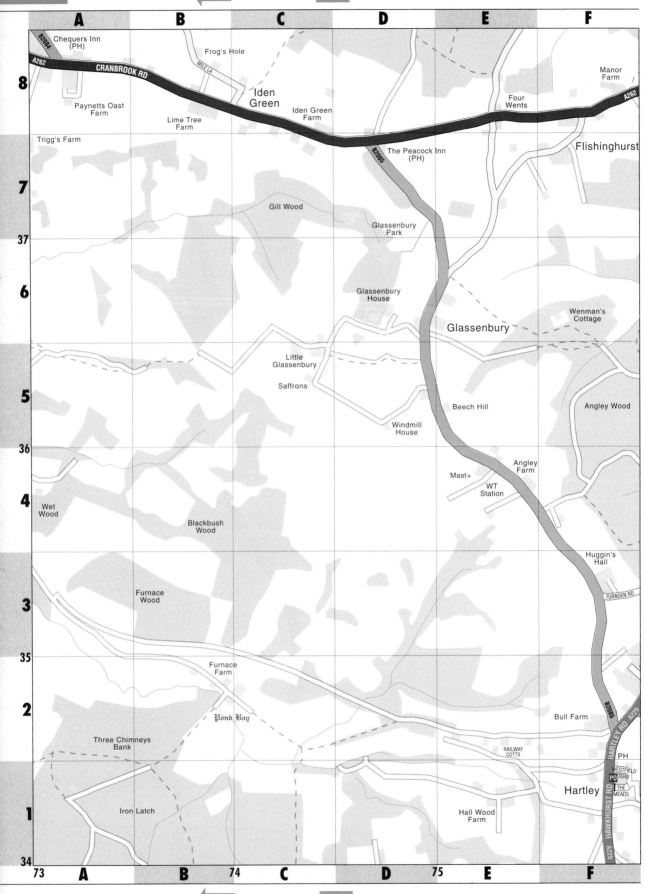

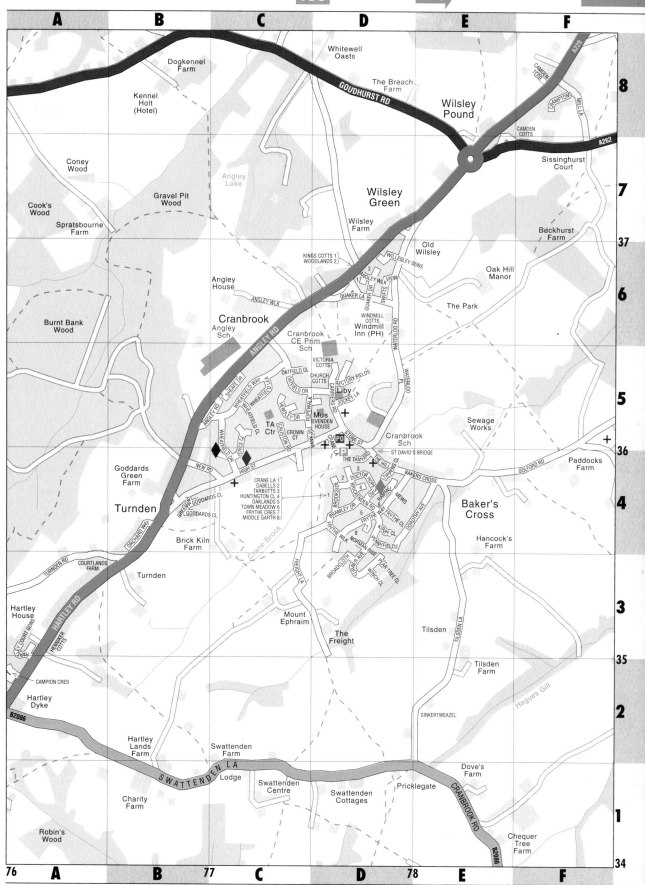

8

7

37

6

5

36

4

3

35

2

1

34

A   B   C   D   E   F

Whitewell Oasts

The Breach Farm

Wilsley Pound

Camden Terr

GOUDHURST RD

A229

Champtons

Mill La

Camden Cotts

A262

Sissinghurst Court

Dogkennel Farm

Kennel Holt (Hotel)

Coney Wood

Angley Lake

Wilsley Green

Wilsley Farm

Old Wilsley

Buckhurst Farm

Cook's Wood

Spratsbourne Farm

Gravel Pit Wood

Kings Cotts 1
Woodlands 2

Willesley Gdns

Angley Wlk View

Quaker La

Swifts

Angley Dr

Oak Hill Manor

The Park

Angley House

Angley Wlk

Cranbrook

Angley Sch

Cranbrook CE Prim Sch

Windmill Cotts

Windmill Inn (PH)

Waterloo Rd

Burnt Bank Wood

ANGLEY RD

Victoria Cotts

Rectory Fields

Church Cotts

Liby

Jockey La

Waterloo Pl

Sewage Works

Oatfield Cl

Oatfield Dr

Carriers Rd

Sheafe Dr

Wheatfield Way

Hedley Dr

Rosewalk

Mus
Evenden House

Crane La

Stone St

Cranbrook Sch

Angley Rd

Wheatfield Cl

Banks Cl

TA Ctr

Crown Ct

PO

The Tanyard

St David's Bridge

Wheatfield Dr

Joyce Cl

Calistori Rd

P

The Hill

Golford Rd

Paddocks Farm

Goddards Green Farm

New Rd

High St

Crane La 1
Dabells 2
Tarbutts 3
Huntington Cl 4
Oaklands 5
Town Meadow 6
Frythe Cres 7
Middle Garth 8

Doctor

Brookside

Big Side

Bramley Dr

Tippens Cl

Bakers Cross

Baker's Cross

Turnden

Greenway

Goddards Cl

Goddards Cl

Crane Brook

Brockloth

Eden Rd

Bramble Mews

Frythe Cl

Frythe

Dorothy Ave

Hancock's Farm

Brick Kiln Farm

ORCHARD WAY

Freight La

Frythe Wlk

Norman Rise

Kirby Cl

Pennyfields

Pear Tree Cl

Turnden Rd

Courtlands Farm

Turnden

HARTLEY RD

Brockloth

Shirley Ave

Winch Cl

Tilsden

Tilsden La

Hartley House

Mount Ephraim

The Freight

Tilsden Farm

Hartley Court Gdns

Henniker Cotts

Sinkertweazel

Hagues Gill

Campion Cres

B2086

Hartley Dyke

Hartley Lands Farm

Swattenden Farm

SWATTENDEN LA

Lodge

Swattenden Centre

Swattenden Cottages

Pricklegate

Dove's Farm

CRANBROOK RD

Charity Farm

Robin's Wood

Chequer Tree Farm

B2086

76   A   B   77   C   D   78   E   F

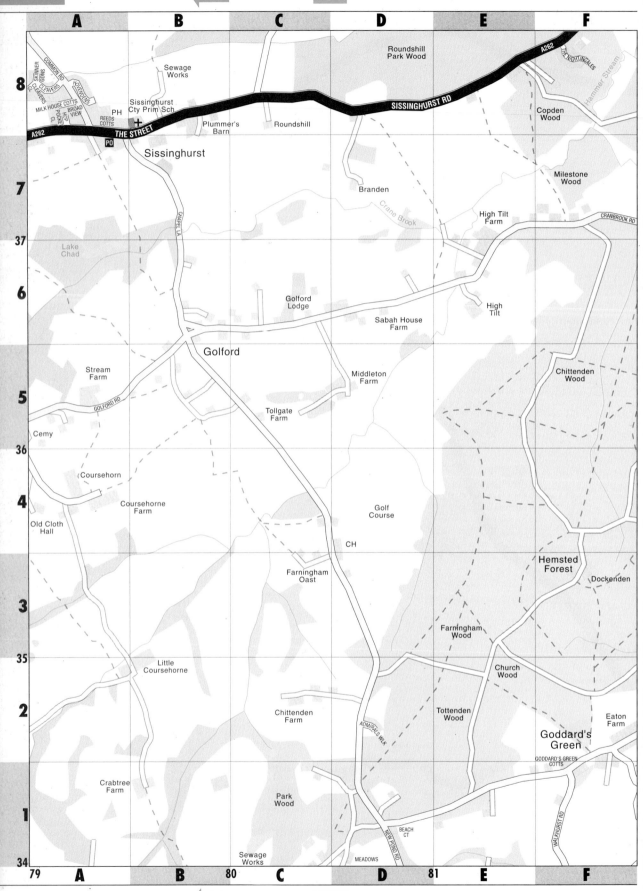
A   B   C   D   E   F

8

COMMON RD
SKINNER
GDNS
CLEAVERS
CL
MILK HOUSE COTTS
HOP
POCKE CL
BROAD VIEW
HOUGHTENS
Sewage Works
Sissinghurst Cty Prim Sch
PH
REEDS COTTS
PO
Plummer's Barn
Roundshill
Roundshill Park Wood
SISSINGHURST RD
A262
THE NIGHTINGALES
Copden Wood
Hammer Stream

A262   THE STREET

Sissinghurst

7

CHAPEL LA
Branden
Crane Brook
Milestone Wood
High Tilt Farm
CRANBROOK RD

37

Lake Chad

6

Golford Lodge
Sabah House Farm
High Tilt

Golford

Stream Farm

Middleton Farm

Chittenden Wood

5

GOLFORD RD

Tollgate Farm

Cemy

36

Coursehorn

4

Coursehorne Farm

Golf Course

Old Cloth Hall

CH

Farningham Oast

Hemsted Forest
Dockenden

3

Farningham Wood

35

Little Coursehorne

Church Wood

2

Chittenden Farm

ADMIRALS WLK

Tottenden Wood

Goddard's Green

GODDARD'S GREEN COTTS

Eaton Farm

Crabtree Farm

1

Park Wood

NEW POND RD
BEACH CT

WALKHURST RD

34

Sewage Works

MEADOWS

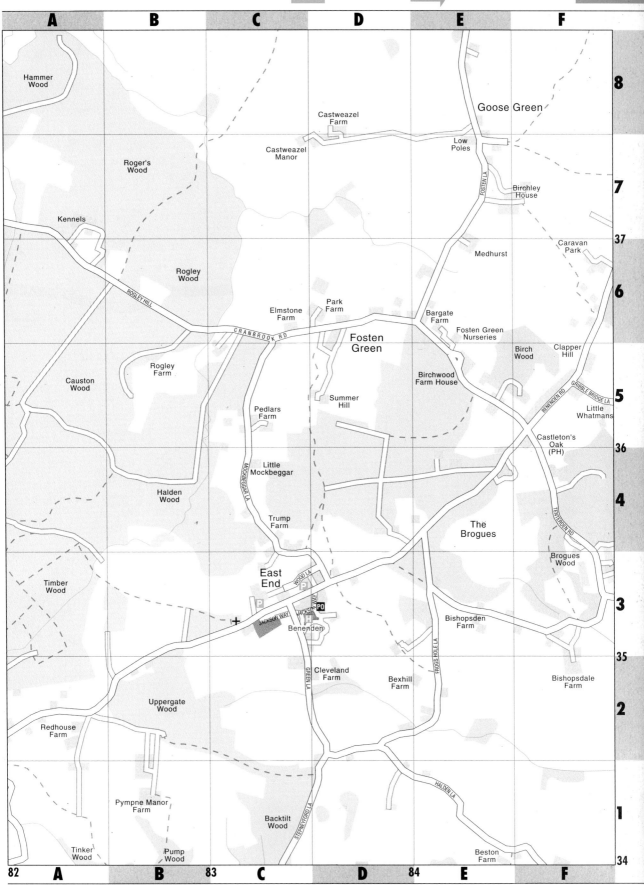

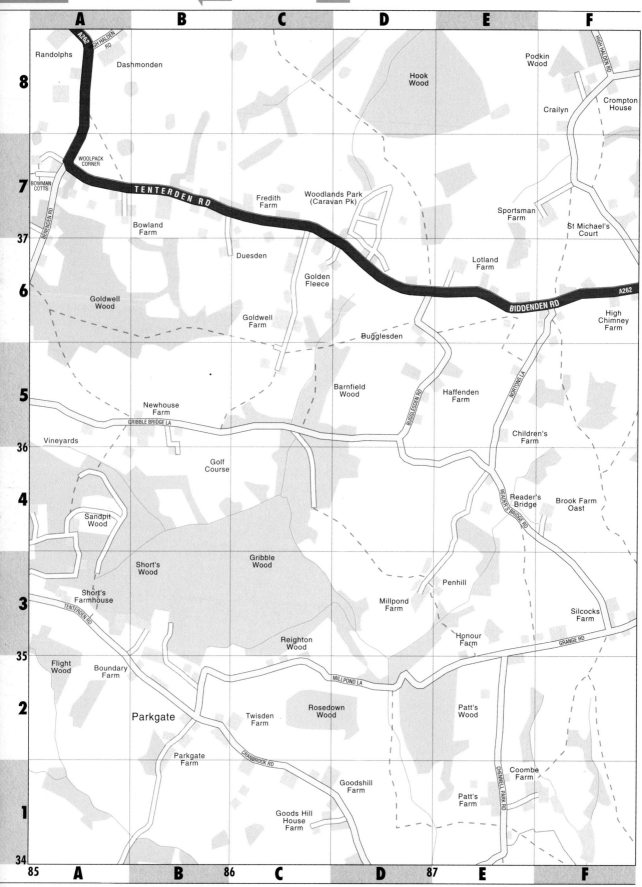

A B C D E F

8

Randolphs
Dashmonden

Hook
Wood

Podkin
Wood

Crailyn

Crompton
House

WOOLPACK
CORNER

7

BOWMAN
COTTS

TENTERDEN RD

Fredith
Farm

Woodlands Park
(Caravan Pk)

Sportsman
Farm

St Michael's
Court

37

Bowland
Farm

Duesden

Golden
Fleece

Lotland
Farm

6

Goldwell
Wood

Goldwell
Farm

Bugglesden

BIDDENDEN RD

A262

High
Chimney
Farm

5

Newhouse
Farm

Barnfield
Wood

Haffenden
Farm

Children's
Farm

GRIBBLE BRIDGE LA

36

Vineyards

Golf
Course

Reader's
Bridge

Brook Farm
Oast

4

Sandpit
Wood

Short's
Wood

Gribble
Wood

Penhill

3

Short's
Farmhouse

TENTERDEN RD

Millpond
Farm

Honour
Farm

Silcocks
Farm

GRANGE RD

35

Flight
Wood

Boundary
Farm

Reighton
Wood

MILLPOND LA

2

Parkgate

Twisden
Farm

Rosedown
Wood

Patt's
Wood

Coombe
Farm

Parkgate
Farm

CRANBROOK RD

Goodshill
Farm

CHENNELL PARK RD

1

Goods Hill
House
Farm

Patt's
Farm

34

85 A 86 C 87 E F
        B   D   F

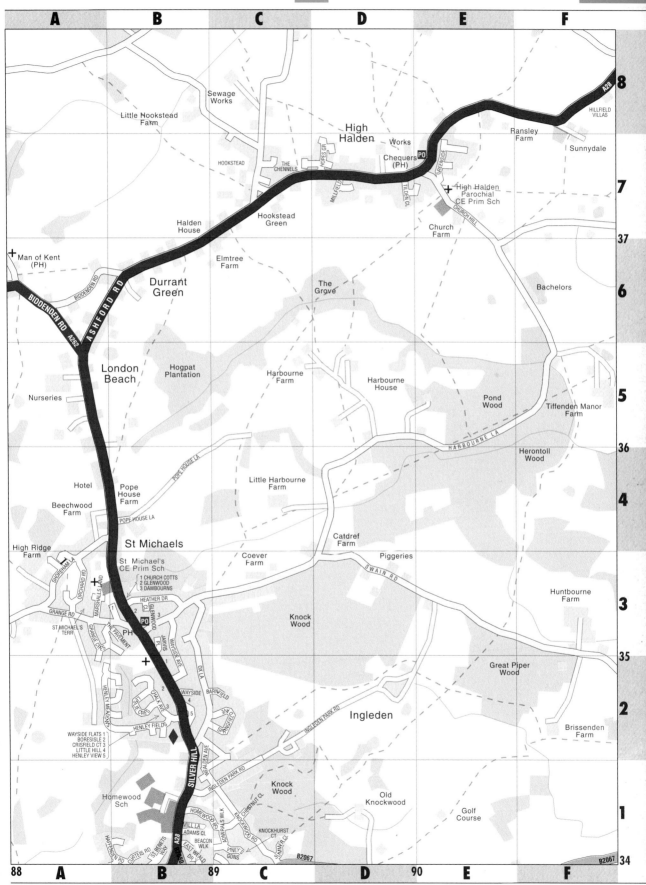

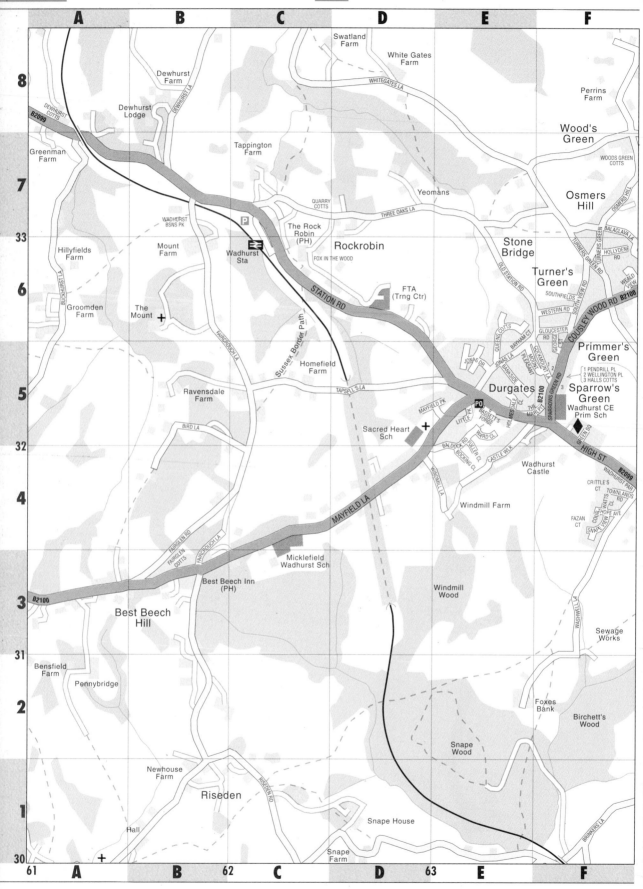

Swatland Farm

White Gates Farm

WHITEGATES LA

Perrins Farm

Dewhurst Farm

Wood's Green

Dewhurst Lodge

DEWHURST LA

WOODS GREEN COTTS

B2099

DEWHURST COTTS

Tappington Farm

Osmers Hill

Greenman Farm

OSMERS HILL

QUARRY COTTS

Yeomans

THREE OAKS LA

BALACLAVA LA

WADHURST BSNS PK

The Rock Robin (PH)

Stone Bridge

TURNERS GREEN GREEN

HOLLYDENE RD

Hillyfields Farm

Mount Farm

Rockrobin

Turner's Green

WEALD VIEW

BUCKHURST LA

Wadhurst Sta

FOX IN THE WOOD

OLD STATION RD

SOUTH VIEW RD

B2100

STATION RD

SOUTHFIELDS

COUSLEY WOOD RD

Groomden Farm

The Mount

FTA (Trng Ctr)

WESTERN RD

GLOUCESTER RD

GEORGE

Primmer's Green

FAIRCROUGH LA

QUEENS COTTS

BAYHAM CT

COCKMOUNT LA

SPARROWS GREEN RD

1 PENDRILL PL
2 WELLINGTON PL
3 HALLS COTTS

Sussex Border Path

Homefield Farm

JONAS DR

JONAS LA

BANKSIDE

MOUNT PLEASANT

Sparrow's Green

Wadhurst CE Prim Sch

Ravensdale Farm

TAPSELL'S LA

Durgates

THE MAPLE

B2100

GREEN SQ

BIRD LA

PO

BASSETT'S FORGE

HOLMESDALE CL

HIGH ST

Sacred Heart Sch

MAYFIELD PK

LITTLE PK

WARD CL

B2099

Wadhurst Castle

Wadhurst Park

CRITTLE'S CT

WADHURST PARK

TOWNLANDS RD

FAIRGLEN RD

FAIRGLEN COTTS

FAIRCROUGH LA

MAYFIELD LA

WINDMILL LA

BALDOCK RD

BOCKING CL

EULER CL

CASTLE WLK

Windmill Farm

FAZAN CT

HOPE AVE

COL

WATTS CL

NEW VIEW

SNAP

Micklefield Wadhurst Sch

Best Beech Inn (PH)

Windmill Wood

B2100

Best Beech Hill

Sewage Works

WASHWELL LA

Bensfield Farm

Pennybridge

Foxes Bank

Birchett's Wood

Newhouse Farm

RISEDEN RD

BEECH RD

Snape Wood

Riseden

BRINKERS LA

Hall

Snape House

Snape Farm

61 A B 62 C D 63 E F

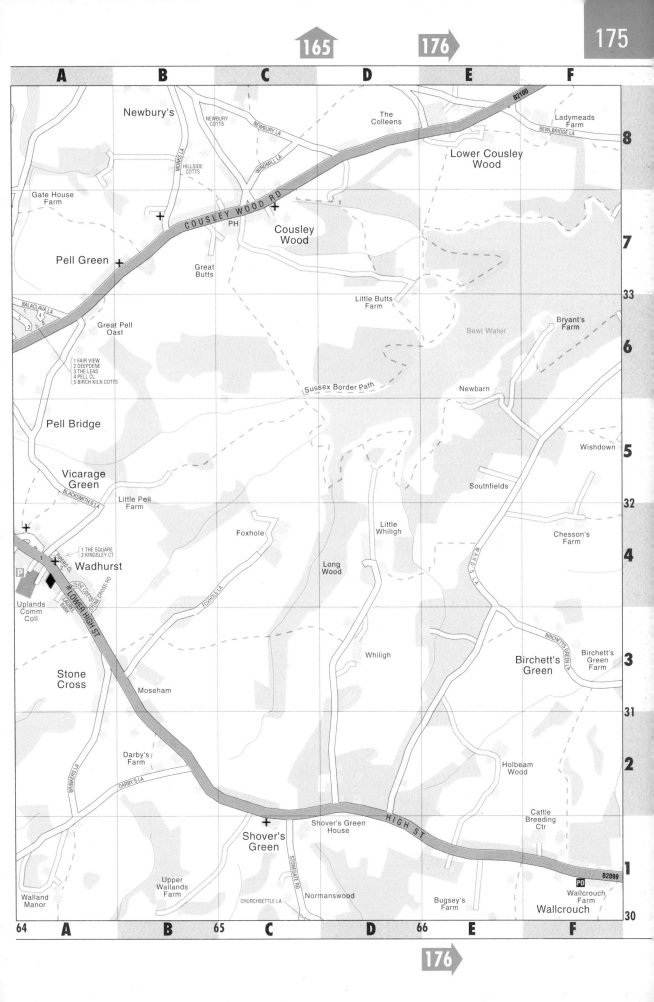

Beal Barn Gardens
BEWLBRIDGE LA
Visitors Ctr
Slipway
Hook Farm
Hook House
Activities Ctr

River Bewl

Cats Wood

Chingley Wood

Chingley Manor

A21

ROSEMARY LA

Stonecrouch

HOOK HILL
WARD'S LA

Beaumans Oast

Bewl Water

Sussex Border Path

CLAPHATCH LA

Greenwoods

Hazelhurst Farm

Rosemary Farmhouse

LOWER HAZELHURST

Nature Reserve

Overy's Farm

Tilehouse Bungalow

LOWER HAZELHURST

Rowley

Bakers & Strakes Farm

Norwoods Farm

Overy's house

LINTON HILL

Borders Farm

HUNTLEY MILL

Burnt Lodge

BOARDERS LA

Walter's Farm

Three Leg Cross

TINKERS LA

CORONATION COTTS

BIRCHETTS LA

Tolhurst

BURNT LODGE LA

Broomden

Windmill Hill

CROSS LA

Landscapes Farm

Pickforde

Steellands Farm

PH
Dale Hill

B2087

Ticehurst House

VINEYARD LA

CROSS LANE GDNS

Newington CT

1 FRONT COTTS
2 CHAPEL PL
3 MARLPIT GDNS
4 REEVES TERR
5 LAVENDER GDNS

CH

Ridgeway Farm

HIGH ST

Inn

HILLBURY GDNS

PICKFORDE LA

FARTHING HILL

Ticehurst

LOWER PLATTS

HORSEGROVE AVE

B2099

LYMDEN LA

Brick Kiln Farm

HAZELWOOD COTTS

PO

SPRINGFIELDS

THE WARREN

ACRES RISE

ST MARY'S LA

CHURCH ST

B2087

MEADOWSIDE COTTS

UPPER PLATTS

B2099

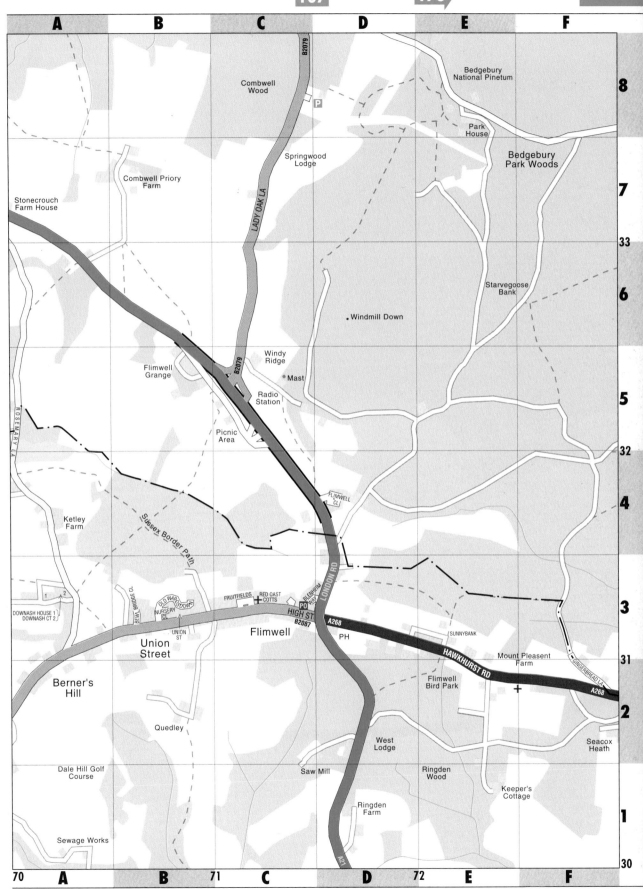

177
168

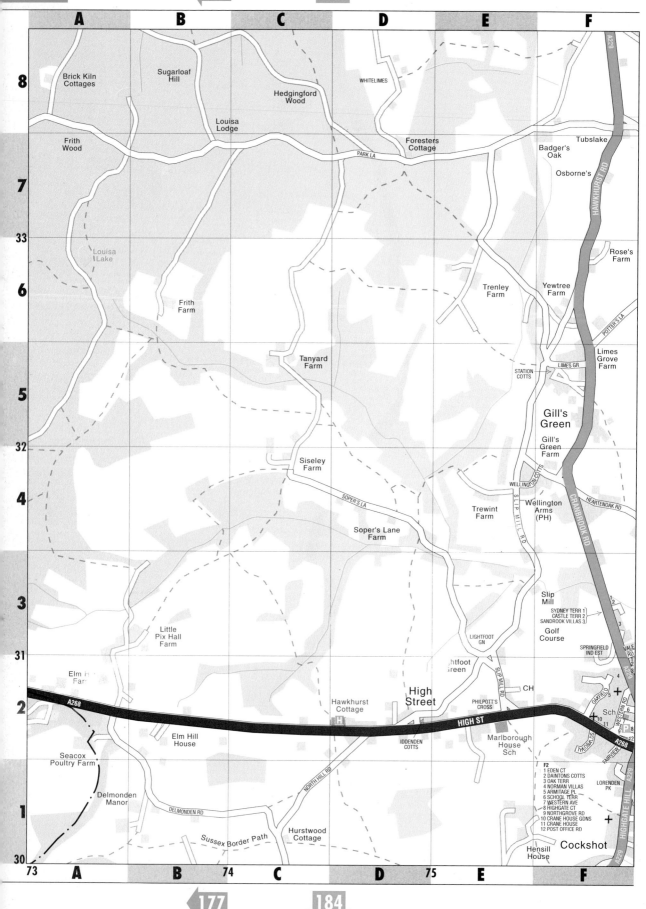

177
184

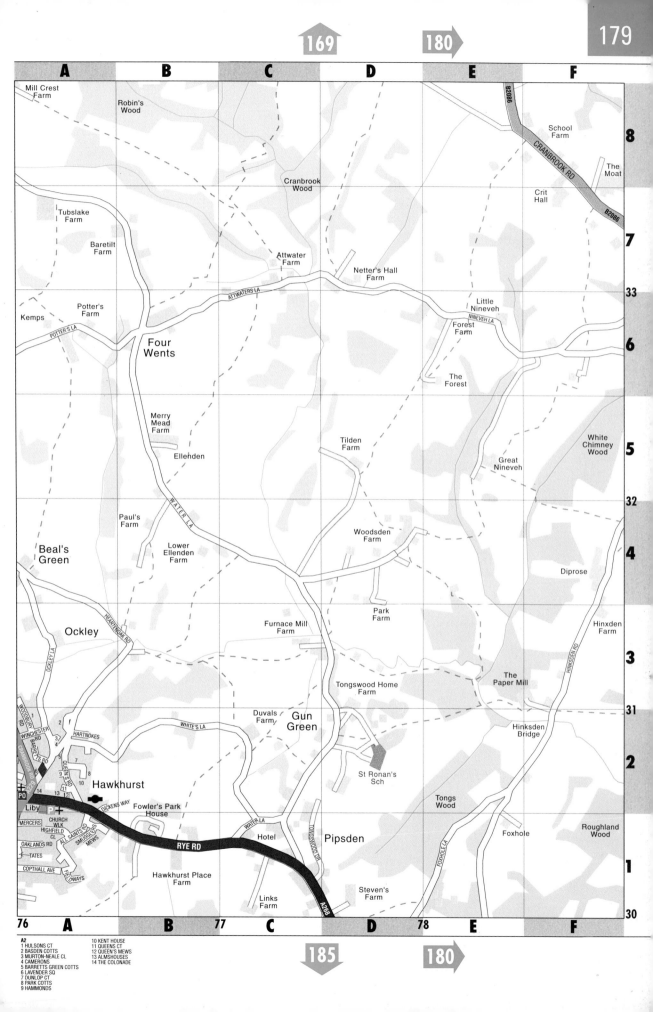

A B C D E F

Mill Crest Farm

Robin's Wood

School Farm

CRANBROOK RD

B2086

The Moat

Cranbrook Wood

Crit Hall

Tubslake Farm

Baretilt Farm

Attwater Farm

Netter's Hall Farm

ATTWATERS LA

Little Nineveh

NINEVEH LA

Kemps

Potter's Farm

POTTER'S LA

Four Wents

Forest Farm

The Forest

Merry Mead Farm

Ellenden

Tilden Farm

Great Nineveh

White Chimney Wood

WATER LA

Paul's Farm

Lower Ellenden Farm

Woodsden Farm

Diprose

Beal's Green

Park Farm

Hinxden Farm

HINXSDEN RD

Ockley

HEARTENOAK RD

OCKLEY LA

Furnace Mill Farm

Tongswood Home Farm

The Paper Mill

Hinksden Bridge

WOODBURY RD

WINCHESTER RD

BARRETTS RD

HARTNOKES

WHITE'S LA

Duvals Farm

Gun Green

St Ronan's Sch

QUEEN'S RD

Hawkhurst

Tongs Wood

PO

Liby

P

Fowler's Park House

DICKENS WAY

WATER LA

TONGSWOOD DR

Pipsden

Foxhole

Roughland Wood

MERCERS

CHURCH WLK

HIGHFIELD CL

ALL SAINTS RD

SMUGGLERS MEWS

Hotel

RYE RD

FOXHOLE LA

Foxhole

OAKLANDS RD

TATES

COPTHALL AVE

FIELDWAYS

Hawkhurst Place Farm

Links Farm

A268

Steven's Farm

A2
1 HULSONS CT
2 BASDEN COTTS
3 MURTON-NEALE CL
4 CAMERONS
5 BARRETTS GREEN COTTS
6 LAVENDER SQ
7 DUNLOP CT
8 PARK COTTS
9 HAMMONDS
10 KENT HOUSE
11 QUEENS CT
12 QUEEN'S MEWS
13 ALMSHOUSES
14 THE COLONADE

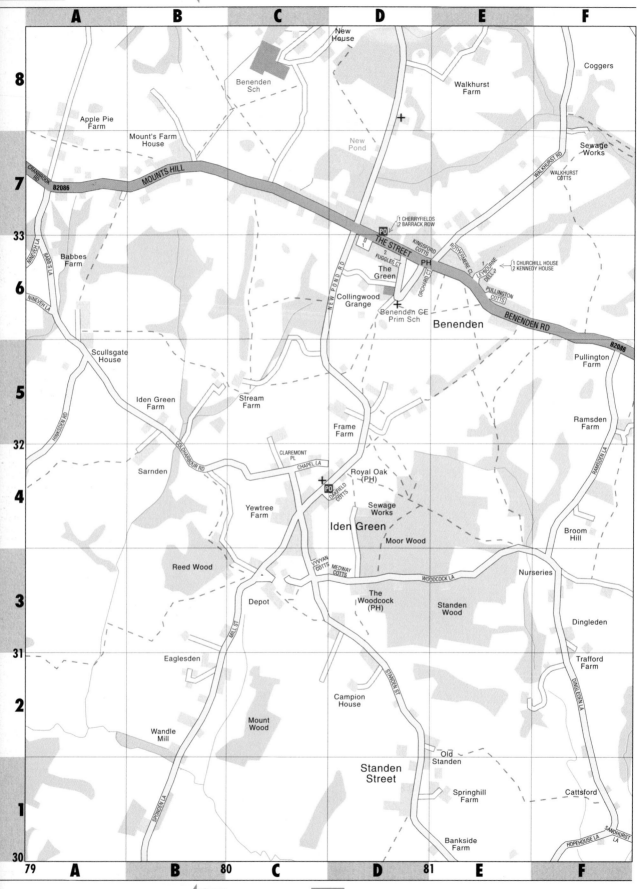

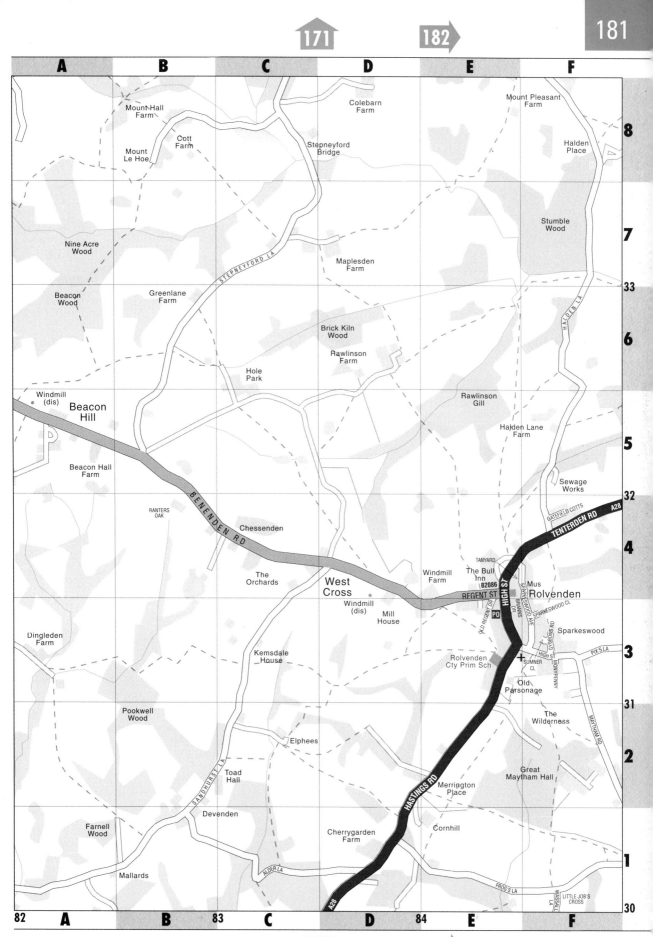

A B C D E F

8

Mount Pleasant Farm

Colebarn Farm

Mount Hall Farm

Cott Farm

Halden Place

Mount Le Hoe

Stepneyford Bridge

7

Stumble Wood

Nine Acre Wood

STEPNEYFORD LA

Maplesden Farm

33

Beacon Wood

Greenlane Farm

HALDEN LA

6

Brick Kiln Wood

Hole Park

Rawlinson Farm

Rawlinson Gill

5

Windmill (dis)

Beacon Hill

Halden Lane Farm

Beacon Hall Farm

Sewage Works

RANTERS OAK

BENENDEN RD

32

GATEFIELD COTTS

TENTERDEN RD

A28

Chessenden

4

TANYARD

The Bull Inn

Mus

The Orchards

Windmill Farm

REGENT ST

HIGH ST

Rolvenden

West Cross

B2086

OLD REGENT DR

SPARKESWOOD AVE

SPARKESWOOD CL

Dingleden Farm

Windmill (dis)

Mill House

PO

BRAINS DR

HIGH ST

Sparkeswood

PIX'S LA

Kemsdale House

Rolvenden Cty Prim Sch

SUMNER CL

MONYPENNY

Old Parsonage

31

MAYTHAM RD

Pookwell Wood

The Wilderness

Elphees

2

SANDHURST LA

Toad Hall

Great Maytham Hall

Devenden

HASLINGS RD

Merrington Place

Farnell Wood

Cherrygarden Farm

Cornhill

1

ALDER LA

Mallards

FROG'S LA

WASSALL LA

LITTLE JOB'S CROSS

82 A B 83 C D 84 E F

A28

30

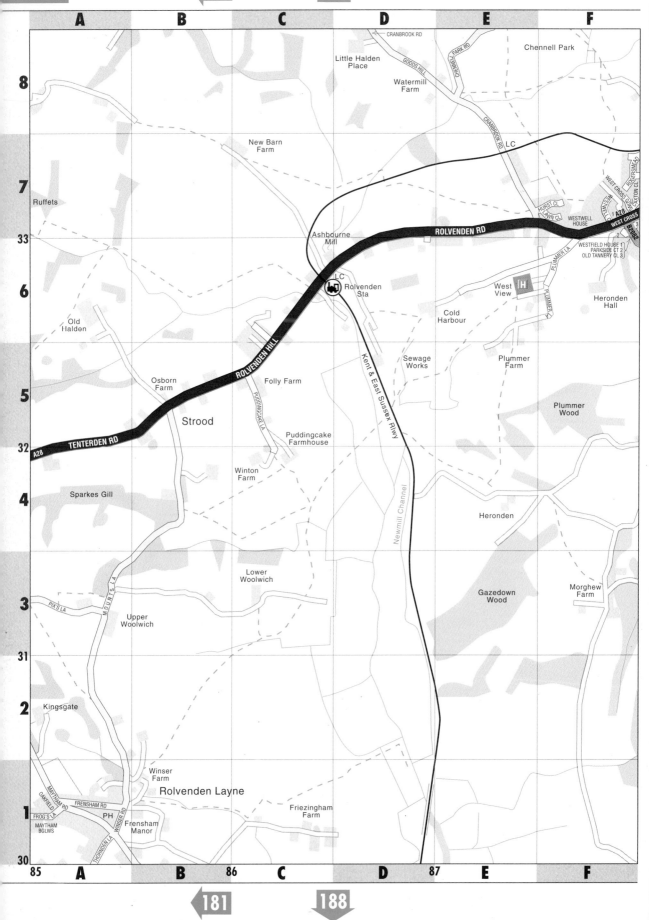

181 188

A B C D E F

8

7

33

6

5

32

4

3

31

2

1

30

85 A B 86 C D 87 E F

Ruffets

New Barn
Farm

Little Halden
Place

CRANBROOK RD

Watermill
Farm

GOODS HILL

Chennell Park

CHENNELL PARK RD

CRANBROOK RD

LC

WEST CROSS

ROGERSMEAD

CAXTON CL

A28

WEST CROSS

B2082

HURST CL

LAWN CL

WEST WELL

WESTWELL
HOUSE

WESTFIELD HOUSE 1
PARKSIDE CT 2
OLD TANNERY CL 3

PLUMMER LA

Ashbourne
Mill

ROLVENDEN RD

LC

Rolvenden
Sta

Cold
Harbour

West
View

IH

PLUMMER

Heronden
Hall

Old
Halden

ROLVENDEN HILL

Osborn
Farm

Strood

Folly Farm

PUDDINGCAKE LA

Sewage
Works

Plummer
Farm

Plummer
Wood

TENTERDEN RD

A28

Puddingcake
Farmhouse

Winton
Farm

Kent & East Sussex Rlwy

Sparkes Gill

Lower
Woolwich

Newmill Channel

Heronden

Morghew
Farm

PIX'S LA

MOUNTS LA

Upper
Woolwich

Gazedown
Wood

Kingsgate

MAYTHAM RD

OAKFIELD

FROG'S

PH

Winser
Farm

Rolvenden Layne

FRENSHAM RD

WINSER RD

Frensham
Manor

Friezingham
Farm

MAYTHAM
BGLWS

THORNDEN LA

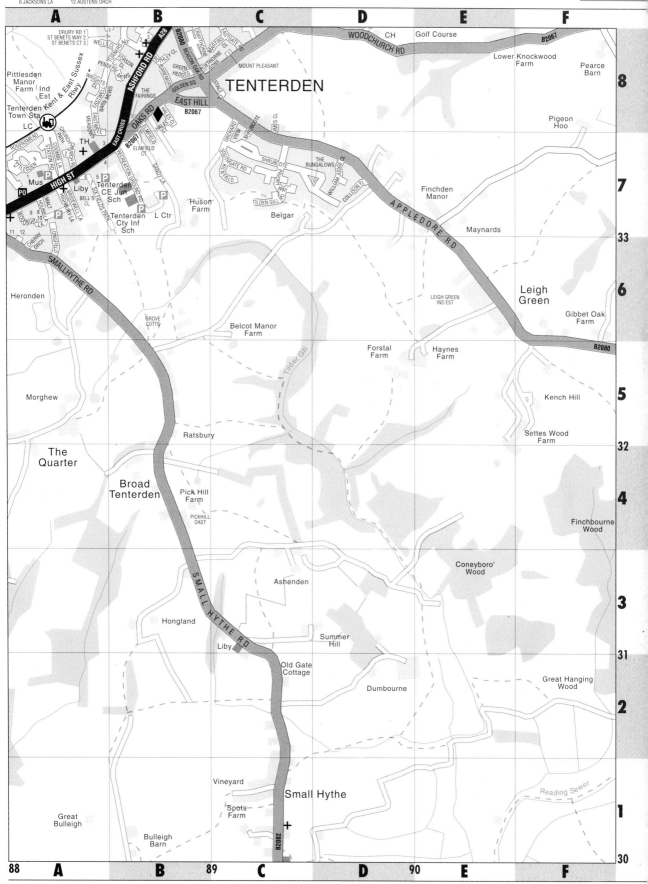

A7
1 PITTLESDEN PL
2 ST MILDRED'S CL
3 EASTWELL
4 SAYERS LA
5 THEATRE SQ
6 JACKSONS LA
7 BELLS LA
8 BURGESS ROW
9 MAYOR'S PL
10 CEDAR CT
11 BENNETTS MEWS
12 AUSTENS ORCH

178

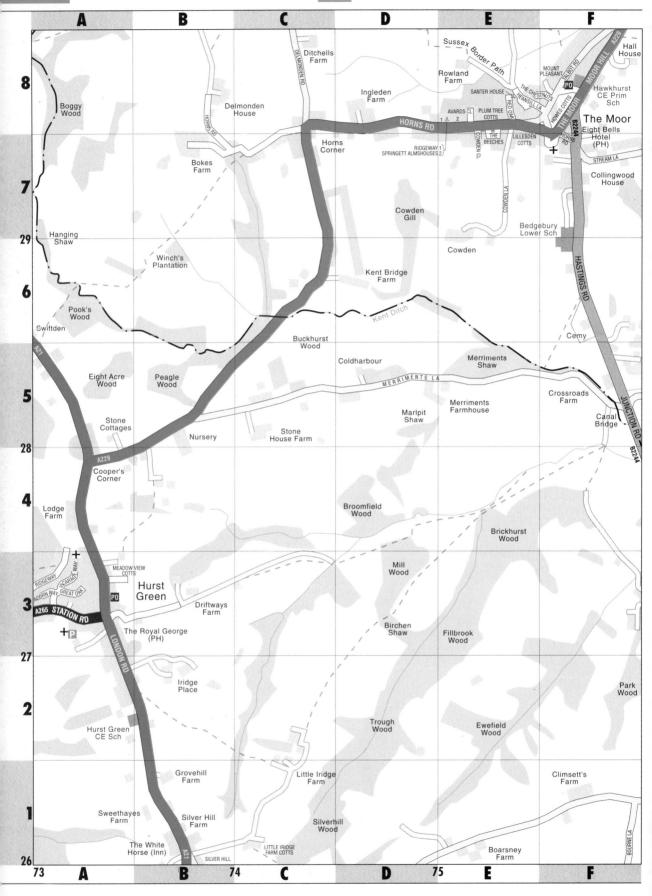

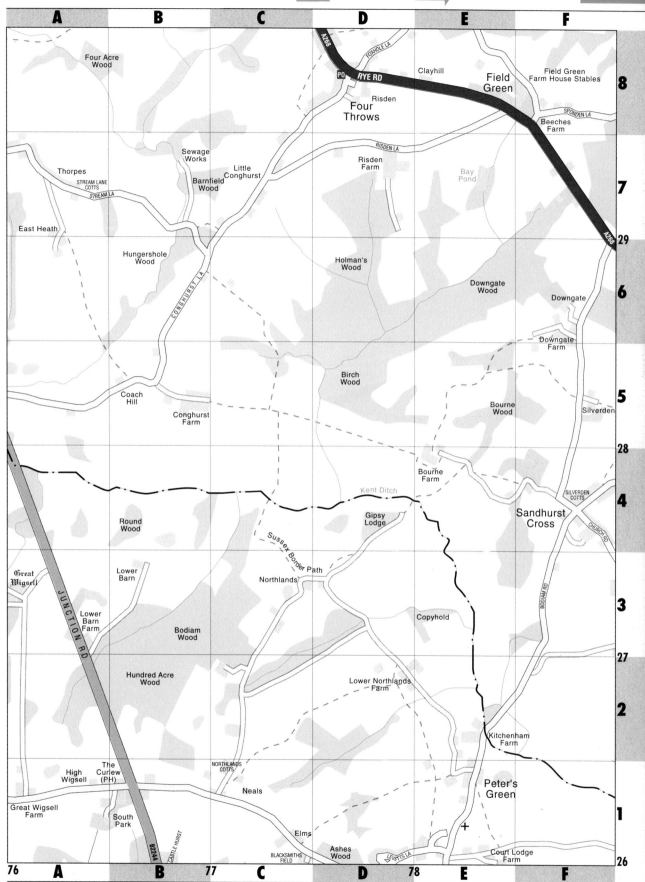

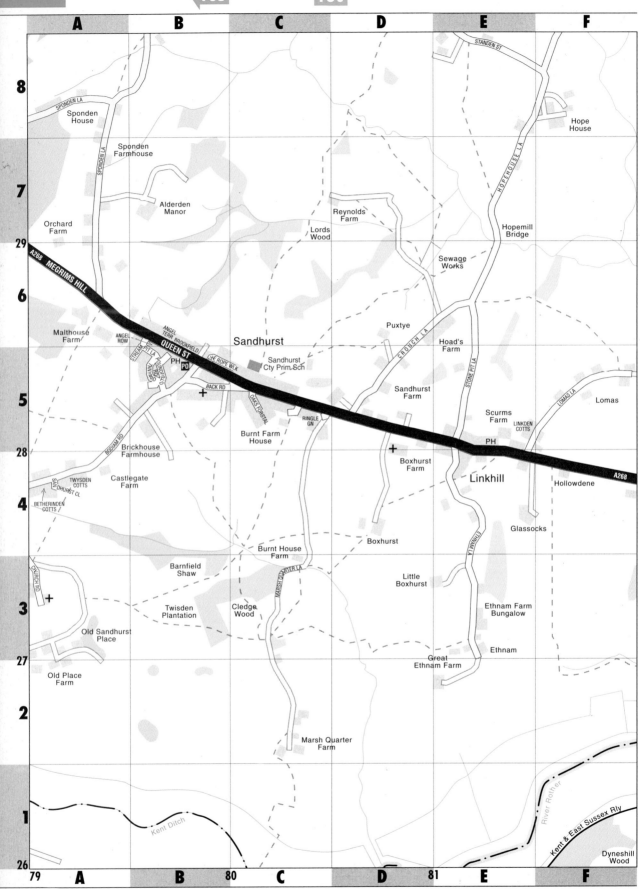

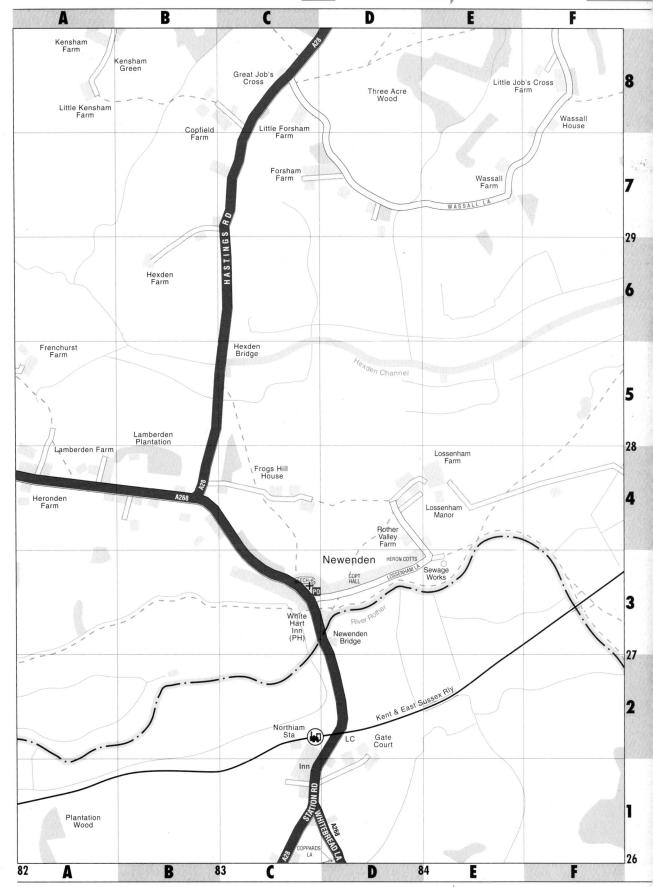

A	B	C	D	E	F

Kensham
Farm

Kensham
Green

8

Great Job's
Cross

Three Acre
Wood

Little Job's Cross
Farm

Little Kensham
Farm

Wassall
House

Copfield
Farm

Little Forsham
Farm

7

Forsham
Farm

Wassall
Farm

WASSALL LA

29

HASTINGS RD

Hexden
Farm

6

Hexden
Bridge

Hexden Channel

Frenchurst
Farm

5

Lamberden
Plantation

28

Lamberden Farm

Lossenham
Farm

Frogs Hill
House

A28

4

Heronden
Farm

A268

Lossenham
Manor

Rother
Valley
Farm

HERON COTTS

Newenden

COPT
HALL

Sewage
Works

LOSSENHAM LA

3

BEECH

PO

River Rother

White
Hart
Inn
(PH)

Newenden
Bridge

27

Kent & East Sussex Rly

2

Northiam
Sta

LC

Gate
Court

Inn

STATION RD

WHITEBREAD LA

Plantation
Wood

1

A28

A268

COPPARDS
LA

26

| A | B | | C | | D | E | F |

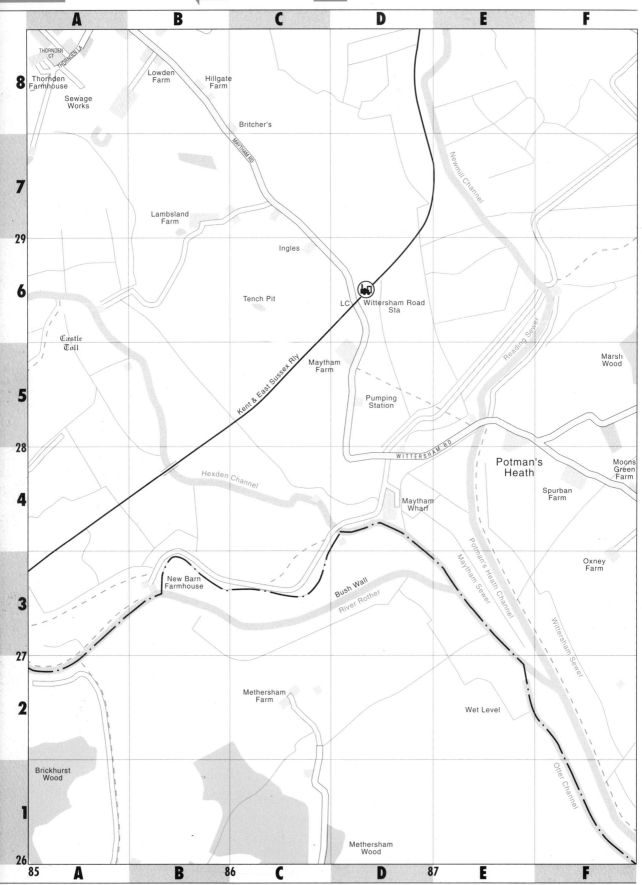

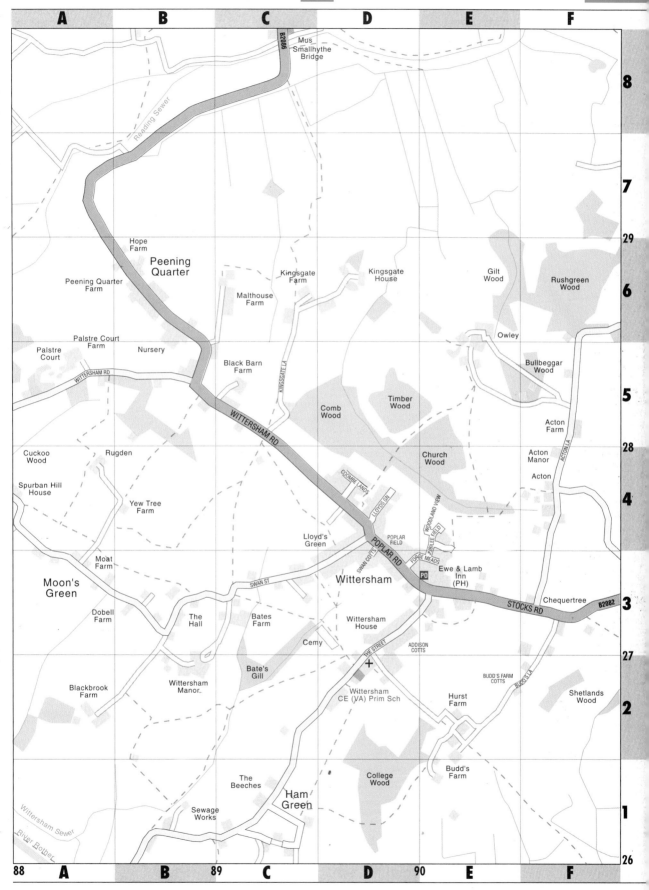

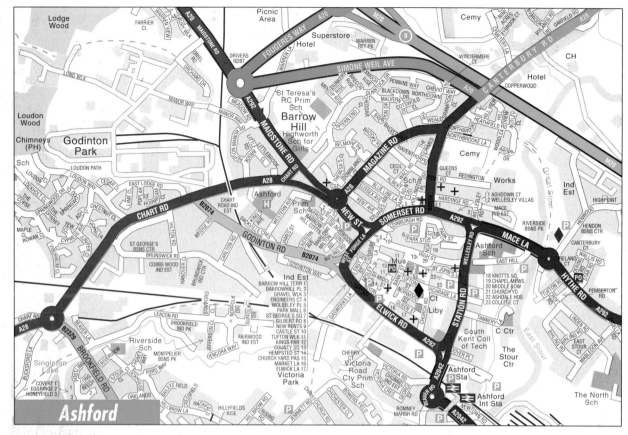

Ashford

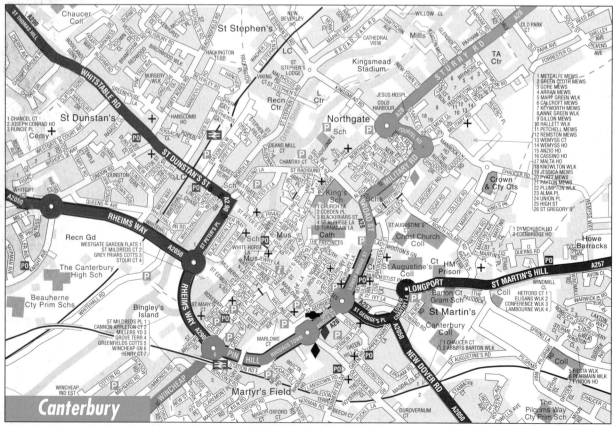

Canterbury

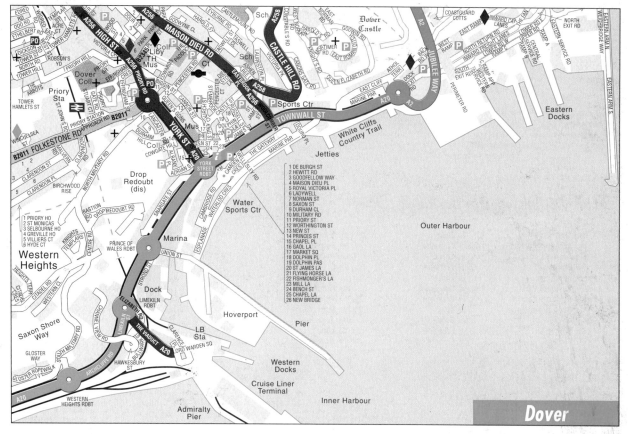

Dover

1 DE BURGH ST
2 HEWITT RD
3 GOODFELLOW WAY
4 MAISON DIEU PL
5 ROYAL VICTORIA PL
6 LADYWELL
7 NORMAN ST
8 SAXON ST
9 DURHAM CL
10 MILITARY RD
11 PRIORY ST
12 WORTHINGTON ST
13 NEW ST
14 PRINCES ST
15 CHAPEL PL
16 GAOL LA
17 MARKET SQ
18 DOLPHIN PL
19 DOLPHIN PAS
20 ST JAMES LA
21 FLYING HORSE LA
22 FISHMONGER'S LA
23 MILL LA
24 BENCH ST
25 CHAPEL LA
26 NEW BRIDGE

1 PRIORY HO
2 ST MONICAS
3 SELBOURNE HO
4 GREVILLE HO
5 VILLIERS CT
6 HYDE CT

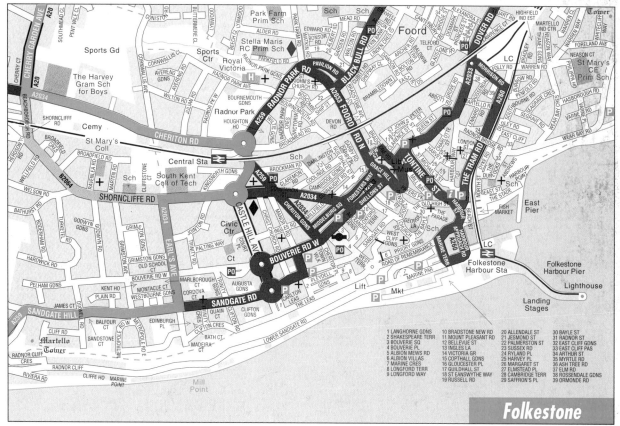

Folkestone

1 LANGHORNE GDNS
2 SHAKESPEARE TERR
3 BOUVERIE SQ
4 BOUVERIE PL
5 ALBION MEWS RD
6 ALBION VILLAS
7 MARINE CRES
8 LONGFORD TERR
9 LONGFORD WAY
10 BRADSTONE NEW RD
11 MOUNT PLEASANT RD
12 BELLEVUE ST
13 INGLES LA
14 VICTORIA GR
15 COPTHALL GDNS
16 GLOUCESTER PL
17 GUILDHALL ST
18 ST EANSWYTHE WAY
19 RUSSELL RD
20 ALLENDALE ST
21 JESMOND ST
22 PALMERSTON ST
23 SUSSEX RD
24 RYLAND PL
25 HARVEY PL
26 MARGARET ST
27 ELMSTEAD PL
28 CAMBRIDGE TERR
29 SAFFRON'S PL
30 BAYLE ST
31 RADNOR ST
32 EAST CLIFF GDNS
33 EAST CLIFF PAS
34 ARTHUR ST
35 MYRTLE RD
36 ASH TREE RD
37 ELM RD
38 ROSSENDALE GDNS
39 ORMONDE RD

Index

Street names are listed alphabetically and show the locality, the Postcode District, the page number and a reference to the square in which the name falls on the map page

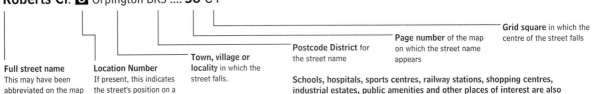

Roberts Cl. 8 Orpington BR5 .... 38 C4

Full street name
This may have been abbreviated on the map

Location Number
If present, this indicates the street's position on a congested area of the map instead of the name

Town, village or locality in which the street falls.

Postcode District for the street name

Page number of the map on which the street name appears

Grid square in which the centre of the street falls

Schools, hospitals, sports centres, railway stations, shopping centres, industrial estates, public amenities and other places of interest are also listed. These are highlighted in

Abbreviations used in the index

App Approach	Cl Close	Espl Esplanade	Orch Orchard	Sq Square
Arc Arcade	Comm Common	Est Estate	Par Parade	Strs Stairs
Ave Avenue	Cnr Corner	Gdns Gardens	Pk Park	Stps Steps
Bvd Boulevard	Cotts Cottages	Gn Green	Pas Passage	St Street, Saint
Bldgs Buildings	Ct Court	Gr Grove	Pl Place	Terr Terrace
Bsns Pk Business Park	Ctyd Courtyard	Hts Heights	Prec Precinct	Trad Est Trading Estate
Bsns Ctr Business Centre	Cres Crescent	Ind Est Industrial Estate	Prom Promenade	Wlk Walk
Bglws Bungalows	Dr Drive	Intc Interchange	Ret Pk Retail Park	W West
Cswy Causeway	Dro Drove	Junc Junction	Rd Road	Yd Yard
Ctr Centre	E East	La Lane	Rdbt Roundabout	
Cir Circus	Emb Embankment	N North	S South	

20/20 Ind Est. ME16 .... 91 C8
Abbess Cl. 11 E6 .... 1 E8
Abbeville House. ME1 .... 47 C4
Abbey Court Sch. ME2 .... 46 E8
Abbey Cres. DA17 .... 4 A2
Abbey Gate Cotts. ME20 .... 76 F2
Abbey Gr. SE2 .... 3 B2
Abbey Pl. DA1 .... 9 D2
Abbey Prim Sch. SE2 .... 3 C3
Abbey Rd. Bexley DA6 & DA7 .... 7 E3
Abbey Rd. Erith DA17 .... 3 E3
Abbey Rd. Gillingham ME8 .... 49 A2
Abbey Rd. Rochester ME2 .... 46 F8
Abbey Rd. Gravesend DA12 .... 30 E7
Abbey Rd. Swanscombe DA9 .... 11 C2
Abbey Terr. SE2 .... 3 C2
Abbey Wood Rd. Kings Hill ME19 89 A5
Abbey Wood Rd. Woolwich SE2 .. 3 C2
Abbey Wood Sch. SE2 .... 3 A3
Abbey Wood Sta. SE2 .... 3 C3
Abbeyhill Rd. DA15 .... 24 C6
Abbots Cl. BR5 .... 37 C1
Abbots Court Rd. ME3 .... 34 F5
Abbots Field. Gravesend DA12 .. 30 C2
Abbots Field. Maidstone ME16 ... 91 B2
Abbotswood Cl. 7 DA17 .... 3 E3
Abbott Rd. TN15 .... 86 F7
Abbott's Wlk. DA7 .... 7 D7
Abbotts Cl. Rochester ME1 .... 47 B3
Abbotts Cl. BR5 .... 37 C1
Abbotts Cl. Swanley BR8 .... 40 A5
Abbotts Cl. Woolwich SE28 .... 3 C6
Aberdeen House. 8 ME15 .... 107 E7
Aberford Gdns. SE18 .... 5 E6
Abergeldie Rd. SE12 .... 5 B1
Abery St. SE18 .... 2 E2
Abigail Cres. ME5 .... 62 A1
Abingdon Rd. ME16 .... 90 F2
Abingdon Way. BR6 .... 52 B6
Abinger Cl. BR1 .... 36 E6
Abinger Dr. ME5 .... 62 D2
Absalom Ct. ME8 .... 49 C2
Acacia Cl. BR5 .... 37 D4
Acacia Rd. Dartford DA1 .... 26 D7
Acacia Rd. Stone DA9 .... 10 E1
Acacia Way. DA15 .... 23 F7
Acacia Wlk. BR8 .... 39 D7
Academy Dr. ME7 .... 48 F1
Academy Pl. SE18 .... 6 A6
Academy Rd. SE18 .... 5 F7
Acer Ave. TN2 .... 163 C8
Achilles Rd. ME5 .... 62 C2
Acland Cl. SE18 .... 6 D7
Acorn Cl. Chislehurst BR7 .... 23 C3
Acorn Cl. Five Oak Green TN12 .. 135 B7
Acorn Gr. ME20 .... 90 D8
Acorn Ind Pk. DA1 .... 9 A2
Acorn Pl. ME15 .... 107 E6
Acorn Rd. ME7 .... 48 F4
Acorn Trad Ctr. RM16 .... 11 E8
Acorn Way. Hurst Green TN19 ...184 A3
Acorn Way. Orpington BR6 .... 51 B6
Acorns The. TN27 .... 142 F1
Acott Fields. ME18 .... 120 F8

Acre Cl. ME4 .... 47 E1
Acres Rise. TN5 .... 176 E1
Acton La. TN30 .... 189 F4
Acton Pl. ME18 .... 105 A1
Acworth House. 1 SE18 .... 6 B8
Acworth Pl. DA1 .... 9 C1
Adam Cl. ME17 .... 106 D3
Adams Cl. TN30 .... 173 B1
Adams Sq. DA6 .... 7 E4
Adamson Rd. E16 .... 1 A7
Adbert Dr. ME15 .... 106 B4
Adcot Wlk. 6 BR6 .... 51 F6
Adderley Gdns. SE9 .... 23 A4
Addington La. ME19 .... 73 B4
Addison Cl. East Malling ME19 .. 74 C1
Addison Cl. Orpington BR5 .... 37 C3
Addison Cotts. TN30 .... 189 D3
Addison Dr. SE12 .... 5 B2
Addison Rd. BR2 .... 36 C4
Addlestead Rd. TN12 .... 119 E6
Adelaide Rd. Chislehurst BR7 .... 23 B3
Adelaide Rd. Gillingham ME7 .... 48 C4
Adelaide Rd. Tilbury RM18 .... 12 F5
Adelaide The. ME3 .... 32 C6
Aden Terr. 1 ME14 .... 92 A7
Adisham Dr. ME16 .... 91 B7
Admaston Rd. SE18 .... 6 C8
Admers Way. DA13 .... 73 B8
Admiral Moore Dr. 3 ME20 ..... 75 F1
Admiral Seymour Rd. SE9 .... 5 F3
Admiral's Wlk. ME4 .... 47 F7
Admirals Wlk. Chatham ME5 ..... 62 B3
Admirals Wlk.
Goddard's Green TN17 .... 170 D2
Admirals Wlk. Swanscombe DA9 11 B2
Admirals Wlk. Tenterden TN30 .173 C1
Admiralty Rd. ME2 .... 33 C2
Admiralty Terr. 1
Gillingham ME4 .... 48 A7
Admiralty Terr. Upper Upton ME2 33 F1
Afghan Rd. ME4 .... 47 E4
Agate Cl. E16 .... 1 D7
Agaton Rd. BR7 & SE9 .... 23 C6
Agnes Cl. E6 .... 2 A6
Ainsdale Cl. BR6 .... 37 D1
Aintree Cl. DA12 .... 30 B5
Aintree House. 1 ME15 .... 107 F6
Aintree Rd. ME5 .... 62 C3
Airedale Cl. DA2 .... 27 C7
Airport Rdbt. E16 .... 1 D5
Aisher Rd. SE28 .... 3 C6
Aisher Way. TN13 .... 83 E6
Ajax Rd. ME1 .... 61 C8
Akehurst La. TN15 .... 84 C2
Alabama St. SE18 .... 6 E7
Alamein Ave. ME5 .... 61 F7
Alamein Gdns. DA2 .... 27 B8
Alamein Rd. DA10 .... 11 D1
Alan Cl. DA1 .... 9 C3
Alanbrooke. DA12 .... 30 C8
Alanbrooke House. SE18 .... 5 E7
Alanthus Cl. SE12 .... 5 A1
Alban Cres. DA4 .... 41 A1

Albany Cl. Sidcup DA5 .... 24 D8
Albany Cl. Tonbridge TN9 .... 133 D7
Albany Hill. TN2 .... 149 C5
Albany Park Sta. DA14 .... 24 D6
Albany Rd. Chatham ME4 .... 48 B2
Albany Rd. Chislehurst BR7 ..... 23 B3
Albany Rd. Erith DA17 .... 7 F8
Albany Rd. Gillingham ME7 ..... 48 D4
Albany Rd. Rochester ME1 .... 47 C4
Albany Rd. Sidcup DA5 .... 24 C8
Albany Rd. Tilbury RM18 .... 13 A6
Albany St. ME14 .... 92 B5
Albany Terr. Chatham ME4 ...... 47 E4
Albany Terr. Gillingham ME7 .... 48 D4
Albatross Ave. ME2 .... 46 C6
Albatross St. SE18 .... 6 E7
Albemarle Rd. ME5 .... 62 C2
Albert Cotts. TN1 .... 149 B4
Albert Manor. ME7 .... 48 B5
Albert Murry Rd. 4 DA12 ...... 30 C8
Albert Pl. ME2 .... 47 B7
Albert Rd. Bromley BR2 .... 36 D4
Albert Rd. Chatham ME4 .... 48 A3
Albert Rd. Chislehurst SE9 ...... 22 E5
Albert Rd. Erith DA17 .... 3 F1
Albert Rd. Gillingham ME7 ...... 48 C4
Albert Rd. Newham E16 .... 1 F5
Albert Rd.
Orpington,Chelsfield BR6 ...... 52 A5
Albert Rd.
Orpington,St Mary Cray BR5 .... 38 B3
Albert Rd. Rochester ME1 .... 47 C3
Albert Rd. Sidcup DA5 .... 25 B8
Albert Rd. 3 Tonbridge TN9 ... 117 B1
Albert Rd. Wilmington DA2 ..... 26 C5
Albert St. Maidstone ME14 ...... 91 F6
Albert St.
Royal Tunbridge Wells TN1 .... 149 B4
Albert Wlk. E16 .... 2 B4
Alberta Rd. DA7 .... 8 C6
Albion Ct. 2 SE7 .... 1 E2
Albion House. E16 .... 2 B5
Albion Pl. Maidstone ME14 ...... 92 B4
Albion Pl. Newington ME9 ...... 65 B6
Albion Rd. Bexley DA6 .... 8 A3
Albion Rd. Chatham ME5 .... 62 B2
Albion Rd. Gravesend DA12 ..... 30 C8
Albion Rd. Marden TN12 .... 138 D5
Albion Rd.
Royal Tunbridge Wells TN1 .... 149 C5
Albion Terr. DA12 .... 13 D1
Albion Way. TN8 .... 112 C4
Albright Ind Est. RM13 .... 4 F8
Albury Ave. DA7 .... 7 E5
Albury Cl. ME5 .... 62 D2
Albyfield. BR1 .... 36 F6
Alchins Cotts. ME17 .... 106 E2
Alconbury. DA6 .... 8 B2
Aldeburgh St. SE18 .... 1 A1
Alder Cl. TN2 .... 133 D1
Alder La. TN17 .... 181 C1
Alder Rd. DA14 .... 23 F5

Alder Way. BR8 .... 39 D7
Aldermary Rd. BR1 .... 36 A8
Alderney Rd. DA8 .... 9 A7
Alders Cotts. TN11 .... 135 A5
Alders Meadow. TN9 .... 116 F2
Alders Rd. TN11 & TN12 .... 134 E6
Alders The. ME18 .... 103 D7
Aldersgrove Ave. SE12 & SE9 .... 22 D5
Aldershot Rd. ME5 .... 62 A7
Alderwood Prim Sch. SE9 .... 6 E1
Alderwood Rd. SE9 .... 6 D1
Aldington Cl. ME5 .... 62 B5
Aldington La. ME14 .... 93 D8
Aldington Rd. Greenwich SE18 ... 1 D3
Aldington Rd. Maidstone ME14 .. 92 F4
Aldon Cl. ME14 .... 92 C6
Aldon Ct. ME14 .... 92 C6
Aldon La. ME19 .... 88 C8
Aldwick Cl. BR7 .... 23 D5
Alen Sq. TN12 .... 139 F4
Alers Rd. DA6 .... 7 D2
Alestan Beck Rd. E16 .... 1 D7
Alexander Cl. Hayes BR2 .... 36 A1
Alexander Cl. Sidcup DA15 .... 6 E1
Alexander Ct. Greenwich SE3 ..... 5 B5
Alexander Ct. Rochester ME2 ..... 47 B8
Alexander Ct. Swanscombe DA9 11 C2
Alexander McLeod Inf Sch. SE2 3 B1
Alexander McLeod Jun Sch. SE2 3 B1
Alexander Rd. Bexley DA16 .... 7 D5
Alexander Rd. Chislehurst BR7 ... 23 B3
Alexander Rd. Swanscombe DA9 11 C2
Alexandra Ave. ME7 .... 48 E4
Alexandra Cl. BR8 .... 39 E7
Alexandra Glen. ME5 .... 62 A1
Alexandra Hospl The. ME5 ...... 77 A8
Alexandra Rd. Chatham ME4 .... 48 B2
Alexandra Rd. Erith DA8 .... 8 F8
Alexandra Rd. Gravesend DA12 .. 30 E8
Alexandra Rd. Tilbury RM18 ..... 12 F5
Alexandra Rd. Tonbridge TN9 .. 133 B8
Alexandra Rd. Maidstone ME14 .. 91 F6
Alexandra St. Newham E16 .... 1 A8
Alfan La. DA2 .... 25 D3
Alford House. 6 SE18 .... 6 B8
Alford Rd. DA8 .... 4 C1
Alfred Cl. ME4 .... 48 B2
Alfred House. 4 DA11 .... 29 F7
Alfred Pl. DA11 .... 29 F7
Alfred Rd. Erith DA17 .... 3 F1
Alfred Rd. Gravesend DA11 ...... 30 B6
Alfred Rd. Hawley DA2 .... 26 F4
Alfred St. RM17 .... 12 C8
Alice Thompson Cl. SE12 .... 22 C6
Alicia House. DA16 .... 7 B6
Alison Cl. E6 .... 2 A7
Alkerden La. DA9 & DA10 .... 11 C1
Alkham Rd. ME14 .... 92 C5
Alkham Tower. 9 BR5 .... 38 C5
All Saints' CE Prim Sch.
Chatham ME4 .... 48 A3
All Saints CE Prim Sch.
Maidstone ME15 .... 92 A3
All Saints Cl. DA10 .... 11 F2

All Saints Hospl. ME4 .... 48 A2
All Saints Rd. Allhallows ME3 .... 19 D8
All Saints Rd. Hawkhurst TN18 .179 A1
All Saints' Rd. Northfleet DA11 .. 29 F7
All Saints Rd.
Royal Tunbridge Wells TN4 ... 149 B6
All Saints Rise. TN4 .... 149 A6
Allan Cl. TN4 .... 148 C4
Allandale Pl. BR6 .... 52 D7
Allandale Rd. TN2 .... 149 D7
Allard Cl. BR5 .... 38 C2
Allen Cl. ME5 .... 62 C6
Allen St. ME14 .... 92 B5
Allendale Cl. DA2 .... 27 D7
Allens. TN12 .... 138 D5
Allens La. TN15 .... 102 A7
Allenswood Rd. SE9 .... 5 F5
Allhallows Cty Prim Sch. ME3 . 19 D8
Allhallows Rd. E6 .... 1 E7
Allhallows-on-Sea Est. ME3 ... 19 E10
Alliance Rd. Newham E16 .... 1 C8
Alliance Rd. Woolwich SE18 ...... 7 A7
Alliance Way. TN12 .... 135 F6
Allington Cl. DA12 .... 30 F7
Allington Dr. Rochester ME2 ..... 46 B8
Allington Dr. Tonbridge TN10 .. 118 A5
Allington Gdns. ME18 .... 104 E3
Allington Prim Sch. ME16 ...... 91 C7
Allington Rd. Gillingham ME8 ... 49 A3
Allington Rd. Orpington BR6 .... 37 E1
Allington Rd.
Paddock Wood TN12 .... 135 F7
Allington Way. ME16 .... 91 B6
Allison Ave. ME7 .... 48 E1
Allnutt Mill Cl. ME15 .... 91 E2
Allotment La. TN13 .... 84 C5
Allsworth Cl. ME9 .... 65 B6
Alma Pl. Hadlow TN11 .... 118 C6
Alma Pl. Rochester ME2 .... 47 A7
Alma Rd. Eccles ME20 .... 75 F6
Alma Rd. New Town ME19 ...... 89 A8
Alma Rd. Orpington BR5 & BR6 .. 52 B8
Alma Rd. Sidcup DA14 .... 24 A5
Alma Rd. Swanscombe DA10 .... 11 F2
Almon Pl. ME1 .... 47 D5
Almond Cl. BR2 .... 37 A2
Almond Dr. BR8 .... 39 D7
Almond Gr. ME7 .... 63 A4
Almond Rd. DA2 .... 27 C8
Almond Way. BR2 .... 37 A2
Almonds The. ME14 .... 93 A4
Alms Row. TN16 .... 82 B3
Almshouses. 13 TN18 .... 179 A2
Alnwick Rd. Eltham SE12 .... 22 B8
Alnwick Rd. Newham E16 .... 1 C7
Alonso House. 3 DA17 .... 4 A1
Alpha Cl. ME5 .... 35 D7
Alpine Bsns Ctr. E6 .... 2 A8
Alpine Copse. 2 BR1 .... 37 A4
Alpine Way. E6 .... 2 A8
Alsike Rd. DA18 .... 3 E3
Altash Way. SE9 .... 23 A6
Altbarn Ind Est. ME5 .... 77 C8

Alton Cl. DA5 .... 24 E7
Alton Cotts. DA4 .... 54 E8
Alverstone Gdns. SE9 .... 23 C7
Alwold Cres. SE12 .... 5 C1
Amanda Cl. ME5 .... 61 F3
Amar Ct. SE18 .... 2 F2
Amardeep Ct. SE18 .... 2 F1
Ambassador Gdns. E6 .... 1 F8
Amber La. ME17 .... 108 A1
Amber Way. ME17 .... 108 B1
Amberleaze Dr. TN2 .... 150 D6
Amberley Cl. 2 Orpington BR6 .. 51 F5
Amberley Cl. Tonbridge TN9 .... 133 A8
Amberley Ct.
  Royal Tunbridge Wells TN4 ...... 149 C8
Amberley Ct. Sidcup DA14 ...... 24 C3
Amberley Rd. SE2 .... 7 D8
Amblecote Cl. SE12 .... 22 B5
Amblecote Meadow. SE12 ...... 22 B5
Amblecote Rd. SE12 .... 22 B5
Ambleside Rd. DA7 .... 8 A5
Ambley Gn. ME7 .... 63 A8
Ambley Rd. ME7 .... 63 B8
Ambrook Rd. DA17 .... 4 A3
Ambrose Cl. Crayford DA1 ...... 9 A3
Ambrose Cl. 6 Newham E6 .... 1 F8
Ambrose Cl. Orpington BR6 ...... 51 F7
Ambrose Hill. ME4 & ME5 ...... 48 C2
Amels Hill. ME5 .... 79 F8
Ames Ave. ME14 .... 93 A4
Ames Rd. DA10 .... 11 E1
Amesbury Rd. BR1 .... 36 D6
Amethyst Ave. ME5 .... 61 E6
Amherst Cl. Maidstone ME16 .... 91 D4
Amherst Cl. Orpington BR5 ...... 38 A5
Amherst Cty Jun Sch. TN13 .... 83 E4
Amherst Dr. BR5 .... 38 A5
Amherst Hill. Chatham ME4 ...... 48 A8
Amherst Hill. Sevenoaks TN13 .. 83 F4
Amherst Rd. Rochester ME1 ...... 47 D3
Amherst Rd.
  Royal Tunbridge Wells TN4 ...... 149 A5
Amherst Rd. Sevenoaks TN13 .. 84 B5
Amherst Redoubt. ME4 ...... 48 A5
Amhurst Bank Rd. TN11 & TN2 .. 138 F4
Amhurst Wlk. SE28 .... 3 A5
Amies House. ME15 .... 106 F3
Ampleforth Rd. SE2 .... 3 C4
Amsbury Rd. ME17 .... 106 B2
Amshurst Villas. ME15 ...... 106 A4
Ancaster St. SE18 .... 6 E7
Anchor and Hope La. SE7 ...... 1 C2
Anchor Bvd. DA9 .... 10 D3
Anchor House. E16 .... 1 C7
Anchor La. ME12 .... 21 F3
Anchor Rd. ME1 .... 47 C1
Anchorage Cl. ME3 .... 19 C3
Ancona Rd. SE18 .... 2 D1
Andace Pk. BR1 .... 36 C8
Anderson Way. DA17 .... 4 B4
Andorra Ct. BR1 .... 36 C8
Andover Ave. E16 .... 1 D7
Andover Rd. BR6 .... 37 E1
Andover Wlk. 12 ME15 ...... 107 F6
Andrew Broughton Way. ME14 92 B4
Andrew Cl. DA1 .... 8 D2
Andrew Manor. ME7 .... 48 C6
Andrew Rd. TN4 .... 149 C8
Andrew Wells House. BR1 ...... 22 B1
Andrewes Gdns. E6 .... 1 E7
Andrews Cl.
  Royal Tunbridge Wells TN2 ...... 149 D5
Andrews Cl. St Paul's Cray BR5 .. 38 D6
Andringham Lodge. 4 BR1 .. 36 B8
Andwell Cl. SE2 .... 3 B4
Anerley Cl. ME16 .... 91 D7
Angel La. TN9 .... 117 B1
Angel Row. TN18 .... 186 B5
Angel Terr. TN18 .... 186 B6
Angel Wlk. 4 TN9 .... 117 B1
Angelica Dr. E6 .... 2 A8
Angerstein Bsns Pk. SE10 ...... 1 A3
Angle Rd. RM16 .... 11 D8
Anglesea Ave. 4 SE18 ...... 2 B2
Anglesea Ctr. 17 DA11 ...... 13 B1
Anglesea Pl. 18 DA11 ...... 13 B1
Anglesea Rd. Orpington BR5 .. 38 C3
Anglesea Rd. Woolwich SE18 .... 2 B2
Anglesey Ave. ME15 .... 107 A7
Anglesey Cl. ME5 .... 62 B7
Anglesey St. SE18 .... 2 C3
Angley Ct. TN12 .... 153 A5
Angley Rd. TN17 .... 169 C5
Angley Sch. TN17 .... 169 C5
Angley Wlk. Cranbrook TN17 .... 169 C6
Angley Wlk. Wilsley Green TN17 169 D6
Anglian Ind Est. E6 .... 1 F4
Ankerdine Cres. SE18 .... 6 B6
Ann St. SE18 .... 2 D2
Ann Stroud Ct. SE12 .... 5 A2
Annandale Rd. DA15 .... 23 F8
Anne of Cleves Rd. DA1 ...... 9 D1
Annesley Rd. SE3 .... 5 B6
Annetts Hall. TN15 .... 87 A8
Annex The. BR8 .... 40 B6
Annie Rd. ME4 .... 74 F6
Ansell Ave. ME4 .... 48 A1
Anson Cl. ME5 .... 62 C6
Anson Rd. ME18 & ME19 ...... 88 E2
Anstridge Rd. SE9 .... 6 D1
Antelope Rd. SE18 .... 1 F3
Anthony Cl. TN13 .... 83 E7
Anthony Roper Cty Prim Sch.
  DA4 .... 54 E8
Anthonys La. BR8 .... 40 A8
Anthonys Way. ME2 .... 47 E8
Aperfield Rd. DA8 .... 8 F8

Apollo Ave. BR1 .... 36 B8
Apollo House. ME5 .... 62 A6
Apollo Way. SE18 .... 2 D3
Apple Cl. ME6 .... 75 A6
Apple Ct. TN12 .... 135 F6
Apple Tree Cl. ME15 ...... 90 F2
Apple Tree La. TN1 & TN2 .. 149 D8
Appleby Cl. ME1 .... 61 D7
Appleby Rd. E16 .... 1 A7
Appledore Ave. DA7 .... 8 D5
Appledore Cl. BR2 .... 36 A4
Appledore Cres. DA15 ...... 23 F5
Appledore Rd. Gillingham ME8 .. 49 A3
Appledore Rd. Tenterden TN30 183 E7
Applegarth Dr. DA1 .... 26 F6
Applegarth House. DA8 ...... 8 F5
Applegarth Rd. SE28 .... 3 C6
Appleshaw Cl. DA11 .... 30 A3
Appleton Rd. SE9 .... 5 E4
Appletons. TN11 .... 118 C8
Appold St. DA8 .... 8 F8
Approach The. BR6 .... 51 F8
April Cl. BR6 .... 51 F5
Apsleden. DA12 .... 30 D2
Apsley St. TN4 .... 148 D4
Aragon Cl. BR2 .... 36 F1
Arbroath Rd. SE9 .... 5 E4
Arbrook Cl. BR5 .... 38 A6
Arbrook Cl. BR5 .... 38 A8
Arbuthnot La. DA5 .... 7 E1
Arcade The. 2 SE9 .... 6 A1
Arcadia Rd. DA13 .... 43 F8
Arcadian Ave. DA5 .... 7 E1
Arcadian Cl. DA5 .... 7 E1
Arcadian Rd. DA5 .... 7 E1
Archer Rd. Chatham ME5 ...... 62 B6
Archer Rd. Orpington BR5 ...... 38 A4
Archer Way. ME8 .... 40 A7
Archery Cl. ME3 .... 33 B7
Archery House Hospl. DA2 .... 10 B1
Archery Rd. SE9 .... 5 F2
Archway Cl. 1 ME2 .... 47 B8
Arden Bsns Pk. ME2 .... 47 E8
Arden Cty Jun Sch. ME7 ...... 48 D6
Arden Gr. BR6 .... 51 B6
Arden St. ME7 .... 48 C6
Ardenlee Dr. ME14 .... 92 B5
Arethusa Rd. ME1 .... 61 C8
Argall House. 3 DA18 ...... 3 E3
Argent St. RM17 .... 12 B7
Argles Cl. DA9 .... 11 A2
Argyle Cl. ME1 .... 61 E8
Argyle Rd. Newham E16 ...... 1 B7
Argyle Rd.
  Royal Tunbridge Wells TN4 .. 133 A2
Argyle Rd. Sevenoaks TN13 .. 84 B2
Argyll Rd. SE18 .... 2 C3
Ariel Cl. DA12 .... 30 F4
Ariel Ct. 4 DA17 .... 4 A1
Arkwright Rd. RM18 .... 13 A5
Arlington Cl. DA15 .... 23 E8
Arlott Cl. ME14 .... 91 F6
Armada Cl. ME4 .... 47 E1
Armada Way. Newham E6 ...... 2 C7
Armitage Pl. 5 TN18 ...... 178 F2
Armoury Dr. DA12 .... 30 C8
Armstrong Cl. Bromley BR1 .. 36 E6
Armstrong Cl. Newham E6 ...... 1 F7
Armstrong Cl.
  Shepham Heath TN14 .... 68 B3
Armstrong Rd. ME15 .... 92 A1
Armytage Cl. ME3 .... 34 E4
Arne Cl. TN10 .... 117 E6
Arne Gr. BR6 .... 51 F7
Arnhem Dr. ME5 .... 61 F7
Arnold Ave. DA13 .... 58 B8
Arnold Pl. RM18 .... 13 C6
Arnold Rd. DA12 .... 30 D6
Arnolde Cl. ME2 .... 47 E7
Arnolds La. DA2 & DA4 ...... 27 A2
Arnott Cl. SE28 .... 3 C5
Arnsberg Way. DA7 .... 8 A3
Arnside Rd. DA7 .... 8 A6
Arran Cl. DA8 .... 8 D8
Arran Gn. ME2 .... 46 C7
Arran Rd. ME15 .... 107 A6
Arrandene House. 3 BR5 .. 38 B7
Arras House. SE2 .... 7 D8
Arsenal Rd. SE9 .... 5 F4
Artemis Cl. DA12 .... 30 E8
Arthur Gr. SE18 .... 2 C2
Arthur Rd. Gillingham ME8 ...... 63 E7
Arthur Rd. Rochester ME1 ...... 47 D3
Arthur Ruxley Est. DA14 ...... 24 D2
Arthur St. Erith DA8 .... 8 F7
Arthur St. Gravesend DA11 .... 30 A8
Arthur St. Grays RM17 ...... 12 C8
Arthur Toft House. 6 RM17 .. 12 B8
Artillery House. SE18 .... 2 A1
Artillery Pl. SE18 .... 2 A2
Artillery Row. DA12 .... 30 C8
Artington Cl. BR6 .... 51 C6
Artisan Cl. E16 .... 2 B6
Arun Ct. BR5 .... 38 C1
Arundel Cl. Chatham ME5 .. 62 D1
Arundel Cl. Sidcup DA5 ...... 24 E6
Arundel Cl. Tonbridge TN9 .. 133 A8
Arundel Ct. 2 DA6 .... 7 E3
Arundel Ct. BR6 .... 52 B5
Arundel Rd. Dartford DA1 ...... 9 C3
Arundel Rd.
  Royal Tunbridge Wells TN1 .. 149 B2
Arundel St. ME14 .... 91 F6
Ascot Cl. Borough Green TN15 .. 87 B7
Ascot Cl. Chatham ME5 .. 62 C2
Ascot Ct. DA5 .... 24 F8

Ascot House. 2 ME15 ...... 107 F6
Ascot Rd. Gravesend DA12 .. 30 B5
Ascot Rd. Orpington BR5 .. 37 F5
Ash Cl. Aylesford ME20 .. 75 E1
Ash Cl. Chatham ME5 .... 48 C1
Ash Cl. Edenbridge TN8 ...... 112 B1
Ash Cl. Gillingham ME8 ...... 49 B3
Ash Cl. Orpington BR5 .... 37 D4
Ash Cl.
  Royal Tunbridge Wells TN2 .. 163 D7
Ash Cl. Sidcup DA14 .... 24 B5
Ash Cl. Swanley BR8 .... 39 D7
Ash Cres. ME3 .... 32 C3
Ash Ct. SE12 .... 22 A8
Ash Gr. Lewisham SE12 ...... 22 A7
Ash Gr. Maidstone ME16 ...... 91 C6
Ash Keys. DA13 .... 73 B8
Ash La. TN15 .... 56 D2
Ash Platt Rd. TN15 .... 84 E6
Ash Rd. Ash TN15 .... 56 D6
Ash Rd. Dartford DA1 ...... 26 D7
Ash Rd. Gravesend DA12 ...... 30 C4
Ash Rd. Hartley DA3 .... 42 F3
Ash Rd. Hawley DA2 .... 26 F4
Ash Rd. Orpington BR6 ...... 51 F3
Ash Rd. Rochester ME2 ...... 46 F6
Ash Rd. Westerham TN16 ...... 81 E2
Ash Row. BR2 .... 37 A3
Ash Tree Cl. TN15 .... 55 F2
Ash Tree Cotts. TN12 ...... 154 B7
Ash Tree Dr. TN15 .... 55 F2
Ash Tree La. ME5 .... 48 D1
Ashbank Cotts. ME17 ...... 109 B7
Ashbee Cl. ME6 .... 75 A7
Ashbourne Ave. DA7 .... 7 E7
Ashbourne Rise. BR6 ...... 51 E6
Ashburn Cl. BR1 .... 22 A1
Ashburnham Cl. TN13 ...... 99 C8
Ashburnham Rd. Erith DA17 .... 4 C2
Ashburnham Rd.
  Maidstone ME14 .... 92 B8
Ashburnham Rd.
  Tonbridge TN10 .... 117 C3
Ashburton Rd. E16 .... 1 A7
Ashby Cl. ME2 .... 60 A4
Ashbys Yd. TN9 .... 117 C1
Ashcombe Dr. TN8 .... 112 B4
Ashcroft Ave. DA15 ...... 7 A1
Ashcroft Cres. DA15 ...... 7 A1
Ashcroft Ct. Dartford DA1 .. 27 A8
Ashcroft Ct. 5 Eltham SE9 ...... 6 A1
Ashcroft Rd. TN12 .... 136 A5
Ashdale Rd. SE12 .... 22 B7
Ashden Wlk. TN10 .... 117 C7
Ashdown Cl. Coldblow DA5 .... 25 C8
Ashdown Cl. Maidstone ME16 .. 91 D3
Ashdown Cl.
  Royal Tunbridge Wells TN4 .. 148 F4
Ashen. E6 .... 2 A7
Ashen Dr. DA1 .... 9 A1
Ashen Grove Rd. DA4 .... 55 B1
Ashenden Cl. ME2 .... 33 C2
Ashenden Wlk. TN2 .... 149 E8
Asher Reeds. TN3 .... 148 A4
Ashes La. TN11 .... 118 B8
Ashfield Gdns. TN27 ...... 141 D6
Ashfield Pl. BR7 .... 23 D1
Ashford Dr. ME17 .... 109 D3
Ashford Rd.
  Durrant Green TN26 & TN30 .. 173 A6
Ashford Rd. Harrietsham ME17 .. 110 C6
Ashford Rd.
  Maidstone,Grove Green
  ME14 & ME15 .... 92 D4
Ashford Rd.
  Maidstone,Silver Hill ME14 .. 93 D3
Ashford Rd. Tenterden TN30 .. 183 B8
Ashgrove Rd. TN13 .... 99 B7
Ashlar Pl. SE18 .... 2 B2
Ashleigh Cl. DA13 .... 57 F1
Ashleigh Gdns. TN27 ...... 141 D6
Ashley Cl. TN13 .... 84 A3
Ashley Gdns. Orpington BR6 .. 51 E5
Ashley Gdns. Rusthall TN4 .. 148 C5
Ashley House. ME5 .... 38 A7
Ashley Park Cl. TN4 .... 148 C5
Ashley Pk. TN4 .... 148 C5
Ashley Rd. Gillingham ME8 ...... 49 C2
Ashley Rd. Hildenborough TN11 .. 116 E5
Ashley Rd. Sevenoaks TN13 .. 84 B3
Ashmead Cl. ME5 .... 62 C3
Ashmead Gate. BR1 .... 36 C8
Ashmore Gr. DA16 .... 6 E4
Ashridge Cres. SE18 .... 6 C7
Ashridge House. DA14 ...... 23 F4
Ashton Way. ME19 .... 89 C6
Ashtree Cl. BR6 .... 51 B6
Ashurst Cl. DA1 .... 8 F4
Ashurst Hill. TN3 .... 146 D2
Ashurst Rd. Maidstone ME14 .. 92 C5
Ashurst Rd. Stone Cross TN3 .. 147 B3
Ashurst Sta. TN3 .... 146 D2
Ashwater Rd. SE12 .... 22 A7
Ashwell Cl. 8 E6 .... 1 E7
Ashwood Cl. ME3 .... 33 C7
Ashwood Pl. DA2 .... 28 B5
Askern Cl. DA6 .... 7 D3
Askews Farm Rd. RM16 ...... 11 E8
Askham Lodge. 8 SE12 .. 22 A8
Aspdin Rd. DA11 .... 29 E5
Aspen Cl. Orpington BR6 .. 52 A5
Aspen Cl. Swanley BR8 ...... 39 D8
Aspen Copse. BR1 .... 36 F7
Aspen Gn. DA18 .... 3 F3
Aspen House. 2 DA15 ...... 24 A5
Aspen Way. 2 Chatham ME5 .. 61 E4

Aspen Way.
  Royal Tunbridge Wells TN2 .. 133 C1
Aspian Dr. ME17 .... 106 D3
Asquith Rd. ME8 .... 63 C6
Association Wlk. ME1 ...... 61 C7
Aster Rd. ME1 .... 34 E3
Astley. RM17 .... 11 F8
Astley St. SE14 .... 92 A4
Aston Cl. Chatham ME5 .. 62 D3
Aston Cl. Sidcup DA14 ...... 24 A5
Astor Ct. E16 .... 1 C7
Astor of Hever Sch The. ME16 .. 91 C3
Astor Rd. TN15 .... 55 E4
Astra Dr. DA12 .... 30 F3
Atcost Rd. IG11 .... 3 A8
Athelstan Gn. ME17 .... 94 C2
Athelstan Rd. ME4 .... 47 F2
Athill Ct. TN13 .... 84 C5
Athol Rd. DA8 .... 4 C1
Atkinson Cl. BR6 .... 52 A5
Atkinson Rd. E16 .... 1 C8
Atlanta Ct. ME1 .... 47 D3
Atlas Gdns. SE7 .... 1 C2
Atlas Rd. DA1 .... 9 F4
Atterbury Cl. TN16 .... 81 D1
Attlee Dr. DA1 .... 10 A2
Attlee Rd. SE28 .... 3 B6
Attwaters La. TN18 .... 179 C6
Atwater Ct. ME17 .... 111 D5
Auckland Cl. RM18 .... 13 A5
Auckland Rd. TN1 .... 149 C5
Auden Rd. ME20 .... 75 A3
Audley Ave. Gillingham ME7 .. 48 E1
Audley Ave. Tonbridge TN9 .. 116 F2
Audley Cl. ME16 .... 91 B5
Audley Rise. TN9 .... 116 F1
Audley Wlk. BR5 .... 38 C3
Audrey Sturley Ct. TN4 .. 148 D4
Augusta Cl. 1 ME7 ...... 48 C7
Augustine Rd. Gravesend DA12 .. 30 C8
Augustine Rd. St Paul's Cray BR5 38 D6
Austell Manor. ME7 .... 48 C6
Austen Cl. Swanscombe DA9 .. 11 C1
Austen Cl. Tilbury RM18 ...... 13 C5
Austen Cl. Woolwich SE28 .. 3 B5
Austen Gdns. DA1 .... 9 F3
Austen Rd. DA8 .... 8 B7
Austen Way. ME20 .... 74 F4
Austens Orch. 12 TN30 .. 183 A7
Austin Ave. B1 & BR2 ...... 36 E4
Austin Cl. ME5 & ME7 .... 48 E2
Austin Rd. Gravesend DA11 .. 29 F7
Austin Rd. Orpington BR5 .. 38 A4
Austral Cl. DA15 .... 23 F5
Autumn Glade. ME14 .... 77 D8
Avalon Cl. ME6 .... 52 D7
Avalon Ctr The. BR6 .... 52 D8
Avalon Gdns. BR5 .... 38 C1
Avalon Rd. BR5 & BR6 .... 52 C8
Avard Gdns. BR6 .... 51 C6
Avards Cl. TN18 .... 184 E8
Avebury Ave. TN9 .... 117 B1
Avebury Rd. BR6 .... 51 D7
Aveling Cl. ME15 .... 34 D6
Aveling Ct. 2 ME2 .... 47 B7
Avenons Rd. 3 E16 ...... 1 A8
Avenue La. ME7 .... 11 C1
Avenue Le Puy. TN9 .... 117 C1
Avenue Rd. Bexley DA7 & DA6 .. 7 E4
Avenue Rd. Erith DA8 .... 8 F8
Avenue Rd. Sevenoaks TN13 .. 84 C3
Avenue The. Aylesford ME20 .. 75 E1
Avenue The. Borough Green TN15 87 A8
Avenue The. Bromley BR1 .. 36 D6
Avenue The. Gravesend DA11 .. 30 A8
Avenue The. Hill Park TN16 .. 81 A4
Avenue The. Keston Mark BR2 .. 50 D7
Avenue The. Orpington BR6 .. 51 F8
Avenue The. St Paul's Cray BR5 .. 24 B1
Avenue The. Swanscombe DA9 .. 11 B2
Avenue The. Tonbridge TN9 .. 117 B2
Averenches Rd. ME14 ...... 92 C5
Avery Cl. Allhallows-on-Sea ME3 .. 19 F7
Avery Cl. Maidstone ME15 .. 91 F1
Avery Hill Rd. SE9 .... 23 D7
Avery La. ME15 .... 108 A3
Avery Way. ME3 .... 19 D8
Aviemore Gdns. ME14 ...... 92 F4
Avington Cl. ME15 .... 91 F1
Avocet Mews. SE28 .... 2 D3
Avocet Wlk. ME5 .... 62 D2
Avon Cl. Gravesend DA12 .. 30 D6
Avon Cl. Tonbridge TN10 .. 117 C5
Avon St. TN1 .... 149 C5
Avondale Mews. BR1 ...... 22 A2
Avondale Pl. ME1 .... 19 C4
Avondale Rd. Bexley DA16 .. 7 C5
Avondale Rd. Bromley BR1 .. 22 A2
Avondale Rd. Chislehurst SE9 .. 22 D6
Avondale Rd. Gillingham ME7 .. 48 D5
Avonmouth Rd. DA1 .... 9 D2
Awliscombe Rd. DA16 .... 6 F5
Axford Ct. ME8 .... 64 A8
Axminster Cres. DA16 ...... 7 C6
Axtaine Rd. BR5 .... 38 D2
Axtane. DA13 .... 28 F1
Axtane Cl. DA4 .... 41 C8
Axton Chase Sch. DA3 .. 42 F6
Aycliffe Cl. BR1 .... 36 F5
Ayelands. DA3 .... 56 E8
Ayelands La. DA3 .... 56 E8
Aylesbury Rd. BR2 .... 36 A6
Aylesford Cres. ME8 .... 49 C2
Aylesford Cty Prim Sch. ME20 .. 75 D1
Aylesford Sch. ME20 .... 75 D1
Aylesford Sta. ME20 .... 75 E2

Aylesham Rd. BR6 .... 37 F2
Aynscombe Angle. BR6 .... 38 A2
Azalea Dr. BR8 .... 39 E5

Babb's La. TN17 .... 180 A6
Babbacombe Rd. BR1 .... 22 B1
Babington House Sch. BR7 .. 22 B2
Babylon La. ME17 & TN12 .. 124 B1
Back La. Godden Green TN15 .. 85 A2
Back La. Goudhurst TN17 ...... 167 E8
Back La. Horsmonden TN12 .. 153 A6
Back La. Marlpit ME17 ...... 107 E1
Back La. Sevenoaks TN13 & TN14 83 C2
Back La. Shipbourne TN11 .. 101 D4
Back La. Sidcup DA5 .... 25 A8
Back Rd. Sandhurst TN18 .. 186 B5
Back Rd. Sidcup DA14 ...... 24 A4
Back St. ME17 .... 108 E6
Backfields. ME1 .... 47 B4
Baden Powell House. 11 DA17 .. 4 A3
Baden Powell Rd. TN13 .. 83 E5
Baden Rd. ME7 .... 48 D7
Bader Cres. ME5 .... 62 A7
Bader Rd. ME5 .... 62 C1
Badgers Copse. BR6 .... 51 E8
Badgers Croft. SE9 .... 23 A5
Badgers Rd. ME14 .... 53 B1
Badgers Rise. TN14 .... 53 A1
Badlow Cl. DA8 .... 8 E7
Badsell Park Farm. TN12 .. 135 C3
Badsell Rd. TN12 .... 135 D6
Baffin Cl. ME4 .... 47 F2
Bailey Dr. ME7 .... 49 A1
Bakenham House. 1 ME1 .. 47 C1
Baker Beall Ct. ME7 .... 8 B4
Baker Hill Cl. DA11 .... 29 F4
Baker La. Headcorn TN27 .. 141 F7
Baker La. Sutton Valence ME17 .. 124 F7
Baker St. SE18 .... 5 E6
Baker St. Burham ME1 ...... 60 F1
Baker St. Rochester ME1 .. 47 C3
Bakers Ave. TN15 .... 55 E3
Bakers Cross. TN17 .... 169 E4
Bakers Mews. 9 BR6 .... 51 F4
Bakery Cl. TN17 .... 156 E2
Balaclava La. TN5 .... 175 A6
Balcaskie Rd. SE9 .... 5 F2
Balcombe Cl. ME6 .... 7 D3
Balcombe Cotts. TN17 ...... 167 E8
Balcombes Hill. TN17 ...... 167 E8
Balder Rise. SE12 .... 22 B6
Baldock Rd. TN5 .... 174 E4
Baldwyn's Pk. DA5 .... 25 D6
Baldwyn's Rd. DA5 .... 25 D6
Balfour Cty Inf Sch. ME4 .. 47 E1
Balfour Cty Jun Sch. ME4 .. 47 E2
Balfour Rd. Bromley BR2 .. 36 C4
Balfour Rd. Chatham ME4 .. 47 E2
Balgowan St. SE18 .... 2 F2
Ball's Gn. TN7 .... 160 B5
Ballamore Rd. BR1 .... 22 A5
Ballard Bsns Pk. ME2 ...... 46 F5
Ballard Cl. TN12 .... 138 C6
Ballard Ind Est. ME5 .... 77 C8
Ballard Way. TN12 .... 136 B7
Ballens Rd. ME5 .... 62 C3
Balliol Rd. DA16 .... 7 B5
Balls Cotts. ME3 .... 33 F4
Balmer Cl. ME8 .... 63 D7
Balmoral Cl. SE12 .... 22 B4
Balmoral Gdns. DA5 .... 24 F8
Balmoral House. 6 ME15 .. 107 F5
Balmoral Rd. Gillingham ME7 .. 48 D5
Balmoral Rd. Sutton at Hone DA4 27 B1
Balmoral Trad Est. E6 .... 2 F8
Baltic Rd. TN9 .... 133 B7
Baltimore Pl. DA16 .... 6 F5
Banbridges Ind Est. TN12 .. 120 A5
Banbury Villas. DA13 ...... 28 F1
Banchory Rd. SE3 .... 5 B7
Banckside. DA3 .... 42 E5
Bancroft Gdns. BR6 .... 37 F1
Bancroft Rd. TN15 .... 71 F3
Bandfield Wlk. DA1 .... 9 F4
Bangor Rd. ME2 .... 46 D6
Bank Cotts. ME17 .... 94 C3
Bank Houses. ME3 .... 27 A3
Bank La. TN11 & TN15 .... 100 A3
Bank St. Chatham ME4 .... 48 B3
Bank St. Cranbrook TN17 .. 169 C5
Bank St. Gravesend DA11 .. 13 B1
Bank St. Maidstone ME14 & ME15 92 A4
Bank St. Sevenoaks TN13 .. 84 C2
Bank St. Tonbridge TN9 .. 117 C2
Bankfield Way. TN17 .... 167 E7
Bankfields. TN27 .... 141 C5
Banks La. DA6 .... 7 F3
Banks Rd. ME2 .... 47 C8
Bankside. Chatham ME5 .... 61 E4
Bankside. Northfleet DA11 .. 12 C1
Bankside. Sevenoaks TN13 .. 83 E6
Bankside. Sparrow's Green TN5 174 E5
Bankside Cl. DA2 .... 25 D4
Banky Meadow. ME16 .... 90 F3
Banner Farm Rd. TN2 .... 149 B2
Banner St. ME2 .... 47 C8
Bannister Gdns. BR5 .... 38 C6
Bannister Rd. ME14 .... 92 A1
Bannockburn Prim Sch. SE18 .. 2 F1
Bannockburn Rd. SE18 .... 2 F2
Banwell Rd. DA5 .... 7 D1

Bapchild Pl. 8 BR5 38 C5
Barbados Terr. 2 ME14 92 A7
Barberry Ave. ME5 61 E5
Barcham Ct. ME15 106 F5
Barchester Way. TN10 117 F6
Barclay Ave. TN10 118 A5
Barcombe Cl. BR5 & BR7 38 A6
Bardell Terr. ME1 47 D5
Barden Ct. ME14 92 B5
Barden Park Rd. TN9 117 A1
Barden Rd. Printstile TN3 131 F2
Barden Rd. Tonbridge TN9 117 B1
Barden St. SE18 6 E7
Bardsley Cl. TN12 120 A7
Barfield. DA4 41 B8
Barfield Rd. BR1 & BR7 37 A6
Barfleur Manor. 6 ME4 48 A6
Barfreston Cl. ME15 91 F2
Bargate Cl. SE18 2 F1
Barge House Rd. E16 2 B4
Bargrove Rd. ME14 92 C5
Barham Cl. Chislehurst BR7 23 B3
Barham Cl. Gravesend DA12 30 F7
Barham Cl. Keston Mark BR2 36 E1
Barham Cl. Park Wood ME15 107 E5
Barham Ct. BR2 36 E1
Barham Mews. ME18 105 B8
Barham Rd. Chislehurst BR7 23 B3
Barham Rd. Dartford DA1 27 A8
Barham's Mill Rd. TN27 127 B3
Baring Cl. SE12 22 A6
Baring Prim Sch. SE12 22 A8
Baring Rd. SE12 22 A6
Bark Hart Rd. BR6 38 B1
Barker Rd. ME16 91 F3
Barking Rd. E16 1 A8
Barkis Cl. ME1 61 D7
Barley Fields. ME14 92 D4
Barleycorn. ME19 74 E1
Barleycorn Dr. ME8 63 E6
Barleymow Cl. ME5 62 C7
Barling Cl. ME5 61 D1
Barlow Cl. ME8 63 E5
Barlow Way. RM13 & RM9 4 E8
Barming Cty Prim Sch. ME16 90 F2
Barming Rd. ME19 89 F2
Barming Sta. ME16 90 F6
Barn End Ctr. DA2 26 C5
Barn End Dr. DA2 26 C5
Barn End La. DA2 26 C4
Barn Hill. ME15 105 E2
Barn Meadow. ME2 59 E4
Barnaby Terr. ME1 47 D2
Barnard Cl. Chislehurst BR7 37 D8
Barnard Cl. Woolwich SE18 2 A3
Barnard Ct. Chatham ME4 48 A2
Barnard Ct. 10 Dartford DA2 10 B1
Barncroft Cl. ME14 92 F4
Barncroft Dr. ME7 62 F4
Barned Ct. ME16 90 F2
Barnehurst Ave. DA7 & DA8 8 C6
Barnehurst Cl. DA8 8 C6
Barnehurst Inf Sch. DA8 8 C6
Barnehurst Jun Sch. DA8 8 C6
Barnehurst Rd. DA7 8 C5
Barnehurst Sta. DA7 8 C5
Barnes Cray Prim Sch. DA1 9 A3
Barnes Cray Rd. DA1 9 A3
Barnes Ct. E16 1 C8
Barnes La. ME17 122 D8
Barnes Wlk. TN12 138 D6
Barnesdale Cres. BR5 38 A4
Barnet Dr. BR2 50 E8
Barnet Wood Rd. BR2 50 C8
Barnett Cl. DA8 8 F5
Barnetts Cl. TN2 & TN4 133 C1
Barnetts Rd. TN11 116 A2
Barnetts Way. TN4 133 C1
Barney Cl. SE7 1 C1
Barnfield. Chatham ME5 62 A8
Barnfield.
Royal Tunbridge Wells TN2 162 F7
Barnfield. St Michaels TN30 173 C2
Barnfield Cl. Crockenhill BR8 39 C2
Barnfield Cl. New Barn DA3 43 D6
Barnfield Cl. Stone DA9 10 F1
Barnfield Cres. TN14 69 E2
Barnfield Gdns. SE18 6 B8
Barnfield Rd. Erith DA17 7 F8
Barnfield Rd. Sevenoaks TN13 83 E4
Barnfield Rd. St Paul's Cray BR5 38 D6
Barnfield Rd. Woolwich SE18 6 B8
Barnhill Ave. BR2 36 A4
Barnhurst Rd. ME14 92 A8
Barnsole Cty Inf Sch. ME7 48 E4
Barnsole Cty Jun Sch. ME7 48 E4
Barnsole Rd. ME7 48 E3
Barnwell Rd. DA1 9 F4
Barnwood Cl. ME1 61 B8
Barnwood Ct. E16 1 B5
Baron Cl. Gillingham ME7 48 E7
Baron Cl. Maidstone ME14 92 F5
Barons Ct. TN4 149 A5
Barr Rd. DA12 30 F6
Barrack Cnr. TN13 84 C4
Barrack Rd. ME4 48 B8
Barrack Row. Benenden TN17 180 D6
Barrack Row. 14
Gravesend DA11 13 B1
Barrel Arch Cl. TN12 138 C6
Barretts Green Cotts. 5 TN18 179 A2
Barretts Rd. Hawkhurst TN18 179 A2
Barretts Rd. Sevenoaks TN13 83 E7
Barrie Dr. 7 ME20 74 F4
Barrier Rd. ME4 47 F5
Barrington Cl. ME5 61 F5
Barrington Prim Sch. DA16 7 D5
Barrington Rd. DA16 7 D5
Barrington Villas. SE18 6 A6
Barrow La. TN3 147 F1
Barrowfields. ME5 62 D1
Barry Ave. DA7 7 E7
Barry Cl. BR6 51 E7
Barry Rd. E6 1 E7
Barth Rd. SE18 2 E2
Bartholomew Way. BR8 39 E6
Bartlett Cl. ME5 62 C1
Bartlett Rd. Gravesend DA11 30 A7
Bartlett Rd. Westerham TN16 81 C1
Bartley Mill. TN3 164 E4
Barton Cl. Bexley DA6 7 E2
Barton Cl. 2 Newham E6 1 F7
Barton Cl. Yalding ME18 104 F1
Barton Cotts. TN11 102 A6
Barton Rd. Maidstone ME15 92 A2
Barton Rd. Rochester ME2 47 A7
Barton Rd. Sidcup DA14 24 E2
Barton Rd. Sutton at Hone DA4 41 B8
Basden Cotts. 2 TN18 179 A2
Baseing Cl. E6 2 A6
Bashford Barn La. ME9 80 F4
Basi Cl. ME2 33 C1
Basildon Rd. SE2 3 A1
Basilon Rd. DA7 7 E5
Basing Cl. ME15 92 B3
Basing Dr. DA5 7 F1
Basket Gdns. SE9 5 E2
Basmere Cl. ME14 92 C6
Bassant Rd. SE18 6 F8
Bassett's Forge. TN5 174 E5
Bassetts Cl. BR6 51 B6
Bassetts La. TN11 & TN8 146 C7
Bassetts Way. BR6 51 B6
Basted La. Basted TN15 86 F5
Basted La. Crouch TN15 87 B4
Bastion Rd. SE18 & SE2 3 A1
Baston Manor Rd. BR2 & BR4 50 B6
Baston Rd. BR2 50 B7
Bat & Ball Sta. TN14 84 C6
Batchelor St. ME4 48 A4
Batchelors. TN2 150 E8
Batchwood Gn. BR5 38 B6
Bates Cl. ME20 75 A3
Bates Hill. TN15 86 C5
Bateson St. SE18 2 E2
Bath Hard. ME1 47 D5
Bath Rd. DA1 26 B8
Bath St. DA11 13 B1
Baths Rd. BR1 & BR2 36 D5
Bathurst Cl. TN12 139 E4
Bathurst Rd. TN12 139 E3
Bathway. 17 SE18 2 A2
Batt's Rd. DA12 & DA13 45 A4
Batten Cl. E6 1 F7
Battery Rd. SE28 2 E4
Battle La. TN12 139 A8
Battle Rd. DA8 & DA17 4 C2
Battle St. DA12 44 F6
Battlefields. TN15 71 F3
Battlesmere Rd. ME3 33 B8
Baugh Rd. DA14 24 C3
Baxter Rd. E16 1 C8
Bay Cl. ME3 34 E3
Bay Manor La. RM16 10 F8
Bay The. DA13 73 A8
Bayard Ct. DA7 8 B3
Bayeux House. 10 SE7 5 C8
Bayfield Rd. SE9 5 D3
Bayhall Rd. TN2 149 C3
Bayham Abbey (rems of). TN3 165 B5
Bayham Ct. TN5 174 E6
Bayham Rd. Royal Tunbridge Wells
TN2 & TN3 163 C7
Bayham Rd. Sevenoaks TN13 84 D4
Bayley's Hill. TN14 98 E3
Bayliss Ave. SE28 3 D6
Bayly Rd. DA1 10 A1
Bayne Cl. E6 1 F7
Baynham Cl. DA5 7 F1
Bayswater Dr. ME8 63 E4
Baytree Cl. Bromley BR1 36 D8
Baytree Cl. Sidcup DA15 23 F7
Baywell. ME19 & ME20 74 E2
Bazes Shaw. DA3 56 F8
Beach Ct. Eltham SE9 5 E1
Beach Ct. Goddard's Green TN17 170 D1
Beacham Cl. SE7 5 D8
Beacon Cl. ME8 63 D7
Beacon Dr. DA2 28 C5
Beacon Hill. ME5 48 D2
Beacon Hill La. ME3 33 F4
Beacon Oak Rd. TN30 183 B8
Beacon Rd. Chatham ME5 48 C2
Beacon Rd. Erith DA8 9 B7
Beacon Rd. Lenham ME17 111 C5
Beacon Rise. TN13 84 A1
Beacon Wlk. TN30 173 B1
Beacon Wood Cty Pk. DA2 28 B4
Beaconfields. TN13 84 A1
Beacons The. ME17 106 C2
Beacons Wlk. 10 E6 1 E8
Beaconsfield Ave. ME7 48 E5
Beaconsfield Cl. SE3 5 A8
Beaconsfield Par. SE9 22 E4
Beaconsfield Rd. Bromley BR1 36 D6
Beaconsfield Rd. Chatham ME4 47 F3
Beaconsfield Rd. Chislehurst SE9 22 E4
Beaconsfield Rd. Greenwich SE3 5 A7
Beaconsfield Rd.
Maidstone ME15 91 E2
Beaconsfield Rd. Maypole DA5 25 E6
Beadon Rd. BR2 36 A4
Beagles Cl. BR5 52 D8
Beagles Wood Rd. TN2 150 E7
Beal Cl. DA16 7 A6
Beamish Rd. BR5 38 C2
Beams The. ME15 92 F1
Bean Cty Prim Sch. DA2 28 C4
Bean Hill Cotts. DA2 28 C4
Bean La. DA2 28 B6
Bean Rd. Bexley DA6 7 D3
Bean Rd. Swanscombe DA9 28 B8
Beanshaw. BR7 & SE9 23 A4
Bearsted Cl. ME8 49 B3
Bearsted Green Bsns Ctr. ME14 93 C4
Bearsted Rd. ME14 92 E6
Bearsted & Thurnham Sta.
ME14 93 B5
Beaton Cl. DA9 11 B2
Beatrice Gdns. DA11 29 E6
Beatty Ave. ME7 48 F4
Beatty Cotts. ME3 19 D7
Beatty Rd. ME1 61 D8
Beaufighter Rd. ME19 88 E3
Beaufort. E6 2 A8
Beaufort Ct. ME2 47 E6
Beaufort Rd. ME2 46 E8
Beaufort Wlk. ME15 107 E4
Beaulieu Rd. TN10 117 B4
Beaulieu Rise. ME1 47 D1
Beaulieu Wlk. ME16 91 C7
Beaumanor Gdns. SE9 23 A4
Beaumont Dr. DA11 29 F8
Beaumont Rd. Maidstone ME16 91 B2
Beaumont Rd. Northfleet DA11 29 E8
Beaumont Rd.
Orpington BR5 & BR6 37 D3
Beauworth Pk. ME15 107 E8
Beaverbank Rd. SE9 23 D7
Beavers Lodge. DA14 23 F3
Beaverwood Rd. BR7 23 E2
Beaverwood Sch for Girls. BR7 23 E2
Bebbington Rd. SE18 2 E2
Beblets Cl. 4 BR6 51 F5
Beckenham Dr. ME16 91 D7
Beckenham La. BR1 & BR2 36 A7
Becket Ct. TN27 141 D5
Beckets Field. TN11 131 A3
Beckett Cl. DA17 3 F3
Becketts Cl. BR6 51 F7
Beckford Dr. BR5 & BR6 37 D2
Beckley Cl. DA12 31 B6
Beckley Mews. ME5 61 F5
Beckman Cl. TN14 68 C4
Becks Rd. DA14 24 A5
Becksbourne Cl. ME14 92 A8
Beckton Park Sta. E16 1 F6
Beckton Rd. E16 1 A8
Beckton Sch. E16 1 D8
Beckton Sta. E6 2 A8
Becton Pl. DA8 8 C6
Bedale Wlk. DA1 27 B7
Beddington Gn. BR5 37 F8
Beddington Rd. BR5 37 F8
Beddow Way. ME20 76 B3
Bedens Rd. DA14 24 E3
Bedford Ave. ME8 49 D1
Bedford Pl. ME16 91 E4
Bedford Rd. Dartford DA1 27 A8
Bedford Rd. Northfleet DA11 29 F6
Bedford Rd. Orpington BR6 38 B1
Bedford Rd.
Royal Tunbridge Wells TN4 133 A1
Bedford Rd. Sidcup DA15 23 E5
Bedford Sq. DA3 42 E6
Bedford Terr. 9 TN1 149 A2
Bedgebury Cl. Chatham ME1 61 D8
Bedgebury Cl. Maidstone ME14 92 C6
Bedgebury Cross. TN17 167 D2
Bedgebury Lower Sch. TN18 184 F7
Bedgebury National Pinetum.
TN17 177 E8
Bedgebury Rd. Eltham SE9 5 D3
Bedgebury Rd. Goudhurst TN17 167 E7
Bedgebury Sch. TN17 167 E1
Bedivere Rd. BR1 22 A5
Bedlam La. TN27 142 E6
Bedonwell Jun Sch. DA17 7 E8
Bedonwell Prim Inf Sch. SE2 7 E8
Bedonwell Rd. Bexley DA7 7 F6
Bedonwell Rd. Erith DA7 & DA17 7 E8
Bedwell Rd. DA17 4 A1
Bedwin Cl. ME1 61 D7
Beeby Rd. E16 1 B8
Beech Ave. Sidcup DA15 24 A8
Beech Ave. Swanley BR8 39 F5
Beech Copse. BR1 36 F7
Beech Ct. DA1 10 A1
Beech Dell. BR2 & BR6 50 F6
Beech Dr. ME16 91 C5
Beech Gr. ME3 32 C4
Beech Green La. Blackham TN7 145 F1
Beech Green La. Withyham TN7 160 B7
Beech Haven Ct. DA1 8 D2
Beech House. 7 DA15 24 A5
Beech Hurst. TN2 150 D7
Beech La. TN12 151 C4
Beech Rd. Dartford DA1 26 D7
Beech Rd. East Malling ME19 89 F7
Beech Rd. Herne Pound ME18 88 D2
Beech Rd. Hoo St Werburgh ME3 34 E3
Beech Rd. Newenden TN18 187 C3
Beech Rd. Orpington BR6 52 A3
Beech Rd. Rochester ME2 46 F6
Beech Rd. Sevenoaks TN13 84 B2
Beech St. TN1 149 B4
Beech Wlk. DA1 9 A3
Beecham Rd. TN10 117 E6
Beechcroft. BR7 23 A1
Beechcroft Ave. DA7 8 D5
Beechcroft Cl. BR6 51 D6
Beechcroft Rd. BR6 51 D6
Beechen Bank Rd. ME5 62 A1
Beechenlea La. BR8 40 B6
Beeches Ct. BR1 22 A2
Beeches The. Aylesford ME20 75 E1
Beeches The. Chatham ME5 62 A4
Beeches The.
Royal Tunbridge Wells TN2 149 D5
Beeches The. Sole Street DA12 44 D5
Beeches The. The Moor TN18 184 E7
Beeches The. Tilbury RM18 13 B5
Beechfield Cotts. 3 BR1 36 C7
Beechfield Rd. Bromley BR1 36 C7
Beechfield Rd. Erith DA8 8 E7
Beechhill Rd. SE9 6 A2
Beechill Dr. RM17 11 F8
Beechin Wood La. TN15 87 D5
Beeching Rd. ME5 62 B3
Beechings Gn. ME8 49 C3
Beechings Way. ME8 49 C3
Beechlands Cl. DA3 43 A4
Beechmont Rd. TN13 99 B6
Beechmont Rise. TN10 117 B6
Beechmore Dr. ME5 62 A2
Beechway. DA5 7 D1
Beechwood Ave. Chatham ME5 48 D2
Beechwood Ave. Orpington BR6 51 E4
Beechwood Cres. DA7 7 E4
Beechwood Dr. Keston BR2 50 D6
Beechwood Dr. Vigo Village DA13 58 A1
Beechwood Gdns. DA13 58 A1
Beechwood Mews. TN2 149 E4
Beechwood Rd. ME16 90 F3
Beechwood Rise. BR7 23 B4
Beechwood Sch (Sacred Heart).
TN2 149 E4
Beechy Lees Rd. TN14 69 E3
Beeken Dene. BR6 51 C6
Beesfield La. DA4 41 A1
Beeston Ct. DA1 10 B1
Begbie Rd. SE3 5 C6
Beggars La. TN16 81 E3
Begonia Ave. ME8 49 C2
Beke Rd. ME8 63 D4
Bekesbourne Tower. 12 BR5 38 D1
Beldam Haw. TN14 68 A8
Belfield Rd. TN2 150 D6
Belford Gr. SE18 2 A2
Belgrave Cl. 5 BR5 38 C5
Belgrave Ct. SE7 5 C7
Belgrave Rd. TN1 149 B4
Belgrave St. ME20 75 F6
Belgrove. 5 TN1 149 A2
Bell Cl. DA9 10 F2
Bell Cres. ME1 75 F8
Bell Gdns. BR5 38 C4
Bell House. SE2 3 D1
Bell La. Burham ME1 75 F8
Bell La. Larkfield ME20 75 B2
Bell La. Lashenden TN27 158 B8
Bell La. Maidstone ME14 93 A5
Bell La. Newham E16 1 A5
Bell La. Staplehurst TN12 139 E3
Bell La. Westfield Sole ME14 77 B7
Bell Rd. ME15 107 E5
Bell Row. TN11 118 F5
Bell Water Gate. SE18 2 A3
Bell Way. ME17 109 E2
Bell Wood Cty Inf Sch. ME15 107 E5
Bell Wood Cty Jun Sch. ME15 107 E5
Bell's Cl. TN30 183 A7
Bell's La. ME3 34 E6
Belle Vue Rd. BR6 51 A1
Bellefield Rd. BR5 38 B4
Bellegrave Par. DA16 6 F4
Bellegrove Cl. DA16 6 F5
Bellegrove Rd. DA16 6 E5
Bellevue Rd. DA6 7 F2
Bellflower Cl. 2 E6 1 E8
Bellgrove Ct. ME5 77 A8
Bellman Ave. DA12 30 E7
Bellmeadow. ME15 107 E6
Bellows La. TN15 86 F7
Bellring Cl. DA17 8 A8
Bells Farm La. TN11 & TN12 119 C8
Bells Farm Rd. TN12 103 D1
Bells La. 7 TN30 183 A7
Bellwood Ct. ME3 18 C3
Belmont Ave. DA16 6 E4
Belmont Cl. ME16 90 F2
Belmont La. BR7 23 C3
Belmont Par. BR7 23 C3
Belmont Prim Sch. DA7 8 A7
Belmont Rd. Chislehurst BR7 23 B3
Belmont Rd. Erith DA8 8 B6
Belmont Rd. Gillingham ME7 48 C4
Belmont Rd. Grays RM17 11 F8
Belnor Ave. ME9 65 F8
Belson Rd. SE18 1 F2
Beltana Dr. DA12 30 E4
Belton Rd. DA14 24 A4
Beltring & Banbridges Halt.
TN12 120 B4
Beltring Hop Farm. TN12 120 A3
Beltring Rd. Beltring TN12 120 B4
Beltring Rd.
Royal Tunbridge Wells TN4 149 A6
Beltwood Rd. DA17 4 C2
Beluncle Villas. ME3 35 C7
Belvedere Cl. DA12 30 C7
Belvedere Ct. DA17 3 F3
Belvedere Cty Prim Jun Sch.
DA17 4 B3
Belvedere Ind Est. DA17 4 D5
Belvedere Link Bsns Pk. DA17 4 C3
Belvedere Rd. Bexley DA7 7 F5
Belvedere Rd. Erith SE28 3 D5
Belvedere Sta. DA17 4 B3
Belvoir Cl. SE9 22 E5
Ben Tillet Cl. E16 1 F5
Benares Rd. SE18 & SE2 2 F2
Benden Cl. TN12 139 F4
Bendmore Ave. SE2 3 A2
Bendon Way. ME8 63 D8
Benedict Cl. 9 Erith DA17 3 E3
Benedict Cl. Halling ME2 60 B4
Benedict Cl. Orpington BR6 51 E7
Benenden CE Prim Sch. TN17 180 D6
Benenden Gn. BR2 36 A4
Benenden Hospl. TN17 171 C3
Benenden Manor. ME8 49 B3
Benenden Rd. Benenden TN17 181 B4
Benenden Rd.
Fosten Green TN17 & TN27 171 F5
Benenden Rd. Rochester ME2 33 C1
Benenden Sch. TN17 180 C8
Beneneden Rd. TN27 172 A7
Benhall Mill Rd. TN2 & TN3 163 D8
Benjamin Ct. 4 DA17 7 F8
Benn House. 7 SE7 1 C1
Bennett Cl. DA16 7 A5
Bennett House. DA11 29 F5
Bennett Memorial Diocesan Sch.
TN4 148 E6
Bennett Way. DA2 27 D3
Bennetts Ave. TN15 71 C7
Bennetts Copse. BR7 22 E2
Bennetts Cotts. ME7 78 A8
Bennetts Mews. 11 TN30 183 A7
Benover Rd. ME18 120 F7
Benson Rd. RM17 12 C8
Bensted Cl. ME15 121 D7
Bentfield Gdns. SE9 22 D5
Bentham Hill. TN3 & TN4 132 D1
Bentham Rd. SE28 3 B5
Bentley Cl. Aylesford ME20 75 F1
Bentley Cl. Chatham ME5 62 D2
Bentley Cl. New Barn DA3 43 C7
Bentley St. DA11 13 C1
Bentley Street Ind Est. DA11 13 C1
Bentley's Meadow. TN15 84 F7
Bentlif Cl. ME16 91 D5
Berber Rd. ME2 47 B8
Bercta Rd. SE9 23 C6
Berengrave La. ME8 49 F2
Berens Ct. DA14 23 F4
Berens Rd. BR5 38 D4
Berens Way. BR5 & BR7 37 F6
Beresford Ave. ME4 47 E2
Beresford Cl. TN17 166 F2
Beresford Dr. BR1 36 E6
Beresford Rd. Gillingham ME7 48 D4
Beresford Rd. Goudhurst TN17 153 F1
Beresford Rd. Kit's Coty ME20 76 D7
Beresford Rd. Northfleet DA11 29 E8
Beresford Square Market Pl. 1
SE18 2 B2
Beresford St. SE18 2 B3
Beresfords Hill. ME17 107 B4
Berger Cl. BR5 37 E3
Bergland Pk. ME2 47 D8
Bering Wlk. E16 1 D7
Berkeley Ave. DA16 7 D6
Berkeley Cl. Chatham ME1 61 D8
Berkeley Cl. Orpington BR5 & BR6 37 E2
Berkeley Cl. Pembury TN2 150 E7
Berkeley Cres. DA1 26 F7
Berkeley Ct. 6 BR8 39 E6
Berkeley Mount. 1 ME4 47 F4
Berkeley Rd. Gravesend DA11 13 B1
Berkeley Rd. 7
Royal Tunbridge Wells TN1 149 A2
Berkeley Terr. RM18 13 A7
Berkhampstead Rd. 8 DA17 4 A1
Berkley Cres. DA11 13 C1
Berkshire Cl. ME5 62 C8
Bermuda Rd. RM18 13 A5
Bernal Cl. SE28 3 D6
Bernard Ashley Dr. SE7 1 B1
Bernard St. 21 DA11 13 B1
Bernersmede. SE3 5 A4
Berry Rd. ME3 34 E3
Berry's Green Rd. TN16 66 B2
Berry's Hill. TN14 & TN16 66 B4
Berryfield Cl. BR1 36 E7
Berryhill. SE9 6 B3
Berryhill Gdns. SE9 6 B3
Berrylands. Hartley DA3 43 A3
Berrylands. Orpington BR6 52 C7
Bert Reilly House. 1 SE18 2 D1
Bertha Hollamby Ct. DA14 24 C3
Bertrand Way. SE28 3 C6
Bertrey Cotts. TN16 66 B3
Berwick Cres. DA15 6 E1
Berwick Rd. Bexley DA16 7 B6
Berwick Rd. Newham E16 1 C7
Berwick Way. TN14 84 B7
Berwyn Gr. ME15 107 A6
Beryl Ave. E6 1 E8
Beryl House. SE18 2 F1
Besant Ct. 15 SE28 3 B6
Bessels Green Rd. TN13 83 D3
Bessels Meadow. TN13 83 D3
Bessels Way. TN13 83 D4
Bessie Lansbury Cl. E6 2 A7
Best St. ME4 47 F4
Beta Rd. ME3 35 D7
Betenson Ave. TN13 83 F5
Bethany Sch. TN17 154 B5
Bethel Rd. Bexley DA16 7 C4
Bethel Rd. Sevenoaks TN13 84 C4
Betherinden Cotts. TN18 186 A4
Bethersden Ct. ME15 107 F7
Bethersden Rd. TN27 & TN26 159 C5
Betjeman Cl. ME20 74 F3
Betony Gdns. ME14 92 F5

Betsham Rd. Betsham DA13 .... 28 D3
Betsham Rd. Erith DA8 .... 8 F7
Betsham Rd. Maidstone ME15 .... 107 F6
Betsham Rd. Swanscombe DA10 .. 28 E8
Betterton Dr. DA14 .... 24 E6
Bettescombe Rd. ME8 .... 63 E7
Betts Rd. E16 .... 1 B6
Beulah Rd. TN1 .... 149 C4
Beult Meadow. TN27 .... 143 A1
Beult Rd. DA1 .... 9 A3
Bevan Pl. BR8 .... 39 F5
Bevan Rd. SE2 .... 3 B1
Bevans Cl. DA9 .... 11 C1
Bevercote Wlk. **1** DA17 .... 7 F8
Beveridge Ct. **1** SE28 .... 3 B6
Beverley Ave. DA15 .... 23 F8
Beverley Cl. ME8 .... 63 F8
Beverley Cres. TN9 .... 132 F7
Beverley Rd. Bexley DA7 .... 8 C5
Beverley Rd. Keston Mark BR2 .... 50 E8
Beverley Rd. Maidstone ME16 .... 90 F2
Bevile House. RM17 .... 12 B7
Bevis Dr. DA2 .... 27 C8
Bewl Bridge Cl. TN5 .... 177 B3
Bewl Water. TN5 .... 176 C6
Bewlbridge La.
    Bewlbridge TN3 & TN5 .... 166 B3
Bewlbridge La.
    Lower Cousley Wood TN5 ...... 175 F8
Bewley La. TN15 .... 86 D2
Bexley Cl. DA1 .... 8 E2
Bexley Coll. Erith DA17 .... 4 B1
Bexley Coll. Erith DA17 .... 4 C2
Bexley Coll (St Joseph's Campus).
    SE2 .... 7 D8
Bexley Gram Sch. DA16 .... 7 B3
Bexley High St. DA5 .... 25 B7
Bexley Hospl. DA5 .... 25 E6
Bexley La. Crayford DA1 .... 8 E2
Bexley La. Sidcup DA14 .... 24 C5
Bexley Rd. Eltham SE9 .... 6 C2
Bexley Rd. Erith DA8 .... 4 F1
Bexley Rd.
    Erith,Northumberland Heath DA8 .. 8 C8
Bexley Sta. DA5 .... 25 A7
Bexley-Erith
    Tech High Sch for Boys. DA5 .. 8 B1
Bexleyheath Golf Course. DA6 .... 7 E2
Bexleyheath St. DA7 .... 7 F4
Bexleyheath Sta. DA7 .... 7 E5
Bexon La. ME9 .... 80 F5
Bickley Cres. ME1 .... 61 C8
Bickley Park Rd. BR1 & BR7 ...... 36 F6
Bickley Park Sch. BR1 .... 36 E6
Bickley Rd. Bromley BR1 .... 36 F6
Bickley Rd. **4** Tonbridge TN9 .. 133 B8
Bickley Sta. BR1 .... 36 E6
Bickmore Way. TN9 .... 117 D3
Bicknor Court Cotts. ME9 .... 80 C2
Bicknor La. ME9 .... 80 D3
Bicknor Rd. Orpington BR6 .... 37 F2
Bicknor Rd. Park Wood ME15 ..... 107 F4
Bidborough CE Prim Sch.
    TN4 .... 132 D3
Bidborough Ridge. TN4 .... 132 E4
Biddenden Cl. ME15 .... 92 F3
Biddenden La. TN27 .... 141 E5
Biddenden Rd.
    Durrant Green TN26 .... 173 A6
Biddenden Rd. Headcorn TN27 ... 141 E2
Biddenden Rd.
    London Beach TN26 & TN27 ... 172 E6
Biddenden Rd. Tylden TN27 ..... 158 F8
Biddenden Way. Eltham SE9 ..... 23 A4
Biddenden Way.
    Istead Rise DA13 .... 29 E1
Biddulph House. **23** SE18 ..... 1 F2
Bideford Rd. DA10 .... 7 B7
Biggin La. RM17 .... 13 B8
Bignell Rd. **28** SE18 .... 2 B1
Bilberry Cl. ME14 .... 92 E5
Bill Hamling Cl. SE9 .... 22 F6
Bill Street Rd. ME2 .... 33 C1
Billet Hill. TN15 .... 56 C6
Billings. DA3 .... 42 F3
Bilsby Gr. SE9 .... 22 D4
Bilsington Cl. ME5 .... 62 B5
Bilton Rd. DA8 .... 9 A8
Binbury La. ME14 .... 79 A5
Bines The. TN12 .... 136 A5
Bingham Point. **11** SE18 ...... 2 B2
Bingham Rd. ME2 .... 33 C1
Bingley Cl. ME6 .... 74 F8
Bingley Rd. Chatham ME1 .... 47 E4
Bingley Rd. Newham E16 .... 1 C7
Binland Gr. ME5 .... 61 D5
Binnacle Rd. ME1 .... 61 C8
Binney Rd. ME3 .... 19 D8
Binsey Wlk. **1** SE2 .... 3 C4
Birbeck Prim Sch. DA14 .... 24 B5
Birbetts Rd. SE9 .... 22 F6
Birch Cl. Eynsford DA4 .... 54 D7
Birch Cl. Hildenborough TN11 ... 116 D4
Birch Cl. Matfield TN12 .... 135 D1
Birch Cl. New Barn DA3 .... 43 C7
Birch Cl.
    Royal Tunbridge Wells TN1 ... 149 D7
Birch Cl. Sevenoaks TN13 .... 84 B4
Birch Cres. ME20 .... 90 D8
Birch Dr. ME5 .... 62 D1
Birch Gr. Bexley DA16 .... 7 A3
Birch Gr. Gillingham ME7 .... 63 A5
Birch Kiln Cotts. TN5 .... 175 A6
Birch Mead. BR2 & BR6 .... 51 A8
Birch Pl. DA9 .... 10 E1
Birch Rd. Hoo St Werburgh ME3 .. 34 E3
Birch Rd. Paddock Wood TN12 ... 136 A6
Birch Row. BR2 .... 37 A3

Birch Tree House. **16** SE7 .... 5 C8
Birch Tree Way. ME15 .... 92 B3
Birch Way. TN1 & TN2 .... 149 D7
Birchden Cotts. TN3 .... 161 C6
Birchdene Dr. SE28 .... 3 A5
Birches The. Greenwich SE7 ...... 5 B8
Birches The. Orpington BR6 ..... 51 A6
Birches The. Swanley BR8 .... 39 E7
Birches The. Tonbridge TN9 .... 133 B7
Birchfield Cl. ME15 .... 107 B6
Birchfields. ME5 .... 62 A3
Birchin Cross Rd. TN15 & TN14 .. 70 A5
Birchington Cl. Bexley DA7 ...... 8 B6
Birchington Cl. Maidstone ME14 . 92 C5
Birchington Cl. Orpington BR5 ... 38 C1
Bircholt Rd. ME15 .... 107 F4
Birchway. TN15 .... 55 F2
Birchwood Ave. Bidborough TN4 . 132 E3
Birchwood Ave. Sidcup DA14 .... 24 C5
Birchwood Cty Prim Sch. BR8 .... 39 D8
Birchwood Dr. DA2 .... 25 E4
Birchwood La. TN14 .... 67 F4
Birchwood Par. DA2 .... 25 E4
Birchwood Park Ave. BR8 .... 39 F6
Birchwood Rd.
    Joyden's Wood DA2 .... 25 D3
Birchwood Rd. Maidstone ME16 ... 91 C5
Birchwood Rd. Orpington BR5 .... 37 E5
Birchwood Terr. BR8 .... 39 C8
Bird House La. BR6 .... 66 A5
Bird in Hand St. TN3 .... 161 B8
Bird-in-Hand La. BR1 .... 36 D7
Birdbrook Rd. SE3 & SE9 .... 5 C4
Birdham Cl. BR1 .... 36 E4
Birkbeck Rd. DA14 .... 24 A5
Birkdale. TN4 .... 149 B6
Birkdale Cl. BR6 .... 37 D2
Birkdale Ct. **3** ME16 .... 91 E4
Birkdale Rd. SE2 .... 3 A2
Birken Rd. TN1 & TN2 .... 149 D6
Birkhall Cl. ME5 .... 62 A5
Birling Ave. Gillingham ME8 .... 49 E1
Birling Ave. Maidstone ME14 ... 93 A4
Birling Cl. ME14 .... 93 A4
Birling Dr. TN2 .... 149 A1
Birling Hill. DA13 & ME6 .... 59 B1
Birling Park Ave. TN2 .... 163 B8
Birling Pk. ME19 .... 74 C5
Birling Rd. Erith DA8 .... 8 E6
Birling Rd. Leybourne ME19 ..... 74 C3
Birling Rd.
    Royal Tunbridge Wells TN2 ... 163 B8
Birling Rd. Ryarsh ME19 .... 74 A5
Birling Rd. Snodland ME6 .... 74 F7
Birling Rd. Snodland ME6 .... 74 F8
Birnam Sq. **1** ME16 .... 91 E4
Birtrick Dr. DA13 .... 43 F4
Bishop Butt Cl. BR6 .... 51 F7
Bishop John Robinson CE Prim Sch.
    SE28 .... 3 C6
Bishop's Down. TN4 .... 148 E3
Bishop's Down Cty Prim Sch.
    TN4 .... 148 E5
Bishop's Down Park Rd. TN4 .... 148 F4
Bishop's Down Rd. TN4 .... 148 F3
Bishop's La. TN5 .... 121 D6
Bishopbourne Gn. ME8 .... 49 B4
Bishops Ave. BR1 .... 36 C6
Bishops Cl. Eltham SE9 .... 23 C6
Bishops Cl. Nettlestead ME18 .. 104 D1
Bishops Ct.
    Royal Tunbridge Wells TN4 ... 148 F3
Bishops Ct. Stone DA9 .... 10 F2
Bishops Gn. BR1 .... 36 C8
Bishops Mews. TN9 .... 133 C8
Bishops Oak Ride. TN10 .... 117 C6
Bishops Way. ME15 .... 91 F4
Bishops Wlk. Chislehurst BR7 ... 37 C8
Bishops Wlk. Rochester ME1 .... 47 C5
Bishopsbourne House. BR1 ...... 22 B1
Black Eagle Cl. TN16 .... 96 C8
Black Horse Ct. TN27 .... 141 E5
Black Horse Mews. TN15 .... 87 A1
Black Horse Rd. DA14 .... 24 A4
Black Mill La. TN27 .... 141 B6
Black Post. ME17 .... 95 E4
Black Rock Gdns. ME7 .... 63 B4
Blackbrook La. BR1 & BR2 .... 37 A5
Blackdale Farm Cotts. DA1 ...... 27 B6
Blackfen Par. DA16 .... 7 A1
Blackfen Rd. DA15 .... 7 B1
Blackhall La. TN15 .... 84 E4
Blackheath Bluecoat CE Sec Sch.
    SE3 .... 5 B7
Blackheath High Sch.
    GPDST (Jun Dept). SE3 .... 5 A5
Blackheath Pk. SE3 .... 5 A5
Blackhurst La. TN2 .... 149 F6
Blacklands. East Malling ME19 .. 89 F8
Blacklands. Mill Street ME19 ... 89 F7
Blacklands Cty Jun Sch. ME19 ... 89 F7
Blacklands Dr. ME19 .... 89 F8
Blackman Cl. ME3 .... 34 D7
Blackman's La. TN11 .... 118 D6
Blackmans Cl. DA1 .... 26 C7
Blackmanstone Way. ME16 .... 91 B7
Blackmead. TN13 .... 83 E6
Blackness. TN13 .... 52 D2
Blacksmith Dr. ME14 .... 92 C5
Blacksmith's La. TN5 .... 175 D4
Blacksmiths Field. TN32 .... 185 C1
Blacksmiths La. BR5 .... 38 C4

Blacksole La. TN15 .... 71 F3
Blacksole Rd. TN15 .... 71 F3
Blackthorn Ave. Chatham ME5 ... 62 A3
Blackthorn Ave.Royal Tunbridge Wells .
    TN2 & TN4 .... 133 C1
Blackthorn Cl. TN15 .... 55 F2
Blackthorn Dr. ME20 .... 75 B2
Blackthorn Gr. DA7 .... 7 E4
Blackthorne Rd. ME8 .... 64 B8
Blackwater Cl. RM13 .... 4 E8
Bladindon Dr. DA5 .... 24 D8
Blair Cl. DA15 .... 6 E2
Blair Dr. TN13 .... 84 B4
Blake Cl. DA16 .... 6 E6
Blake Dr. **3** DA5 .... 74 F4
Blake Gdns. DA1 .... 9 F3
Blake Way.
    Royal Tunbridge Wells TN1 ... 149 D7
Blake Way. Tilbury RM18 .... 13 C5
Blakemore Way. DA17 .... 3 E3
Blakeney Cl. ME14 .... 93 B4
Blaker Ave. ME1 .... 47 E1
Blaker Ct. SE7 .... 5 C7
Blanchard Cl. SE9 .... 22 E5
Bland St. SE9 .... 5 D3
Blanmerle Rd. SE9 .... 23 B7
Blann Cl. SE9 .... 5 D1
Blatchford Cl. SE9 .... 74 D1
Blatchington Rd. TN1 .... 149 B1
Bleak Hill La. SE18 .... 6 F8
Bleakwood Rd. ME5 .... 61 F4
Blean Rd. ME8 .... 49 C2
Blean Sq. ME14 .... 92 C6
Bleddyn Cl. DA15 .... 7 C1
Bledlow Cl. SE28 .... 3 C5
Blendon Dr. DA5 .... 7 D1
Blendon Rd. Maidstone ME14 .... 92 C5
Blendon Rd. Sidcup DA5 .... 7 D1
Blendon Terr. SE18 .... 6 C8
Blenheim Ave. ME1 & ME4 .... 47 E2
Blenheim Cl. Dartford DA1 ...... 9 C1
Blenheim Cl. Maidstone ME15 ... 92 F3
Blenheim Cl. Meopham DA13 .... 58 B8
Blenheim Ct. DA15 .... 23 D5
Blenheim Dr. DA16 .... 6 F6
Blenheim Gr. DA12 .... 30 C8
Blenheim Inf Sch. BR6 .... 52 C8
Blenheim Jun Sch. BR6 .... 52 C8
Blenheim Rd. Bromley BR1 & BR2 36 E5
Blenheim Rd. Dartford DA1 ...... 9 C1
Blenheim Rd.
    Orpington BR5 & BR6 .... 52 C8
Blenheim Rd. Sidcup DA15 ...... 24 C7
Blenheim Way. TN5 .... 177 C3
Bletchington Ct. **3** DA17 .... 4 A2
Blewbury House. **3** SE2 .... 3 C4
Bligh Cty Prim Inf Sch The.
    ME2 .... 46 C7
Bligh Rd. DA11 .... 13 A1
Bligh Way. ME2 .... 46 D6
Bligh's Rd. TN13 .... 84 B2
Blind La. Bredhurst ME7 .... 63 A1
Blind La. Lidsing ME7 .... 62 F1
Blind Mary's La. ME9 .... 80 E4
Bliss Way. TN10 .... 117 C5
Blithdale Rd. SE2 .... 3 A2
Blockhouse Rd. **5** RM17 ..... 12 C8
Blockmakers Ct. ME4 .... 48 A3
Bloomfield Rd. Bromley BR2 .... 36 D4
Bloomfield Rd. Woolwich SE18 ... 2 B1
Bloomfield Terr. TN16 .... 81 E2
Bloors Cl. ME9 .... 49 D1
Bloors La. Gillingham ME8 ...... 49 E1
Bloors Wharf Rd. ME7 .... 49 F4
Blowers Grove Wood. ME7 .... 63 B3
Blowers Hill. Cowden TN8 ...... 145 D8
Blowers Hill. Speldhurst TN3 .. 148 B8
Bloxam Gdns. SE9 .... 5 E2
Blue Anchor La. RM18 .... 13 B7
Blue Boar La. ME1 .... 47 D5
Blue Chalet Ind Pk. TN15 .... 55 D4
Bluebell Cl. Gillingham ME7 .... 48 F6
Bluebell Cl. Orpington BR6 ..... 51 D8
Blueberry La. TN14 .... 67 C4
Bluecoat La. TN17 .... 167 C6
Bluett St. ME14 .... 92 A5
Blunden La. ME18 .... 105 A1
Blunts Rd. SE9 .... 6 A2
Blyth Rd. SE28 .... 3 C6
Blythe Hill. BR5 .... 38 A8
Blythe Rd. ME15 .... 92 A3
Boakes Meadow. TN14 .... 68 F8
Boarders La. TN5 .... 176 C3
Boarley Ct. ME14 .... 76 F1
Boarley La. ME14 .... 76 F2
Boathouse Rd. ME12 .... 21 F3
Bobbing Hill. ME9 .... 65 F5
Bocking Cl. TN5 .... 174 E4
Bockingford La. ME15 .... 106 F8
Bodiam Cl. ME8 .... 49 C3
Bodiam Rd. TN18 & TN32 .... 185 F3
Bodle Ave. DA10 .... 11 E1
Bodsham Cres. ME15 .... 93 B3
Boevey Path. **2** SE2 .... 7 F8
Bognor Rd. DA16 .... 7 D6
Boley Hill. ME1 .... 47 C6
Boleyn Rd. TN14 .... 69 E2
Boleyn Way. DA10 .... 28 E8
Bolner Cl. ME5 .... 61 F2
Bombay House. **1** ME15 ..... 107 E5
Bombers La. TN16 .... 81 D7
Bonar Pl. BR7 .... 22 F1
Bonaventure Ct. DA12 .... 30 F4
Bonchester Cl. BR7 .... 37 A8
Bond Cl. TN14 .... 67 D4
Bond Rd. ME3 .... 63 E5
Bond St. RM17 .... 12 C8

Bondfield Rd. East Malling ME19 89 F8
Bondfield Rd. **4** Newham E6 .. 1 E8
Boneashe La. TN15 .... 87 D6
Boneta Rd. DA17 .... 3 F3
Bonflower La. ME17 .... 122 C7
Bonney Way. BR8 .... 39 E6
Bonnington Gn. ME8 .... 49 C3
Bonnington Rd. ME14 .... 92 C6
Bonnington Tower. BR2 .... 36 E3
Booth Cl. SE28 .... 3 B6
Booth Rd. ME4 .... 47 F2
Bootham Cl. ME2 .... 46 D5
Borden CE Cty Prim Sch. ME9 ... 65 F3
Bordyke. TN9 .... 117 C2
Boreham Rd. E16 .... 1 A7
Boresisle. TN30 .... 173 B2
Borgard House. SE18 .... 5 E7
Borgard Rd. SE18 .... 1 F2
Borough Green Prim Sch. TN15 .. 87 A7
Borough Green &
    Borough Green Sta.
        Borough Green TN15 ...... 86 E7
Borough Green &
    Borough Green Sta.
        Ightham TN15 .... 86 D6
Borough Green Rd.
    Wrotham TN15 .... 72 A1
Borough Green Rd.
    Wrotham TN15 .... 72 A2
Borough Green & Wrotham Sta.
    TN15 .... 86 F7
Borough Rd. ME7 .... 48 D4
Borstal HM Prison &
    Youth Custody Ctr. ME1 ..... 47 B1
Borstal Manor Cty Jun Sch.
    ME1 .... 46 F2
Borstal Rd. ME1 .... 47 B3
Borstal St. ME1 .... 47 A2
Bosley Cl. TN13 .... 84 A4
Bostall Hill. SE2 .... 3 B1
Bostall La. SE2 .... 3 B1
Bostall Manorway. SE2 .... 3 B2
Bostall Park Ave. DA7 .... 7 E7
Bostall Rd. BR5 .... 24 B1
Boston Gdns. ME8 .... 49 C1
Boston Rd. ME5 .... 62 C2
Boston Sch. BR2 .... 50 B8
Bosville Ave. TN13 .... 84 A4
Bosville Dr. TN13 .... 84 A4
Bosville Rd. TN13 .... 84 A4
Boswell Cl. BR5 .... 38 C3
Boswell House. BR2 .... 36 D4
Bosworth House. DA8 .... 4 E1
Botany. TN9 .... 117 C1
Botany Bay La. BR7 .... 37 C7
Botha Rd. E13 .... 1 C8
Bothwell Cl. **7** E16 .... 1 A8
Botsom La. TN15 .... 55 D4
Bott Rd. DA2 .... 26 F4
Bottle House Cotts. TN11 ...... 130 F1
Bottlescrew Hill. ME17 .... 107 A8
Boucher Dr. DA11 .... 29 F4
Boughton Cl. ME8 .... 49 B3
Boughton La. ME15 .... 107 B6
Boughton Monchelsea
    Cty Prim Sch. ME17 .... 107 B2
Boughton Par. ME15 .... 107 A7
Boughton Place Cotts. ME17 ... 127 A8
Boughton Rd.
    Boughton Malherbe ME17 .... 111 B2
Boughton Rd. Woolwich SE28 .... 2 E3
Boultwood Rd. E6 .... 1 F7
Boundary House. **3** DA11 ..... 29 F7
Boundary Rd.
    Chatham ME1 & ME4 .... 47 E3
Boundary Rd.
    Royal Tunbridge Wells TN2 ... 149 D1
Boundary Rd. Sidcup DA15 .... 6 E2
Boundary St. **2** DA8 .... 8 F7
Boundary The. TN3 & TN4 ...... 148 B3
Bounds Cross. TN27 .... 157 F7
Bounds Oak Way. TN4 .... 132 E3
Bounds The. ME20 .... 75 E1
Bourdillon Ct. SE9 .... 22 E6
Bournbrook Rd. SE3 & SE9 .... 5 E4
Bourne Cl. TN9 .... 117 D3
Bourne Ent Ctr. TN15 .... 87 A7
Bourne Grange La. TN11 .... 118 D8
Bourne Ind Pk. DA1 .... 8 E2
Bourne La. Silver Hill TN32 ... 184 F1
Bourne La. Tonbridge TN9 ...... 117 D3
Bourne La. Yopps Green TN15 .... 86 F1
Bourne Mead. DA5 .... 8 D2
Bourne Par. DA5 .... 25 B8
Bourne Pk. TN11 .... 118 F5
Bourne Place Sch. TN11 .... 116 A7
Bourne Rd. Bexley DA1 & DA5 ... 8 D2
Bourne Rd. Bromley BR2 .... 36 D5
Bourne Rd. Gravesend DA12 ..... 30 F6
Bourne Rd. Sidcup DA5 .... 25 B8
Bourne Row. TN8 .... 130 D6
Bourne Vale. Hayes BR2 .... 36 A2
Bourne Vale.
    Plaxtol Spoute TN15 .... 102 A8
Bourne Way. Hayes BR2 .... 50 A8
Bourne Way. Swanley BR8 .... 39 C6
Bourner Cotts. TN17 .... 156 D4
Bourneside Terr. ME17 .... 94 D2
Bournewood Cl. ME15 .... 92 F1
Bournewood Rd.
    Bexley SE18 & SE2 .... 7 A7
Bournewood Rd. Orpington BR5 .. 38 C2
Bournville Ave. ME4 .... 47 F1
Bow Arrow La. DA2 .... 10 B1
Bow Hill. ME18 .... 104 D5
Bow Rd. ME18 .... 104 E7
Bow Terr. ME18 .... 104 E7
Bowater Pl. SE3 .... 5 B7

Bet – Bra 195

Bowater Rd. SE18 .... 1 D3
Bowen Rd. TN4 .... 148 B4
Bower Cl. ME6 .... 91 E4
Bower Gr. ME5 .... 62 C1
Bower Grove Sch. ME16 .... 91 B2
Bower La. Eynsford DA4 .... 54 F6
Bower La. Maidstone ME16 ...... 91 E3
Bower La. Maidstone ME16 ...... 91 E3
Bower Mount Rd. ME16 .... 91 D4
Bower Pl. ME16 .... 91 E4
Bower Rd. BR8 .... 26 A2
Bower St. ME16 .... 91 E4
Bower Terr. ME16 .... 91 E3
Bower Wlk. TN12 .... 139 E3
Bowers Ave. DA11 .... 29 F4
Bowers House. ME7 .... 48 C7
Bowers Rd. TN14 .... 68 F8
Bowers Wlk. **1** E6 .... 1 F7
Bowes Cl. DA15 .... 7 B1
Bowes Rd. ME2 .... 47 B8
Bowes Wood. DA3 .... 56 F7
Bowesden La.
    Shorne Ridgeway DA12 .... 31 F1
Bowesden La.
    Shorne Ridgeway ME2 .... 46 A8
Bowford Ave. DA7 .... 7 E6
Bowley La. ME17 .... 127 D8
Bowling Green Row. **1** SE18 .. 1 F2
Bowls Pl. TN12 .... 136 A7
Bowman Ave. E16 .... 1 A6
Bowman Cl. ME5 .... 62 C5
Bowman Cotts. TN27 .... 172 A7
Bowmans Rd. DA1 .... 25 F8
Bowmead. SE9 .... 22 F6
Bown Cl. RM18 .... 13 B5
Bowness Rd. DA7 .... 8 B5
Bowyer Cl. E6 .... 1 F8
Bowzell Rd. TN14 .... 99 A2
Box Tree Wlk. **20** BR5 .... 38 D1
Boxgrove Prim Sch. SE2 .... 3 C3
Boxgrove Rd. SE2 .... 3 C3
Boxley Cl. ME14 .... 92 B8
Boxley Cotts. DA4 .... 41 C5
Boxley Rd. Chatham ME5 .... 62 A2
Boxley Rd. Maidstone ME14 .... 92 B7
Boxley St. E16 .... 1 B5
Boxmend Ind Est. ME15 .... 107 F3
Boxshall House. **7** SE18 ...... 6 B8
Boy Court La. TN27 .... 125 F1
Boyard Rd. SE18 .... 2 B1
Boyces Hill. ME9 .... 65 D6
Boyle House. **12** DA17 .... 4 A3
Boynton Court Rd. ME17 .... 125 A6
Brabourne Ave. ME8 .... 49 C3
Brabourne Cres. DA7 .... 7 F8
Bracken Cl. Newham E6 .... 1 F7
Bracken Cl.
    Royal Tunbridge Wells TN2 ... 149 E5
Bracken Hill. ME5 .... 62 A1
Bracken Lea. ME5 .... 48 C1
Bracken Rd. TN2 .... 149 E5
Bracken Wlk. TN10 .... 117 B6
Brackendene. DA2 & DA5 .... 25 E4
Brackens The. BR6 .... 52 A5
Brackley Cl. ME14 .... 92 C5
Brackwood Cl. ME8 .... 63 D5
Bracondale Ave. DA13 .... 43 F8
Bracondale Rd. SE2 .... 3 A2
Bradbourne Ct. TN13 .... 84 B6
Bradbourne La. ME19 .... 75 B1
Bradbourne Park Rd. TN13 ...... 84 A4
Bradbourne Rd. Grays RM17 .... 12 B8
Bradbourne Rd.
    Sevenoaks TN13 & TN14 ..... 84 B5
Bradbourne Rd. Sidcup DA5 ..... 25 A8
Bradbourne Sch The. TN14 ...... 84 A6
Bradbourne Vale Rd.
    TN13 & TN14 .... 84 A5
Bradbury Ct. **3** Greenwich SE3 . 5 A7
Bradbury Ct. **2** Northfleet DA11 29 F7
Braddick Cl. ME15 .... 107 B6
Bradenham Ave. DA16 .... 7 A3
Bradfield Rd. E16 .... 1 B4
Bradfields Ave. ME5 .... 61 F5
Bradfields Ave W. ME5 .... 61 F5
Bradfields Sch. ME5 .... 62 A6
Bradford Cl. BR2 .... 36 F1
Bradford St. TN9 .... 117 B1
Bradley House. ME3 .... 19 C4
Bradley Rd. Upper Halling ME2 . 59 E5
Bradley Rd. White Post TN3 ... 146 D5
Bradley Stone Rd. E6 .... 1 F8
Bradymead. E6 .... 2 B7
Braemar Ave. DA7 .... 8 C3
Braemar Gdns. DA15 .... 23 D5
Braes The. ME3 .... 32 C3
Braeside. TN13 .... 83 F3
Braeside Ave. DA7 .... 8 C3
Braeside Cres. DA7 .... 8 C3
Braeside Cl. DA17 .... 8 C3
Brake Ave. ME5 .... 61 E5
Brakefield Rd. DA13 .... 29 B1
Bramble Ave. DA2 .... 28 C5
Bramble Bank. DA13 .... 72 F7
Bramble Cl. Hilden Park TN11 . 116 F4
Bramble Cl. Maidstone ME16 .... 91 B3
Bramble Croft. DA8 .... 4 C2
Bramble La. TN13 .... 99 B7
Bramble Reed La. TN12 .... 151 B7
Bramble Wlk. TN1 .... 149 D7
Brambleberry Rd. SE18 .... 6 C8
Brambledown. Chatham ME5 ...... 62 B8
Brambledown. Hartley DA3 ...... 42 F5
Bramblefield Cl. DA3 .... 42 E6

Brambletree Cotts. ME1 46 E2
Brambletree Cres. ME1 46 F2
Bramdean Cres. SE12 22 A7
Bramdean Gdns. SE12 22 A7
Bramhope La. SE7 5 B8
Bramley Cl. Gillingham ME8 64 B8
Bramley Cl. Istead Rise DA13 29 F1
Bramley Cl. Orpington BR6 37 B1
Bramley Cl. Swanley BR8 39 E5
Bramley Cres. ME15 92 F3
Bramley Ct. Bexley DA16 7 B6
Bramley Ct. Marden TN12 138 B6
Bramley Dr. TN17 169 D4
Bramley Gdns. Coxheath ME17 106 C3
Bramley Gdns.
Paddock Wood TN12 135 E7
Bramley Pl. DA1 9 A3
Bramley Rd. East Peckham TN12 119 F6
Bramley Rd. Snodland ME6 75 A8
Bramley Rise. ME2 46 E8
Bramleys. TN27 141 D5
Brampton Prim Sch. DA16 7 D5
Brampton Rd. DA7 7 E6
Bramshot Ave. SE3 & SE7 5 B8
Bramshott Cl. ME16 91 C6
Branbridges Rd. TN12 120 B4
Brandon Rd. DA1 27 A8
Brandon St. DA11 30 B8
Brandreth Rd. E6 1 F7
Brands Hatch Circuit. DA3 55 F6
Brands Hatch Cotts. TN15 56 A6
Brands Hatch Rd. TN15 56 A7
Branham House. 1 SE18 2 B1
Branns Dr. TN17 181 E3
Bransell Cl. BR8 39 C3
Bransgore Cl. ME8 63 D7
Branston Cres. BR5 37 D1
Branstone Ct. RM16 10 B8
Brantingham Cl. TN9 132 F7
Branton Rd. DA9 10 F1
Brantwood Ave. DA8 8 C7
Brantwood Rd. DA7 8 B4
Brantwood Way. BR5 38 C6
Brasenose Rd. ME7 48 E4
Brassey Dr. ME20 90 D8
Brasted Cl. Bexley DA6 7 D2
Brasted Cl. Orpington BR6 52 A8
Brasted Ct. Brasted TN14 82 D2
Brasted Ct. Rochester ME2 33 A1
Brasted Hill. TN14 82 A7
Brasted Hill Rd. TN14 & TN16 82 C5
Brasted La. TN14 67 A1
Brasted Rd. Erith DA8 8 E7
Brasted Rd. Westerham TN16 81 E1
Brattle Farm Mus. TN12 139 D1
Brattle Wood. TN13 99 C6
Braundton Ave. DA15 23 F7
Bray Dr. E16 1 A6
Bray Gdns. ME15 106 F5
Braywood Rd. SE9 6 D3
Breach La. ME9 64 F8
Breach Rd. RM16 10 F8
Breakneck Hill. DA9 11 B2
Breakspears Dr. BR5 38 A8
Breaside Prep Sch. BR1 36 D8
Breckonmead. BR1 36 C7
Brecon Ct. 7 SE9 6 A1
Bredgar Cl. ME14 92 C5
Bredgar House. 1 BR5 38 D1
Bredgar Rd. ME8 49 B4
Bredhurst CE Prim Sch. ME7 63 B1
Bredhurst Rd. Gillingham ME8 63 B4
Bredhurst Rd. Gillingham ME8 63 C5
Breedon Ave. TN4 132 F1
Bremner Cl. BR8 40 A5
Brenchley Ave. DA11 30 B3
Brenchley Cl. Chatham ME1 47 D2
Brenchley Cl. Chislehurst BR7 37 A8
Brenchley Cl. Hayes BR2 36 A4
Brenchley & Matfield
CE (VA) Prim Sch. TN12 152 A8
Brenchley Rd. Gillingham ME8 49 B2
Brenchley Rd.
Horsmonden. TN12 152 F6
Brenchley Rd. Maidstone ME15 91 F2
Brenchley Rd. Matfield TN12 151 F8
Brenchley Rd. St Paul's Cray BR5 37 F7
Brenda Terr. DA10 28 E8
Brendon Ave. ME5 62 A3
Brendon Cl. Erith DA8 8 E6
Brendon Cl.
Royal Tunbridge Wells TN2 149 D5
Brendon Rd. BR7 23 D6
Brenley Gdns. SE9 5 D3
Brennan Rd. RM18 13 B5
Brent Cl. Chatham ME5 61 E5
Brent Cl. Dartford DA2 10 B1
Brent Cl. Sidcup DA5 24 E7
Brent Cty Prim Inf Sch The.
DA2 27 C8
Brent Cty Prim Jun Sch The.
DA2 27 C8
Brent La. DA1 27 A7
Brent Rd. Newham E16 1 A8
Brent Rd. Woolwich SE18 6 B7
Brent The. Dartford DA1 & DA2 27 B8
Brent The. Tonbridge TN10 117 C6
Brent Way. DA2 10 B1
Brentfield Rd. DA1 27 B8
Brentlands Dr. DA1 27 A7
Brentor Ct. TN2 149 D6
Brentwood Cl. SE9 23 C7
Brentwood House. SE18 5 D7
Brenzett Cl. ME5 62 B5
Brenzett House. 6 BR5 38 C4
Bretland Rd. TN4 148 D4
Breton Rd. ME1 47 C2
Brett Wlk. ME8 63 D4
Brewer Rd. ME3 33 B7
Brewer St. Lamberhurst TN3 166 A5
Brewer St. Maidstone ME14 92 A5
Brewers Field. DA2 26 C4
Brewers Rd. DA12 45 C8
Brewery La. TN13 84 C2
Brewery Rd. Keston Mark BR2 36 E1
Brewery Rd. Woolwich SE18 2 D1
Brewhouse Rd. 3 SE18 1 F2
Brewhouse Yd. 13 DA11 13 B1
Brian Cres. TN4 149 B8
Briar Cl. Larkfield ME20 75 A2
Briar Cl. 8 Marlpit Hill TN8 112 D3
Briar Dale. ME3 32 B4
Briar Fields. ME14 92 E5
Briar Rd. DA5 25 D5
Briar Wlk. TN10 117 C6
Briars The. TN15 55 D4
Briars Way. DA3 43 A4
Briarswood Way. BR6 51 F5
Briary Ct. DA14 24 B3
Briary Gdns. BR1 22 B3
Brice Rd. ME3 32 B3
Brick Ct. RM17 12 A8
Brick Field View. ME2 33 C1
Brick Kiln La. Broad Ford TN12 153 B2
Brick Kiln La. Ulcombe ME17 125 D5
Brickenden Rd. TN17 169 D4
Brickfield Cotts. SE18 6 F8
Brickfield Farm Gdns. BR6 51 C6
Brickfields. Pembury TN2 150 E8
Brickfields. West Malling ME19 74 B1
Brickwell Cotts. TN17 156 F6
Brickworks Cl. TN9 133 B7
Bridewell La. TN30 183 A7
Bridge Bsns Pk. TN12 135 C7
Bridge Cl. TN9 133 C8
Bridge Cotts. TN12 153 A6
Bridge Ct. 14 Dartford DA2 10 B1
Bridge Ct. 2 Grays RM17 12 B8
Bridge House. TN4 149 B5
Bridge Mill Way. ME15 91 D2
Bridge Rd. Bexley DA7 7 E5
Bridge Rd. Erith DA8 8 F6
Bridge Rd. Gillingham ME7 48 C7
Bridge Rd. Grays RM17 12 B8
Bridge Rd. Orpington BR5 38 B3
Bridge Rd. Rochester ME1 47 C2
Bridge St. ME15 106 F5
Bridgeland Rd. E16 1 A6
Bridgen Rd. DA5 24 E8
Bridges Dr. DA1 10 B2
Bridgewater Cl. BR5 & BR7 37 E6
Bridgewater Pl. ME19 & ME20 74 E2
Bridle Way. BR6 51 C6
Brier Cl. ME5 62 C8
Bright Cl. DA17 3 D2
Bright Ct. 8 SE28 3 C5
Bright Rd. ME4 48 B2
Bright Ridge. TN4 148 E8
Brightlands. DA11 29 E4
Brigstock Rd. DA17 4 B2
Brimpsfield Cl. SE2 3 B3
Brimstone Cl. BR6 52 C3
Brimstone Hill. DA13 58 D8
Brindle Gate. DA15 23 E7
Brindle Way. ME5 62 C1
Brindle's Field. TN9 133 A7
Brindley Cl. DA7 8 A4
Brindley Way. BR1 22 B3
Brinkburn Cl. SE2 3 A2
Brinkers La. TN5 175 A2
Brinklow Cres. SE18 6 B7
Brionne Gdns. TN9 133 D8
Brisbane House. RM18 12 F6
Brisbane Rd. ME4 48 A3
Briset Prim Sch. SE9 5 D3
Briset Rd. SE9 5 D3
Brishing Cl. ME15 107 E5
Brishing La. ME17 107 D4
Brishing Rd. ME15 & ME17 107 F3
Brisley's Row. ME1 60 F1
Brissenden Cl. ME2 34 A3
Bristol Cl. ME2 46 D5
Bristol Rd. DA12 30 D5
Bristow Rd. DA7 7 E6
Britannia Bsns Pk. ME20 90 E7
Britannia Cl. ME2 60 A4
Britannia Dr. DA12 30 F3
Britannia Gate. E16 1 A5
Brittain Ct. SE9 22 E7
Brittain House. SE9 22 E7
Brittains La. TN13 83 F2
Britten Cl. TN10 117 F6
Brittenden Cl. 1 BR6 51 F4
Brittenden Par. BR6 51 F4
Britton St. ME7 48 B5
Brixham Rd. DA16 7 D6
Brixham St. E16 2 A5
Broad Bridge Cl. SE3 5 A7
Broad Ditch Rd. DA13 29 D1
Broad Gr. TN2 149 A1
Broad La. Heath Side DA2 26 B4
Broad La. Stone Cross TN3 147 A4
Broad Lawn. SE9 23 A7
Broad Oak. Brenchley TN12 152 C8
Broad Oak. Groombridge TN3 161 C6
Broad Oak Cl. Brenchley TN12 152 C8
Broad Oak Cl.
Royal Tunbridge Wells TN2 148 F1
Broad Oak Cl. St Paul's Cray BR5 38 A7
Broad Rd. DA10 11 E1
Broad St. ME17 124 E7
Broad Street Hill. ME14 & ME17 94 D7
Broad View. TN17 170 A8
Broad Wlk.
Eltham SE18 & SE3 & SE9 5 E5
Broad Wlk.
Greenwich SE18 & SE3 & SE9 5 E5
Broad Wlk. Orpington BR6 52 D7
Broad Wlk. Sevenoaks TN15 99 F7
Broadcloth. TN17 169 D3
Broadcroft. TN2 162 F8
Broadcroft Rd. BR5 37 D2
Broader La. ME14 78 B2
Broadfield Rd. ME15 107 A8
Broadgate Rd. E16 1 D7
Broadheath Dr. BR7 22 F3
Broadhoath. TN15 85 E1
Broadlands Dr. ME5 62 B4
Broadlands Rd. BR1 22 B4
Broadmead. TN2 162 F8
Broadmead Ave. TN2 162 F8
Broadoak. ME19 74 E2
Broadoak Ave. ME15 107 A8
Broadoak Cl. DA2 & DA4 27 A2
Broadoak Rd. DA8 8 D7
Broadview. DA13 57 F6
Broadview Ave. ME8 63 E8
Broadwater Ct. TN2 162 E8
Broadwater Down. TN2 162 F8
Broadwater Down Cty Prim Sch.
TN2 162 F8
Broadwater Gdns. BR6 51 C6
Broadwater House. DA12 13 D1
Broadwater La.
Royal Tunbridge Wells TN2 & TN4 148 F1
Broadwater La.
Royal Tunbridge Wells TN2 162 F8
Broadwater Rd. Well Street ME19 89 D6
Broadwater Rd. Woolwich SE18 2 D3
Broadwater Rise. TN2 148 F1
Broadway. Bexley DA6 7 F3
Broadway. Bexley DA6 & DA7 8 A3
Broadway. Crockenhill BR8 39 C3
Broadway. Gillingham ME8 49 A3
Broadway. Grays RM17 12 C8
Broadway. Maidstone ME16 91 F4
Broadway. Tilbury RM18 12 F5
Broadway Sh Ctr. 5 DA6 8 A3
Broadway The. Hadlow TN11 118 E8
Broadway The.
Lamberhurst TN3 166 B5
Broadwood. DA11 30 B3
Broadwood Rd. ME3 34 A4
Brock Rd. E13 1 B8
Brockenhurst Ave. ME15 92 C1
Brockenhurst Cl. ME8 63 C7
Brocklebank House. 7 E16 2 A5
Brocklebank Rd. SE7 1 B2
Brockway. TN15 87 A7
Brockwell Cl. BR5 37 F4
Brodrick Gr. SE2 3 B2
Brogden Cres. ME17 108 F7
Broke Farm Dr. BR6 52 C2
Brokes Way. TN4 149 B8
Brome House. SE18 5 E6
Brome Rd. SE9 5 F4
Bromhedge. SE9 22 F5
Bromholm Rd. SE2 3 B3
Bromley. RM17 11 F8
Bromley Cl. Chatham ME5 62 B4
Bromley Cl. Newington ME9 65 A5
Bromley Col
of Further & Higher Ed. BR2 36 D3
Bromley Comm. BR2 36 D3
Bromley General Hospl. BR1 36 B5
Bromley High Sch for Girls.
BR1 37 A5
Bromley Ind Est. BR1 36 D6
Bromley La. BR7 23 D1
Bromley Manor Mansions. 3
BR1 36 A6
Bromley North Sta. BR1 36 A8
Bromley Public Golf Course.
BR2 36 E2
Bromley Rd. BR7 37 B8
Bromley South Sta. BR2 36 A6
Bromley Valley Gymnastics Ctr.
BR5 38 A7
Brompton Dr. DA8 9 B7
Brompton Farm Rd. ME2 33 A2
Brompton Hill. ME4 47 F6
Brompton La. ME2 47 A8
Brompton Rd. ME7 48 B6
Brompton-Westbrook
Cty Prim Sch. ME7 48 A5
Bronington Cl. ME5 62 A5
Bronte Cl. Erith DA8 8 B7
Bronte Cl. Lunsford ME20 74 F3
Bronte Cl. Tilbury RM18 13 C5
Bronte Gr. DA1 9 F3
Bronte Sch. DA12 30 C7
Bronte View. DA12 30 C7
Brook. ME4 48 A4
Brook Cotts. Collier Street TN12 137 F8
Brook Cotts. Dean Street ME15 106 C7
Brook Ct. 10 TN8 112 D3
Brook General Hospl. SE18 5 E6
Brook Hill Cl. SE18 2 B1
Brook La. Bexley DA5 7 D2
Brook La. Bromley BR1 22 A2
Brook La. Greenwich SE3 5 B5
Brook La. Plaxtol Spoute TN15 102 A8
Brook La. Snodland ME6 75 A6
Brook La. Tonbridge TN9 117 D2
Brook Rd. Lunsford ME20 74 F4
Brook Rd. Northfleet DA11 29 E7
Brook Rd.
Royal Tunbridge Wells TN1 149 D7
Brook Rd. Swanley BR8 39 D7
Brook St. Erith DA8 8 B7
Brook St. Snodland ME6 75 B8
Brook St. Tonbridge TN9 133 A8
Brook Vale. DA8 8 B6
Brookbank. ME14 92 A8
Brookdale Rd. DA5 7 E1
Brookdene Rd. SE18 & SE2 2 F2
Brooke Dr. DA12 31 B7
Brookend Rd. DA15 23 E7
Brookes Pl. ME9 65 B6
Brookfield. Four Elms TN8 113 B5
Brookfield. Kemsing TN14 69 E2
Brookfield. Sandhurst TN18 186 B5
Brookfield Ave. ME20 75 A4
Brookfields. TN11 102 E1
Brookhill Rd. SE18 2 B1
Brookhurst Gdns. TN4 132 E3
Brooklands. Dartford DA1 26 E7
Brooklands. Headcorn TN27 141 C6
Brooklands.
Royal Tunbridge Wells TN1 149 D7
Brooklands Ave. DA15 23 D6
Brooklands Farm Cl. TN3 147 A6
Brooklands Pk. SE3 5 A4
Brooklands Prim Sch. SE3 5 A4
Brooklands Rd. ME20 75 A4
Brooklyn Paddock. ME7 48 D6
Brooklyn Rd. BR2 36 D4
Brooklyn Villas. TN12 138 C5
Brookmead. TN11 116 E4
Brookmead Ave. BR1 & BR2 36 F4
Brookmead Cl. BR6 38 B3
Brookmead Rd. ME3 33 B7
Brookmead Way. BR5 & BR6 38 B3
Brooks Cl. Eltham SE9 23 A6
Brooks Cl. Staplehurst TN12 139 E4
Brooks Pl. ME14 92 A4
Brookside. Cranbrook TN17 169 D4
Brookside. Hoo St Werburgh ME3 34 E5
Brookside. Orpington BR6 37 F2
Brookside Rd. DA13 29 F1
Brookway. SE3 5 A4
Broom Ave. BR5 38 B7
Broom Cl. BR2 36 E3
Broom Hill Rd. ME2 46 F8
Broom La. TN3 147 E2
Broom Mead. DA6 8 A2
Broom Pk. TN3 147 E3
Broomcroft Rd. ME8 49 F2
Broomfield House. 4 BR5 38 B7
Broomfield Rd. Bexley DA6 8 A2
Broomfield Rd.
Broomfield ME17 109 D4
Broomfield Rd. Sevenoaks TN13 83 F5
Broomfield Rd.
Swanscombe DA10 11 E2
Broomfields. DA3 42 E4
Broomhill Bank Sch. TN3 148 C6
Broomhill Park Rd. TN4 148 F8
Broomhill Rd. Dartford DA1 9 B1
Broomhill Rd. Orpington BR6 38 A2
Broomhill Rd.
Royal Tunbridge Wells TN3 148 D7
Broomhill Rise. DA6 8 A2
Broomhills. DA13 28 E4
Broomleigh. BR1 36 A8
Broomscroft Cotts. ME18 89 C1
Broomshaw Rd. ME16 90 F3
Broomwood Rd. BR5 38 B7
Brougham Ct. 2 DA2 10 B1
Broughton Rd. Orpington BR6 51 D8
Broughton Rd. Otford TN14 69 A3
Brow Cl. BR5 38 D2
Brow Cres. BR5 38 D2
Brown Rd. DA12 30 E7
Brown St. ME8 49 F1
Browndens Rd. ME2 59 E4
Brownelow Copse. ME5 62 B1
Brownhill Cl. ME5 62 A4
Browning Cl. Bexley DA16 6 E6
Browning Cl. 6 Lunsford ME20 74 F4
Browning Rd. DA1 9 F3
Browning Wlk. RM18 13 C5
Brownings. TN8 112 C4
Brownspring Dr. SE9 23 B5
Broxbourne Rd. BR6 37 F2
Bruce Cl. DA16 7 B6
Bruce Ct. DA15 23 F4
Bruce Gr. BR6 38 A1
Bruces Wharf Rd. RM17 12 A8
Brucks The. ME18 104 E7
Brummel Cl. DA7 8 C4
Brunel Cl. RM18 13 B4
Brunel Way. ME4 48 A7
Brungers Wlk. TN10 117 B5
Brunswick Cl. DA6 7 D3
Brunswick House Cty Prim Sch.
ME16 91 E5
Brunswick Rd. DA6 7 E3
Brunswick St. ME15 92 A3
Brunswick St E. ME15 92 A3
Brunswick Terr. TN1 149 A2
Brunswick Wlk. 1 DA12 30 D8
Brushwood Lodge. 1 DA17 4 A2
Bruton Cl. BR7 22 F1
Bryanston Rd. RM18 13 C5
Bryant Cl. ME18 104 D6
Bryant Rd. ME2 47 A7
Bryant St. ME4 48 A3
Bryony Sch (private). ME8 63 F5
Bubblestone Rd. TN14 69 B3
Buckden Cl. SE12 5 A1
Buckham Thorns Rd. TN16 81 C1
Buckhole Farm Rd. ME23 17 C4
Buckhurst Ave. TN15 87 A7
Buckhurst La. Rockrobin TN5 174 A6
Buckhurst La.
Sevenoaks TN13 & TN15 84 C2
Buckhurst Rd. TN16 81 B7
Buckingham Ave. DA16 6 E3
Buckingham Cl. BR5 37 E2
Buckingham Dr. BR7 23 C3
Buckingham Rd. Gillingham ME7 48 D5
Buckingham Rd. Northfleet DA11 29 D8
Buckingham Rd.
Royal Tunbridge Wells TN1 149 B2
Buckingham Row. ME15 107 E7
Buckland Cl. ME5 62 A2
Buckland Hill. ME16 91 E5
Buckland La. ME16 91 D6
Buckland Pl. ME16 91 E4
Buckland Rd. Cliffe Woods ME3 33 A8
Buckland Rd.
Lower Luddesdown DA13 59 A7
Buckland Rd. Maidstone ME16 91 E4
Buckland Rd. Orpington BR6 51 E6
Buckler Gdns. SE9 22 F5
Bucklers Cl. TN2 149 C3
Buckles Ct. SE2 3 D2
Buckley Cl. DA1 8 F5
Buckmore Park (Scout Camp).
ME5 61 C3
Bucks Cross Rd. Chelsfield BR6 52 E5
Bucks Cross Rd. Northfleet DA11 29 F5
Buckthorn House. DA15 23 F5
Buckwheat Ct. SE2 3 D3
Budd's Farm Cotts. TN30 189 F2
Budd's La. TN30 189 F2
Budgin's Hill. BR6 & TN14 67 C8
Budleigh Cres. DA16 7 C6
Bugglesden Rd. TN27 172 D5
Bugsby's Way. SE10 & SE7 1 A2
Bull Alley. DA16 7 B4
Bull Fields. ME6 75 A8
Bull Hill. ME17 127 F8
Bull La. Chislehurst BR7 23 D1
Bull La. Eccles ME20 75 F5
Bull La. Lower Higham ME3 32 D7
Bull La. Stockbury ME9 64 E2
Bull La. Wrotham TN15 72 A3
Bull Lane Cotts. TN3 165 C4
Bull Orch. ME16 90 F1
Bull Rd. ME19 74 C5
Bull Yd. 5 DA11 13 B1
Bullbanks Rd. DA17 4 C2
Bulldog Rd. ME5 62 B2
Bullen La. TN12 119 E7
Buller Rd. ME4 47 F2
Bullers Cl. DA14 24 E3
Bullers Wood Dr. BR7 22 F1
Bullers Wood Sch for Girls.
BR7 36 F8
Bullfinch Cl.
Paddock Wood TN12 136 A5
Bullfinch Cl. Sevenoaks TN13 83 D5
Bullfinch Cnr. TN13 83 E5
Bullfinch Dene. TN13 83 D5
Bullfinch La. TN13 83 E5
Bullingstone Cotts. TN3 147 E7
Bullingstone La. TN3 147 F7
Bullion Cl. TN12 135 F6
Bullivant Cl. DA9 11 A2
Bulls Pl. TN2 150 D6
Bulrush Cl. ME5 61 F3
Bumbles Cl. ME1 61 D7
Bungalows The. TN30 183 D7
Bunker's Hill. Erith DA17 4 A2
Bunker's Hill. Ridley TN15 57 B4
Bunkers Hill. DA14 24 F5
Bunny La. TN3 162 E5
Bunters Hill Rd. ME3 33 B4
Bunton St. SE18 2 A3
Burberry La. ME17 109 B5
Burch Rd. DA11 12 F1
Burcharbro Rd. SE2 7 D8
Burdett Ave. DA12 31 F4
Burdett Cl. DA14 24 E3
Burdett Rd. TN4 148 B4
Burford Rd. BR1 36 E5
Burgate Cl. DA1 8 F4
Burgess Hall Dr. ME17 108 F6
Burgess Rd. ME2 47 B7
Burgess Row. 8 TN30 183 A7
Burghclere Dr. ME16 91 B2
Burghfield Rd. DA13 29 F1
Burgoyne Ct. ME14 91 F7
Burham CE Prim Sch. ME1 75 F8
Burham Rd. ME1 60 E8
Burial Ground La. ME15 91 E1
Burleigh Ave. DA15 6 F2
Burleigh Cl. ME2 46 E8
Burleigh Dr. ME14 76 F1
Burley Rd. E16 1 C8
Burlings La. TN14 66 F2
Burlington Cl. 5 Newham E6 1 E7
Burlington Cl. Orpington BR6 51 B8
Burlington Gdns. ME8 63 E4
Burlington Lodge. BR7 22 F1
Burma Way. ME5 61 F6
Burman Cl. DA2 27 C8
Burmarsh Cl. ME5 62 B5
Burn's Rd. ME7 48 C7
Burnaby Rd. DA11 12 E1
Burnell Ave. DA16 7 A5
Burnett Rd. DA8 9 D8
Burnham Cres. DA1 9 C3
Burnham Rd. Dartford DA1 9 C3
Burnham Rd. Sidcup DA14 24 E6
Burnham Terr. DA1 9 D2
Burnham Trad Est. DA1 9 D3
Burnham Wlk. ME8 63 E3
Burnley Rd. RM16 11 A6
Burns Ave. DA15 7 B1
Burns Cl. Bexley DA16 6 F6
Burns Cl. Erith DA8 8 F6
Burns Cres. TN9 133 A7
Burns Pl. RM18 13 B6
Burns Rd. ME16 91 C2

Burnt Ash Hill. SE12 .... 22 A7
Burnt Ash La. BR1 & SE12 ...... 22 B3
Burnt Ash Prim Sch. BR1 .... 22 A3
Burnt House Cl. ME2 .... 33 C2
Burnt House La. Dartford DA1 .. 26 F5
Burnt House La. Hawley DA2 .... 26 F4
Burnt House La. Speldhurst TN3 148 A5
Burnt Lodge La. TN5 .... 176 B2
Burnt Oak Jun Mix Sch. DA15 ... 24 A7
Burnt Oak La. Sidcup DA15 ..... 7 A1
Burnt Oak La. Sidcup DA15 ..... 24 B7
Burnt Oak Terr. ME7 .... 48 D6
Burntash Rd. ME20 .... 90 F8
Burnthouse La. TN27 .... 142 D1
Burntwood Gr. TN13 .... 99 B8
Burntwood Rd. TN13 .... 99 B7
Burr Bank Terr. DA2 .... 26 C4
Burr Cl. DA7 .... 7 F4
Burrage Gr. SE18 .... 2 C2
Burrage Pl. SE18 .... 2 B1
Burrage Rd. SE18 .... 2 C1
Burrard Rd. E16 .... 1 B7
Burrfield Dr. BR5 .... 38 D4
Burrows La. ME3 .... 19 C3
Burrswood Villas. TN3 .... 161 B7
Bursdon Cl. DA15 .... 23 F6
Burslem Rd. TN2 .... 149 E7
Bursted Wood Prim Sch. DA7 .... 8 B5
Burston Rd. ME17 .... 106 B2
Burt Rd. E16 .... 1 C5
Burwash Ct. BR5 .... 38 C4
Burwash Rd. SE18 .... 2 D1
Burwood Ave. BR2 .... 50 B8
Busbridge Rd. Loose ME15 ...... 106 E6
Busbridge Rd. Snodland ME6 .... 74 E7
Bush Cl. ME9 .... 80 F5
Bush Rd. Cuxton ME2 .... 46 B2
Bush Rd. East Peckham TN12 .... 119 E8
Bush Row. ME20 .... 76 A3
Bushell Way. BR7 .... 23 A3
Bushey Ave. BR5 .... 37 D2
Bushey House. SE12 .... 22 C5
Bushey Lees. DA15 .... 6 F1
Bushfield Wlk. DA10 .... 28 E8
Bushmeadow Rd. ME8 .... 49 F2
Bushmoor Cres. SE18 .... 6 B6
Bushy Gill. TN3 .... 148 A3
Bushy Gr. ME17 .... 109 D2
Buston Farm Cotts. ME18 .... 105 B2
Busty La. TN15 .... 86 D6
Butcher Cl. TN12 .... 139 E3
Butcher Wlk. DA10 .... 28 E8
Butcher's La. ME19 .... 88 D1
Butchers La. TN15 .... 56 D8
Butchers Cl. E16 .... 1 A7
Butchers Yd. BR6 .... 66 A8
Butler House. RM17 .... 12 B8
Butler's Cotts. DA7 .... 8 A5
Butler's Pl. ME3 .... 56 E7
Butt Green La. ME17 .... 123 A7
Butt Law Cl. ME3 .... 34 E5
Butterfield Sq. E6 .... 1 F7
Butterfly Ave. DA1 .... 26 F6
Butterfly La. SE9 .... 6 B1
Buttermere Cl. ME7 .... 49 A5
Buttermere Rd. BR5 .... 38 D5
Buttmarsh Cl. SE18 .... 2 B1
Button Dr. ME3 .... 19 C5
Button House. ME3 .... 33 F6
Button La. ME15 .... 93 B2
Button St. BR8 .... 40 C5
Butts The. TN14 .... 69 B2
Buttway La. ME3 .... 16 A6
Buxton Cl. Chatham ME5 .... 62 D1
Buxton Cl. Maidstone ME15 ..... 107 A8
Buxton Rd. DA8 .... 8 B7
Buzzard Creek Ind Est. IG11 ... 3 A8
Bychurch Pl. ME15 .... 92 A3
Bycliffe Mews. DA11 .... 29 F8
Bycliffe Terr. DA11 .... 29 F8
Byland Cl. SE2 .... 3 B3
Byng Rd. TN4 .... 148 F5
Bynon Ave. DA7 .... 7 F4
Byrneside. TN11 .... 116 E4
Byron Cl. SE28 .... 3 C5
Byron Cty Prim Sch. ME7 .... 48 C3
Byron Dr. DA8 .... 8 B7
Byron Gdns. RM18 .... 13 C6
Byron Rd. Dartford DA1 .... 10 B3
Byron Rd. Gillingham ME7 ...... 48 C3
Byron Rd. Maidstone ME14 ...... 92 B7

Cabbage Stalk La. TN4 .... 148 E2
Cacket's La. TN14 .... 66 E4
Cade La. TN13 .... 99 C7
Cadlocks Hill. TN14 .... 52 F1
Cadnam Cl. ME8 .... 46 E8
Cadogan Ave. DA2 .... 27 D8
Cadogan Gdns. TN1 .... 149 B4
Cadogan Rd. ME18 .... 2 C3
Cadwallon Rd. SE9 .... 23 C6
Caerleon Cl. DA14 .... 24 C3
Cage Green Cty Prim Sch.
  TN10 .... 117 D5
Cage Green Rd. TN10 .... 117 C5
Cage La. TN27 .... 142 F1
Cairns Cl. DA1 .... 9 D2
Caistor Rd. TN9 .... 117 A1
Caithness Gdns. DA15 .... 6 F1
Calais Cotts. ME3 .... 56 A8
Calcott Wlk. SE9 .... 22 D4
Calcutta House. ME15 .... 107 E5
Calcutta Rd. RM18 .... 13 A5
Calder Rd. ME14 .... 91 E7
Calderwood. DA12 .... 30 E2
Calderwood St. SE18 .... 2 A2
Caldew Ave. ME8 .... 49 C1

Caldy Rd. DA17 .... 4 B3
Caledonian Ct. ME8 .... 63 E8
Calehill Cl. ME14 .... 92 C6
Caley Rd. TN1 .... 149 D7
Calfstock La. DA4 .... 40 F5
Caling Croft. DA3 .... 42 F1
Caliph Cl. DA12 .... 30 F5
Callaways La. ME9 .... 65 B6
Callams Cl. ME8 .... 63 D6
Calshot Ct. [5] DA2 .... 10 B1
Calton Rd. TN2 .... 149 C3
Calverley Park Cres. [1]
  TN1 & TN2 .... 149 B3
Calverley Park Gdns.
  TN1 & TN2 .... 149 B3
Calverley Pk. TN1 & TN2 ...... 149 C4
Calverley Rd. TN1 & TN2 ...... 149 B3
Calverley St. TN1 .... 149 B4
Calvert Cl. Erith DA17 .... 4 B2
Calvert Cl. Sidcup DA14 ...... 24 E2
Calverton Prim Sch. E16 ...... 1 D7
Calvin Cl. BR5 .... 38 D6
Calydon Rd. SE7 .... 1 B1
Cambert Way. SE9 .... 5 B3
Camberwell La. TN14 .... 97 F4
Camborne Manor. ME7 .... 48 C6
Camborne Rd. Bexley DA16 ..... 6 F5
Camborne Rd. Sidcup DA14 ..... 24 C5
Cambray Rd. BR6 .... 37 F2
Cambria Ave. ME1 .... 46 F2
Cambria Cl. DA15 .... 23 E7
Cambria Cres. DA12 .... 30 F4
Cambria House. [2] DA8 .... 8 E7
Cambrian Gr. DA11 .... 30 A8
Cambrian Rd. TN4 .... 149 C7
Cambridge Barracks Rd. [12]
  SE18 .... 1 F2
Cambridge Cres. ME15 .... 107 D7
Cambridge Dr. SE12 .... 5 A2
Cambridge Gdns. ME7 .... 149 B2
Cambridge Gn. SE9 .... 23 B7
Cambridge House. [3] ME15 .... 107 D7
Cambridge Rd. Bromley BR1 .... 22 A1
Cambridge Rd. Gillingham ME8 .. 63 C6
Cambridge Rd. Rochester ME2 .. 47 A8
Cambridge Rd. Sidcup DA14 .... 23 E4
Cambridge Row. SE18 .... 2 B2
Cambridge Terr. ME4 .... 47 F4
Cambus Rd. E16 .... 1 A8
Camdale Rd. SE18 .... 6 F7
Camden Ave. TN2 .... 150 C6
Camden Cl. Chatham ME5 .... 62 B5
Camden Cl. Chislehurst BR7 ... 37 C8
Camden Cl. Northfleet DA11 ... 29 C7
Camden Cotts. ME17 .... 169 F8
Camden Cl. [9] Erith DA17 .... 4 A1
Camden Cl. Pembury TN2 .... 150 D6
Camden Cl. [2]
  Royal Tunbridge Wells TN1 .. 149 B4
Camden Gr. BR7 .... 23 B2
Camden Hill. TN1 & TN2 .... 149 B3
Camden Park (Golf Course).
  BR7 .... 23 B1
Camden Park Rd. BR7 .... 23 A1
Camden Pk. TN2 .... 149 C2
Camden Rd. Gillingham ME7 .... 48 D7
Camden Rd.
  Royal Tunbridge Wells TN1 .. 149 B4
Camden Rd. Sevenoaks TN13 .... 84 B5
Camden Rd. Sidcup DA5 .... 24 F8
Camden St. ME14 .... 92 A5
Camden Terr. ME17 .... 169 F8
Camden Way. BR7 .... 23 A1
Camel Rd. E16 .... 1 D5
Camellia Cl. ME8 .... 63 D7
Camelot Cl. SE18 .... 2 D4
Camer Gdns. DA13 .... 44 C3
Camer Park (Ctry Pk). DA13 ... 44 C2
Camer Park Rd. DA13 .... 44 C2
Camer Rd. DA13 .... 44 C3
Camer St. DA13 .... 44 C3
Cameron Cl. Chatham ME5 ...... 62 B8
Cameron Cl. Joyden's Wood DA5 25 E5
Cameron Rd. ME2 .... 36 A4
Camerons. [4] TN18 .... 179 A2
Camomile Dr. ME14 .... 92 F5
Camp Hill. TN11 .... 115 A3
Camp Site The. BR8 .... 25 A1
Camp Way. ME15 .... 107 C6
Campbell Cl. SE18 .... 6 A6
Campbell Rd. Gravesend DA11 .. 29 F8
Campbell Rd. Maidstone ME15 .. 92 A3
Campbell Rd.
  Royal Tunbridge Wells TN4 .. 149 A6
Campfield Rd. SE9 .... 22 D8
Campion Cl. Chatham ME5 ...... 61 E3
Campion Cl. Newham E6 .... 1 F6
Campion Cl. Northfleet DA11 .. 29 E4
Campion Cres. TN17 .... 169 A2
Campion Cl. [5] RM17 .... 12 D8
Campion Pl. SE28 .... 3 B5
Campleshon Rd. ME8 .... 63 D5
Campus Way. ME7 .... 63 A8
Camrose Ave. DA8 .... 8 B8
Camrose St. SE2 .... 3 A2
Canada Farm Rd. DA4 .... 42 A6
Canada Rd. DA8 .... 9 B7
Canada Terr. [3] ME15 .... 92 A7
Canadian Ave. ME7 .... 48 F4
Canal Basin. DA12 .... 13 D1
Canal Rd. Gravesend DA12 ..... 13 D1
Canal Rd. Lower Higham ME3 ... 32 C6
Canal Road Ind Pk. [2] DA12 .. 30 D8
Canberra Rd. Erith DA7 .... 7 D8
Canberra Rd. Greenwich SE7 ... 5 D8

Canberra Sq. RM18 .... 13 A5
Canbury Path. BR5 .... 38 A5
Canning St. ME14 .... 92 A6
Cannock Sch. ME5 .... 62 F5
Cannon Bridge Works. TN9 ..... 117 D2
Cannon La. TN9 .... 117 D2
Cannon Pl. SE7 .... 1 E1
Cannon Rd. DA7 .... 7 F5
Canon Cl. ME1 .... 47 B2
Canon La. ME18 .... 89 C1
Canon Rd. BR1 .... 36 D6
Cansiron La. TN7 & TN8 .... 144 E2
Canterbury Ave. DA14 & DA15 .. 24 C5
Canterbury Cl. Dartford DA1 .. 27 A8
Canterbury Cl. [7] Newham E6 .. 1 F7
Canterbury Cres. TN10 .... 117 C5
Canterbury House. Erith DA8 .. 8 F7
Canterbury House. [2]
  Maidstone ME15 .... 107 D7
Canterbury Rd. Gravesend DA12 30 C6
Canterbury Rd. Pembury TN2 ... 150 E6
Canterbury St. ME7 .... 48 B2
Canterbury Way. RM16 & DA1 ... 10 D5
Cantwell House. SE18 .... 6 B7
Cantwell Rd. SE18 .... 6 B7
Capel Cl. Gillingham ME8 ..... 63 D4
Capel Cl. Keston Mark BR2 .... 36 E1
Capel Cty Prim Sch. TN12 ..... 134 F7
Capel Pl. DA2 .... 26 C4
Capelands. DA3 .... 57 A8
Capell Cl. ME17 .... 106 C3
Capetown House. [1] RM17 ..... 107 F5
Capstan Ct. DA9 .... 10 C3
Capstan Ctr. RM17 .... 12 E7
Capstone Farm Country Pk.
  ME7 .... 62 D5
Capstone Rd. Chatham ME5 ..... 48 D1
Capstone Rd. Gillingham ME7 .. 62 F6
Capstone Rd. Lewisham BR1 .... 22 A4
Captain's Cl. ME17 .... 124 E6
Captain's Wlk The. TN15 ...... 87 C7
Caraway Cl. E13 .... 1 B8
Cardens Rd. ME3 .... 33 B8
Cardiff St. SE18 .... 6 E7
Cardinal Cl. Chislehurst BR7 . 37 D8
Cardinal Cl. Tonbridge TN9 ... 133 D8
Cardwell Prim Sch. SE18 ...... 1 F2
Cardwell Rd. SE18 .... 2 A2
Carew House. [24] SE18 .... 1 F2
Carey Ct. DA6 .... 8 A2
Carhaven House. [3] DA8 ...... 8 E7
Caring La. ME15 .... 93 E1
Caring Rd. ME15 .... 93 C1
Carisbrooke Ave. DA5 .... 24 D7
Carisbrooke Cl. [9] DA5 ...... 10 B1
Carisbrooke Dr. ME16 .... 91 D4
Carisbrooke Rd. Bromley BR2 .. 36 C5
Carisbrooke Rd. Rochester ME2 32 E1
Carl Ekman House. DA11 .... 29 D8
Carleton Pl. DA4 .... 41 C5
Carleton Rd. DA1 .... 27 A8
Carlisle Cl. ME2 .... 46 C6
Carlisle Rd. DA1 .... 10 A1
Carlton Ave. Gillingham ME7 .. 48 E4
Carlton Ave. Stone DA9 .... 10 E1
Carlton Cres. Chatham ME5 .... 62 D8
Carlton Cres.
  Royal Tunbridge Wells TN2 .. 149 C4
Carlton Gdns. ME15 .... 107 B8
Carlton Gn. DA14 .... 23 F4
Carlton Par. BR5 .... 38 B2
Carlton Rd. Bexley DA16 ...... 7 B4
Carlton Rd. Erith DA8 .... 8 C8
Carlton Rd.
  Royal Tunbridge Wells TN2 .. 149 C4
Carlton Rd. Sidcup DA14 ...... 23 F3
Carlyle Ave. BR1 .... 36 D6
Carlyle Rd. SE28 .... 3 C6
Carman's Cl. ME15 & ME17 ..... 106 F3
Carmelite Way. DA3 .... 42 F4
Carnation Cl. ME19 & ME20 .... 75 A1
Carnation Cres. ME19 .... 74 F1
Carnation Rd. ME2 .... 46 D7
Carnation St. SE2 .... 3 B1
Carnbrook Rd. SE3 .... 5 D4
Carnecke Gdns. SE9 .... 5 E2
Caroline Cres. ME16 .... 91 D7
Carolyn Dr. BR6 .... 52 A7
Carpeaux Cl. ME4 .... 48 A4
Carpenters Cl. ME4 .... 48 A4
Carpenters La. Hadlow TN11 ... 102 D2
Carpenters La.
  Staplehurst TN12 .... 139 C8
Carpinus Cl. ME5 .... 62 B1
Carr Gr. SE18 .... 1 E2
Carrack House. DA8 .... 4 E1
Carriage Mus. ME15 .... 92 A3
Carriageway The. TN14 .... 82 D3
Carrick Dr. TN13 .... 84 B4
Carrie House. ME16 .... 91 E5
Carriers Pl. ME15 .... 91 E5
Carriers Rd. TN17 .... 169 D5
Carrill Way. DA17 .... 3 D3
Carrington Rd. DA1 .... 10 A1
Carroll Gdns. ME20 .... 74 F3
Carronade Pl. SE18 .... 2 C3
Carsington Gdns. DA1 .... 26 D6
Carson Rd. E16 .... 1 A7
Carston Cl. SE12 & SE13 ...... 5 A2
Carters Hill. TN15 .... 100 B6
Carters Hill Cl. SE9 .... 22 C7
Carters Hill La. DA13 .... 57 F2
Carters Row. DA11 .... 30 B8
Cartmel Rd. DA7 .... 8 A6
Carton Cl. ME1 .... 47 B2
Carton Rd. ME3 .... 32 B3
Carville Ave. TN4 .... 132 F1
Carvoran Way. ME8 .... 63 C5

Cascade Cl. BR5 .... 38 C6
Cascades L Ctr. DA12 .... 31 A4
Caspian Wlk. E16 .... 1 D7
Cassilda Rd. SE2 .... 3 A2
Casstine Cl. BR8 .... 25 F1
Castalia Ct. DA1 .... 9 F4
Casterbridge Rd. SE3 .... 5 A4
Castile Rd. SE18 .... 2 A2
Castilion Prim Sch. SE28 ..... 3 C7
Castilla House. BR1 .... 22 B1
Castle Ave. ME1 .... 47 C4
Castle Dene. ME14 .... 91 F8
Castle Dr. TN14 .... 69 E2
Castle Farm Rd. TN14 .... 54 A3
Castle Fields. TN9 .... 117 B2
Castle Hill. Hartley DA3 ..... 42 E4
Castle Hill. Rochester ME1 ... 47 C6
Castle Hill. Thurnham ME14 ... 78 D1
Castle Hill. Tonbridge TN11 .. 133 F5
Castle Hurst. TN32 .... 185 B1
Castle La. DA12 .... 31 B6
Castle Rd. Chatham ME4 .... 48 B2
Castle Rd. Eynsford DA4 ...... 54 C5
Castle Rd. Grays RM17 .... 11 F8
Castle Rd. Gravesend DA12 .... 30 B5
Castle Rd.
  Royal Tunbridge Wells TN4 .. 149 A3
Castle St. Royal Tunbridge Wells,
  Mount Sion TN1 .... 149 A2
Castle St. Royal TunbridgeWells,
  Southborough TN4 .... 132 F2
Castle St. Stone DA9 .... 11 A2
Castle St. Swanscombe DA10 ... 11 F1
Castle St. Tonbridge TN9 ..... 117 C2
Castle St. Upper Upton ME1 ... 33 E1
Castle Terr. Hawkhurst TN18 .. 178 F3
Castle Terr. Wouldham ME1 .... 60 C4
Castle View Rd. ME2 .... 47 A7
Castle Way. ME19 .... 74 D2
Castle Wlk. TN5 .... 174 E4
Castlecombe Prim Sch. SE9 .... 22 E3
Castlecombe Rd. SE9 .... 22 E4
Castlefields. DA3 .... 43 F8
Castleford Ave. SE9 .... 23 B7
Castlemaine Ave. ME7 .... 48 F6
Castleton Ave. DA7 .... 8 D5
Castleton Rd. SE12 & SE9 ..... 22 E4
Castlewood Day Hospl. SE18 ... 6 A6
Castlewood Rd. SE9 .... 5 E6
Cates Ct. TN12 .... 120 A7
Cathcart Dr. BR6 .... 37 F1
Catherine Cl. ME16 .... 91 A3
Catherine Cl. [7] TN1 .... 149 B4
Catherine St. ME1 .... 47 D3
Catkin Cl. ME5 .... 61 F1
Catterick Rd. ME5 .... 62 D2
Cattistock Rd. SE9 .... 22 E3
Causton Rd. TN17 .... 169 C5
Cave Hill. ME15 .... 91 F1
Cavell Cres. DA1 .... 10 B3
Cavendish Ave. Bexley DA16 ... 6 F4
Cavendish Ave. Erith DA8 ..... 8 C8
Cavendish Ave. Gillingham ME7 48 E6
Cavendish Ave. Sevenoaks TN13 84 A5
Cavendish Ave. Sidcup DA15 ... 24 A8
Cavendish Cl. TN10 .... 117 D7
Cavendish Ct. TN9 .... 117 D3
Cavendish Dr. TN2 .... 149 B1
Cavendish Rd. ME1 .... 47 D3
Cavendish Sq. DA3 .... 42 D6
Cavendish Way. ME15 .... 93 B3
Caverley Rd. TN1 .... 149 B4
Caversham Cl. ME8 .... 49 F1
Caveside Cl. BR7 .... 37 A8
Caxton Cl. Hartley DA3 .... 42 F5
Caxton Cl. Tenterden TN30 .... 182 F7
Caxton La. TN11 .... 118 E8
Cayser Dr. ME17 .... 109 E2
Cazeneuve St. ME1 .... 47 C5
Cecil Ave. Gillingham ME8 .... 49 A2
Cecil Ave. Rochester ME2 ..... 47 B8
Cecil Rd. Gravesend DA11 ..... 29 F7
Cecil Rd. Rochester ME1 ...... 47 C5
Cecil Road Cty Prim Sch. DA11 29 F7
Cecil Way. BR2 .... 36 A1
Cedar Ave. Gravesend DA12 .... 30 C4
Cedar Ave. Sidcup DA15 .... 24 A8
Cedar Cl. Ditton ME20 .... 90 D8
Cedar Cl. Keston Mark BR2 .... 50 E7
Cedar Cl. Meopham Station DA13 44 A3
Cedar Cl. Swanley BR8 .... 39 C7
Cedar Copse. BR1 .... 36 F7
Cedar Cres. Keston Mark BR2 .. 50 E7
Cedar Cres. Tonbridge TN10 ... 117 C7
Cedar Ct. Eltham SE9 .... 5 E1
Cedar Ct. [10] Greenwich SE7 . 5 C1
Cedar Ct.
  Royal Tunbridge Wells TN4 .. 149 A5
Cedar Ct. [10] Tenterden TN30 183 A7
Cedar Dr. Edenbridge TN8 ..... 112 B2
Cedar Dr. Maidstone ME16 ..... 90 C2
Cedar Dr. Sutton at Hone DA4 . 41 B7
Cedar Gdns. ME9 .... 79 E8
Cedar Gr. Gillingham ME7 ..... 63 A5
Cedar Gr. Sidcup DA5 .... 7 D1
Cedar Lodge. TN4 .... 148 F3
Cedar Mount. SE9 .... 22 D7
Cedar Pl. [3] SE7 .... 1 C1
Cedar Rd. Bromley BR1 .... 36 C6
Cedar Rd. Dartford DA1 .... 26 D7
Cedar Rd. Erith DA8 .... 9 B7
Cedar Rd. Hoo St Werburgh ME3 34 E3
Cedar Rd. Rochester ME2 ...... 46 D7
Cedar Ridge. TN2 .... 149 D5

Cedar Terrace Rd. TN13 .... 84 C4
Cedarhurst Dr. SE9 .... 5 C2
Cedarmore Ct. BR7 .... 23 C2
Cedars Sch The. Maidstone ME16 91 D4
Cedars Sch The. Rochester ME1 47 C4
Cedars The. TN12 .... 136 A4
Cedarwood House. ME15 .... 106 B6
Cedric Rd. SE9 .... 23 C5
Celandine Dr. SE28 .... 3 B5
Celestine Cl. ME5 .... 62 A1
Cement Block Cotts. RM17 ..... 12 C8
Cement Industry Heritage Ctr.
  DA11 .... 12 B2
Cemetery La. Hadlow TN11 ..... 103 A1
Cemetery Rd. Halling ME2 ..... 60 A4
Cemetery Rd. Snodland ME6 .... 59 F1
Cemetery Rd. Woolwich SE2 .... 7 B7
Centenary Ct. DA4 .... 41 A2
Central Ave. Bexley DA16 ..... 7 A5
Central Ave. Gillingham ME4 .. 48 B8
Central Ave. Gravesend DA12 .. 30 B5
Central Ave. Tilbury RM18 .... 13 A6
Central Bsns Pk. ME2 .... 47 E2
Central Cl. SE28 .... 2 B2
Central Lodge. TN15 .... 72 E6
Central Par. ME1 .... 47 D2
Central Par Villas. BR5 ...... 38 C7
Central Park Gdns. ME1 .... 47 E2
Central Rd. Dartford DA1 ..... 9 E2
Central Rd. New Hythe ME20 ... 75 B4
Central Rd. Rochester ME2 .... 47 A7
Central Sta. TN1 .... 149 A3
Central Terr. ME3 .... 33 F6
Central Way. SE28 .... 3 B6
Centre 2000. ME16 .... 91 C8
Centre Common Rd. BR7 .... 23 C1
Centre Ct. ME2 .... 47 E7
Centre Rd. DA3 .... 56 E7
Centurian Way. DA18 .... 4 A1
Centurion Ct. ME7 .... 48 F1
Century Rd. ME8 .... 63 D8
Ceres Rd. SE18 .... 2 F2
Cerne Rd. DA12 .... 30 E5
Cervia Way. DA12 .... 30 F5
Chada Ave. ME7 .... 48 E3
Chadd Dr. BR1 .... 36 E6
Chadfields. RM18 .... 13 A7
Chadwell Hill. RM17 .... 13 A8
Chadwick Cl. DA11 .... 29 E5
Chadwick Ct. [4] SE28 .... 3 B5
Chadwick Way. SE28 .... 3 C6
Chadwin Rd. E13 .... 1 B8
Chaffey House. [6] SE7 .... 1 C1
Chaffinch Cl. ME5 .... 62 A7
Chaffinch Way. TN12 .... 136 A5
Chafford Cotts. TN3 .... 146 F5
Chafford La. TN3 .... 146 F5
Chain Gate. TN27 .... 127 A8
Chalcombe Rd. SE2 .... 3 B3
Chalet Cl. DA2 .... 25 D4
Chalfont Dr. ME8 .... 63 D6
Chalice Way. DA9 .... 10 F2
Chalk Ave. TN30 .... 173 B2
Chalk Ct. RM17 .... 12 A8
Chalk Pit Ave. BR5 .... 38 C6
Chalk Pit Hill. ME4 .... 48 A3
Chalk Rd. Chalk DA12 .... 31 A6
Chalk Rd. Lower Higham ME3 ... 32 C6
Chalk Rd. Newham E13 .... 1 C8
Chalkenden Ave. ME8 .... 49 A2
Chalket La. TN2 .... 150 C5
Chalkpit Cotts. TN15 .... 31 E5
Chalkstone Cl. DA16 .... 7 A6
Chalkways. TN14 .... 69 F3
Chalky Bank. DA11 .... 30 A3
Chalky Rd. ME9 .... 79 C6
Challenge Cl. DA12 .... 30 F4
Challenger Cl. TN12 .... 135 F6
Challock House. [3]
  Orpington BR5 .... 38 D1
Challock Wlk. ME14 .... 92 C6
Chamberlain Ave. ME16 .... 91 C2
Chamberlain Cl. SE18 .... 2 D3
Chamberlain Ct. ME8 .... 63 B5
Chamberlain Rd. ME4 .... 48 B2
Chancel Cl. TN15 .... 55 E3
Chancellor House. TN4 .... 148 F3
Chancellor Way. TN13 .... 84 A5
Chancelot Rd. SE2 .... 3 B2
Chancery Cl. DA1 .... 27 A7
Chancery La. ME15 .... 92 B3
Chanctonbury Cl. SE9 .... 23 B5
Chandler Ave. E16 .... 1 A8
Chandler's Hill. DA13 .... 58 C5
Chandlers Rd. DA13 .... 58 C5
Chandlers Dr. DA8 .... 4 E2
Chandos Rd. TN1 .... 149 C5
Chantler's Hill. TN12 .... 136 A4
Chantlers Mead. TN8 .... 145 A5
Chantrey Cl. DA14 .... 24 E3
Chantry Ave. DA3 .... 42 E3
Chantry Ct. DA11 .... 13 C1
Chantry Cty Prim Schs. DA12 .. 13 C1
Chantry La. BR2 .... 36 D4
Chantry Pl. TN12 .... 138 C6
Chantry Rd. TN12 .... 138 C6
Chapel Alley Cotts. TN14 ..... 69 A8
Chapel Cl. Crayford DA1 ...... 8 E2
Chapel Cl. Ryarsh ME6 .... 73 F5
Chapel Cl. West Thurrock RM16 11 B8
Chapel Cotts. ME17 .... 108 F5
Chapel Ct. DA10 .... 11 E1

Chapel Farm Rd. SE9 .... 22 F6
Chapel Field Cotts. DA4 .... 41 B8
Chapel Hill. DA1 .... 8 E2
Chapel Houses. ME2 .... 59 E4
Chapel La.
Gillingham,Hempstead ME7 .... 63 A4
Chapel La. Gillingham,Lidsing ME7 63 A2
Chapel La. Iden Green TN17 .... 180 C4
Chapel La. Maidstone ME14 .... 93 A5
Chapel La. Potter's Forstal TN27 127 B2
Chapel La. Sissinghurst TN17 .... 170 B7
Chapel La. Staplehurst TN12 .... 139 F3
Chapel La. Upper Halling ME2 .... 59 C4
Chapel Pl. 8
Royal Tunbridge Wells TN1 .... 149 A2
Chapel Pl. Ticehurst TN5 .... 176 E1
Chapel Rd. Bexley DA7 .... 8 A3
Chapel Rd. Grain ME3 .... 21 B5
Chapel Rd. Snodland ME6 .... 75 A8
Chapel Rd. Sutton Valence ME17 124 E7
Chapel Row. Ightham TN15 .... 86 C6
Chapel Row. Lower Stoke ME3 .... 19 C4
Chapel St. East Malling ME19 .... 90 A6
Chapel St. Ryarsh ME19 .... 73 F5
Chapel View. TN15 .... 86 C6
Chapel Wlk. TN14 .... 98 B5
Chapel Wood. DA3 .... 56 E8
Chapel Wood Rd. DA3 .... 56 E8
Chaplin Dr. TN27 .... 141 D5
Chapman Ave. ME15 .... 107 F8
Chapman Rd. DA17 .... 4 B1
Chapman Way. East Malling ME19 89 F4
Chapman Way.
Royal Tunbridge Wells TN4 .... 149 C8
Chapman's Hill. DA13 & TN15 .... 57 E4
Chapman's La. Hockenden BR8 .... 39 A7
Chapman's La. St Paul's Cray BR5 538 D7
Chapmans End. BR5 .... 38 E7
Chapmans Rd. TN14 .... 82 E3
Chapter Rd. ME2 .... 46 F8
Chapter Sch. ME2 .... 46 E8
Chardwell Cl. E6 .... 1 F7
Charford Rd. E16 .... 1 A8
Charing Cl. BR6 .... 51 F6
Charing House. 5 DA8 .... 8 F7
Charing Rd. ME8 .... 49 B3
Chariot Way. ME2 .... 46 F4
Charity Farm Cotts. TN17 .... 156 F7
Charlbury Cl. ME16 .... 91 C3
Charldane Rd. SE9 .... 23 B5
Charlecote Ct. ME8 .... 63 D8
Charles Busby Ct. 3 ME20 .... 75 F1
Charles Cl. Sidcup DA14 .... 24 B4
Charles Cl. Snodland ME6 .... 75 A8
Charles Ct. Erith DA8 .... 8 E8
Charles Ct.
Royal Tunbridge Wells TN2 .... 149 C3
Charles Dickens Ave. ME2 .... 32 C2
Charles Dr. ME2 .... 46 B2
Charles Grinling Wlk. SE18 .... 2 A2
Charles Rd. TN14 .... 53 B1
Charles St. Chatham ME4 .... 47 E3
Charles St. Grays RM17 .... 12 C8
Charles St. Maidstone ME16 .... 91 E3
Charles St. Newham E16 .... 1 C5
Charles St. Rochester ME2 .... 47 A7
Charles St.
Royal Tunbridge Wells TN4 .... 149 A8
Charles St. Stone DA9 .... 10 F2
Charlesfield. SE12 .... 22 C5
Charlesford Ave. ME17 .... 109 D3
Charlieville Rd. DA8 .... 8 C7
Charlotte Cl. Bexley DA6 .... 7 E2
Charlotte Cl. Chatham ME5 .... 62 B6
Charlotte Dr. ME8 .... 49 C1
Charlotte Park Ave. BR1 .... 36 E6
Charlotte Pl. RM16 .... 11 B8
Charlottes Cotts. TN11 .... 115 F1
Charlton Church La. SE7 .... 1 C1
Charlton Dene. SE7 .... 5 D7
Charlton La.
Chartway Street ME17 .... 125 C4
Charlton La. Greenwich SE7 .... 1 D1
Charlton La. West Farleigh ME15105 E6
Charlton Manor. ME7 .... 48 B5
Charlton Manor Prim Sch. SE7 .. 5 D7
Charlton Park La. SE7 .... 5 E8
Charlton Park Rd. SE7 .... 5 D8
Charlton Park Sch. SE7 .... 5 E8
Charlton Rd. SE3 & SE7 .... 5 B8
Charlton St. Grays RM16 .... 11 D8
Charlton St. Maidstone ME16 .... 91 C2
Charlton's Way. TN4 .... 148 E1
Charminster Rd. SE12 & SE9 .... 22 D4
Charmouth Rd. DA16 .... 7 C6
Charnwood La. BR6 .... 52 B1
Charnwood Villas. BR6 .... 52 C1
Charne The. TN14 .... 69 A2
Charnock. BR8 .... 39 E5
Chart Cnr. ME17 .... 108 B1
Chart Hill Rd. ME17 .... 124 A7
Chart Hills Golf Course. TN27 158 A5
Chart La. TN16 .... 97 B7
Chart Pl. ME8 .... 63 C3
Chart Rd. ME17 .... 123 E7
Chart View. TN15 .... 70 B2
Charter Dr. DA5 .... 24 E8
Charter St. Chatham ME4 .... 47 F2
Charter St. Gillingham ME7 .... 48 C7
Charterhouse Dr. TN13 .... 84 A4
Charterhouse Rd. BR6 .... 52 A6
Charton Cl. 5 DA17 .... 7 F8
Chartway. TN13 & TN15 .... 84 C3
Chartway St. ME17 .... 109 C1
Chartwell Cl. Rochester ME2 .... 33 B1

Chartwell Cl. Sidcup BR7 .... 23 D6
Chartwell Dr. BR6 .... 51 D5
Chartwell (National Trust).
TN16 .... 96 F4
Chase Sq. 12 DA11 .... 13 B1
Chase The. Bexley DA7 .... 8 B4
Chase The. Bromley BR1 .... 36 B6
Chase The. Chatham ME1 .... 47 D2
Chase The. Gillingham ME8 .... 49 A2
Chase The. Kemsing TN14 .... 69 E3
Chase The.
Pratt's Bottom BR6 & TN14 .... 52 A1
Chase The. Tonbridge TN10 .... 117 C5
Chase The. West Thurrock RM16 .. 11 D8
Chastilian Rd. DA1 .... 26 A8
Chatham Ave. BR2 .... 36 A2
Chatham Gr. ME4 .... 47 F1
Chatham Gram Sch for Boys.
ME4 .... 61 F8
Chatham Gram Sch for Girls.
ME5 .... 48 C2
Chatham Hill. ME4 .... 48 B3
Chatham Hill Rd. TN14 .... 84 C6
Chatham Historic Dockyard.
ME4 .... 48 A7
Chatham House. 22 SE18 .... 1 F2
Chatham Rd. Chatham ME20 .... 76 D8
Chatham Rd. Kit's Coty ME20 .... 76 D6
Chatham Rd. Kit's Coty ME20 .... 76 D6
Chatham Rd. Maidstone ME14 .... 76 E1
Chatham Rd. Sandling ME14 .... 76 E4
Chatham Rd. Sandling ME14 .... 76 E4
Chatham Ski Ctr. ME7 .... 62 E6
Chatham South Sec Sch. ME4 .. 61 F8
Chatham St. SE18 .... 2 B3
Chatham Sta. ME4 .... 47 E4
Chatsworth Ave. Bromley BR1 .. 22 B4
Chatsworth Ave. Sidcup DA15 .. 24 A7
Chatsworth Dr. ME2 .... 33 B1
Chatsworth House. 8 BR2 .... 36 A5
Chatsworth Inf Sch. DA15 .... 24 A7
Chatsworth Par. BR5 .... 37 C4
Chatsworth Rd. Dartford DA1 .... 9 C3
Chatsworth Rd. Gillingham ME7 . 48 C6
Chattenden Barracks Royal Sch of
Military Engineering. ME3 .... 33 F5
Chattenden Ct. ME14 .... 92 B6
Chattenden Cty Prim Sch.
ME3 .... 33 F4
Chattenden La. ME3 .... 33 F5
Chattenden Terr. ME3 .... 33 F4
Chatterton Rd. BR2 .... 36 D4
Chaucer Cl. Rochester ME2 .... 47 E8
Chaucer Cl. Tilbury RM18 .... 13 C5
Chaucer Gdns. TN9 .... 132 F7
Chaucer Ind Pk. TN15 .... 85 D8
Chaucer Pk. DA1 .... 26 F8
Chaucer Rd. Bexley DA16 .... 6 F6
Chaucer Rd. Gillingham ME7 .... 48 D3
Chaucer Rd. Northfleet DA11 .... 29 D5
Chaucer Rd. Sidcup DA15 .... 24 C7
Chaucer Way. ME20 .... 75 A3
Chaundrye Cl. SE9 .... 5 F1
Chauntler Cl. E16 .... 1 B6
Chauser Way. 2 DA1 .... 10 A3
Chave Rd. DA1 .... 26 E5
Cheeselands. TN27 .... 157 F2
Cheffins House. ME7 .... 48 E7
Chegwell Dr. ME5 .... 62 B4
Chegworth La. ME17 .... 110 A6
Chegworth Rd. ME17 .... 109 F5
Chelmar Rd. ME7 .... 48 B4
Chelmsford Cl. E6 .... 2 A1
Chelmsford Rd. ME2 .... 46 D6
Chelsfield Cl. ME8 .... 49 E2
Chelsfield La.
Badgers Mount BR6 & TN14 .... 53 B2
Chelsfield La.
Chelsfield BR5 & BR6 .... 52 D7
Chelsfield La. Orpington BR5 .... 38 D2
Chelsfield Lakes Golf Course.
BR6 .... 52 E3
Chelsfield Park Hospl. BR6 .... 52 F5
Chelsfield Prim Sch. BR6 .... 52 E5
Chelsfield Rd. BR5 .... 38 C3
Chelsfield Sta. BR6 .... 52 B5
Chelsiter Ct. DA14 .... 23 F4
Chelsworth Dr. SE18 .... 6 D8
Cheltenham Cl. Gravesend DA12 30 C3
Cheltenham Cl.
Maidstone ME15 .... 107 F6
Cheltenham Rd. BR6 .... 52 A7
Cheney Cl. ME8 .... 63 D5
Cheney's Cotts. DA12 .... 31 A2
Chenies Cl. TN2 .... 163 A8
Chenies The. Joyden's Wood DA2 25 E4
Chenies The.
Orpington BR5 & BR6 .... 37 E3
Chennell Park Rd. TN30 .... 172 E1
Chennels The. TN26 .... 173 C7
Chepstow House. 3 ME15 .... 107 F6
Chequer's Cotts. TN17 .... 153 F1
Chequers Cl. Chatham ME5 .... 77 A8
Chequers Cl. Istead Rise DA13 .. 43 F7
Chequers Cl. St Paul's Cray BR5 . 37 F5
Chequers Ctr. ME15 .... 92 A4
Chequers Hill Cotts. TN8 .... 114 A2
Chequers La. RM9 .... 3 F8
Cherbourg Cres. ME5 .... 61 F7
Cherbury Cl. SE28 .... 3 D7
Cheriton Ave. BR2 .... 36 A4
Cheriton Cl. 7 SE12 .... 22 A8
Cheriton Dr. SE18 .... 6 D8
Cheriton Rd. SE18 .... 63 D8
Cheriton Way. ME16 .... 91 C7
Cherries The. ME16 .... 91 A2
Cherry Amber Cl. ME8 .... 63 F8
Cherry Ave. BR8 .... 39 D5

Cherry Ct. DA14 .... 24 B5
Cherry Gr. TN10 .... 117 E5
Cherry Hill Ct. ME9 .... 65 B6
Cherry Lodge Golf Course.
TN16 .... 66 A2
Cherry Orch. Ditton ME19 .... 90 C8
Cherry Orch. Greenwich SE7 .... 5 C8
Cherry Orch. Tenterden TN30 .. 183 A6
Cherry Orch The. TN11 .... 102 E5
Cherry Orchard Cl. BR5 .... 38 C4
Cherry Orchard Inf Sch. SE7 ...... 5 C7
Cherry Orchard Rd. BR2 .... 50 E8
Cherry Orchard Way. ME16 .... 91 B3
Cherry Rd. ME3 .... 34 E3
Cherry Tree Cl. RM17 .... 12 C8
Cherry Tree Cl. 17 SE7 .... 5 C8
Cherry Tree Gr. DA2 .... 55 B1
Cherry Tree La. DA2 .... 25 F5
Cherry Tree Rd. Gillingham ME8 . 63 F8
Cherry Tree Rd.
Royal Tunbridge Wells TN2 .... 148 E1
Cherry Trees. DA3 .... 42 F4
Cherry View. ME17 .... 107 B3
Cherry Wlk. BR2 .... 36 A1
Cherrycot Hill. BR6 .... 51 D6
Cherrycot Rise. BR6 .... 51 C6
Cherrydown Rd. DA14 .... 24 D6
Cherryfields. TN17 .... 180 D6
Cherrywood Dr. DA11 .... 29 E5
Chervil Mews. SE28 .... 3 B5
Chervilles. ME16 .... 91 A2
Cherwell Cl. TN10 .... 117 B4
Chesfield Cl. TN11 .... 102 F1
Chesham Ave. BR2 & BR5 .... 37 B3
Chesham Dr. ME8 .... 63 E6
Cheshire Rd.
Maidstone,Shepway ME15 .... 107 E7
Cheshire Rd.
Maidstone,Willington ME15 .... 92 C2
Cheshunt Cl. DA13 .... 44 A3
Cheshunt Rd. DA17 .... 4 A1
Chessenden La. TN27 .... 143 A1
Chessington Ave. DA7 .... 7 E7
Chester Ave. TN2 .... 149 D2
Chester Cl. ME2 .... 46 D6
Chester Rd. Gillingham ME7 .... 48 D2
Chester Rd. Sidcup DA15 .... 6 E2
Chesterfield Cl. BR5 .... 38 D5
Chesterfield Dr. Dartford DA1 .... 9 B2
Chesterfield Dr. Sevenoaks TN13 83 D5
Chesterfield Dr. Sevenoaks TN13 83 E5
Chesterford House. SE18 .... 5 D7
Chesterton Rd. 5 ME20 .... 74 F4
Chesterton Way. RM18 .... 13 C5
Chestfield Cl. ME8 .... 49 E2
Chestnut Ave. Chatham ME5 .... 61 F3
Chestnut Ave. Hill Park TN16 .... 81 A6
Chestnut Ave.
Royal Tunbridge Wells TN4 .... 149 B8
Chestnut Ave. Staplehurst TN12 139 F4
Chestnut Cl. Edenbridge TN8 .... 112 B2
Chestnut Cl. Frittenden TN17 .. 156 E6
Chestnut Cl. Kings Hill ME19 .... 89 A2
Chestnut Cl. Northfleet DA11 .... 12 F1
Chestnut Cl. Orpington BR6 .... 52 A5
Chestnut Cl.
Royal Tunbridge Wells TN4 .... 149 B8
Chestnut Cl. Tenterden TN30 .. 173 C1
Chestnut Dr. Bexley DA7 .... 7 E4
Chestnut Dr. Coxheath ME17 .... 106 B3
Chestnut Dr. Kingswood ME17 . 109 D2
Chestnut Gr. DA2 .... 25 E4
Chestnut La. Matfield TN12 .... 135 D1
Chestnut La. Sevenoaks TN13 .. 84 B3
Chestnut La. Vigo Village DA13 .. 73 B8
Chestnut Pl. TN8 .... 145 A5
Chestnut Rd. Dartford DA1 .... 26 D7
Chestnut Rd. Rochester ME2 .... 46 E6
Chestnut Rise. SE18 .... 2 E1
Chestnut St. ME9 .... 65 E4
Chestnut Wlk. Larkfield ME20 .. 75 B2
Chestnut Wlk. Sevenoaks TN15 .. 99 F6
Chestnut Wlk. Tonbridge TN9 .. 116 F2
Chestnut Wood La. ME9 .... 65 E3
Chestnuts The. Addington TN19 . 73 C3
Chestnuts The. 10 Erith DA17 .... 4 A1
Chestnuts The. The Moor TN18 . 184 F8
Chestnuts The. Woolwich SE18 .. 6 B6
Cheswick Cl. DA1 .... 8 F3
Chesworth Cl. DA8 .... 8 E5
Chetney Cl. ME2 .... 46 C7
Chetwood Wlk. 14 E6 .... 1 E8
Cheveney Wlk. 2 BR2 .... 36 A6
Chevening CE Prim Sch. TN13 83 B5
Chevening Cl. ME5 .... 62 A5
Chevening Cl. ME2 .... 52 A8
Chevening House. BR5 .... 38 A8
Chevening La. TN14 .... 67 E3
Chevening Rd. 2 Greenwich SE10 1 A1
Chevening Rd.
Sevenoaks TN13 & TN14 .... 83 B6
Chevening Rd. Sundridge TN14 .. 82 F4
Chevenings The. DA14 .... 24 C5
Cheviot Cl. Erith DA7 .... 8 E5
Cheviot Cl. Tonbridge TN9 .... 117 C4
Cheviot Gdns. ME15 .... 93 A1
Chevron Cl. E16 .... 1 A7
Chevron House. RM17 .... 12 B7
Cheyne Cl. BR2 .... 50 E7
Cheyne Wlk. Longfield DA3 .... 42 D6
Cheyne Wlk. Meopham DA13 .... 58 A8
Chicago Ave. ME7 .... 48 F5
Chichester Cl. Gillingham ME8 ... 64 A8
Chichester Cl. Greenwich SE3 .... 5 C6
Chichester Cl. Newham E6 .... 1 E7
Chichester Ct. 3 DA5 .... 25 A8
Chichester Dr. TN13 .... 83 F2

Chichester Rd. Stone DA9 .... 10 F1
Chichester Rd. Tonbridge TN9 . 133 A8
Chichester Rise. DA12 .... 30 D4
Chichester Rd. ME5 .... 48 C2
Chicks La. TN17 .... 167 A2
Chiddingstone Ave. DA7 .... 7 F7
Chiddingstone Castle. TN8 .. 130 B7
Chiddingstone CE Prim Sch.
TN8 .... 130 C7
Chiddingstone Cl. ME15 .... 107 F6
Chidley Cross Rd. TN12 .... 119 E6
Chieftain Cl. ME7 .... 49 B1
Chieveley Dr. TN2 .... 149 D1
Chieveley Par. DA7 .... 8 B4
Chieveley Rd. DA7 .... 8 B3
Chiffinch Gdns. DA11 .... 29 E5
Childs Cres. DA10 .... 11 D1
Childs Way. TN15 .... 71 F3
Childsbridge La. TN14 & TN15 .. 84 F7
Childsbridge Way. TN15 .... 84 F7
Childscroft Rd. ME8 .... 49 F2
Chilham Cl. Chatham ME4 .... 47 E3
Chilham Cl. Sidcup DA5 .... 24 F8
Chilham House. ME2 .... 33 C1
Chilham Rd. Chislehurst SE9 .... 22 E4
Chilham Rd. Gillingham ME8 .... 49 A3
Chilham Rd. Maidstone ME16 .. 91 C7
Chilham Way. BR2 .... 36 A2
Chillington Cl. ME2 .... 59 E4
Chillington St. ME14 .... 91 F6
Chilliwack Rd. ME3 .... 33 F5
Chilston Cl. TN4 .... 149 A5
Chilston Rd. Lenham ME17 .... 111 D5
Chilston Rd.
Royal Tunbridge Wells TN4 .... 149 A5
Chiltern Cl. Erith DA7 .... 8 E6
Chiltern Cl. Maidstone ME15 .... 92 F1
Chiltern Ct. 11 SE9 .... 6 A1
Chiltern Rd. DA11 .... 29 E5
Chiltern Way. TN9 .... 117 C4
Chiltern Wlk. TN2 .... 149 D4
Chilton Ct. ME8 .... 49 E1
Chilton Dr. ME3 .... 32 B3
Chimes The. ME1 .... 47 C5
Chinbrook Cres. SE12 .... 22 B5
Chinbrook Rd. SE12 .... 22 B5
Chippendale Cl. ME5 .... 61 F1
Chippendale Dr. ME17 .... 110 D6
Chipperfield Rd. BR5 .... 38 A7
Chipstead Cl. ME16 .... 91 D6
Chipstead La. TN13 .... 83 D5
Chipstead Park. TN13 .... 83 C5
Chipstead Place Gdns. TN13 .. 83 D5
Chipstead Rd. Gillingham ME8 .. 63 D4
Chipstead Sq. TN13 .... 83 D5
Chislehurst CE Prim Sch. BR7 . 23 C1
Chislehurst Cl. ME15 .... 107 F6
Chislehurst High St. BR7 .... 23 B2
Chislehurst Rd.
Bromley BR1 & BR7 .... 36 E8
Chislehurst Rd.
Orpington,Broom Hill BR6 .... 38 A2
Chislehurst Rd.Orpington,Petts Wood
BR5 & BR6 & BR7 .... 37 E4
Chislehurst Rd. Sidcup DA14 .... 24 A3
Chislehurst & Sidcup Gram Sch.
DA15 .... 24 B6
Chislehurst Sta. BR7 .... 37 A7
Chislet Wlk. ME8 .... 63 D5
Chiswell Sq. SE3 .... 5 B5
Chorleywood Cres. BR5 .... 38 A7
Christ Church Ave. Erith DA8 .... 8 E8
Christ Church Ave. 1
Royal Tunbridge Wells TN1 .... 149 A2
Christ Church CE Sch. SE18 .... 6 A6
Christ Church Cres. 2 DA12 .... 30 C8
Christ Church Rd. 3 DA12 .... 30 C8
Christ's Coll for Boys. SE3 .... 5 A6
Christchurch Ct. ME5 .... 48 C2
Christchurch House. 9 ME15 107 E5
Christchurch Rd. Dartford DA1 .... 9 C1
Christchurch Rd. Sidcup DA15 .. 23 F5
Christchurch Rd. Tilbury RM18 .. 13 A6
Christen Way. ME15 & ME17 .... 107 F3
Christian Fields Ave. DA12 .... 30 C4
Christie Cl. ME 62 B6
Christie Dr. 8 ME20 .... 74 F4
Christie House. DA6 .... 8 B2
Christies Ave. TN14 .... 53 B1
Christmas La. ME23 .... 17 F3
Christmas St. ME7 .... 48 E7
Christopher Cl. DA15 .... 6 F2
Chudleigh. DA14 .... 24 B4
Chulkhurst. TN27 .... 157 F1
Church Alley. 9 DA11 .... 13 B1
Church Ave. DA14 .... 24 B3
Church Cl. Brenchley TN12 .... 152 C8
Church Cl. Cliffe ME3 .... 16 B6
Church Cl. Mereworth ME18 .... 103 D8
Church Cotts. Cranbrook TN17 169 D5
Church Cotts. Crockenhill BR8 .. 39 D2
Church Cotts. Shoreham TN14 .. 69 A8
Church Cotts. St Michaels TN30 173 B3
Church Cres. ME17 .... 124 C8
Church Farm Cl. Crockenhill BR8 39 D3
Church Farm Cl.
Hoo St Werburgh ME3 .... 34 E4
Church Field. Dartford DA1 .... 26 D6
Church Field. Edenbridge TN8 . 112 D1
Church Field. Snodland ME6 .... 60 B1
Church Field Cotts. TN15 .... 87 A3
Church Fields. New Town ME19 . 89 B8
Church Fields. Sevenoaks TN13 . 83 F5
Church Gn. Marden TN12 .... 138 C6
Church Gn. Rochester ME2 .... 47 C8
Church Gn. Staplehurst TN12 .. 139 E2

Church Hill.
Boughton Monchelsea ME17 .. 123 B7
Church Hill. Chatham ME5 .... 48 C2
Church Hill. Crayford DA1 .... 8 E3
Church Hill. Cudham TN14 .... 66 C4
Church Hill. Dartford DA1 .... 26 D6
Church Hill. High Halden TN26 .. 173 E1
Church Hill. Leigh TN11 .... 115 F2
Church Hill. Orpington BR6 .... 38 A2
Church Hill. Plaxtol TN15 .... 101 E8
Church Hill. Stockbury ME9 .... 79 F7
Church Hill. Stone DA9 .... 10 E2
Church Hill. Woolwich SE18 .... 1 F3
Church Hill Wood. BR5 .... 37 F4
Church Hyde. SE18 .... 6 E8
Church La. Capel TN11 .... 134 F6
Church La. Chalk DA12 .... 31 C6
Church La.
Chartway Street ME17 .... 125 B8
Church La. Chatham ME4 .... 47 F6
Church La. Chislehurst BR7 .... 37 C8
Church La. East Peckham TN12 .. 119 F7
Church La. Frant TN3 .... 163 B4
Church La. Harrietsham ME17 .. 110 E6
Church La. Kemsing TN15 .... 70 B2
Church La. Keston Mark BR2 .... 36 E1
Church La. Maidstone ME14 .... 93 B4
Church La. Newington ME9 .... 65 B6
Church La. Stockbury ME9 .... 79 E8
Church La. Tonbridge TN9 .... 117 C3
Church La. Trottiscliffe ME19 .. 73 B5
Church La. West Farleigh ME15 105 D7
Church Manor Way. SE18 & SE2 .. 3 A2
Church Manorway. DA8 .... 4 D3
Church Meadow. TN12 .... 153 A7
Church Mews. ME8 .... 63 F8
Church Path. Gillingham ME7 .... 48 E6
Church Path. Northfleet DA11 .. 12 C1
Church Path. Stone DA9 .... 10 F1
Church Rd. Bexley, DA7 & DA6 .... 7 F4
Church Rd. Bexley,Welling DA16 ... 7 B5
Church Rd. Brasted TN16 .... 82 B3
Church Rd. Bromley BR1 & BR2 .. 36 A7
Church Rd. Chart Sutton ME17 .. 124 C8
Church Rd. Chelsfield BR6 .... 52 D4
Church Rd. Crockenhill BR8 .... 39 D2
Church Rd. Erith DA8 .... 4 D1
Church Rd. Goudhurst TN17 .... 167 F8
Church Rd. Grafty Green ME17 . 126 F7
Church Rd. Gravesend DA12 .... 30 C2
Church Rd. Harrietsham ME17 .. 110 E6
Church Rd. Hartley DA3 .... 43 A2
Church Rd. Henhurst DA13 .... 44 C8
Church Rd. Hildenborough TN11 116 D6
Church Rd. Hucking ME17 .... 79 E1
Church Rd. Keston BR2 .... 50 D3
Church Rd. Lamberhurst TN3 .. 166 C6
Church Rd. Low Street RM18 .... 13 E8
Church Rd.
Maidstone,Shepway ME15 .... 107 F7
Church Rd. Maidstone,Tovil ME15 91 E2
Church Rd. Offham ME18 .... 88 D8
Church Rd. Orpington BR6 .... 51 D5
Church Rd. Paddock Wood TN12 136 B6
Church Rd. Royal Tunbridge Wells
TN1 & TN4 .... 149 A3
Church Rd. Royal Tunbridge Wells,
Southborough TN4 .... 132 C2
Church Rd. Ryarsh ME19 .... 74 A3
Church Rd. Sandhurst Cross
TN18 .... 185 F4
Church Rd. Seal TN15 .... 84 F6
Church Rd. Sevenoaks Weald
TN14 .... 99 B3
Church Rd. Sidcup DA14 .... 24 A4
Church Rd. Stone DA9 .... 10 F2
Church Rd. Stone Street TN15 .. 85 E3
Church Rd. Sundridge TN14 .... 82 E2
Church Rd. Sutton at Hone DA4 .. 26 F1
Church Rd. Sutton at Hone DA4 .. 27 A2
Church Rd. Swanley Village BR8 . 40 D8
Church Rd. Swanscombe DA10 .. 11 F1
Church Rd. Tenterden TN30 .... 183 A7
Church Rd. Tilbury RM18 .... 12 F6
Church Rd. West Kingsdown TN15 55 E3
Church Rd. West Peckham ME18 103 A6
Church Row. Chislehurst BR7 .... 37 C8
Church Row. Plaxtol TN15 .... 101 E8
Church Row.
West Malling ME18 .... 103 B6
Church Row Mews. BR7 .... 23 C1
Church Sq. ME17 .... 111 D5
Church St.
Boughton Monchelsea ME17 .. 107 B2
Church St. Burham ME1 .... 60 F1
Church St. Chatham ME4 .... 48 A4
Church St. Cliffe ME3 .... 16 B5
Church St. Cowden TN8 .... 145 B5
Church St. Edenbridge TN8 .... 112 D1
Church St. Gillingham ME7 .... 48 E6
Church St. Gravesend DA11 .... 13 B1
Church St. Grays RM17 .... 12 C8
Church St. Hadlow TN11 .... 118 E3
Church St. Hoo St Werburgh ME3 34 E5
Church St. Loose ME15 .... 106 F5
Church St. Lower Higham ME3 .. 32 D7
Church St. Maidstone ME14 .... 92 A4
Church St. Maidstone,Tovil ME15 91 E2
Church St. Newham E16 .... 2 B5
Church St. Rochester ME1 .... 47 D4
Church St. Seal TN15 .... 85 A7
Church St. Shoreham TN14 .... 69 A8
Church St. Southfleet DA13 .... 29 A3
Church St. Teston ME18 .... 105 A8
Church St. Ticehurst TN5 .... 176 D1
Church St. Tonbridge TN9 .... 117 C2
Church Terr. ME5 .... 48 C2
Church View. Biddenden TN27 .. 157 F2

Church View. Swanley BR8 ...... 39 D6
Church Wlk. Dartford DA1 ...... 26 D5
Church Wlk. East Malling ME19 .... 90 A7
Church Wlk. Eynsford DA4 ...... 54 E7
Church Wlk. Gravesend DA12 .... 30 D8
Church Wlk. Hawkhurst TN18 .. 179 A1
Church Wlk. Headcorn TN27 ..... 141 C5
Churchbury Rd. SE9 .... 22 C8
Churchfield. ME19 .... 73 D3
Churchfield Rd. DA16 .... 7 A4
Churchfield Sch. SE2 .... 3 A2
Churchfields Terr. ME1 .... 47 B4
Churchill Ave. ME5 .... 62 A7
Churchill CE Prim Sch. TN16 .... 81 C2
Churchill Cl. DA1 .... 27 B7
Churchill Cotts. ME17 .... 108 F6
Churchill Ct. 4 BR6 .... 51 C5
Churchill House.
  Benenden TN18 .... 180 E6
Churchill House.
  Maidstone ME16 .... 91 B2
Churchill Pk. DA1 .... 10 A2
Churchill Rd. Gravesend DA11 .. 29 F7
Churchill Rd. Grays RM17 ...... 12 D8
Churchill Rd. Horton Kirby DA4 .. 41 C5
Churchill Rd. Newham E16 .... 1 C7
Churchill Sq. ME19 .... 89 A3
Churchill Way. BR1 .... 36 A7
Churchills Ropewalk. TN17 .... 167 E8
Churchside. DA13 .... 73 A8
Churchyard Cotts. TN3 .... 148 A8
Churn La. TN12 .... 137 A2
Chute Cl. ME8 .... 63 D4
Chyngton Cl. DA15 .... 23 F5
Cimba Wood. DA12 .... 30 E4
Cinder Hill La. TN11 .... 115 C1
Cinderhill Wood. TN12 .... 135 C2
Cinnabar Cl. ME5 .... 62 A1
Circle The. RM18 .... 13 A6
Circuit Rd. SE28 .... 3 A4
Circular Way. SE18 .... 6 A8
Cirrus Cres. DA12 .... 30 E3
City Way. ME1 .... 47 D2
Civic Sq. RM18 .... 13 A5
Civic Way. TN1 .... 149 A3
Clacket La. TN16 .... 96 A8
Claire House. ME16 .... 91 B5
Clandon Cl. BR1 .... 22 A2
Clandon Rd. ME5 .... 62 D2
Clanricarde Gdns. 1 TN1 ..... 149 A3
Clanricarde Rd. 2 TN1 .... 149 A3
Claphatch La. TN5 .... 176 A5
Clapper La. TN12 .... 139 D6
Clapton Ct. ME8 .... 63 D8
Clara Pl. SE18 .... 2 A2
Clare Ave. TN9 .... 116 F1
Clare Cnr. SE9 .... 23 B8
Clare Ct. BR7 .... 36 F8
Clare La. ME19 .... 89 E8
Clare Way. Bexley DA6 .... 7 E6
Clare Way. Sevenoaks TN13 ...... 99 C8
Claremont Cl. Newham E16 .... 2 A5
Claremont Cl. Orpington BR6 .... 51 A6
Claremont Cres. DA1 .... 8 E3
Claremont Cty Prim Sch. TN2 149 B2
Claremont Gdns. TN1 & TN2 .. 149 B2
Claremont Pl. 1
  Gravesend DA11 .... 30 B8
Claremont Pl. Iden Green TN17 180 C4
Claremont Rd. Bromley BR1 ..... 36 F5
Claremont Rd. Hextable BR8 .... 25 E1
Claremont Rd. Maidstone ME14 . 92 B5
Claremont Rd.
  Royal Tunbridge Wells TN1 .. 149 B2
Claremont St. E16 .... 2 A4
Claremont Way. 1 ME4 .... 47 F3
Clarence Ave.
  Bromley BR1 & BR2 .... 36 E5
Clarence Ave. Rochester ME1 ... 47 C4
Clarence Cres. DA14 .... 24 B5
Clarence Ct. ME14 .... 92 E4
Clarence Pl. DA11 .... 30 B7
Clarence Rd. Bexley DA6 .... 7 E3
Clarence Rd. Bromley BR1 & BR2 36 E6
Clarence Rd. Chatham ME4 .... 48 B2
Clarence Rd. Chislehurst SE9 ... 22 C6
Clarence Rd. 2 Grays RM17 .... 12 A8
Clarence Rd. Royal Tunbridge Wells
  TN1 & TN4 .... 149 A3
Clarence Rd. Sidcup DA14 .... 24 B4
Clarence Row. Gravesend DA11 . 30 B8
Clarence Row.
  Royal Tunbridge Wells TN1 .. 149 A3
Clarendon Cl. Maidstone ME14 .. 93 A4
Clarendon Cl. St Paul's Cray BR5 38 C6
Clarendon Gdns. Dartford DA2 .. 27 D8
Clarendon Gdns. Rochester ME2 33 A1
Clarendon Gdns.
  Royal Tunbridge Wells TN2 .. 149 A1
Clarendon Gr. BR5 .... 38 A5
Clarendon Gr. BR5 .... 38 A5
Clarendon Mews. DA5 .... 25 B7
Clarendon Path. BR5 .... 38 A6
Clarendon Pl.
  Joyden's Wood DA2 .... 25 E3
Clarendon Pl. Maidstone ME14 .. 92 A4
Clarendon Pl. Sevenoaks TN13 .. 84 A2
Clarendon Rd. Gravesend DA11 . 13 C1
Clarendon Rd. Sevenoaks TN13 . 84 A2
Clarendon Way.
  Royal Tunbridge Wells TN2 .. 149 A1
Clarendon Way.
  St Paul's Cray BR5 & BR7 ..... 37 F6
Clareville Rd. BR5 & BR6 .... 51 C8
Clarewood Dr. ME19 .... 89 E8
Claridge. TN4 .... 149 B6
Claridge Cl. ME7 .... 62 F4

Clark Cl. DA8 .... 9 A6
Clark Mews. ME20 .... 75 F1
Clarkbourne Dr. RM17 .... 12 D8
Clarkes Green Rd. TN15 .... 70 B5
Clarks La. TN14 .... 67 F7
Claston Cl. DA1 .... 8 E3
Clavadal Rd. TN12 .... 136 A7
Clavell Cl. ME8 .... 63 E4
Clay Cotts. TN17 .... 167 E8
Clay Hill Rd. TN3 .... 165 D6
Clay Wood Cl. BR6 .... 37 E2
Claybridge Rd. SE12 .... 22 C4
Clayfarm Rd. SE9 .... 23 C6
Claygate. ME15 .... 92 D1
Claygate Cross. TN15 .... 87 A3
Claygate La. TN11 .... 101 F4
Claygate Rd. TN12 .... 121 B2
Clayhill. TN17 .... 167 D8
Clayhill Cres. SE12 & SE9 ...... 22 D4
Claymill House. 2 SE18 .... 2 C1
Clayton Cl. 3 E6 .... 1 F7
Clayton Croft Rd. DA2 .... 26 A6
Clayton's La. TN3 .... 146 E2
Claytonville Terr. DA17 .... 4 A2
Claywood La. DA13 & DA2 ..... 28 D5
Clayworth Cl. DA15 .... 7 B1
Cleanthus Cl. SE18 .... 6 B6
Cleanthus Rd. SE18 .... 6 B6
Clearway. TN15 .... 73 A1
Clearways Bsns Est. TN15 .... 55 E3
Cleave Ave. BR6 .... 51 E4
Cleave Rd. ME7 .... 48 E3
Cleavers. TN17 .... 170 A8
Cleavers Cl. TN17 .... 170 A8
Cleavesland. ME18 .... 120 E5
Cleeve Ct. 2 DA1 .... 9 D1
Cleeve Park Gdns. DA14 .... 24 B6
Cleeve Park Sch. DA14 .... 24 C5
Clegg House. SE3 .... 5 B6
Clematis Ave. ME8 .... 63 B5
Clement Cl. ME16 .... 91 D5
Clement St. ME8 .... 26 E2
Clements Ave. E16 .... 1 A6
Clenches Farm La. TN13 .... 84 A1
Clenches Farm Rd. TN13 .... 84 A1
Clendon Way. SE18 .... 2 D2
Clerks Field. TN27 .... 141 D5
Clermont Cl. ME7 .... 63 A4
Cleve Rd. DA14 .... 24 D5
Cleveland. TN2 .... 149 D4
Cleveland House.
  Maidstone ME16 .... 91 B2
Cleveland House.
  Northfleet DA11 .... 12 D1
Cleveland Rd. Bexley DA16 .... 6 F5
Cleveland Rd. Gillingham ME7 .. 48 D6
Clevely Cl. SE7 .... 1 D2
Cleves Rd. TN14 .... 69 E2
Clewer House. 8 SE2 .... 3 D4
Clewson Rise. ME14 .... 92 B8
Cliff Hill. ME17 .... 107 D4
Cliff Hill Rd. ME17 .... 107 C4
Cliffe Rd. ME2 .... 33 B2
Cliffe Woods Cty Prim Fst Sch.
  ME3 .... 33 C8
Clifford Ave. BR7 .... 22 F2
Clifton Cl. Maidstone ME14 ..... 92 B5
Clifton Cl. 8 Orpington BR6 .... 51 C5
Clifton Cl. Rochester ME2 .... 46 F7
Clifton Cotts. TN1 .... 149 D8
Clifton Ct. DA1 .... 8 E1
Clifton Marine Par. DA11 .... 12 F1
Clifton Pl. TN1 .... 149 B2
Clifton Rd. Bexley DA16 .... 7 C4
Clifton Rd. Gillingham ME7 ..... 48 C7
Clifton Rd. Gravesend DA11 .... 13 A1
Clifton Rd.
  Royal Tunbridge Wells TN1 .. 149 C7
Clifton Rd. Sidcup DA14 .... 23 E4
Cliftonville Ct. SE12 .... 22 A7
Clinch Cl. 15 E16 .... 1 A8
Clinch St. ME3 .... 18 A4
Clinton Ave. Bexley DA16 .... 7 A3
Clinton Ave. Rochester ME2 .... 46 E8
Clinton Cl. ME17 .... 106 B3
Clinton La. TN8 .... 113 E3
Clipper Bvd. DA9 .... 10 E3
Clipper Bvd W. DA9 .... 10 D4
Clipper Cl. ME2 .... 47 E7
Clipper Cres. DA12 .... 30 F4
Clipper Ct. ME2 .... 47 E7
Clive Ave. DA1 .... 8 F1
Clive House. ME20 .... 90 F8
Clive Rd. Erith DA17 .... 4 B2
Clive Rd. Gravesend DA11 .... 13 B1
Clive Rd. Rochester ME1 .... 47 C3
Clock House La. TN13 .... 84 A4
Clock Tower Mews. ME6 .... 60 A1
Clockhouse. TN2 .... 149 F6
Cloisterham Rd. ME1 .... 61 D7
Cloisters Ave. BR1 & BR2 .... 36 F4
Cloisters Ct. DA7 .... 8 B4
Cloisters The. 1 Dartford DA1 ... 9 E1
Cloisters The. Lenham ME17 .. 111 C5
Cloonmore Ave. BR6 .... 51 F6
Close The. Addington ME19 ..... 73 C2
Close The. Birling ME19 .... 74 B5
Close The. Borough Green TN15 87 A8
Close The. Groombridge TN3 . 161 C6
Close The. Ightham TN15 .... 86 D6
Close The. New Barn DA3 .... 43 B7
Close The. Orpington BR5 .... 37 F2
Close The. Rochester ME1 .... 47 C4
Close The. Sevenoaks TN13 ..... 83 E3
Close The. Sidcup DA14 .... 24 B3

Close The. 1
  Sidcup,Old Bexley DA5 .... 25 A8
Close The. Wilmington DA2 ..... 26 D5
Cloth Hall Gdns. TN27 .... 158 A2
Clothier House. SE7 .... 1 E1
Clothworkers Rd. SE18 .... 6 D7
Cloudesley Cl. ME1 .... 47 B1
Cloudesley Rd. Bexley DA7 .... 7 F6
Cloudesley Rd. Erith DA8 .... 8 F6
Clovelly Rd. DA7 .... 7 E8
Clovelly Way. BR6 .... 37 F3
Clover Bank View. ME5 .... 62 B6
Clover Ct. 11 RM17 .... 12 D8
Clover Rd. ME3 .... 34 E3
Clover St. ME4 .... 47 F4
Clover Wlk. 13 TN8 .... 112 D3
Cloverdale Gdns. DA15 .... 6 F1
Clovers The. DA11 .... 29 E4
Club Gardens Rd. BR2 .... 36 A2
Clyde Rd. TN10 .... 117 C6
Clydesdale House. DA18 .... 3 E4
Clydon Cl. DA8 .... 8 E8
Coach Dr The. DA13 .... 72 E7
Coach & Horses Pas. 15 TN2 .. 149 A2
Coach La. Egerton TN27 .... 127 E6
Coach Rd. Ightham Common TN15 86 B2
Coalhouse Fort. RM18 .... 14 E6
Coastguard Cotts. Cliffe ME3 .. 15 C8
Coastguard Cotts. Grain ME3 .. 21 B5
Coates Hill Rd. BR1 .... 37 A7
Cob Cl. TN15 .... 86 C6
Cob Dr. DA12 .... 31 E3
Cobb Cl. ME2 .... 46 D8
Cobbett Cl. ME19 .... 89 F8
Cobbett Rd. SE9 .... 5 E4
Cobbett's Ride. TN2 .... 148 F1
Cobbs Cl. Paddock Wood TN12 135 F6
Cobbs Cl. Wateringbury ME18 .. 104 E7
Cobden Ct. 9 SE28 .... 3 C5
Cobden Rd. Orpington BR6 ...... 51 D6
Cobden Rd. Sevenoaks TN13 ... 84 C4
Cobdown Cl. ME20 .... 75 C2
Cobfield. ME17 .... 108 A1
Cobham Cl. Bromley BR2 .... 36 E2
Cobham Cl. Maidstone ME16 ... 91 E4
Cobham Cl. Rochester ME2 ...... 46 E7
Cobham Cl. 1 Sidcup DA16 .... 7 B1
Cobham Cty Prim Sch. DA12 .... 45 A5
Cobham Hall. DA12 .... 45 C6
Cobham House. 4 DA8 .... 8 F7
Cobham Pl. DA6 .... 7 D2
Cobham Terr. DA9 .... 11 B1
Cobhambury Rd. DA12 & DA13 . 45 B4
Cobhams. TN3 .... 148 A8
Cobland Rd. SE12 .... 22 C4
Cobsdene. DA12 .... 30 D2
Cobtree Cl. ME5 .... 62 C8
Cobtree Rd. ME17 .... 106 C3
Cobtree Wharf. ME20 .... 76 C2
Cockerhurst Rd. TN14 .... 53 E2
Cockmannings La. BR5 .... 38 E1
Cockmannings Rd. BR5 .... 38 D2
Cockmount La. TN5 .... 174 F5
Cockpit The. TN12 .... 138 C5
Cocksett Ave. BR6 .... 51 E4
Cocksure La. DA14 .... 25 A4
Codrington Cres. DA12 .... 30 D3
Codrington Gdns. DA12 .... 30 D3
Cogate Rd. TN12 .... 135 E6
Colchester Cl. ME5 .... 62 A7
Cold Arbor Rd. TN13 .... 83 D3
Cold Blow Cres. DA5 .... 25 D7
Cold Harbour La. ME9 .... 65 F6
Coldbridge La. TN27 .... 127 B5
Coldharbour La. Aylesford ME20 76 A1
Coldharbour La.
  Hildenborough TN11 .... 116 E7
Coldharbour La. Hucking ME14 . 79 B1
Coldharbour La. Rainham RM13 . 4 F6
Coldharbour Rd.
  Iden Green TN17 .... 180 B4
Coldharbour Rd. Northfleet DA11 29 F5
Coldharbour Rd.
  White Post TN11 .... 146 A3
Coldharbour Sports Ctr. SE9 .... 23 A6
Coldred Rd. ME15 .... 107 F4
Coldrum La. ME19 .... 73 C6
Cole Cl. SE28 .... 3 B5
Cole Terr. ME17 .... 111 C4
Colebrook Ind Est. TN2 .... 133 E1
Colebrook Rd. TN4 .... 149 C8
Colebrooke Ct. DA14 .... 24 B4
Colegate Dr. ME14 .... 93 C4
Coleman Rd. DA17 .... 4 A2
Colemans Heath. SE9 .... 23 B5
Colepits Wood Rd. SE9 .... 6 D2
Coleraine Rd. 1 SE3 .... 5 A8
Coleridge Cl. 4 ME20 .... 74 F4
Coleridge Rd. Dartford DA1 ..... 10 B3
Coleridge Rd. Tilbury RM18 .... 13 C5
Coleridge Way. BR6 .... 38 A3
Coles Ct. TN2 .... 149 C3
Coles La. TN16 .... 82 C4
Coleshall Cl. ME15 .... 107 F6
Colets Orch. TN14 .... 69 B3
Colewood Dr. ME2 .... 46 B8
Colfe's Prep Sch. SE12 .... 5 B1
Colin Blythe Rd. TN10 .... 117 C5
Colin Chapman Way. SE9 .... 55 E6
Colin Cl. DA2 .... 10 B1
Coll of Guidance Studies. BR8 . 25 F1
College Ave. Gillingham ME7 ... 48 B4
College Ave. Maidstone ME15 ... 91 F3
College Ave. Tonbridge TN9 .. 133 A7

College Cotts. ME16 .... 91 F3
College Ct. 5 ME15 .... 92 A3
College Dr. TN2 .... 149 D4
College Gn. BR1 .... 36 B3
College Rd. Bromley BR1 .... 22 A1
College Rd. Chatham ME4 .... 48 A7
College Rd. Hextable BR8 .... 25 F1
College Rd. Maidstone ME15 ... 91 F2
College Rd. New Hythe ME20 ... 75 D3
College Rd. Northfleet DA11 ... 12 B2
College View. SE9 .... 22 D7
College Yd. ME1 .... 47 C6
Coller Cres. DA2 .... 27 E3
Collet Rd. TN14 .... 69 E2
Collet Wlk. ME8 .... 63 D4
Collier Cl. E16 .... 2 B6
Collier Street CE Prim Sch.
  TN12 .... 121 D1
Colliers' Green CE Prim Sch.
  TN17 .... 154 F2
Colliers Wood. BR2 .... 50 D5
Collindale Ave. Erith DA8 .... 8 B8
Collindale Ave. Sidcup DA15 .... 24 A7
Collings Wlk. ME8 .... 63 D4
Collington Cl. DA11 .... 29 E8
Collington House. SE7 .... 5 B8
Collington Terr. ME15 .... 107 E4
Collingwood House. DA9 .... 11 D2
Collingwood Ind Ctr. ME17 ... 108 E2
Collingwood Rd. ME20 .... 76 C7
Collis St. ME7 .... 47 A8
Collison Pl. TN30 .... 183 D7
Colman House. 2 ME14 .... 92 A4
Colman Rd. E16 .... 1 C7
Colne Rd. TN10 .... 117 B5
Colney Rd. DA1 .... 9 F1
Colonade The. 14 TN18 .... 179 A2
Colonel's Way. TN4 .... 133 A2
Coltness Cres. SE2 .... 3 B1
Colts Hill Pl. TN12 .... 135 B5
Coltsfoot La. TN17 .... 155 F2
Coltsfoot Dr. ME14 .... 92 F4
Coltstead. DA3 .... 56 E7
Columbia Wharf Rd. RM17 ..... 12 A8
Columbine Ave. E6 .... 1 E8
Columbine Cl. East Malling ME19 74 F1
Columbine Cl. Rochester ME2 .. 46 E7
Columbine Rd. East Malling ME19 89 F8
Columbine Rd. Rochester ME2 . 46 E7
Colverne Cl. DA8 .... 8 F8
Colview Ct. SE9 .... 22 D7
Colyer Cl. SE9 .... 23 B6
Colyer House. SE2 .... 3 D1
Colyer Rd. DA11 .... 29 D6
Colyers Cl. DA8 .... 8 D6
Colyers La. DA8 .... 8 D6
Colyers Prim Sch. DA7 .... 8 D6
Colyton Cl. ME16 .... 7 D6
Combe Bank Cotts. TN14 .... 82 D5
Combe Bank Sch. TN14 .... 82 E4
Combedale Rd. SE10 .... 1 A1
Combeside. SE18 .... 6 F7
Combwell Cres. SE2 .... 3 A3
Comfrey Ct. RM17 .... 12 D8
Command Rd. ME14 .... 91 F8
Commercial Pl. DA11 .... 13 C1
Commercial Rd.
  Paddock Wood TN12 .... 135 F6
Commercial Rd. Rochester ME2 . 47 A7
Commercial Rd.
  Royal Tunbridge Wells TN1 . 149 B5
Commercial Rd. Tonbridge TN9 133 C8
Commissioner's Rd. ME2 .... 47 C8
Commodore Rd. ME14 .... 92 C5
Common La. Heath Side DA2 ... 26 A4
Common Rd. Burham ME1 ...... 61 B1
Common Rd. Cliffe Woods ME3 . 33 B6
Common Rd. Hadlow TN11 .... 102 E2
Common Rd.
  Ightham Common TN15 ...... 86 B3
Common Rd. Sissinghurst TN17 170 A8
Common The. ME1 .... 47 C6
Common View. TN4 .... 148 C4
Common Wlk. ME3 .... 16 D6
Commonside. BR2 .... 50 C6
Commonwealth House. 5
  RM18 .... 13 A5
Commonwealth Way. SE2 .... 3 C1
Commority Rd. DA13 .... 73 B8
Comp La. TN15 .... 87 E6
Compass Cl. ME1 .... 47 C1
Compass Ctr. ME4 .... 48 B8
Compasses Rd. TN12 .... 115 B2
Compasses The. TN11 .... 115 B2
Compton Cl. ME5 .... 62 D2
Compton Pl. DA8 .... 8 F8
Concord Ave. ME5 .... 61 E5
Concord Cl. Paddock Wood TN12 135 E7
Concord Cl.
  Royal Tunbridge Wells TN2 . 149 C4
Concorde Dr. E6 .... 1 F8
Concrete Cotts. ME3 .... 15 E4
Condover Cres. SE18 .... 6 B7
Conduit Rd. SE18 .... 2 B1
Coneyburrow Rd. TN2 .... 149 E5
Conference Rd. SE2 .... 3 C2
Conghurst La. TN18 .... 185 B6
Congleton Gr. SE18 .... 2 C1
Congo Rd. SE18 .... 2 D1
Congress Rd. SE2 .... 3 C2
Congreve Rd. SE9 .... 5 F4
Conifer Ave. 6 E16 .... 2 B7
Conifer Cl. BR6 .... 51 D6
Conifer Dr.
  Culverstone Green DA13 ...... 57 F2

Conifer Way. BR8 .... 39 C8
Coniscliffe Cl. BR7 .... 37 A8
Coniston Ave. Bexley DA16 .... 6 E4
Coniston Ave.
  Royal Tunbridge Wells TN4 . 148 E5
Coniston Cl. Bexley DA7 .... 8 C6
Coniston Cl. Dartford DA1 ...... 26 B7
Coniston Cl. Erith DA8 .... 8 E7
Coniston Cl. Gillingham ME7 ... 49 A6
Coniston Rd. DA7 .... 8 C6
Connaught Br. E16 .... 1 D6
Connaught Cl. ME15 .... 107 F4
Connaught Mews. Chatham ME4 48 C4
Connaught Mews. Chatham ME4 2 A1
Connaught Rd. Chatham ME4 .. 48 C2
Connaught Rd. Gillingham ME7 . 48 D5
Connaught Rd.
  Newham,Custom House E16 ... 1 C6
Connaught Rd.
  Newham,Silvertown E16 .... 1 D5
Connaught Rd. Woolwich SE18 .. 2 B1
Connaught Way. TN4 .... 148 F5
Conquest Ind Est. ME2 .... 47 A6
Conrad Cl. ME8 .... 63 D4
Consort Cl. ME14 .... 92 B5
Constable Rd. Northfleet DA11 . 29 E7
Constable Rd. Tonbridge TN10 117 E5
Constance St. E16 .... 1 F5
Constitution Hill. Chatham ME4 . 48 B3
Constitution Hill.
  Gravesend DA12 .... 30 C7
Constitution Hill. Snodland ME6 75 A8
Constitution Hill Rd. TN4 ...... 132 F1
Constitution Rise. SE18 .... 6 A6
Constitutional Hill Rd. TN4 ... 132 F1
Consul Gdns. BR8 .... 26 A1
Contessa Cl. BR6 .... 51 E5
Convalescent La. TN17 .... 155 F2
Convent Prep Sch. DA12 .... 30 C6
Conway Cl. ME2 .... 32 E1
Conway Gdns. RM17 .... 12 B7
Conway Inf & Jun Sch. SE18 ..... 2 F2
Conway Mews. ME7 .... 48 A6
Conway Rd. Maidstone ME16 .. 91 C6
Conway Rd. Woolwich SE18 ...... 2 E2
Conyerd Rd. TN15 .... 86 F6
Conyers Wlk. ME8 .... 63 D4
Cooden Cl. BR1 .... 22 B1
Cook Cl. ME5 .... 62 C6
Cook Sq. DA8 .... 8 F7
Cookham Dene Cl. BR7 .... 37 D8
Cookham Hill. ME1 .... 47 A2
Cookham Rd. BR8 .... 39 A8
Cookham Wood Rd. ME1 .... 61 B8
Cookhill Rd. SE2 .... 3 B3
Coolfin Rd. E16 .... 1 B7
Cooling Cl. ME14 .... 92 C6
Cooling Comm. ME3 .... 33 D8
Cooling Rd. Cliffe ME3 .... 16 C4
Cooling Rd. Cooling ME3 .... 16 E4
Cooling Rd. High Halstow ME23 17 C3
Cooling Rd. Rochester ME2 ..... 33 B2
Cooling St. ME3 .... 16 D1
Coomb Field. TN8 .... 128 C8
Coombe Ave. TN14 .... 84 B7
Coombe Cl. Chatham ME5 .... 62 B3
Coombe Cl. Snodland ME6 ...... 75 A7
Coombe Farm La. ME18 .... 18 E6
Coombe La. TN30 .... 183 A7
Coombe Lands. TN30 .... 189 D4
Coombe Lea. BR1 .... 36 E6
Coombe Lodge. SE7 .... 5 C8
Coombe Rd. Gravesend DA12 .. 30 C4
Coombe Rd.
  Hoo St Werburgh ME3 .... 34 E5
Coombe Rd. Maidstone ME15 .. 91 F2
Coombe Rd. Otford TN14 .... 69 C4
Coombfield Dr. DA2 .... 27 D4
Cooper Cl. DA9 .... 10 F2
Cooper Ct. SE18 .... 6 B8
Cooper Rd. Chatham ME5 .... 62 B3
Cooper Rd. Snodland ME6 .... 74 F6
Cooper Shaw Rd. RM18 .... 13 E7
Cooper's Rd. DA11 .... 29 F7
Coopers Cl. DA4 .... 41 D8
Coopers Cotts. DA2 .... 27 A4
Coopers La. Lewisham SE12 .... 22 B6
Coopers La.
  Poundsbridge TN11 & TN3 . 147 C7
Coopers' Lane Prim Sch. SE12 22 B6
Coopers Sch. BR7 .... 37 C8
Coote Rd. DA7 .... 7 F6
Copenhagen Rd. ME7 .... 48 C4
Copley Dene. BR1 .... 36 D8
Coppards La. TN31 .... 187 D1
Copper Beech Cl.
  Gravesend DA12 .... 30 D8
Copper Beech Cl. 7
  Orpington BR5 .... 38 C4
Copper La. TN12 .... 138 E5
Copper Tree Ct. ME15 .... 107 A5
Copper Tree Wlk. ME5 .... 62 C1
Copperfield Cl. Chalk DA12 .... 31 A7
Copperfield Cl. Erith SE28 .... 3 C7
Copperfield Cres. ME2 .... 32 C2
Copperfield Dr. DA1 .... 8 E2
Copperfield Rd. ME7 .... 108 E4
Copperfield Rd. ME1 .... 47 C2
Copperfield Wlk. 6 E16 .... 2 B7
Copperfields. 2 Dartford DA1 ... 9 E1
Copperfields. Kemsing TN15 ... 69 F2
Copperfields Cl. TN15 .... 69 F2
Copperfields Orch. TN15 .... 69 F2
Copperfields The. ME1 .... 47 B4

Copperfields Wlk. TN15 .... 69 F2
Coppergate. ME7 .... 62 F5
Coppergate Cl. BR1 .... 36 B8
Copperhouse La. ME7 .... 49 B6
Copperhouse Rd. ME2 .... 46 C7
Coppice Ct. ME7 .... 63 B4
Coppice Rd. ME5 .... 62 C2
Coppice The. Aylesford ME20 ..... 75 E1
Coppice The. Bitchet Green TN15 85 D1
Coppice The. Pembury TN2 ...... 150 D7
Coppice The. Vigo Village DA13 .. 73 B8
Coppice View. ME4 .... 92 E6
Copping's Rd. TN11 .... 115 C4
Copse Bank. TN15 .... 84 F7
Copse Cl. SE7 .... 5 B8
Copse Rd. TN11 .... 116 E4
Copse Side. DA3 .... 42 E6
Copse The. ME3 .... 34 E3
Copsehill. ME2 .... 74 E2
Copsewood Way. ME15 .... 93 A3
Copt Hall. TN18 .... 187 D3
Copt Hall Rd.
  Ightham Common TN15 .... 86 A4
Copt Hall Rd. Sole Street DA13 ... 44 B5
Coptefield Dr. DA17 .... 3 E3
Copthall Ave. TN18 .... 179 A1
Copthorne Ave. BR2 .... 50 F8
Coraline Wlk. 4 SE2 .... 3 C4
Corbyland Rd. DA15 .... 23 E7
Corbylands Rd. DA15 .... 23 E8
Cordelia Cres. ME1 .... 46 F2
Corelli Rd. SE18 & SE3 .... 5 E6
Corinthian Ct. ME3 .... 21 B5
Corinthian Manorway. DA8 .... 4 D2
Corinthian Rd. DA8 .... 4 D2
Cork House. BR5 .... 38 B6
Cork La. TN12 .... 155 D8
Cork St. ME20 .... 75 F6
Corkwell St. ME4 .... 47 E3
Cormorant Cl. ME2 .... 46 C7
Corn Mill Dr. BR6 .... 38 A2
Cornel House. 4 DA15 .... 24 A5
Cornelia Pl. 8 E8
Cornell Cl. DA14 .... 24 E2
Corner Farm Rd. TN12 .... 139 E4
Corner Gn. SE3 .... 5 A5
Cornfield Way. TN10 .... 117 D6
Cornflower Cl. ME14 .... 92 E4
Cornford Cl. Hayes BR2 .... 36 A4
Cornford Cl. Pembury TN2 ...... 150 B6
Cornford Pk. TN2 .... 150 C6
Cornforth Cl. TN12 .... 139 F4
Cornwall Ave. DA16 .... 6 F4
Cornwall Cl. ME15 .... 107 E7
Cornwall Cres. ME1 .... 60 D4
Cornwall Dr. BR5 .... 24 C1
Cornwall Rd. Dartford DA1 .... 9 F4
Cornwall Rd. Gillingham ME7 ... 48 D6
Cornwall Rd. Rochester ME1 ..... 47 C3
Cornwallis Ave. Chatham ME4 ... 47 E1
Cornwallis Ave. Gillingham ME8 . 49 A4
Cornwallis Ave. Linton ME17 ... 122 E8
Cornwallis Ave. Sidcup DA15 .... 23 D6
Cornwallis Ave. Tonbridge TN10 117 F4
Cornwallis Cl. DA8 .... 8 F8
Cornwallis Cotts. ME17 .... 106 E2
Cornwallis Rd. Maidstone ME16 .. 91 D4
Cornwallis Sch The. ME15 ...... 106 F2
Cornwallis Wlk. SE9 .... 5 F4
Cornwell Ave. DA12 .... 30 C5
Corona Rd. SE12 .... 22 A8
Corona Terr. ME6 .... 74 F6
Coronation Cl. DA5 .... 7 E1
Coronation Cotts.
  Berner's Hill TN5 .... 176 F2
Coronation Cotts. Stoke ME3 .... 19 A3
Coronation Ct. DA8 .... 8 D7
Coronation Flats. 2 ME4 .... 47 F3
Coronation Rd. Chatham ME5 .... 48 C2
Coronation Rd. Grain ME3 .... 21 B5
Corporation Rd. ME7 .... 48 D7
Corporation St. ME1 .... 47 C6
Corral Cl. ME5 .... 48 D2
Corrall Almshouses. 4 ME15 ... 92 A3
Corrance Gn. ME15 .... 107 A8
Correnden Rd. TN11 .... 117 A3
Corseley Rd. TN3 .... 161 B5
Cossack St. ME1 .... 47 D3
Cossington Rd. ME5 .... 62 B1
Costells Meadow. TN16 .... 81 D1
Cot La. TN27 .... 158 B3
Cotleigh Ave. DA5 .... 24 D6
Cotman Way. TN12 .... 119 E6
Cotman's Ash La. TN15 .... 70 D4
Cotmandene Cres. ME5 .... 38 A7
Coton Rd. DA16 .... 7 A4
Cotswold Cl. DA7 .... 8 E5
Cotswold Gdns. ME15 .... 93 A2
Cotswold Rd. DA11 .... 29 E5
Cotswold Rise. BR6 .... 37 F3
Cottage Ave. BR2 .... 36 E1
Cottage Field Cl. DA5 & DA14 .. 24 C7
Cottage Rd. ME4 .... 47 F6
Cottall Ave. ME4 .... 47 F2
Cottenham Cl. ME19 .... 89 F7
Cotton La. DA9 .... 10 D2
Coulman St. ME7 .... 48 D5
Coulter House. DA9 .... 11 C2
Coulters Cl. ME14 .... 92 D5
Coulton Ave. DA11 .... 29 E7
Council Ave. DA11 .... 12 C1
Council Cotts. Coxheath ME15 .. 106 A4
Council Cotts. Key's Green TN12151 C4

Council Houses. TN15 .... 102 A8
Countess of Thanet's Almshouses.
  TN8 .... 144 F3
County Gate. BR7 .... 23 C5
County Gr. ME19 .... 89 B8
County Rd. Maidstone ME14 ..... 92 A6
County Rd. Newham E6 .... 2 B8
Coupland Pl. SE18 .... 2 C1
Course The. SE9 .... 23 A5
Court Ave. DA17 .... 3 F1
Court Broomes. ME17 .... 125 C8
Court Cres. BR8 .... 39 E5
Court Dr. ME16 .... 91 D4
Court Farm Rd. SE9 .... 22 E5
Court La. Detling ME14 .... 78 C5
Court La. Hadlow TN11 .... 119 B7
Court Lane Pl. TN11 .... 118 F8
Court Lodge. DA17 .... 4 A1
Court Lodge Cotts.
  East Farleigh ME15 .... 106 A7
Court Lodge Cotts.
  Horton Kirby DA4 .... 41 C6
Court Lodge Rd. ME7 .... 48 F6
Court Meadow. Wateringbury ME8 . 49 B2
Court Meadow. Wrotham TN15 .. 71 F3
Court Rd. Burham ME1 .... 75 E8
Court Rd. Eltham SE9 .... 22 F7
Court Rd. Lane End DA2 .... 27 E3
Court Rd.
  Royal Tunbridge Wells TN4 ... 148 F4
Court Road (Orpington By-Pass).
  Chelsfield BR6 & TN14 .... 52 D5
Court Road (Orpington By-Pass).
  Orpington BR5 & BR6 .... 38 B2
Court St. BR1 .... 36 A7
Court Yd. SE9 .... 5 F1
Courtaulds Cl. SE28 .... 3 A5
Courtenay Rd. ME15 .... 91 F2
Courteney Rd. ME8 .... 63 B8
Courtenwell. TN3 .... 147 E4
Courtfield Ave. ME5 .... 62 B3
Courthope. TN12 .... 136 A6
Courthope Ave. TN5 .... 174 F4
Courtland Gr. SE28 .... 3 D6
Courtlands. Hilden Park TN11 ... 117 A3
Courtlands Ave. SE12 .... 5 B2
Courtlands Cl. ME18 .... 105 A8
Courtlands Farm. TN17 .... 169 A3
Courtleet Dr. DA7 .... 8 B6
Courtwood Dr. TN13 .... 84 A3
Courtyard Gdns. TN15 .... 71 F3
Courtyard The. ME7 .... 63 A8
Cousley Wood Rd. TN5 .... 175 C2
Couthurst Rd. SE3 .... 5 B7
Coutts Ave. DA12 .... 31 E4
Coutts House. SE7 .... 5 C8
Covelees Wall. E6 .... 2 A7
Coventry Cl. 9 Newham E6 .... 1 A7
Coventry Rd. Rochester ME2 .... 46 D6
Coventry Rd. TN10 .... 117 D5
Coverdale Ave. ME15 .... 107 D6
Coverdale Cl. ME5 .... 62 B7
Covert The. Chatham ME5 .... 62 B7
Covert The. Orpington BR5 & BR6 37 E3
Covert The. Vigo Village DA13 .... 72 F2
Covet Wood Cl. BR5 .... 37 F3
Covey Hall Rd. ME6 .... 60 A1
Cow La. TN8 .... 129 D1
Cow Leaze. E6 .... 2 A7
Cowan Cl. E6 .... 1 E8
Cowbeck Cl. ME8 .... 63 D6
Cowden Cl. TN18 .... 184 E8
Cowden Cross. TN8 .... 145 C7
Cowden Mews. TN8 .... 145 A5
Cowden Rd. Maidstone ME14 .... 92 C5
Cowden Rd. Orpington BR6 ..... 37 F2
Cowden Sta. TN8 .... 145 D8
Cowdrey Cl. Maidstone ME16 .... 91 B2
Cowdrey Rd. Rochester ME1 .... 47 B2
Cowdrey Ct. DA1 .... 26 B8
Cowen House. 4 SE18 .... 6 B8
Cowley Ave. DA9 .... 11 A2
Cowper Ave. RM18 .... 13 B6
Cowper Cl. Bexley DA16 .... 7 A2
Cowper Cl. Bromley BR2 .... 36 D5
Cowper Rd. Bromley BR2 .... 36 D5
Cowper Rd. Erith DA17 .... 4 A1
Cowper Rd. Gillingham ME7 ..... 48 D3
Cowstead Rd. ME9 .... 64 D2
Cox St. ME14 .... 78 E6
Cox's Cl. ME6 .... 74 F8
Coxheath Cty Prim Sch. ME17 106 C3
Coxmount Rd. SE7 .... 1 D1
Coxwell Rd. SE18 .... 2 D1
Cozenton Cl. ME8 .... 49 E1
Crabbs Croft Cl. 7 BR6 .... 51 C5
Crabtree Cl. ME18 & ME19 ...... 89 A2
Crabtree Manorway. Erith DA17 .. 4 C3
Crabtree Manorway. Erith DA17 .. 4 C5
Crabtree Rd. ME8 .... 63 D8
Craddock Way. ME8 .... 63 D5
Cradducks La. TN12 .... 140 B4
Cradles Rd. ME9 .... 64 C2
Cradley Rd. SE9 .... 23 D7
Cragie Wlk. ME8 .... 63 E4
Craigerne Rd. SE3 & SE7 .... 5 B7
Craigholm. SE18 .... 6 A6
Craigton Rd. SE9 .... 5 F3
Crampton's Rd. TN14 .... 84 B7
Cramptons. TN17 .... 169 F8
Cranborne Ave. ME15 .... 92 C1
Cranbourne Ave. ME15 .... 107 B8
Cranbrook CE Prim Sch. TN17 169 C3
Cranbrook Cl. Gillingham ME8 ... 49 C3
Cranbrook Cl. Hayes BR2 .... 36 A3
Cranbrook Cl. Maidstone ME15 107 F7

Cranbrook House. 1 DA8 .... 8 F7
Cranbrook Point. E16 .... 1 B5
Cranbrook Rd. Benenden TN17 179 F8
Cranbrook Rd. Erith DA7 .... 7 F6
Cranbrook Rd.
  Fosten Green TN27 & TN17 ... 171 C6
Cranbrook Rd. Gill's Green TN18178 F4
Cranbrook Rd. Goudhurst TN17 168 A8
Cranbrook Rd.
  Knox Bridge TN12 & TN17 .... 155 F7
Cranbrook Rd.
  Parkgate TN27 & TN30 .... 172 C1
Cranbrook Rd. Tenterden TN30 182 E7
Cranbrook Sch. TN17 .... 169 D5
Crandalls. TN11 .... 115 F1
Crane House. 11 TN18 .... 178 F2
Crane House Gdns. 10 TN18 ... 178 F2
Crane La. Cranbrook TN17 ...... 169 D4
Crane La. Cranbrook TN17 ...... 169 D5
Cranford Cl. ME8 .... 49 D1
Cranford Rd. Dartford DA1 ...... 26 E7
Cranford Rd. Tonbridge TN10 ... 118 A5
Cranham Sq. TN12 .... 138 C5
Cranleigh Cl. Bexley DA5 .... 8 B1
Cranleigh Cl. Orpington BR6 .... 52 A7
Cranleigh Dr. BR8 .... 39 E5
Cranleigh Gdns. Chatham ME1 .. 47 D3
Cranleigh Gdns. Maidstone ME16 91 C7
Cranley Par. SE9 .... 22 E4
Cranley Rd. E13 .... 1 B8
Cranmer Ct. ME15 .... 107 B8
Cranmer Rd. TN13 .... 83 E4
Cranmore Rd. BR7 & SE9 .... 22 F3
Cranwell Rd. TN4 .... 148 C4
Crathie Rd. SE12 .... 5 B1
Craven Rd. BR6 .... 52 D7
Crawfords. BR8 .... 25 E1
Crawley Cl. 1 DA11 .... 13 B1
Crawshay Cl. TN13 .... 84 A4
Cray Ave. BR5 .... 38 B4
Cray Cl. DA1 .... 9 A3
Cray Rd. Crockenhill BR8 .... 39 C3
Cray Rd. Erith DA17 .... 8 A8
Cray Rd. Sidcup DA14 .... 24 C2
Cray Valley Golf Course. BR5 .. 38 B4
Cray Valley Rd. BR5 .... 38 B4
Craybrooke Rd. DA14 .... 24 B4
Crayburne. DA13 .... 28 F4
Craybury End. SE9 .... 23 C6
Craydene Rd. DA8 .... 8 F6
Crayfields Ind Pk. BR5 .... 38 C7
Crayford Cl. ME14 .... 92 C6
Crayford Commercial Ctr. DA1 . 8 E1
Crayford High St. DA1 .... 8 E2
Crayford Ind Est. DA1 .... 8 F2
Crayford L Ctr. DA1 .... 8 E1
Crayford Rd. DA1 .... 8 F2
Crayford Sta. DA1 .... 8 E1
Crayford Way. DA1 .... 9 A3
Craylands. BR5 .... 38 C6
Craylands La. DA10 .... 11 D2
Craylands Sq. DA10 .... 11 D2
Craymill Sq. DA1 .... 8 F5
Crays Par The. BR5 .... 38 C7
Crayside Ind Est. DA1 .... 9 B3
Craythorne. TN30 .... 183 B8
Creasey's Row. TN14 .... 97 E5
Credenhall Dr. BR2 .... 36 F1
Crediton Rd. E16 .... 1 A7
Credo Way. RM16 .... 11 B8
Creek The. DA11 .... 12 B2
Cremorne Rd. DA11 .... 29 F8
Crendon Pk. TN4 .... 149 A8
Crescent Ave. RM17 .... 12 D8
Crescent Cotts. TN13 .... 83 E7
Crescent Cl. 1 RM17 .... 12 D8
Crescent Dr. BR5 .... 37 C3
Crescent Gdns. BR8 .... 39 C7
Crescent Rd. Bromley BR1 ...... 22 A1
Crescent Rd. Erith DA8 .... 8 F8
Crescent Rd. Royal Tunbridge Wells
  TN1 & TN2 .... 149 B3
Crescent Rd. Sidcup DA15 ...... 23 F5
Crescent Rd. Woolwich SE18 ..... 2 B2
Crescent The. Bexley DA5 .... 24 F8
Crescent The. Bidborough TN4 . 132 E4
Crescent The.
  Borough Green TN15 .... 87 A8
Crescent The. Groombridge TN3 161 C7
Crescent The. Longfield DA3 .... 42 E6
Crescent The. Maidstone ME14 .. 91 F8
Crescent The. Northfleet DA11 .. 29 F6
Crescent The. Sevenoaks TN13 .. 84 D6
Crescent The. Sidcup DA14 ..... 23 F4
Crescent The. Swanscombe DA9 11 C2
Crescent The. Tonbridge TN9 .... 117 B3
Crescent Way. Chatham ME5 .... 61 D5
Crescent Way. Orpington BR6 .. 51 E5
Cressey Cl. ME4 .... 47 E4
Cressingham Ct. 1 DA17 .... 4 A3
Crest Ave. RM17 .... 12 B7
Crest Cl. TN14 .... 68 B8
Crest Ind Est. TN12 .... 138 C6
Crest Rd. ME1 .... 47 C1
Crest View. DA9 .... 11 A3
Crest View Dr. BR5 .... 37 C4
Crestway. ME5 .... 62 B8
Crete Hall Rd. DA11 .... 12 E1
Creton St. SE18 .... 2 A3
Creve Coeur Cl. ME4 .... 93 A5
Cricket Ground Rd. BR7 .... 37 B8
Cricketers Cl. Erith DA8 .... 4 E1
Cricketers Cl.
  Harrietsham ME17 .... 110 D6
Cricketers Dr. DA13 .... 58 A7
Cripple Hill. TN26 .... 159 D1
Cripple St. ME15 .... 107 A7
Crisfield Ct. TN30 .... 173 B2

Crismill La. ME14 .... 93 F4
Crismill Rd. ME14 .... 93 F3
Crispe Cl. ME8 .... 63 D4
Crispin Ct. ME17 .... 106 C3
Crispin Dr. ME2 .... 46 E8
Crispin Rd. ME14 .... 24 C1
Crittall's Cnr. DA14 .... 24 C1
Crittenden Bglws. ME15 .... 106 A4
Crittenden Cotts. ME15 .... 106 A4
Crittenden Rd. TN12 .... 135 D3
Crittle's Ct. TN5 .... 174 F4
Crocken Hill Rd. TN27 .... 127 C2
Crockenhall Way. DA13 .... 29 E1
Crockenhill La. BR8 .... 39 C3
Crockenhill Hill. BR5 .... 38 D4
Crockenhill La. BR8 .... 40 C2
Crockenhill Rd. BR5 & BR8 .... 38 D4
Crockers Hatch Cnr. TN2 ...... 147 D2
Crockham Hill CE Prim Sch.
  TN8 .... 96 C2
Crockham Way. SE9 .... 23 A4
Croft Cl. Chatham ME5 .... 62 C1
Croft Cl. Chislehurst BR7 .... 22 F3
Croft Cl. Erith DA17 .... 3 F1
Croft Cl. Tonbridge TN10 .... 117 F5
Croft Ct. TN8 .... 112 C1
Croft Gdns. ME17 .... 111 D4
Croft La. TN8 .... 112 C1
Croft Rd. Bromley BR1 .... 22 A2
Croft Rd. Westerham TN16 ..... 81 C1
Croft The. Leybourne ME20 .... 74 E2
Croft The. Swanley BR8 .... 39 F6
Croft Way. Sevenoaks TN13 .... 83 F2
Croft Way. Sidcup DA15 .... 23 E5
Crofters The. ME8 .... 63 F7
Crofton Ave. Orpington BR6 .... 51 C8
Crofton Ave. Sidcup DA5 .... 24 D8
Crofton Inf Sch. BR5 .... 37 D2
Crofton Jun Sch. BR5 .... 37 D2
Crofton La. BR5 & BR6 .... 37 D2
Crofton Rd. BR6 .... 51 B8
Croftside. DA13 .... 73 A8
Cromarty Ct. 5 BR1 .... 36 C7
Crombie Rd. DA15 .... 23 D7
Cromer Pl. 5 BR6 .... 37 D1
Cromer Rd. ME2 .... 47 B8
Cromer St. TN9 .... 117 A1
Cromford Cl. BR6 .... 51 E7
Cromlix Cl. BR7 .... 37 B7
Cromwell Ave. BR2 .... 36 B5
Cromwell Ave. Maidstone ME14 .. 92 B5
Cromwell Rd.
  Royal Tunbridge Wells TN2 ... 149 C3
Cromwell Terr. ME4 .... 48 A3
Cronin Cl. 2 ME20 .... 74 F4
Crook Log. DA6 .... 7 D3
Crook Log Prim Sch. DA6 .... 7 D3
Crook Log Sports Ctr. DA16 .... 7 F4
Crook Rd. TN12 .... 136 D1
Crooked La. DA11 .... 13 B1
Crookston Rd. SE9 .... 6 A4
Croombs Rd. E16 .... 1 C8
Crosby House. 9 A1
Crosby Rd. ME7 .... 48 D3
Cross Ct. 11 SE28 .... 3 B6
Cross Dr. ME7 .... 109 B1
Cross Keys. Maidstone ME14 .... 93 C4
Cross Keys. Sevenoaks TN13 .... 99 A8
Cross Keys Cl. TN13 .... 99 A8
Cross La. Sidcup DA5 .... 24 F8
Cross La. E. DA12 .... 30 B6
Cross La W. DA11 .... 30 B6
Cross Lane Gdns. TN5 .... 176 D1
Cross Rd. Dartford DA1 .... 9 C1
Cross Rd. Hawley DA2 .... 26 F4
Cross Rd. Keston Mark BR2 .... 50 E8
Cross Rd. Northfleet DA11 ...... 12 F1
Cross Rd. Orpington BR5 .... 38 B4
Cross Rd. Sidcup DA14 .... 24 B4
Cross St. Chatham ME4 .... 48 A4
Cross St. Erith DA8 .... 8 E8
Cross St. Gillingham ME7 .... 48 C6
Cross St. 24 Gravesend DA11 .. 13 B1
Cross St. Maidstone ME14 ...... 92 A6
Cross St. Rochester ME2 .... 47 B8
Cross Way. ME1 .... 47 C3
Crossbrook Rd. SE3 .... 5 E4
Crossmead. SE9 .... 22 F7
Crossway. Chatham ME5 .... 61 E6
Crossway. Erith SE28 .... 3 D7
Crossway. Orpington BR5 .... 37 D4
Crossway. Chislehurst SE9 ..... 22 D6
Crossway The.
  Royal Tunbridge Wells TN4 ... 148 D2
Crossways. Chart Sutton ME17 .. 108 B1
Crossways. Dartford DA9 .... 10 C3
Crossways Bvd. DA9 .... 10 C3
Crouch Croft. SE9 .... 23 A5
Crouch House Cotts. TN8 .... 112 B2
Crouch House Rd. TN8 .... 112 B2
Crouch La. Crouch TN15 .... 87 B6
Crouch La. Linkhill TN18 .... 186 D6
Crouch The. ME1 .... 47 C5
Crow Dr. TN14 .... 68 C4
Crow Hill. TN15 .... 87 A7
Crow Hill Rd. TN15 .... 87 A7
Crow La. ME1 .... 47 C5
Crowden Way. SE28 .... 3 C6
Crowhurst La. Basted TN15 .... 86 E4
Crowhurst La.
  West Kingsdown TN15 .... 56 B4
Crowhurst Oast. TN12 .... 103 D1
Crowhurst La. TN15 .... 86 F6
Crowhurst Way. BR5 .... 38 C4
Crown Acres. TN12 .... 120 A6
Crown Cl. BR6 .... 52 A6
Crown Ct. Bromley BR1 .... 36 A4
Crown Ct. Cranbrook TN17 ..... 169 C5

Crown Ct. Eltham SE12 .... 5 B1
Crown Ct. Tilbury RM18 .... 13 A5
Crown Gn. DA12 .... 31 E3
Crown La. Bromley BR2 .... 36 D4
Crown La. Chislehurst BR7 ...... 37 C8
Crown La. Shorne DA12 .... 31 E4
Crown Lane Spur. BR2 .... 36 D3
Crown Rd. Grays RM17 .... 12 A8
Crown Rd. Marlpit Hill TN8 .... 112 D4
Crown Rd. Orpington BR6 ...... 52 A5
Crown Rd. Shoreham TN14 .... 53 F1
Crown St. ME7 .... 48 D6
Crown Woods Sch. SE9 .... 6 C2
Crown Woods Way. SE9 .... 6 D2
Crownfields. Maidstone ME14 .. 92 A5
Crownfields. Sevenoaks TN13 .. 84 B2
Crowther Cl. TN12 .... 139 E4
Croxley Cl. BR5 .... 38 B7
Croxley Gn. BR5 .... 38 B8
Croyde Cl. SE9 .... 23 D8
Croydon Cl. ME5 .... 62 C4
Croydon Rd.
  Keston Mark BR2 & BR4 & BR6 .. 50 C7
Croydon Rd. Westerham TN16 .. 81 B2
Crozier House. SE3 .... 5 B4
Cruden Rd. DA12 .... 30 F6
Crump's La. ME17 .... 126 B4
Crumpsall St. SE2 .... 3 C2
Crundale. 2 ME14 .... 92 A5
Crundale Rd. ME8 .... 49 C3
Crundale Tower. BR5 .... 38 C1
Crundwell Rd. TN4 .... 132 F1
Crusader Cl. ME7 .... 63 B8
Crusader Dr. DA1 .... 9 F3
Crusoe Rd. DA8 .... 4 D1
Crutches La. ME2 .... 32 E1
Cryals Ct. TN12 .... 151 E5
Cryals Rd. TN12 .... 151 D5
Crystal House. SE18 .... 2 F1
Cuckmere St. 10 BR5 .... 38 D1
Cuckmere House. 3 ME15 ..... 107 E8
Cuckold's Cnr. ME3 .... 32 C6
Cuckolds Cnr. DA3 .... 57 B7
Cuckolds Green Rd. ME3 .... 19 B5
Cuckoo La. Lamberhurst Quarter
  TN12 & TN3 .... 152 A2
Cuckoo La.
  Tonbridge TN10 & TN11 ...... 118 A7
Cuckoowood Ave. ME14 .... 76 F1
Cudham CE Prim Sch. TN16 .... 66 A2
Cudham Cl. ME14 .... 92 C6
Cudham La N. TN14 & BR6 .... 66 D7
Cudham La S. TN14 & TN16 .... 66 C2
Cudham Park Rd. TN14 .... 51 E1
Cudham Rd. BR6 .... 66 B7
Cuff Cres. SE9 .... 5 D1
Cugley Rd. DA2 .... 27 C8
Culcroft. DA3 .... 42 F6
Culpeper Cl. Hollingbourne ME17 94 F2
Culpeper Cl. Rochester ME2 .... 47 E6
Culpepers. TN17 .... 167 E7
Culpepper Rd. Coxheath ME17 .. 106 B3
Culpepper Rd. Gillingham ME8 .. 63 D4
Culverden Ave. TN4 .... 149 A6
Culverden Down. TN4 .... 148 F5
Culverden Park Rd. TN4 .... 148 F5
Culverden Pk. TN4 .... 148 F5
Culverden Sq. TN1 & TN4 ...... 149 A5
Culverden St. TN1 .... 149 A4
Culverstone Green Cty Prim Sch.
  DA13 .... 57 F3
Culverstone House. BR5 .... 38 B6
Culverton Ct. 5 DA14 .... 24 A4
Culvey Cl. DA3 .... 42 E4
Cumberland Ave. Bexley DA16 .. 6 F3
Cumberland Ave.
  Gravesend DA12 .... 30 C8
Cumberland Ave.
  Maidstone ME15 .... 107 D1
Cumberland Cl. TN11 .... 117 A4
Cumberland Dr. Dartford DA1 .. 26 F8
Cumberland Dr. Erith DA7 .... 7 E7
Cumberland Gdns. 10 TN1 ... 149 A2
Cumberland Mews. 12 TN1 ... 149 A2
Cumberland Rd.
  Gillingham ME4 & ME7 .... 48 B7
Cumberland Rd. Gillingham ME7 48 C7
Cumberland Rd. Newham E13 .. 1 B8
Cumberland Sch. E16 .... 1 A8
Cumberland Wlk. TN1 .... 149 A2
Cumberland Yd. 11 TN1 .... 149 A2
Cumbrian Ave. DA7 .... 8 E5
Cundy Rd. E16 .... 1 C7
Cunningham Cl. TN4 .... 149 B7
Cunningham Cres. ME5 .... 62 A8
Cunningham House. ME1 .... 47 B4
Cunningham Rd. TN4 .... 149 B7
Cupola Cl. BR1 .... 22 B3
Curlew Cl. SE28 .... 3 D6
Curlew Cres. ME2 .... 46 C6
Curlews The. DA12 .... 30 D6
Curran Ave. DA15 .... 6 F2
Currie Rd. TN4 .... 149 A5
Curteis Rd. TN30 .... 173 B1
Curtis Way. 7 SE28 .... 3 B6
Curtismill Cl. BR5 .... 38 B6
Curtismill Way. BR5 .... 38 B6
Curzon Cl. BR6 .... 51 D6
Curzon Cl. SE9 .... 23 C5
Curzon Dr. RM17 .... 12 C7
Curzon Rd. Chatham ME4 .... 47 F3
Curzon Rd. Maidstone ME14 .... 92 A6
Custom House Sta. E16 .... 1 C7
Cut The. TN27 .... 158 E8
Cutbush Almshouses. 2 ME15 92 A3
Cutbush and Corrall Ct. ME14 .. 92 B4
Cutmore St. DA11 .... 30 B8
Cutter Ridge Rd. DA13 .... 45 A1

Cutty Sark Ct. DA9 .... 11 A2
Cuxton. BR5 .... 37 C4
Cuxton Cl. DA6 .... 7 E2
Cuxton Cty Inf Sch. ME2 .... 46 B2
Cuxton Cty Jun Sch. ME2 .... 46 B2
Cuxton Ind Est. ME2 .... 46 C2
Cuxton Rd. Park Wood ME15 .... 107 F5
Cuxton Rd. Rochester ME2 .... 46 F5
Cuxton Sta. ME2 .... 46 C2
Cyclamen Rd. BR8 .... 39 D5
Cygnet Cl. ME20 .... 75 A2
Cygnet Gdns. DA11 .... 29 F6
Cygnet L Ctr. DA11 .... 29 C8
Cygnet Rd. ME5 .... 62 C2
Cypress Ave. ME3 .... 34 E3
Cypress Ct. ME7 .... 48 F6
Cypress Gr. TN2 .... 163 C8
Cypress Rd. ME2 .... 33 C1
Cypress Tree Cl. DA15 .... 23 F7
Cyprus Pl. E6 .... 2 A6
Cyprus Sta. E6 .... 2 A6
Cyril Lodge. DA14 .... 24 A4
Cyril Rd. Bexley DA7 .... 7 E5
Cyril Rd. Orpington BR6 .... 38 A2

D'arcy Pl. BR2 .... 36 A5
Dabbling Cl. DA8 .... 9 B7
Dabells. TN17 .... 169 D4
Daerwood Cl. BR2 .... 36 F1
Daffodil Rd. ME2 .... 46 E7
Dagmar Rd. ME4 .... 48 B2
Dagonet Gdns. BR1 .... 22 A5
Dagonet Rd. BR1 .... 22 A5
Dahlia Dr. BR8 .... 39 F7
Dahlia Rd. SE2 .... 3 B2
Dainton Cl. 2 BR1 .... 36 B8
Daintons Cotts. 2 TN18 .... 178 F2
Dairsie Ct. 2 BR1 .... 36 C7
Dairsie Rd. SE9 .... 6 A4
Dairy Cl. DA1 .... 27 B1
Dairy La. Chainhurst TN12 .... 121 F4
Dairy La. Crockham Hill TN8 .... 96 B1
Dairy La. Woolwich SE18 .... 1 F2
Dairy Pl. TN12 .... 121 F4
Dakota Gdns. E6 .... 1 E8
Dalberg Way. SE2 .... 3 D3
Dale Cl. Crayford DA1 .... 8 F1
Dale Cl. Greenwich SE3 .... 5 A4
Dale End. DA1 .... 8 F1
Dale Rd. Crayford DA1 .... 8 F1
Dale Rd. Rochester ME1 .... 47 C3
Dale Rd. Southfleet DA13 .... 29 A4
Dale Rd. Swanley BR8 .... 39 C6
Dale St. Chatham ME4 .... 47 E2
Dale St.
  Royal Tunbridge Wells TN1 .... 149 B4
Dale The. BR2 .... 50 D6
Dale View. DA8 .... 8 F5
Dale Wlk. DA2 .... 27 C7
Dale Wood Rd. BR6 .... 37 E1
Daleside. BR6 .... 52 A5
Daleside Cl. BR6 .... 52 A4
Dalison Rd. ME2 .... 60 A4
Dallin Rd. Bexley DA6 .... 7 D3
Dallin Rd. Woolwich SE18 .... 6 B7
Dalmeny Rd. DA7 & DA8 .... 8 B6
Dalton Cl. BR6 .... 51 F7
Dalton St. ME7 .... 48 C6
Daltons Rd. BR6 & BR8 .... 53 C7
Damiem Cl. ME4 .... 48 A2
Damigos Rd. DA12 .... 30 F7
Damon Cl. DA14 .... 24 B5
Damon Ct. DA14 .... 24 B5
Damson Dr. BR8 .... 39 C5
Damson Dr. ME3 .... 34 E3
Danaway Cotts. ME9 .... 65 C3
Dando Cres. SE3 .... 5 B4
Dandridge Cl. SE10 .... 1 A1
Dane Cl. Chatham ME5 .... 62 C2
Dane Cl. Hartlip ME9 .... 64 D6
Dane Cl. Orpington BR6 .... 51 D5
Dane Cl. Sidcup DA5 .... 25 A8
Dane Ct. ME17 .... 106 C2
Dane La. ME9 .... 64 D6
Dane Rd. TN14 .... 68 F2
Danecourt Sch The. ME8 .... 49 A2
Danefield Ct. Maidstone ME14 .... 93 B4
Danefield Ct. Sevenoaks TN13 ... 83 C4
Danehill Wlk. DA14 .... 24 A5
Danemore. TN30 .... 183 B8
Danes Cl. DA11 .... 29 C5
Danes Hill. ME7 .... 49 A6
Danescombe. SE12 .... 22 A7
Danns La. ME18 .... 89 A1
Dansington Rd. DA16 .... 7 A3
Danson Cres. DA16 .... 7 B4
Danson La. DA16 .... 7 B3
Danson Mead. DA16 .... 7 C4
Danson Prim Sch. DA16 .... 7 A3
Danson Rd. Bexley DA6 .... 7 D2
Danson Rd. Sidcup DA6 .... 7 D1
Danson Underpass. DA5 .... 7 C1
Danson Way. ME8 .... 49 D2
Danvers Rd. TN9 .... 117 B1
Darby Gdns. ME3 .... 32 B3
Darby's La. TN5 .... 175 E2
Darent Cl. TN13 .... 83 C5
Darent Ind Pk. ME2 .... 9 D8
Darent Mead. DA4 .... 41 B8
Darent Valley Golf Course.
  TN14 .... 69 A6
Darenth Ave. TN10 .... 117 C5
Darenth Cotts. TN13 .... 68 F8
Darenth Ct. 19 BR5 .... 38 D1
Darenth Cty Prim Sch. DA2 ... 27 E2
Darenth Dr. DA12 .... 31 B7
Darenth Gdns. TN16 .... 81 D1
Darenth Hill. DA2 & DA4 .... 27 C3

Darenth House. 2 ME15 .... 107 D8
Darenth La. TN13 .... 83 E6
Darenth Rd. Bexley DA16 .... 7 A6
Darenth Rd. Dartford DA1 .... 26 F7
Darenth Rd S. DA2 .... 27 B4
Darenth Rise. ME5 .... 62 B3
Darenth Way. TN14 .... 69 A8
Darenth Wood Rd. Dartford DA2 .. 27 E6
Darenth Wood Rd. Lane End DA2 27 E5
Dargate Cl. ME15 .... 91 D7
Dargets Rd. ME5 .... 62 A3
Daria Dr. DA10 .... 30 F5
Darland Ave. ME7 .... 48 E1
Darlton Cl. DA1 .... 8 F4
Darman La. TN12 .... 120 D3
Darnets Field. TN14 .... 68 F2
Darnley Cl. ME2 .... 46 D6
Darnley Dr. TN4 .... 132 E4
Darnley Rd. Gravesend DA11 ..... 30 A8
Darnley Rd. 1 Grays RM17 ..... 12 B8
Darnley Rd. Rochester ME2 ..... 46 E6
Darnley St. DA11 .... 30 A8
Darns Hill. BR8 .... 39 C2
Darrick Wood House. BR6 ..... 51 C7
Darrick Wood Inf Sch. BR6 ... 51 B7
Darrick Wood Jun Sch. BR6 .... 51 B7
Darrick Wood Rd. BR6 .... 51 D8
Darrick Wood Sch. BR6 .... 51 B7
Darrick Wood Sports Ctr. BR6 51 C8
Dart Cl. ME2 .... 46 F7
Dartford Golf Club. DA1 .... 26 B6
Dartford Gram Sch. 9 C1
Dartford Gram Sch for Girls.
  DA1 .... 26 C8
Dartford Rd. Coldblow DA5 ..... 25 C7
Dartford Rd. Dartford DA1 .... 9 C1
Dartford Rd. Farningham DA4 ... 41 A5
Dartford Rd. Sevenoaks TN13 .... 84 C3
Dartford Sta. DA1 .... 9 E1
Dartford Trad Pk. DA1 .... 26 F6
Dartmouth Rd. BR2 .... 36 A2
Darwin Cl. BR6 .... 51 D5
Darwin Cl. SE9 .... 6 A1
Darwin Dr. TN10 .... 117 D6
Darwin Rd. Bexley DA16 .... 6 F4
Darwin Rd. Tilbury RM18 ..... 12 F6
Dashmonden Cl. ME2 .... 33 C2
Dashwood Cl. DA6 .... 8 A2
Dashwood Rd. DA11 .... 30 A6
Davall House. 10 RM17 .... 12 B8
Davenport Ave. ME7 .... 48 E7
Davenport Rd. DA14 .... 24 E6
David Coffer Ct. DA17 .... 4 B2
David Saloman's House. TN3 148 D8
Davidson Tower. BR1 .... 22 B3
Davis Ave. DA11 .... 29 E7
Davis Cl. TN13 .... 84 C5
Davy's Pl. DA12 .... 30 E2
Dawbourns. TN30 .... 173 B3
Dawes Cl. DA9 .... 10 F2
Dawes St. ME7 .... 48 C5
Dawson Ave. BR5 .... 38 B7
Dawson Dr. BR8 .... 25 E1
Days La. DA15 .... 23 E8
Days Lane Prim Sch. DA15 ..... 6 F1
Dayton Dr. DA9 .... 9 D8
De Lapre Cl. BR5 .... 38 D2
De Luci Rd. DA8 .... 4 C1
De Lucy Prim Sch. SE2 .... 3 B4
De Lucy St. SE2 .... 3 B2
De Mere Cl. ME8 .... 63 D6
De Warren House. DA11 .... 12 D1
Deacon Cl. ME2 .... 46 E8
Deacon Est The. ME20 .... 76 A2
Deacon Trad Ctr. ME2 .... 47 A6
Deacon Trad Est. TN9 .... 117 D1
Deacons Leas. BR6 .... 51 D6
Deakin Leas. TN11 & TN9 ..... 133 B7
Dean & Chapter Cotts. DA13 ... 29 B2
Dean La. DA13 .... 58 C5
Dean Rd. Luddesdown DA13 ..... 58 E8
Dean Rd. Rochester ME2 .... 46 F8
Dean St. ME15 .... 106 C6
Dean Wood Cty Prim Inf Sch.
  ME8 .... 63 D3
Dean Wood Cty Prim Jun Sch.
  ME8 .... 63 D4
Deanery Rd. TN8 .... 96 C1
Deangate Ridge Sports Ground.
  ME3 .... 34 D8
Deans Ct. 6 TN9 .... 133 B8
Deans Hill Rd. ME9 .... 80 D5
Deansfield Inf Sch. SE9 .... 6 A4
Deansfield Jun Sch. SE9 .... 6 A4
Deanwood Cl. ME8 .... 63 D6
Deanwood Dr. ME8 .... 63 E4
Debrabant Cl. ME8 .... 8 D8
Decoy Hill Rd. ME23 .... 17 F6
Deepdene. TN5 .... 175 A6
Deepdene Rd. DA16 .... 7 A4
Deerhurst Cl. DA3 .... 43 C6
Deerhurst Gdns. ME16 .... 91 D4
Deerleap La. TN14 .... 67 E6
Defiance Wlk. SE18 .... 1 F3
Defiant Cl. ME5 .... 62 B6
Defoe Cl. Chatham ME5 .... 62 B6
Defoe Cl. Erith DA8 .... 4 F1
Degema Rd. BR7 .... 23 B3
Deidre Chapman House. DA10 11 E1
Delacourt Rd. SE3 .... 5 B7
Delafield Rd. SE7 .... 1 C1
Delagarde Rd. TN16 .... 81 C1
Delamere Gdns. 3 ME6 .... 75 A8
Delamere Rd. 3 ME6 .... 75 A8
Delaware Cotts. TN8 .... 128 F8
Delce Cty Inf Sch. ME1 .... 47 D2
Delce Cty Jun Sch. ME1 .... 47 C2

Delce Rd. ME1 .... 47 D4
Delius Dr. TN10 .... 117 F6
Dell Dr. TN2 .... 149 D4
Dell The. Maypole DA5 .... 25 E7
Dell The. Woolwich SE2 .... 3 A1
Delme Cres. SE3 .... 5 B5
Delmonden Rd. TN18 .... 178 B1
Delves Ave. TN2 .... 149 C1
Delvon Cl. SE18 .... 6 A7
Den Cross. TN8 .... 128 D6
Den La. TN12 .... 121 C3
Denbeigh Dr. TN10 .... 117 D6
Denberry Dr. DA14 .... 24 B5
Denbigh Ave. ME8 .... 49 D1
Denbigh Cl. BR7 .... 22 F2
Denbigh Rd. TN4 .... 149 C7
Denbridge Rd. BR1 & BR7 ..... 36 F7
Dene Ave. DA15 .... 24 B8
Dene Cl. DA2 .... 25 E4
Dene Dr. New Barn DA3 .... 43 B7
Dene Dr. Orpington BR6 .... 52 B7
Dene Holm Rd. DA11 .... 29 E5
Dene Lodge Cl. TN15 .... 86 F7
Dene Rd. DA1 .... 26 F8
Dene The. TN13 .... 84 B1
Dene Way. TN3 .... 148 A7
Dene Wlk. DA3 .... 42 E6
Denecourt. BR5 .... 38 C1
Denesway. DA13 .... 44 B3
Denham Rd. ME9 .... 65 B7
Denham St. SE10 .... 1 A1
Denison Mews. ME3 .... 19 C4
Deniston Ave. DA5 .... 24 E7
Denmark House. 9 SE7 .... 1 E2
Denmark Rd. BR1 .... 36 B8
Denmark St. E13 .... 1 B8
Dennard Way. BR6 .... 51 A6
Dennettsland Rd. TN8 .... 96 C1
Dennington Ct. TN4 .... 133 A2
Dennis Cadman House. 4
  ME20 .... 75 F1
Dennis Rd. DA11 .... 30 B5
Dennis Willocks Cl. ME9 ..... 65 B6
Denny Cl. 12 E6 .... 1 E8
Denny Ct. 1 DA2 .... 10 B1
Denstead Wlk. 11 ME15 ..... 107 E8
Denton Cl. ME15 .... 107 E8
Denton Court Rd. DA12 .... 30 E8
Denton Rd. Bexley DA16 .... 7 E4
Denton Rd. Dartford DA1 ..... 25 E8
Denton Rd. Maypole DA5 .... 25 E7
Denton St. DA12 .... 30 E8
Denton Terr. DA5 .... 25 E6
Denver Cl. BR6 .... 37 E3
Denver Ind Est. RM13 .... 4 E8
Denver Rd. DA1 .... 26 A8
Derby Rd. TN11 .... 116 E6
Derby Rd. Chatham ME5 .... 48 E2
Derby Rd. Gillingham ME5 ..... 48 E2
Derby Rd. Grays RM17 .... 12 B8
Derby Rd. Maidstone ME15 ..... 107 C8
Derby Road Bridge. RM17 ..... 12 B8
Derifall Cl. E6 .... 1 F8
Dering Way. DA12 .... 30 F7
Deringwood Dr. ME15 .... 92 F1
Dernier Rd. TN10 & TN9 ..... 117 C4
Derrick Gdns. SE7 .... 1 C2
Derry Downs. BR5 .... 38 C3
Derwent Cl. DA1 .... 26 B7
Derwent Cres. DA7 .... 8 A5
Derwent Dr. Orpington BR5 ... 37 D2
Derwent Dr.
  Royal Tunbridge Wells TN4 ..... 148 F5
Derwent House. 5 ME15 ..... 107 E7
Derwent Lodge Sch. TN1 ..... 149 B4
Derwent Rd. TN10 .... 117 C5
Derwent Way. ME8 .... 63 D8
Detling CE Prim Sch. ME14 ... 78 A1
Detling Cl. ME8 .... 49 C2
Detling Hill. ME14 .... 78 B2
Detling Rd. Bromley BR1 ..... 22 A3
Detling Rd. Northfleet DA11 ... 29 D7
Devalls Cl. E6 .... 2 A6
Devema Cl. BR7 .... 37 A8
Devenish Rd. SE2 .... 3 A4
Devon Cl. Chatham ME5 .... 62 C7
Devon Cl. Gillingham ME8 ..... 49 F1
Devon Cl. ME4 .... 41 B8
Devon Rd. Maidstone ME15 ..... 107 C8
Devon Rd. Sutton at Hone DA4 ... 41 C8
Devonshire Ave. DA1 .... 9 B1
Devonshire Cl. TN2 .... 162 F8
Devonshire Rd. Bexley DA6 ..... 7 F3
Devonshire Rd. Chislehurst SE9 .. 22 E6
Devonshire Rd. Gillingham ME7 .. 48 D7
Devonshire Rd. Gravesend DA12 30 B6
Devonshire Rd. Newham E16 ... 1 B7
Devonshire Rd. Orpington BR6 .. 38 A2
Devonshire Sq. BR2 .... 36 B5
Dewberry Gdns. E6 .... 1 E8
Dewhurst Cotts. TN5 .... 174 A7
Dewhurst La. TN5 .... 174 B8
DeWinter House. TN13 .... 84 A3
Dewlands Ave. DA2 .... 27 B8
Dexter House. 2 DA18 .... 3 E3
Dhekelia Cl. ME14 .... 92 A7
Dial Cl. DA11 .... 30 B7
Dial Cl. Swanscombe DA9 .... 11 D2
Dial Rd. ME7 .... 48 F6
Diameter Rd. BR5 .... 37 C3
Diamond Field. TN12 .... 152 F3
Diana Cl. DA8 .... 8 E8
Dianne Ct. SE12 .... 22 A7
Dianthus Cl. SE2 .... 3 B1
Dibden La. TN13 & TN14 ..... 98 E8
Dickens Ave. Dartford DA1 ..... 10 A3
Dickens Ave. Tilbury RM18 ..... 13 B6

Dickens Cl. Erith DA8 .... 8 B7
Dickens Cl. Hartley DA3 .... 42 F4
Dickens Cl. Langley Heath ME17 108 E4
Dickens Cl. ME2 .... 47 D8
Dickens Dr. Chislehurst BR7 ..... 23 C2
Dickens Dr. East Malling ME19 ... 74 F1
Dickens House. 3 DA17 ..... 3 F1
Dickens Rd. Gravesend DA12 ... 30 E7
Dickens Rd. Rochester ME1 ..... 47 C2
Dickens Way. TN18 .... 179 A2
Dickensian Cl. ME3 .... 19 A2
Dickley La. ME17 .... 111 A6
Dickson House. SE18 .... 5 E6
Dickson Rd. SE9 .... 5 E4
Digdoga La. TN17 .... 156 D3
Dignals Cl. ME8 .... 49 F2
Dilhorne Cl. SE12 .... 22 B5
Dillon Way. TN1 .... 149 D6
Dillywood Cotts. ME3 .... 32 F2
Dillywood La. ME3 .... 32 F2
Dimmock Cl. TN12 .... 136 B7
Dingleden La. TN17 .... 180 F2
Dippers Cl. TN15 .... 69 F2
Dislingbury Rd. TN11 .... 134 C4
Disraeli Cl. Park Wood ME15 .. 107 E5
Disraeli Cl. Woolwich SE28 ..... 3 C5
Dittisham Rd. SE9 .... 22 E4
Ditton CE Jun Sch. ME20 ..... 75 C1
Ditton Court Rd. ME19 .... 75 B1
Ditton Cty Inf Sch. ME20 ..... 75 C1
Ditton Pl. ME19 & ME20 .... 75 B1
Ditton Rd. DA6 .... 7 E2
Dixon Cl. Maidstone ME15 ..... 91 F2
Dixon Cl. 4 Newham E6 ..... 1 F7
Dixon House. SE9 .... 3 C1
Dixwell Cl. ME8 .... 63 D5
Dobell Rd. SE9 .... 5 F2
Dobson Rd. DA12 .... 30 E3
Dock Approach Rd. RM17 ..... 12 E8
Dock Head Rd. ME4 .... 48 A8
Dock Rd. Chatham ME4 .... 47 F6
Dock Rd. Gillingham ME4 ..... 48 A7
Dock Rd. Grays RM17 .... 12 D8
Dock Rd. Tilbury RM18 .... 12 E5
Dock Rd. Tilbury RM18 .... 13 A4
Dockland St. Newham E16 ..... 2 A4
Dockland St. Newham E16 ..... 2 A5
Doctor Hope's Rd. TN17 ..... 169 D4
Dodd Rd. TN10 .... 117 E5
Doddington Ct. ME16 .... 91 E5
Doddington Rd. ME8 .... 49 D3
Doebury Wlk. SE18 .... 6 F7
Dog Cotts. RH19 .... 144 B1
Doggett's Sq. ME2 .... 47 C7
Doggetts Row. ME3 .... 19 A2
Dogwood Cl. Chatham ME5 ... 62 D1
Dogwood Cl. Northfleet DA11 ... 29 F4
Dolphin Cl. SE28 .... 3 D7
Dolphin Dr. ME8 .... 63 E5
Dombey Cl. Higham ME3 ..... 32 C3
Dombey Cl. Rochester ME1 ..... 47 C3
Domonic Dr. SE9 .... 23 B5
Donaldson Rd. SE18 .... 6 A6
Doncaster Cl. 7 ME15 .... 107 F6
Donet Cl. ME8 .... 63 C5
Dongola Rd. ME2 .... 33 B1
Donkey Field. TN11 .... 115 E1
Donkey La. DA4 .... 55 B8
Donnington Rd. TN13 .... 83 D8
Doon Brae. TN4 .... 133 A2
Dorado Gdns. BR6 .... 52 D7
Doran Gr. SE18 .... 6 E7
Dorchester. TN4 .... 149 B6
Dorchester Ave. DA5 .... 24 D8
Dorchester Cl. Cliffe Woods ME3 33 B7
Dorchester Cl. Dartford DA1 ..... 26 F7
Dorchester Cl. St Paul's Cray BR5 24 B1
Dorchester Rd. DA12 .... 30 D5
Dorcis Ave. DA7 .... 7 E5
Doric Ave. TN4 .... 132 F1
Doric Cl. TN4 .... 132 F1
Dorin Ct. TN2 .... 149 C3
Doris Ave. DA7 .... 8 C6
Dorking Rd. TN1 .... 149 C6
Dorland Rd. SE9 .... 6 D1
Dormers Dr. DA13 .... 44 B2
Dormers Cl. SE3 .... 5 A7
Dornberg Rd. SE3 .... 5 B7
Dornden Dr. TN3 .... 148 A4
Dornden Gdns. ME5 .... 62 B2
Dorne Cotts. TN27 .... 127 E6
Dorney Rise. BR5 .... 37 F5
Dorothy Ave. TN17 .... 169 E4
Dorothy Evans Cl. DA7 .... 8 B3
Dorrit Way. Chislehurst BR7 ..... 23 C2
Dorrit Way. Rochester ME1 ..... 47 D2
Dorset Ave. DA16 .... 6 F3
Dorset Cotts. TN7 .... 160 B4
Dorset Cres. DA12 .... 30 F7
Dorset Rd. Chislehurst SE9 ..... 22 E6
Dorset Rd.
  Royal Tunbridge Wells TN2 ..... 149 D2
Dorset Road Inf Sch. SE9 ..... 22 E6
Dorset Sq. ME8 .... 49 D1
Dorset St. TN13 .... 84 C1
Dorset Way. ME15 .... 107 C8
Dorton Coll. TN15 .... 84 F5
Dorton Dr. TN15 .... 84 F5
Dorton House
  (Royal London Society
  Sch for the Blind). TN15 ... 84 F5
Dorville Rd. SE12 & SE13 ..... 5 A2
Dothill Rd. SE18 .... 6 C7
Dotterel Cl. ME5 .... 62 C2
Doubleton La. TN11 .... 131 A5
Doug Siddons Ct. 7 RM17 ... 12 C8

Douglas Almshouses. ME17 .. 111 D5
Douglas Bldgs. TN12 .... 139 E5
Douglas Rd. TN9 .... 7 B6
Douglas Rd. Lenham ME17 ..... 111 D5
Douglas Rd. Maidstone ME16 ... 91 E3
Douglas Rd. 6 Newham E16 ... 1 A8
Douglas Rd. Tonbridge TN9 ..... 133 A8
Dove App. E6 .... 1 E8
Dove Cl. ME5 .... 62 B6
Dove Rd. TN10 .... 117 C6
Dovedale Cl. DA16 .... 7 A5
Dovedale Rd. DA2 .... 27 C7
Doveney Cl. BR5 .... 38 D6
Dover House. ME2 .... 33 C1
Dover Patrol. SE3 .... 5 C5
Dover Rd. Northfleet DA11 ..... 29 D8
Dover Rd. Woolwich SE18 ..... 6 C5
Dover Rd E. DA11 .... 29 F7
Dover Road Cty Prim Jun Sch.
  DA11 .... 29 E7
Dover St. ME16 .... 91 C2
Doves Cl. BR2 .... 50 E8
Dowding Way. TN2 .... 133 E1
Dowding Wlk. 3 DA11 ..... 29 E5
Dower House Cres. TN4 ..... 132 E3
Dowgate Cl. TN9 .... 133 D7
Dowlerville Rd. BR6 .... 51 F4
Dowling Cl. ME6 .... 74 E7
Dowling House. DA17 .... 3 F3
Down Ave. TN3 .... 166 A4
Down House. BR6 .... 66 A7
Down La. TN3 .... 163 C1
Down's Cl. TN27 .... 141 E5
Downage The. DA11 .... 30 A6
Downash Ct. TN5 .... 177 A3
Downash House. TN5 .... 177 A3
Downbank Ave. DA7 .... 8 D5
Downderry Way. ME19 ..... 75 B1
Downderry Rd. BR1 & SE12 ... 22 A4
Downe Ave. TN14 .... 66 D8
Downe Cl. DA16 .... 7 C7
Downe House. 9 SE7 .... 5 C8
Downe Prim Sch. BR6 .... 66 B7
Downe Rd. Cudham BR6 & TN14 ... 66 C5
Downe Rd. Farthing Street BR2 ... 50 E2
Downend. SE18 .... 6 B7
Downer Ct. ME4 .... 61 E8
Downham Way. BR1 & SE12 ... 22 A4
Downings. E6 .... 2 A7
Downlands. ME17 .... 110 F6
Downleys Cl. SE9 .... 22 F6
Downman Rd. SE9 .... 5 E4
Downs Ave. Chislehurst BR7 ... 22 F3
Downs Ave. Dartford DA1 ..... 27 A8
Downs Cl. ME14 .... 92 B8
Downs Rd. Istead Rise DA13 ... 29 D3
Downs Rd. Maidstone ME14 ... 92 B8
Downs Rd. Yalding ME18 ..... 105 A1
Downs The. ME5 .... 61 D1
Downs Valley. DA3 .... 42 E5
Downs View. Burham ME1 ..... 60 F1
Downs View. West Malling ME19 89 B8
Downs View. BR6 .... 52 C1
Downs View Rd. ME14 .... 92 B8
Downs Wood. DA13 .... 72 F8
Downside. ME2 .... 47 A7
Downsview. Chatham ME5 ..... 62 C8
Downsview. Trottiscliffe ME19 ... 73 A5
Downsview Ct. TN13 .... 83 F2
Downsview Cty Prim Sch. BR8 40 A6
Downsview Rd. TN13 .... 83 F2
Downsway. BR6 .... 51 E5
Doyle Cl. DA8 .... 8 E6
Doyle Way. RM18 .... 13 C5
Drage Rd. TN12 .... 119 E6
Drake Cres. SE28 .... 3 C7
Drake Cl. BR5 .... 38 B3
Drake's Ave. ME2 .... 46 F8
Draper Cl. DA17 .... 3 F2
Draper Ct. BR1 .... 36 E5
Draper St. 3 TN4 .... 132 F2
Drawell Cl. SE18 .... 2 E1
Dray Corner Rd. TN27 .... 140 F7
Dray Ct. TN11 .... 118 E3
Drays Cotts. DA4 .... 41 B5
Drayton Ave. BR6 .... 37 B1
Drayton Rd. TN9 .... 133 C8
Drew Prim Sch. E16 .... 1 E5
Drew Rd. Newham E16 .... 1 D5
Drew Rd. Newham E16 .... 1 E5
Drewery Dr. ME8 .... 63 C5
Driffield Gdns. TN9 .... 132 F7
Drift The. BR2 .... 50 D7
Drive The. Bexley DA5 .... 24 D8
Drive The. Chislehurst BR7 ..... 37 B8
Drive The. Erith DA8 .... 8 B8
Drive The. Gravesend DA12 ... 30 E4
Drive The. New Barn DA3 ..... 43 B6
Drive The. Orpington BR6 ..... 51 F8
Drive The.
  Royal Tunbridge Wells TN2 ..... 149 B1
Drive The. Sevenoaks TN13 ..... 84 B3
Drive The. Sidcup DA14 .... 24 B4
Drive The. St Paul's Cray BR7 ... 37 C6
Drive The. Tonbridge TN9 ..... 133 B7
Drove Way The. DA13 .... 29 E1
Drudgeon Way. DA2 .... 28 C5
Drummond Cl. DA8 .... 8 F6
Drummond House. 11 SE18 ... 2 A2
Drury Rd. TN30 .... 183 B8
Dry Bank Ct. TN10 .... 117 C4
Dry Bank Rd. TN10 .... 117 C4
Dry Hill Park Cres. TN10 ..... 117 B3
Dry Hill Park Rd. TN10 .... 117 B3
Dry Hill Rd. TN10 .... 117 B3
Dryden House. BR2 .... 36 D4

Dryden Pl. RM18 13 B6
Dryden Rd. DA16 6 F6
Dryden Way. BR6 38 A1
Dryhill La. TN14 83 B3
Dryhill Rd. DA17 7 F8
Dryland Ave. 5 BR6 51 F6
Dryland Rd. Borough Green TN15 86 F6
Dryland Rd. Snodland ME6 74 F8
Duchess Cl. ME2 46 E8
Duchess of Kent Ct The. 1 ME20 75 F1
Duchess of Kent Dr. ME5 62 B3
Duchess' Wlk. TN15 84 E2
Ducie House. 8 SE7 5 C8
Ducketts Rd. DA1 8 F2
Duddington Cl. SE9 22 D4
Dudely Rd. DA11 29 E8
Dudley Lodge. TN2 149 C4
Dudley Rd. TN1 149 A4
Dudsbury Rd. DA1 9 B2
Dukes Meadow. TN11 114 F2
Dukes Meadow Dr. ME7 62 F6
Dukes Orch. DA5 25 C7
Dukes Rd. TN1 149 C5
Dukes Wlk. 5 ME15 92 A4
Dulverton Prim Sch. DA15 23 D6
Dulverton Rd. SE9 23 D6
Dumbreck Rd. SE9 6 A4
Dunblane Rd. SE9 5 E5
Duncan Rd. ME7 48 D5
Duncans Cotts. 3 TN16 81 D1
Duncroft. SE18 6 E7
Dundale Rd. TN12 & TN3 151 A3
Dundonald Cl. 6 E6 1 E7
Dunedin House. 2 RM18 13 A5
Dunera Dr. ME14 92 A7
Dunk's Green Rd. TN11 102 A5
Dunkery Rd. SE12 & SE9 22 E5
Dunkin Rd. DA1 10 A3
Dunkirk Cl. DA12 30 C3
Dunkirk Dr. ME5 61 F6
Dunkley Villas. TN15 72 F1
Dunlop Ct. 7 TN18 179 A2
Dunlop Point. E16 1 A5
Dunlop Rd. RM18 12 F6
Dunn Street Rd. ME7 78 A8
Dunning's La. ME1 47 C4
Dunnings The. ME16 91 A2
Dunnock Rd. E6 1 E7
Dunnose Ct. RM16 10 B8
Dunoon Cotts. BR6 66 A5
Dunorlan Farm Cotts. TN2 149 E4
Dunstable Ct. 4 SE3 5 A7
Dunstall Welling Est. DA16 7 B5
Dunstan Glade. BR5 37 D3
Dunstan Gr. TN4 149 B6
Dunstan Rd. TN4 149 B6
Dunster Ct. 4 DA2 10 B1
Dunton Green Cty Prim Sch. TN13 83 E7
Dunton Green Sta. TN13 83 E7
Dunvegan Rd. SE9 5 F3
Dunwich Rd. DA7 7 F6
Dupree Rd. SE7 1 B1
Durant Rd. BR8 26 A2
Durban House. 7 ME15 107 E5
Durham Cl. ME15 92 E1
Durham Rd. Bromley BR2 36 A5
Durham Rd. Gillingham ME8 63 C7
Durham Rd. Sidcup DA14 24 B3
Durham Rise. SE18 2 D1
Duriun Way. DA8 9 B7
Durley Gdns. BR6 52 B7
Durndale La. Northfleet DA11 29 E4
Durndale La. Northfleet DA11 29 F5
Durrant Way. Orpington BR6 51 D5
Durrant Way. Swanscombe DA10 28 E8
Durrell Gdns. ME5 48 C1
Dursley Cl. SE3 5 C5
Dursley Gdns. SE3 5 D6
Dursley Rd. SE3 5 C5
Duval Dr. ME1 61 E8
Duvard's Pl. ME9 65 F1
Dux Hill. TN15 101 F8
Dux La. TN15 86 F1
Duxberry Cl. BR2 36 E4
Duxford House. 12 SE2 3 D4
Dyke Dr. BR5 38 C2
Dykewood Cl. DA5 25 E5
Dylan Rd. DA17 4 A3
Dymchurch Cl. BR6 51 E6
Dyneley Rd. SE12 22 C5
Dynes Rd. TN14 & TN15 69 E2
Dynevor Rd. TN4 149 C7

Eagle Cl. ME20 75 A2
Eagle House. RM17 11 F8
Eagle Way. DA11 12 A2
Eagles Rd. DA9 11 B2
Eaglesfield Rd. SE18 6 B6
Eaglesfield Sch. SE18 6 A6
Eaglestone Cl. TN15 87 A8
Ealdham Prim Sch. SE9 5 C3
Ealdham Sq. SE9 5 C3
Ealing Cl. ME5 62 C4
Eardemont Cl. DA1 8 F3
Eardley Point. 9 SE18 2 B2
Eardley Rd. Erith DA17 4 A1
Eardley Rd. Sevenoaks TN13 84 B3
Earl Cl. ME5 62 B4
Earl Rd. DA11 29 E6
Earl Rise. SE18 2 D2
Earl St. ME14 91 F4
Earl's Rd. TN4 148 F4
Earlshall Rd. SE9 6 A3
Eason Villas. TN12 138 D6
East Becton District Ctr. E16 1 F8
East Borough Cty Prim Sch. ME14 92 B5
East Cliff Rd. TN4 149 A6
East Crescent Rd. DA11 13 C1
East Cross. TN30 183 B7
East Dr. BR5 38 B3
East Farleigh Cty Prim Sch. ME15 106 B6
East Farleigh Sta. ME16 106 B8
East Hall Hill. ME17 123 E7
East Hall Rd. BR5 38 F2
East Ham Ind Est. E16 1 E8
East Ham Manor Way. E6 2 A7
East Hill. Dartford DA1 26 F8
East Hill. South Darenth DA4 41 D7
East Hill. Tenterden TN30 183 B8
East Hill Dr. DA1 26 F8
East Hill Rd. TN15 70 B7
East Holme. DA8 8 D6
East Kent Ave. DA11 12 C1
East Malling Research Sta (Horticultural). ME19 90 C6
East Malling Sta. ME19 90 A6
East Mascalls. 15 SE7 5 C8
East Mill. DA11 12 F1
East Milton Rd. DA12 30 D8
East Park Rd. ME20 91 A8
East Peckham Cty Prim Sch. TN12 119 F6
East Rd. Bexley DA16 7 B5
East Rd. Chatham ME4 48 A7
East Rd. Gillingham ME4 48 A8
East Rochester Way. Coldblow DA1 25 D8
East Rochester Way. Sidcup SE9 7 C1
East Row. ME1 47 C5
East St. Addington ME19 73 D3
East St. Bexley DA7 8 A3
East St. Bromley BR1 36 A7
East St. Chatham ME4 48 A3
East St. Gillingham ME7 48 D6
East St. Grays RM16 11 E8
East St. Harrietsham ME17 110 E5
East St. Hunton ME15 121 F7
East St. Snodland ME6 75 B8
East St. Tonbridge TN9 117 C2
East Street N. ME19 73 D3
East Sutton Park (HM Young Offender Inst & Prison). ME17 125 B7
East Sutton Rd. Hearnden Green ME17 125 C4
East Sutton Rd. Sutton Valence ME17 125 A7
East Terr. Gravesend DA11 13 C1
East Terr. Sidcup DA15 23 E7
East Thurrock Rd. RM17 12 C8
East Weald Dr. TN30 173 B1
East Wickham Inf Sch. DA16 6 F6
East Wickham Jun Sch. DA16 7 A6
East Woodside. DA5 24 E7
Eastbrook Rd. SE3 5 B6
Eastbury Rd. Newham E6 2 A8
Eastbury Rd. Orpington BR5 37 D3
Eastcombe Ave. SE7 5 B8
Eastcote. BR6 37 F1
Eastcote Prim Sch. DA16 6 D4
Eastcote Rd. DA16 6 D5
Eastcourt Gn. ME8 49 B4
Eastcourt La. Gillingham ME8 49 B3
Eastcourt La. Gillingham,Lower Twydall ME7 & ME8 49 B4
Easterfields. ME16 & ME19 90 C5
Eastern Rd. ME7 48 F6
Eastern Way. Erith SE28 3 D5
Eastern Way. 1 Grays RM17 12 A8
Eastfield Gdns. TN10 117 E5
Eastfield House. ME16 91 B2
Eastgate. ME1 47 D5
Eastgate Cl. SE28 3 D7
Eastgate Ct. ME1 47 C5
Eastgate Rd. TN30 183 C8
Eastgate Terr. ME1 47 C5
Eastlands Cl. TN2 & TN4 162 E8
Eastlands Rd. TN4 148 E1
Eastleigh Rd. DA7 8 C4
Eastling Cl. ME8 49 D3
Eastling House. 8 BR5 38 D1
Eastmead Cl. BR1 36 E7
Eastmoor Pl. SE18 & SE7 1 D3
Eastmoor St. SE7 1 D3
Eastnor Rd. SE9 23 C7
Eastry Cl. ME16 91 C7
Eastry Rd. DA8 8 A7
Eastview Ave. SE18 6 E7
Eastway. BR2 36 A2
Eastwell. 3 TN30 183 A7
Eastwell Barn Mews. TN30 183 A8
Eastwell Cl. Maidstone ME14 92 C5
Eastwell Cl. Paddock Wood TN12 135 E6
Eastwell Meadows. TN30 183 A8
Eaton Ct. BR7 23 C2
Eaton Rd. DA14 24 D6
Eaton Sq. DA3 42 D6
Ebbsfleet Ind Est. DA11 12 B2
Ebbsfleet Wlk. DA11 12 B1
Ebdon Way. SE3 5 B4
Ebury Cl. BR2 50 E7
Eccles Row. ME20 75 F6
Eccleston Cl. BR6 37 D1
Eccleston Rd. ME15 91 F2
Echo Cl. ME15 107 F6
Echo Ct. DA12 30 C6
Eclipse Rd. E13 1 B8
Edam Ct. 11 DA14 24 A5
Eddington Cl. ME15 107 B6
Eden Ave. ME5 62 A7
Eden Cl. DA5 25 D4
Eden Ct. 1 Hawkhurst TN18 178 F2
Eden Ct. 17 Orpington BR5 38 D1
Eden Pl. DA11 30 B8
Eden Rd. High Halstow ME23 17 E4
Eden Rd. Joyden's Wood DA5 25 D4
Eden Rd. Royal Tunbridge Wells TN1 149 A2
Eden Valley Sch. TN8 112 C2
Eden Villas. TN8 128 D7
Edenbridge Cl. BR5 38 D5
Edenbridge Cty Prim Sch. TN8 112 D1
Edenbridge & District War Meml Hospl. TN8 128 D7
Edenbridge Golf & Country Club. TN8 112 A2
Edenbridge Rd. TN8 & TN7 145 E2
Edenbridge Sta. TN8 112 C3
Edenbridge Town Sta. TN8 112 D2
Edenbridge Trad Ctr. TN8 128 D8
Edendale Rd. DA7 8 D5
Edensmuir Ct. SE3 5 A7
Edgar Cl. BR8 39 F6
Edgar Rd. TN14 69 E2
Edge Hill. SE18 6 B8
Edge Hill Ct. DA14 23 F4
Edgeborough Way. BR1 36 D8
Edgebury. BR7 & SE9 23 B4
Edgebury Prim Sch. BR7 23 C4
Edgebury Wlk. BR7 23 C5
Edgefield Cl. DA1 27 B7
Edgehill Gdns. DA13 43 F8
Edgehill Rd. BR7 23 C4
Edger Pl. 3 ME15 92 A4
Edgewood Dr. BR6 52 A5
Edgeworth Rd. SE9 5 D3
Edgington Way. DA14 24 D1
Edinburgh Ct. DA8 8 D7
Edinburgh Mews. RM18 13 B5
Edinburgh Rd. Chatham ME4 48 C2
Edinburgh Rd. Gillingham ME7 48 D5
Edinburgh Rd. Grain ME3 21 B5
Edinburgh Sq. Maidstone ME15 107 C7
Edinburgh Sq. Maidstone ME15 107 D6
Edington Rd. SE2 3 B3
Edison Gr. SE18 6 F7
Edison Rd. Bexley DA16 6 F6
Edison Rd. Bromley BR2 36 A7
Edith Pond Ct. SE9 23 B6
Edith Rd. BR6 52 A5
Ediva Rd. DA13 44 A4
Edmund Cl. Maidstone ME16 91 A3
Edmund Cl. Meopham Station DA13 44 A4
Edmund Rd. Bexley DA16 7 A4
Edmund Rd. Orpington BR5 38 C3
Edmunds Ave. BR5 38 D6
Edmundson House. 10 SE18 2 A2
Edna Rd. ME14 91 F8
Edward Ct. Chatham ME5 48 C1
Edward Ct. 2 Newham E16 1 A8
Edward Harvey Ct. DA17 3 F1
Edward Rd. Bromley BR1 22 C1
Edward Rd. Chislehurst BR7 23 B3
Edward St. Chatham ME4 48 A3
Edward St. Rochester ME2 47 B7
Edward St. Royal Tunbridge Wells TN4 148 F8
Edward St. Rusthall TN4 148 C4
Edward Tyler Rd. SE12 22 C6
Edward Wlk. ME19 89 F8
Edwards Cl. ME8 63 C5
Edwards Gdns. BR8 39 D5
Edwards Rd. DA17 4 A2
Edwin Arnold Ct. DA15 23 F4
Edwin Cl. DA7 7 F8
Edwin Petty Pl. DA2 27 C8
Edwin Rd. Gillingham ME8 63 C8
Edwin Rd. Wilmington DA2 26 C5
Edwin St. Gravesend DA11 30 B8
Edwin St. Newham E16 1 A8
Edwina Pl. ME9 65 C7
Egdean Wlk. TN13 84 C4
Egerton Ave. BR8 39 F8
Egerton CE Prim Sch. TN27 127 F3
Egerton Cl. DA1 26 B7
Egerton House Rd. TN27 127 E4
Egerton Rd. ME14 91 E7
Eggpie La. TN11 115 E7
Egham Rd. E13 1 B8
Eglantine La. DA4 41 B3
Eglinton Hill. SE18 6 B7
Eglinton Inf Sch. SE18 6 A8
Eglinton Jun Mix Sch. SE18 6 A8
Eglinton Rd. Swanscombe DA10 11 F1
Eglinton Rd. Woolwich SE18 6 B8
Egremont Rd. ME15 92 F2
Eight Dock East Rd. ME4 34 A1
Eileen Ct. BR7 23 A3
Eisenhower Dr. E6 1 E8
Elaine Ave. ME2 46 E7
Elaine Ct. ME2 46 E6
Elaine Prim Sch. ME2 46 E6
Elbourne Trad Est. DA17 4 B3
Elbury Dr. E16 1 A7
Elder Cl. Hoo St Werburgh ME3 34 E3
Elder Cl. Kingswood ME17 109 D2
Elder Cl. Sidcup DA15 23 F7
Elder Ct. ME8 63 B6
Elderslie Rd. SE9 6 A2
Eldon St. ME4 48 A4
Eldon Way. TN12 135 F7
Eldred Dr. BR5 52 D8
Eleanor Wlk. 25 SE18 1 F2
Elford Cl. SE9 5 C3
Elgal Cl. BR6 51 B5
Elgar Cl. TN10 117 E6
Elgar Gdns. RM18 13 B6
Elgin Gdns. ME2 46 D5
Elham Cl. Bromley BR1 22 D1
Elham Cl. Gillingham ME8 49 B3
Elibank Rd. SE9 6 A3
Eling Ct. ME15 107 A8
Eliot Rd. DA1 10 B2
Elizabeth Cl. RM18 13 B5
Elizabeth Ct. Chatham ME5 62 A7
Elizabeth Ct. Erith DA8 8 D7
Elizabeth Ct. Gillingham ME8 49 C1
Elizabeth Ct. Gravesend DA11 13 A1
Elizabeth Garlick Ct. 1 TN1 149 B4
Elizabeth Garrett Anderson House. 9 DA17 4 A3
Elizabeth House. ME14 92 A6
Elizabeth Huggins Cotts. DA11 30 B6
Elizabeth Pl. DA4 40 E3
Elizabeth Raybould Ctr (Univ of Greenwich)The. DA2 10 B1
Elizabeth Smith's Ct. ME19 89 F7
Elizabeth St. DA9 10 E2
Elizabeth Terr. SE9 5 F1
Elizabeth Way. BR5 38 C4
Ellen Cl. BR1 36 D6
Ellen Wilkinson Prim Sch. E16 1 E8
Ellen's Pl. ME9 65 C6
Ellenborough Rd. DA14 24 E3
Ellenswood Cl. ME15 93 A1
Ellerman Rd. RM18 12 F5
Ellerslie. DA12 30 D8
Ellesmere Ct. SE12 22 A7
Ellingham Leas. ME15 107 C7
Elliott Rd. BR2 36 D5
Elliott St. DA12 30 D8
Elliotts La. TN14 & TN16 82 C3
Ellis Cl. SE9 23 C6
Ellis Ct. DA1 27 B7
Ellis Way. DA1 26 F6
Elliscombe Mount. 11 SE7 5 C8
Elliscombe Rd. SE7 5 C8
Ellison Rd. DA15 23 D7
Elliston House. 14 SE18 2 A2
Elm Ave. Chatham ME4 47 F1
Elm Ave. Chattenden ME3 34 A4
Elm Cl. Dartford DA1 26 C7
Elm Cl. Egerton TN27 127 F3
Elm Cl. Higham ME3 32 C3
Elm Cotts. BR8 40 B8
Elm Court Ind Est. ME7 62 E3
Elm Cres. ME19 89 F8
Elm Dr. BR8 39 D7
Elm Gr. Erith DA8 8 D7
Elm Gr. Hildenborough TN11 116 F5
Elm Gr. Maidstone ME15 92 B3
Elm Gr. Orpington BR6 37 F1
Elm La. TN10 & TN9 117 C3
Elm Rd. Dartford DA1 26 D7
Elm Rd. Erith DA8 9 A6
Elm Rd. Gillingham ME7 48 E6
Elm Rd. Gravesend DA12 30 C5
Elm Rd. Grays RM17 12 C8
Elm Rd. Hoo St Werburgh ME3 34 E3
Elm Rd. Orpington BR6 52 A3
Elm Rd. Royal Tunbridge Wells TN4 132 F1
Elm Rd. Sidcup DA14 24 A4
Elm Rd. Stone DA9 10 E1
Elm Rd. Westerham TN16 81 E2
Elm Terr. 3 Eltham SE9 6 A1
Elm Terr. West Thurrock RM16 11 B8
Elm Tree Cotts. ME3 19 A3
Elm Tree Ct. 18 SE7 5 C8
Elm Tree Dr. ME1 47 A2
Elm Wlk. Aylesford ME20 75 E1
Elm Wlk. Orpington BR6 50 F7
Elmbank Dr. BR1 36 D7
Elmbourne Dr. DA17 4 B2
Elmbrook Gdns. SE9 5 E3
Elmcroft Ave. DA15 7 A1
Elmcroft Rd. BR6 38 A2
Elmdene Rd. SE18 2 B1
Elmfield. Gillingham ME8 49 A3
Elmfield. Tenterden TN30 183 B8
Elmfield Cl. Gravesend DA11 30 B7
Elmfield Cl. Sevenoaks Weald TN14 99 B2
Elmfield Ct. Bexley DA16 7 B6
Elmfield Ct. Coxheath ME17 106 C3
Elmfield Ct. Tenterden TN30 183 B8
Elmfield Pk. BR1 36 A6
Elmfield Rd. BR1 36 A6
Elmhurst. Erith DA17 7 E8
Elmhurst. Swanscombe DA9 11 B1
Elmhurst Ave. TN2 150 D8
Elmhurst Gdns. ME1 47 E3
Elmhurst Rd. SE9 22 E5
Elmington Cl. DA5 8 B1
Elmlee Cl. BR7 22 F2
Elmley Cl. 15 E6 1 E8
Elmley St. SE18 2 D2
Elmshurst Gdns. TN10 117 C7
Elmslie Ct. SE9 6 A1
Elmstead Ave. BR7 22 F3
Elmstead Cl. TN13 83 E5
Elmstead Glade. BR7 22 F2
Elmstead La. BR7 & SE9 22 F3
Elmstead Rd. DA8 8 E6
Elmstead Woods Sta. BR7 22 E2
Elmsted Cres. DA16 7 C8
Elmstone Cl. ME16 91 B2
Elmstone Hole Rd. ME17 126 D8
Elmstone La. ME16 91 B2
Elmstone Rd. ME8 63 D7
Elmstone Terr. 3 BR5 38 C5
Elmtree Cotts. TN14 67 D4
Elmwood Dr. DA5 24 E8
Elmwood Rd. ME3 33 F6
Elphick's Pl. TN2 163 B8
Elrick Cl. DA8 8 E8
Elsa Rd. DA16 7 C5
Elsinore House. 7 SE7 1 E2
Elstow Cl. Eltham SE9 5 F2
Elstow Cl. Eltham SE9 6 A2
Elstree Gdns. DA17 3 E2
Eltham CE Prim Sch. SE9 5 F2
Eltham Coll. SE9 22 D6
Eltham Green Rd. SE9 5 C3
Eltham Green Sch. SE9 5 D1
Eltham High St. SE9 5 F1
Eltham Hill. SE9 5 E2
Eltham Hill Sch. SE9 5 E1
Eltham & Mottingham Hospl (General). SE9 5 F1
Eltham Palace. SE9 22 E8
Eltham Palace Rd. SE12 & SE9 5 D1
Eltham Park Gdns. SE9 6 A3
Eltham Rd. SE12 & SE9 5 B2
Eltham Sta. SE9 5 F2
Eltham Warren Golf Course. SE9 6 B2
Elvington Cl. ME16 91 D5
Elwick Ct. DA1 9 A3
Elwill Way. DA13 43 F8
Elwyn Gdns. SE12 22 A8
Ely Cl. Erith DA8 8 F5
Ely Cl. Gillingham ME8 49 E2
Ely Ct. TN2 149 B4
Ely Gdns. TN10 & TN9 117 D4
Elysian Ave. BR5 37 F3
Embassey Ct. DA14 24 B5
Embassy Cl. ME7 48 F1
Embassy Ct. DA16 7 B4
Ember Cl. BR5 37 C2
Emerald Cl. Chatham ME1 61 D7
Emerald Cl. Newham E16 1 E7
Emersons Ave. BR8 25 F1
Emerton Cl. DA6 7 E3
Emes Rd. DA8 8 C7
Emily Jackson Cl. TN13 84 B3
Emily Rd. ME5 62 B6
Emmett Hill La. ME18 120 F5
Emmetts Garden (NT). TN14 97 D5
Emmetts Rd. TN14 & TN16 97 D6
Empress Dr. BR7 23 B2
Empress Rd. DA12 30 E8
Emsworth Gr. ME14 92 D6
Enderfield Ct. BR7 37 A8
Engineer Cl. SE18 6 A8
Englefield Cl. BR5 37 F5
Englefield Cres. Cliffe Woods ME3 33 B7
Englefield Cres. Orpington BR5 38 A5
Englefield Path. BR5 38 A5
English Martyrs' RC Prim Sch. ME2 47 B8
Ennerdale Rd. DA7 8 A6
Ennis Rd. SE18 6 C8
Ensfield Rd. Leigh TN11 115 E1
Ensfield Rd. Upper Hayesden TN11 & TN3 132 A6
Ensign House. RM17 11 F8
Enslin Rd. SE9 23 A8
Enterprise Bsns Est. ME2 47 E7
Enterprise Cl. ME2 47 D8
Enterprise Ctr The. ME5 77 C8
Enterprise Rd. ME15 92 A1
Enterprise Way. TN8 112 C3
Epaul La. ME1 47 C6
Epsom Cl. Bexley DA7 8 B4
Epsom Cl. Maidstone ME15 107 F6
Epsom Cl. New Town ME19 89 B8
Epstein Rd. SE28 3 B5
Erica Ct. BR8 39 E5
Eridge Green Cl. BR5 38 C1
Eridge Rd. TN2 & TN4 148 E1
Eridge Sta. TN3 161 E2
Erindale. SE18 6 D8
Erindale Terr. SE18 6 D8
Erith Cl. ME14 92 A8
Erith & District Hospl. DA8 8 D8
Erith High St. Erith DA8 4 E1
Erith High St. Erith DA8 8 F8
Erith Rd. Bexley DA7 8 B4
Erith Rd. Erith DA17 4 B1
Erith Sch. DA8 8 D7
Erith Sch West. DA8 8 B7
Erith Sta. DA8 4 E1
Ermington Rd. BR7 & SE9 23 C6
Ernest Dr. ME16 91 B5
Ernest Rd. ME4 48 A3
Erskine House. 7 SE7 5 C8
Erskine Park Rd. TN4 148 C4
Erskine Rd. DA13 73 B8
Erwood Rd. SE7 1 E1
Escott Gdns. SE9 22 E4
Escreet Gr. SE18 2 A2
Eshcol Rd. ME3 35 C6
Esher Cl. DA5 24 F7
Eskdale Cl. DA2 27 C7
Eskdale Rd. DA7 8 A6
Esplanade. ME1 47 B5
Essenden Rd. DA17 4 A1
Essex Cl. TN2 162 F8
Essex Rd. 1 Dartford DA1 9 D1
Essex Rd. Gravesend DA11 30 A7
Essex Rd. Halling ME2 60 A6
Essex Rd. Longfield DA3 42 D7
Essex Rd. Maidstone ME15 107 E6
Essex Rd. West Thurrock RM16 11 A8
Essex St. SE18 2 C3
Estelle Cl. ME1 61 D7
Estridge Way. TN10 117 F5
Etfield Gr. DA14 24 B3

Ethel Brooks House. SE18 .... 6 B8
Ethel Rd. E16 .... 1 B7
Ethel Terr. BR6 .... 52 C2
Ethel-Maud Ct. ME7 .... 48 D7
Ethelbert Cl. BR1 .... 36 A6
Ethelbert Rd. Bromley BR1 & BR2 36 A6
Ethelbert Rd. Erith DA8 .... 8 C7
Ethelbert Rd. Rochester ME1 .... 47 C4
Ethelbert Rd. St Paul's Cray BR5 . 38 D6
Ethelbery Rd. DA2 .... 26 E3
Etherington Hill. TN3 .... 148 C8
Ethnam La. TN18 .... 186 E4
Ethronvi Rd. DA7 .... 7 E4
Eton Cl. ME5 .... 61 F4
Eton Rd. BR6 .... 52 B6
Eton Way. DA1 .... 9 C3
Europa Trad Est. DA8 .... 4 D1
Europe Rd. SE18 .... 1 F3
Euroway. ME20 .... 90 E8
Eustace Pl. SE18 .... 1 F2
Eva Rd. ME7 .... 48 D3
Evans Cl. DA9 .... 11 A2
Evelyn Denington Rd. E6 .... 1 F8
Evelyn Rd. Maidstone ME16 .... 91 E3
Evelyn Rd. Newham E16 .... 1 B5
Evelyn Rd. Otford TN14 .... 69 C2
Evenden House. TN17 .... 169 D5
Evenden Rd. DA13 .... 44 A2
Evenlode House. 5 SE2 .... 3 C4
Everard Ave. BR2 .... 36 A1
Everest Cl. 1 DA11 .... 29 E5
Everest Ct. SE9 .... 22 E6
Everest Dr. ME3 .... 34 E4
Everest La. ME2 .... 33 B1
Everest Mews. ME3 .... 34 E4
Everest Pl. BR8 .... 39 D5
Everest Rd. SE9 .... 5 F2
Everett Wlk. DA17 .... 3 F1
Everglades Cl. DA3 .... 42 F5
Everglades The. ME7 .... 62 F6
Evergreen Cl. Gillingham ME7 ...... 63 A5
Evergreen Cl. Higham ME3 .... 32 B3
Evergreen Cl. Leybourne ME19 ... 74 E2
Eversfield Ct. SE12 .... 22 B6
Eversley Ave. DA7 & DA8 .... 8 E5
Eversley Cl. ME16 .... 91 C6
Eversley Cross. DA7 .... 8 E5
Eversley Rd. SE7 .... 5 B8
Evesham Rd. DA12 .... 30 D6
Evry Rd. DA14 .... 24 C2
Ewart Rd. ME4 .... 47 E1
Ewehurst La. TN3 .... 147 F6
Ewell Ave. ME19 .... 89 A8
Ewell La. ME15 .... 105 D5
Ewins Cl. TN12 .... 136 A6
Exedown Rd. TN15 .... 71 C4
Exeter Cl. Newham E6 .... 1 F7
Exeter Cl. Tonbridge TN10 & TN9 117 D4
Exeter Rd. Bexley DA16 .... 6 F5
Exeter Rd. Gravesend DA12 .... 30 D5
Exeter Rd. Newham E16 .... 1 A8
Exeter Wlk. ME1 .... 61 C7
Exford Gdns. SE12 .... 22 B7
Exford Rd. SE12 .... 22 B7
Exmouth Rd. Bexley DA16 .... 7 C7
Exmouth Rd. Bromley BR2 .... 36 B6
Exmouth Rd. Gillingham ME7 .... 48 C7
Exmouth Rd. Grays RM17 .... 12 B8
Exton Cl. ME5 .... 62 C2
Exton Gdns. ME14 .... 92 F5
Eyhorne St. ME17 .... 94 D2
Eylesden Court Sch. ME14 .... 93 B4
Eynsford Castle. DA4 .... 54 E8
Eynsford Cl. BR5 .... 37 C3
Eynsford Cres. DA5 .... 24 D7
Eynsford Rd. Crockenhill BR8 ...... 39 E3
Eynsford Rd. Eynsford DA4 .... 40 F1
Eynsford Rd. Maidstone ME16 ...... 91 D7
Eynsford Rd. Swanscombe DA9 ... 11 C2
Eynsford Rise. DA4 .... 54 D6
Eynsford Sta. DA4 .... 54 D6
Eynsham Dr. SE2 .... 3 B3
Eynswood Dr. DA14 .... 24 C3

F Ave. SE18 .... 2 B3
Fackenden La. TN14 .... 69 C7
Factory Rd. Newham E16 .... 1 E5
Factory Rd. Northfleet DA11 .... 12 C1
Faesten Way. DA5 .... 25 E5
Fagus Cl. ME5 .... 62 B1
Fair Acres. BR2 .... 36 A4
Fair View. TN5 .... 175 A6
Fair View Jun & Inf Schs. ME8 63 C5
Fairacre Pl. DA3 .... 42 E6
Fairbank Ave. BR6 .... 51 B8
Fairbourne Heath Cotts. ME17 110 B1
Fairbourne La. ME17 .... 110 C4
Fairby La. DA3 .... 42 E3
Fairby Rd. SE12 .... 5 B2
Faircrouch La. TN5 .... 174 B5
Fairfax Bsns Ctr. ME15 .... 107 F4
Fairfax Cl. ME8 .... 63 D5
Fairfax Gdns. SE3 .... 5 C6
Fairfax Rd. RM18 .... 12 F6
Fairfield Ave. TN1 & TN2 .... 149 C5
Fairfield Cl. Kemsing TN15 .... 70 A1
Fairfield Cl. Sidcup DA15 .... 6 F1
Fairfield Cres. TN9 .... 133 C8
Fairfield Gr. SE7 .... 5 D8
Fairfield Rd. Bexley DA7 .... 7 F5
Fairfield Rd. Borough Green TN15 86 F8
Fairfield Rd. Bromley BR1 .... 22 A1
Fairfield Rd. Orpington BR5 .... 37 D3
Fairfield Way. TN11 .... 116 F5
Fairfields. DA12 .... 30 E3
Fairford Ave. DA7 .... 8 D6
Fairglen Cotts. TN5 .... 174 B4
Fairglen Rd. TN5 .... 174 B4
Fairhurst Dr. ME15 .... 106 B4
Fairings The. TN30 .... 183 B8
Fairland House. BR2 .... 36 B5
Fairlands Ct. 6 SE9 .... 6 A1
Fairlawn. SE7 .... 5 C8
Fairlawn Ave. DA16 .... 7 D5
Fairlawn Cl. ME18 .... 105 A8
Fairlawn Ct. SE7 .... 5 C7
Fairlead Rd. ME1 .... 47 D1
Fairlight Cl. TN4 .... 133 A2
Fairlight Cross. DA3 .... 43 C6
Fairlight Ct. TN10 .... 117 B4
Fairman's La. TN12 .... 152 B6
Fairmead. BR1 .... 36 F5
Fairmead Cl. BR1 .... 36 F5
Fairmead Rd. TN8 .... 112 C5
Fairmeadow. ME14 .... 91 F4
Fairmile House. BR5 .... 38 A7
Fairmile Rd. TN2 .... 149 E5
Fairmont Cl. DA17 .... 3 F1
Fairoak Cl. BR5 .... 37 B2
Fairoak Dr. SE9 .... 6 D2
Fairseat La. Fairseat TN15 .... 72 B5
Fairseat La. Stansted TN15 .... 57 A1
Fairthorn Rd. SE10 & SE7 .... 1 A1
Fairtrough Rd. BR6 .... 67 B7
Fairview. Erith DA8 .... 8 F7
Fairview. Fawkham Green DA3 ..... 56 B7
Fairview. Hawkhurst TN18 .... 178 F2
Fairview Ave. ME8 .... 63 B5
Fairview Cl. TN9 .... 133 B7
Fairview Cotts. ME15 .... 106 F5
Fairview Dr. Higham ME3 .... 32 B4
Fairview Dr. Orpington BR6 .... 51 D6
Fairview Gdns. DA13 .... 44 A4
Fairview Ind Est. RM9 .... 4 D8
Fairview Rd. DA13 .... 29 E1
Fairwater Ave. DA16 .... 7 A3
Fairway. Bexley DA6 .... 7 E2
Fairway. Orpington BR5 .... 37 D4
Fairway Cl. ME1 .... 47 C1
Fairway Ct. 12 SE9 .... 6 A1
Fairway Dr. DA2 .... 27 B8
Fairway The. Bromley BR1 & BR2 36 F4
Fairway The. Gravesend DA11 ...... 30 B6
Fairway The. Rochester ME1 .... 47 C1
Fairways The. TN4 .... 149 A7
Falcon Ave. Bromley BR1 .... 36 E5
Falcon Ave. Grays RM17 .... 12 C7
Falcon Cl. DA1 .... 9 F2
Falcon Gn. ME20 .... 74 F1
Falcon Mews. DA11 .... 29 E7
Falconwood Ave. DA16 .... 6 E5
Falconwood Par. DA16 .... 6 F3
Falconwood Sta. SE9 .... 6 D3
Falkland Pl. ME5 .... 61 E1
Fallowfield. ME5 .... 62 B8
Fallowfield Cl. ME14 .... 92 E4
Falmouth Pl. TN12 .... 135 C7
Fanconi Rd. ME5 .... 62 B3
Fancy Row. ME14 .... 93 C5
Fane Way. ME8 .... 63 D4
Fant La. ME16 .... 91 B2
Faraday Ave. DA14 .... 24 B6
Faraday Rd. Bexley DA16 .... 7 A4
Faraday Rd. Maidstone ME14 .... 92 C7
Faraday Ride. TN10 .... 117 D7
Faraday Way. Greenwich SE18 ...... 1 D3
Faraday Way. Orpington BR5 ...... 38 B5
Fareham Wlk. 10 ME15 .... 107 F6
Faringdon Ave. BR2 .... 37 A3
Farjeon Rd. SE18 & SE3 .... 5 D6
Farleigh Ave. BR2 .... 36 A2
Farleigh Ct. ME16 .... 91 A2
Farleigh Hill. ME15 .... 91 E1
Farleigh Hill Ret Pk. ME15 .... 91 E1
Farleigh La. ME16 .... 91 A1
Farleigh Trad Est. ME15 .... 91 E1
Farley Cl. ME5 .... 62 D2
Farley La. TN16 .... 96 B8
Farley Rd. DA12 .... 30 F7
Farleycroft. TN16 .... 81 C1
Farlow Cl. DA11 .... 29 F5
Farm Ave. BR8 .... 39 C6
Farm Holt. DA3 .... 42 F1
Farm La. TN11 .... 117 A4
Farm Pl. DA1 .... 9 A3
Farm Rd. Chatham ME5 .... 61 E3
Farm Rd. Sevenoaks TN14 .... 84 C7
Farm Vale. DA5 .... 8 B1
Farmcombe Cl. TN1 .... 149 B2
Farmcombe La. TN1 .... 149 B2
Farmcombe Rd. TN1 & TN2 .... 149 C2
Farmcote Rd. SE12 .... 22 A7
Farmcroft. DA11 .... 30 A6
Farmdale. ME1 .... 46 F3
Farmdale Ave. ME1 .... 46 F2
Farmdale Rd. SE10 .... 1 A1
Farmer Cl. ME17 .... 109 A6
Farmland Wlk. BR7 .... 23 B3
Farmstead Dr. TN8 .... 112 D3
Farnaby Dr. TN13 .... 84 A1
Farnaby Rd. SE9 .... 5 C3
Farnborough Cl. ME16 .... 91 C2
Farnborough Comm.
Keston Mark BR2 & BR6 .... 50 F7
Farnborough Comm.
Orpington BR6 .... 51 A6
Farnborough Ct. 2 BR6 .... 51 C5
Farnborough Hill. BR6 .... 51 E5
Farnborough Hospl. BR6 .... 51 A6
Farnborough Prim Sch. BR6 ...... 51 C5
Farnborough Way. BR6 .... 51 D5
Farne Cl. ME15 .... 107 A6
Farnham Beeches. TN3 .... 148 A4
Farnham Cl. Gillingham ME8 ...... 64 A8
Farnham Cl. Langton Green TN3 148 A3
Farnham La. TN3 .... 148 A4
Farnham Rd. DA16 .... 7 C5
Farningham Cl. ME14 .... 92 C6
Farningham Hill Rd. DA4 .... 40 D3
Farningham Road Sta. DA4 .... 41 B7
Farnol Rd. DA1 .... 10 A3
Faro Cl. BR1 .... 37 A7
Farraday Cl. ME1 .... 61 D8
Farrant Cl. BR6 .... 52 A3
Farrier Cl. ME14 .... 92 E5
Farriers Cl. DA12 .... 30 F7
Farriers Ct. ME8 .... 64 C8
Farrington Ave. BR5 .... 38 B6
Farrington House. 12 SE18 .... 2 A2
Farrington Pl. BR7 .... 23 D1
Farringtons Sch. BR7 .... 23 D1
Fartherwell Ave. ME19 .... 89 A8
Fartherwell Rd. ME19 .... 89 A8
Farthing Cl. DA1 .... 9 F3
Farthing Cnr. ME9 .... 63 E3
Farthing Hill. TN5 .... 176 E1
Farthing St. BR6 .... 50 F2
Farthingfield. TN15 .... 72 A3
Farthings Cotts. ME14 .... 76 F1
Farwell Rd. DA14 .... 24 C4
Farwig La. BR1 .... 36 A8
Fashoda Rd. BR2 .... 36 D5
Fauchon's Cl. ME14 .... 92 F3
Fauchon's La. ME14 .... 92 F4
Faversham Rd. ME17 .... 111 E7
Fawkham Ave. DA3 .... 43 C6
Fawkham CE Prim Sch. DA3 ...... 42 B1
Fawkham Green Rd. TN15 .... 56 B7
Fawkham House. 10 BR5 .... 38 D1
Fawkham Manor Hospl. DA3 ...... 42 C1
Fawkham Rd. Longfield DA3 .... 42 D6
Fawkham Rd.
West Kingsdown TN15 .... 56 A4
Fawley Cl. ME14 .... 91 E7
Faygate Cres. DA6 .... 8 A2
Fazan Ct. TN5 .... 174 F4
Fearon St. SE10 .... 1 A1
Featherby Cty Prim Inf Sch.
ME8 .... 49 A3
Featherby Jun Sch. ME8 .... 49 A3
Featherby Rd.
Gillingham,Lower Twydall ME7 ..... 49 A5
Featherby Rd.
Gillingham,Twydall ME8 .... 49 A3
Federation Rd. SE2 .... 3 C2
Feenan Highway. RM18 .... 13 B6
Felderland Cl. ME17 .... 107 E5
Felderland Dr. ME17 .... 107 E5
Felderland Rd. ME17 .... 107 E5
Feldspar Cl. ME5 .... 62 A1
Felhampton Rd. SE9 .... 23 B5
Felix Manor. BR7 .... 23 E2
Felixstowe Rd. SE2 .... 3 B3
Fell Mead. TN12 .... 119 F6
Fellowes Way. TN11 .... 116 E5
Fellows Cl. ME8 .... 63 B6
Felltram Way. SE7 .... 1 A1
Felspar Cl. SE18 .... 2 F1
Felstead Rd. BR6 .... 52 B8
Felsted Rd. E16 .... 1 D7
Felton Cl. BR5 .... 37 B3
Felton House. SE9 .... 5 C3
Felton Lea. DA14 .... 23 F3
Fen Gr. DA15 .... 6 F1
Fen Meadow. TN15 .... 71 C1
Fen Pond Rd. TN15 .... 86 C7
Fendyke Rd. SE2 .... 3 D3
Fenn Cl. BR1 .... 22 A2
Fennell St. SE18 .... 6 A8
Fens Way. BR8 .... 26 A2
Fenton Cl. BR7 .... 22 F3
Fenwick Cl. 16 SE18 .... 6 A8
Ferbies. TN3 .... 148 A7
Ferbies Cotts. TN3 .... 148 A7
Ferby Ct. DA15 .... 23 F4
Ferdinand Terr. TN3 .... 161 C7
Ferguson Ave. DA12 .... 30 C4
Fern Cl. DA8 .... 9 B6
Fern Down. DA13 .... 73 B8
Fern Hill Pl. 3 BR6 .... 51 C5
Fernbank Cl. ME5 .... 61 F2
Ferndale. Bromley BR1 .... 36 C7
Ferndale.
Royal Tunbridge Wells TN2 .... 149 D5
Ferndale. Sevenoaks TN13 .... 84 C5
Ferndale Cl. Bexley DA7 .... 7 E6
Ferndale Cl.
Royal Tunbridge Wells TN2 .... 149 C4
Ferndale Point. TN2 .... 149 C4
Ferndale Rd. Gillingham ME7 ...... 48 E5
Ferndale Rd. Gravesend DA12 ..... 30 B6
Ferndale St. E6 .... 2 B7
Ferndale Way. BR6 .... 51 D5
Ferndell Ave. DA5 .... 25 D5
Ferndene. DA3 .... 43 D6
Ferndown Cl. Gillingham ME7 ..... 63 A5
Ferndown Cl. Orpington BR6 ...... 37 D1
Ferndown Rd. SE9 .... 22 D8
Fernheath Way. DA2 .... 25 D3
Fernhill Rd. ME16 .... 91 A2
Fernhill St. E16 .... 1 F5
Fernholt. TN10 .... 117 C7
Fernhurst Cres. TN4 .... 133 A2
Fernleigh Rise. ME20 .... 75 B2
Ferns The. Larkfield ME20 .... 75 B1
Ferns The. Platt TN15 .... 87 C7
Ferns The.
Royal Tunbridge Wells TN1 .... 149 C4
Fernside La. TN13 .... 99 D6
Fernwood Cl. BR1 .... 36 C7
Ferranti Cl. SE18 .... 1 D3
Ferrier Cl. ME8 .... 63 E4
Ferrier Point. 8 E16 .... 1 A8
Ferry La. Rainham RM13 .... 4 E7
Ferry La. Wouldham ME1 .... 60 C4
Ferry Rd. Halling ME2 .... 60 B4
Ferry Rd. Tilbury RM18 .... 13 A4
Festival Ave. DA3 .... 43 D6
Festival Cl. Erith DA8 .... 8 F7
Festival Cl. Sidcup DA5 .... 24 D7
Ffinch Cl. ME20 .... 90 D8
Fiddlers Cl. DA9 .... 11 B3
Field Cl. Bromley BR1 .... 36 C7
Field Cl. Chatham ME5 .... 61 E6
Field Dr. TN8 .... 112 D3
Field Rd. DA13 & TN15 .... 57 E6
Fieldfare Rd. SE28 .... 3 C6
Fielding Ave. RM18 .... 13 B6
Fielding Dr. ME20 .... 75 A3
Fields La. ME18 .... 104 E7
Fieldside Cl. BR6 .... 51 C6
Fieldway. BR5 .... 37 D3
Fieldways. TN18 .... 179 A1
Fieldworks Rd. ME4 & ME7 .... 48 A7
Fiennes Way. TN13 .... 99 C8
Fiesta Dr. RM9 .... 4 C8
Fife Rd. E16 .... 1 A8
Fifteenpenny Fields. SE9 .... 6 A2
Fifth Ave. RM16 .... 11 A8
Fiji Terr. ME14 .... 92 A7
Filborough Way. DA12 .... 31 B6
Filmer La. TN13 & TN14 & TN15 .. 84 E6
Filston La. TN13 & TN14 .... 68 E5
Filston Rd. DA8 .... 4 C1
Finch Ct. ME14 .... 91 E7
Finchale Rd. SE2 .... 3 A3
Finchley Cl. DA1 .... 10 A1
Finchley Rd. RM17 .... 12 B8
Findlay Cl. ME8 .... 63 D6
Finglesham Cl. BR5 .... 38 D1
Finglesham Ct. ME15 .... 107 C8
Finsbury Way. DA5 .... 7 F1
Fintonagh Dr. ME14 .... 92 B6
Finucane Dr. BR5 .... 38 C2
Fir Dene. BR6 .... 51 A8
Fir Tree Cl. Hildenborough TN11 116 E5
Fir Tree Cl. 5 Orpington BR6 ..... 51 F5
Fir Tree Cl. Staplehurst TN12 ..... 139 F3
Fir Tree Gr. Bredhurst ME7 .... 63 B1
Fir Tree Gr. Chatham ME5 .... 62 D1
Fir Tree Rd. TN4 .... 148 F3
Firbank Cl. E16 .... 1 D8
Fircroft Way. TN8 .... 112 C3
Firecrest Cl. DA3 .... 43 B6
Firethorn Cl. ME7 .... 48 E6
Firmin Rd. DA1 .... 9 C2
Firmingers Rd. BR6 .... 53 C5
Firs Cl. ME20 .... 75 E1
Firs Ct. TN4 .... 148 F6
Firs The. Coldblow DA5 .... 25 D7
Firs The. Sidcup DA15 .... 23 F5
Firside Gr. DA15 .... 23 F7
First Ave. Bexley DA7 .... 7 C7
First Ave. Chatham ME4 .... 48 C2
First Ave. Gillingham ME7 .... 48 E3
First Ave. Northfleet DA11 .... 29 E7
First Ave. West Thurrock RM16 .... 11 A8
First La. ME15 .... 93 E2
First St. TN3 .... 147 F3
Fisher House. 13 SE18 .... 2 A2
Fisher Rd. ME5 .... 62 B7
Fisher St. Maidstone ME14 .... 92 A6
Fisher St. Newham E16 .... 1 A8
Fisher's Gate Cotts. TN7 .... 160 A1
Fisher's Way. DA17 .... 4 C5
Fishermans Wlk. SE28 .... 2 E4
Fishermen's Hill. DA11 .... 12 B2
Fishers Cl. TN12 .... 139 F5
Fishers Rd. TN12 .... 139 F5
Fishponds Rd. BR2 .... 50 D5
Fisons Rd. E16 .... 1 A5
Fitzroy Ct. DA1 .... 27 B7
Fitzthorold House. ME7 .... 48 E7
Fitzwilliam Mews. E16 .... 1 A5
Fitzwilliam Rd. ME14 .... 92 F5
Five Acre Wood Sch. ME15 .... 107 B7
Five Bells La. ME1 .... 47 D4
Five Elms Rd. BR2 .... 50 C7
Five Oak Green Rd.
Five Oak Green TN11 & TN12 .... 134 D6
Five Oak Green Rd.
Tonbridge TN9 .... 133 F7
Five Oak La. TN12 .... 139 B1
Five Wents. BR8 .... 40 A7
Fiveash Rd. DA11 .... 29 F8
Fiveways. TN1 .... 149 A4
Fiveways L Ctr. ME4 .... 48 A4
Flack Gdns. ME3 .... 34 E5
Flamingo Cl. ME5 .... 62 A7
Flamsteed Rd. SE7 .... 1 E1
Flats The. DA9 .... 11 C2
Flaxman Ct. Erith DA17 .... 4 A1
Flaxman Ct. 7 Gillingham ME7 . 48 A6
Flaxman Dr. ME16 .... 91 C6
Flaxmore Ct. DA7 .... 8 B4
Flaxmore Pl. TN4 .... 133 A2
Flaxton Rd. SE18 .... 6 E7
Fleet Ave. DA2 .... 27 C7
Fleet Dale Par. DA2 .... 27 C7
Fleet Rd. Dartford DA2 .... 27 C7
Fleet Rd. Northfleet DA11 .... 29 C6
Fleet Rd. Rochester ME1 .... 47 D1
Fleetdown Cty Prim Sch. DA2 . 27 C6
Fleetwood Cl. E16 .... 1 D8
Fleetwood Ct. 1 Newham E6 .... 1 F8
Fleetwood Ct. Orpington BR6 ...... 51 A6
Fleming Gdns. RM18 .... 13 C6
Fleming Way. Erith SE28 .... 3 D6
Fleming Way. Tonbridge TN10 .. 117 E7
Fletcher Rd. TN12 .... 139 E3
Fletchers Cl. BR2 .... 36 B5
Fletching Rd. SE7 .... 5 D8
Flimwell Bird Pk. TN19 .... 177 E2
Flimwell Cl. TN5 .... 177 D4
Flint Cl. 8 BR6 .... 51 F4
Flint Gn. ME5 .... 62 C3
Flint La. ME17 .... 111 C8
Flint St. RM16 .... 11 B8
Flintmill Cres. SE3 & SE9 .... 5 E5
Floats The. TN13 .... 83 E6
Flood Hatch. ME15 .... 91 D2
Flora St. DA17 .... 3 F1
Florance La. TN3 .... 161 B6
Florence Cl. RM17 & RM16 .... 11 E8
Florence Cotts. TN8 .... 112 C1
Florence Farm Mobile Home Pk.
TN15 .... 55 D4
Florence House. SE18 .... 5 F6
Florence Rd. Bromley BR1 .... 36 A8
Florence Rd. Erith SE2 .... 3 C2
Florence Rd. Maidstone ME16 ..... 91 E3
Florence St. ME2 .... 47 B8
Flower Rise. ME14 .... 91 F7
Flowerfield. TN14 .... 68 F2
Flowerhill Way. DA13 .... 29 E1
Floyd Rd. SE7 .... 1 C1
Flume End. ME16 .... 91 D2
Flyers Way The. TN16 .... 81 D1
Foalhurst Cl. TN10 .... 117 E4
Foley Ct. DA1 .... 27 B7
Foley St. ME14 .... 92 A5
Folkstone House. 4 ME15 ...... 107 F6
Fontwell Cl. 6 ME15 .... 107 F6
Fontwell Dr. BR2 .... 37 A4
Foord Almshouses. ME1 .... 47 B3
Foord Rd. ME17 .... 111 D5
Foord St. ME1 .... 47 D4
Footbury Hill Rd. BR6 .... 38 A2
Foots Cray High St. DA14 .... 24 D2
Foots Cray La. DA5 & DA14 .... 24 C7
Footscray Rd. BR7 & SE9 .... 23 C7
Force Green La. TN16 .... 81 E4
Ford House. 2 SE18 .... 2 B1
Ford La. Trottiscliffe ME19 .... 73 A4
Ford La. Wrotham Heath TN15 ..... 72 F2
Ford Rd. DA11 .... 12 B2
Fordcombe CE Prim Sch. TN3 147 B5
Fordcombe Cl. ME15 .... 107 F7
Fordcombe La. TN3 .... 147 C5
Fordcombe Rd. Fordcombe TN3 147 C4
Fordcombe Rd. Penshurst TN11 131 A3
Fordcroft Rd. BR5 .... 38 B4
Forde Ave. BR1 .... 36 C6
Fordingbridge Cl. ME16 .... 91 B5
Fords Park Rd. E16 .... 1 A7
Fordwich Cl. Maidstone ME16 ..... 91 B7
Fordwich Cl. Orpington BR6 .... 37 F2
Fordwich Gn. ME8 .... 49 C3
Foreland St. SE18 .... 2 D2
Foremans Barn Rd. ME15 .... 105 F3
Forest Cl. BR7 .... 37 A8
Forest Dr. Chatham ME5 .... 61 F2
Forest Dr. Keston Mark BR2 .... 50 E7
Forest Gr. TN10 .... 117 C5
Forest Hill. ME15 .... 91 F1
Forest Lawns. BR1 .... 36 C8
Forest Rd. Erith DA8 .... 9 A6
Forest Rd. Paddock Wood TN12 . 136 A6
Forest Rd.
Royal Tunbridge Wells,Hawkenbury
TN2 .... 149 C1
Forest Rd.
Royal Tunbridge Wells,
Rumbers Hill TN2 .... 163 A8
Forest Ridge. BR2 .... 50 F6
Forest Way. Kings Hill ME19 ...... 89 A3
Forest Way. Orpington BR5 .... 38 A4
Forest Way. Pembury TN2 .... 150 D8
Forest Way.
Royal Tunbridge Wells TN2 ...... 149 D1
Forest Way. Sidcup SE9 .... 23 D8
Forestdale Rd. ME5 .... 77 A8
Foresters Cl. ME5 .... 61 F2
Foresters Cres. DA7 .... 8 B3
Forge Cl. Hayes BR2 .... 36 A1
Forge Cl. Penshurst TN11 .... 131 B4
Forge Cotts. ME18 .... 104 C2
Forge Croft. TN8 .... 112 D1
Forge La. Benover ME18 .... 121 B4
Forge La. Boxley ME14 .... 77 C2
Forge La. Bredhurst ME7 .... 63 A1
Forge La. Dean Street ME15 ...... 106 C7
Forge La. Egerton Forstal TN27 .. 127 C1
Forge La. Gillingham ME7 .... 48 E7
Forge La. Gravesend DA12 .... 30 F6
Forge La. Headcorn TN27 .... 141 D5
Forge La. High Halstow ME23 ...... 17 E3
Forge La. Higham ME3 .... 32 C3
Forge La. Horton Kirby DA4 .... 41 C5
Forge La. Leeds ME17 .... 108 F7
Forge La. Rabbit's Cross TN12 ... 123 F3
Forge La. Shorne DA12 .... 31 E3
Forge La. West Kingsdown TN15 . 56 A1
Forge La. West Peckham ME18 .. 103 A6
Forge Lane Cty Inf Sch. ME7 ..... 48 E6
Forge Meadow. ME17 .... 110 D6
Forge Meadows. TN27 .... 141 D5
Forge Meads. TN30 .... 189 E3
Forge Rd.
Groombridge TN3 & TN6 .... 161 C2
Forge Rd.
Royal Tunbridge Wells TN4 .... 133 A1
Forge Sq. TN11 .... 115 F2
Forge The. TN12 .... 135 B7
Forge View. TN15 .... 100 B5
Forge Way. Paddock Wood TN12 136 A7
Forge Way. Shoreham TN14 .... 68 F8

Forgefield Ct. BR5 .... 38 C4
Formby Rd. ME2 .... 60 A7
Formby Terr. ME2 .... 60 A6
Forsham La. ME17 .... 124 C5
Forson Cl. TN30 .... 183 B8
Forstal Cl. BR2 .... 36 A6
Forstal Cotts. ME20 .... 76 B2
Forstal La. ME17 .... 106 D4
Forstal Rd. Egerton Forstal TN27 127 C1
Forstal Rd. Forstal ME20 .... 76 C2
Forstal The. Cobbarn TN3 ..... 161 F3
Forstal The. Hadlow TN11 .... 118 F8
Forstal The. Pembury TN2 .... 150 E8
Forstall. TN3 .... 148 A4
Forstall The. TN11 .... 116 A2
Forsters. ME17 .... 108 E4
Fort Luton (Mus). ME4 .... 48 A1
Fort Pitt Gram Sch. ME1 .... 47 E4
Fort Pitt Hill. ME1 & ME4 ...... 47 E4
Fort Pitt St. ME4 .... 47 E3
Fort Rd. Shepham Heath TN14 .. 68 C4
Fort Rd. Tilbury RM18 .... 13 C5
Fort St. Newham E16 .... 1 B5
Fort St. Rochester ME1 .... 47 D4
Fortis Cl. E16 .... 1 C7
Fortrye Cl. DA11 .... 29 E6
Fortuna Cl. DA3 .... 42 F5
Forty Acre La. E16 .... 1 A8
Fossdene Prim Sch. SE7 .... 1 B1
Fossdene Rd. SE7 .... 1 B1
Fosse Bank. TN9 .... 133 A7
Fosse Bank Cl. TN9 .... 133 A7
Fosse Bank New Sch. TN11 ... 116 E7
Fosse Rd. TN9 .... 117 B2
Fossington Rd. DA17 .... 3 D2
Fosten La. TN27 .... 171 E7
Foster Clark Est. ME15 .... 92 B2
Foster St. ME15 .... 92 A3
Fosters Cl. BR7 .... 22 F3
Fosters VC Prim Sch. DA16 ..... 7 B5
Fostington Way. ME5 .... 61 F1
Foulds Cl. ME8 .... 63 B5
Founder Cl. E6 .... 2 B7
Fountain Cl. Eynsford DA4 ..... 54 E8
Fountain Cl. Sidcup DA15 .... 7 B1
Fountain Ent Pk. ME15 .... 92 A1
Fountain La. ME16 .... 91 A2
Fountain Rd. ME2 .... 32 E1
Fountain Wlk. DA11 .... 12 F1
Four Acres. ME19 .... 90 B5
Four Elms Cty Prim Sch. TN8 .. 113 B5
Four Elms Hill. ME3 .... 33 E4
Four Elms Rd. TN8 .... 112 D4
Four Oaks Rd. TN12 & TN27 ... 140 E7
Four Wents. Langley Heath ME17 108 E3
Four Wents. Marlpit ME17 .... 107 F2
Fouracre Cotts. ME9 .... 64 F6
Fourth Ave. Gillingham ME7 ... 48 E4
Fourth Ave. West Thurrock RM16 11 A8
Fourwents Rd. ME3 .... 34 D7
Fowey Cl. ME5 .... 62 C5
Fowler Cl. Gillingham ME8 .... 63 C3
Fowler Cl. Sidcup DA14 .... 24 E3
Fox Cl. Newham E16 .... 1 A8
Fox Cl. Orpington BR6 .... 52 A5
Fox Hollow Dr. DA16 .... 7 D4
Fox House Rd. DA17 .... 4 B1
Fox In The Wood. TN5 .... 174 C6
Fox La. BR2 .... 50 C5
Fox St. ME7 .... 48 C6
Foxburrow Cl. ME8 .... 63 D5
Foxbury. DA3 .... 56 E7
Foxbury Ave. BR7 .... 23 D2
Foxbury Cl. Bromley BR1 .... 22 B2
Foxbury Cl. Orpington BR6 ..... 52 A5
Foxbury Dr. BR6 .... 52 A4
Foxbury Rd. BR1 .... 22 B2
Foxbush. TN11 .... 116 C6
Foxcroft Rd. SE18 .... 6 B6
Foxden Dr. ME15 .... 92 F1
Foxendown La. DA13 .... 44 B1
Foxes Dale. SE3 .... 5 A4
Foxfield Prim Sch. SE18 .... 2 C2
Foxfield Rd. BR6 .... 51 D8
Foxglove Cl. TN8 .... 112 D3
Foxglove Cres. ME5 .... 61 E4
Foxglove Rise. ME14 .... 91 E7
Foxhole La. Four Throws TN18 .. 179 E1
Foxhole La. Matfield TN12 ..... 151 C8
Foxhole La. Wadhurst TN5 .... 175 B4
Foxhole Rd. SE9 .... 5 E2
Foxhome Cl. BR7 .... 23 A2
Foxton House. E16 .... 2 A4
Foxton Rd. RM16 .... 11 D8
Foxwood Gr. BR6 .... 52 C1
Foxwood Rd. DA2 .... 28 B5
Foxwood Way. DA3 .... 43 D7
Framley Rd. TN10 .... 117 F5
Framlingham Cres. SE9 .... 22 F4
Frances St. SE18 .... 1 F2
Francis Ave. DA7 .... 8 A5
Francis Dr. ME5 .... 62 A2
Francis La. ME15 .... 107 F5
Francis Rd. Dartford DA1 .... 9 D2
Francis Rd. Hildenborough TN11 116 D6
Francis Rd. St Paul's Cray BR5 .. 38 D6
Frank Burton Cl. SE7 .... 1 B1
Frank Woolley Rd. TN10 ...... 117 F5
Frank's Hollow Rd. TN3 & TN4 132 C2
Frankapps Cl. ME9 .... 65 B6
Frankfield Rise. TN2 .... 149 A1
Franklin Dr. ME14 .... 91 F7
Franklin Rd. Bexley DA7 .... 7 E6
Franklin Rd. Gillingham ME7 .... 48 D5
Franklin Rd. Gravesend DA12 ... 30 D3

Franklins Cotts. ME15 .... 106 C5
Franks Ct. ME8 .... 49 B2
Franks La. DA4 .... 41 B4
Franks Wood Ave. BR2 & BR5 ... 37 C4
Frant CE Prim Sch. TN3 ...... 163 B4
Frant Field. TN8 .... 112 C1
Frant Rd. TN2 & TN3 .... 163 A7
Frant Sta. TN3 .... 163 F5
Fraser Cl. Coldblow DA5 .... 25 C7
Fraser Cl. Newham E6 .... 1 E7
Fraser House. SE18 .... 2 A2
Fraser Rd. DA8 .... 4 D1
Frederic House. SE7 .... 1 E1
Frederick Andrews Ct. RM17 ... 12 D8
Frederick Pl. SE18 .... 2 B1
Frederick Rd. ME7 .... 48 C4
Free Heath Rd. TN3 & TN5 .... 165 C3
Freehold. TN12 .... 119 F6
Freehold The. TN11 .... 102 D1
Freeland Way. DA8 .... 9 A6
Freelands Gr. BR1 .... 36 B8
Freelands Rd. Bromley BR1 ... 36 B8
Freelands Rd. Snodland ME6 ... 74 F8
Freeman Gdns. ME4 .... 47 F2
Freeman Rd. DA12 .... 30 E5
Freeman Way. ME15 .... 107 E7
Freemasons Rd. E16 .... 1 B7
Freesia Cl. Gillingham ME7 .... 48 F6
Freesia Cl. Orpington BR6 ..... 51 F5
Freight La. TN17 .... 169 C3
Fremantle House. RM18 .... 12 F6
Fremantle Rd. DA17 .... 4 A2
Fremlin Cl. TN4 .... 148 B4
Fremlins Rd. ME14 .... 93 C4
Frensham Rd.
   Rolvenden Layne TN17 ..... 182 A1
Frensham Rd. Sidcup DA15 .... 23 D6
Frensham Wlk. ME5 .... 61 F1
Freshland Rd. ME16 .... 91 B4
Freshwater Rd. ME5 .... 62 B7
Freta Rd. DA6 .... 7 F2
Frewing Cl. BR7 .... 23 A3
Friar Rd. BR5 .... 38 A4
Friars Ave. ME5 .... 61 F2
Friars Mews. SE9 .... 6 A2
Friars Way. TN2 .... 149 D6
Friars Wlk. SE2 .... 3 D1
Friary Pl. ME2 .... 47 B7
Friary Prec. ME2 .... 47 B7
Friday Rd. DA8 .... 4 D1
Friday St. ME17 .... 125 B6
Friezland Rd. TN4 .... 148 D1
Friezley La. TN17 .... 155 C1
Frimley Cl. ME14 .... 24 C3
Frindsbury Hill. ME2 .... 33 C1
Frindsbury Rd. ME2 .... 47 B8
Frinstead Cl. BR5 .... 38 D5
Frinstead Wlk. ME16 .... 91 B7
Frinsted Cl. ME8 .... 49 C3
Frinsted Rd. DA8 .... 8 D7
Frinton Rd. DA14 .... 24 E6
Friston Way. ME1 .... 61 D8
Friswell Pl. DA7 .... 8 A3
Frithwood Cl. ME15 .... 92 F1
Frittenden Rd. Rochester ME2 .. 33 D2
Frittenden Rd. Staplehurst TN12 140 B2
Frobisher Gdns. ME1 .... 47 C2
Frobisher Rd. Erith DA8 .... 9 A7
Frobisher Rd. Newham E6 .... 2 A7
Frobisher Way. DA12 .... 30 E3
Frog La. Rainham ME9 .... 4 D8
Frog La.
   Royal Tunbridge Wells TN1 ... 149 A2
Frog La. West Malling ME19 ... 89 C8
Frog's La. TN17 .... 181 E1
Froghole La. TN16 & TN8 ...... 96 D3
Frogmore Wlk. ME17 .... 111 C5
Frognal Ave. DA14 .... 24 A2
Frognal Pl. DA14 .... 24 A3
Frognall Cnr. BR7 .... 23 F2
Frogs Hole La. TN17 .... 171 E3
Froissart Rd. SE9 .... 5 E2
Fromandez Dr. TN12 .... 152 F5
Frome Ct. TN10 .... 117 B5
Front Cotts. TN5 .... 176 E1
Frost Cres. ME5 .... 62 A7
Froyle Cl. ME16 .... 91 C6
Fruitfields. TN5 .... 177 C3
Fry Cl. ME3 .... 21 A6
Fry's Cotts. ME3 .... 19 C4
Frythe Cl. TN17 .... 169 D4
Frythe Cres. TN17 .... 169 D4
Frythe Way. TN17 .... 169 D4
Frythe Wlk. TN17 .... 169 D4
FTA (Trng Ctr). TN5 .... 174 D6
Fuchsia St. SE2 .... 3 B1
Fuggles Cl. TN12 .... 135 E6
Fuggles Cl. TN17 .... 180 D6
Fulbert Dr. ME14 .... 92 F5
Fuller Cl. Durgates TN5 .... 174 E5
Fuller Cl. Orpington BR6 .... 51 F5
Fullers Cl. ME14 .... 93 A4
Fullers Hill. TN16 .... 81 D1
Fulmar Rd. ME2 .... 46 D6
Fulmer Rd. E16 .... 1 D8
Fulthorp Rd. SE3 .... 5 A5
Fulwich Rd. DA1 .... 9 F1
Furfield Cl. ME17 .... 107 E5
Furnace Ave. TN3 .... 166 A3
Furnace La. Hook Green TN3 ... 165 E4
Furnace La. Horsmonden TN12 . 152 F7
Furner Cl. DA1 .... 8 F4
Furness Sch. BR8 .... 25 F2
Furnival Ct. TN2 .... 162 F8
Furrell's Rd. ME1 .... 47 D5
Furze Bank. TN8 .... 113 B6
Furzefield Ave. TN3 .... 148 A8
Furzefield Cl. BR7 .... 23 B2

Furzefield Rd. SE3 & SE7 .... 5 B7
Furzehill Sq. BR5 .... 38 B5
Fyfe Way. BR1 .... 36 A7

Gable Cl. DA1 .... 9 A2
Gables Cl. SE12 .... 22 A7
Gables The. Bromley BR1 ...... 22 B1
Gables The. New Barn DA3 ..... 43 C6
Gabriel Gdns. DA12 .... 30 E3
Gabriel Spring Road (East).
   DA3 & DA4 .... 55 F8
Gabriel's Hill. ME14 & ME15 ... 92 A4
Gabrielspring Rd. DA4 .... 55 D8
Gads Hill. ME7 .... 48 F6
Gads Hill Sch. ME2 .... 32 C2
Gadsby La. TN27 .... 159 F3
Gadwall Cl. E16 .... 1 B7
Gadwall Way. SE28 .... 2 D4
Gafford's Bridge Cotts. TN12 . 137 C4
Gagetown Terr. ME14 .... 91 F7
Gainsborough Ave. Dartford DA1 . 9 C2
Gainsborough Ave. Tilbury RM18 13 B6
Gainsborough Cl. ME8 .... 63 D6
Gainsborough Dr.
   Maidstone ME16 .... 91 B4
Gainsborough Dr.
   Northfleet DA11 .... 29 D5
Gainsborough Gdns. TN10 .... 117 E5
Gainsborough House. ME1 ..... 47 D5
Gainsborough Sq. DA7 .... 7 D4
Gaitskell Rd. SE9 .... 23 C7
Galahad Ave. ME2 .... 46 E6
Galahad Rd. BR1 .... 22 A4
Galena Cl. ME5 .... 62 A1
Galena House. SE18 .... 2 F1
Gallants La. ME15 .... 105 F6
Galleon Bvd. DA9 .... 10 D3
Galleon Cl. Chatham ME1 ..... 61 C8
Galleon Cl. Erith DA8 .... 4 D2
Galley Hill Rd. DA11 .... 11 F2
Galley Hill Trad Est. DA10 .... 11 E2
Gallions Mount Prim Sch. SE18 . 2 F1
Gallions Rd. Greenwich SE7 ..... 1 A2
Gallions Rd. Newham E16 .... 2 C6
Gallions Reach Sta. E16 .... 2 B6
Gallon Cl. SE7 .... 1 C2
Gallops The. DA13 .... 72 F7
Gallosson Rd. SE18 .... 2 E2
Gallus Sq. SE3 .... 5 B4
Galsworthy Cl. SE28 .... 3 B5
Galsworthy Cres. SE3 .... 5 C6
Galsworthy Rd. RM18 .... 13 C6
Galton House. SE18 .... 5 F6
Games House. SE7 .... 5 C8
Gamma Rd. SE28 .... 35 D7
Gandy's La. ME17 .... 107 C2
Garden Ave. DA7 .... 8 A3
Garden Cl. Lewisham SE12 .... 22 B5
Garden Cl. Maidstone ME15 .. 107 E7
Garden Cl. Toy's Hill TN16 .... 97 C3
Garden Cotts. Leigh TN11 .... 116 A2
Garden Cotts. St Paul's Cray BR5 38 C7
Garden Ct. SE9 .... 6 A1
Garden Pl. ME4 .... 48 A7
Garden Rd. Bromley BR1 ...... 22 B2
Garden Rd.
   Royal Tunbridge Wells TN1 ... 149 B4
Garden Rd. Sevenoaks TN13 .. 84 D5
Garden Rd. Tonbridge TN9 ... 117 D2
Garden Row. DA11 .... 29 F5
Garden St. Gillingham ME7 .... 48 A6
Garden St.
   Royal Tunbridge Wells TN1 ... 149 B4
Garden Terr. TN15 .... 85 A6
Garden Way. ME18 .... 88 F2
Gardenia Cl. ME2 .... 33 B2
Gardens The. ME17 .... 106 C3
Gardiner Cl. BR5 .... 38 C7
Gardiner House. SE18 .... 5 F7
Gardiner St. ME7 .... 48 C6
Gardyne Mews. TN9 .... 133 B8
Gareth Br. DA12 .... 22 A4
Garfield Rd. ME7 .... 48 D6
Gargany Wlk. SE28 .... 3 D6
Garibaldi St. SE18 .... 2 E2
Garland Rd. SE18 .... 6 D7
Garlands. TN11 .... 116 D8
Garlinge Rd. TN4 .... 133 A1
Garnet Wlk. E6 .... 1 E8
Garnett Cl. SE9 .... 5 F4
Garrard Cl. Bexley DA7 .... 8 A4
Garrard Cl. Chislehurst BR7 .... 23 B3
Garrick Dr. SE18 .... 2 D3
Garrick St. DA11 .... 13 B1
Garrington Cl. ME14 .... 92 C6
Garrison Cl. SE18 .... 6 A7
Garrison Rd. ME12 .... 21 F3
Garrolds Cl. BR8 .... 39 D7
Garrow. DA3 .... 43 B6
Garside Cl. SE28 .... 2 D3
Garth Rd. TN13 .... 99 C7
Garvary Rd. E16 .... 1 B7
Garvock Dr. TN13 .... 84 A1
Gas House Rd. ME1 .... 47 C6
Gascoyne Dr. DA1 .... 8 F1
Gasoline Alley. TN15 .... 72 D2
Gasson Rd. DA10 .... 11 E1
Gassons Rd. ME6 .... 74 E8
Gatcombe Cl. Chatham ME5 .... 62 A5
Gatcombe Cl. Maidstone ME16 . 91 B5
Gate Farm Rd. TN3 & TN4 ... 132 C4
Gateacre Ct. DA14 .... 24 A5
Gatefield Cotts. TN17 .... 181 F4
Gatehouse Farm Cotts. TN4 .. 132 C4
Gates Green Rd. BR2 & BR4 ... 50 A6

Gateway Par. DA12 .... 30 F4
Gatland La. ME16 .... 91 B2
Gatling St. SE18 & SE2 .... 3 A1
Gaton Rd. SE2 .... 3 C3
Gattons Way. DA14 .... 24 F4
Gatwick Farm Cotts. RH19 ... 144 A4
Gatwick Rd. DA12 .... 30 B6
Gault Cl. ME15 .... 93 A2
Gautrey Sq. E6 .... 1 F7
Gavestone Cres. SE12 .... 22 B8
Gavestone Rd. SE12 .... 22 B8
Gavin House. SE18 .... 2 E2
Gayhurst Cl. ME8 .... 63 D6
Gaylor Rd. RM18 .... 12 F6
Gaza Trad Est. TN11 .... 115 D7
Gazelle Glade. DA12 .... 30 F3
Gean Cl. ME5 .... 77 A8
Geddes Pl. DA7 .... 8 A3
Gedge's Hill. TN12 .... 135 F3
Geffery's Ct. SE9 .... 22 E5
General Gordon Pl. SE18 .... 2 B2
Genesta Glade. DA12 .... 31 A3
Genesta Rd. SE18 .... 6 C8
Geneva Ave. ME8 .... 49 A2
Gentian Cl. Chatham ME5 ..... 61 E4
Gentian Cl. Maidstone ME14 .. 92 E5
George Akass House. SE18 ..... 2 C1
George Crooks House. RM17 12 B8
George La. Hayes BR2 .... 36 B1
George La. Leeds ME17 .... 109 B7
George La. Rochester ME1 ..... 47 C6
George Marsham House.
   ME15 .... 106 F3
George St. Chainhurst ME15 .. 122 A4
George St. Grays RM17 .... 12 A8
George St. Maidstone ME15 ... 92 A3
George St.
   Royal Tunbridge Wells TN2 ... 149 C3
George St. Sparrow's Green TN5 174 F5
George St. Staplehurst TN12 .. 139 E6
George St. Tonbridge TN9 .... 133 B8
George Summers Cl. ME2 ..... 47 E8
Georges Cl. BR5 .... 38 C6
Georgian Cl. BR2 .... 36 B1
Georgian Dr. ME17 .... 106 D3
Georgian Way. ME8 .... 63 C4
Geraint Rd. BR1 .... 22 A4
Gerald Ave. ME4 .... 47 F2
Gerald Rd. DA12 .... 30 E8
Gerda Rd. SE9 .... 23 C6
Gerdview Dr. DA2 .... 26 C4
Gerrard Ave. ME1 .... 61 E8
Gertrude Rd. DA17 .... 4 A2
Gibbet La. TN12 .... 152 F6
Gibbetts. TN3 .... 147 F3
Gibbs Hill. Headcorn TN27 ... 141 D6
Gibbs Hill. Nettlestead ME18 . 104 B5
Gibraltar Ave. ME7 .... 48 B7
Gibraltar Hill. ME4 .... 47 F4
Gibraltar La. ME14 .... 91 F8
Gibson Cl. DA11 .... 29 F5
Gibson Dr. ME19 .... 88 F4
Gidd's Pond Cotts. ME14 ..... 92 E6
Giddyhorn La. ME16 .... 91 C5
Gideon Cl. DA17 .... 4 B2
Gifford Cl. ME8 .... 49 C3
Giggs Hill. BR5 .... 38 A8
Gighill Rd. ME20 .... 74 F4
Gilbert Cl. Eltham SE18 .... 5 F6
Gilbert Cl. Gillingham ME7 .... 63 A5
Gilbert Cl. Swanscombe DA10 .. 11 D1
Gilbert Rd. Bromley BR1 .... 22 A1
Gilbert Rd. Erith DA17 .... 4 A3
Gilbert Rd. SE18 .... 6 F8
Gilbert Terr. ME14 .... 91 F7
Gilbourne Rd. SE18 .... 6 F8
Gilchrist Cotts. TN14 .... 99 C2
Gildenhill Rd. BR8 .... 26 C1
Gildersome St. SE18 .... 6 A8
Gill Ave. Newham E16 .... 1 A7
Gill Ave. Rochester ME2 .... 33 D2
Gill Cres. DA11 .... 29 F5
Gill Ct. SE18 .... 2 C2
Gill The. TN2 .... 150 E8
Gill's Rd. Green Street Green DA2 28 B1
Gill's Rd. South Darenth DA4 .. 41 F8
Gillan Ct. SE12 .... 22 B5
Gilletts La. ME19 .... 90 A6
Gillies Ct. DA14 .... 23 E4
Gillies Rd. TN15 .... 55 E5
Gillingham Gn. ME7 .... 48 E6
Gillingham Rd. ME7 .... 48 D5
Gillingham Sta. ME7 .... 48 D5
Gillmans Rd. BR5 & BR6 ...... 38 B1
Gilroy Way. BR5 .... 38 B2
Gimble Way. TN2 .... 134 D1
Gingerbread La. TN18 .... 177 F2
Ginsbury Cl. ME2 .... 47 E6
Gipps Cross La. TN3 .... 147 F3
Gipsy Cl. RM17 .... 12 C8
Gipsy Rd. DA16 .... 7 D5
Giralda Cl. E16 .... 1 D8
Glade Bsns Ctr The. RM16 .... 10 F8
Glade The. Bromley BR1 ...... 36 D7
Glade The. Chatham ME5 ..... 62 A2
Glade The. Greenwich SE7 ...... 5 C7
Glade The. Sevenoaks TN13 ... 84 B4
Glades Sh Ctr The. BR1 .... 36 A7
Glades The. DA12 .... 30 D2
Gladeswood Rd. DA17 .... 4 B2
Gladstone Rd. Chatham ME4 ... 47 F2
Gladstone Rd. Dartford DA1 .... 9 F1
Gladstone Rd. Maidstone ME14 . 92 A6
Gladstone Rd. Orpington BR6 .. 51 C5
Gladstone Rd. Rusthall TN4 .. 148 B4
Gladstone Rd. Tonbridge TN9 . 117 B1
Gladwell Rd. BR1 .... 22 A1
Gladwyn Cl. ME8 .... 63 D4
Glamford Rd. ME2 .... 46 D5

Glamis Cl. ME5 .... 62 A5
Glanville Rd. Bromley BR2 .... 36 B6
Glanville Rd. Gillingham ME7 .. 48 D5
Glanville Rd. Rochester ME2 ... 47 A8
Glasbrook Rd. SE9 .... 22 D8
Glasgow House. ME15 .... 107 E7
Glass Yd. SE18 .... 2 A3
Glassmill La. BR2 .... 36 A7
Glebe Cl. TN27 .... 143 B2
Glebe Cotts. TN16 .... 82 B4
Glebe Gdns. ME17 .... 111 E5
Glebe House. SE18 .... 2 A2
Glebe House Dr. BR2 .... 36 B1
Glebe La. Maidstone ME16 .... 91 A1
Glebe La. Sevenoaks TN13 .... 84 B1
Glebe Meadow. ME18 .... 104 E7
Glebe Pl. DA4 .... 41 C5
Glebe Rd. Bromley BR1 .... 36 A8
Glebe Rd. Gillingham ME7 .... 48 E3
Glebe Rd. Gravesend DA11 .... 29 F7
Glebe Rd. Sevenoaks Weald TN14 99 B3
Glebe The. Bidborough TN4 .. 132 D3
Glebe The. Chislehurst BR7 ... 37 C8
Glebe The. Cuxton ME2 .... 46 C2
Glebe The. Pembury TN2 .... 150 D8
Glebe The. Penshurst TN11 .. 131 A3
Glebe Way. SE9 .... 8 E8
Glebefield The. TN13 .... 83 F4
Glebeland. TN27 .... 127 F4
Glebelands.
   Bidborough TN3 & TN4 .... 132 C3
Glebelands. Biddenden TN27 . 157 F3
Glebelands. Crayford DA1 .... 8 F3
Glebelands. Penshurst TN11 .. 131 A3
Gleeson Dr. BR6 .... 51 F6
Glen Ct. DA14 .... 24 A4
Glen Dunlop House The. TN13 84 C5
Glen House. E16 .... 2 A5
Glen The. SE1 .... 51 A7
Glen View. DA12 .... 30 C7
Glen View Rd. BR1 .... 36 D7
Glenalvon Way. SE7 .... 1 E2
Glenbarr Cl. SE9 .... 6 B4
Glencairne Cl. E16 .... 1 D8
Glencoe Cty Inf Sch. ME4 ..... 48 A2
Glencoe Cty Prim Sch. ME4 ... 48 A2
Glencoe Rd. ME4 .... 48 A2
Glendale. BR8 .... 39 F4
Glendale Cl. SE9 .... 6 A4
Glendale Ct. TN1 .... 149 D6
Glendale Rd. Erith DA8 .... 4 C2
Glendale Rd. Northfleet DA11 .. 29 E5
Glendale Way. SE28 .... 3 C6
Glendower Cres. BR5 & BR6 .. 38 A3
Glendown Rd. SE2 .... 3 A1
Gleneagles Cl. BR6 .... 37 D1
Gleneagles Ct. ME5 .... 61 F2
Gleneagles Dr. ME15 .... 92 A1
Gleneagles Gn. BR6 .... 37 D1
Glenesk Rd. SE9 .... 6 B3
Glengall Rd. DA7 .... 7 E4
Glenhead Cl. SE9 .... 6 B4
Glenhouse Rd. SE9 .... 6 A4
Glenhurst Ave. DA5 .... 24 F7
Glenister St. E16 .... 2 A5
Glenlea Rd. SE9 .... 6 A3
Glenluce Rd. SE3 .... 5 A8
Glenlyon Rd. SE9 .... 6 A2
Glenmore Pk. TN2 .... 162 F8
Glenmore Rd. DA16 .... 6 F6
Glenmount Path. SE18 .... 2 C1
Glenrosa Gdns. DA12 .... 30 F3
Glenrose Ct. DA14 .... 24 B3
Glenshiel Rd. SE9 .... 6 A2
Glentrammon Ave. BR6 .... 51 F4
Glentrammon Cl. BR6 .... 51 F5
Glentrammon Gdns. BR6 .... 51 F4
Glentrammon Rd. BR6 .... 51 F4
Glenure Rd. SE9 .... 6 A2
Glenview. SE2 .... 7 D8
Glenwood. TN30 .... 173 B3
Glenwood Cl. Chatham ME5 .. 48 C1
Glenwood Cl. Gillingham ME7 .. 63 A7
Glenwood Cl. Maidstone ME16 . 91 C5
Glenwood Cl. St Michaels TN30 173 B3
Glenwood Ct. DA14 .... 24 A4
Glimpsing Gn. DA18 .... 3 E3
Glistening Glade. ME8 .... 63 E6
Gload Cres. BR5 .... 52 D8
Globe La. ME4 .... 47 F5
Globe Yd. DA11 .... 13 B1
Gloucester Ave. Bexley DA16 ... 6 F3
Gloucester Ave. Sidcup DA15 .. 23 E6
Gloucester Cl. ME8 .... 64 A8
Gloucester Ct. RM18 .... 12 F5
Gloucester Par. DA15 .... 7 A2
Gloucester Rd. Dartford DA1 .. 26 B8
Gloucester Rd. Erith DA17 ...... 3 F1
Gloucester Rd. Gravesend DA12 30 C4
Gloucester Rd. Maidstone ME15 107 D8
Gloucester Rd.
   Sparrow's Green TN5 ...... 174 F6
Glover Cl. SE2 .... 3 C2
Gloxinia Rd. DA13 .... 29 B2
Glyn Davies Cl. TN13 .... 83 F7
Glyn Dr. DA14 .... 24 B4
Glynde Rd. DA7 .... 7 E4
Glyndebourne Pk. BR6 .... 51 B8
Glyndon Rd. SE18 .... 2 D2
Goad Ave. ME5 .... 62 C2
Goddard's Green Cotts. TN17 170 F1
Goddards Cl. TN17 .... 169 B4
Godden Rd. ME6 .... 74 F8
Goddings Dr. ME1 .... 47 A3
Goddington Chase. BR6 .... 52 B6
Goddington House. BR6 ...... 52 C7

Goddington La. Harrietsham ME17 ... 110 B6
Goddington La. Orpington BR6 ... 52 A7
Goddington Rd. ME2 ... 47 B8
Godfrey Cl. ME2 ... 32 F1
Godfrey Evans Cl. TN10 ... 117 F5
Godfrey Hill. SE18 ... 1 E2
Godfrey Rd. SE18 ... 1 F2
Godstow Rd. SE2 ... 3 C4
Godwin House. SE18 ... 5 F6
Godwin Rd. BR1 & BR2 ... 36 C6
Gold St. DA12 ... 44 E4
Goldace. RM17 ... 11 F8
Goldcrest Cl. Newham E16 ... 1 D8
Goldcrest Cl. Woolwich SE28 ... 3 C6
Golden Plover Cl. E16 ... 1 A7
Golden Sq. TN30 ... 183 B8
Golden Wood Cl. ME5 ... 77 D8
Goldfinch Cl. Larkfield ME20 ... 75 A2
Goldfinch Cl. Orpington BR6 ... 52 A5
Goldfinch Cl. Paddock Wood TN12 ... 136 A5
Goldfinch Rd. SE28 ... 2 D3
Goldie Leigh Hospl. SE2 ... 7 C8
Golding Cl. ME20 ... 75 C1
Golding Gdns. TN12 ... 120 A6
Golding Rd. TN13 ... 84 C5
Goldings. TN12 ... 135 E5
Goldings The. ME8 ... 63 C8
Goldmark House. SE3 ... 5 B4
Goldsel Rd. BR8 ... 39 E5
Goldsmid Rd. TN9 ... 133 C8
Goldsmith St. SE18 ... 2 E1
Goldsmith. RM17 ... 11 F8
Goldsmith Rd. ME8 ... 63 E5
Goldsmith's Bottom. TN14 ... 98 E7
Goldstone Wlk. ME5 ... 62 A1
Goldsworth Dr. ME2 ... 33 A1
Goldthorne Cl. ME14 ... 92 C5
Goldwing Cl. E16 ... 1 A7
Golf Links Ave. DA11 ... 30 B3
Golf Rd. BR1 ... 37 A6
Golford Rd. TN17 ... 169 F4
Gollogly Terr. 9 SE7 ... 1 C1
Goodall Cl. ME8 ... 63 E5
Goodbury Rd. TN15 ... 70 B6
Gooding House. 4 SE7 ... 1 C1
Goodley Stock. TN16 & TN8 ... 96 F6
Goodmead Rd. BR6 ... 38 A2
Goods Hill. TN30 ... 182 D8
Goods Station Rd. TN1 ... 149 B4
Goodtrees La. TN8 ... 145 B2
Goodwin Dr. Maidstone ME14 ... 92 B8
Goodwin Dr. Sidcup DA14 ... 24 D6
Goodwin Rd. ME3 ... 33 B7
Goodwins The. TN2 ... 148 F1
Goodwood Cl. High Halstow ME23 ... 17 E4
Goodwood Cl. Maidstone ME15 ... 107 F6
Goodwood Cres. DA12 ... 30 C2
Goodworth Rd. TN15 ... 71 F3
Goosander Way. SE18 & SE28 ... 2 D3
Goose Cl. ME5 ... 62 A7
Goose Green Cl. BR5 ... 38 A7
Goose Sq. 6 E6 ... 1 F7
Gooseneck La. TN27 ... 141 C5
Gordon Cl. ME17 ... 106 E3
Gordon City Jun Sch. ME2 ... 47 B8
Gordon House. SE12 ... 22 A8
Gordon Pl. DA11 ... 13 C1
Gordon Prim Sch. SE9 ... 5 F3
Gordon Rd. Chatham ME4 ... 48 B2
Gordon Rd. Dartford DA1 ... 26 D8
Gordon Rd. Erith DA7 ... 4 C2
Gordon Rd. Gillingham ME7 ... 48 E5
Gordon Rd. Gillingham,Brompton ME4 ... 48 A7
Gordon Rd. Hoo St Werburgh ME3 ... 34 D5
Gordon Rd. Northfleet DA11 ... 29 E8
Gordon Rd. Rochester ME2 ... 47 A8
Gordon Rd. Royal Tunbridge Wells TN4 ... 149 C7
Gordon Rd. Sevenoaks TN13 ... 84 B2
Gordon Rd. Sidcup DA15 ... 6 E2
Gordon Terr. ME1 ... 47 C4
Gordon Way. BR1 ... 36 A8
Gore Cotts. DA2 ... 27 C4
Gore Court Rd. ME15 ... 107 F5
Gore Farm Cotts. DA2 ... 27 C5
Gore Green Rd. ME3 ... 32 E7
Gore La. TN17 ... 153 E4
Gore Rd. Dartford DA2 ... 27 D6
Gore Rd. Silver Street ME9 ... 80 F5
Gorham Cl. ME6 ... 74 F7
Gorham Dr. Maidstone ME15 ... 93 A1
Gorham Dr. Tonbridge TN9 ... 133 E8
Gorman Rd. SE18 ... 1 F2
Gorringe Ave. DA4 ... 41 D7
Gorse Ave. ME5 ... 61 F5
Gorse Cl. E16 ... 1 A7
Gorse Cres. ME20 ... 90 D8
Gorse Rd. Orpington BR5 ... 53 A8
Gorse Rd. Rochester ME2 ... 46 F8
Gorse Rd. Royal Tunbridge Wells TN2 ... 149 E5
Gorse Way. DA3 ... 43 A4
Gorse Wood Rd. Hartley DA3 ... 43 A5
Gorse Wood Rd. New Barn DA3 ... 43 A6
Goss Hill. BR8 ... 26 C2
Gossage Rd. SE18 ... 2 D1
Gosshill Rd. BR7 ... 37 A7
Gossington Cl. BR7 ... 23 B4
Gothic Cl. DA1 ... 26 D5
Goudhurst Cl. ME16 ... 91 E4
Goudhurst & Kilndown CE Prim Sch. TN17 ... 167 E8
Goudhurst Rd. Gillingham ME8 ... 49 B3
Goudhurst Rd. Horsmonden TN12 ... 153 B5

Goudhurst Rd. Knox Bridge TN12 & TN17 ... 155 C6
Goudhurst Rd. Wilsley Pound TN17 ... 169 D8
Gouge Ave. DA11 ... 29 E7
Gould Rd. ME5 ... 62 B3
Goulburst Rd. TN12 ... 138 B5
Gourock Rd. SE9 ... 6 A2
Gover Hill. TN11 ... 102 E6
Grace Ave. Bexley DA7 ... 7 F5
Grace Ave. Maidstone ME16 ... 91 D6
Grace Cl. SE9 ... 22 D5
Gracious La. TN13 ... 99 B5
Gracious Lane Bridge. TN13 ... 99 A6
Gracious Lane End. TN14 ... 98 F5
Grafton Ave. ME1 ... 61 E8
Graham Ct. BR1 ... 22 B1
Graham House. SE18 ... 6 B7
Graham Rd. DA7 ... 8 A3
Grain Rd. Gillingham ME8 ... 63 C3
Grain Rd. Grain ME3 ... 20 D3
Grainey Field. ME9 ... 64 E4
Grainger Wlk. TN10 ... 117 E6
Gram Sch for Girls Wilmington. DA2 ... 26 B5
Grampian Cl. Orpington BR6 ... 37 F3
Grampian Cl. Royal Tunbridge Wells TN2 ... 149 D5
Grampian Way. ME15 ... 93 A1
Granada House. 6 ME15 ... 92 A4
Granada St. 7 ME15 ... 92 A4
Granary. TN12 ... 136 B6
Granary Cl. Gillingham ME8 ... 49 F1
Granary Cl. Maidstone ME14 ... 92 E5
Granby House. 14 SE18 ... 1 F2
Granby Rd. Eltham SE9 ... 5 F4
Granby Rd. Northfleet DA11 ... 12 D1
Granby Rd. Woolwich SE18 ... 2 B3
Grand Depot Rd. SE18 ... 2 A1
Grandshire Gdns. ME3 ... 34 E6
Grandshore La. TN17 ... 156 B5
Grange Cl. Edenbridge TN8 ... 112 C1
Grange Cl. Leybourne ME19 ... 74 C2
Grange Cl. Sidcup DA15 ... 24 A5
Grange Cl. Westerham TN16 ... 81 C1
Grange Cotts. TN11 ... 101 D5
Grange Cres. Erith SE28 ... 3 C7
Grange Cres. Rochester ME3 ... 173 A3
Grange Dr. Chislehurst BR7 ... 22 F2
Grange Dr. Pratt's Bottom BR6 ... 52 C2
Grange Gdns. SE25 ... 148 D4
Grange Hill. Chatham ME4 ... 48 B3
Grange Hill. Plaxtol TN15 ... 101 E8
Grange House. Erith DA8 ... 9 A5
Grange House. Gravesend DA11 ... 30 A8
Grange House. Maidstone ME16 ... 91 A4
Grange La. Hartley DA3 ... 43 B2
Grange La. Maidstone ME5 ... 77 A1
Grange Rd. Gillingham ME7 ... 49 B5
Grange Rd. Gravesend DA11 ... 30 A8
Grange Rd. Platt TN15 ... 87 C7
Grange Rd. Grays RM17 ... 12 B8
Grange Rd. Orpington BR6 ... 51 C8
Grange Rd. Rochester ME2 ... 47 B7
Grange Rd. Rusthall TN4 ... 148 D4
Grange Rd. Sevenoaks TN13 ... 99 A8
Grange Rd. St Michaels TN30 ... 172 B1
Grange The. East Malling ME19 ... 90 A7
Grange The. South Darenth DA4 ... 41 D8
Grange The. West Kingsdown TN15 ... 55 F2
Grange The. Westerham TN16 ... 81 C1
Grange Way. Erith DA8 ... 9 B7
Grange Way. Hartley DA3 ... 42 A3
Grange Way. Rochester ME1 ... 47 C3
Grangehill Pl. SE9 ... 5 F4
Grangehill Rd. SE9 ... 5 F3
Grangeways Cl. DA11 ... 29 F4
Grangewood. DA5 ... 24 F7
Granite St. SE18 ... 2 F1
Grant Cl. ME7 ... 49 B1
Grant's Cotts. ME17 ... 111 B5
Granton Rd. DA14 ... 24 C2
Granville Ct. TN13 ... 84 A3
Granville Mews. DA14 ... 24 A4
Granville Rd. Bexley DA16 ... 7 C4
Granville Rd. Gillingham ME7 ... 48 E5
Granville Rd. Gravesend DA11 ... 29 F7
Granville Rd. Maidstone ME14 ... 92 A6
Granville Rd. Royal Tunbridge Wells TN1 ... 149 C5
Granville Rd. Sevenoaks TN13 ... 84 A3
Granville Rd. Sidcup DA14 ... 24 B4
Granville Rd. Westerham TN16 ... 81 C1
Granville Sch The. TN13 ... 84 A3
Grapple Rd. ME14 ... 92 A7
Grasdene Rd. SE18 & SE2 ... 7 A7
Grasmere Ave. BR6 ... 51 B7
Grasmere Gdns. BR6 ... 51 B7
Grasmere Gr. ME2 ... 33 C2
Grasmere Rd. Bexley DA7 ... 8 C5
Grasmere Rd. Orpington BR6 ... 51 B7
Grassington Rd. DA14 ... 24 A4
Grasslands. ME17 ... 108 E4
Grassmere. ME20 ... 74 F2
Grassy Glade. ME7 ... 63 B6
Grassy La. TN13 ... 99 B8
Gravel Hill. DA6 ... 8 B2
Gravel Hill Cl. DA6 ... 8 B2
Gravel Hill Prim Sch. DA6 ... 8 B3
Gravel Pit Way. BR6 ... 38 A1
Gravel Rd. Keston Mark BR2 ... 50 E8
Gravel Rd. Sutton at Hone DA4 ... 27 B1
Gravel Wlk. ME7 ... 47 D5
Gravelly Bottom Rd. ME17 ... 109 B2
Gravelly Ways. TN12 ... 120 D3
Gravelwood Cl. BR7 ... 23 C5
Graveney Cl. ME3 ... 33 C7

Graveney Rd. ME15 ... 107 F7
Graves Est. DA16 ... 7 B5
Gravesend Gram Sch for Boys. ... 30 D8
Gravesend Gram Sch for Girls. Gravesend DA11 ... 30 A7
Gravesend Gram Sch for Girls. Gravesend DA11 ... 30 A8
Gravesend & North Kent Hospl. DA11 ... 13 A1
Gravesend Rd. Gadshill ME2 & ME3 & DA12 ... 32 C2
Gravesend Rd. Rochester ME2 ... 46 F8
Gravesend Rd. Shorne DA12 ... 31 D5
Gravesend Rd. Vigo Village TN15 ... 72 D6
Gravesend Sta. DA11 ... 13 B1
Gravesham Ct. 8 DA11 ... 30 B8
Grayland Cl. BR1 ... 36 D8
Graylands. RM17 ... 11 E8
Grayne Ave. ME3 ... 21 B5
Grays Farm Prim Sch. BR5 ... 38 B8
Grays Farm Production Village. BR5 ... 38 B8
Grays Farm Rd. BR5 ... 38 B8
Grays Rd. TN14 & TN16 ... 81 D7
Grays Sh Ctr. RM17 ... 12 A8
Grays Sta. RM17 ... 12 A8
Grazeley Cl. DA6 ... 8 C2
Great Basin Rd. ME12 ... 21 F2
Great Bounds Dr. TN4 ... 132 E3
Great Brooms Rd. TN4 ... 149 C8
Great Courtlands. TN3 ... 148 A3
Great Elms. TN11 ... 102 E1
Great Elms Rd. BR2 ... 36 C5
Great Footway. TN3 ... 147 F3
Great Hall Arc. 3 TN1 ... 149 B3
Great Harry Dr. SE9 ... 23 A5
Great Ivy Mill Cotts. ME15 ... 106 F7
Great Lines. ME7 ... 48 B5
Great Lodge Cotts. TN2 ... 133 C2
Great Maytham Hall. TN17 ... 181 F2
Great Oak. TN19 ... 184 A3
Great Queen St. DA1 ... 9 F1
Great South Ave. ME4 ... 48 A1
Great Thrift. BR5 ... 37 C5
Greatness La. TN14 ... 84 C6
Greatness Rd. TN13 & TN14 ... 84 C6
Grebe Apartments. 13 ME15 ... 107 E5
Grebe Cl. ME3 ... 19 C4
Grebe Cl. ME20 ... 74 F1
Grecian Rd. TN1 ... 149 B6
Grecian St. ME2 ... 92 A6
Green Acres. DA14 ... 23 F4
Green Bank Cl. ME7 ... 63 A5
Green Cl. ME1 ... 47 D2
Green Court Rd. BR8 ... 39 F5
Green Farm Cl. BR6 ... 51 F5
Green Farm La. DA12 ... 31 E5
Green Gdns. BR6 ... 51 C5
Green Hedges. TN30 ... 183 B8
Green Hill. Maidstone ME15 ... 93 B1
Green Hill. Woolwich SE18 ... 1 F1
Green Hill La. ME17 ... 110 D1
Green La. Boughton Monchelsea ME17 ... 107 C3
Green La. Cliffe ME3 ... 16 B6
Green La. Collier Street TN12 ... 137 E8
Green La. Devil's Den ME17 ... 124 B4
Green La. East End TN17 ... 171 C2
Green La. Eltham BR7 & SE9 ... 23 B5
Green La. Four Elms TN8 ... 113 C7
Green La. Grain ME3 ... 21 B5
Green La. Langley Heath ME17 ... 108 E3
Green La. Meopham Station DA13 ... 44 B2
Green La. Platt's Heath ME17 ... 110 F2
Green La. Smarden TN27 ... 143 A1
Green La. Stockbury ME9 ... 64 F1
Green La. Trottiscliffe ME19 ... 73 A5
Green La. Withyham TN26 ... 159 F3
Green La The. TN11 ... 115 F1
Green Lane Cotts. Collier Street TN12 ... 121 D1
Green Lane Cotts. Langley Heath ME17 ... 108 E3
Green Lawns. 8 SE18 ... 2 B2
Green Pl. DA1 ... 8 E2
Green Rd. TN12 ... 153 A6
Green Sands. ME14 ... 77 C8
Green Sq. TN5 ... 174 F5
Green St. ME7 ... 48 C5
Green Street Green Prim Sch. BR6 ... 51 F4
Green Street Green Rd. DA1 & DA2 ... 27 D4
Green The. Bexley,Bexley Heath DA7 ... 8 A6
Green The. Bexley,Falconwood DA16 ... 6 F4
Green The. East Farleigh ME15 ... 106 B7
Green The. Hayes BR2 ... 36 A2
Green The. Langton Green TN3 ... 147 E3
Green The. Leigh TN11 ... 115 F1
Green The. Lewisham BR1 ... 22 A5
Green The. Sevenoaks TN13 ... 84 D5
Green The. Sidcup DA14 ... 24 A4
Green The. St Paul's Cray BR5 ... 24 B1
Green The. Westerham TN16 ... 81 D1
Green Vale. DA6 ... 7 D2
Green View Ave. TN11 ... 116 A1
Green Way. Bromley BR2 ... 36 E5
Green Way. Eltham SE9 ... 5 D2
Green Way. Hartley DA3 ... 42 E4
Green Way. Maidstone ME16 ... 91 B3
Green Way. Royal Tunbridge Wells TN2 ... 149 E8

Green Wlk. DA1 ... 8 F3
Green's Cotts. ME15 ... 106 A1
Greenacre. DA1 ... 26 C6
Greenacre Cl. Chatham ME5 ... 62 A5
Greenacre Cl. Swanley BR8 ... 39 E5
Greenacre Sch. ME5 ... 61 F5
Greenacres. SE9 ... 6 A1
Greenacres Cl. BR6 ... 51 C6
Greenacres Prim Sch & Language Impairment Unit. SE9 ... 23 A6
Greenbank. ME5 ... 62 B8
Greenbank Lodge. 2 BR7 ... 37 A8
Greenbanks. DA1 ... 26 E6
Greenbay Rd. SE7 ... 5 D7
Greenborough Cl. ME15 ... 107 E6
Greencourt Rd. BR5 ... 37 E4
Greencroft Cl. E16 ... 1 D8
Greendale Wlk. 4 DA11 ... 29 E5
Greenfield. TN8 ... 112 D1
Greenfield Cl. Eccles ME20 ... 76 A6
Greenfield Cl. Rusthall TN4 ... 148 C5
Greenfield Cotts. ME14 ... 77 C3
Greenfield Gdns. BR5 ... 37 D2
Greenfield Rd. Gillingham ME7 ... 48 D6
Greenfield Rd. Joyden's Wood DA2 ... 25 D3
Greenfields. ME15 ... 107 E8
Greenfields Cl. ME3 ... 33 D3
Greenfinches. Gillingham ME7 ... 62 F6
Greenfinches. New Barn DA3 ... 43 B6
Greenfrith Dr. TN10 ... 117 B6
Greenhill Cts. SE7 ... 1 F1
Greenhill La. TN27 ... 143 F7
Greenhill Rd. Northfleet DA11 ... 29 F6
Greenhill Rd. Otford TN14 ... 69 C5
Greenhill Terr. SE18 ... 1 F1
Greenhithe. 3 ME15 ... 92 A3
Greenhithe Cl. SE9 ... 23 E8
Greenhithe Sta. DA9 ... 11 A2
Greenholm Rd. SE9 ... 6 B2
Greening St. SE2 ... 3 C2
Greenlands. TN15 ... 87 C7
Greenlands Rd. TN15 ... 85 B8
Greenlaw St. SE18 ... 2 A3
Greenleas. TN2 ... 150 C6
Greenleigh Ave. BR5 ... 38 B5
Greens End. SE18 ... 2 B2
Greensand Rd. ME15 ... 93 A2
Greenshields Ind Est. E16 ... 1 B5
Greenside. High Halden TN26 ... 173 E7
Greenside. Maidstone ME15 ... 92 B3
Greenside. Swanley BR8 ... 39 D7
Greenslade Prim Sch. SE18 ... 6 D8
Greentrees Ave. TN10 ... 117 F5
Greenvale Gdns. ME8 ... 49 B2
Greenvale Rd. SE9 ... 6 A3
Greenview Cres. TN11 ... 116 A4
Greenview Wlk. ME8 ... 49 A4
Greenway. Chatham ME5 ... 61 D6
Greenway. Chislehurst BR7 ... 23 B3
Greenway. Cranbrook TN17 ... 169 B4
Greenway Court Farm Cotts. ME17 ... 95 A1
Greenway Court Rd. ME17 ... 95 A1
Greenway La. ME17 ... 110 A7
Greenway The. BR5 ... 38 B3
Greenways. Maidstone ME14 ... 92 F5
Greenways. South Barn DA3 ... 43 D6
Greenways The. TN12 ... 135 F5
Greenwich Cl. Chatham ME5 ... 62 B6
Greenwich Cl. Maidstone ME16 ... 91 D4
Greenwich Com Coll. SE9 ... 5 E1
Greenwich Cres. E6 ... 1 E8
Greenwich Educ Tuition Ctr (Foxhill Ctr). SE18 ... 6 B8
Greenwich Ind Est. SE7 ... 1 B2
Greenwood Cl. Orpington BR5 & BR6 ... 37 E3
Greenwood Cl. Sidcup DA15 ... 24 A2
Greenwood House. 8 RM17 ... 12 B8
Greenwood Pl. TN15 ... 72 A2
Greenwood Rd. DA5 ... 24 D4
Greenwood Sch. SE18 ... 6 E6
Greenwood Way. TN15 ... 83 F2
Greggs Wood Rd. TN1 & TN2 ... 149 E7
Gregor Mews. SE3 ... 5 A7
Gregory Cres. SE9 ... 22 D8
Gregory House. SE3 ... 5 B5
Grenada Rd. SE7 ... 5 C8
Grenadier St. E16 ... 2 A5
Grenville Cl. DA13 ... 58 A8
Gresham Ave. DA3 ... 42 F4
Gresham Cl. DA5 ... 7 F1
Gresham Rd. Coxheath ME17 ... 106 D3
Gresham Rd. Hartley DA3 ... 42 F5
Gresham Rd. Newham E16 ... 1 B7
Gresswell Cl. DA14 ... 24 A5
Grey Wethers. ME14 ... 76 E4
Greybury La. TN8 ... 128 B3
Greyfriars Cl. ME16 ... 91 D5
Greyhound Way. DA1 ... 8 E1
Greys Park Cl. BR2 ... 50 D5
Greystone Pk. TN14 ... 82 E2
Greystones Cl. TN14 & TN15 ... 69 E2
Greystones Rd. ME15 ... 93 A3
Gribble Bridge La. TN27 ... 172 B5
Grieves Rd. DA11 ... 29 F5
Grieveson House. ME4 ... 48 A4
Griffin Manor Sch. SE18 ... 6 E6
Griffin Manor Way. SE28 ... 2 D3
Griffin Rd. SE18 ... 2 E1
Griffin Way. SE28 ... 2 E1
Griffiths House. 2 SE18 ... 6 B8
Grigg La. TN27 ... 142 C1
Grigg's Cross. BR5 ... 38 D3

Griggs Way. TN15 ... 87 A7
Grinling House. 6 SE18 ... 2 A2
Grizedale Cl. ME1 ... 61 D8
Gromenfield. TN3 ... 161 C7
Groombridge Cl. DA16 ... 7 A2
Groombridge Hill. TN3 ... 147 D1
Groombridge Place. TN3 ... 161 C8
Groombridge Rd. TN3 ... 147 A1
Groombridge Sq. 13 ME15 ... 107 F6
Grosmont Rd. SE18 ... 2 F1
Grosvenor Ave. ME1 & ME4 ... 47 E3
Grosvenor Bridge. TN1 & TN4 ... 149 B5
Grosvenor Cres. DA1 ... 9 D2
Grosvenor Pk. TN1 & TN4 ... 149 A4
Grosvenor Rd. Bexley DA6 ... 7 E2
Grosvenor Rd. Erith DA17 ... 8 A8
Grosvenor Rd. Gillingham ME7 ... 49 A1
Grosvenor Rd. Orpington BR5 & BR6 ... 37 E3
Grosvenor Rd. Royal Tunbridge Wells TN1 ... 149 A4
Grosvenor Sq. TN4 ... 42 E6
Grosvenor Wlk. TN1 ... 149 A4
Grove Ave. TN1 ... 149 A2
Grove Cl. BR2 ... 50 A8
Grove Cotts. TN30 ... 183 B6
Grove Green La. ME14 ... 92 E5
Grove Green Rd. ME14 ... 92 F5
Grove Hill Gdns. TN1 ... 149 B2
Grove Hill Rd. TN1 & TN2 ... 149 B3
Grove Market Pl. SE9 ... 5 F1
Grove Park Rd. SE12 & SE9 ... 22 D6
Grove Park Sta. SE12 ... 22 B5
Grove Rd. Bexley DA7 ... 8 C3
Grove Rd. Chatham ME4 ... 48 B2
Grove Rd. Erith DA17 ... 7 F8
Grove Rd. Gillingham ME7 ... 49 A6
Grove Rd. Grays RM17 ... 12 C8
Grove Rd. Maidstone ME15 ... 107 C7
Grove Rd. Northfleet DA11 ... 12 B8
Grove Rd. Penshurst TN11 & TN8 ... 130 E2
Grove Rd. Rochester ME2 ... 47 B8
Grove Rd. Seal TN15 ... 85 B5
Grove Rd. Sevenoaks TN13 & TN14 ... 84 C6
Grove Rd. Upper Halling ME2 ... 59 E5
Grove The. Bexley DA6 ... 7 D3
Grove The. Gravesend DA11 ... 30 B8
Grove The. Maidstone ME14 ... 93 A3
Grove The. Pembury TN2 ... 150 D8
Grove The. Sidcup DA14 ... 24 E4
Grove The. Swanley BR8 ... 39 F6
Grove The. Swanscombe DA10 ... 11 F2
Grove The. West Kingsdown TN15 ... 55 F1
Grove Vale. BR7 ... 23 A2
Grove Wood Cotts. TN11 ... 100 A1
Grovebury Cl. DA8 ... 8 D8
Grovebury Cl. DA6 ... 8 B2
Grovebury Rd. SE2 ... 3 B4
Grovehurst La. TN12 ... 153 C5
Grovelands. ME17 ... 111 E5
Grovelands Rd. BR5 ... 24 A1
Grovelands Way. RM17 ... 11 F8
Grover St. 3 TN1 ... 149 B4
Groves The. ME6 ... 74 F7
Grovewood Dr. ME14 ... 92 F4
Guardian Cl. ME8 ... 49 C1
Guardian Ind Est. TN12 ... 138 C2
Guestwick. TN10 ... 117 F5
Guibal Rd. SE12 ... 22 B7
Guild Cl. Erith DA8 ... 8 F7
Guild Rd. Greenwich SE7 ... 5 D8
Guildford Gdns. ME2 ... 46 C6
Guildford Rd. Newham E6 ... 1 F7
Guildford Rd. 7 Royal Tunbridge Wells TN1 & TN2 ... 149 B3
Gullands. ME17 ... 108 E4
Gulliver Rd. DA15 ... 23 E6
Gumley Rd. RM16 ... 11 E8
Gumping Rd. BR5 ... 51 C8
Gun Hill. RM18 ... 13 D8
Gun La. Horsmonden TN12 ... 153 A5
Gun La. Rochester ME2 ... 47 B7
Gundulph Rd. Bromley BR2 ... 36 C6
Gundulph Rd. Chatham ME1 & ME4 ... 47 E4
Gundulph Sq. ME1 ... 47 C6
Gunfleet Cl. DA12 ... 30 E8
Gunlands. TN12 ... 153 A6
Gunn Rd. DA10 ... 11 E1
Gunner La. SE18 ... 2 A1
Gunning St. SE18 ... 2 E2
Gunnis Cl. ME8 ... 63 D4
Gurdon Rd. SE7 ... 1 A1
Guston Rd. ME14 ... 92 C6
Guy Barnett Gr. SE3 ... 5 A4
Gwillim Cl. DA15 ... 7 A2
Gwynn Rd. DA11 ... 29 C6
Gybbon Rise. TN12 ... 139 E3
Gybbons Rd. TN17 ... 181 F3

Ha-Ha Rd. SE18 & SE7 ... 5 F8
Hackney Rd. ME16 ... 91 C2
Hadden Rd. SE28 ... 2 E3
Haddon Gr. DA15 ... 24 A8
Haddon Rd. BR5 ... 38 C4
Hadleigh Ct. ME7 ... 63 B3
Hadleigh Wlk. 6 E6 ... 1 E7
Hadley Cl. DA13 ... 58 B8
Hadley Ct. TN4 ... 148 F6
Hadley Gdns. ME17 ... 94 E3
Hadley House. BR5 ... 38 C4
Hadley Rd. DA17 ... 3 F2
Hadlow Coll of Agriculture & Horticulture. TN11 ... 118 D8

Hadlow Cty Prim Sch. TN11 ... 118 E8
Hadlow Pk. TN11 .... 102 E1
Hadlow Rd. Bexley DA16 .... 7 C7
Hadlow Rd. Maidstone ME14 ...... 92 C5
Hadlow Rd. Sidcup DA14 .... 24 A4
Hadlow Rd. Tonbridge TN9 ...... 117 D3
Hadlow Rd.
  Tonbridge,Higham Wood TN10 ... 118 A5
Hadlow Stair Rd. TN10 .... 117 F4
Hadlow Way. DA13 .... 29 E1
Haffenden Cl. TN12 .... 138 D6
Haffenden Rd. TN30 .... 173 B1
Haig Ave. Chatham ME1 .... 47 D1
Haig Ave. Chatham,Luton ME4 .... 48 A2
Haig Ave. Gillingham ME7 .... 48 E4
Haig Ct. BR7 .... 23 B3
Haig Gdns. DA12 .... 30 C8
Haig Villas. ME3 .... 34 A5
Hailey Rd. DA18 .... 4 A4
Haileybury Rd. BR6 .... 52 A6
Hailstone Cl. TN11 .... 118 E8
Haimo Prim Sch. SE9 .... 5 D2
Haimo Rd. SE9 .... 5 D2
Hainault St. SE9 .... 23 B7
Halcot Ave. DA6 .... 8 C2
Haldane Gdns. DA11 .... 29 C7
Haldane Rd. SE28 .... 3 D6
Halden Cl. ME15 .... 107 F6
Halden La. TN17 .... 181 F6
Hale Cl. BR6 .... 51 C6
Hale Cotts. DA9 .... 11 C2
Hale Ct. TN12 .... 120 A7
Hale La. TN14 .... 68 F2
Hale Oak Rd.
  Hall's Green TN14 & TN8 ...... 114 E4
Hale Oak Rd.
  Sevenoaks Weald TN14 .... 99 B1
Hale Rd. ME3 .... 33 C7
Hale St. TN12 .... 120 A7
Hales Cl. TN30 .... 183 B8
Hales Ct. TN30 .... 183 B8
Haleys Pl. ME1 .... 76 A8
Half Moon La. TN11 .... 116 D6
Halfpence La. DA12 .... 45 B7
Halfpenny Cl. ME16 .... 91 A2
Halfway St. DA15 .... 23 E7
Halifax Cl. ME5 .... 62 B6
Halifield Dr. DA17 .... 3 E3
Hall Hill. TN15 .... 85 C4
Hall Place Cres. DA1 & DA5 .... 8 D7
Hall Rd. Aylesford ME20 .... 75 F1
Hall Rd. Chatham ME5 .... 62 C3
Hall Rd. Dartford DA1 .... 9 F3
Hall Rd.
  Northfleet,Pepper Hill
  DA11 &DA13 .... 29 C5
Hall Rd.
  Northfleet,Wombwell Park DA11 .. 29 D6
Hall Rd. St Mary Hoo ME3 .... 18 C6
Hall Rd. Wouldham ME1 .... 60 C3
Hall The. SE3 .... 5 A4
Hall View. SE9 .... 22 D6
Hall's Grove Rd. TN2 .... 149 D2
Hall's Hole Rd. TN2 .... 149 E4
Hallam Cl. BR7 .... 22 F3
Hallford Way. DA1 .... 9 C2
Hallgate. SE3 .... 5 A4
Halling Cty Prim Sch. ME2 .... 59 F5
Halling Sta. ME2 .... 60 A5
Halls Cotts. TN5 .... 174 F5
Hallsfield Rd. ME5 .... 61 D2
Hallsville Prim Sch. E16 .... 1 A7
Hallwards. TN12 .... 139 F2
Hallwood Cl. ME8 .... 63 D5
Hallwood House. ME5 .... 62 C2
Hallywell Cres. E6 .... 1 F8
Halons Rd. SE9 .... 23 A8
Halsbrook Rd. SE3 .... 5 D4
Halstead Cty Prim Sch. TN14 .... 67 F7
Halstead La. TN14 .... 67 E8
Halstead Place Sch. TN14 .... 67 E8
Halstead Rd. DA8 .... 8 E6
Halstead Wlk. ME16 .... 91 C7
Halstow Cl. ME15 .... 107 B6
Halstow Prim Sch. SE10 .... 1 A1
Halstow Rd. SE10 & SE3 .... 1 A1
Halt Robin La. DA17 .... 4 B2
Halt Robin Rd. Erith DA17 .... 4 A2
Halt Robin Rd. Erith DA17 .... 4 B2
Ham La. Gillingham ME5 .... 62 E3
Ham La. Lenham ME17 .... 111 C5
Ham River Hill. ME3 .... 33 A6
Ham Shades Cl. DA15 .... 24 A5
Hamble Rd. TN10 .... 117 B5
Hambledon Ct. ME16 .... 91 B3
Hambledown Rd. SE9 .... 23 E8
Hambro Ave. BR2 .... 36 A1
Hamelin Rd. ME7 .... 62 F8
Hamerton Rd. DA11 .... 12 B2
Hamilton Ct. TN4 .... 149 A5
Hamilton House.
  Coxheath ME17 .... 106 C3
Hamilton House.
  Royal Tunbridge Wells TN4 .... 149 A5
Hamilton Rd. Bexley DA7 .... 7 F5
Hamilton Rd. Gillingham ME7 .... 48 D7
Hamilton Rd. Sidcup DA15 .... 24 A4
Hamilton Wlk. DA8 .... 8 F5
Hamlea Cl. SE12 .... 5 A2
Hamlet House. Eltham SE9 .... 6 A2
Hamlet House. Erith DA8 .... 8 E7
Hamlin Rd. TN13 .... 83 E6
Hamlyn Ct. TN13 .... 83 E6
Hammelton Rd. BR1 .... 36 A8
Hammerwood Pk. RH19 .... 144 C2

Hammond Way. SE28 .... 3 B6
Hammonds. TN18 .... 179 A2
Hammonds Sq. ME6 .... 75 A8
Hamond Hill. ME4 .... 47 E4
Hampden Way. ME19 .... 88 F3
Hampshire Cl. ME5 .... 62 C7
Hampshire Dr. ME15 .... 107 C8
Hampson Way. ME14 .... 93 A4
Hampstead Cl. SE28 .... 3 B5
Hampstead La. ME18 .... 104 C1
Hampton Cl. ME5 .... 62 A5
Hampton Cotts. TN14 .... 67 F4
Hampton Cres. DA12 .... 30 E6
Hampton House. DA7 .... 8 B5
Hampton Rd. ME14 .... 92 C6
Hamptons Rd. TN11 .... 102 B5
Hamwick Gn. ME5 .... 62 C1
Hanameel St. E16 .... 1 B5
Hanbury Cl. ME18 .... 104 E7
Hanbury Wlk. DA5 .... 25 E5
Handel Cres. ME5 .... 62 A7
Handel Wlk. TN10 .... 117 E6
Hands Wlk. E16 .... 1 A7
Hang Grove Hill. BR6 .... 66 B6
Hangmans Cnr. BR7 .... 37 B8
Hanmer Way. TN12 .... 139 E2
Hanover Ave. E16 .... 1 A5
Hanover Ct. ME14 .... 92 B5
Hanover Dr. Chislehurst BR7 ...... 23 C4
Hanover Dr. Gillingham ME8 ...... 63 C4
Hanover Gn. ME20 .... 74 F3
Hanover Pl. DA3 .... 56 F8
Hanover Rd. Coxheath ME17 .... 106 C3
Hanover Rd.
  Royal Tunbridge Wells TN1 .... 149 A4
Hanover Way. DA7 .... 7 D4
Hansol Rd. DA6 .... 7 E2
Hansom Terr. BR1 .... 36 B8
Hanway. ME4 .... 49 A2
Harbex Cl. DA5 .... 25 B8
Harbledown Manor. ME8 .... 49 B3
Harbledown Pl. BR5 .... 38 C5
Harborough Ave. DA15 .... 23 F8
Harbour The. ME17 .... 124 E5
Harbourland Cl. ME14 .... 92 B8
Harbourne La. TN26 & TN30 .. 173 E5
Harcourt Ave. DA5 & DA15 ...... 24 C8
Harcourt Gdns. ME8 .... 63 E4
Harcourt Rd. DA6 & DA7 .... 7 E3
Harden Ct. SE7 .... 1 E2
Harden Rd. DA11 .... 29 F6
Hardens Manorway. SE18 .... 1 D2
Hardie Cl. ME19 .... 74 F1
Harding House. SE18 .... 1 F2
Harding Rd. DA7 .... 7 F5
Hardinge Ave. TN4 .... 132 E3
Hardinge Cl. ME8 .... 63 D4
Hardinge St. SE18 .... 2 C3
Hardman Rd. SE7 .... 1 B1
Hardres Terr. BR5 .... 52 D8
Hards Town. ME4 .... 48 A4
Hardwick Cres. DA2 .... 10 B1
Hardwick Ct. DA8 .... 8 D8
Hardwick House. ME15 .... 107 E8
Hardwick Rd. TN11 .... 116 E6
Hardy Ave. DA11 .... 29 E6
Hardy Cl. ME5 .... 62 B6
Hardy Gr. DA1 .... 10 A3
Hardy Rd. SE3 .... 5 A8
Hardy St. ME14 .... 92 A6
Hare St. Chatham ME4 .... 48 B3
Hare St. Woolwich SE18 .... 2 A3
Harebell Cl. Chatham ME5 .... 61 F4
Harebell Cl. Maidstone ME14 .... 92 E5
Harebell Dr. E6 .... 2 A8
Haredale Cl. ME1 .... 61 D7
Harefield Rd. DA14 .... 24 D5
Harenc Sch Trust. DA14 .... 24 C3
Harescroft. TN2 .... 162 F7
Harfst Way. BR8 .... 39 C8
Hargate. TN2 .... 162 F8
Hargood Rd. SE3 .... 5 C6
Harland Ave. DA15 .... 23 E6
Harland Rd. SE12 .... 22 A7
Harland Way. TN4 .... 132 F4
Harlands Gr. BR6 .... 51 B6
Harlech Cl. ME2 .... 32 F1
Harlequin House. DA18 .... 3 E3
Harley Gdns. BR6 .... 51 E6
Harleyford. BR1 .... 36 C8
Harlington Rd. DA7 .... 7 E4
Harman Ave. DA11 .... 30 B3
Harman Ct. ME5 .... 62 B3
Harman Dr. DA15 .... 6 F1
Harmer Ct. TN4 .... 133 A2
Harmer Rd. DA10 .... 11 F1
Harmer St. DA11 .... 13 C1
Harmers Way. TN27 .... 127 F3
Harmony St. TN4 .... 148 D4
Harness Rd. SE28 .... 3 A4
Harold Ave. Erith DA17 .... 3 F1
Harold Ave. Gillingham ME7 ...... 48 E4
Harold Gibbons Ct. SE7 .... 5 C8
Harold Rd. Cuxton ME2 .... 46 C3
Harold Rd. Hawley DA2 .... 26 F4
Harp Farm Rd. ME14 .... 77 C6
Harper Rd. E6 .... 1 F7
Harple La. ME14 .... 77 F1
Harpswood. ME17 .... 94 F1
Harptree Dr. ME5 .... 61 F5
Harraden Rd. SE3 .... 5 C6
Harrier Mews. SE28 .... 2 D4
Harrier Way. E6 .... 1 F8
Harries Rd. TN1 & TN2 .... 149 E1
Harrietsham Sta. ME17 .... 110 D6
Harrington Way. SE18 .... 1 D3
Harris Cl. DA11 .... 29 F5
Harris Ct. DA7 .... 7 F6

Harrison Dr. ME23 .... 17 E4
Harrison Rd. TN15 .... 86 F7
Harrison Way. TN13 .... 84 A5
Harrow Cl. TN8 .... 112 D3
Harrow Ct. Chatham ME5 .... 62 C4
Harrow Ct. Stockbury ME9 .... 79 D8
Harrow Gdns. BR6 .... 52 B6
Harrow Manor Way. SE2 .... 3 C3
Harrow Rd. Gillingham ME7 ...... 62 F6
Harrow Rd. Knockholt Pound TN14 67 E4
Harrow Way. ME14 .... 92 E5
Harrowby Gdns. DA11 .... 29 E6
Hart Dyke Cres. BR8 .... 39 D6
Hart Dyke Rd. Orpington BR5 .... 38 C1
Hart Dyke Rd. Swanley BR8 ...... 39 D6
Hart Shaw. DA3 .... 43 B7
Hart St. ME16 .... 91 F3
Hart St Commercial Ctr. ME16 .. 91 F3
Hartfield Cl. TN10 .... 117 E5
Hartfield Cres. BR4 .... 50 A7
Hartfield Pl. DA11 .... 29 D8
Hartfield Rd. Hayes BR4 .... 50 A6
Hartfield Rd. Stick Hill TN8 .... 129 A4
Hartford Rd. DA5 .... 8 A1
Hartford Wlk. DA17 .... 4 A1
Harting Rd. SE9 .... 22 E5
Hartington Cl. BR6 .... 51 C5
Hartington Rd. E16 .... 1 B7
Hartington St. ME4 .... 48 A3
Hartlake Rd. TN11 .... 118 D3
Hartlands Cl. DA5 .... 7 F1
Hartley Bottom Rd. DA3 .... 43 C2
Hartley Cl. Bromley BR1 .... 36 F7
Hartley Cl. Maidstone ME15 .... 107 F6
Hartley Court Gdns. TN17 ...... 169 A3
Hartley Cty Prim Sch. DA3 .... 42 E3
Hartley Hill. DA3 .... 43 A1
Hartley Rd. Bexley DA16 .... 7 C7
Hartley Rd. Hartley TN17 .... 169 A3
Hartley Rd. Longfield DA3 .... 42 E7
Hartley Rd. Westerham TN16 .... 81 D2
Hartlip Endowed CE Prim Sch.
  ME9 .... 64 D5
Hartlip Hill. ME9 .... 64 F7
Hartmann Rd. E16 .... 1 E5
Hartnokes. TN18 .... 179 A2
Hartnup St. ME16 .... 91 C2
Harton Cl. BR1 .... 36 D8
Hartpiece Cl. ME8 .... 49 F2
Hartshill Rd. TN13 .... 84 C4
Hartslock Dr. SE2 .... 3 D4
Hartsmead Rd. SE9 .... 22 F6
Hartville Rd. SE18 .... 2 E2
Hartwell House. SE7 .... 1 B1
Harty Ave. ME8 .... 63 C3
Harvard Ct. SE9 .... 6 A1
Harvel Ave. ME2 .... 46 F7
Harvel Cl. BR5 & BR7 .... 38 A6
Harvel Cres. SE2 .... 3 D1
Harvel La. DA13 .... 58 B2
Harvel Rd. DA13 .... 73 A8
Harvel St. DA13 .... 58 C3
Harvest Bank Rd. BR4 .... 50 A7
Harvest Rd. TN10 .... 117 D6
Harvest Ridge. ME19 .... 74 D2
Harvest Way. BR8 .... 39 D2
Harvesters Cl. ME8 .... 63 E7
Harvesters Way. ME14 .... 92 D4
Harvey Gdns. SE7 .... 1 C1
Harvey Point. E16 .... 1 A8
Harvey Rd. ME8 .... 63 E8
Harvill Rd. DA14 .... 24 E3
Harwood Ave. BR1 .... 36 B7
Harwood Ct. RM17 .... 12 C8
Harwood Est. ME15 .... 107 F5
Haslemere Ave. DA7 .... 8 A5
Haslemere Rd. DA7 .... 8 A5
Hasler Cl. SE28 .... 3 C6
Hasletts Cl. TN4 .... 149 B6
Haslewood Cl. TN27 .... 143 B2
Hassendean Rd. SE3 & SE7 .... 5 B7
Hassock Wood. BR2 .... 50 E6
Hassop Wlk. SE9 .... 22 E4
Haste Hill Cl. ME17 .... 107 B3
Haste Hill Rd. ME17 .... 107 B3
Hasted Cl. DA9 .... 11 C1
Hasted Rd. Greenwich SE7 .... 1 D1
Hasted Rd. Newington ME9 ...... 65 B7
Hasteds. ME17 .... 94 D2
Hastings Cl. RM16 .... 11 E8
Hastings Rd. Keston Mark BR2 .. 50 E8
Hastings Rd.
  Kipping's Cross TN12 .... 150 F5
Hastings Rd. Maidstone ME15 .. 92 B3
Hastings Rd.
  Newenden TN17 & TN18 ...... 187 C6
Hastings Rd. Pembury TN2 .... 150 D6
Hastings Rd. The Moor TN18 .. 184 F6
Hastings St. SE18 .... 2 C3
Hatch Rd. ME17 .... 111 C5
Hatches La. TN11 & TN12 ...... 119 D6
Hatfield Cl. SE3 .... 5 A7
Hatfield Rd. ME2 .... 47 A8
Hatham Green La. TN15 .... 56 D1
Hathaway Cl. BR2 .... 50 E8
Hathaway Ct. Gillingham ME8 .. 63 D8
Hathaway Ct. Rochester ME1 .... 47 B5
Hatherall Rd. ME14 .... 92 B6
Hatherley Cres. DA14 .... 24 A6
Hatherley Rd. DA14 .... 24 A5
Hathern Gdns. SE9 .... 23 A4
Hatmill La. TN12 .... 152 A7
Hattersfield Cl. DA17 .... 3 F2
Hatton Cl. Northfleet DA11 ...... 29 E5
Hatton Cl. Woolwich SE18 .... 6 D7
Hatton Ct. BR7 .... 22 F1
Hatton Rd. ME5 .... 62 C3

Havant Wlk. ME15 .... 107 F6
Havelock Rd. Bromley BR2 .... 36 C5
Havelock Rd. Dartford DA1 .... 9 B1
Havelock Rd. Erith DA8 .... 8 F7
Havelock Rd. Gravesend DA11 .. 29 F7
Havelock Rd. Tonbridge TN9 .. 117 B2
Haven Cl. Chislehurst SE9 .... 22 F5
Haven Cl. Istead Rise DA13 ...... 43 F8
Haven Cl. Rochester ME1 .... 47 C2
Haven Cl. Sidcup DA14 .... 24 C2
Haven Cl. Swanley BR8 .... 39 F7
Haven Hill. TN15 .... 57 A3
Haven Lodge. SE18 .... 2 B2
Haven St. ME3 .... 33 C5
Haven Way. ME4 .... 34 B1
Havengore Ave. DA12 .... 30 E8
Haverstock Ct. BR5 .... 38 B7
Haverthwaite Rd. BR6 .... 51 D7
Havisham Cl. ME1 .... 47 D2
Havisham Rd. DA12 .... 31 A7
Havock La. ME14 .... 91 F4
Hawbeck Rd. ME8 .... 63 C3
Hawden Cl. TN11 .... 116 F4
Hawden La. TN11 .... 116 F4
Hawden Rd. TN9 .... 117 B2
Hawes Rd. BR1 .... 36 B8
Hawfield Bank. BR6 .... 52 D7
Hawkenbury Cl. TN2 .... 149 D2
Hawkenbury Mead. TN2 .... 149 D1
Hawkenbury Rd.
  Hawkenbury TN12 .... 140 C6
Hawkenbury Rd.
  Royal Tunbridge Wells TN2 & TN3 149 E1
Hawkes Cl. RM17 .... 12 B8
Hawkes Rd. ME20 .... 75 F5
Hawkhurst CE Prim Sch.
  Hawkhurst TN18 .... 178 F2
Hawkhurst CE Prim Sch.
  The Moor TN18 .... 184 F8
Hawkhurst Cottage Hospl.
  TN18 .... 178 D2
Hawkhurst Rd.
  Flimwell TN18 & TN19 & TN5 .... 177 E2
Hawkhurst Rd. Gillingham ME8 .. 49 B3
Hawkhurst Rd.
  Hartley TN17 & TN18 .... 178 F7
Hawkinge Wlk. BR5 .... 38 B6
Hawkins Ave. DA12 .... 30 C4
Hawkins Cl. ME4 .... 48 A6
Hawksmoor Cl. Newham E6 ...... 1 E7
Hawksmoor Cl. Woolwich SE18 .. 2 E1
Hawksmoor Prim Sch. SE28 ...... 3 B6
Hawkwell Cotts. TN2 .... 134 F2
Hawkwood. ME16 .... 91 B5
Hawkwood Cl. ME1 .... 47 D5
Hawkwood La. BR7 .... 37 C8
Hawley Ct. ME16 .... 91 E4
Hawley Rd. DA1,DA2&DA4 ...... 27 A4
Hawley Terr. DA2 .... 27 A4
Hawley Vale. DA2 .... 27 A4
Hawser Rd. ME1 .... 47 C1
Hawstead La. BR6 .... 52 A4
Hawthorn Cl. Edenbridge TN8 .. 112 C2
Hawthorn Cl. Gravesend DA12 .. 30 C4
Hawthorn Cl. Orpington BR5 .... 37 D3
Hawthorn House. ME5 .... 61 F5
Hawthorn La. TN13 .... 83 F5
Hawthorn Pl. DA8 .... 4 C1
Hawthorn Rd. Bexley DA6 .... 7 F3
Hawthorn Rd. Dartford DA1 ...... 26 D7
Hawthorn Rd. Rochester ME2 .... 46 E6
Hawthorn Terr. DA15 .... 6 F2
Hawthorn Wlk.
  Royal Tunbridge Wells TN2 .... 149 E8
Hawthorn Wlk. Tonbridge TN10 117 C7
Hawthorndene Cl. BR2 .... 50 A8
Hawthorndene Rd. BR2 .... 50 A8
Hawthorne Ave. ME8 .... 49 C2
Hawthorne Cl. BR1 .... 36 F6
Hawthorne Rd. BR1 .... 36 F6
Hawthorns. Chatham ME5 .... 61 F1
Hawthorns. Hartley DA3 .... 42 F5
Hawthorns The. ME20 .... 75 E1
Haxted Rd. BR1 .... 36 B8
Hay's Mead. DA13 .... 44 F3
Hayday Rd. E16 .... 1 A8
Haydens Cl. BR5 .... 38 C3
Haydens Mews. TN9 .... 117 C3
Haydens The. TN9 .... 117 C3
Hayes Cl. Hayes BR2 .... 50 A8
Hayes Cl. Higham ME3 .... 32 C3
Hayes Cl. West Thurrock RM16 .. 11 C8
Hayes Garden. BR2 .... 36 A1
Hayes La. Hayes BR2 .... 36 A4
Hayes La. Stockbury ME9 .... 79 F6
Hayes Prim Sch. BR2 .... 36 B1
Hayes Rd. Hayes BR2 .... 36 A5
Hayes Rd. Stone DA2 .... 27 E8
Hayes Sch. BR2 .... 50 B8
Hayes St. BR2 .... 36 B1
Hayes Sta. BR2 .... 36 A1
Hayes Terr. DA12 .... 31 E3
Hayes Wood Ave. BR2 .... 36 B5
Hayesbrook Sch. TN9 .... 133 A8
Hayesden La. TN11 & TN3 & TN4 132 B3
Hayesford Park Dr. BR2 .... 36 A4
Hayfield. ME19 .... 74 E2
Hayfield Rd. BR5 .... 38 A4
Hayfields. ME5 .... 62 D3
Hayle Mill Cotts. ME15 .... 106 F3
Hayle Mill Rd. ME15 .... 106 F8
Hayle Rd. ME15 .... 92 A3
Hayley Cl. ME2 .... 46 C2
Hayman Wlk. ME20 .... 75 F6
Haymans Hill. TN12 .... 153 C7
Haymen St. ME4 .... 47 E3
Haynes Rd. DA11 .... 29 F5
Hayrick Cl. ME14 .... 92 E5

Hays Rd. ME6 .... 74 F6
Haysden Ctry Pk. TN11 .... 132 D8
Haywain Cl. Maidstone ME14 .... 92 F4
Haywain Cl. Paddock Wood TN12 136 A5
Hayward Ave. ME2 .... 47 B8
Hayward Cl. DA1 .... 8 D2
Hayward Dr. DA1 .... 26 F6
Haywood Rd. BR2 .... 36 D5
Haywood Rise. BR6 .... 51 B8
Hazel Ave. Hoo St Werburgh ME3 34 E3
Hazel Ave. Maidstone ME16 .... 91 C5
Hazel Cotts. TN14 .... 68 A6
Hazel Dr. DA8 .... 9 B6
Hazel End. BR8 .... 39 E4
Hazel Gr. Chatham ME5 .... 62 B8
Hazel Gr. Orpington BR6 .... 51 B8
Hazel Rd. Dartford DA1 .... 26 D6
Hazel Rd. Erith DA8 .... 9 A6
Hazel Shaw. TN10 .... 117 D7
Hazel Street Rd. ME9 .... 80 A4
Hazel Wlk. BR2 .... 37 A3
Hazelbank. TN3 .... 147 F3
Hazelden Cl. TN15 .... 56 A2
Hazeldene Rd. DA16 .... 7 C5
Hazelmere Rd. BR5 .... 37 D5
Hazelmere Way. BR2 .... 36 A3
Hazels The. ME8 .... 63 B5
Hazelwood Cl. TN2 .... 149 E8
Hazelwood Cotts. TN5 .... 176 D1
Hazelwood Dr. ME16 .... 91 B4
Hazelwood Rd. TN14 .... 66 D8
Hazlemere Dr. ME7 .... 49 A5
Hazlitt Ct. SE28 .... 3 C5
Hazlitt Dr. ME15 .... 91 D5
Head Race The. ME15 .... 91 D2
Headcorn Cty Prim Sch. TN27 141 C5
Headcorn Rd. Bromley BR1 ...... 22 A3
Headcorn Rd. Gillingham ME8 .. 49 B4
Headcorn Rd. Platt's Heath
  ME17 .... 110 F1
Headcorn Rd.
  Smarden Bell TN27 .... 142 C3
Headcorn Rd. Standen TN27 .... 158 A5
Headcorn Rd. Staplehurst TN12 140 B4
Headcorn Rd. The Harbour
  ME17 .... 124 E4
Headcorn Rd. Ulcombe ME17 .... 125 C7
Headcorn Sta. TN27 .... 141 D4
Headingley Rd. ME16 .... 91 B4
Headley Ct. TN8 .... 112 C2
Headley House. BR5 .... 38 B7
Healy Dr. BR6 .... 51 F6
Heansill La. TN18 .... 184 E8
Hearns Cl. BR5 .... 38 C5
Hearns Rd. BR5 .... 38 C5
Hearns Rise. BR5 .... 38 D5
Heartenoak Rd. TN18 .... 179 B3
Heath Ave. DA7 .... 7 D8
Heath Cl. Orpington BR5 .... 38 C3
Heath Cl. Swanley BR8 .... 39 E7
Heath Gdns. DA1 .... 26 C7
Heath Gr. ME16 .... 91 A2
Heath House. DA15 .... 23 F4
Heath La. Dartford DA1 .... 26 C7
Heath La.
  Dartford,Dartford Heath DA1 .... 26 B7
Heath Park Dr. BR1 .... 36 E6
Heath Rd. Coldblow DA5 .... 25 C7
Heath Rd. Coxheath ME17 ...... 106 C3
Heath Rd. Crayford DA1 .... 8 F1
Heath Rd. Langley Heath ME17 .. 108 E4
Heath Rd. Maidstone ME16 ...... 90 F3
Heath Rise. BR2 .... 36 A3
Heath Side. BR5 .... 37 C2
Heath St. DA1 .... 26 D8
Heath Terr. TN12 .... 153 A6
Heath The. ME19 .... 89 F5
Heath View Dr. SE2 .... 7 D8
Heath Villas. SE18 .... 2 F1
Heath Way. DA7 & DA8 .... 8 D6
Heathclose Ave. DA1 .... 26 B8
Heathclose Rd. DA1 .... 26 B7
Heathcote Cl. ME20 .... 75 F2
Heathdene Dr. DA17 .... 4 B2
Heathend Rd. DA5 .... 25 E7
Heather Cl. Chatham ME5 .... 61 F4
Heather Cl. Newham E6 .... 2 A7
Heather Dr. Dartford DA1 .... 26 A8
Heather Dr. Maidstone ME15 .... 92 B2
Heather Dr. St Michaels TN30 .. 173 B3
Heather End. BR8 .... 39 D5
Heather Rd. SE12 .... 22 A7
Heather Wlk. TN10 .... 117 B6
Heatherbank. Chislehurst BR7 .. 37 A7
Heatherbank. Eltham SE9 .... 5 F5
Heatherbank Cl. DA1 .... 8 E1
Heatherside Rd. DA14 .... 24 C5
Heatherwood Cl. ME17 .... 109 E2
Heathfield. Chislehurst BR7 ...... 23 C2
Heathfield. Langley Heath ME17 108 E4
Heathfield Ave. ME14 .... 92 C7
Heathfield Cl. Chatham ME5 .... 62 B7
Heathfield Cl. Keston BR2 .... 50 C5
Heathfield Cl. Maidstone ME14 .. 92 B7
Heathfield Cl. Newham E16 .... 1 D1
Heathfield Ct. DA14 .... 24 B3
Heathfield La. BR7 .... 23 C2
Heathfield Rd. Bexley DA6 .... 7 F3
Heathfield Rd. Keston BR2 .... 50 D5
Heathfield Rd. Maidstone ME14 92 C7
Heathfield Rd. Sevenoaks TN13 .. 83 F5
Heathfield Terr. Swanley BR8 .... 39 D7
Heathfield Terr. Woolwich SE18 .. 6 F8
Heathfields. TN2 .... 149 D3
Heathlands Rise. DA1 .... 9 B1
Heathlee Rd. DA1 .... 8 E1
Heathley End. BR7 .... 23 C2
Heathorn St. ME14 .... 92 B5

Heathside Ave. Bexley DA7 .... 7 E5
Heathside Ave. Coxheath ME17 .. 106 C4
Heathview. TN4 .... 132 F2
Heathview Ave. DA1 .... 8 E1
Heathview Cres. DA1 .... 26 B7
Heathway. SE3 .... 5 A7
Heathwood Gdns. Swanley BR8 .. 39 C7
Heathwood Gdns. Woolwich SE7 .. 1 E1
Heathwood Wlk. DA5 .... 25 E7
Heaverham Rd. TN15 .... 70 C2
Heavitree Cl. SE18 .... 2 D1
Heavitree Rd. SE18 .... 2 D1
Hector St. SE18 .... 2 E2
Hectorage Rd. TN9 .... 133 D8
Hedge Place Rd. DA9 .... 11 A1
Hedgerow The. ME14 .... 92 E5
Hedgerows The. DA11 .... 29 E6
Hedges The. ME14 .... 92 A7
Hedley Ave. RM16 .... 11 C8
Hedley St. ME14 .... 92 A5
Heights The. SE7 .... 1 C1
Helen Allison Sch The. DA13 ..... 44 B2
Helen Cl. DA1 .... 26 B8
Helen Keller Ct. TN10 .... 117 D4
Helen St. SE18 .... 2 B2
Helverswood. TN14 .... 53 A2
Hemmings Cl. DA14 .... 24 B3
Hempstead Cty Jun Sch. ME7 .... 63 A5
Hempstead Cty Prim Sch. ME7 .. 63 A5
Hempstead Rd. Gillingham ME7 .. 63 A5
Hempstead Rd. Gillingham ME7 .. 63 B6
Hempstead Valley Dr. ME7 .... 63 A4
Hempstead Valley Sh Ctr. ME7 .. 63 A3
Hemsted Rd. DA8 .... 8 E7
Henbane Cl. ME14 .... 92 E5
Henderson Dr. DA1 .... 10 A3
Hendley Dr. TN17 .... 169 C5
Hendry House. ME3 .... 33 F6
Hendy Rd. ME6 .... 75 B8
Henfield Cl. DA5 .... 8 A1
Hengist Rd. Eltham SE12 .... 22 B8
Hengist Rd. Erith DA8 .... 8 C7
Hengrove Ct. DA5 .... 24 E7
Henham Gdns. TN12 .... 120 A6
Henhurst Hill. DA13 .... 44 D8
Henhurst Rd. Gravesend DA13 .... 30 E1
Henhurst Rd. Henhurst DA12 ...... 44 E8
Heniker La. ME17 .... 125 A4
Henley Bsns Pk. ME2 .... 47 D7
Henley Cl. Chatham ME5 .... 62 A6
Henley Cl. Gillingham ME8 .... 63 D8
Henley Cl.
  Royal Tunbridge Wells TN2 ..... 149 C4
Henley Deane. DA11 .... 29 E4
Henley Fields. Maidstone ME14 .. 92 E6
Henley Fields. St Michaels TN30 173 B2
Henley Meadows. TN30 .... 173 A2
Henley Rd. Newham E16 .... 1 F4
Henley Rd. Paddock Wood TN12 136 A4
Henley St. DA13 .... 44 F3
Henley View. TN30 .... 173 B2
Henniker Cotts. TN17 .... 169 A3
Henry Cooper Way. SE12 .... 22 D4
Henry St. Bromley BR1 .... 36 B8
Henry St. Chatham ME4 .... 48 B3
Henry St. 9 Grays RM17 .... 12 C8
Henson Cl. BR6 .... 51 B8
Henville Rd. BR1 .... 36 B8
Henwick Prim Sch. SE9 .... 5 E4
Henwick Rd. SE9 .... 5 E4
Henwood Green Rd.
  TN12 & TN2 .... 150 E6
Henwoods Cres. TN2 .... 150 D6
Henwoods Mount. TN2 .... 150 E6
Herald Wlk. DA1 .... 9 F2
Herbert Pl. SE18 .... 6 B8
Herbert Rd. Bexley DA7 .... 7 E5
Herbert Rd. Bromley BR2 .... 36 A4
Herbert Rd. Chatham ME4 .... 48 A3
Herbert Rd. Gillingham ME8 .... 63 E8
Herbert Rd. Hextable BR8 .... 26 B2
Herbert Rd. Swanscombe DA10 .. 11 F1
Herbert Rd. Woolwich SE18 .... 6 B8
Herdsdown. ME3 .... 34 D5
Hereford Cl. ME8 .... 49 D2
Hereford House. 7 SE18 .... 1 F2
Hereford Rd. ME15 .... 107 D7
Heritage Dr. ME7 .... 48 F1
Heritage Hill. BR2 .... 50 C5
Heritage Rd. ME5 .... 62 A6
Heritage The. BR6 .... 38 A2
Herman Terr. ME4 .... 48 A3
Hermitage Ct. ME16 .... 90 F5
Hermitage La. Detling ME14 .... 78 A4
Hermitage La.
  Maidstone ME16 & ME20 .... 90 F6
Hermitage La.
  Rabbit's Cross ME17 .... 123 E6
Hermitage Rd. ME3 .... 32 E4
Herne Rd. ME8 .... 49 C2
Hero Wlk. ME1 .... 47 F5
Heron Apartments. 3 ME15 .... 107 F5
Heron Cl. TN8 .... 112 C3
Heron Cotts. TN18 .... 187 D3
Heron Cres. DA14 .... 23 E4
Heron Ct. BR2 .... 36 C5
Heron Hill. DA17 .... 3 F2
Heron Hill La. DA13 .... 58 A4
Heron Rd. ME20 .... 74 F1
Heron Way. Chatham ME5 .... 62 B7
Heron Way. Lower Stoke ME3 .... 19 C4
Heronden Rd. ME15 .... 107 F4
Herongate Rd. BR8 .... 25 E1
Herons Way. TN2 .... 150 E8
Heronsgate Prim Sch. SE28 .... 2 C7
Herringham Rd. SE7 .... 1 C3
Herts Cres. ME15 .... 106 F3
Hervey Rd. SE3 & SE7 .... 5 B6

Hesketh Ave. DA2 .... 27 B7
Heskett Pk. TN2 .... 150 E6
Hever Ave. TN15 .... 55 E4
Hever Castle. TN8 .... 129 D7
Hever Cl. ME15 .... 107 F6
Hever Court Rd. DA12 .... 30 D2
Hever CE Prim Sch. TN8 .... 129 D6
Hever Croft. Eltham SE9 .... 23 A4
Hever Croft. Rochester ME2 .... 46 F5
Hever Gdns. Bromley BR1 .... 37 A7
Hever Gdns. Maidstone ME16 .... 91 E3
Hever House. ME2 .... 33 C1
Hever Rd. Hever TN8 .... 129 B7
Hever Rd. West Kingsdown TN15 55 E4
Hever Road Cotts. TN8 .... 113 E2
Hever Sta. TN8 .... 129 B6
Hever Wood Rd. TN15 .... 55 E4
Heversham Rd. SE18 .... 2 E2
Heversham Rd. DA7 .... 8 A6
Hewett House. 7 SE18 .... 2 B1
Hewett Pl. BR8 .... 39 D5
Hewitt Cl. ME7 .... 48 F6
Hewitts Rd. BR6 & TN14 .... 52 F3
Hextable Cl. ME16 .... 91 D7
Hextable Cty Inf Sch. BR8 .... 25 F2
Hextable Cty Jun Sch. BR8 .... 25 F2
Hextable Sch. BR8 .... 39 F8
Hibbs Cl. BR8 .... 39 D7
Hibernia Dr. DA12 .... 30 F5
Hibernia Point. 11 SE2 .... 3 D4
Hickin Cl. SE7 .... 1 D2
Hickman Cl. E16 .... 1 D8
Hickory Dell. ME7 .... 63 A5
Hide. E6 .... 2 A7
Higgins' La. ME4 .... 47 F5
High Banks. Loose ME15 .... 106 F5
High Banks. Rochester ME1 .... 47 D2
High Beeches.
  Royal Tunbridge Wells TN2 ..... 149 D6
High Beeches. Sidcup DA14 .... 24 E3
High Broom Ind Pk. TN4 .... 149 C8
High Brooms Rd. TN4 .... 149 C7
High Brooms Sta. TN1 .... 149 C7
High Croft Cotts. BR8 .... 40 A5
High Cross Rd. TN15 .... 86 B1
High Dewar Rd. ME8 .... 64 A8
High Elms. ME8 .... 49 E1
High Elms Public Golf Course.
  BR6 .... 51 D3
High Elms Rd. BR6 .... 51 C2
High Firs. BR8 .... 39 E5
High Firs Cty Prim Sch. BR8 ..... 39 F5
High Gr. Bromley BR1 .... 36 D8
High Gr. Woolwich SE18 .... 6 D6
High Halden Parochial
  CE Prim Sch. TN26 .... 173 E7
High Halden Rd. TN27 .... 158 C2
High Halstow Cty Prim Sch.
  ME23 .... 17 E3
High Hilden Cl. TN11 .... 117 A4
High House La. TN11 .... 102 C2
High Meads Rd. E16 .... 1 D7
High Oak Hill. ME9 .... 65 D8
High Point. SE9 .... 23 B5
High Rd. DA2 .... 26 C5
High Ridge. TN17 .... 167 E8
High Rocks. TN3 .... 148 B1
High Rocks La. TN3 & TN4 ...... 148 C1
High St. Aylesford ME20 .... 75 F3
High St. Bean DA2 .... 28 B5
High St. Bidborough TN4 .... 132 C3
High St. Biddenden TN27 .... 157 F1
High St. Borough Green TN15 .... 86 F7
High St. Brasted TN16 .... 82 C3
High St. Brenchley TN12 .... 152 B8
High St. Bromley BR1 .... 36 A7
High St. Chatham ME4 .... 47 E4
High St. Chatham ME4 .... 48 A4
High St. Cowden TN8 .... 145 B5
High St. Cranbrook TN17 .... 169 C4
High St. Dartford DA1 .... 9 E1
High St. Downe BR6 .... 66 A8
High St. East Malling ME19 .... 90 A6
High St. Edenbridge TN8 .... 112 C1
High St. Eynsford DA4 .... 54 E8
High St. Farningham DA4 .... 40 F2
High St. Flimwell TN5 .... 177 C3
High St. Frant TN3 .... 163 C4
High St. Gillingham ME7 .... 48 B6
High St. Gillingham ME7 .... 48 B6
High St. Gillingham,Brompton ME4 48 A6
High St. Gillingham,Rainham ME8 . 63 F8
High St. Goudhurst TN17 .... 167 E8
High St. Grain ME3 .... 21 B6
High St. Gravesend DA11 .... 13 B1
High St. 3 Grays RM17 .... 12 A8
High St. Hadlow TN11 .... 118 E8
High St. Halling ME2 .... 60 A4
High St. Headcorn TN27 .... 141 C5
High St. High Street TN18 .... 178 E2
High St. Kemsing TN15 .... 70 B2
High St. Lamberhurst TN3 .... 166 B5
High St. Leigh TN11 .... 115 F1
High St. Lenham ME17 .... 111 D5
High St. Maidstone ME14 .... 91 F4
High St. Marden TN12 .... 138 D6
High St. Newington ME9 .... 65 C6
High St. Northfleet DA11 .... 12 C1
High St. Orpington BR6 .... 38 A1
High St.
  Orpington,Farnborough BR6 .... 51 C5
High St.
  Orpington,Green Street Green BR6 51 F4
High St. Otford TN14 .... 69 A3

High St. Pembury TN2 .... 150 C6
High St. Penshurst TN11 .... 131 B4
High St. Rochester ME2 .... 47 B7
High St. Rochester ME1 .... 47 C6
High St. Rochester ME4 .... 47 E4
High St. Rolvenden TN17 .... 181 E4
High St.
  Royal Tunbridge Wells TN1 ..... 149 A2
High St. Seal TN15 .... 84 F6
High St. Sevenoaks TN13 .... 84 C3
High St. Sevenoaks,Chipstead
  TN13 .... 83 C5
High St. Shoreham TN14 .... 53 F1
High St. Sidcup DA14 .... 24 A4
High St. Smarden TN27 .... 143 A1
High St. Snodland ME6 .... 75 A8
High St. Staplehurst TN12 .... 139 F3
High St. Sutton Valence ME17 .. 124 E7
High St. Swanley BR8 .... 39 F5
High St. Swanscombe DA10 .... 11 F2
High St.
  Swanscombe,Greenhithe DA9 ... 11 B3
High St. Tenterden TN30 .... 183 A7
High St. Ticehurst TN5 .... 176 C1
High St. Tonbridge TN9 .... 117 C2
High St. Upper Upton ME2 .... 33 F1
High St. Wadhurst TN5 .... 174 F4
High St. West Malling ME19 .... 89 C8
High St. Westerham TN16 .... 96 C8
High St. Wouldham ME1 .... 60 C5
High St. Wrotham TN15 .... 72 A3
High St. Yalding ME18 .... 104 F1
High Tor Cl. BR1 .... 22 B1
High View. ME3 .... 32 C4
High Woods La. TN2 .... 150 B3
Higham Cl. ME15 .... 91 E2
Higham Cty Prim Sch. ME3 .... 32 C5
Higham Gdns. TN10 .... 117 F5
Higham La. TN10 .... 117 F6
Higham Rd. Cliffe ME3 .... 16 A4
Higham Rd. Rochester ME3 .... 33 D3
Higham School Rd. TN10 .... 117 E6
Higham Sta. ME3 .... 32 D6
Higham View. ME14 .... 76 E4
Highbanks Cl. DA16 .... 7 B7
Highberry. ME19 .... 74 E2
Highbrook Rd. SE3 .... 5 D4
Highbury La. TN30 .... 183 A7
Highcombe. SE7 .... 5 B8
Highcombe Cl. SE9 .... 22 E7
Highcroft Gn. ME15 .... 107 F4
Highcross Rd. DA13 .... 28 D2
Highdown Cotts. TN17 .... 166 F3
Highfield Ave. Erith DA8 .... 8 B8
Highfield Ave. Orpington BR6 .... 51 F5
Highfield Cl. Gillingham ME8 ..... 63 D7
Highfield Cl. Hawkhurst TN18 .. 179 A1
Highfield Cl. Pembury TN2 .... 150 D6
Highfield Rd. Bexley DA6 .... 7 F2
Highfield Rd. Bromley BR1 .... 36 F5
Highfield Rd. Dartford DA1 .... 26 D8
Highfield Rd. Gillingham ME8 .... 63 D7
Highfield Rd. Kemsing TN14 ...... 69 F3
Highfield Rd.
  Royal Tunbridge Wells TN4 ..... 149 C7
Highfield Rd.
  St Paul's Cray BR5 & BR7 .... 37 F6
Highfield Rd N. DA1 .... 9 D1
Highfield Rd S. DA1 .... 26 D7
Highfields Rd. TN8 .... 112 C4
Highgate Ct. 8 TN18 .... 178 F2
Highgate Hill. TN18 .... 178 F1
Highgrove. TN2 .... 163 A8
Highgrove Cl. BR7 .... 36 E8
Highgrove Rd. ME5 .... 62 A5
Highland Rd. Badgers Mount
  TN14 .... 68 B8
Highland Rd. Bexley DA6 .... 8 A3
Highland Rd. Maidstone ME15 .. 107 E6
Highlands Cl. ME2 .... 46 D5
Highlands Hill. BR8 .... 40 A8
Highlands Pk. TN15 .... 84 E6
Highlands Rd. BR5 .... 38 C2
Highmead. SE18 .... 6 F7
Highridge. ME7 .... 48 F1
Highridge Rd. ME14 .... 92 F5
Highstead Cres. DA8 .... 8 E7
Highview. Vigo Village DA13 ...... 73 B8
Highview. Woolwich SE18 .... 6 F7
Highview Cl. ME15 .... 107 A8
Highview Dr. ME5 .... 61 D5
Highview Rd. DA14 .... 24 B4
Highway Prim Sch. BR6 .... 52 C5
Highway The. BR6 .... 52 C5
Highwood Cl. BR6 .... 51 C8
Highwood Dr. BR6 .... 51 C8
Highwoods Cl. ME3 .... 32 C4
Hilary Cl. DA7 .... 8 C6
Hilary Gdns. ME1 .... 46 F1
Hilbert Cl. TN2 .... 149 C5
Hilborough Way. BR6 .... 51 D5
Hilda May Ave. BR8 .... 39 E7
Hilda Rd. ME4 .... 48 A3
Hilda Vale Cl. BR6 .... 51 A6
Hilda Vale Rd. BR6 .... 51 A6
Hilden Ave. TN11 .... 116 F4
Hilden Dr. DA8 .... 9 B7
Hilden Grange Sch. TN10 .... 117 B4
Hilden Oaks Sch. TN10 .... 117 B3
Hilden Park Rd. TN11 .... 116 F4
Hildenborough CE Prim Sch.
  TN11 .... 116 D6
Hildenborough Cres. ME16 ...... 91 C7
Hildenborough Rd. Leigh TN11 116 A3
Hildenborough Rd.
  Shipbourne TN11 & TN15 ...... 100 E4
Hildenborough Sta. TN11 .... 116 B6

Hilders Cl. TN8 .... 112 B4
Hilders La. TN8 .... 112 A4
Hill Brow. Bromley BR1 .... 36 D8
Hill Brow. Crayford DA1 .... 8 F1
Hill Brow. Maidstone ME14 .... 93 A5
Hill Chase. ME5 .... 61 E3
Hill Cl. Chislehurst BR7 .... 23 B3
Hill Cl. Istead Rise DA13 .... 29 E1
Hill Cres. Coldblow DA5 .... 25 C7
Hill Cres. Lenham ME17 .... 111 D5
Hill Crest.
  Royal Tunbridge Wells TN4 ..... 149 B8
Hill Crest. Sevenoaks TN13 .... 84 A5
Hill Crest. Sidcup DA15 .... 24 B8
Hill Ct. ME3 .... 33 F4
Hill End. Orpington BR6 .... 51 F8
Hill End. Woolwich SE18 .... 6 A6
Hill Farm Ave. ME2 .... 32 F1
Hill Farm Cl. ME23 .... 17 E3
Hill Green Rd. ME9 .... 79 D8
Hill House Rd. DA2 .... 27 C8
Hill Rd. Dartford DA1 .... 26 E6
Hill Rd. Rochester ME1 .... 47 A2
Hill Rd. Wouldham ME1 .... 60 F5
Hill Rise. DA2 .... 27 E3
Hill Sch The. TN16 .... 81 B4
Hill Shaw. DA3 .... 42 F3
Hill St. TN1 .... 149 B5
Hill The. Cranbrook TN17 .... 169 D4
Hill The. Northfleet DA11 .... 12 C1
Hill Top. TN17 .... 154 E5
Hill Top Cotts. ME17 .... 106 E2
Hill View. Basted TN15 .... 86 F4
Hill View. Borough Green TN15 .. 87 A7
Hill View Cl. TN15 .... 87 A7
Hill View Dr. DA16 .... 6 E5
Hill View Rd.
  Hildenborough TN11 .... 116 F5
Hill View Rd. New Barn DA3 ...... 43 B6
Hill View Rd. Orpington BR6 ...... 51 F8
Hill View Rd. Rusthall TN4 .... 148 C4
Hill View Way. ME5 .... 61 E5
Hill's Terr. ME4 .... 47 F3
Hillary Ave. DA11 .... 29 E5
Hillary Ct. SE9 .... 22 E6
Hillary Rd. ME14 .... 92 A7
Hillbert Rd. TN1 & TN2 .... 149 C5
Hillborough Ave. TN13 & TN15 .. 84 B5
Hillborough Gr. ME5 .... 62 A3
Hillbrow Cl. DA5 .... 25 D4
Hillbury Gdns. TN5 .... 176 D1
Hillcrest. TN8 .... 113 B5
Hillcrest Ave. ME16 .... 11 A8
Hillcrest Dr. Cuxton ME2 .... 46 C2
Hillcrest Dr.
  Royal Tunbridge Wells TN1 ..... 149 D7
Hillcrest Dr. Swanscombe DA9 .. 11 A2
Hillcrest Rd. Bromley BR1 .... 22 A4
Hillcrest Rd. Chatham ME4 .... 47 F2
Hillcrest Rd. Dartford DA1 .... 25 F8
Hillcrest Rd. Marlpit Hill TN8 .. 112 C4
Hillcrest Rd. Orpington BR6 ...... 52 A8
Hillcroft Rd. ME2 .... 2 B8
Hilden Shaw. ME15 .... 107 A8
Hilldown Lodge. BR6 .... 52 B8
Hilldrop Rd. BR1 .... 22 B2
Hillfield Rd. TN13 .... 83 E7
Hillfield Villas. TN26 .... 173 F8
Hillgarth. TN1 .... 149 A8
Hillingdon Ave. TN13 .... 84 D6
Hillingdon Rd. Bexley DA7 .... 8 B5
Hillingdon Rd. Gravesend DA11 30 B6
Hillingdon Rise. TN13 .... 84 D5
Hillreach. SE18 & SE7 .... 1 F1
Hills La. TN15 .... 70 C2
Hillsgrove Cl. DA16 .... 7 C7
Hillsgrove Prim Sch. DA16 .... 7 C7
Hillshaw Cres. ME2 .... 46 D5
Hillside. Erith DA17 .... 4 C2
Hillside. Farningham DA4 .... 40 F2
Hillside. Lane End DA2 .... 27 E3
Hillside. Tonbridge TN9 .... 133 A7
Hillside Ave. Gravesend DA12 .... 30 D6
Hillside Ave. Rochester ME2 ...... 47 B8
Hillside Cotts. TN5 .... 174 D1
Hillside Ct. Swanley BR8 .... 40 A5
Hillside Ct. Wateringbury ME18 104 E7
Hillside Dr. DA12 .... 30 D6
Hillside La. BR2 .... 50 A8
Hillside Rd. Chatham ME4 .... 48 A4
Hillside Rd. Crayford DA1 .... 9 A1
Hillside Rd. Kemsing TN14 .... 69 F3
Hillside Rd. Sevenoaks TN13 ..... 84 D4
Hillside The. BR6 .... 52 B2
Hilltop. Tonbridge TN9 .... 133 B7
Hilltop. West Farleigh ME15 .... 105 D3
Hilltop Gdns. Dartford DA1 .... 9 F2
Hilltop Gdns. Orpington BR6 .... 51 E8
Hilltop Prim Sch. ME2 .... 33 C1
Hilltop Rd. Rochester ME2 .... 33 C1
Hilltop Rd. West Thurrock RM16 . 11 B8
Hillview Cres. BR6 .... 37 F1
Hillview Rd. BR7 & SE9 .... 23 A4
Hillview Sch for Girls. TN9 ..... 133 D8
Hillydeal Rd. TN14 .... 69 C4
Hillyfield Cl. ME2 .... 32 F1
Hillyfields Cty Jun Sch. ME7 .... 48 E6
Hilton Rd. ME3 .... 33 B7
Hind Cres. DA8 .... 8 D7
Hines Terr. ME5 .... 61 E4
Hinksden Rd. TN17 & TN18 ..... 179 F3
Hinksey Path. SE2 .... 3 D3
Hinstock Rd. SE18 .... 6 C1
Hinton Cl. SE9 .... 22 E7
Hinton Cres. ME7 .... 63 A6
Hitchen Hatch La. TN13 .... 84 B4
Hither Chantlers. TN3 .... 148 A2

Hive La. DA11 .... 12 B2
Hive The. DA11 .... 12 B1
Hoath Cl. ME7 .... 63 B7
Hoath La. ME8 .... 63 B7
Hoath Meadow. TN12 .... 153 A6
Hoath Way. ME7 & ME8 .... 63 B5
Hobart Rd. RM18 .... 13 A6
Hoblands End. BR7 .... 23 E2
Hockenden La. BR5 & BR8 .... 39 B7
Hockers Cl. ME14 .... 93 A8
Hockers La. ME14 .... 93 A7
Hoddesdon Rd. DA17 .... 4 A1
Hodgkins Cl. SE28 .... 3 D6
Hodgson Cres. ME6 .... 60 A1
Hodsoll Ct. BR5 .... 38 D4
Hodsoll St. TN15 .... 57 D1
Hodson Cres. BR5 .... 38 D3
Hog Hill. ME14 .... 93 B5
Hog La. DA11 .... 29 D5
Hogarth Cl. E16 .... 1 D8
Hogbarn La. ME17 .... 95 F2
Hoghole La. TN3 .... 165 F2
Hognore La. TN15 .... 72 D6
Hogtrough Hill. TN16 & TN14 ... 82 A5
Holbeach Gdns. DA15 .... 6 F1
Holborn La. ME4 .... 47 F5
Holborn Rd. E13 .... 1 B8
Holborough Rd. ME6 .... 60 A1
Holbrook House. BR7 .... 37 D8
Holbrook La. BR7 .... 23 D1
Holbrook Way. BR2 .... 36 F4
Holburne Cl. SE3 .... 5 C6
Holburne Gdns. SE3 .... 5 D6
Holburne Rd. SE3 .... 5 D6
Holcombe Rd. Chatham ME4 ..... 47 F2
Holcombe Rd. Rochester ME1 .... 47 C3
Holcote Cl. DA17 .... 3 E3
Holden Cnr. TN4 .... 132 F1
Holden Park Rd. TN4 .... 149 A8
Holden Rd. TN4 .... 132 F1
Holder Cl. ME5 .... 62 C6
Holding St. ME8 .... 49 F1
Hole La. TN15 .... 112 A6
Holford St. 1 TN9 .... 117 B1
Holgate St. SE7 .... 1 D3
Holland House. ME1 .... 47 D5
Holland Rd. Chatham ME5 .... 61 E4
Holland Rd. Maidstone ME14 .... 92 B5
Hollands Cl. DA12 .... 31 E3
Hollies Ave. DA15 .... 23 F7
Hollies The. DA12 .... 30 D2
Holligrave Rd. BR1 .... 36 A8
Hollin Cl. TN4 .... 148 F4
Hollingbourne Ave. DA7 .... 7 F6
Hollingbourne Cty Prim Sch.
  ME17 .... 94 E2
Hollingbourne Hill. ME17 .... 94 F4
Hollingbourne Rd. ME8 .... 49 C2
Hollingbourne Sta. ME17 .... 94 C3
Hollingbourne Tower. 4 BR5 .. 38 D1
Hollington Ct. BR7 .... 23 B2
Hollingworth Rd.
  Orpington BR2 & BR5 .... 37 B2
Hollingworth Rd.
  Park Wood ME15 .... 107 F5
Hollingworth Way. TN16 .... 81 D1
Hollow La. Hartlip ME9 .... 64 C5
Hollow La. Snodland MC6 .... 74 F6
Hollow Trees Dr. TN11 .... 116 A1
Holly Bank. TN12 .... 152 B8
Holly Bush La. TN13 .... 84 C3
Holly Cl. Chatham ME5 .... 62 C8
Holly Cl. Gillingham ME7 .... 48 E6
Holly Cotts. TN12 .... 112 B2
Holly Ct. DA14 .... 24 B4
Holly Farm Rd. ME15 .... 108 C6
Holly Hill. DA13 .... 58 F3
Holly Hill Rd. DA17 .... 4 B1
Holly Rd. Dartford DA1 .... 26 D7
Holly Rd. Orpington BR6 .... 52 A3
Holly Rd. Rochester,Strood ME2 46 E5
Holly Rd. Rochester,Wainscott
  ME2 .... 33 D2
Holly Tree Cl. ME17 .... 109 E2
Hollybrake Cl. BR7 .... 23 D1
Hollybush Cl. TN13 .... 84 C3
Hollybush Ct. TN13 .... 84 C3
Hollybush La. BR6 .... 53 A4
Hollybush Rd. DA12 .... 30 C6
Hollycroft. ME2 .... 46 C2
Hollydale Dr. BR2 .... 50 F7
Hollydene Rd. TN5 .... 174 F6
Hollyshaw Terr. TN2 .... 149 C2
Hollytree Ave. BR8 .... 39 E7
Hollytree Dr. ME3 .... 32 B3
Hollywood La. Knockmill TN15 .. 70 F8
Hollywood La. Rochester ME2 ... 33 C2
Hollywood Manor. TN15 .... 70 F7
Hollywood Way. DA8 .... 9 B6
Holm Ct. SE12 .... 22 B5
Holm Mill La. ME7 .... 110 B6
Holmbury Manor. 6 DA14 .... 24 A4
Holmbury Pk. BR7 .... 22 E1
Holmcroft Way. BR2 .... 36 F4
Holmdale Rd. BR7 .... 23 C3
Holmdene Cl. BR1 .... 36 E6
Holmes Ct. ME19 .... 73 F4
Holmesdale Com Sch. ME6 .... 74 F7
Holmesdale Hill.
  South Darenth DA4 .... 41 C8
Holmesdale Rd. Bexley DA16 ...... 7 D5
Holmesdale Rd. Sevenoaks TN13 84 D4
Holmesdale Rd.
  South Darenth DA4 .... 41 C8

Holmesdale Sch (Farm Annex). ME6 ... 74 F6
Holmewood House. TN3 ... 148 A2
Holmewood Rd. TN4 ... 149 C7
Holmewood Ridge. TN3 ... 147 F3
Holmhurst Cl. TN4 ... 148 F4
Holmhurst Rd. DA17 ... 4 B1
Holmleigh Ave. DA1 ... 9 E2
Holmoaks. Gillingham ME8 ... 49 E2
Holmoaks. Maidstone ME14 ... 92 C5
Holmsdale Gr. DA1 & DA7 ... 8 E4
Holmside. ME7 ... 48 E3
Holmwood Cotts. BR6 ... 52 C1
Holmwood Ct. DA14 ... 23 F3
Holstein Way. 6 DA18 ... 3 C6
Holt Cl. SE28 ... 3 C6
Holt Rd. E16 ... 1 E5
Holt Wood Ave. ME20 ... 90 E8
Holtwood Cl. ME8 ... 63 D6
Holtye Cres. ME15 ... 92 B2
Holtye Golf Club. TN8 ... 144 F3
Holtye Rd. RH19 ... 144 A3
Holwood Park Ave. BR2 & BR6 ... 50 F6
Holy Family RC Prim Sch. SE9 ... 5 C3
Holy Family RC Prim Sch The. ME15 ... 107 F4
Holy Innocents RC Prim Sch. BR6 ... 51 F7
Holy Trinity CE Prim Sch. Dartford DA1 ... 9 C2
Holy Trinity CE Prim Sch. Dartford DA1 ... 9 D1
Holy Trinity Coll & Prep Sch. BR1 ... 36 C8
Holy Trinity Lamorbey CE Prim Sch. DA15 ... 24 A7
Holyhead Rd. 3 E6 ... 1 F8
Holyoake Terr. TN13 ... 84 A3
Holywell Cl. SE3 ... 5 A8
Home Farm La. TN11 ... 116 A3
Home Farm Cotts. BR5 ... 38 D8
Home Farm Ct. TN3 ... 163 C4
Home Farm La. Royal Tunbridge Wells TN11 & TN2 ... 133 F1
Home Farm La. Royal Tunbridge Wells TN2 ... 149 E8
Home Gdns. DA1 ... 9 E1
Home Hill. BR8 ... 25 F1
Home Lea. BR6 ... 51 F5
Home Mead Cl. 6 DA11 ... 30 B8
Homedean Rd. TN13 ... 83 C4
Homefield Cl. St Paul's Cray BR5 ... 38 B5
Homefield Cl. Swanley BR8 ... 39 F6
Homefield Rd. Bromley BR1 ... 36 C8
Homefield Rd. Sevenoaks TN13 ... 83 E5
Homefield Rise. BR6 ... 38 A1
Homemead. 7 Gravesend DA11 ... 30 B8
Homemead. Swanscombe DA9 ... 11 B1
Homemead Rd. BR2 ... 36 F4
Homer Cl. DA7 ... 8 C6
Homesdale Rd. Bromley BR1 & BR2 ... 36 C6
Homesdale Rd. Orpington BR5 & BR6 ... 37 E2
Homestead Rd. Marlpit Hill TN8 ... 112 B5
Homestead Rd. Orpington BR6 ... 38 A2
Homestead The. Crayford DA1 ... 8 E2
Homestead The. Dartford DA1 ... 9 C1
Homestead The. Groombridge TN3 ... 161 C7
Homevale Cotts. TN14 ... 67 E4
Homewards Rd. ME3 ... 19 B8
Homewood Cotts. DA12 ... 31 E1
Homewood Cres. BR7 ... 23 E2
Homewood Rd. Langton Green TN3 ... 147 F3
Homewood Rd. Tenterden TN30 ... 173 B1
Homewood Sch. TN30 ... 173 B1
Homoepathic Hospl. TN1 ... 149 A3
Honduras Terr. 8 ME14 ... 92 A7
Hone St. ME2 ... 47 B8
Honey Bee Glade. ME8 ... 63 E6
Honey Cl. ME7 ... 63 A5
Honey La. ME15 ... 108 B6
Honeybourne Way. BR5 ... 37 D1
Honeycrock Hill. ME9 ... 79 F8
Honeyden Rd. DA14 ... 24 E2
Honeypot Cl. ME2 ... 47 B8
Honeypot La. Hodsoll Street TN15 ... 57 D2
Honeypot La. North Ash TN15 ... 85 C8
Honeysuckle Cl. 3 Chatham ME5 ... 61 E4
Honeysuckle Cl. Gillingham ME7 ... 62 F4
Honeysuckle Ct. 4 SE12 ... 22 A8
Honiton Rd. DA16 ... 6 F5
Honywood Rd. ME17 ... 111 C4
Hoo Comm Rd. ME3 ... 34 A4
Hoo Rd. ME2 & ME3 ... 33 D3
Hoo St Werburgh Cty Prim Sch. ME3 ... 34 D5
Hoo St Werburgh Mid Sch. ME3 ... 34 C5
Hood Ave. BR5 ... 38 B4
Hook Cl. ME5 ... 61 E5
Hook Farm Rd. ME2 ... 36 D4
Hook Green La. DA13 ... 44 A4
Hook Green La. DA2 ... 25 F5
Hook Green Rd. DA13 ... 28 F1
Hook Hill. TN5 ... 176 A6
Hook La. Bexley DA16 ... 7 A4
Hook La. Harrietsham ME17 ... 110 C6
Hook Lane Prim Sch. DA16 ... 7 A4
Hook Rd. ME6 ... 74 F8
Hook St. ME17 ... 127 F8
Hookfields. DA11 ... 29 E5

Hookstead. TN26 ... 173 C7
Hookwood Cotts. TN14 ... 67 C8
Hookwood Rd. BR6 & TN14 ... 67 C7
Hooper Rd. E16 ... 1 A7
Hooper's Pl. ME1 ... 47 C4
Hooper's Rd. ME1 ... 47 C4
Hoopers La. ME3 ... 18 F5
Hoopers Yd. TN15 ... 84 C1
Hop Pocket Cl. TN17 ... 170 A8
Hop Pocket La. TN17 ... 135 F7
Hope Ave. TN11 ... 102 E1
Hope Cl. SE12 ... 22 B5
Hope Cotts. DA2 ... 28 B6
Hope Rd. DA10 ... 11 F1
Hope St. Chatham ME4 ... 48 A3
Hope St. Maidstone ME14 ... 91 F6
Hope Terr. ME3 ... 32 D7
Hopedale Rd. SE7 ... 5 B8
Hopehouse La. TN17 & TN18 ... 186 F1
Hopes Gr. TN26 ... 173 D7
Hopewell Dr. Chatham ME5 ... 62 C8
Hopewell Dr. Gravesend DA12 ... 30 F3
Hopgarden Cl. 12 TN8 ... 112 D3
Hopgarden Rd. TN13 ... 99 A8
Hopgarden Oast. ME18 ... 104 F1
Hopgarden Rd. TN10 ... 117 D6
Hoppers Cnr. ME15 ... 105 D7
Hopton Cl. BR2 ... 36 B1
Hopton Rd. SE18 ... 2 C3
Hopwood Gdns. TN4 ... 149 A6
Horizon Cl. TN4 ... 149 B8
Horley Cl. DA6 ... 8 A2
Horley Rd. SE9 ... 22 E4
Horn La. SE10 ... 1 A2
Horn Park La. SE12 ... 5 B2
Horn Park La. SE12 ... 5 B1
Horn Park Prim Sch. SE12 ... 22 B8
Horn Yd. 6 DA11 ... 13 B1
Horn's Oak Rd. DA13 ... 58 B6
Hornbeam Ave. Chatham ME5 ... 62 B2
Hornbeam Ave. Royal Tunbridge Wells TN2 ... 133 D1
Hornbeam Cl. Larkfield ME20 ... 75 B2
Hornbeam Cl. Putlands TN12 ... 135 F5
Hornbeam House. 6 DA15 ... 24 A5
Hornbeam La. DA7 ... 8 C5
Hornbeam Way. DA7 ... 37 A3
Hornbeams. DA13 ... 73 B8
Horncastle Cl. SE12 ... 22 A8
Horncastle Rd. SE12 ... 22 A8
Horne House. SE18 ... 5 E6
Hornetts Cl. BR8 ... 39 D2
Hornfair Rd. SE7 ... 5 D7
Hornfield Cotts. DA13 ... 58 C3
Horning Cl. SE9 ... 22 E4
Horns La. ME18 ... 88 D1
Horns Lodge La. TN11 ... 117 A8
Horns Rd. TN18 ... 184 D8
Horsa Rd. Eltham SE12 ... 22 C8
Horsa Rd. Erith DA8 ... 8 C7
Horse Leaze. ME6 ... 2 A7
Horsecroft Cl. BR6 ... 38 B1
Horsegrove Ave. TN5 ... 176 F1
Horsell Rd. BR5 ... 38 B8
Horseshoe Cl. Gillingham ME7 ... 62 F5
Horseshoe Cl. Maidstone ME14 ... 92 E5
Horseshoes La. ME17 ... 108 E4
Horsewash La. ME1 ... 47 C6
Horsfeld Gdns. SE9 ... 5 E2
Horsfeld Rd. SE9 ... 5 D2
Horsfield Cl. DA2 ... 27 C8
Horsham Rd. DA6 ... 8 A2
Horsley Rd. Bromley BR1 ... 36 B8
Horsley Rd. Rochester ME1 ... 47 B4
Horsmonden Cl. BR6 ... 37 F2
Horsmonden Cty Prim Sch. TN12 ... 153 A6
Horsmonden Rd. TN12 ... 152 D6
Horsted Ave. ME4 ... 47 E1
Horsted Cty Inf Sch. ME4 ... 61 D5
Horsted Cty Jun Sch. ME5 ... 61 D5
Horsted Way. ME1 ... 61 D7
Horton Downs. ME15 ... 92 F1
Horton Kirby CE Prim Sch. DA4 ... 41 C6
Horton Pl. TN16 ... 81 D1
Horton Rd. DA4 ... 41 C6
Horton Tower. 2 BR5 ... 38 C5
Horton Way. DA4 ... 40 F2
Hortons Way. 1 TN16 ... 81 D1
Horwood Cl. ME1 ... 61 B8
Hoselands View. DA13 ... 42 E5
Hoser Ave. SE12 ... 22 A6
Hosey Common La. TN16 ... 96 F5
Hosey Common Rd. TN16 & TN8 ... 96 D5
Hosey Hill. TN16 ... 96 E8
Hoskin's Cl. E16 ... 1 C7
Hospital La. ME1 ... 47 E4
Hospital Rd. Hollingbourne ME17 ... 109 E8
Hospital Rd. Sevenoaks TN13 ... 84 C6
Hotel Rd. ME8 ... 49 A2
Hotham Cl. Sutton at Hone DA4 ... 27 B1
Hotham Cl. Swanley Village BR8 ... 40 B8
Hothfield Rd. ME8 ... 49 F1
Hottsfield. DA3 ... 42 E6
Hougham House. 11 BR5 ... 38 D1
Houghton Ave. ME7 ... 63 B3
Houselands Rd. TN9 ... 117 B2
Hove Cl. RM17 ... 12 A8
Hovendens. TN17 ... 170 A8
Hoveton Rd. SE28 ... 3 C7
How Green La. TN8 ... 113 C2
Howard Ave. Rochester ME1 ... 47 D3
Howard Ave. Sidcup DA5 ... 24 C8
Howard Dr. ME16 ... 91 B5
Howard Gdns. TN2 ... 149 A1
Howard Rd. Bromley BR1 ... 22 A1
Howard Rd. Dartford DA1 ... 10 A1
Howard Rd. East Malling ME19 ... 89 F8

Howard Sch The. ME8 ... 63 D8
Howarth Rd. SE2 ... 3 A2
Howbury La. DA8 ... 9 A5
Howbury Rd. DA1 & DA8 ... 9 A5
Howbury Wlk. ME8 ... 63 D4
Howden Cl. SE28 ... 3 D6
Howells Cl. TN15 ... 55 E4
Howes Cotts. TN18 ... 184 F8
Howick Rd. ME20 ... 90 F8
Howland Rd. TN12 ... 138 E6
Howlsmere Cl. ME4 ... 48 A2
Hubbard's Hill. TN13 & TN14 ... 99 B4
Hubbard's La. ME15 ... 107 A3
Hubble Dr. ME15 ... 107 E7
Huckleberry Cl. ME5 ... 62 B3
Hudson Cl. ME8 ... 49 C1
Hudson Pl. SE18 ... 2 C1
Hudson Rd. DA7 ... 7 F6
Hugh Christie Tech Coll The. TN10 ... 117 D6
Hughes Dr. ME2 ... 33 D2
Hulsewood Cl. DA2 ... 26 B5
Hulsons Cl. 1 TN18 ... 179 A2
Humber Cres. ME2 ... 46 F7
Humber House. 5 ME15 ... 107 E8
Humber Rd. Dartford DA1 ... 9 D2
Humber Rd. 4 Greenwich SE10 ... 1 A1
Humber Rd. Greenwich SE3 ... 5 A8
Humboldt Ct. TN2 ... 149 D5
Hume Ave. RM18 ... 13 B5
Hume Cl. RM18 ... 13 A4
Humphreys. TN12 ... 151 F6
Hundred of Hoo Sch. ME3 ... 34 C5
Hungershall Pk. TN4 ... 148 E2
Hunsdon Dr. TN13 ... 84 B4
Hunstanton Cl. ME8 ... 63 E3
Hunt Rd. Northfleet DA11 ... 29 F5
Hunt Rd. Tonbridge TN10 ... 117 E6
Hunt St. Nettlestead ME18 ... 104 F5
Hunt St. West Farleigh ME15 & ME18 ... 105 B5
Hunter's Gr. BR6 ... 51 C6
Hunters Cl. SE25 ... 25 E5
Hunters Ct. 4 ME7 ... 48 C7
Hunters Lodge. 10 DA15 ... 24 A5
Hunters Way. Gillingham ME7 ... 48 E1
Hunters Way. Royal Tunbridge Wells TN2 ... 148 F1
Hunters Way W. ME5 & ME7 ... 48 E1
Hunters Wlk. TN14 ... 67 E5
Huntersfield Cl. ME5 ... 62 C1
Huntingdon Wlk. 4 ME15 ... 107 E7
Huntingfield Rd. DA13 ... 44 A2
Huntington Cl. TN17 ... 169 D4
Huntington Rd. ME17 ... 106 B3
Huntley Ave. DA11 ... 12 C1
Huntley Mill Rd. TN5 ... 176 E3
Huntleys Pk. TN4 ... 148 F5
Hunton CE Prim Sch. ME15 ... 121 D7
Hunton Hill. ME15 ... 105 F1
Hunton House. 4 BR5 ... 38 C4
Hunton Rd. TN12 ... 122 A3
Hunts Cl. SE3 ... 5 A5
Hunts Farm Cl. TN15 ... 87 A7
Hunts Mede Cl. ME7 ... 22 F1
Huntsman La. Maidstone ME14 ... 92 B4
Huntsman La. Wrotham Heath TN15 ... 72 E1
Huntsman's Cnr. ME4 ... 61 E8
Huntsmans Cl. ME4 ... 47 E1
Huntsmoor House. BR5 ... 38 B5
Hurlfield. DA2 ... 26 C5
Hurlingham Rd. DA7 ... 7 F7
Huron Cl. 5 BR6 ... 51 F4
Hurst Cl. Chatham ME5 ... 61 E6
Hurst Cl. Staplehurst TN12 ... 139 F4
Hurst Cl. Tenterden TN30 ... 182 F7
Hurst Farm Rd. TN14 ... 99 B3
Hurst Green CE Sch. TN19 ... 184 A2
Hurst Hill. ME5 ... 61 E2
Hurst House. SE2 ... 3 D1
Hurst La. Chatham ME5 ... 61 E6
Hurst La. Sevenoaks Weald TN14 ... 99 B2
Hurst Pl. Erith SE2 ... 7 D8
Hurst Pl. Gillingham ME8 ... 63 F8
Hurst Rd. Chatham ME5 ... 24 D7
Hurst Rd. Erith DA8 ... 8 C7
Hurst Rd. Sidcup DA5 ... 24 D7
Hurst Springs. DA5 ... 24 E7
Hurst The. Crouch ME18 ... 102 D7
Hurst The. Plaxtol Spoute TN15 ... 87 C1
Hurst The. Royal Tunbridge Wells TN2 ... 149 E7
Hurst Way. Maidstone ME16 ... 90 F2
Hurst Way. Sevenoaks TN13 ... 99 C8
Hurstbourne Cotts. DA5 ... 25 B8
Hurstfield. BR2 ... 36 A4
Hurstings The. ME16 ... 91 D2
Hurstmere Sch. DA15 ... 24 C7
Hurstwood. ME5 ... 61 E4
Hurstwood Ave. Erith DA7 & DA8 ... 8 E6
Hurstwood Ave. Sidcup DA5 ... 24 E7
Hurstwood Dr. BR1 ... 36 F6
Hurstwood La. TN4 ... 148 F3
Hurstwood Pk. TN4 ... 148 F3
Hurstwood Rd. Bredhurst ME7 ... 63 B1
Hurstwood Rd. Detling ME14 ... 78 B7
Husheath Hill. TN17 ... 154 F6
Husseywell Cres. BR2 ... 36 A1
Hutsford Cl. ME8 ... 63 D5
Hutson Terr. RM16 ... 10 D8
Huxley Cl. ME1 ... 47 A4
Huxley House. ... 3 D1
Huxley Rd. DA16 ... 6 F4
Hyacinth Rd. ME2 ... 46 E6
Hybrid Cl. ME1 ... 47 D1
Hyde Dr. BR5 ... 38 B5

Hyde Rd. Bexley DA7 ... 7 F5
Hyde Rd. Maidstone ME16 ... 91 D6
Hyde's Orch. TN27 ... 141 E5
Hylton St. SE18 ... 2 F2
Hyperion Dr. ME2 ... 32 F1
Hythe Ave. DA7 ... 7 F7
Hythe Cl. Orpington BR5 ... 38 C5
Hythe Cl. Royal Tunbridge Wells TN4 ... 133 A1
Hythe St. DA1 ... 9 E1

Ickleton Rd. SE9 ... 22 E4
Icough Ct. SE3 ... 5 B7
Iddenden Cotts. TN18 ... 178 D2
Ide Hill CE Prim Sch. TN14 ... 97 F4
Ide Hill Rd. TN14 ... 97 F2
Idenwood Cl. ME8 ... 63 D6
Idleigh Court Rd. DA3 & DA13 ... 57 C8
Ifield Cl. ME15 ... 107 F7
Ifield Cotts. DA12 ... 31 C2
Ifield Sch. DA12 ... 30 C3
Ifield Way. DA12 ... 30 D2
Ightham By-Pass. TN15 ... 86 C7
Ightham Cotts. DA2 ... 28 B6
Ightham Cty Prim Sch. TN15 ... 86 B6
Ightham Mote (NT). TN15 ... 101 A7
Ightham Rd. Erith DA8 ... 8 A7
Ightham Rd. Shipbourne TN11 & TN15 ... 101 C5
Ilkley Rd. E16 ... 1 C8
Illustrious Cl. ME5 ... 62 A6
Imber Ct. 4 SE9 ... 6 A1
Impala Gdns. TN4 ... 149 B6
Imperial Bsns Pk. DA11 ... 12 F1
Imperial Dr. 2 DA12 ... 30 F3
Imperial Rd. ME7 ... 48 C3
Imperial Ret Pk. DA11 ... 13 A1
Imperial Way. BR7 & SE9 ... 23 C5
Impton Cl. ME5 ... 62 A1
Inca Dr. SE9 ... 23 B8
Indus Rd. SE7 ... 5 C7
Ingle Rd. ME4 ... 47 F2
Ingleby Way. BR7 ... 23 A3
Ingledew Rd. SE18 ... 2 D1
Ingleside Gr. 3 SE3 ... 5 A8
Ingleton Ave. DA16 ... 7 A2
Inglewood. Chislehurst BR7 ... 23 D2
Inglewood. Swanley BR8 ... 39 E7
Inglewood Copse. BR1 ... 36 F7
Inglewood Rd. DA7 ... 8 D3
Ingoldsby Rd. DA12 ... 30 F7
Ingram Rd. Dartford DA1 ... 26 E7
Ingram Rd. Gillingham ME7 ... 48 E6
Ingress Gdns. DA9 & DA10 ... 11 D2
Ingress Terr. DA13 ... 28 F4
Inigo Jones Rd. SE7 ... 5 E7
Institute Rd. ME4 ... 48 A4
Instone Rd. DA1 ... 26 D8
Inverary Pl. SE18 ... 6 D8
Inverine Rd. SE7 ... 1 B1
Invermore Pl. SE18 ... 2 C2
Inverness House. 6 ME15 ... 107 E7
Invicta Cl. BR7 ... 23 A3
Invicta Gram Sch for Girls. ME14 ... 92 C4
Invicta Inf Sch. SE3 ... 5 A7
Invicta Rd. Dartford DA2 ... 10 B1
Invicta Rd. Greenwich SE3 & SE7 ... 5 A8
Invicta Villas. ME14 ... 93 C4
Iona Cl. ME5 ... 62 D1
Iona Rd. ME15 ... 107 A7
Ireland Cl. E6 ... 1 F8
Irene Rd. BR6 ... 37 F2
Iris Ave. DA5 ... 7 E1
Iris Cl. ME5 ... 77 A8
Iris Cres. DA7 ... 7 F8
Iron Mill La. DA1 ... 8 F3
Iron Mill Pl. DA1 ... 8 F3
Ironside Cl. ME5 ... 62 A8
Ironstones. TN3 ... 148 B3
Irvine Rd. ME3 ... 32 B3
Irvine Way. BR6 ... 37 F2
Irving House. TN1 ... 149 B5
Irving Way. BR8 ... 39 D7
Irving Wlk. DA10 ... 28 E8
Irwin Ave. SE18 ... 6 F7
Isabella Dr. BR6 ... 51 C6
Isham Rd. SE6 ... 6 C8
Islehurst Cl. BR7 ... 37 A8
Ismays Rd. TN15 ... 86 C3
Istead Rise. DA13 ... 29 F1
Istead Rise Cty Prim Sch. DA13 ... 43 E8
Ivedon Rd. DA16 ... 7 C5
Ivens Way. ME17 ... 110 D6
Iverhurst Cl. DA6 ... 7 D2
Iversgate Cl. ME8 ... 49 F2
Ives Rd. TN9 ... 116 F1
Ivor Gr. SE9 ... 23 B7
Ivorydown. BR1 ... 22 A4
Ivy Bower Cl. DA9 ... 11 B2
Ivy Cl. Dartford DA1 ... 27 A8
Ivy Cl. Gravesend DA12 ... 30 C3
Ivy Cl. Kingswood ME17 ... 109 D2
Ivy House La. TN13 ... 68 E2
Ivy La. TN14 ... 67 E3
Ivy Rd. E16 ... 1 A7
Ivy St. ME8 ... 63 F8
Ivy Villas. DA9 ... 11 A2
Ivybridge Ct. 1 BR7 ... 37 A8
Izane Rd. DA6 ... 7 F3

Jack Lobley Cty Prim Sch. RM18 ... 12 F6
Jackass La. BR2 ... 50 C4
Jacklin Cl. ME5 ... 61 F2

Jackson Ave. ME1 ... 61 E8
Jackson Cl. Gillingham ME8 ... 49 C1
Jackson Cl. Stone DA9 ... 11 A2
Jackson Rd. BR2 ... 50 F8
Jackson St. SE18 ... 6 A8
Jackson Way. ME7 ... 171 C3
Jacksons La. 6 TN30 ... 183 A7
Jacob House. 5 DA18 ... 3 D4
Jacob's La. ME3 ... 35 B6
Jade Cl. E16 ... 1 D7
Jaffray Rd. BR2 ... 36 D5
Jaggard Way. TN12 ... 139 E3
Jagger Cl. DA2 ... 27 C8
Jago Cl. SE18 ... 6 C8
Jail La. TN16 ... 66 A3
Jamaica Terr. ME14 ... 92 A7
James Newman Ct. SE9 ... 23 A5
James Rd. Cuxton ME2 ... 46 C2
James Rd. Dartford DA1 ... 26 A8
James St. Chatham ME4 ... 47 F4
James St. Gillingham ME7 ... 48 C6
James St. Maidstone ME14 ... 92 A5
James St. Rochester ME1 ... 47 C4
James Whatman Way. ME14 ... 91 F5
Janet Ct. 4 ME7 ... 8 A3
Japonica Cl. ME5 ... 62 C2
Jaquets Ct. DA5 ... 25 A6
Jarrah Cotts. RM16 ... 10 D8
Jarrett Ave. ME2 ... 33 C2
Jarvis La. TN17 ... 154 B3
Jarvis Pl. TN30 ... 173 B3
Jashada House. SE18 ... 2 A1
Jasmine Cl. 2 Chatham ME5 ... 61 F4
Jasmine Cl. East Malling ME19 ... 89 F8
Jasmine Cl. Orpington BR6 ... 51 B8
Jasmine Cotts. TN3 ... 161 C7
Jasmine Rd. ME19 ... 89 F8
Jason Wlk. SE9 ... 23 A4
Jasper Ave. ME1 ... 47 D2
Jasper Rd. E16 ... 1 D7
Javelin Rd. ME19 ... 88 F3
Jay Gdns. BR7 ... 22 F4
Jefferson Dr. ME8 ... 49 C1
Jefferson Wlk. 13 SE18 ... 6 A8
Jeffery St. ME7 ... 48 C6
Jeffrey Cl. TN12 ... 139 E4
Jeffrey Row. SE12 ... 5 B2
Jeffrey St. ME14 ... 92 A5
Jeken Rd. SE9 ... 5 C3
Jellicoe Ave. DA12 ... 30 C5
Jellicoe Ave W. DA12 ... 30 C5
Jenkins' Dale. ME4 ... 47 F3
Jenkins Dr. ME15 ... 107 E5
Jenner House. 4 DA17 ... 4 A3
Jenner Rd. ME1 ... 47 C4
Jenner Way. ME20 ... 75 F6
Jennifer Cl. ME3 ... 34 F5
Jenningtree Rd. DA8 ... 9 B7
Jenningtree Way. DA17 ... 4 C4
Jenton Ave. DA7 ... 7 E5
Jerome Rd. ME20 ... 74 F4
Jersey Dr. BR5 ... 37 D3
Jersey Rd. Newham E16 ... 1 C7
Jersey Rd. Rochester ME2 ... 47 A8
Jeskyns Rd. DA12 ... 44 E6
Jessamine Pl. DA2 ... 27 C8
Jessamine Terr. BR8 ... 39 C8
Jessup Cl. SE18 ... 2 C2
Jetty Rd. Kingsnorth ME3 ... 35 D7
Jetty Rd. Sheerness ME12 ... 21 F3
Jetty Wlk. 4 RM17 ... 12 A8
Jevington Way. SE12 ... 22 B7
Jewell Gr. TN12 ... 138 D5
Jeyes Rd. ME7 ... 48 C4
Jezreels Rd. ME7 ... 48 D3
Jim Bradley Cl. 16 SE18 ... 2 A2
Jiniwin Rd. ME1 ... 61 D7
Joan Cres. SE9 ... 22 D8
Jockey La. TN17 ... 169 D5
Johannesburg House. 2 ME15 ... 107 F4
John Mayne CE Prim Sch. TN7 ... 157 F1
John Newton Ct. DA16 ... 7 A4
John Spare Ct. TN4 ... 149 A6
John St. Grays RM17 ... 12 C8
John St. Maidstone ME14 ... 92 A6
John St. Rochester ME1 ... 47 C4
John St. R Tunbridge Wells TN4 ... 149 A5
John Wilson St. SE18 ... 2 A2
John's Rd. DA13 ... 43 F4
Johns Cl. DA3 ... 42 F4
Johnson Ave. ME7 ... 48 C7
Johnson Cl. DA11 ... 29 D5
Johnson Rd. BR2 ... 36 D4
Johnsons Ave. TN14 ... 53 B1
Johnsons Way. DA9 ... 11 C1
Joiners Ct. ME4 ... 48 B2
Jonas Dr. TN5 ... 174 E5
Jonas La. TN5 ... 174 E5
Jones Rd. E13 ... 1 B8
Jordan Cl. ME15 ... 107 E5
Joy Rd. DA12 ... 30 C7
Joyce Cl. TN17 ... 169 C5
Joyce Dawson Way. SE28 ... 3 A6
Joyce Green Hospl. DA1 ... 9 F5
Joyce Green La. Dartford DA1 ... 9 E6
Joyce Green La. Dartford,Temple Hill DA1 ... 9 F4
Joyce Green Wlk. DA1 ... 9 F3
Joyce Page Cl. SE7 ... 5 D8
Joyden's Wood Rd. DA5 ... 25 E5
Joydens Wood Cty Jun Sch. DA5 ... 25 E4
Joydens Wood Cty Prim Inf Sch. DA5 ... 25 E4
Jubilee Ctry Pk. BR2 ... 37 B4
Jubilee Cl. DA9 ... 11 C1

Jubilee Cnr. ME17 125 E3
Jubilee Cres. Gravesend DA12 30 E6
Jubilee Cres. Ightham TN15 86 C6
Jubilee Ct. DA1 26 D8
Jubilee Field. TN30 189 E4
Jubilee Prim Sch. SE28 3 C6
Jubilee Rd. Maypole BR6 53 A4
Jubilee Rd. West Thurrock RM16 11 B8
Jubilee Rise. TN15 84 F6
Jubilee Terr. ME7 48 C6
Jubilee Way. DA14 24 A6
Judd Rd. TN9 133 B7
Judd Sch The. TN9 133 A8
Judeth Gdns. DA12 30 E3
Judkins Cl. ME5 62 C6
Juglans Rd. BR6 38 A1
Julian Rd. BR6 52 A4
Julians Cl. TN13 99 A8
Julians Way. TN13 99 A8
Junction Rd.
Bodiam TN18 & TN32 185 A3
Junction Rd. Dartford DA1 9 D1
Junction Rd. Gillingham ME7 48 D4
Juniper Cl. Chatham ME5 62 A4
Juniper Cl.
Royal Tunbridge Wells TN2 113 D1
Juniper La. E6 1 E8
Juniper Wlk. BR8 39 D7
Jury St. 10 DA11 13 B1
Jutland Cl. ME3 19 D7
Jutland House. 10 SE7 1 E2

Kale Rd. DA18 3 E4
Kashgar Rd. SE18 2 F2
Kashmir Rd. SE7 5 D7
Katherine Ct. ME5 62 B2
Katherine Gdns. SE9 5 D3
Katherine Rd. TN8 128 C8
Katie Rance Ct. 8 SE18 1 F2
Kay St. DA16 7 B6
Keary Rd. DA10 28 F8
Keats Gdns. RM18 13 B5
Keats House. DA1 8 E2
Keats Rd. Bexley DA16 6 F6
Keats Rd. Erith DA17 4 C3
Keats Rd. Lunsford ME20 74 F3
Kechill Gdns. BR2 36 A2
Kedleston Dr. BR5 37 F4
Keeble Cl. SE18 6 B8
Keedonwood Rd. BR1 22 A3
Keefe Cl. ME5 61 D1
Keel Gdns. TN4 148 E8
Keeling Rd. SE9 5 D2
Keemor Cl. SE18 6 A7
Keep The. SE3 5 A5
Keightley Dr. SE9 23 C7
Keir Hardy House. 7 DA17 4 A3
Keith Ave. DA4 27 B2
Keith Sutton House. SE9 23 C6
Kelbrook Rd. SE3 & SE9 5 E4
Kelchers La. TN11 118 F5
Kelham House. 10 SE18 6 B8
Kellaway Rd. Chatham ME5 62 A2
Kellaway Rd. Greenwich SE3 5 D5
Kellner Rd. SE28 2 F3
Kelly Dr. ME7 48 C7
Kelly House. ME1 61 C7
Kelsall Cl. SE3 5 B5
Kelsey Rd. BR5 38 B7
Kelso Dr. DA12 30 F4
Kelvin Cl. TN10 117 D7
Kelvin House. 3 DA17 4 A3
Kelvin Par. BR6 37 E1
Kelvin Rd. Bexley DA16 7 A4
Kelvin Rd. Tilbury RM18 13 A5
Kemble Cl. TN2 149 E7
Kemble Dr. BR2 50 E7
Kemnal Rd. BR7 23 D3
Kemnal Tech Coll. BR5 24 B1
Kemnal Warren. BR7 23 D2
Kemp Cl. ME5 61 E4
Kempley Ct. 2 RM17 12 D8
Kempt St. SE18 6 A8
Kempton Cl. Chatham ME5 62 C2
Kempton Cl. Erith DA8 8 C8
Kemsing Cl. DA5 24 E8
Kemsing Cty Prim Sch. TN15 70 A2
Kemsing Rd. Greenwich SE10 1 A1
Kemsing Rd. Wrotham TN15 71 C3
Kemsing Sta. TN15 85 D8
Kemsley Cl. Northfleet DA11 29 F4
Kemsley Cl. Swanscombe DA9 11 B1
Kemsley Street Rd. ME14 63 C1
Kendal Dr. TN9 117 C2
Kendal Pk. TN4 148 E5
Kendal Way. ME8 63 D8
Kendall Ct. DA15 24 A5
Kendall Lodge. 5 BR1 36 B8
Kendon Bsns Pk. ME2 47 D8
Kenia Wlk. DA12 30 F5
Kenilworth Dr. ME8 63 D6
Kenilworth Gdns. Gillingham
ME8 63 D7
Kenilworth Gdns. Woolwich SE18 6 B5
Kenilworth House. ME16 91 B2
Kenilworth Rd. BR5 37 C3
Kenley Cl. Sidcup DA5 25 A8
Kenley Cl. St Paul's Cray BR7 37 E6
Kenley House. 6 BR5 38 B7
Kenmere Rd. DA16 7 C5
Kennard Cl. ME1 46 F2
Kennard St. E16 1 F5
Kennedy Cl. BR5 37 D1
Kennedy Gdns. TN13 84 D5
Kennedy House. TN17 180 E6
Kennel Barn Rd. ME9 80 C5
Kennet Ct. 2 BR8 39 E6
Kennet Rd. Crayford DA1 9 A4
Kennet Rd. Tonbridge TN10 117 C5
Kennett Ct. 16 BR5 38 D1
Kennington Cl. Gillingham ME8 49 B4
Kennington Cl. Maidstone ME15 107 F7
Kensington Ct. 4 RM17 12 C8
Kensington House. ME16 91 A2
Kent Ave. Bexley DA16 6 F2
Kent Ave. Maidstone ME15 92 C1
Kent Cl. Chatham ME1 61 C8
Kent Cl. Orpington BR6 51 E4
Kent Cl. Paddock Wood TN12 136 A6
Kent Coll. TN2 134 D3
Kent County Opthalmic
& Aural Hospl. ME14 92 A4
Kent County Show Gd. ME14 78 C3
Kent & East Sussex Rly. TN17 188 D5
Kent Hatch Rd. TN8 & RH8 96 B4
Kent House. 10 TN18 179 A2
Kent Inst of Art & Design.
Chatham ME1 47 E4
Kent Inst of Art & Design.
Maidstone ME16 91 C3
Kent Kraft Ind Est. DA11 11 F2
Kent Music Sch. TN9 133 B8
Kent Rd. Dartford DA1 9 E1
Kent Rd. Gravesend DA11 30 A7
Kent Rd. Grays RM17 12 C8
Kent Rd. Halling ME2 60 A6
Kent Rd. Longfield DA3 42 D7
Kent Rd. Orpington BR5 38 B3
Kent Rd. R Tunbridge Wells TN4 149 A6
Kent Rd. Snodland ME6 75 A6
Kent St. ME18 88 E2
Kent & Sussex Hospl. TN4 149 A4
Kent Terr. Lower Higham ME3 32 D7
Kent Terr. Meopham Green DA13 58 A7
Kentish Gdns. TN2 162 E8
Kentish Rd. DA17 4 A2
Kentish Way. BR1 & BR2 36 B6
Kentmere Rd. SE18 2 E2
Kenward Ct. TN11 118 E8
Kenward Rd. Eltham SE9 5 D2
Kenward Rd. Maidstone ME16 91 C5
Kenward Rd. Yalding ME18 104 E2
Kenwood Ave. Chatham ME5 62 A4
Kenwood Ave. New Barn DA3 43 C6
Kenwyn Rd. DA1 9 D2
Kenya Rd. SE7 5 D7
Kenya Terr. 7 ME14 92 A7
Kenyon Wlk. ME8 63 B3
Kerry Cl. E16 1 B7
Kersey Gdns. SE9 22 E4
Kesteven Cl. ME2 60 B5
Kestlake Rd. DA5 7 C1
Kestner Ind Est. DA9 11 A3
Keston Ave. BR2 50 C5
Keston CE Prim Sch. BR2 50 D5
Keston Cl. DA16 7 C7
Keston Ct. DA5 24 F8
Keston Gdns. BR2 50 C6
Keston Park Cl. BR2 50 F7
Kestrel Ave. E6 1 E8
Kestrel Cl. TN8 112 D3
Kestrel House. 9 ME7 48 B6
Kestrel Rd. ME5 62 C2
Keswick Cl. TN9 117 C2
Keswick Dr. ME16 91 B5
Keswick Rd. Bexley DA7 8 A6
Keswick Rd. Orpington BR6 38 A2
Ketridge La. ME19 89 D2
Kettle La. ME15 105 E6
Kettlewell Ct. BR8 39 F7
Kevington Cl. BR5 37 F5
Kevington Dr. BR5 & BR7 37 F5
Kevington Prim Sch. BR5 38 D4
Kewlands. ME14 92 C6
Keycol Hill. ME9 65 F5
Keycol Hospl. ME9 65 E6
Keyes Ave. ME4 47 F2
Keyes Gdns. TN9 132 F7
Keyes Rd. DA1 10 A3
Keynes Ct. 9 SE28 3 B6
Keynsham Gdns. SE9 5 E2
Keynsham Rd. SE9 5 E2
Keyworth Cl. TN12 135 F6
Khartoum Rd. Chatham ME4 47 F5
Khartoum Rd. Gillingham ME4 48 A6
Khyber Rd. ME4 & ME7 48 B7
Kibbles La. TN4 148 E8
Kidbrooke Gdns. SE3 5 A6
Kidbrooke Gr. SE3 5 B6
Kidbrooke La. SE9 5 E3
Kidbrooke Park Cl. SE3 5 B6
Kidbrooke Park Prim Sch. SE3 5 C6
Kidbrooke Park Rd. SE3, 9 & 12 5 B4
Kidbrooke Sch. SE3 5 D5
Kidbrooke Sta. SE3 5 B4
Kidbrooke Way. SE3 5 B5
Kidd Pl. SE7 1 E1
Kiddens. BR8 39 B7
Kildare Rd. E16 1 A8
Killewarren Way. BR5 38 C3
Killick Cl. TN13 83 E6
Killick Rd. ME3 34 D5
Killicks Cotts. ME18 120 F8
Kiln Barn Rd.
ME16 & ME19 & ME20 90 C7
Kiln Field. TN30 183 C7
Kiln La. TN11 115 F1
Kiln Way. TN12 136 A5
Kilndown. DA12 30 D2
Kilndown Cl. ME16 91 C7
Kilnfields. BR6 53 A4
Kilnwood. TN14 67 F6
Kimber House. 11 SE18 6 B8
Kimberley Dr. DA14 24 D6
Kimberley Rd. ME7 48 D3
Kimmeridge Gdns. SE9 22 E4
Kimmeridge Rd. SE9 22 E4
Kincraig. BR7 37 A8
Kincraig Dr. TN13 84 B4
Kinder Cl. SE28 3 D6
King and Queen Cl. SE9 22 E4
King Arthur's Dr. ME2 33 A1
King Edward Ave. DA1 9 D1
King Edward Rd. Chatham ME4 47 F2
King Edward Rd. Gillingham ME7 48 F6
King Edward Rd. Maidstone ME15 91 F2
King Edward Rd. Rochester ME1 47 C5
King Edward Rd. Stone DA9 11 A2
King George Ave. E16 1 D7
King George Rd. ME5 61 E4
King George V Hill. TN1 149 C5
King George V Memorial Houses.
ME8 49 C2
King Harolds Way. DA7 7 E7
King Henry Mews. 7 BR6 51 F5
King Hill. ME19 89 A5
King John's Wlk. SE9 5 E1
King St. Chatham ME4 48 A4
King St. Gillingham ME7 48 C6
King St. Gravesend DA11 13 B1
King St. Maidstone ME14 & ME15 92 A4
King St. Rochester ME1 47 C5
King St. West Malling ME19 89 C8
King William Rd. 5 ME7 48 C7
King's Ave. ME1 47 C3
King's Bastion. ME7 48 A5
King's Cotts. ME18 104 D6
King's Highway. SE18 & SE2 6 F8
King's Orch. Eltham SE9 5 E1
King's Orch. Rochester ME1 47 C5
King's Rd. Chatham ME5 48 D1
King's Rd. Tonbridge TN9 133 D7
King's Sch. ME1 47 C5
King's Standing Ind Est. TN2 133 F2
Kingfisher Apartments. 11
ME15 107 E5
Kingfisher Cl. Erith SE28 3 C6
Kingfisher Cl. St Paul's Cray BR5 38 D5
Kingfisher Ct. TN15 55 E3
Kingfisher Dr. ME5 62 C7
Kingfisher Drive Cty Prim Sch.
ME5 62 B7
Kingfisher Pl. DA4 41 C7
Kingfisher Rd. ME20 75 A2
Kingfisher St. E6 1 E8
Kings Acre. ME15 93 A1
Kings Ave. BR1 22 A2
Kings Cl. DA1 8 E3
Kings Cotts. Leeds ME17 108 F6
Kings Cotts. Wilsley Green TN17 169 D6
Kings Ct. TN12 153 A6
Kings Dr. DA12 30 B5
Kings Farm Cty Prim Sch. DA12 30 C3
Kings Hill Ave. ME19 89 A4
Kings La. TN12 137 C7
Kings Pk. TN2 149 D3
Kings Rd. Headcorn TN27 141 C5
Kings Rd. Orpington BR6 51 F6
Kings Standing Way. TN2 133 F1
Kings Toll Rd. TN12 & TN2 151 A6
Kings Wlk. RM17 12 A8
Kingsand Rd. SE12 22 A6
Kingsdale Ct. Chatham ME5 48 C1
Kingsdale Ct. Swanscombe DA10 11 E1
Kingsdale Rd. SE18 6 F8
Kingsdown Cl. Gillingham ME7 63 B4
Kingsdown Cl. Gravesend DA12 30 F7
Kingsdown Cl. Maidstone ME16 91 C4
Kingsdown Way. BR2 36 A3
Kingsfield House. SE9 22 D5
Kingsford Cotts. TN17 180 D6
Kingsford Way. E6 1 F8
Kingsgate Cl. Bexley DA7 7 E6
Kingsgate Cl. Maidstone ME16 91 C4
Kingsgate Cl. St Paul's Cray BR5 38 C6
Kingsgate La. TN30 189 C5
Kingsground. SE9 5 E1
Kingshill Dr. ME3 34 D6
Kingsholm Gdns. SE9 5 E3
Kingshurst Rd. SE12 22 A8
Kingsingfield Cl. TN15 55 E3
Kingsingfield Rd. TN15 55 E2
Kingsland Gr. TN27 141 D5
Kingsland La. TN27 127 E1
Kingsley Ave. DA1 10 A2
Kingsley Ct. Bexley DA6 8 A3
Kingsley Ct. Wadhurst TN5 175 A4
Kingsley Ct. 1 Woolwich SE28 3 C5
Kingsley Mews. BR7 23 B2
Kingsley Rd. Maidstone ME15 92 A3
Kingsley Rd. Orpington BR6 51 F3
Kingsley Wood Dr. SE9 22 F5
Kingsman Par. SE18 1 F3
Kingsman St. SE18 1 F2
Kingsmead Cl. DA15 24 A6
Kingsmere. BR7 36 E8
Kingsnorth Ct. BR8 39 C3
Kingsnorth Rd. ME8 49 C4
Kingsridge Gdns. DA1 9 D1
Kingston Cres. ME5 62 C4
Kingston Ct. DA11 12 B1
Kingston Dr. ME15 107 A8
Kingsway. Chatham ME5 48 D1
Kingsway. Gillingham ME7 48 E1
Kingsway. Orpington BR5 37 D4
Kingswood Ave. Chatham ME4 47 F2
Kingswood Ave. Erith DA17 3 F2
Kingswood Ave. Swanley BR8 39 F6
Kingswood Cl. Dartford DA1 9 C1
Kingswood Cl. Orpington BR6 37 D2
Kingswood Cl.
Royal Tunbridge Wells TN2 149 C3
Kingswood Cty Prim Sch.
ME17 109 E2
Kingswood Rd. Gillingham ME7 48 D6
Kingswood Rd.
Kit's Coty ME1 & ME20 76 D8
Kingswood Rd.
Royal Tunbridge Wells TN2 149 C3
Kingswood Rd. Sevenoaks TN13 83 E7
Kinlet Rd. SE18 6 C6
Kinnings Row. TN9 117 C2
Kinross Cl. ME5 62 B7
Kinveachy Gdns. SE7 1 E1
Kipling Ave. RM18 13 C6
Kipling Dr. ME20 74 F4
Kipling Rd. Bexley DA7 7 E6
Kipling Rd. Dartford DA1 10 B2
Kippington Cl. TN13 83 F3
Kippington Dr. SE9 22 D7
Kippington Rd. TN13 84 A2
Kirby Cl. TN17 169 D4
Kirby Rd. Chattenden ME3 33 F5
Kirby Rd. Dartford DA2 27 D8
Kirk La. SE18 6 C8
Kirkcourt. TN13 84 A4
Kirkdale. ME15 106 F5
Kirkdale Cl. ME5 62 D1
Kirkdale Cotts. ME15 106 F5
Kirkdale Rd. Maidstone ME15 106 F6
Kirkdale Rd.
Royal Tunbridge Wells TN1 149 B4
Kirkham Rd. E6 1 E7
Kirkham St. SE18 6 E8
Kirkins Cl. TN12 153 A6
Kirkland Cl. DA15 6 E1
Kirkman Ct. TN12 139 E3
Kirkside Rd. SE3 5 A8
Kit Hill Ave. ME5 61 E3
Kit's Coty House. ME20 76 C6
Kitchener Ave. Chatham ME4 48 A1
Kitchener Ave. Gravesend DA12 30 C5
Kitchener Cotts. ME3 19 C4
Kitchener Rd. Chattenden ME3 33 F4
Kitchener Rd. Rochester ME2 47 A8
Knatts La. TN15 70 E8
Knatts Valley Rd. TN15 55 D1
Knave Wood Rd. TN14 69 E2
Knaves Acre. TN27 141 D5
Knavesacre Ct. ME8 63 D5
Knee Hill. SE2 3 C1
Knee Hill Cres. SE2 3 C2
Knight Ave. ME7 48 D7
Knight Rd. Rochester ME2 47 A6
Knight Rd. Tonbridge TN10 117 E6
Knight's Ct. DA8 8 F7
Knight's Ridge. TN2 150 D7
Knight's Way. TN27 141 D6
Knighton Rd. TN14 68 F2
Knightrider Ct. ME15 92 A3
Knightrider St. 1 ME15 92 A3
Knights Cl. Hoo St Werburgh ME3 34 E5
Knights Cl. Pembury TN2 150 D7
Knights Croft. DA3 56 F7
Knights Manor Way. DA1 9 F1
Knights Pk. ME2 47 A6
Knights Rd. Hoo St Werburgh ME3 34 D5
Knights Rd. Newham E16 1 A4
Knights Ridge. BR6 52 B5
Knightsbridge Cl. TN4 148 F5
Knightsbridge Mews. BR7 22 F1
Knock Mill La. TN15 71 A5
Knockhall Chase. DA9 11 C2
Knockhall Cty Prim Sch. DA9 11 C2
Knockhall Rd. DA9 11 C2
Knockholt CE Prim Sch. TN14 67 B2
Knockholt Rd. Eltham SE9 5 D2
Knockholt Rd. Halstead TN14 67 F6
Knockholt Sta. TN14 52 E2
Knockhurst Ct. TN30 173 C1
Knockwood Rd. TN30 173 C1
Knole. TN15 84 D1
Knole Cl. TN14 99 B2
Knole Gate. DA15 23 E5
Knole La. TN13 & TN15 84 C1
Knole Park Golf Course. TN15 84 E2
Knole Rd. Chatham ME5 62 C3
Knole Rd. Dartford DA1 26 B8
Knole Rd. Sevenoaks TN13 84 D4
Knole The. Eltham SE9 23 A4
Knole The. Istead Rise DA13 29 E1
Knole Way. TN15 84 C2
Knoll Rd. Sidcup DA14 24 B4
Knoll Rd. Sidcup,Old Bexley DA5 8 A1
Knoll Rise. BR6 37 F1
Knoll The. BR2 36 A1
Knotley Hall Cotts. TN11 115 A2
Knott Ct. ME14 91 F6
Knotts Pl. TN13 84 A3
Knowle Ave. DA7 7 F7
Knowle Cl. TN3 147 F3
Knowle Cotts. TN3 163 E1
Knowle La. TN12 136 C3
Knowle Rd. Castle Hill TN12 136 D3
Knowle Rd. Keston Mark BR2 50 E8
Knowle Rd. Maidstone ME14 92 B6
Knowle Rd. Wouldham ME1 60 D4
Knowles Gdns. TN27 141 D5
Knowles Wlk. TN12 139 F3
Knowlton Gdns. ME16 91 B2
Knowlton Gn. BR2 36 A4
Knowsley Way. TN11 116 D6
Knox Ct. TN15 84 F6
Kydbrook Cl. BR5 37 C2
Kyetop Wlk. ME8 63 D6
Kynaston Rd. Bromley BR1 22 A3
Kynaston Rd. Orpington BR5 38 B2

La Tourne Gdns. BR6 51 C7
Labour-in-Vain Rd. TN15 71 E5
Laburnham Pl. SE9 6 A2
Laburnum Ave. Dartford DA1 26 D7
Laburnum Ave. Swanley BR8 39 D6
Laburnum Ct. TN1 149 C7
Laburnum Dr. ME20 75 A2
Laburnum Gr. DA11 29 D8
Laburnum Rd. ME2 46 E5
Laburnum Way. BR2 37 B2
Lacebark Cl. DA15 23 F8
Lacey Cl. ME17 108 E4
Laceys La. ME17 122 C7
Ladbrooke Cres. DA14 24 D5
Laddingford CE Prim Sch.
ME18 120 E4
Laddingford Farm Ind Est.
ME18 120 D4
Ladds Cnr. ME7 49 B5
Ladds La. ME6 60 A2
Ladds Way. BR8 39 D5
Ladham Rd. TN17 154 A2
Ladies Mile. TN3 160 D4
Lady Amherst's Dr. TN14 98 A4
Lady Boswell's CE Prim Sch.
TN15 84 C2
Lady Oak La.
TN17 & TN18 & TN5 177 C7
Lady Vane Cl. TN11 101 C5
Lady's Gift Rd. TN4 148 F8
Ladyclose Ave. ME3 33 A7
Ladycroft Gdns. 6 BR6 51 C5
Ladycroft Way. BR6 51 C5
Ladyfern Ct. TN2 149 C4
Ladyfields. Chatham ME5 62 D2
Ladyfields. Northfleet DA11 29 F4
Ladysmith Rd. SE9 6 A1
Ladywell House. BR5 38 B7
Ladywood Ave. BR5 37 E4
Ladywood Rd. Cuxton ME2 46 B2
Ladywood Rd. Lane End DA2 27 E3
Lagonda Way. DA1 9 C3
Lagoon Rd. BR5 38 B4
Lake Ave. BR1 22 A2
Lake Dr. ME3 32 C6
Lake Rd. Ditton ME20 90 E8
Lake Rd.
Royal Tunbridge Wells TN4 148 E4
Lake View Rd. TN13 84 A4
Lakedale Rd. SE18 2 E1
Lakelands. Harrietsham ME17 110 E6
Lakelands. Maidstone ME15 107 A7
Laker Rd. ME1 61 C6
Lakes Rd. BR2 50 C5
Lakeside.
Royal Tunbridge Wells TN2 149 E6
Lakeside. Snodland ME6 74 F6
Lakeside Ave. SE28 3 A5
Lakeside Cl. Bough Beech TN8 113 F4
Lakeside Cl. Sidcup DA15 7 C2
Lakeside Dr. BR2 50 E7
Lakeside Pk. ME2 47 E7
Lakeswood Rd. BR5 37 C3
Lakeview Cl. ME6 75 A6
Lakeview Rd. DA16 7 B3
Lakewood Dr. ME8 63 C6
Lamb Cl. RM18 13 C5
Lamb's Cross. ME17 124 A5
Lambard House. 6 ME14 92 A5
Lambarde Ave. SE9 23 A4
Lambarde Cl. ME2 46 C6
Lambarde Dr. TN13 84 A4
Lambarde Rd. TN13 84 A5
Lambardes. DA3 56 F7
Lamberhurst CE Prim Sch.
TN3 166 B6
Lamberhurst Cl. 14 BR5 38 D1
Lamberhurst Gn. ME8 49 B3
Lamberhurst Golf Course. TN3 166 C5
Lamberhurst Rd.
Horsmonden TN12 & TN3 152 E3
Lamberhurst Rd. Maidstone
ME16 91 B7
Lambersart Cl. TN2 & TN4 113 D1
Lambert Ct. DA8 8 C8
Lambert Mews. 4 ME6 75 A8
Lambert Rd. E16 1 B7
Lambert's Yd. TN9 117 B1
Lamberts Rd. TN1 & TN2 149 D8
Lambeth Cl. ME5 62 B4
Lambourn Dr. ME18 & ME19 89 A2
Lambourn Way. Chatham ME5 62 C2
Lambourn Way.
Royal Tunbridge Wells TN2 149 D1
Lambourne Pl. SE3 5 B6
Lambourne Rd. ME15 92 F2
Lambs Bank. TN9 133 B7
Lambscroft Ave. SE12 & SE9 22 D5
Lambsfrith Gr. ME7 63 B3
Lamorbey Cl. DA15 23 F6
Lamorna Ave. DA12 30 D6
Lamorna Cl. BR6 38 A2
Lampington Row. TN3 147 E3
Lamplighters Cl. 2 Dartford DA1 9 F1
Lamplighters Cl. Gillingham ME7 62 F5
Lamport Cl. SE18 1 F2
Lamson Rd. RM13 4 F8
Lancashire Rd. ME15 107 E7
Lancaster Ct. Gillingham ME8 63 C7
Lancaster Ct. Gravesend DA12 30 C5
Lancaster Way. ME19 88 F3
Lance Croft. DA3 56 F8
Lancelot Ave. ME2 46 E7
Lancelot Cl. ME2 46 E6
Lancelot Ct. BR6 52 B8
Lancelot Rd. DA16 7 A4
Lances Cl. DA13 44 A2
Lancet La. ME15 107 A6
Lancey Cl. SE7 1 E2

Lancing Rd. BR6 .... 52 B8
Land Way. ME3 .... 32 D5
Landale Gdns. DA1 .... 26 C8
Landor Ct. ME7 .... 63 A3
Landseer Ave. DA11 .... 29 D5
Landseer Cl. TN10 .... 117 E6
Landstead Rd. SE18 .... 6 D7
Landway. TN15 .... 84 F7
Landway The.
  Borough Green TN15 .... 86 F7
Landway The. Kemsing TN15 .... 70 A2
Landway The. Maidstone ME14 . 93 A4
Landway The. St Paul's Cray BR5 38 C6
Lane End. DA7 .... 8 B4
Lane The. SE3 .... 5 A4
Lanes Ave. DA11 .... 30 A5
Laneside. BR7 .... 23 C3
Langafel CE (VC) Prim Sch.
  DA3 .... 43 A6
Langafel Cl. DA3 .... 42 F7
Langbrook Rd. SE3 .... 5 D5
Langdale Cl. Gillingham ME8 ... 49 D1
Langdale Cl. Orpington BR6 ..... 51 B7
Langdale Cres. DA7 .... 8 A6
Langdale Rise. ME16 .... 91 C5
Langdale Wlk. DA11 .... 29 E5
Langdon Rd. Bromley BR2 .... 36 B6
Langdon Rd. Rochester ME1 ..... 47 C4
Langdon Shaw. DA14 .... 23 F3
Langford Pl. DA14 .... 24 A5
Langham Gr. ME16 .... 91 C4
Langholm Rd. TN3 .... 147 F3
Langhorne House. SE7 .... 5 C8
Langlands Dr. DA2 .... 27 E3
Langley Gdns. BR5 .... 37 B3
Langley House. BR1 .... 22 B1
Langley Rd. DA16 .... 7 C8
Langmore Ct. DA7 .... 7 D4
Langton Cl. ME14 .... 92 C5
Langton Green Cty Prim Sch.
  TN3 .... 147 E4
Langton Rd. Rusthall TN3 & IN4 148 C3
Langton Rd. Speldhurst TN3 ... 148 A7
Langton Ridge. TN3 .... 148 B3
Langton Way. SE3 .... 5 B7
Langworth Cl. DA2 .... 26 C5
Lankester Parker Rd. ME1 ...... 61 C6
Lannoy Rd. SE9 .... 23 C7
Lanridge Rd. SE2 .... 3 D3
Lansbury Cres. DA1 .... 10 A2
Lansbury Ct. SE28 .... 3 B6
Lansbury Gdns. RM18 .... 13 A6
Lansbury House. DA17 .... 3 F1
Lansdown Rd. Northfleet DA11 .. 29 F7
Lansdown Rd. Sidcup DA14 ..... 24 B5
Lansdown Rd. Tilbury RM18 .... 12 F5
Lansdowne Ave.
  Bexley DA7 .... 7 D7
Lansdowne Ave.
  Maidstone ME15 .... 107 C6
Lansdowne Ave. Orpington BR6 . 37 B1
Lansdowne Ct. ME4 .... 47 F4
Lansdowne La. SE7 .... 1 D1
Lansdowne Mews. SE7 .... 1 D1
Lansdowne Prim Sch. RM18 .... 12 F5
Lansdowne Rd. Bromley BR1 ... 22 B1
Lansdowne Rd. Chatham ME4 ... 47 E2
Lansdowne Rd. Royal Tunbridge Wells
  TN1 & TN2 .... 149 B4
Lansdowne Rd. Sevenoaks TN13 84 D5
Lansdowne Rd. Tonbridge TN9 . 117 B2
Lansdowne Sq. Northfleet DA11 . 12 F1
Lansdowne Sq.
  Royal Tunbridge Wells TN1 .. 149 B4
Lapins La. ME18 .... 88 F2
Lapis Cl. DA12 .... 31 B7
Lapwing Cl. DA8 .... 9 B7
Lapwing Rd. ME3 .... 21 B5
Lapwings The. DA12 .... 30 D6
Lapworth Cl. BR6 .... 52 C8
Larch Cl. ME20 .... 75 B2
Larch Cres. Hoo St Werburgh ME3 34 E3
Larch Cres. Tonbridge TN10 ... 117 C6
Larch Dene. BR6 .... 52 C8
Larch Gr. Paddock Wood TN12 .. 135 F6
Larch Gr. Sidcup DA15 .... 23 F7
Larch Rd. DA1 .... 26 D7
Larch Way. BR2 .... 37 A2
Larch Wlk. ME8 .... 39 D7
Larch Wood Cl. ME5 .... 62 D1
Larchcroft. ME5 .... 62 A4
Larches The. ME3 .... 32 C3
Larchwood Rd. SE9 .... 23 B6
Larkfield. TN12 .... 135 A7
Larkfield Ave. ME7 .... 48 E4
Larkfield Brookfield Cty Prim Schs.
  ME20 .... 75 A2
Larkfield Cl. Hayes BR2 .... 50 A8
Larkfield Cl. Larkfield ME20 .... 75 B1
Larkfield Rd. Larkfield ME20 ... 75 B1
Larkfield Rd. Sevenoaks TN13 . 83 C4
Larkfield Rd. Sidcup DA14 ...... 23 F5
Larkfield Trad Est. ME20 .... 75 B5
Larkfields. DA11 .... 29 E5
Larkin Cl. ME2 .... 33 B2
Larks Field. DA3 .... 42 F5
Larkspur Cl. East Malling ME19 . 75 A1
Larkspur Cl. Newham E16 .... 1 E8
Larkspur Cl. Orpington BR6 ..... 52 C7
Larkspur Rd. Chatham ME5 ..... 61 E4
Larkspur Rd. East Malling ME19 . 74 F1
Larkstore Pk. TN12 .... 139 E5
Larkwell La. DA3 .... 42 F5
Larner Rd. DA8 .... 8 E7

Laser Quay. ME2 .... 47 D6
Lashenden Air Warfare Mus.
  TN27 .... 142 A2
Lassa Rd. SE9 .... 5 F2
Latham Cl. E6 .... 1 E7
Latham Rd. DA6 .... 8 A2
Latimer Pl. 8 ME7 .... 48 C7
Latona Dr. DA12 .... 30 F3
Latymers. TN11 .... 131 B4
Launcelot Prim Sch. BR1 .... 22 A4
Launcelot Rd. BR1 & SE12 ...... 22 A4
Launder Way. ME15 .... 91 E2
Laura Dr. BR8 .... 26 A1
Laurel Ave. DA12 .... 30 C6
Laurel Bank.
  Royal Tunbridge Wells TN4 .. 149 B8
Laurel Bank. Wadhurst TN5 .... 175 A4
Laurel Cl. Dartford DA1 .... 26 C7
Laurel Cl. Sidcup DA14 .... 24 A5
Laurel Gr. ME7 .... 109 D2
Laurel Rd. Gillingham ME7 ...... 48 C7
Laurel Rd.
  Royal Tunbridge Wells TN1 .. 149 D7
Laurel Way. TN1 .... 149 D7
Laurel Wlk. ME8 .... 63 E6
Laurel Way. 8
Laurels The. Bromley BR2 .... 36 A5
Laurels The. Maidstone ME16 .. 91 C2
Laurels The. New Barn DA3 ..... 43 D6
Laurels The. Wilmington DA2 .. 26 C5
Laurie Gray Ave. ME5 .... 61 D1
Lavenda Cl. ME7 .... 63 A4
Lavender Cl. Bromley BR2 ...... 36 E3
Lavender Cl. 1 Chatham ME5 .. 61 E4
Lavender Cl. East Malling ME19 . 89 F8
Lavender Gdns. TN5 .... 176 E1
Lavender Hill. Swanley BR8 ..... 39 D6
Lavender Hill. Tonbridge TN9 . 133 C8
Lavender Rd. ME19 .... 89 F8
Lavender Sq. 6 TN18 .... 179 A2
Lavenders Rd. ME19 .... 89 C6
Lavernock Rd. DA7 .... 8 A5
Lavidge Rd. SE9 .... 22 F6
Lavinia Rd. 1 DA1 .... 9 F1
Lavisham House. BR1 .... 22 B3
Lawford Gdns. DA1 .... 9 C2
Lawn Cl. Bromley BR1 .... 22 B1
Lawn Cl. Chatham ME4 .... 48 B2
Lawn Cl. Swanley BR8 .... 39 C7
Lawn Cl. Tenterden TN30 ...... 182 F7
Lawn Cty Prim Sch. DA11 .... 12 C1
Lawn Pk. TN13 .... 99 B8
Lawn Rd. Northfleet DA11 .... 12 C1
Lawn Rd. Tonbridge TN9 ...... 133 B8
Lawns Cres. RM17 .... 12 D8
Lawns The. Brenchley TN12 ... 152 B8
Lawns The. Sidcup DA14 .... 24 B4
Lawrance Sq. DA11 .... 29 F5
Lawrence Cl. ME15 .... 107 A7
Lawrence Dr. DA2 .... 45 A5
Lawrence Gdns. RM18 .... 13 B7
Lawrence Hill Gdns. DA1 .... 9 C1
Lawrence Hill Rd. DA1 .... 9 C1
Lawrence Rd. Erith DA8 .... 8 B7
Lawrence Rd. Hayes BR4 .... 50 A6
Lawrence Rd. Tonbridge TN10 . 117 E6
Lawrence St. ME7 .... 48 C5
Lawson Cl. E16 .... 1 C8
Lawson Gdns. DA1 .... 9 D3
Lawson House. 1 SE18 .... 6 A8
Lawson Rd. DA1 .... 9 D3
Laxey Rd. BR6 .... 51 F4
Laxey The. ME15 .... 91 E1
Laxton Cl. ME15 .... 92 F3
Laxton Dr. ME17 .... 108 A1
Laxton Gdns. TN12 .... 135 E7
Layfield House. 1 SE10 .... 1 A1
Layfield Rd. ME7 .... 48 F7
Layhams Rd. BR2 .... 50 A3
Laymarsh Cl. DA17 .... 3 F3
Layzell Wlk. SE9 .... 22 D7
Le May Ave. SE12 .... 22 B5
Le Temple Rd. TN12 .... 136 B6
Lea Cl. ME4 .... 47 E1
Lea Rd. TN13 .... 99 C8
Lea Vale. DA1 & DA7 .... 8 D3
Leafield La. DA14 .... 24 F5
Leafy Glade. ME8 .... 63 B6
Leafy Gr. BR2 .... 50 C5
Leafy La. DA13 .... 58 A3
Leafy Oak Rd. SE12 .... 22 C5
Lealands Ave. TN11 .... 116 A1
Lealands Cl. TN3 .... 161 C6
Leamington Ave. Bromley BR1 .. 22 C3
Leamington Ave. Orpington BR6 51 E6
Leamington Cl. BR1 .... 22 C3
Leamouth Rd. E6 .... 1 E8
Leander Dr. DA12 .... 30 F4
Leander Rd. ME1 .... 61 C7
Learoyd Gdns. E6 .... 2 A6
Leas Dale. SE9 .... 23 A5
Leas Gn. BR7 .... 23 F2
Leas The. Turner's Green TN5 .. 175 A6
Leas The. Woolwich SE18 .... 6 B6
Leatherbottle Gn. DA18 .... 3 F3
Leaves Green Rd. BR2 .... 50 D1
Lebrun Sq. SE3 .... 5 B4
Leckwith Ave. DA17 .... 7 E8
Leclair House. SE3 .... 5 B4
Leconfield Cl. TN9 .... 132 F7
Leda Rd. SE18 .... 1 F3
Lee Gn. BR5 .... 38 A4
Lee Green Rd. ME3 .... 33 D4
Lee Rd. ME6 .... 75 A8
Lee Sta. SE12 .... 5 A1
Leechcroft Ave. Sidcup DA15 .... 6 F2

Leechcroft Ave. Swanley BR8 ... 39 F6
Leeds & Broomfield CE Prim Sch.
  ME17 .... 109 A7
Leeds Castle. ME17 .... 109 D7
Leeds Cl. BR6 .... 52 D8
Leeds House. ME17 .... 33 C1
Leeds Rd. ME17 .... 108 E3
Leeds Sq. ME8 .... 49 B3
Lees Rd. ME18 .... 120 E7
Leesons Hill. BR5 & BR7 .... 38 A6
Leesons Prim Sch. BR5 .... 38 B6
Leesons Way. BR5 .... 37 F7
Leet Cl. ME7 .... 48 E6
Leeward Rd. ME1 .... 47 C1
Leewood Cl. SE12 .... 5 A1
Leewood Pl. BR8 .... 39 D5
Legatt Rd. SE9 .... 5 D2
Legge La. ME19 .... 74 D6
Leggs' La. TN3 .... 147 E5
Leghorn Rd. SE18 .... 2 D1
Leicester Dr. TN2 .... 162 F8
Leicester Rd. Maidstone ME15 . 107 D7
Leicester Rd. Tilbury RM18 ..... 12 F6
Leigh Ave. ME15 .... 107 B6
Leigh City Tech Coll The. DA1 . 27 A7
Leigh Cty Prim Sch. TN11 .... 115 F1
Leigh Green Ind Est. TN30 .... 183 E6
Leigh Halt. TN11 .... 115 F1
Leigh Pl. DA16 .... 7 A5
Leigh Rd. Gravesend DA11 ...... 30 B6
Leigh Rd. Powder Mills TN11 .. 116 D3
Leigh Terr. 2 St Paul's Cray BR5 38 B6
Leigh Terr. Teston ME18 .... 90 A1
Leighton Cl. TN4 .... 149 A7
Leighton Gdns. RM18 .... 13 A7
Leila Parnell Pl. 14 SE7 .... 5 C8
Leith Hill. BR5 .... 38 A8
Leith Hill Gn. BR5 .... 38 A8
Leith Park Rd. DA11 & DA12 ... 30 B7
Lelland House. 8 SE7 .... 1 E2
Lemonwell Ct. SE9 .... 6 C2
Lemonwell Dr. SE9 .... 6 C2
Len Clifton House. 3 SE18 .... 1 F2
Len Valley Wlk. ME15 .... 92 F1
Lenderyou Ct. DA1 .... 9 F1
Lendon Rd. TN15 .... 86 F6
Leneda Dr. TN2 .... 162 E8
Leney Rd. ME18 .... 104 E7
Lenfield Ave. ME14 .... 92 B4
Lenham Cty Prim Sch. ME17 . 111 C5
Lenham Heath Rd. ME17 .... 111 C2
Lenham House. Lenham ME17 . 111 E5
Lenham House. 13
Lenham Rd.
  Broadstone TN27 & ME17 ... 126 D3
Lenham Rd. Erith DA7 .... 7 F8
Lenham Rd.
  Fairbourne Heath ME17 ...... 110 C1
Lenham Sta. ME17 .... 111 C4
Lenham Way. ME8 .... 49 A3
Lennard Rd. Keston Mark BR2 .. 36 F1
Lennard Rd. Sevenoaks TN13 ... 83 E7
Lennox Ave. DA11 .... 13 A1
Lennox House. 6 DA17 .... 4 A3
Lennox Rd. DA1 .... 29 F8
Lennox Rd E. DA1 .... 30 A8
Lenor Cl. ME7 .... 7 E3
Lensbury Way. SE2 .... 3 D3
Lenside Dr. ME15 .... 93 A2
Lenton St. SE18 .... 2 D2
Leonard Ave. Otford TN14 .... 69 B3
Leonard Ave. Swanscombe DA10 28 E8
Leonard Cl. ME16 .... 91 B6
Leonard Judge House. DA2 ..... 27 E3
Leonard Rd. ME4 .... 48 B3
Leonard Robbins Path. 3 SE28 . 3 B6
Leonard St. E16 .... 1 E5
Leopold Rd. 2 ME4 .... 48 A3
Lesley Cl. Istead Rise DA13 ..... 43 F8
Lesley Cl. Sidcup DA5 .... 25 B8
Lesley Cl. Swanley BR8 .... 39 D6
Lesley Tew Ct. TN10 .... 117 C5
Leslie Cres. TN30 .... 173 B2
Leslie Pl. ME15 .... 91 E5
Leslie Rd. Gillingham ME7 ...... 48 D7
Leslie Rd. Newham E16 .... 1 B7
Leslie Smith Sq. 7 SE18 .... 6 A8
Lesnes Abbey (remains of). SE2 3 C2
Lesney Park Prim Sch. DA8 .... 8 D8
Lesney Park Rd. DA8 .... 8 D8
Lesney Pk. DA8 .... 8 D8
Lessness Ave. DA7 .... 7 D7
Lessness Heath Prim Sch. DA17 . 4 A1
Lessness Pk. DA17 .... 4 A1
Lessness Rd. 11 DA17 .... 4 A1
Lested La. ME17 .... 108 B2
Lester Rd. ME4 .... 48 A3
Lestock House. SE3 .... 5 D6
Letchworth Ave. ME4 .... 47 F1
Letchworth Cl. BR2 .... 36 A4
Letchworth Dr. BR2 .... 36 A4
Letter Box La. TN13 .... 99 C6
Leverholme Gdns. SE9 .... 23 A4
Levett Cl. ME3 .... 21 B6
Levetts La. TN32 .... 185 D1
Lewd La. TN27 .... 143 A3
Lewes Cl. RM17 .... 12 A8
Lewes Rd. BR1 .... 36 D7
Lewin Rd. DA6 .... 7 E3
Lewing Cl. BR6 .... 37 E1
Lewis Ave. ME6 .... 49 B2
Lewis Court Dr. ME17 .... 107 C3
Lewis Cl. DA11 .... 29 F6
Lewis King House. BR1 .... 22 B1
Lewis Rd. Bexley DA16 .... 7 C4
Lewis Rd. Istead Rise DA13 .... 43 F8

Lewis Rd. Sidcup DA14 .... 24 C5
Lewis Rd. Swanscombe DA10 .. 11 E1
Leybank. TN11 .... 116 F4
Leybourne CE (VA) Prim Sch.
  ME19 .... 74 E2
Leybourne Cl. Chatham ME5 ... 62 A2
Leybourne Cl. Hayes BR2 .... 36 A3
Leybourne Dell. TN17 .... 180 E6
Leybourne Rd. ME2 .... 46 F8
Leybourne Way. ME20 .... 74 F4
Leybridge Ct. SE12 .... 5 A2
Leyburn House. SE18 .... 5 E7
Leycroft Gdns. DA8 .... 9 B6
Leydenhatch La. BR8 .... 39 D8
Leyes Rd. E16 .... 1 D7
Leyhill Cl. BR8 .... 39 E4
Leyland Rd. SE12 .... 5 A2
Leysdown Ave. DA7 .... 8 C3
Leysdown Rd. SE9 .... 22 F6
Leyton Ave. ME7 .... 48 E1
Leyton Cross. DA2 .... 26 A6
Leyton Cross Rd. DA2 .... 25 F5
Leywood Rd. DA13 .... 58 D3
Lezayre Rd. BR6 .... 51 F4
Libya Terr. 6 ME14 .... 92 A7
Lichdale Cl. 7 BR6 .... 51 F6
Lichfield Cl. ME8 .... 49 D2
Liddon Rd. BR1 .... 36 D6
Lidsing Rd. ME14 .... 77 E6
Lidwells La. TN17 .... 153 E1
Lieth Park Rd. DA12 .... 30 C7
Liffler Rd. SE18 .... 2 E1
Lightfoot Gn. TN18 .... 178 E3
Lila Pl. BR8 .... 39 E5
Lilac Cres. ME2 .... 46 E6
Lilac Gdns. BR8 .... 39 D6
Lilac Pl. DA13 .... 44 B2
Lilac Rd. ME2 .... 46 E5
Lilburne Gdns. SE9 .... 5 E2
Lilburne Rd. SE9 .... 5 E2
Lilian Barker Cl. SE12 .... 5 A2
Lilk Hill. ME14 .... 93 C3
Lillechurch Rd. ME3 .... 32 F7
Lillesden Cotts. TN18 .... 184 E8
Lilliebunn. TN17 .... 174 D2
Limavady House. 18 SE18 .... 2 A2
Lime Ave. DA11 .... 29 D8
Lime Cl. Bromley BR1 .... 36 E5
Lime Cl. Frant TN3 .... 163 B3
Lime Cl. Marden TN12 .... 138 C6
Lime Cotts. TN12 .... 139 F3
Lime Cres. ME19 .... 90 A7
Lime Ct. ME8 .... 63 C3
Lime Gr. Orpington BR6 .... 51 B8
Lime Gr. Sidcup DA15 .... 6 F1
Lime Hill Rd. TN1 .... 149 A4
Lime Kiln Dr. SE7 .... 5 B8
Lime Pit La. TN14 .... 68 C2
Lime Rd. BR8 .... 39 D6
Lime Row. DA18 .... 3 F3
Lime Tree Cl. TN9 .... 117 C2
Lime Tree Wlk. TN13 .... 84 B2
Limecroft Cl. ME19 .... 74 D7
Limes Cl. TN30 .... 183 C8
Limes Gr. TN18 .... 178 F5
Limes Row. BR6 .... 51 B5
Limes The. Edenbridge TN8 ... 112 C1
Limes The. Frittenden TN17 .. 156 E6
Limes The. Keston Mark BR2 ... 50 E8
Limes The. Lenham ME17 ...... 111 D5
Limetree Cl. ME5 .... 62 B8
Limetree Terr. ME17 .... 111 E6
Limewood Rd. DA8 .... 8 C7
Linchmere Rd. SE12 .... 22 A8
Linclon Cl. BR8 .... 8 F5
Lincoln Cl. ME2 .... 46 D6
Lincoln Ct. SE12 .... 22 C5
Lincoln Green Rd. BR5 .... 37 F4
Lincoln Rd. Erith DA8 .... 8 F5
Lincoln Rd. Maidstone ME15 .. 107 D8
Lincoln Rd. Sidcup DA14 .... 24 B3
Lincolnshire Terr. DA2 .... 27 D4
Lincon Rd. ME7 .... 48 D7
Linden Ave. DA1 .... 26 C7
Linden Chase Rd. TN13 .... 84 B5
Linden Cl. Orpington BR6 .... 52 A5
Linden Cl. Paddock Wood TN12 .136 A6
Linden Cl. Purfleet RM16 .... 10 C8
Linden Cl.
  Royal Tunbridge Wells TN2 . 149 A2
Linden Ct. Sidcup DA14 .... 23 E4
Linden Ct. Tonbridge TN10 ... 117 B7
Linden Gdns. TN2 .... 148 F1
Linden House. 5 ME5 .... 61 F4
Linden Park Rd. TN2 .... 149 A2
Linden Rd. Coxheath ME17 ... 106 C4
Linden Rd. Gillingham ME7 .... 48 E5
Linden Sq. TN13 .... 83 E5
Lindenfield. BR7 .... 37 B7
Lindens The. ME20 .... 75 E1
Lindisfarne Cl. DA12 .... 30 E6
Lindridge La. TN12 .... 139 C5
Lindsay House. 2 SE18 .... 2 A2
Lindsey Cl. BR1 .... 36 E5
Lindwood Cl. 8 E6 .... 1 F8
Lineacre Cl. ME8 .... 63 D6
Lines Terr. ME4 .... 48 A4
Ling Rd. Erith DA8 .... 8 C8
Ling Rd. Newham E16 .... 1 A8
Lingey Cl. DA15 .... 23 F6
Lingfield Ave. DA2 .... 27 B8
Lingfield Cres. SE9 .... 6 D3
Lingfield Rd. Borough Green TN15 87 B7
Lingfield Rd. Edenbridge TN8 . 128 A8
Lingfield Rd. Gravesend DA12 .. 30 B6
Lingley Dr. ME2 .... 33 C2
Lingwood. DA7 .... 8 B5

Link Hill La. TN27 .... 127 D3
Link The. Eltham SE9 .... 23 A5
Link The. New Ash Green DA3 .. 56 F8
Link Way. Bromley BR2 .... 36 E2
Link Way.
  Royal Tunbridge Wells TN2 . 149 B8
Linkden Cotts. TN18 .... 186 A5
Links The. Addington ME19 .... 73 E2
Links The. Chatham ME5 .... 62 B8
Links View. Dartford DA1 .... 26 C7
Links View. Woolwich SE18 ...... 6 B6
Linkway. ME20 .... 75 C1
Linley Cl. RM18 .... 14 D7
Linnet Ave. TN12 .... 136 A5
Linnet Cl. SE28 .... 3 C6
Linslade Rd. BR6 .... 52 A4
Linsted Ct. SE9 & DA15 .... 6 E1
Linton Cl. Bexley DA16 .... 7 B6
Linton Cl. 2 Greenwich SE7 ...... 1 C1
Linton Dann Cl. ME3 .... 34 D6
Linton Gdns. E6 .... 1 E7
Linton Gore. ME17 .... 106 D3
Linton Hill. TN12 .... 122 F6
Linton Hospl. ME17 .... 106 C2
Linton Mead Prim Sch. SE28 ... 3 B6
Linton Rd. ME15 .... 106 F4
Lintorn Symonds Rd. ME3 ...... 33 F5
Linwood Ave. ME2 .... 46 E8
Lion Rd. Bexley DA6 .... 7 F3
Lion Rd. Newham E6 .... 1 F8
Lionel Gdns. SE9 .... 5 D2
Lionel Oxley House. 5 RM17 ... 12 B8
Lionel Rd. Eltham SE9 .... 5 D2
Lionel Rd. Tonbridge TN9 ...... 133 A8
Lions Cl. SE12 .... 22 D5
Liphook Way. ME16 .... 91 C8
Lipscombe Rd. TN2 .... 149 D6
Lipton Cl. SE28 .... 3 C6
Liptraps La. TN1 & TN2 .... 149 D7
Lipwell Hill. ME23 .... 17 B4
Liskeard Cl. BR7 .... 23 C2
Liskeard Gdns. SE3 .... 5 A6
Lisle Cl. DA12 .... 31 B6
Lismore Cl. ME15 .... 107 A7
Lister Cl. ME19 .... 89 F8
Lister House. SE2 .... 3 D1
Lister Rd. RM18 .... 13 A5
Lister Wlk. SE28 .... 3 D6
Listmas Rd. ME4 .... 48 B3
Little Alley. TN8 .... 128 B5
Little Bayham Cotts. TN3 ...... 164 F4
Little Birches. ME3 .... 23 E6
Little Bounds Cl. TN4 .... 132 F3
Little Browns La. TN8 .... 112 A4
Little Buckland Ave. ME16 ..... 91 D6
Little Ct. ME16 .... 91 D2
Little Footway. TN3 .... 147 F3
Little Heath. SE7 .... 1 E1
Little Heath Rd. DA7 .... 7 F7
Little Hill. TN30 .... 173 B2
Little Iridge Farm Cotts. TN19 184 C1
Little Job's Cross. TN17 .... 181 F1
Little John Ave. ME5 .... 61 F2
Little Julians Hill. TN13 .... 99 B8
Little Kit's Coty House. ME20 .. 76 C5
Little Mallett. TN3 .... 147 F3
Little Market Row. ME19 .... 74 D2
Little Mount Sion. TN1 .... 149 A2
Little Oakham Ct. ME3 .... 19 C4
Little Orch. ME17 .... 106 D3
Little Oxley. ME20 .... 74 E2
Little Pk. TN5 .... 174 E5
Little Queen St. DA1 .... 26 F8
Little Redlands. BR1 .... 36 E7
Little Sheepfurst Cotts. TN12 137 E5
Little Thrift. BR5 .... 37 C5
Little Wood. TN13 .... 84 D5
Littlebourne Ave. ME8 .... 49 B4
Littlebourne Rd. ME14 .... 92 C6
Littlebrook Manor Way. DA1 .. 10 A2
Littlecombe. SE7 .... 5 B8
Littlecourt Rd. TN13 .... 84 A3
Littlecroft. SE9 .... 6 A4
Littlecroft. Istead Rise DA13 ... 29 E5
Littledale. Darenth DA2 .... 27 C5
Littledale. Woolwich SE2 .... 7 A8
Littlefield. TN11 .... 118 E8
Littledale Rd. TN13 .... 84 D5
Littlejohn Rd. BR5 .... 38 B4
Littlemede. SE9 .... 22 F5
Littlemore Rd. SE2 .... 3 A4
Livesey St. ME18 .... 90 A1
Livingstone Circ. ME7 .... 48 D5
Livingstone Gdns. DA12 .... 30 D3
Livingstone Hospl. DA1 .... 26 F8
Livingstone Rd. Gillingham ME7 . 48 E5
Livingstone Rd. Gravesend DA12 30 D3
Livingstone Wlk. 4 ME15 ..... 107 F5
Lizban St. SE3 .... 5 B7
Llanover Rd. SE18 .... 6 A7
Lloyd House. 10 SE18 .... 1 F2
Lloyds Gn. TN30 .... 189 D4
Loaland Bsns Ctr. ME2 .... 47 D8
Loam Ct. DA1 .... 26 E7
Loampits Cl. TN9 .... 117 D3
Lobelia Cl. Gillingham ME7 ..... 48 E6
Lobelia Cl. 5 Newham E6 .... 1 E8
Locarno Ave. ME8 .... 49 A2
Lochat Rd. ME3 .... 33 E6
Lochmere Cl. DA8 .... 8 B8
Lock La. ME14 & ME16 .... 76 D1
Lock St. ME7 .... 48 C5
Lock's Yd. TN15 .... 84 C2
Lockesley Dr. BR5 .... 38 A3
Lockington Cl. TN9 .... 132 F7
Lockington Gr. ME1 .... 47 C5
Locknut Cotts. TN3 .... 57 E2
Lockside. TN9 .... 117 C2
Locksley Cl. ME5 .... 61 E2

Lockswood. ME16 .... 91 D7
Lockyer Rd. RM16 .... 10 C8
Lockyers Hill. DA13 .... 58 F5
Lodden Ct. 15 BR5 .... 38 D1
Loddington La. ME17 .... 123 A8
Loder Cl. ME17 .... 111 B5
Lodge Ave. DA1 .... 9 C1
Lodge Cl. Orpington BR6 .... 38 B1
Lodge Cl. Wateringbury ME18 .. 104 D8
Lodge Cres. BR6 .... 38 B1
Lodge Ct. DA12 .... 31 E2
Lodge Gdns. ME17 .... 125 F6
Lodge Hill. DA16 .... 7 B7
Lodge Hill La. ME3 .... 33 F7
Lodge La. Cobham DA12 .... 45 B5
Lodge La. Sidcup DA5 .... 7 D1
Lodge La. Westerham TN16 .... 96 C8
Lodge Oak La. TN9 .... 133 D8
Lodge Rd. Bromley BR1 .... 22 C1
Lodge Rd. Maidstone ME14 .... 92 D5
Lodge Rd. Staplehurst TN12 .... 139 E5
Lodge Rd. Tonbridge TN9 .... 117 B2
Lodgewood Cotts. TN8 .... 113 D2
Logs Hill. BR1 & BR7 .... 36 E8
Logs Hill Cl. BR7 .... 36 E8
Lomaria Ct. TN2 .... 149 C4
Lomas La. TN18 .... 186 F5
Lombard St. DA4 .... 41 C5
Lombard Trad Est. SE7 .... 1 B2
Lombard Wall. SE7 .... 1 B2
Lombardy Cl. ME7 .... 63 A6
Lombardy Dr. ME14 .... 92 C5
London City Airport. E16 .... 1 E5
London Golf Course. TN15 ...... 56 D4
London La. Bromley BR1 .... 22 A1
London La.
Cranbrook Common TN17 ...... 156 A2
London Rd. Addington ME19 ...... 73 D2
London Rd. Bidborough TN4 ...... 132 F3
London Rd. Bromley BR1 .... 36 A8
London Rd. Crayford DA1 .... 8 D2
London Rd. Ditton ME20 .... 75 C1
London Rd. Farningham DA4 ...... 40 D3
London Rd. Flimwell TN5 .... 177 D3
London Rd. Gillingham ME8 ...... 49 C1
London Rd. Grays RM17 & RM16 .. 11 E8
London Rd.
Hartlip Hill ME8 & ME9 .... 64 D7
London Rd. Hurst Green TN19 .. 184 A3
London Rd. Knockholt Pound TN14 67 E4
London Rd. Maidstone ME16 ...... 91 C6
London Rd. Maypole BR6 & TN14 52 F2
London Rd. Newington ME9 ...... 65 A6
London Rd. Northfleet DA11 ...... 12 E1
London Rd. Rochester ME2 ...... 47 A7
London Rd.
Royal Tunbridge Wells,Mount Sion
TN1 & TN2 & TN4 .... 149 A3
London Rd. Sevenoaks TN13 ...... 84 B2
London Rd.
Sevenoaks,Dunton Green TN13 ... 83 E7
London Rd. Shepham Heath TN14 68 C6
London Rd. Swanley BR8 .... 39 E6
London Rd.
Swanley,White Oak BR8 .... 39 D7
London Rd. Swanscombe DA9 ... 11 C2
London Rd. Tilbury RM18 .... 13 B5
London Rd.
Tonbridge TN10 & TN11 .... 117 B3
London Rd. Twitton TN13 & TN14 68 D1
London Rd.Watt's Cross
TN11 & TN13 & TN15 .... 116 B7
London Rd. West Kingsdown TN15 56 A1
London Rd. Westerham TN16 ...... 81 D3
London Rd. Wrotham TN15 ...... 72 B3
London Rd. Wrotham Heath TN15 72 F1
London Rd E. ME2 .... 90 F8
London Road Purfleet. RM16 ... 10 C8
London Road West Thurrock.
RM16 .... 11 A8
Londonderry Par. DA8 .... 8 D7
Lonewood Way. TN11 .... 102 F2
Long Acre. BR5 & BR6 .... 52 D8
Long Barn Rd. TN14 .... 99 B2
Long Catlis Rd. ME8 .... 63 D4
Long La. Bexley DA7 .... 7 E6
Long La. Rabbit's Cross ME17 ... 123 D5
Long Mark Rd. 5 E16 .... 1 D8
Long Mead Cty Prim Sch.
TN10 .... 117 B5
Long Mead Way. TN10 .... 117 B4
Long Meads. TN3 & TN4 .... 148 B4
Long Mill La. Crouch TN15 ...... 87 B3
Long Mill La. Platt TN15 .... 87 C7
Long Rede La. ME16 .... 90 F3
Long Slip. TN3 .... 148 A3
Long Wlk. SE18 .... 6 B8
Longbury Cl. BR5 .... 38 B6
Longbury Dr. BR5 .... 38 B7
Longcroft. SE9 .... 23 A5
Longdon Wood. BR2 .... 50 E6
Longfellow Rd. ME7 .... 48 C3
Longfield. TN30 .... 183 A6
Longfield Ave.
High Halstow ME23 .... 17 E4
Longfield Ave. New Barn DA3 ... 43 D7
Longfield Pl. ME15 .... 107 C8
Longfield Rd.
Meopham Station DA13 .... 43 E3
Longfield Rd.Royal Tunbridge Wells
TN1 & TN2 & TN11 .... 133 E1
Longfields Dr. ME14 .... 93 A5
Longford Cl. ME8 .... 64 A8
Longford Ct. ME8 .... 64 A8
Longham Copse. ME15 .... 92 F1
Longhill Ave. ME7 .... 48 B3

Longhurst Dr. ME5 .... 61 F2
Longlands Ct. DA15 .... 23 F5
Longlands Park Cres. DA15 ...... 23 E6
Longlands Prim Sch. DA15 ...... 23 E5
Longlands Rd. DA15 .... 23 F5
Longleat Ct. DA15 .... 23 E6
Longleat Villas. 3 DA6 .... 7 E3
Longleigh La. SE2 .... 7 C8
Longley Rd. Gillingham ME8 ... 49 F1
Longley Rd. Rochester ME1 ...... 47 C4
Longmarsh View. DA4 .... 41 B8
Longmead. ME7 .... 37 A7
Longmead Dr. DA14 .... 24 D6
Longmeadow Rd. DA15 .... 23 E7
Longparish Cl. ME15 .... 107 F6
Longreach Rd. DA8 .... 9 B7
Longshaw Rd. ME15 .... 107 F5
Longspring Wood. TN13 .... 99 A6
Longten's Cotts. DA12 .... 31 E6
Longtown Ct. 7 DA2 .... 10 B1
Longview Way. TN1 .... 149 D7
Longwalk. DA13 .... 43 E8
Longwood. ME2 .... 62 B1
Longworth Cl. SE28 .... 3 D7
Lonsdale Cl. SE12 & SE9 .... 22 D5
Lonsdale Cres. DA2 .... 27 C7
Lonsdale Dr. ME8 .... 63 E7
Lonsdale Gdns. TN1 & TN2 ...... 149 A3
Lonsdale Rd. DA7 .... 7 F5
Loop Rd. BR7 .... 23 C2
Loose Cty Prim Sch. ME15 ...... 107 A6
Loose Rd. ME15 .... 107 A7
Loraine Ct. BR7 .... 23 B3
Lord Chatham's Ride. TN14 ...... 67 D2
Lord Roberts Terr. SE18 .... 2 A1
Lord Romney's Hill. ME14 ...... 92 F3
Lord St. Gravesend DA11 .... 30 B8
Lord St. Newham E16 .... 1 E5
Lord Warwick St. SE18 .... 1 F3
Lords Wood Cl. ME5 .... 62 B2
Lords Wood La. ME5 .... 62 B3
Lordswood Cl. DA2 .... 27 E4
Lordswood Cty Prim Sch. ME5 62 B3
Lordswood Ind Est. ME5 .... 77 C8
Lorenden Pk. TN18 .... 178 F1
Lorton Cl. DA12 .... 30 E6
Lossenham La. TN18 .... 187 D3
Louisville Ave. ME7 .... 48 D4
Louvain Rd. DA2 .... 27 E8
Lovage App. ME4 .... 47 F3
Lovelace Ave. BR2 .... 37 A3
Lovelace Cl. Gillingham ME8 ... 63 D4
Lovelace Cl.
West Kingsdown TN15 .... 55 E4
Lovelace Gn. SE9 .... 5 F4
Lover's La. DA9 .... 11 D3
Lovers La. TN17 .... 153 F1
Lovibonds Ave. BR6 .... 51 B7
Low Cl. DA9 .... 11 A2
Low Meadow. ME2 .... 60 B5
Low Street La. RM18 .... 13 F8
Lowe Ave. E16 .... 1 A8
Lower Bell La. ME20 .... 75 B2
Lower Boxley Rd. 8 ME14 ...... 92 A5
Lower Camden. BR7 .... 36 F8
Lower Church Hill. DA9 .... 10 E2
Lower Croft. SE9 .... 39 F5
Lower East Rd. ME4 .... 48 B8
Lower Fant Rd. ME16 .... 91 D2
Lower Farm Rd. ME17 .... 123 D5
Lower Gn. TN11 .... 115 F1
Lower Gravel Rd. BR2 .... 36 F1
Lower Green Rd. Pembury TN2 150 D7
Lower Green Rd.
Rusthall TN3 & TN4 .... 148 C6
Lower Hartlip Rd. ME9 .... 64 E5
Lower Haysden La.
TN11 & TN4 & TN9 .... 132 D8
Lower Hazelhurst. TN5 .... 176 A4
Lower High St. TN5 .... 175 A4
Lower Higham Rd. DA12 .... 31 B7
Lower Park Rd. DA17 .... 4 A2
Lower Platts. TN5 .... 176 F1
Lower Rainham Rd. ME7 .... 49 D5
Lower Range Rd. DA12 .... 30 E8
Lower Rd. Erith DA8 .... 4 D2
Lower Rd. Erith,Belvedere DA17 ... 4 B3
Lower Rd. Hextable ME8 .... 26 B1
Lower Rd.
Lower Higham DA12 & ME3 ...... 32 B6
Lower Rd. Maidstone ME15 ...... 92 B6
Lower Rd. Northfleet DA11 ...... 12 A3
Lower Rd. Orpington BR5 & BR6 ... 38 B3
Lower Rd. Sutton Valence ME17 124 E7
Lower Rd. Tilbury RM18 .... 13 A3
Lower Rd. West Farleigh ME15 .. 105 D7
Lower Rochester Rd. ME3 ...... 32 E6
Lower St. Leeds ME17 .... 109 A7
Lower St. Stocks Green TN11 ... 115 F5
Lower Station Rd. DA1 .... 8 E1
Lower Stone St. ME15 .... 92 A3
Lower Tovil. ME15 .... 91 E2
Lower Twydall La. ME7 & ME8 .. 49 C4
Lower Warren Rd. ME5 & ME14 74 A6
Lower Woodlands Rd. ME7 ...... 49 A6
Lowfield St. DA1 .... 26 E7
Lownds Ct. BR1 .... 36 A7
Loxwood Cl. BR5 & BR6 .... 52 D8
Lubbock Cl. ME15 .... 107 E5
Lubbock Ct. BR7 .... 22 F1
Lubbock Rd. BR7 .... 22 F1

Lubbock Wlk. ME8 .... 63 D5
Lucas Rd. ME6 .... 74 E7
Lucerne Ct. 5 DA18 .... 3 E3
Lucerne Rd. BR6 .... 37 F1
Lucerne St. ME14 .... 92 A5
Lucknow Rd. TN12 .... 136 A8
Lucknow St. SE18 .... 6 E1
Lucks Hill. ME19 .... 89 D8
Lucks La. Paddock Wood TN12 .. 136 B8
Lucks La. Rabbit's Cross ME17 .. 123 F6
Lucks Way. TN12 .... 138 B6
Luddenham Cl. ME14 .... 92 C6
Luddesdon Rd. DA8 .... 8 E5
Luddesdown House. 5 BR5 ...... 38 C4
Luddesdown Rd. DA13 .... 45 A2
Ludham Cl. SE28 .... 3 C7
Ludlow Cl. BR2 .... 36 A6
Luffield Rd. SE2 .... 3 B3
Luffman Rd. SE12 .... 22 B5
Lughorse La. ME15 & ME18 ...... 105 C1
Lugilina Dr. TN8 .... 128 C3
Lullingstone Ave. ME8 .... 39 F6
Lullingstone Castle. DA4 .... 54 B5
Lullingstone Cl. Gillingham ME7 . 63 B3
Lullingstone Cl.
St Paul's Cray BR5 .... 24 B1
Lullingstone Cres. BR5 .... 24 B1
Lullingstone La. DA4 .... 54 C8
Lullingstone Pk. DA4 .... 53 F6
Lullingstone Rd. 3 Erith DA17 ... 7 F8
Lullingstone Rd. Maidstone ME16 91 C7
Lulworth Rd. Bexley DA16 ...... 6 F5
Lulworth Rd. Chislehurst SE9 ... 22 E6
Lumley Cl. DA17 .... 4 A1
Lumsden Terr. ME4 .... 47 E4
Lunedale Rd. DA2 .... 27 C7
Lunsford Cty Prim Sch. ME20 .. 75 A2
Lunsford La. ME20 .... 74 F2
Lupton Cl. SE12 .... 22 B4
Lurkins Rise. TN17 .... 167 D7
Lushington Rd. ME14 .... 91 E7
Lusted Rd. TN13 .... 83 E7
Luton City Inf Sch. ME5 .... 48 C2
Luton Cty Jun Sch. ME4 .... 48 C2
Luton High St. ME5 .... 48 C2
Luton Rd. Chatham ME4 .... 48 B2
Luton Rd. Sidcup DA14 .... 24 C5
Luxfield Rd. SE9 .... 22 E7
Luxon Rd. DA13 .... 58 E4
Luxted Rd. BR6 .... 66 A6
Lyall Way. ME8 .... 63 E4
Lych Gate Rd. BR6 .... 38 A1
Lychfield Dr. ME2 .... 47 A8
Lydd Cl. DA15 .... 23 E5
Lydd Rd. Chatham ME5 .... 62 B5
Lydd Rd. Erith DA7 .... 7 F7
Lydden Ct. SE9 .... 6 E1
Lydens La. TN8 .... 128 F6
Lydford Ct. 6 DA2 .... 10 B1
Lydia Cotts. 2 DA11 .... 30 B8
Lydia Rd. DA8 .... 8 F8
Lydstep Rd. BR7 .... 23 A4
Lyford St. SE18 & SE7 .... 1 E2
Lyle Cl. ME2 .... 47 B8
Lyle Ct. ME16 .... 91 C5
Lyle Pk. TN13 .... 84 B4
Lymden La. TN5 .... 176 A1
Lyme Farm Rd. SE12 & SE3 ...... 5 B3
Lyme Rd. DA16 .... 7 B6
Lyminge Cl. Gillingham ME8 ... 49 C2
Lyminge Cl. Sidcup DA14 .... 23 F4
Lymington Cl. 2 E6 .... 1 F8
Lymington Ct. ME15 .... 107 F4
Lyndean Ind Est. SE2 .... 3 C3
Lynden Way. BR8 .... 39 D6
Lyndhurst. BR7 .... 23 B2
Lyndhurst Ave. ME8 .... 63 C7
Lyndhurst Cl. Bexley DA7 .... 8 B4
Lyndhurst Cl. Orpington BR6 ... 51 B6
Lyndhurst Dr. TN13 .... 83 E4
Lyndhurst Rd. Maidstone ME15 107 C8
Lyndhurst Rd. DA13 .... 43 F8
Lyndon Ave. DA15 .... 6 F2
Lyndon Rd. DA17 .... 4 A2
Lynette Ave. ME2 .... 33 A1
Lyngs Cl. ME18 .... 120 F8
Lynmead Cl. TN8 .... 112 B4
Lynmere Rd. DA16 .... 7 B5
Lynmouth Rise. BR5 .... 38 B5
Lynne Cl. 7 BR6 .... 51 F4
Lynors Ave. ME2 .... 33 A1
Lynstead Cl. BR1 .... 36 C7
Lynstead House. ME16 .... 91 A1
Lynsted Cl. DA6 .... 8 B2
Lynsted Gdns. SE9 .... 5 D4
Lynsted Rd. ME8 .... 49 B3
Lynton Ave. BR5 .... 38 B5
Lynton Dr. ME5 .... 62 B3
Lynton Rd. DA11 .... 30 A7
Lynton Rd S. DA11 .... 30 A7
Lynwood. TN3 .... 161 C6
Lynwood Gr. BR6 .... 37 E1
Lyons Cres. TN9 .... 117 C2
Lyoth Rd. BR5 .... 51 C8
Lysander Rd. ME19 .... 88 F3
Lysander Way. BR6 .... 51 C7
Lytchet Rd. BR1 .... 22 B1
Lytton Strachy Path. 8 SE28 ... 3 B6
Lyveden Rd. SE3 .... 5 B7

Mabbett House. 2 SE18 .... 6 A8
Mabel Cotts. DA3 .... 43 A6
Mabel Rd. BR8 .... 26 A2
Mabledon Rd. TN9 .... 133 A8
Macallister House. 8 SE18 ...... 6 B8
Macaulay Cl. ME20 .... 75 A4
Macaulay Way. 2 SE28 .... 3 B5

Macbean St. SE18 .... 2 B3
Macdonald Ct. TN12 .... 136 A6
Macdonald Rd. ME7 .... 48 D6
Mace Ct. RM17 .... 12 E8
Mace Farm Cotts. TN14 .... 66 E6
Mace La. TN14 .... 66 D6
Macgregor Rd. E16 .... 1 C8
Mackenders Cl. ME20 .... 76 A6
Mackenders Gn. ME20 .... 76 A6
Mackenders La. ME20 .... 76 A6
Mackenzie Way. DA12 .... 30 D2
Maclean House. 9 SE18 .... 1 F2
Macleod House. SE18 .... 5 E6
Macmillan Gdns. 3 DA1 .... 10 A3
Macoma Rd. SE18 .... 6 D8
Macoma Terr. SE18 .... 6 D8
Mada Rd. BR6 .... 51 B7
Madan Rd. TN16 .... 81 E2
Madden Ave. ME5 .... 61 E5
Madden Cl. DA10 .... 11 E1
Maddocks Cl. DA14 .... 24 E3
Madeira Pk. TN1 .... 149 B2
Madginford Cl. ME15 .... 93 A2
Madginford Park Cty Inf Sch.
ME15 .... 93 A2
Madginford Park Cty Jun Sch.
ME15 .... 93 A2
Madginford Rd. ME15 .... 92 F2
Madison Cres. DA7 .... 7 C7
Madison Gdns. DA7 .... 7 C7
Madison Way. TN13 .... 83 F4
Madras House. 2 ME15 .... 107 E5
Mafeking Rd. ME15 .... 61 F3
Magdalen Cl. ME7 .... 63 A4
Magdalen Gr. BR6 .... 52 B6
Magnolia Ave. ME8 .... 63 B5
Magnolia Cl. TN9 .... 133 C7
Magpie Bottom. TN14 & TN15 .. 69 E6
Magpie Gn. ME20 .... 75 A1
Magpie Gn. 3 TN8 .... 112 D3
Magpie Hall Cl. BR2 .... 36 E3
Magpie Hall La. BR2 .... 36 F3
Magpie Hall Rd. ME4 .... 48 A2
Magpie La. ME9 & ME14 .... 63 F1
Magwitch Cl. ME1 .... 47 B4
Maida Rd. Chatham ME4 .... 48 B2
Maida Rd. Erith DA17 .... 4 A3
Maidstone Barracks Sta. ME16 91 E5
Maidstone East Sta. ME14 ...... 91 F5
Maidstone Gram Sch. ME14 ... 92 B2
Maidstone Gram Sch for Girls.
ME16 .... 91 E5
Maidstone Hospl The. ME16 .... 91 A4
Maidstone Ind Ctr. ME14 ...... 91 F5
Maidstone Mus & Art Gallery.
ME14 .... 91 F5
Maidstone Rd. Chatham ME4 ... 47 F2
Maidstone Rd.
Chatham,Walderslade ME5 ...... 61 D4
Maidstone Rd.
Chestnut Street ME9 .... 65 D4
Maidstone Rd.
Colt's Hill TN12 & TN2 .... 135 B4
Maidstone Rd. Five Wents ME17 108 C2
Maidstone Rd. Gillingham ME8 ... 63 C6
Maidstone Rd.
Gillingham,Bredhurst ME7 ...... 63 B2
Maidstone Rd.
Goose Green TN11 .... 103 C3
Maidstone Rd. Grays RM17 ...... 12 A8
Maidstone Rd. Headcorn TN27 . 141 B7
Maidstone Rd. Lenham ME17 ... 111 D5
Maidstone Rd. Lower Green TN2 134 E1
Maidstone Rd. Matfield TN12 ... 151 C6
Maidstone Rd.
Nettlestead Green ME18 ...... 104 C3
Maidstone Rd.
Paddock Wood TN12 .... 136 A8
Maidstone Rd. Platt TN15 ...... 87 C7
Maidstone Rd. Rochester ME1 ... 47 C3
Maidstone Rd. Ruxley DA14 ... 24 F1
Maidstone Rd. Sevenoaks TN13 . 83 E5
Maidstone Rd. Sidcup DA14 ... 24 D2
Maidstone Rd. Staplehurst TN12 139 E7
Maidstone Rd.
Styants Bottom TN15 .... 85 C5
Maidstone Rd. Swanley BR8 ... 39 B8
Maidstone Rd.
Underling Green TN12 .... 122 F2
Maidstone Rd.
Yewtree Green TN12 .... 137 C3
Maidstone St Francis Sch.
ME14 .... 92 A5
Maidstone West Sta. ME16 ...... 91 F4
Mailyns The. ME8 .... 63 D7
Main Gate Rd. Chatham ME4 ... 47 F7
Main Gate Rd. Chatham ME4 ... 48 A8
Main Rd. Chattenden ME3 ...... 33 F4
Main Rd. Crockenhill BR8 .... 39 D3
Main Rd. Farningham DA4 ...... 40 D3
Main Rd. Hextable BR8 .... 39 F8
Main Rd. Hoo St Werburgh ME3 .. 34 C5
Main Rd. Kingsnorth ME3 .... 35 D7
Main Rd. Knockholt TN14 ...... 67 C3
Main Rd. Longfield DA3 .... 42 E7
Main Rd. Marlpit Hill TN8 ...... 112 B6
Main Rd. Sidcup DA14 & DA15 .. 23 E5
Main Rd. South Street TN16 ... 81 A7
Main Rd. St Paul's Cray BR5 ... 38 D7
Main Rd. Sundridge TN14 ...... 82 E3
Main Rd. Sutton at Hone DA4 ... 27 B1
Main Road Gorse Hill. DA4 ...... 55 D7

Major York's Rd. TN4 .... 148 F2
Malden Dr. ME14 .... 92 A8
Mall The. 6 Bexley DA6 .... 8 A3
Mall The. 4 Bromley BR1 ...... 36 A6
Mallard Apartments. 12
ME15 .... 107 E5
Mallard Cl. DA1 .... 9 F2
Mallard Path. SE28 .... 2 D7
Mallard Way. Lower Stoke ME3 .. 19 C4
Mallard Way. Marlpit Hill TN8 .. 112 C3
Mallard Wlk. Larkfield ME20 ... 74 F2
Mallard Wlk. Sidcup DA14 ...... 24 C2
Mallards Way. ME15 .... 93 A1
Malling Rd. Kent Street ME18 ... 88 D7
Malling Rd. Lunsford ME20 ...... 74 F5
Malling Rd. Snodland ME6 ...... 75 A7
Malling Rd. Teston ME18 .... 90 A1
Malling Sch The. ME19 .... 89 F7
Malling Terr. ME16 .... 91 C4
Mallingdene Cl. ME3 .... 33 B8
Mallings Dr. ME14 .... 93 C4
Mallings La. ME14 .... 93 C4
Mallow Cl. DA11 .... 29 E4
Mallow Ct. RM17 .... 12 D8
Mallow Way. 1 ME5 .... 61 F4
Mallows The. ME14 .... 91 E7
Mallys Pl. DA4 .... 41 C8
Malmaynes Hall Rd. ME3 ...... 18 D3
Malory Sch. BR1 .... 22 A4
Malt House La. TN30 .... 183 A7
Malta Ave. ME5 .... 62 A7
Malta Rd. RM18 .... 12 F5
Malta Terr. 5 ME14 .... 92 A7
Maltby Cl. BR6 .... 38 A1
Malthouse Cl. ME17 .... 111 D5
Malthouse Hill. ME15 .... 106 F4
Malthouse La. DA12 .... 31 E3
Malthouse Rd. TN15 .... 56 F2
Malthus Path. 7 SE28 .... 3 C5
Maltings Cl. TN11 .... 118 E8
Maltings Ent Ctr The. DA12 ... 30 F7
Maltings The. Gillingham ME8 .. 64 A8
Maltings The. Gravesend DA12 ... 31 E3
Maltings The. Maidstone ME14 .. 92 E5
Maltings The. Orpington BR6 ... 37 F1
Maltings The.
The Quarries ME17 .... 107 B4
Malton Mews. SE18 .... 6 E8
Malton St. SE18 .... 6 E8
Malton Way. TN2 .... 149 F7
Malus Cl. ME5 .... 62 B1
Malvern Ave. DA7 .... 7 E7
Malvern House. DA11 .... 12 D1
Malvern Rd. Gillingham ME7 ... 48 E3
Malvern Rd. Orpington BR6 ...... 52 B6
Malvina Ave. DA12 .... 30 C6
Malyons Rd. BR8 .... 25 F1
Mamignot Cl. ME14 .... 93 A5
Manchester Cl. ME5 .... 62 C6
Mandela Rd. E16 .... 1 A7
Mandeville Cl. 1 SE3 .... 5 A7
Mandeville Ct. 1 ME14 .... 92 A5
Manford Ind Est. DA8 .... 9 B8
Mangold Way. 4 DA18 .... 3 E3
Mangravet Ave. ME15 .... 107 C7
Manister Rd. SE2 .... 3 A3
Manitoba Gdns. 6 BR6 .... 51 F4
Mann Sq. TN13 .... 133 D7
Manning Ct. 3 SE28 .... 3 B5
Manning Rd. BR5 .... 38 D4
Manningham House. ME19 ...... 90 A6
Mannock Rd. DA1 .... 9 F4
Manor Cl. Chalk DA12 .... 31 B6
Manor Cl. Crayford DA1 .... 8 E3
Manor Cl. Erith SE28 .... 3 C7
Manor Cl. Heath Side DA2 ...... 26 A5
Manor Cl. Maidstone ME14 ...... 93 B3
Manor Cl.
Royal Tunbridge Wells TN4 ...... 148 E3
Manor Cotts. Lamberhurst TN3 . 166 B5
Manor Cotts. Langley ME17 ...... 108 C5
Manor Ct. Gillingham ME7 ...... 49 C4
Manor Ct. Maidstone ME14 ...... 93 B3
Manor Ct. Sole Street DA13 ...... 44 D4
Manor Cty Inf Sch. RM18 ...... 13 B7
Manor Dr. DA3 .... 43 A3
Manor Farm Cotts. TN15 .... 86 A6
Manor Field. DA12 .... 31 E3
Manor Forstal. DA3 .... 56 F7
Manor Gdns. ME5 .... 61 F4
Manor Gr. TN10 .... 117 C3
Manor House. 8 ME7 .... 48 A6
Manor House Dr. ME16 .... 91 D3
Manor House Gdns. TN8 ...... 112 C1
Manor La. Fawkham Green DA3 ... 42 C2
Manor La. Hartley DA3 .... 43 A3
Manor La. Rochester ME1 ...... 46 F3
Manor Park Ctry Pk. ME19 ...... 89 B7
Manor Park Rd. BR7 .... 37 D8
Manor Pk. Chislehurst BR7 ...... 37 D8
Manor Pk. Erith DA8 .... 9 A8
Manor Pk.
Royal Tunbridge Wells TN4 ...... 148 E3
Manor Rd. BR7 .... 37 D7
Manor Rd. Chatham ME4 ...... 47 F4
Manor Rd. Crayford DA1 .... 8 E3
Manor Rd. Edenbridge TN8 ...... 112 B1
Manor Rd. Grays RM17 .... 12 C8
Manor Rd. Longfield Hill DA3 ... 43 C4
Manor Rd.
Royal Tunbridge Wells TN4 ...... 132 E1
Manor Rd. Rusthall TN4 .... 148 C4
Manor Rd. Sidcup DA15 .... 24 A5

Manor Rd. Sidcup,Old Bexley DA5 **25** B7
Manor Rd. Sole Street DA13 .... **44** D4
Manor Rd. Sundridge TN14 .... **82** D3
Manor Rd. Swanscombe DA10 ..... **28** E8
Manor Rd. Tilbury RM18 .... **13** A5
Manor Rd. West Thurrock RM16 ... **11** C8
Manor Rise. ME14 .... **93** B3
Manor Road Cty Inf Sch. DA10 **28** E8
Manor St. ME7 .... **48** A6
Manor Way. Bexley DA5 .... **8** D4
Manor Way. Bromley BR2 .... **36** E3
Manor Way. Grays RM17 .... **12** D7
Manor Way. Grays RM17 .... **12** D7
Manor Way. Greenwich SE3 .... **5** A3
Manor Way. Northfleet DA11 ...... **12** A3
Manor Way. Orpington BR5 .... **37** C5
Manor Way. Rainham RM13 .... **4** A7
Manor Way. Sidcup DA5 .... **25** A7
Manor Way. Swanscombe DA10 ... **11** E3
Manor Way Bsns Ctr. RM9 .... **4** D8
Manorbrook. SE12 & SE3 .... **5** A3
Manordene Rd. SE28 .... **3** D7
Manorfields Cl. BR7 .... **37** F6
Manorside Cl. SE2 .... **3** D2
Manse Dr. DA14 .... **24** C3
Manse Par. BR8 .... **40** A5
Manse Way. BR8 .... **40** A5
Mansel Dr. ME1 .... **47** A2
Mansergh Cl. SE18 .... **5** E7
Mansfield Cl. BR5 .... **38** D3
Mansfield Rd. BR8 .... **25** F2
Mansfield Wlk. ME16 .... **91** E2
Mansion House Cl. TN27 .... **158** A2
Mansion Row. ME7 .... **48** A6
Manthorpe Rd. SE18 .... **2** C1
Manton Rd. SE2 .... **3** A2
Manwarings The. TN12 .... **153** A6
Manwood St. E16 .... **1** F5
Maple Ave. Gillingham ME7 .... **48** E6
Maple Ave. Maidstone ME16 ...... **91** C6
Maple Cl. Larkfield ME20 .... **75** A2
Maple Cl. Orpington BR5 .... **37** D4
Maple Cl.
  Royal Tunbridge Wells TN2 .... **149** A1
Maple Cl. Swanley BR8 .... **39** E7
Maple Cres. DA15 .... **7** A1
Maple Ct. Newham E6 .... **2** A8
Maple Ct. Stone DA2 .... **27** E8
Maple Leaf Dr. DA15 .... **23** F7
Maple Rd. Dartford DA1 .... **26** C7
Maple Rd. Gravesend DA12 .... **30** C4
Maple Rd. Grays RM17 .... **12** C8
Maple Rd. Hoo St Werburgh ME3 .. **34** E3
Maple Rd. Rochester ME2 .... **46** F6
Maplecroft Cl. E6 .... **1** E7
Mapledene. BR7 .... **23** C3
Maples The. DA3 .... **43** B6
Maplescombe La. DA4 .... **55** B6
Maplesden Cl. ME16 .... **90** F3
Maplesden Noakes Sch The.
  ME16 .... **91** E6
Mapleton. TN8 .... **113** A7
Mapleton Cl. BR2 .... **36** A3
Mapleton Rd. TN16 & TN8 .... **96** E3
Maplin House. SE2 .... **3** D4
Maplin Rd. E16 .... **1** B7
Maplins Cl. ME8 .... **49** F1
Mar House. ME7 .... **5** C8
Maran Way. DA18 .... **3** D3
Marathon Paddock. ME7 .... **48** D4
Marble House. SE18 .... **2** F1
Marbrook Ct. SE12 .... **22** C5
Marcellina Way. BR6 .... **51** F7
Marcet Rd. DA1 .... **9** C2
Marconi Rd. DA11 .... **29** D5
Marcus Rd. DA1 .... **26** A8
Marden Ave. BR2 .... **36** A3
Marden Cres. DA5 .... **8** C2
Marden Cty Prim Sch. TN12 .. **138** B5
Marden Rd. Rochester ME2 .... **33** C1
Marden Rd. Staplehurst TN12 .. **139** C5
Marden Sta. TN12 .... **138** C6
Marechal Niel Ave. DA15 .... **23** D5
Marechal Niel Par. DA15 .... **23** D5
Margaret Gardner Dr. SE9 .... **22** F6
Margaret Rd. DA5 .... **7** D1
Margate Cl. ME7 .... **48** E6
Margetts La. ME1 .... **60** D1
Margetts Pl. ME4 .... **34** A3
Marian Sq. TN12 .... **139** F4
Marina Cl. BR2 .... **36** A6
Marina Dr. Bexley DA16 .... **6** E5
Marina Dr. Dartford DA1 .... **27** A7
Marina Dr. Northfleet DA11 ...... **12** F1
Marine Dr. Hoo St Werburgh ME3 **34** E3
Marine Dr. Woolwich SE18 .... **1** F2
Marine View. **34** B1
Mariners Ct. DA9 .... **11** B3
Mariners Wlk. DA8 .... **8** F8
Marion Cl. ME5 .... **62** A2
Marion Cres. Maidstone ME15 .. **107** B8
Marion Cres. Orpington BR5 ..... **38** B4
Maritime Cl. Rochester ME2 ..... **47** D8
Maritime Cl. Swanscombe DA9 .. **11** B2
Maritime Ind Est. SE7 .... **1** C7
Maritime Way. ME4 .... **48** A8
Marjorie McClure Sch. BR7 ..... **37** C8
Mark Cl. Bexley DA7 .... **7** E6
Mark Cl. Keston BR2 .... **50** E6
Mark La. DA12 .... **13** E1
Mark Way. BR8 .... **40** A4
Market Alley. B DA11 .... **13** B1
Market Bldgs. B ME14 .... **91** F4
Market Colonnade. B ME14 .... **91** F4
Market Meadow. BR5 .... **38** C5

Market Pl. B Bexley DA7 .... **8** A3
Market Pl. Dartford DA1 .... **26** E8
Market Pl. B
  Royal Tunbridge Wells TN2 .... **149** A2
Market Pl. B Tilbury RM18 .... **13** A5
Market Sq. Bromley BR1 .... **36** A7
Market Sq.
  Royal Tunbridge Wells TN2 .... **149** B4
Market Sq. Westerham TN16 ...... **81** D1
Market St. Dartford DA1 .... **26** E8
Market St. B Maidstone ME14 ... **91** F4
Market St. B
  Royal Tunbridge Wells TN2 .... **149** A2
Market St. Staplehurst TN12 .... **139** F5
Market St. Woolwich SE18 .... **2** A2
Market Way. B TN16 .... **81** D1
Marks Sq. DA11 .... **29** F4
Marlborough Cl. Orpington BR6 . **37** F3
Marlborough Cl.
  Royal Tunbridge Wells TN4 .... **148** E4
Marlborough Cres. TN13 .... **83** E3
Marlborough Ct. TN16 .... **81** C1
Marlborough House. ME8 .... **63** F8
Marlborough House Sch.
  TN18 .... **178** E2
Marlborough La. SE7 .... **5** C7
Marlborough Park Ave. DA15 ... **24** A7
Marlborough Rd. Bexley DA16 .... **7** A4
Marlborough Rd. Bromley BR2 .. **36** C5
Marlborough Rd. Dartford DA1 ... **9** C1
Marlborough Rd. Gillingham ME7 **48** B5
Marlborough Rd. Woolwich SE18 **2** E3
Marlborough Sch. DA15 .... **24** A8
Marle Place Rd. TN12 .... **152** C4
Marler House. DA8 .... **8** F5
Marley Ave. DA7 .... **7** D8
Marley La. TN27 .... **142** C3
Marley Rd. Harrietsham ME17 .. **110** F6
Marley Rd. Hoo St Werburgh ME3 **34** E3
Marley Way. ME1 .... **47** C2
Marlhurst. TN8 .... **112** B4
Marling Way. DA12 .... **30** E3
Marlings Cl. BR7 .... **37** E5
Marlings Park Ave. BR7 .... **37** E6
Marlow Copse. ME5 .... **61** F1
Marlowe Cl. BR7 .... **23** D2
Marlowe Gdns. SE9 .... **6** A1
Marlowe Rd. ME20 .... **75** A3
Marlowes The. DA1 .... **8** D3
Marlpit Cl. TN8 .... **112** C4
Marlpit Cotts. ME17 .... **107** E2
Marlpit Gdns. TN5 .... **176** E1
Marlpit The. TN5 .... **174** E5
Marlwood Cl. DA15 .... **23** E6
Marmadon Rd. SE18 & SE2 .... **2** F2
Marne Ave. DA16 .... **7** A4
Marquis Dr. ME7 .... **63** B3
Marrabon Cl. DA15 .... **24** A7
Marram Ct. RM17 .... **12** E8
Marriott Rd. DA1 .... **27** A8
Marsden Way. B BR6 .... **51** F6
Marsh Cres. ME23 .... **17** E4
Marsh Green Rd. TN8 .... **128** C5
Marsh La. ME2 .... **16** B6
Marsh Quarter La. TN18 .... **186** C3
Marsh Rd. Gillingham ME8 .... **60** B5
Marsh St. Dartford DA1 .... **10** A5
Marsh St. Rochester ME2 .... **47** B7
Marsh Way. New Hythe ME20 ..... **75** A4
Marsh Way. Rainham RM9 .... **4** D8
Marshall Gdns. TN11 .... **102** E1
Marshall Path. B SE28 .... **3** B6
Marshall Rd. ME8 .... **63** C8
Marshalls Gr. SE18 .... **1** E2
Marshalls Land. TN30 .... **173** A3
Marsham Cl. BR7 .... **23** B3
Marsham Cres. ME17 .... **108** B1
Marsham St. ME14 .... **92** A4
Marsham Way. ME2 .... **60** A5
Marshbrook Cl. SE3 .... **5** D4
Marshland View. ME3 .... **19** C5
Marston Cl. ME5 .... **61** E3
Marston Ct. DA14 .... **23** F4
Marston Dr. ME14 .... **92** C5
Marston House. RM17 .... **12** A8
Marston Wlk. ME5 .... **61** E3
Martens Ave. DA7 .... **8** C3
Martens Cl. DA7 .... **8** C3
Martham Cl. SE28 .... **3** D6
Martin Bowes Rd. SE9 .... **5** F4
Martin Cl. ME7 .... **63** A3
Martin Dene. DA6 .... **7** F2
Martin Dr. DA2 .... **10** C1
Martin Hardie Way. TN10 .... **117** E5
Martin House. DA11 .... **29** F6
Martin Rd. Rochester ME2 .... **47** B8
Martin Rd. Wilmington DA2 ...... **26** C5
Martin Rise. **7** F2
Martin Sq. ME20 .... **75** A2
Martin's Shaw. TN13 .... **83** C5
Martindale Ave. Newham E16 ..... **1** A6
Martindale Ave. Orpington BR6 . **52** A5
Martins Cl. Lower Higham ME3 .. **32** D6
Martins Cl. St Paul's Cray BR5 .. **38** D6
Martins Cl. Tenterden TN30 .... **183** C8
Martins La. TN12 .... **103** E2
Martyn House. SE2 .... **7** D8
Marvels Cl. SE12 .... **22** B6
Marvels La. SE12 .... **22** C5
Marvels Lane Prim Sch. SE12 .. **22** D4
Marvillion Ct. TN12 .... **119** F6
Marvin House. B SE18 .... **6** B8
Marwell. TN16 .... **81** B1
Marwood Cl. DA16 .... **7** B4
Mary Burrows Gdns. TN15 .... **70** B2
Mary Day's. TN17 .... **167** E7
Mary Lawrenson Pl. B SE3 .... **5** A7
Mary Macarthur House. B DA17 **4** A3

Mary Magdalene House. B
  TN9 .... **133** B8
Mary Rose Hall. E6 .... **1** F8
Marybank. SE18 .... **1** F2
Maryfield Cl. DA5 .... **25** E5
Maryland Cl. ME8 .... **63** E5
Maryland Dr. ME16 .... **90** F2
Maryland Rd. TN9 .... **133** D1
Maryon Ct. BR5 .... **38** B5
Maryon Gr. SE7 .... **1** E2
Maryon Rd. SE7 .... **1** E2
Maryville. DA16 .... **6** F5
Mascall's Court La. TN12 .... **136** B4
Mascall's Court Rd. TN12 .... **136** A4
Mascalls Ct. B SE7 .... **5** C8
Mascalls Pk. TN12 .... **135** F5
Mascalls Rd. SE7 .... **5** C8
Mascalls Sch. TN12 .... **136** A4
Masefield Cl. DA8 .... **8** F6
Masefield Dr. ME8 .... **33** B8
Masefield Rd. Dartford DA1 ..... **10** B2
Masefield Rd. Lunsford ME20 ... **74** F4
Masefield Rd. Northfleet DA11 .. **29** D5
Masefield View. BR6 .... **51** C7
Masham House. B DA18 .... **3** D4
Mason Cl. DA2 .... **8** B4
Masons Hill. Bromley BR2 .... **36** B5
Masons Hill. Woolwich SE18 ...... **2** B2
Master Gunners' Pl. SE18 .... **5** E7
Masters La. ME19 .... **74** B5
Masthead Cl. DA9 .... **10** C3
Matchless Dr. SE18 .... **6** A7
Mate Hall Villas. ME14 .... **93** C4
Matfield Cl. BR2 .... **36** A4
Matfield Cres. ME14 .... **92** C5
Matfield Rd. DA17 .... **8** A8
Matilda Cl. ME7 .... **63** B8
Matrix Bsns Ctr. ME1 .... **9** E2
Matterdale Gdns. ME16 .... **90** E2
Matthews La. TN11 .... **102** F4
Mattinson Pl. ME9 .... **95** F7
Matts Hill Rd. ME9 .... **63** E2
Maud Cashmore Way. SE18 .... **1** F3
Maude Rd. SE18 .... **26** A2
Maudslay Rd. SE9 .... **6** A1
Maundene Cty Prim Sch. ME5 .. **62** B5
Maunder Cl. ME5 .... **62** C8
Mavelstone Cl. BR1 .... **36** E8
Mavelstone Rd. BR1 .... **36** E8
Mavis Wlk. B E6 .... **1** E8
Maxey Rd. SE18 .... **2** C2
Maxim Rd. Crayford DA1 .... **8** E2
Maxim Rd. Erith DA8 .... **4** E2
Maximfeldt Rd. DA8 .... **4** E8
Maximilian Dr. ME2 .... **60** B4
Maxton Cl. ME14 .... **92** F5
Maxwell Dr. ME16 .... **91** B6
Maxwell Gdns. BR6 .... **51** F7
Maxwell House. Chislehurst BR7 **23** B1
Maxwell House. B
  Woolwich SE18 .... **6** B8
Maxwell Rd. Bexley DA16 .... **7** A4
Maxwell Rd. Gillingham ME7 ..... **48** A6
May Ave. Northfleet DA11 .... **29** F7
May Ave. Orpington BR5 .... **38** B4
May Avenue Est. B DA11 .... **29** F7
May Ct. RM17 .... **12** E8
May Pl. DA13 .... **44** D4
May Rd. Gillingham ME7 .... **48** C4
May Rd. Hawley DA2 .... **26** F4
May Rd. Rochester ME1 .... **47** C3
May St. Cuxton ME2 .... **46** B2
May St. Snodland ME6 .... **75** B8
May Terr. B ME4 .... **48** A7
May Wynne House. E16 .... **1** B7
Maybury Ave. DA2 .... **27** C7
Maybury Cl. BR5 .... **37** B4
Maycotts La. TN12 .... **135** D1
Mayday Gdns. SE3 .... **5** E5
Mayerne Rd. SE9 .... **5** D2
Mayes Cl. BR8 .... **40** A5
Mayeswood Rd. SE12 .... **22** C4
Mayfair. ME2 .... **47** C8
Mayfair Ave. Bexley DA6 .... **7** D6
Mayfair Ave. Maidstone ME15 .. **107** A8
Mayfair Rd. DA1 .... **9** D2
Mayfield. Bexley DA7 .... **7** F4
Mayfield. Swanscombe DA10 ..... **11** E1
Mayfield Ave. BR6 .... **37** F2
Mayfield Cl. Chatham ME5 .... **62** A1
Mayfield Cl. Gillingham ME8 .... **49** E2
Mayfield La. TN5 .... **174** D4
Mayfield Pk. TN5 .... **174** E5
Mayfield Rd. Bromley BR1 .... **36** E4
Mayfield Rd. Erith DA17 .... **4** C2
Mayfield Rd. Northfleet DA11 ... **29** F8
Mayfield Rd.
  Royal Tunbridge Wells TN4 ... **148** F4
Mayfield Villas. DA14 .... **24** C2
Mayford Rd. ME5 .... **62** D2
Mayhill Rd. SE7 .... **5** B8
Maylam Ct. TN10 .... **117** C4
Maylands Dr. DA14 .... **24** D4
Maynard Cl. DA8 .... **8** F7
Maynard House. SE18 .... **2** A2
Maynard Pl. ME5 .... **48** D2
Maynard's La. TN12 .... **135** E1
Maynards. TN12 .... **138** C5
Mayor's Pl. B TN30 .... **183** A7
Mayors La. DA2 .... **26** C3
Mayplace Ave. DA1 .... **9** A3
Mayplace Cl. DA7 .... **8** B4
Mayplace La. Woolwich SE18 ..... **6** B7
Mayplace Prim Sch. DA7 .... **8** D3
Mayplace Rd E. DA7 .... **8** C4
Mayplace Rd W. DA7 .... **8** A3

Maypole Cotts. BR6 .... **53** A4
Maypole Cres. DA8 .... **9** D8
Maypole Cty Prim Sch. DA5 .. **25** E6
Maypole La. TN17 .... **167** F8
Maypole Rd. Gravesend DA12 ... **30** F7
Maypole Rd. Maypole BR6 .... **52** F4
Maytham Bglws. TN17 .... **182** A1
Maytham Rd. TN17 .... **182** A1
Mayweed Ave. ME5 .... **61** E4
Mc Call Cres. SE7 .... **1** E1
Mc Dowall Cl. B E16 .... **1** A8
Mc Kenzie Rd. ME5 .... **62** A3
McAlpine Cres. ME15 .... **106** F3
McAuley Cl. SE9 .... **6** A2
McCabe Ct. TN12 .... **139** E2
McCudden Rd. DA1 .... **9** F4
McCudden Row. B ME4 .... **48** A6
McDermott Rd. TN15 .... **86** F7
McKenzie Cl. ME20 .... **90** F8
McLeod Rd. SE2 .... **3** B2
Mcmillan Cl. DA12 .... **30** C4
Mead Cl. BR8 .... **26** D7
Mead Cres. DA1 .... **26** D7
Mead Rd. Chislehurst BR7 .... **23** C2
Mead Rd. Dartford DA1 .... **26** D7
Mead Rd. Edenbridge TN8 ...... **128** D2
Mead Rd. Gravesend DA11 ...... **30** B6
Mead Road Inf Sch. BR7 .... **23** C2
Mead The. Leybourne ME19 ..... **74** E2
Mead The. New Ash Green DA3 . **56** E8
Mead The.
  Royal Tunbridge Wells TN2 .... **149** C2
Mead Wall. ME3 .... **15** F8
Mead Way. BR2 .... **36** A3
Meades Cl. TN12 .... **138** B6
Meadfield Rd. DA13 .... **58** A8
Meadow Bank. Leigh TN11 ...... **115** F1
Meadow Bank.
  West Malling ME19 .... **89** C8
Meadow Bank Cl. TN15 .... **55** F2
Meadow Cl. Bexley DA6 .... **7** F2
Meadow Cl. Chatham ME5 .... **61** F5
Meadow Cl. Chislehurst BR7 .... **23** B2
Meadow Cl. Sevenoaks TN13 ... **84** A4
Meadow Cl. Upper Halling ME2 . **59** E4
Meadow Cres. ME5 .... **59** E4
Meadow Croft. BR1 .... **36** F6
Meadow Ct. TN15 .... **55** C1
Meadow Hill Rd. B TN1 & TN2 **149** B3
Meadow La. Marlpit Hill TN8 .. **112** E3
Meadow La. Vigo Village DA13 .. **58** A1
Meadow Rd. Gravesend DA11 ... **30** A6
Meadow Rd. Groombridge TN3 **161** C7
Meadow Rd. Northfleet DA11 ... **29** C7
Meadow Rd.
  Royal Tunbridge Wells TN1 .... **149** A4
Meadow Rd.Royal Tunbridge Wells,
  Southborough TN4 .... **132** F1
Meadow Rd. Rusthall TN4 .... **148** C4
Meadow Rd. Tonbridge TN9 .... **133** B8
Meadow The. Chislehurst BR7 .. **23** C2
Meadow The. Pembury TN2 ..... **150** E8
Meadow View. DA15 .... **24** B8
Meadow View Cotts.
  Hurst Green TN19 .... **184** A3
Meadow View Cotts.
  Laddingford ME18 .... **120** E5
Meadow View Rd. ME17 .... **107** B3
Meadow Way. Dartford DA2 ..... **27** C8
Meadow Way. Marden TN12 ... **138** E6
Meadow Way. Orpington BR6 ... **51** A7
Meadow Wlk. Maidstone ME15 . **92** B3
Meadow Wlk. Snodland ME6 ... **74** F7
Meadow Wlk. Wilmington DA2 . **26** C4
Meadowbank Rd. ME4 .... **48** A4
Meadowdown. ME14 .... **92** E4
Meadowdown Cl. ME7 .... **63** A4
Meadowlands. TN15 .... **84** F7
Meadows. TN17 .... **170** D1
Meadows Ct. DA14 .... **24** B2
Meadows Sch (Barnados).
  TN4 .... **132** F2
Meadows The. Biddenden TN27 **157** F2
Meadows The. Halstead TN14 .. **67** F6
Meadows The. Maidstone ME15 . **91** E2
Meadows The. Orpington BR6 ... **52** C4
Meadowside. Dartford DA1 ...... **26** E7
Meadowside. Eltham SE9 .... **5** C3
Meadowside Cotts. TN5 .... **176** F1
Meadowsweet Cl. B E16 .... **1** D8
Meadowview. BR5 .... **38** C6
Meadowview Rd. DA5 .... **7** F1
Meads The. TN17 .... **168** F1
Meadside Wlk. ME5 .... **61** F6
Meadway. Halstead TN14 .... **67** F6
Meadway. Hildenborough TN11 .. **116** E5
Meadway The. Orpington BR6 ... **52** B4
Meadway The. Sevenoaks TN13 . **83** F5
Meath Cl. BR5 .... **38** B4
Medbury Rd. DA12 .... **30** F7
Mede House. BR1 .... **22** B3
Medebourne Cl. SE3 .... **5** A4
Medhurst Cres. DA12 .... **30** F6
Medhurst Gdns. DA12 .... **30** F5
Medick Ct. RM17 .... **12** E8
Medina House. B DA8 .... **8** E7
Medina Rd. Ditton ME20 .... **75** C1
Medina Rd. Tonbridge TN10 .. **117** C6
Medlar Gr. ME7 .... **63** A4
Medlar House. B DA15 .... **24** A5
Medlar Rd. RM17 .... **12** E8
Medlars The. Maidstone ME14 .. **92** D6
Medlars The.
  Meopham Station DA13 .... **44** A3
Medway Ave. High Halstow ME23 **17** F4
Medway Ave. Yalding ME18 .... **104** F1
Medway Com Coll. ME4 .... **48** A1
Medway Cotts. TN17 .... **180** D3

Medway Ct. B BR5 .... **38** D1
Medway Ent Ctr. ME2 .... **47** D8
Medway Gdns. ME4 .... **47** F7
Medway Heritage Ctr. ME4 ..... **47** F5
Medway Hospl. ME7 .... **48** B4
Medway House. B ME15 .... **107** D8
Medway Meadows. TN12 .... **120** A6
Medway Rd. Crayford DA1 .... **9** A4
Medway Rd. Gillingham ME7 .... **48** C7
Medway Rd.
  Gillingham,Rainham ME8 .... **49** F1
Medway Rd.
  Royal Tunbridge Wells TN1 .... **149** B5
Medway Service Area. ME8 ..... **63** F3
Medway St. Chatham ME4 .... **47** F5
Medway St. Maidstone ME14 ... **91** F4
Medway Trad Est. ME16 .... **91** F3
Medway View.
  Barnes Street TN11 .... **119** A5
Medway View. Lower Stoke ME3 **19** C3
Medway Villas. ME15 .... **106** B7
Medway Wharf Rd. TN9 .... **117** C1
Meerbank Rd. SE3 & SE9 .... **5** C4
Meeson's La. RM17 .... **11** F8
Meeting House La. ME4 .... **47** F4
Megby Cl. ME8 .... **63** D6
Megrims Hill. TN18 .... **186** A6
Meirs Court Rd. ME8 .... **63** E6
Melanda Cl. ME7 .... **22** F3
Melanie Cl. DA7 .... **7** E6
Melba Gdns. RM18 .... **13** A7
Melbourne Cl. BR6 .... **37** E2
Melbourne Ct. B DA11 .... **13** B1
Melbourne Rd. Chatham ME4 ... **48** A3
Melbourne Rd. Tilbury RM18 ... **12** E6
Melbury Ct. ME7 .... **22** F2
Meldrum Cl. BR5 .... **38** C3
Melford Dr. ME16 .... **91** C4
Melliker La. DA13 .... **44** A3
Melling St. SE18 .... **6** E8
Mellish Ind Est. E16 .... **1** D3
Mells Cres. SE9 .... **22** F4
Melody Cl. ME8 .... **63** C4
Melrose Cl. Lewisham SE12 ..... **22** B7
Melrose Cl. Maidstone ME15 .. **107** A7
Melrose Cres. BR6 .... **51** D5
Melthorpe Gdns. SE3 .... **5** E6
Melville Cl. ME4 .... **47** F6
Melville Rd. Maidstone ME15 ... **92** A3
Melville Rd. Sidcup DA14 .... **24** C6
Memess Path. B SE18 .... **6** A8
Memorial Hospl. SE18 .... **6** A5
Mendip Rd. DA7 .... **8** E6
Mendip Wlk. TN2 .... **149** D5
Mennie House. SE18 .... **5** F6
Meon Ct. B BR5 .... **38** D1
Meopham Cty Prim Sch. DA13 **44** A2
Meopham Sch. DA13 .... **58** A8
Meopham Sta. DA13 .... **44** A4
Mera Dr. DA7 .... **8** A3
Merbury Rd. SE28 .... **2** E2
Merbury St. SE18 .... **2** B3
Mercer Dr. ME17 .... **110** F6
Mercer St. TN1 .... **149** B5
Mercer Way. ME17 .... **108** B1
Mercers. Hawkhurst TN18 ..... **179** A1
Mercers. Langton Green TN3 .. **148** A3
Mercer's Cl. TN12 .... **135** E6
Merchant Pl. TN12 .... **138** C5
Merchland Rd. SE9 .... **23** C7
Mercury Cl. ME1 .... **47** A3
Mere Cl. BR6 .... **51** B8
Meresborough Cotts. ME8 ...... **63** F5
Meresborough La. ME8 & ME9 . **64** B5
Meresborough Rd. ME8 .... **64** A7
Mereside. BR6 .... **51** A8
Merewood Cl. B BR1 .... **37** A7
Merewood Rd. DA7 .... **8** C5
Mereworth Cl. ME8 .... **49** A3
Mereworth Cty Prim Sch.
  ME18 .... **103** C8
Mereworth Dr. SE18 .... **6** C7
Mereworth House. ME2 .... **33** C1
Mereworth Rd.
  Mereworth ME18 .... **103** C7
Mereworth Rd.
  Royal Tunbridge Wells TN4 .... **149** A6
Meriden Cl. BR1 .... **22** D1
Meridian Pk. ME2 .... **47** E6
Meridian Rd. SE7 .... **5** D7
Meridian Trad Est. SE7 .... **1** B2
Merifield Rd. SE9 .... **5** C3
Merino Pl. DA15 .... **7** A2
Merivale Gr. ME5 .... **62** B4
Merlewood. TN13 .... **84** B4
Merlewood Dr. BR7 .... **36** F8
Merlin Ave. ME20 .... **74** F2
Merlin Cl. TN10 .... **117** E4
Merlin Gdns. BR1 .... **22** A5
Merlin Prim Sch. BR1 .... **22** A5
Merlin Rd. DA16 .... **7** A3
Merlin Rd N. DA16 .... **7** A3
Mermaid Cl. ME5 .... **62** A6
Mermerus Gdns. DA12 .... **30** F4
Merrals Wood Rd. ME2 .... **46** D5
Merrilees Rd. DA15 .... **23** E8
Merriman Rd. SE3 .... **5** C6
Merriments La. TN18 & TN19 .. **184** D5
Merrion Cl. TN4 .... **149** B7
Merrion Way. TN4 .... **149** B7
Merry Boys Rd. ME3 .... **33** B8
Merrydown Way. BR7 .... **36** F8
Merryfield. SE3 .... **5** A5
Merryfield Cl. B TN9 .... **133** B8
Merryfield House. SE12 .... **22** C5
Merryfields. ME2 .... **33** A1
Merryweather Cl. DA1 .... **9** F1
Mersey Rd. TN10 .... **117** B5

Merton Ave. DA3 .... 42 F5
Merton Cl. ME5 .... 62 C5
Merton Court Prep Sch. DA14 . 24 C4
Merton Ct. DA16 .... 7 B5
Merton Gdns. BR5 .... 37 B4
Merton Rd. ME15 .... 92 F2
Mervyn Ave. BR7 & SE9 .... 23 C6
Mervyn Stockwood House. SE9 23 C6
Mesne Way. TN14 .... 68 F7
Messent Rd. SE9 .... 5 D2
Messeter Pl. SE9 .... 6 A1
Meteor Rd. ME19 .... 88 F3
Methuen Rd. Bexley DA6 .... 7 F3
Methuen Rd. Erith DA17 .... 4 B2
Metro Ctr The. BR5 .... 38 B3
Mews The. Longfield DA3 .... 42 E6
Mews The. Maidstone ME16 .... 91 E5
Mews The. Pembury TN2 .... 150 C6
Mews The. Rochester ME2 .... 46 F7
Mews The. 5
  Royal Tunbridge Wells TN1 .... 149 B3
Mews The. Sevenoaks TN13 .... 84 A3
Meyer Rd. DA8 .... 8 D8
Micawber Cl. ME8 .... 62 A1
Michael Gdns. DA12 .... 30 E3
Michael Marshall House. SE9 .. 23 C6
Michael Tetley Hall
  (Nursery Trng Coll,
  Dr Barnardo's Home). TN2 149 D6
Michaels La. DA3 .... 56 C8
Michele Cotts. ME4 .... 32 C6
Micklefield Wadhurst Sch.
  TN5 .... 174 C4
Mickleham Cl. BR5 .... 38 A7
Mickleham Rd. BR5 .... 38 A7
Mid Comp Cotts. TN15 .... 87 E6
Mid Kent Coll (City Way Ctr).
  ME1 .... 47 E4
Mid Kent Coll of H & F Ed.
  Chatham ME1 & ME4 .... 61 E6
Mid Kent Coll of H & F Ed.
  Maidstone ME16 .... 91 E3
Mid Kent Coll of H & F Ed.
  Maidstone,Cherry Orchard ME16 . 91 C3
Mid Kent Golf Course. DA11 ... 30 B5
Mid Kent Sch for Girls. ME14 .. 92 A5
Mid Kent Sh Ctr The. ME16 ... 91 C7
Middle Field. TN3 .... 150 E8
Middle Garth. TN17 .... 169 D4
Middle La. TN15 .... 84 F6
Middle Mill Rd. ME19 .... 89 F7
Middle Park Ave. SE9 .... 22 E8
Middle Park Inf & Jun Sch.
  SE9 .... 22 D8
Middle Rd. TN3 .... 164 A5
Middle Row. 6 ME15 .... 91 F4
Middle St. 5 ME4 .... 48 A6
Middle Wlk. TN2 .... 149 E8
Middlefields. ME8 .... 64 A8
Middleham Ct. 12 DA2 .... 10 B1
Middlesex Rd. ME15 .... 107 D7
Middleton Ave. DA14 .... 24 C3
Middleton Cl. ME8 .... 63 E4
Middleton Ct. BR1 .... 22 B1
Middlings Rise. TN13 .... 83 F1
Middlings The. TN13 .... 83 F2
Middlings Wood. TN13 .... 84 A2
Midfield Ave. Bexley DA7 .... 8 C4
Midfield Ave. Hextable BR8 ... 26 B2
Midfield Way. BR5 .... 38 B8
Midhurst Cl. ME15 .... 92 A3
Midhurst Hill. DA6 .... 8 A2
Midley Cl. ME16 .... 91 C7
Midsummer Ct. SE12 .... 5 A3
Midsummer Rd. ME6 .... 74 E8
Midway The. TN4 .... 148 D2
Midwinter Cl. 3 DA16 .... 7 A4
Miers Court Cty Prim Sch. ME8 63 F7
Mierscourt Cl. ME8 .... 64 A8
Mierscourt Rd. ME8 .... 63 E6
Mike Spring Ct. DA12 .... 30 F4
Milburn Rd. ME7 .... 48 C7
Mildmay Pl. TN14 .... 68 F8
Mildred Cl. DA1 .... 10 A1
Mildred Rd. DA8 .... 4 E1
Mile La. TN17 .... 168 B8
Mile Oak Rd. TN12 .... 136 C3
Mile Stone Rd. DA2 .... 10 B1
Milebush La. TN12 .... 122 E1
Miles Pl. ME1 .... 47 D3
Milestone Sch. DA12 .... 10 B1
Milford Cl. Erith SE2 .... 7 E8
Milford Cl. Maidstone ME16 ... 91 D5
Military Rd. ME4 .... 47 F5
Milk House Cotts. TN17 .... 170 A8
Milk St. Bromley BR1 .... 22 B2
Milk St. Newham E16 .... 2 B5
Mill Bank. TN27 .... 141 C6
Mill Brook Rd. BR5 .... 38 C5
Mill Cl. Lenham ME17 .... 111 C4
Mill Cl. Rochester ME2 .... 33 B1
Mill Cotts. ME8 .... 105 B6
Mill Cres. TN9 .... 117 C2
Mill Ct. Sutton at Hone DA4 ... 41 C7
Mill Ct. 14 Woolwich SE28 ... 3 B6
Mill Hall Bsns Est The. ME20 ... 75 C2
Mill Hall Rd. New Hythe ME20 ... 75 C2
Mill Hall Rd. New Hythe ME20 ... 75 C3
Mill Hill. TN8 .... 128 D7
Mill Hill La. DA12 .... 31 D3
Mill House Cl. DA4 .... 40 E1
Mill La. Benover ME18 .... 121 A7
Mill La. Biddenden Green TN27 .. 143 A2
Mill La. Chatham,Bluebell Hill ME5 61 D1
Mill La. Chatham,Luton ME5 ... 48 C1
Mill La. Coxheath ME17 .... 106 D4
Mill La. Eynsford DA4 .... 40 E1
Mill La. Farthing Street BR6 ... 51 B1
Mill La. Frittenden TN12 & TN17 156 D8
Mill La. Hartlip ME9 .... 64 E6
Mill La. Ightham TN15 .... 86 D5
Mill La. Maidstone ME14 .... 91 F6
Mill La. Sevenoaks TN13 & TN14 .. 84 D6
Mill La. Shoreham TN14 .... 53 F1
Mill La. Sissinghurst TN17 .... 169 F8
Mill La. Snodland ME6 .... 75 B8
Mill La. Tenterden TN30 .... 173 B1
Mill La. Tonbridge TN9 .... 117 C2
Mill La. Wateringbury ME18 ... 104 D7
Mill La.
  Watt's Cross TN11 & TN15 ...... 100 C2
Mill La. West Thurrock RM16 ...... 11 D8
Mill La. Westerham TN16 .... 96 C8
Mill La. Woolwich SE18 .... 2 A1
Mill La. Yewtree Green TN12 ... 137 B1
Mill Pl. Chislehurst BR7 .... 37 B8
Mill Pl. Crayford DA1 .... 9 A3
Mill Pond Cl. TN13 .... 84 D6
Mill Pond Rd. DA1 .... 9 E1
Mill Rd. Erith DA8 .... 8 C7
Mill Rd. Gillingham ME7 .... 48 C6
Mill Rd. Hawley DA2 .... 26 F4
Mill Rd. Newham E16 .... 1 B5
Mill Rd. Northfleet DA11 .... 29 E8
Mill Rd. Purfleet RM16 .... 10 B8
Mill Rd. Rochester ME2 .... 47 B8
Mill Rd. Sevenoaks TN13 .... 83 E6
Mill St. Iden Green TN17 & TN18 180 C3
Mill St. Loose ME15 .... 106 F5
Mill St. Maidstone ME15 .... 91 F4
Mill St. Mill Street ME19 .... 89 F7
Mill St. Snodland ME6 .... 75 B8
Mill St. Westerham TN16 .... 96 D8
Mill Stone Cl. DA4 .... 41 C7
Mill Vale. BR2 .... 36 A7
Mill View. TN11 .... 102 D1
Mill Wlk. ME16 .... 91 A3
Millais Pl. RM18 .... 13 A7
Millbank Way. SE12 .... 5 A2
Millbro. BR8 .... 40 A8
Millbrook. ME19 .... 74 D1
Millbrook Ave. DA16 .... 6 D3
Millbrook Cl. ME15 .... 91 F1
Millcroft Rd. ME3 .... 16 B4
Miller Cl. DA7 .... 8 B4
Miller Rd. DA12 .... 31 A6
Miller Way. ME2 .... 33 D2
Millers Cotts. TN11 .... 134 C6
Millers Wharf. ME16 .... 91 E2
Millers Wlk. DA13 .... 58 A7
Millfield. High Halden TN26 ... 173 D7
Millfield. New Ash Green DA3 ... 56 B8
Millfield Dr. ME14 .... 91 E6
Millfield La. DA3 .... 56 E8
Millfield Rd. TN15 .... 55 D4
Millfields. ME5 .... 62 D2
Millfields Cl. BR5 .... 38 B5
Millfields Cotts. BR5 .... 38 B5
Millfordhope Rd. ME2 .... 46 C7
Millhall. ME20 .... 75 E2
Millhouse La. ME19 .... 73 D3
Millman Ct. SE3 .... 5 B7
Millpond Cl. ME2 .... 47 B8
Millpond La. TN27 & TN30 ... 172 D2
Mills Cres. TN15 .... 84 F8
Mills Rd. ME20 .... 90 E8
Mills Terr. ME4 .... 48 A3
Millside Ind Est. DA1 .... 9 D3
Millstone Terr. ME15 .... 91 E2
Millstone Mews. DA4 .... 41 C8
Millstream Ct. TN3 .... 146 D2
Millward Wlk. 14 SE18 .... 6 A8
Millwood Rd. BR5 .... 38 C6
Milne Gdns. SE9 .... 5 E2
Milne House. 15 SE18 .... 1 F2
Milner Rd. ME7 .... 48 D7
Milroy Ave. DA11 .... 29 E6
Milstead Cl. ME14 .... 92 C5
Milsted Rd. ME8 .... 49 C3
Milton Ave. Badgers Mount TN14 53 B1
Milton Ave. Cliffe Woods ME3 ... 33 B8
Milton Ave. Gravesend DA12 ... 30 C7
Milton Ct. DA12 .... 30 C6
Milton Dr. TN1 & TN2 .... 149 D7
Milton Gdns. Tilbury RM18 ... 13 B6
Milton Gdns. Tonbridge TN9 ... 132 F7
Milton Hall Rd. DA12 .... 30 D7
Milton House. DA1 .... 8 E2
Milton Lodge. 3 DA14 .... 24 A4
Milton Pl. DA12 .... 13 C1
Milton Rd. Bexley DA16 .... 6 F6
Milton Rd. Erith DA17 .... 4 A2
Milton Rd. Gillingham ME7 ... 48 C3
Milton Rd. Gravesend DA12 ... 30 C8
Milton Rd. Sevenoaks TN13 ... 83 E6
Milton Rd. Swanscombe DA10 ... 11 E1
Milton St. Maidstone ME16 ... 91 C2
Milton St. Swanscombe DA10 ... 11 D1
Milverton Way. SE9 .... 23 A4
Mimosa Cl. BR6 .... 52 C8
Mincers Cl. ME5 .... 62 C2
Mineral St. SE18 .... 2 E2
Minerva Cl. DA14 .... 23 E4
Minerva Rd. ME2 .... 47 A8
Ministry Way. SE9 .... 22 F6
Minshaw Cl. DA14 .... 23 F4
Minster Rd. Bromley BR1 .... 22 B1
Minster Rd. Gillingham ME8 ... 49 C3
Minters Orch. TN15 .... 87 B7
Miranda House. 5 DA14 .... 4 A1
Mirfield St. SE7 .... 1 D3
Miriam Ct. DA14 .... 24 B4
Miriam Rd. SE18 .... 2 E1
Mirror Path. SE12 .... 22 C5
Miskin Cotts. ME3 .... 16 B6
Miskin Rd. Dartford DA1 .... 26 D8
Miskin Rd. Hoo St Werburgh ME3 34 E5
Miskin Way. DA12 .... 30 D2
Mitchell Ave. Chatham ME4 ... 47 F2
Mitchell Ave. Northfleet DA11 ... 29 C6
Mitchell Cl. Dartford DA1 .... 26 E6
Mitchell Cl. Erith DA17 .... 4 C3
Mitchell Cl. Lenham ME17 .... 111 C5
Mitchell Cl. Woolwich SE2 .... 3 C2
Mitchell Rd. Bromley BR1 .... 36 A8
Mitchell Rd. Orpington BR6 ... 51 F6
Mitchell Wlk. Newham E6 .... 1 F8
Mitchell Wlk. Swanscombe DA10 28 E8
Mitcham Cl. TN15 .... 55 E3
Mitre Cl. 5 Erith DA17 .... 4 A2
Mitre Ct. 5 Tonbridge TN9 ... 117 C2
Mitre Rd. ME1 .... 47 B4
Moat Cl. BR6 .... 51 F4
Moat Croft. DA16 .... 7 C4
Moat Ct. Eltham SE9 .... 5 F1
Moat Ct. Sidcup DA15 .... 23 F5
Moat Farm. TN2 .... 163 A7
Moat Farm Rd. ME3 .... 18 D6
Moat La. Cowden TN8 .... 145 E7
Moat La. Erith DA8 .... 9 A6
Moat Rd. TN27 .... 141 B5
Moatbridge Sch. SE9 .... 5 D1
Mockbeggar La. TN17 & TN27 .171 C4
Model Farm Cl. SE9 .... 22 E5
Modest Cnr. TN4 .... 132 E1
Moira Rd. SE9 .... 5 F3
Molash Rd. BR5 .... 38 D5
Molehill Copse Cty Prim Sch.
  ME15 .... 107 D7
Moles Mead. TN8 .... 112 C2
Molescroft. SE9 .... 23 C5
Molescroft Way. TN9 .... 132 F7
Mollison Rise. DA12 .... 30 E3
Molyneux Almshouses. TN4 .. 148 B4
Molyneux Ct. TN4 .... 148 F4
Molyneux Park Rd. TN4 .... 148 F4
Monarch Cl. Chatham ME5 ... 62 A6
Monarch Cl. Hayes BR4 .... 50 A6
Monarch Cl. Tilbury RM18 .... 13 B5
Monarch Dr. E16 .... 1 D8
Monarch Mews. 8 DA17 .... 4 A3
Monckton's Ave. ME14 .... 91 F7
Monckton's Dr. ME14 .... 91 F7
Moncktons La. ME14 .... 91 F7
Moncrieff Cl. 4 E6 .... 1 E7
Moncrif Cl. ME14 .... 93 B4
Monds Cotts. TN14 .... 82 E3
Monica James House. 12
  DA14 .... 24 A5
Monk Dr. E16 .... 1 A6
Monk St. SE18 .... 2 A2
Monkdown. ME15 .... 93 A1
Monkreed Villas. DA3 .... 43 D4
Monks Cl. SE2 .... 3 D2
Monks La. TN5 .... 175 B8
Monks Orch. DA1 .... 26 D6
Monks Way. BR5 .... 37 D1
Monks Wlk. Southfleet DA13 ... 29 A2
Monks Wlk. 5 Tonbridge TN9 .. 133 B8
Monkton Rd. Bexley DA16 .... 6 F5
Monkton Rd. Borough Green TN15 86 F7
Monkwood Cl. ME1 .... 61 B8
Monmouth Cl. Bexley DA16 ... 7 A3
Monmouth Cl. Gillingham ME8 ... 49 D2
Mons Way. BR2 .... 36 E3
Monson Rd. TN1 .... 149 B4
Monson Way. 5 TN1 .... 149 B4
Montacute Gdns. TN2 .... 148 F2
Montacute Rd. TN2 .... 149 A1
Montague Cl. BR8 .... 39 F5
Montague Terr. 1 BR2 .... 36 A5
Montbelle Prim Sch. SE9 .... 23 B5
Montbelle Rd. SE9 .... 23 B5
Montbretia Cl. BR5 .... 38 C5
Montcalm Cl. BR2 .... 36 A3
Montcalm Rd. SE7 .... 5 D7
Monteith Cl. TN3 .... 148 A3
Monterey Cl. DA5 .... 25 C6
Montfort Cl. Chatham ME5 ... 61 F2
Montfort Rd. Kemsing TN15 ... 69 E2
Montfort Rd. Rochester ME2 ... 47 A8
Montgomery Ave. ME5 .... 62 A7
Montgomery Cl. DA15 .... 6 F1
Montgomery Rd. Gillingham ME7 48 C3
Montgomery Rd.
  Royal Tunbridge Wells TN4 ... 149 B7
Montgomery Rd.
  South Darenth DA4 .... 41 D8
Montpelier Ave. DA5 .... 24 D8
Montpelier Gate. ME16 .... 91 B5
Montreal Rd. Sevenoaks TN13 ... 83 E4
Montreal Rd. Tilbury RM18 ... 13 A5
Montrose Ave. Bexley DA16 ... 6 E4
Montrose Ave. Chatham ME5 ... 48 E2
Montrose Ave. Sidcup DA15 ... 24 A8
Montrose Cl. DA16 .... 6 F4
Monypenny. TN17 .... 181 F3
Moon Cl. SE12 .... 5 A3
Moon's La. TN18 .... 128 A1
Moonstone Dr. ME5 .... 62 B2
Moor Hill. TN18 .... 184 F8
Moor La. TN8 .... 128 A4
Moor Park Cl. ME8 .... 64 A8
Moor Rd The. TN14 .... 84 C7
Moor St. ME8 .... 64 B8
Moor The. TN18 .... 184 F8
Moorcroft Gdns. BR1 .... 36 E4
Moorden La. TN11 .... 115 A1
Moordown. SE18 .... 6 B6
Moore Ave. Grays RM16 .... 11 E8
Moore Ave. Tilbury RM18 .... 13 B5
Moore Rd. DA10 .... 11 E1
Moore St. ME2 .... 47 A8
Moorfield Rd. BR6 .... 38 A2
Moorhead Way. SE3 .... 5 B4
Moorhouse Rd. RH8 .... 96 A6
Mooring Rd. ME1 .... 47 D1
Moorings The. E16 .... 1 C8
Moorside Rd. BR1 .... 22 A4
Morants Court Cross. TN14 ... 68 C1
Morants Court Rd. TN13 & TN14 83 C8
Morden Rd. SE3 .... 5 A5
Morden Road Mews. SE3 .... 5 A5
Morden St. ME1 .... 61 C8
More Park RC Prim Sch. ME19 89 D8
Morel Cl. TN13 .... 84 B5
Morella Wlk. ME17 .... 111 C5
Morello Cl. BR8 .... 39 D5
Morement Rd. ME3 .... 34 D6
Moreton Almshouses. TN16 ... 81 D1
Moreton Cl. BR1 .... 8 E4
Morewood Cl. TN13 .... 83 F4
Morgan Dr. DA2 .... 27 E8
Morgan Rd. BR1 .... 22 A1
Morgan St. E16 .... 1 A8
Morhen Cl. ME6 .... 74 E7
Morland Ave. DA1 .... 9 B2
Morland Dr. Lamberhurst TN3 .. 166 B5
Morland Dr. Rochester ME2 ... 33 A1
Morley Cl. BR6 .... 51 B8
Morley Dr. TN12 .... 153 A6
Morley Rd. Chislehurst BR7 ... 37 C8
Morley Rd. Tonbridge TN9 ... 117 C1
Morley's Rd. TN14 .... 99 D2
Morne Cotts. TN14 .... 68 F8
Morning Cross Cotts. ME3 ... 16 B4
Mornington Ave. BR1 .... 36 D6
Mornington Cl. DA5 .... 25 D7
Morris Cl. East Malling ME19 ... 74 F1
Morris Cl. Orpington BR6 .... 51 E7
Morris Gdns. DA1 .... 10 A2
Morry La. ME17 .... 125 D7
Morstan Gdns. SE9 .... 22 F4
Mortimer Rd. Erith DA8 .... 8 D8
Mortimer Rd. Orpington BR6 ... 38 A1
Mortimers Ave. ME3 .... 33 A8
Mortlake Rd. E16 .... 1 B7
Morton Cl. BR8 .... 39 E7
Morvale Cl. DA17 .... 3 F2
Mosquito Rd. ME19 .... 88 F3
Mossbank. ME5 .... 62 A3
Mossdown Cl. DA17 .... 4 A2
Mosslea Rd. Bromley BR2 .... 36 B4
Mosslea Rd. Orpington BR6 ... 51 C7
Mossy Glade. ME8 .... 63 C6
Mostyn Rd. ME14 .... 92 C4
Mosul Way. BR2 .... 36 E3
Mosyer Dr. BR5 & BR6 .... 52 D8
Mote Ave. ME15 .... 92 B3
Mote Cotts. TN15 .... 101 A7
Mote Pk. ME15 .... 92 C4
Mote Rd. Ivy Hatch TN15 & TN11 101 A7
Mote Rd. Maidstone ME15 .... 92 A3
Mote The. DA3 .... 56 F8
Motherwell Way. RM16 .... 11 A8
Mottingham Ct. SE9 .... 22 F7
Mottingham Gdns. SE9 .... 22 D7
Mottingham La. Eltham SE12 ... 22 C8
Mottingham La.
  Lewisham SE12 & SE9 .... 22 C7
Mottingham Prim Sch. SE9 ... 22 F5
Mottingham Rd. SE9 .... 22 F5
Mottingham Sta. SE9 .... 22 F7
Mottisfont Rd. SE2 .... 3 B2
Mouat Ct. ME5 .... 62 A3
Moultain Hill. BR8 .... 40 A5
Mound The. SE9 .... 23 A5
Mount Ave. ME18 .... 105 A1
Mount Cl. Bromley BR1 .... 36 E6
Mount Cl. Sevenoaks TN13 ... 83 F4
Mount Culver Ave. DA14 .... 24 D2
Mount Dr. Bexley DA6 .... 7 E2
Mount Dr. Maidstone ME14 ... 93 A6
Mount Edgcumbe Rd. TN4 ... 149 A3
Mount Ephraim. TN1 & TN4 ... 149 A4
Mount Ephraim Ct. TN4 .... 148 F4
Mount Ephraim Rd. TN1 .... 149 A4
Mount Harry Rd. TN13 .... 84 B4
Mount La. Hartlip ME9 .... 64 D4
Mount La. Maidstone ME14 ... 93 A6
Mount Lodge. ME1 .... 47 B2
Mount Pleasant. Aylesford ME20 76 A3
Mount Pleasant. Gillingham ME4 48 B3
Mount Pleasant.
  Hildenborough TN11 .... 116 D6
Mount Pleasant.
  Hook Green TN12 .... 165 C6
Mount Pleasant. Ide Hill TN14 ... 97 F4
Mount Pleasant.
  Paddock Wood TN12 .... 135 F6
Mount Pleasant.
  Sparrow's Green TN5 .... 174 E5
Mount Pleasant.
  Tenterden TN30 .... 183 C8
Mount Pleasant Ave. 2 TN2 .. 149 B3
Mount Pleasant Cl. TN11 .... 116 D6
Mount Pleasant Dr. ME14 .... 93 A5
Mount Pleasant La. ME3 .... 166 A6
Mount Pleasant Rd. Dartford DA1 9 F1
Mount Pleasant Rd.
  R Tunbridge Wells TN1 & TN2 .. 149 A3
Mount Pleasant Rd.
  Sevenoaks Weald TN14 .... 99 B2
Mount Pleasant Terr. ME17 ... 110 E2
Mount Pleasant Wlk. DA5 .... 7 F2
Mount Rd. Bexley DA6 .... 7 E2
Mount Rd. Chatham ME4 .... 47 F2
Mount Rd. Crayford DA1 .... 8 F1
Mount Rd. Rochester ME1 .... 47 B2
Mount Sion. TN1 .... 149 A2
Mount The. DA6 .... 8 B2
Mountain Cl. TN15 .... 71 F3
Mountbatten Ave. Chatham ME5 62 A7
Mountbatten Ave. Higham ME3 . 32 C4
Mountbatten Cl. SE18 .... 6 E8
Mountfield. TN15 .... 87 A7
Mountfield Cl. DA13 .... 57 F2
Mountfield Ct. 4 TN1 .... 149 B3
Mountfield Gdns. TN2 .... 149 B3
Mountfield Pk. TN2 .... 133 C8
Mountfield Rd. TN2 .... 149 B3
Mountfield Way. 1 BR5 .... 38 C5
Mounthurst Rd. BR2 .... 36 A2
Mountjoy Cl. SE2 .... 3 B4
Mounts Hill. TN17 .... 180 B7
Mounts La. TN17 .... 182 A3
Mounts Rd. DA9 .... 11 B1
Mountsfield Cl. ME16 .... 91 D5
Mountview Rd. BR6 .... 38 A2
Moyle Cl. ME8 .... 63 D4
Mozart Ct. ME4 .... 47 E3
Muir Rd. ME15 .... 92 A2
Muir St. E16 .... 1 E5
Mulbarton Ct. BR7 .... 23 D2
Mulberry Cl. Gillingham ME7 ... 63 A4
Mulberry Cl. Greenwich SE7 ... 5 C8
Mulberry Cl. Meopham Sta DA13 44 B3
Mulberry Cl.
  Royal Tunbridge Wells TN2 ... 133 D1
Mulberry Rd. DA11 .... 29 E4
Mulberry Way. DA17 .... 4 C4
Mulgrave House. 20 SE18 .... 1 F2
Mulgrave Prim Sch. SE18 .... 2 A2
Mullein Cl. 6 RM17 .... 12 D8
Mullender Ct. DA12 .... 31 A7
Muller House. SE18 .... 2 A1
Multon Rd. TN15 .... 55 E4
Munday Bois Cotts. TN27 .... 143 F8
Munday Bois Rd. TN27 .... 127 E1
Munday Rd. E16 .... 1 A6
Munday Works Est. TN9 .... 117 C1
Munford Dr. DA10 .... 28 E8
Mungeam House. ME1 .... 47 C4
Mungo Park Rd. DA12 .... 30 D3
Mungo Park Way. BR5 .... 38 D2
Munn's La. ME9 .... 64 E6
Munnery Way. BR6 .... 51 B8
Murchison Ave. DA5 .... 24 E7
Murrain Dr. ME15 .... 93 A1
Murray Ave. BR1 .... 36 B7
Murray Bsns Ctr. BR5 .... 38 B6
Murray House. 21 SE18 .... 1 F2
Murray Rd. Rochester ME2 .... 47 C8
Murray Rd. St Paul's Cray BR5 .... 38 B6
Murray Sq. E16 .... 1 B6
Murton-Neale Cl. 3 TN18 .... 179 A2
Muscovy House. 3 SE28 .... 3 E4
Museum of Kent Rural Life.
  ME14 .... 76 D1
Museum St. ME14 .... 91 F4
Musket Ct. Eyhorne Street ME17 . 94 B2
Musket La. Silver Hill ME17 .... 94 A2
Mussenden La. DA3 & DA4 ... 41 E3
Mustang Rd. ME19 .... 88 F3
Mycenae Rd. SE3 .... 5 A8
Mynn Cres. ME14 .... 93 A4
Myra St. SE2 .... 3 A2
Myrtle Alley. SE18 .... 2 A3
Myrtle Cl. DA8 .... 8 E6
Myrtle Cres. ME5 .... 61 F5
Myrtle Pl. DA2 .... 27 D8
Myrtle Rd. DA1 .... 26 D6
Myrtledene Rd. SE2 .... 3 A1

Nadine St. SE7 .... 1 C1
Nag's Head La. Bexley DA16 ... 7 B4
Nag's Head La. Chatham ME1 ... 47 D4
Nagpur House. 4 ME15 .... 107 E5
Nairn Ct. RM18 .... 12 F5
Nansen Rd. DA12 .... 30 D4
Napier Ct. Lewisham SE12 .... 22 B5
Napier Ct. Maidstone ME14 ... 91 F7
Napier Cty Prim Sch. ME7 .... 48 D4
Napier Rd. Bromley BR2 .... 36 B5
Napier Rd. Erith DA17 .... 3 F2
Napier Rd. Gillingham ME7 .... 48 D4
Napier Rd. Northfleet DA11 .... 29 F7
Napier Rd.
  Royal Tunbridge Wells TN2 ... 149 D2
Napoleon Dr. TN12 .... 138 D5
Napoleon Wlk. ME17 .... 111 C5
Napwood Cl. ME8 .... 63 D6
Nares Rd. ME8 .... 63 D4
Narrow Way. BR2 .... 36 E3
Naseby Ct. DA14 .... 23 F4
Nash Bank. DA13 .... 43 F7
Nash Cl. ME5 .... 62 C2
Nash Croft. DA11 .... 29 E4
Nash Gn. BR1 .... 22 A2
Nash La. BR2 .... 50 A4
Nash St. DA13 .... 44 A7
Nashenden Farm La. ME1 .... 61 A8
Nashenden La. ME1 .... 46 F1
Nassau Path. 6 SE28 .... 3 C5
Natal Rd. ME4 .... 48 A3
Nathan Way. SE28 & SE18 .... 2 E3
National Sea Trng Coll. DA12 .. 14 A1
Naylor's Cotts. ME7 .... 63 B1
Neal Rd. TN15 .... 55 E5
Neale St. ME4 .... 48 A3
Neath Ct. 2 ME15 .... 107 E8
Neatscourt Rd. E16 .... 1 B6
Neills Rd. TN3 .... 165 D2
Nellington Ct. TN4 .... 148 B4
Nellington Rd. TN3 & TN4 .... 148 B4

Nelson Ave. TN9 .... 117 A1
Nelson House. **5**
  Park Wood ME15 .... 107 F5
Nelson House. Swanscombe DA9 11 D2
Nelson Mandela Rd. SE3 .... 5 C4
Nelson Pl. DA14 .... 24 A4
Nelson Rd. Bromley BR2 .... 36 C5
Nelson Rd. Dartford DA1 .... 9 C1
Nelson Rd. Erith DA17 .... 3 F1
Nelson Rd. Gillingham ME7 ..... 48 D4
Nelson Rd. Northfleet DA11 .... 29 F6
Nelson Rd.
  Royal Tunbridge Wells TN2 .... 149 D2
Nelson Rd. Sidcup DA14 .... 24 A4
Nelson Rd. Wouldham ME1 ...... 60 C5
Nelson Terr. ME5 .... 48 C1
Nepicar La. TN15 .... 72 D3
Neptune Bsns Pk. ME2 .... 47 E7
Neptune Cl. ME2 .... 47 E7
Neptune Wlk. DA8 .... 4 D2
Nesbit Rd. SE9 .... 5 D3
Nesbitt House. DA6 .... 8 B2
Ness Rd. DA8 .... 9 D8
Nestor Ct. ME18 .... 105 A8
Nethercombe House. **4** SE3 .. 5 A8
Nethewode Ct. DA17 .... 4 B2
Netley Cl. ME14 .... 92 D6
Nettlestead La. ME18 .... 104 A6
Nevill Cl. ME19 .... 74 C1
Nevill Gate. TN2 .... 149 B1
Nevill Golf Course. TN2 & TN3 163 D7
Nevill Lodge. TN2 .... 149 C4
Nevill Pk. TN4 .... 148 E3
Nevill Pl. ME6 .... 75 A7
Nevill Rd. ME6 .... 75 A7
Nevill Ridge. TN4 .... 148 D3
Nevill St. TN1 & TN2 .... 149 A2
Nevill Terr. TN2 .... 148 F2
Neville Cl. Maidstone ME14 ... 92 B8
Neville Cl. Sidcup DA15 .... 23 F4
Neville Rd. ME4 .... 47 E2
New Ash Green Cty Prim Sch.
  DA3 .... 56 F8
New Ash Jun & Inf Sch. DA3 .. 42 F1
New Barn Pk. BR8 .... 39 E8
New Barn Rd.
  Hawkenbury ME17 .... 124 E2
New Barn Rd.
  Northfleet Green DA13 .... 29 C3
New Barn Rd. Swanley BR8 .... 39 F8
New Barn St. E13 .... 1 B8
New Barns Rd. ME14 .... 92 A8
New Bassetts Cotts. TN12 .... 153 B5
New Beacon Sch The. TN13 .... 99 A8
New Cotts. Bean DA2 .... 28 B5
New Cotts. Shipbourne TN11 .. 101 D5
New Cotts. Shorne DA12 .... 31 E5
New Covenant Pl. ME1 .... 47 D4
New Ct. **2** TN9 .... 117 C2
New Cut. Chatham ME4 .... 47 F4
New Cut. Dean Street ME15 ... 106 D7
New Cut Rd. ME14 .... 92 D5
New Delhi House. **5** ME15 .. 107 E5
New Eltham Sta. SE9 .... 23 C7
New England Rd. TN4 .... 149 A7
New Farm Ave. BR2 .... 36 A5
New Hall Farm La. ME3 .... 19 B6
New House La. DA11 .... 30 A6
New Hythe La. ME20 .... 75 B3
New Hythe Sta. ME20 .... 75 C4
New Inn Cotts. ME15 .... 106 C7
New Lydenburg Commercial Est.
  E16 .... 1 C3
New Lydenburg St. SE7 .... 1 C3
New Mill Rd. BR5 .... 38 C8
New Pond Rd. TN17 .... 180 D6
New Pound La. ME18 .... 88 C1
New Rd. Bexley DA16 .... 7 B5
New Rd. Burham ME1 .... 60 F1
New Rd. Chatham ME4 .... 47 D4
New Rd. Chatham ME4 .... 47 F4
New Rd. Cliffe ME3 .... 16 A4
New Rd. Cranbrook TN17 ...... 169 B4
New Rd. Ditton ME19 & ME20 .. 75 C1
New Rd. East Malling ME19 ... 90 A8
New Rd. Egerton TN27 .... 127 F3
New Rd. Erith SE2 .... 3 D1
New Rd. Gravesend DA11 .... 13 B1
New Rd. Grays RM17 .... 12 A8
New Rd. Grays RM17 .... 12 B8
New Rd. Headcorn TN27 ...... 141 D5
New Rd. Hextable BR8 .... 25 F1
New Rd. Langley ME17 .... 108 C5
New Rd. Meopham Station DA13 43 F4
New Rd. Orpington BR6 .... 38 A2
New Rd. Paddock Wood TN12 .. 136 A6
New Rd. Saint's Hill TN11 .... 131 A1
New Rd. South Darenth DA4 ... 41 D7
New Rd. Sundridge TN14 .... 82 E2
New Rd. Swanley BR8 .... 39 F6
New Road Ave. ME4 .... 47 E4
New Road Cty Prim Sch. ME4 .. 48 A3
New Road Hill. BR2 & BR6 .... 50 F2
New St. Chatham ME4 .... 47 E3
New St. New Street TN15 .... 57 D4
New St. Westerham TN16 .... 96 C8
New Street Hill. BR1 .... 22 C3
New Street Rd. DA13 & TN15 .. 57 C6
New Strs. ME4 .... 47 F6
New Swan Yd. **7** DA11 .... 13 B1
New Villas. ME15 .... 106 C7
New Wharf Rd. TN9 .... 117 B1
New Wlk. TN15 .... 71 F3
New Years La. BR6 & TN14 ... 67 A5
Newark Ct. **1** ME4 .... 47 B7

Newark Knok. E6 .... 2 A8
Newark Yd. ME2 .... 47 B7
Newbarn La. TN14 & TN16 ..... 66 C2
Newborough Ct. TN10 .... 117 C6
Newbury Ave. ME15 .... 91 C6
Newbury Cl. ME3 .... 33 B8
Newbury Cotts. TN5 .... 175 B8
Newbury Ct. DA14 .... 23 F4
Newbury La. TN5 .... 175 C8
Newbury Rd. BR2 .... 36 A6
Newchurch Rd. ME15 .... 92 A1
Newcomen Rd. TN4 .... 149 A5
Newenden Cl. ME14 .... 92 D6
Newenden Rd. ME2 .... 33 C2
Newham Coll of FE
  (Royal Docks Campus). E16 ..... 2 C5
Newham Way. E13 .... 1 B8
Newhaven Gdns. SE9 .... 5 D3
Newhaven La. **4** E16 .... 1 A8
Newhouse Terr. TN8 .... 112 C3
Newick Cl. DA5 .... 8 B1
Newing Gn. BR1 .... 22 D1
Newington CE Prim Sch. ME9 . 65 B7
Newington Ct. TN5 .... 176 E1
Newington Ent Ctr. ME9 .... 65 C8
Newington House. **9** BR5 .. 38 D1
Newington Ind Est. ME9 .... 64 F6
Newington Wlk. ME14 .... 92 C6
Newitt Rd. ME3 .... 34 E5
Newland Green La. TN27 ..... 143 D8
Newland St. E16 .... 1 F5
Newlands. TN3 .... 148 A3
Newlands Cl. **8** SE9 .... 6 A1
Newlands La. ME3 .... 33 C8
Newlands Rd. TN4 .... 149 B7
Newlands Rise. TN4 .... 149 A6
Newlands Way. TN4 .... 149 B7
Newling Cl. E6 .... 1 F7
Newlyn Ct. **1** ME14 .... 92 A4
Newlyn Dr. TN12 .... 139 F5
Newlyn Rd. DA16 .... 6 F5
Newman Rd. BR1 .... 36 A8
Newman's Rd. DA11 .... 29 F6
Newmarket Gn. SE9 .... 22 D8
Newnham Cl. ME8 .... 49 C2
Newnham Lodge. DA17 .... 4 A1
Newnhams Cl. BR1 .... 36 F2
Newports. BR8 .... 39 D2
Newstead Ave. BR6 .... 51 E8
Newstead Woods Sch for Girls.
  BR6 .... 51 D7
Newton Abbot Rd. DA11 .... 29 F6
Newton Ave. TN10 .... 117 E7
Newton Cl. Chatham ME5 .... 62 C2
Newton Cl. **1** Maidstone ME16 . 91 E3
Newton Gdns. TN12 .... 135 F7
Newton Rd. Bexley DA16 .... 7 A4
Newton Rd.
  Royal Tunbridge Wells TN1 .. 149 B4
Newton Rd. Tilbury RM18 ...... 13 A5
Newton Terr. BR2 .... 36 D3
Newton Willows. TN3 .... 161 C7
Newton's Ct. DA9 .... 10 D3
Newtown Cotts. TN12 .... 139 E6
Nichol La. BR1 .... 22 A1
Nicholas Cl. ME16 .... 91 A3
Nicholas Ct. SE12 .... 22 A7
Nicholas Stacey House. **3** SE7 . 1 B1
Nicholson House. SE18 .... 5 E7
Nickelby Cl. SE28 .... 3 C7
Nicklaus Dr. ME5 .... 61 F3
Nickleby Cl. ME1 .... 47 C2
Nickleby Rd. DA12 .... 31 A7
Nicola Terr. DA7 .... 7 E6
Nicolson Rd. BR5 .... 38 D2
Nicolson Way. TN13 .... 84 D5
Nigeria Rd. SE7 .... 5 D7
Nightingale Cl. Gillingham ME8 . 63 E6
Nightingale Cl. Larkfield ME20 . 74 F2
Nightingale Cl. Northfleet DA11 . 29 E4
Nightingale Cnr. BR5 .... 38 D5
Nightingale Gr. **4** DA1 .... 10 A3
Nightingale House. SE18 .... 2 A1
Nightingale La. Bromley BR1 .. 36 D7
Nightingale La.
  Goathurst Common TN14 ...... 98 B5
Nightingale Pl. SE18 .... 6 B8
Nightingale Prim Sch. SE18 ..... 2 B1
Nightingale Rd. Kemsing TN14 . 69 E2
Nightingale Rd. Orpington BR5 . 37 C3
Nightingale Vale. SE18 .... 6 A8
Nightingale Way. Newham E6 ... 1 E8
Nightingale Way. Swanley BR8 . 39 E6
Nightingales The.
  Royal Tunbridge Wells TN4 .. 149 A5
Nightingales The.
  Sissinghurst TN17 .... 170 F8
Nile Path. **6** SE18 .... 6 B8
Nile Rd. ME7 .... 48 C4
Nine Acres Rd. ME2 .... 46 B3
Nine Acres Sch. SE18 .... 2 D1
Nine Elms Gr. DA11 .... 30 A8
Nineveh La. TN17 & TN18 .... 179 E6
Ninhams Wood. BR6 .... 51 A6
Nita Ct. SE12 .... 22 A7
Nithdale Rd. SE18 .... 6 C7
Nizels La. TN11 .... 115 F8
No 1 St. SE18 .... 2 B3
No 2 St. SE18 .... 2 B3
Noah's Ark. TN15 .... 70 B1
Noble Tree Cross. TN11 .... 116 B6
Noble Tree Rd. TN11 .... 116 B6
Nook The. ME18 .... 104 F2
Norah La. ME3 .... 32 B3
Nordenfeldt Rd. DA8 .... 4 D1

Nore Cl. ME7 .... 48 E1
Norfield Rd. DA2 & DA5 .... 25 D3
Norfolk Cl. Chatham ME5 .... 62 C3
Norfolk Cl. Dartford DA1 .... 10 A1
Norfolk Cl. Gillingham ME8 .... 49 D2
Norfolk Cres. DA15 .... 23 E8
Norfolk Gdns. DA7 .... 7 F6
Norfolk Pl. DA16 .... 7 A5
Norfolk Rd. Gravesend DA12 .. 30 D8
Norfolk Rd. Maidstone ME15 .. 107 C8
Norfolk Rd.
  Royal Tunbridge Wells TN1 .. 149 B2
Norfolk Rd. Tonbridge TN9 ... 117 A1
Norham Ct. **11** DA2 .... 10 B1
Norlands Cres. BR7 .... 37 B8
Norman Cl. Gillingham ME8 .... 63 B5
Norman Cl. Kemsing TN14 ..... 69 D2
Norman Cl. Maidstone ME14 .. 92 B6
Norman Cl. Orpington BR6 ..... 51 C7
Norman Rd. Dartford DA1 ...... 26 E7
Norman Rd. Erith DA17 .... 4 B3
Norman Rd. Erith DA17 .... 4 B5
Norman Rd. New Town ME19 .. 89 B8
Norman Rd.
  Royal Tunbridge Wells TN1 .. 149 B5
Norman Rd. Snodland ME6 ..... 75 A6
Norman Rise. TN17 .... 169 D4
Norman St. TN14 .... 97 F5
Norman Villas. **4** TN18 ..... 178 F4
Normandy Prim Sch. DA7 .... 8 D6
Normandy Terr. E16 .... 1 B7
Normandy Way. DA7 & DA8 ..... 8 E6
Normanhurst Ave. DA16 .... 7 D6
Normanhurst Rd.
  Borough Green TN15 .... 87 A7
Normanhurst Rd.
  St Paul's Cray BR5 .... 38 B7
Normans Cl. DA11 .... 30 A8
Norreys Rd. ME8 .... 63 E7
Norrington Rd. ME15 .... 107 B6
Norris Way. DA1 .... 8 F4
Norstead Gdns. TN4 .... 149 B7
Norsted La. BR6 .... 67 B8
North Ash Rd. DA3 .... 56 F7
North Bank Cl. ME2 .... 46 F5
North Beckton Prim Sch. E16 ... 1 F8
North Borough Cty Jun Sch.
  ME14 .... 92 A6
North Cl. DA6 .... 7 D3
North Cray Prim Schs. DA14 .. 24 E2
North Cray Rd.
  North Cray DA5 & DA14 .... 25 A6
North Cray Rd. Sidcup DA14 ... 24 E4
North Cres. ME17 .... 106 D4
North Dane Way. ME5 .... 62 C4
North Down. TN12 .... 139 E4
North Downs Bsns Pk. TN14 .. 68 C3
North Downs Terr. ME19 .... 73 A5
North End La. BR6 .... 51 B2
North End Trad Est. DA8 .... 8 E6
North Farm La.
  Royal Tunbridge Wells TN2 .. 133 E2
North Farm La.
  Royal Tunbridge Wells
  TN1 & TN2 .... 149 D8
North Farm Rd. TN1 & TN4 ... 149 C8
North Folly Rd. ME15 .... 105 F3
North Glade. DA5 .... 24 F7
North Hill Rd. TN18 .... 178 C1
North Kent Ave. DA11 .... 12 C1
North Lockside Rd. ME4 .... 48 D8
North Meadow. ME19 .... 88 D7
North Pasley Rd. ME4 .... 48 B7
North Pk. SE9 .... 6 A1
North Pole La. BR2 .... 50 A4
North Pole Rd.
  ME16 & ME8 & ME19 .... 90 C2
North Pondside Rd. ME4 .... 48 A8
North Rd. Bromley BR1 .... 36 B8
North Rd. Cliffe ME3 .... 16 B6
North Rd. Dartford DA1 .... 9 A1
North Rd. Erith DA17 .... 4 B4
North Rd. Gillingham ME4 & ME7 . 48 A7
North Rd. Goudhurst TN17 ... 153 E1
North Rd. Woolwich SE18 .... 2 E1
North Riding. DA3 .... 43 D6
North Side Three Rd. ME4 ..... 48 C8
North St. Bexley DA7 .... 8 A3
North St. Biddenden TN27 .... 158 A2
North St. Bromley BR1 .... 36 A8
North St. Cowden TN8 .... 145 A6
North St. Dartford DA1 .... 26 D8
North St. Gravesend DA11 ..... 30 B8
North St. Headcorn TN27 ..... 141 C5
North St. Maidstone ME16 ..... 90 F2
North St. Rochester ME2 .... 47 B7
North St.
  Royal Tunbridge Wells TN2 .. 149 C3
North St. Sutton Valence ME17 . 124 E8
North Terr. ME3 .... 33 F6
North View. ME15 .... 92 B1
North View Ave. RM18 .... 13 A6
North View Cotts. ME15 ...... 106 C7
North View Rd. TN13 .... 84 C6
North Way. ME14 .... 92 B7
North West Kent Coll of Tech.
  DA12 .... 30 F7
North Woolwich Rd. E16 .... 1 B5
North Woolwich Rdbt. E16 ...... 1 D5
North Woolwich Sta. E16 .... 2 A4
Northall Rd. DA7 .... 8 C5
Northbourne. BR2 .... 36 A2
Northbourne Rd. ME8 .... 49 B4
Northcote Rd. Gravesend DA11 . 29 F7
Northcote Rd. Rochester ME2 . 47 A7

Northcote Rd. Sidcup DA14 .... 23 E4
Northcote Rd. **2** Tonbridge TN9117 B1
Northcourt Cty Prim Sch. DA12 30 E7
Northdown. ME9 .... 79 D8
Northdown Cl. Maidstone ME14 . 92 B7
Northdown Cl.
  Paddock Wood TN12 .... 135 F6
Northdown Rd. Bexley DA16 ... 7 C8
Northdown Rd. Kemsing TN14 . 69 E2
Northdown Rd. Longfield DA3 .. 42 E7
Northdown View. ME17 .... 110 F6
Northend Prim Sch. DA8 .... 8 F6
Northend Rd. DA8 .... 8 F6
Northesk House. **6** ME1 ..... 47 C6
Northgrove Rd. **9** TN18 .... 178 F2
Northiam Sta. TN31 .... 187 C2
Northlands Ave. BR6 .... 51 E6
Northlands Cotts. TN32 .... 185 C1
Northleigh Cl. ME15 .... 107 A6
Northolme Rise. BR6 .... 51 E8
Northover. BR1 .... 22 A4
Northpoint Bsns Est. ME2 ..... 47 D8
Northridge Rd. DA12 .... 30 C5
Northside Rd. BR1 .... 36 A8
Northumberland Ave.
  Bexley DA16 .... 6 E4
Northumberland Ave.
  Gillingham ME8 .... 49 E1
Northumberland Cl. DA8 .... 8 C7
Northumberland Ct. ME15 .... 107 D7
Northumberland Gdns. BR1 ... 37 A5
Northumberland Heath Inf Sch.
  DA8 .... 8 B7
Northumberland Heath Jun Sch.
  DA8 .... 8 C7
Northumberland Pk. DA8 .... 8 C7
Northumberland Rd.
  Istead Rise DA13 .... 29 F1
Northumberland Rd.
  Maidstone ME15 .... 107 D8
Northumberland Rd. Newham E6 1 E7
Northumberland Way. DA7 & DA8 8 D6
Northview. BR8 .... 39 E7
Northward Hill Nature Reserve.
  ME23 .... 17 E5
Northwood Ave. ME23 .... 17 E4
Northwood Pl. DA18 .... 3 F3
Northwood Prim Sch. DA18 ..... 3 F3
Northwood Rd. TN10 .... 117 C6
Norton Cres. TN10 .... 117 B7
Norton Gr. ME5 .... 61 E3
Norton House. **8** SE18 .... 2 A2
Norton Rd. Five Wents ME17 .. 108 D1
Norton Rd.
  Royal Tunbridge Wells TN4 .. 133 A1
Nortons La. TN27 & TN30 .... 172 E5
Nortons Way. TN12 .... 135 B7
Norvic House. DA8 .... 8 F7
Norway Terr. **4** ME14 .... 92 A7
Norwich Ave. TN10 .... 117 D5
Norwich Cl. ME2 .... 46 D6
Norwich Pl. **7** DA6 .... 8 A3
Norwood Cl. ME3 .... 16 B4
Norwood Ct. **6** DA1 .... 10 A3
Norwood La. DA13 .... 44 B8
Notre Dame RC Prim Sch. SE18 . 6 B8
Nottidge Rd. TN4 .... 148 D1
Nottingham Ave.
  Maidstone ME15 .... 107 D7
Nottingham Ave. Newham E16 .. 1 C7
Nottingham Wlk. ME2 .... 46 D6
Novar Cl. BR6 .... 37 F2
Novar Rd. SE9 .... 23 C7
Nower The. TN14 .... 81 F8
Nuffield Hospl. TN2 .... 149 C3
Nuffield Rd. BR8 .... 26 A2
Nugent Ind Pk. BR5 .... 38 C5
Nunnery Cl. ME1 .... 47 C1
Nunnington Cl. SE9 .... 22 E5
Nursery Ave. Bexley DA7 .... 7 F4
Nursery Ave. Maidstone ME16 . 91 B6
Nursery Ave.
  Maidstone,Bearsted ME14 .... 93 B3
Nursery Cl. Dartford DA2 .... 27 C8
Nursery Cl. Orpington BR6 .... 38 A2
Nursery Cl. Sevenoaks TN13 .. 84 C5
Nursery Cl. Swanley BR8 .... 39 C7
Nursery Cl. Tonbridge TN10 .. 117 E7
Nursery Cl. Union Street TN5 . 177 B3
Nursery Gdns. BR7 .... 23 B2
Nursery Pl. TN13 .... 83 D4
Nursery Rd. Ditton ME20 .... 75 C1
Nursery Rd. Gillingham ME8 ... 63 D8
Nursery Rd.
  Meopham Station DA13 .... 44 A4
Nursery Rd. Paddock Wood TN12 135 F8
Nursery Rd.
  Royal Tunbridge Wells TN4 .. 149 B8
Nursery The. Erith DA8 .... 8 F7
Nursery The. Westerham TN16 . 96 C8
Nurstead Ave. DA3 .... 43 D6
Nurstead Church La. DA13 ..... 44 A5
Nurstead La. DA3 .... 43 D5
Nurstead Rd. DA8 .... 8 A7
Nut Tree Cl. ME6 .... 52 D7
Nutfield Cl. ME5 .... 62 B8
Nutfield Way. BR6 .... 51 B8
Nutfields. TN15 .... 86 B4

Nuthatch. DA3 .... 43 B7
Nuthatch Gdns. SE28 .... 2 D4
Nutley Cl. BR8 .... 39 F8
Nutmead Cl. DA5 .... 25 C7
Nutwood Cl. ME14 .... 92 E4
Nuxley Rd. DA17 .... 4 A1
NW Kent Coll of Tech. DA1 .... 26 D8
Nyanza St. SE18 .... 6 D8

O'Neill Path. **11** SE18 .... 6 A8
Oak Ave. Gillingham ME7 .... 48 E6
Oak Ave. Sevenoaks TN13 ..... 99 B7
Oak Cl. Crayford DA1 .... 8 F3
Oak Cl. Hoo St Werburgh ME3 . 34 E3
Oak Cotts. TN8 .... 113 B6
Oak Dr. Higham ME3 .... 32 B4
Oak Dr. Larkfield ME20 .... 75 B2
Oak End Cl. TN4 .... 133 A2
Oak Farm Gdns. TN27 .... 141 D6
Oak Farm La. TN15 .... 57 E1
Oak Hill Rd. TN13 .... 84 A2
Oak House. **6** Chatham ME5 . 61 F4
Oak House. Sidcup DA15 .... 24 A5
Oak La. Headcorn TN27 .... 141 D5
Oak La. Moor Street ME8 & ME9 . 64 D8
Oak La. Sevenoaks TN13 .... 99 A8
Oak Lodge La. TN16 .... 81 D2
Oak Rd.
  Erith,Northumberland Heath DA8 . 8 C7
Oak Rd. Erith,Slade Green DA8 . 9 A5
Oak Rd. Five Oak Green TN12 .. 135 B7
Oak Rd. Gravesend DA12 .... 30 C4
Oak Rd. Grays RM17 .... 12 C8
Oak Rd. Hoo St Werburgh ME3 . 34 E3
Oak Rd. Orpington BR6 .... 52 A3
Oak Rd. Rochester ME2 .... 46 E6
Oak Rd.
  Royal Tunbridge Wells TN1 .. 149 D7
Oak Rd. Stone DA9 .... 10 E1
Oak Rd. Westerham TN16 ...... 81 D2
Oak Terr. **3** ME18 .... 178 F2
Oak Tree Cl. ME15 .... 107 C6
Oak Tree Cl. Marden TN12 ... 138 D5
Oak Tree Cl.
  Royal Tunbridge Wells TN1 .. 149 A1
Oak Tree Gdns. BR1 .... 22 B3
Oak Trees Cty Prim Sch.
  ME15 .... 107 C7
Oak View. TN8 .... 112 B2
Oakapple La. ME16 .... 91 A3
Oakbrook Cl. BR1 & SE12 ...... 22 B4
Oakcroft. SE12 .... 22 B5
Oakdale La. ME3 .... 96 C2
Oakdale Rd. TN4 .... 148 F4
Oakdene Ave. Chislehurst BR7 . 23 A3
Oakdene Ave. Erith DA8 .... 8 C8
Oakdene Rd. Orpington BR5 ... 38 A3
Oakdene Rd. Sevenoaks TN13 . 84 A5
Oakenden Rd. DA13 .... 44 E1
Oakenholt House. **1** SE2 ..... 3 D4
Oakfield. Hawkhurst TN18 .... 178 F2
Oakfield. Rolvenden Layne TN17 . 182 A1
Oakfield Cotts. TN17 .... 180 D4
Oakfield Court Rd. TN2 .... 149 C3
Oakfield Cty Prim Sch. DA1 ... 26 E6
Oakfield La. Dartford DA2 ...... 26 C6
Oakfield La. Keston BR2 .... 50 D6
Oakfield Park Rd. DA1 .... 26 D6
Oakfield Pl. DA1 .... 26 D6
Oakfield Rd. Marlpit Hill TN8 .. 112 B5
Oakfield Rd. Matfield TN12 ... 151 D8
Oakfields. TN13 .... 84 B1
Oakham Dr. BR2 .... 36 A5
Oakhill House. BR5 .... 38 A8
Oakhill Rd. BR6 .... 51 F8
Oakhouse Rd. DA6 .... 8 A2
Oakhurst Ave. DA7 .... 7 E7
Oakhurst Cl. ME5 .... 61 F3
Oakhurst Gdns. DA7 .... 7 E7
Oakland Cl. ME5 .... 61 F3
Oakland Villas. TN3 .... 161 B7
Oaklands. TN17 .... 169 D4
Oaklands Ave. DA15 .... 23 F6
Oaklands Cl. Bexley DA6 .... 7 F2
Oaklands Cl. Orpington BR5 ... 37 E3
Oaklands Cl.
  West Kingsdown TN15 .... 55 E4
Oaklands Cty Prim Sch. ME5 .. 61 F4
Oaklands La. Bexley DA6 .... 7 F2
Oaklands Rd. Dartford DA2 .... 27 C7
Oaklands Rd. Groombridge TN3 161 B6
Oaklands Rd. Hawkhurst TN18 . 179 A1
Oaklands Rd. Northfleet DA11 . 29 F4
Oaklands Way. TN11 .... 116 F4
Oaklea Rd. TN12 .... 135 F6
Oakleigh Cl. Chatham ME5 ..... 61 E2
Oakleigh Cl. Swanley BR8 ...... 39 E6
Oakleigh Gdns. BR6 .... 51 E6
Oakleigh Park Ave. BR7 .... 37 A8
Oakley Cl. **7** Newham E6 ...... 1 E7
Oakley Cl. West Thurrock RM16 . 11 C8
Oakley Ct. DA1 .... 27 B7
Oakley Dr. Keston Mark BR2 ... 50 F7
Oakley Dr. Sidcup SE9 .... 23 D7
Oakley Pk. DA5 & DA15 .... 24 D7
Oakley Rd. BR2 .... 50 E8
Oakmead. Meopham DA13 ..... 58 A8
Oakleigh Cl. **7** Newham E6 ... 1 E7
Oakmead Ave. BR2 .... 36 A3
Oakmere Rd. SE2 .... 7 A8
Oakmont Pl. BR6 .... 37 D1
Oaks Bsns Village The. ME5 ... 62 F1
Oaks Dene. ME5 .... 61 F1
Oaks Forstal. TN18 .... 186 C5
Oaks Rd. TN30 .... 183 B8

Oaks The. Aylesford ME20 ...... 75 E1
Oaks The. Smarden Bell TN27 .. 142 F2
Oaks The. Swanley BR8 .... 39 E7
Oaks The. Woolwich SE18 .... 2 C1
Oakum Ct. ME4 .... 48 B2
Oakway. DA5 .... 7 E1
Oakways. SE9 .... 6 B1
Oakwood Ave. ME6 .... 36 B6
Oakwood Cl. Chislehurst BR7 .... 23 A2
Oakwood Cl. Dartford DA1 .... 27 B7
Oakwood Ct. Maidstone ME16 .. 91 D3
Oakwood Ct. Swanley BR8 .... 39 C7
Oakwood Dr. Bexley DA7 .... 8 C3
Oakwood Dr. Sevenoaks TN13 .. 84 B4
Oakwood Gdns. BR6 .... 51 C8
Oakwood Hospl. ME16 .... 91 B3
Oakwood Park Gram Sch.
ME16 .... 91 C3
Oakwood Rd. Maidstone ME16 .. 91 D3
Oakwood Rd. Orpington BR6 .... 51 C8
Oakwood Rise. Longfield DA3 .. 42 E6
Oakwood Rise.
Royal Tunbridge Wells TN2 .. 149 E7
Oasis The. 4 BR1 .... 36 C7
Oast Cl. TN1 .... 149 D7
Oast Ct. ME18 .... 104 F1
Oast House Way. BR5 .... 38 B5
Oast La. TN11 .... 117 A4
Oast View. TN12 .... 153 A6
Oast Way. DA3 .... 42 E3
Oastfield Ct. TN15 .... 84 C2
Oasts The. ME14 .... 93 C4
Oastview. ME8 .... 64 A8
Oatfield Cl. TN17 .... 169 C5
Oatfield Dr. TN17 .... 169 C5
Oatfield Rd. BR6 .... 37 F1
Occupation La. SE18 .... 6 B6
Ockham Dr. BR5 .... 24 A1
Ockley La. TN18 .... 179 A3
Ockley Rd. TN18 .... 179 A2
Octavia Ct. ME5 .... 62 B3
Octavia Way. 12 SE28 .... 3 B6
Odeon Ct. 1 E16 .... 1 A8
Odeon Par. SE9 .... 5 E3
Odiham Dr. ME16 .... 91 C7
Offen's Dr. TN12 .... 139 E3
Offenham Rd. BR7 & SE9 .... 22 F4
Offham Cty Prim Sch. ME19 .... 88 D8
Offham Rd. ME19 .... 89 A7
Officers' Rd. ME4 .... 48 B8
Ogilby St. SE18 .... 1 F2
Okehampton Cres. DA16 .... 7 C6
Okemore Gdns. BR5 .... 38 C5
Old Ashford Rd. ME17 .... 111 E5
Old Barn Rd. Gillingham ME7 .... 62 F6
Old Barn Cl. Kemsing TN15 ...... 70 A2
Old Barn Rd. Tonbridge TN9 .... 132 F8
Old Barn Rd. ME19 .... 74 E2
Old Barn Way. DA8 .... 8 D4
Old Bexley CE Prim Sch. DA5 .. 25 A7
Old Bexley CE Sch. DA5 .... 24 F7
Old Bexley La. Dartford DA1 .... 25 F7
Old Bexley La. Maypole DA5 .... 25 E6
Old Carriageway The.
Gillingham ME7 .... 62 F4
Old Carriageway The.
Sevenoaks TN13 .... 83 C5
Old Castle Wlk. ME8 .... 63 D4
Old Chapel Rd. BR8 .... 39 C2
Old Chatham Rd. Kit's Coty ME20 76 D6
Old Chatham Rd.
Maidstone ME14 .... 76 F1
Old Church La. ME18 .... 103 E4
Old Church Rd. Burham ME1 .... 60 C1
Old Church Rd. Matfield TN2 .. 134 D2
Old Church Rd.
Mereworth ME18 .... 103 D5
Old Church Rd. Pembury TN2 .. 150 D8
Old Clem Sq. 12 SE18 .... 6 A8
Old Coach Rd. TN15 .... 71 E5
Old Ctyd The. BR1 .... 36 B8
Old Dartford Rd. DA4 .... 40 F3
Old Dover Rd. SE3 & SE7 .... 5 B7
Old Downs. DA3 .... 42 E4
Old Dr. ME15 .... 106 F6
Old Farm Ave. DA15 .... 23 E6
Old Farm Gdns. BR6 .... 39 F6
Old Farm Rd E. DA15 .... 24 A6
Old Farm Rd W. DA15 .... 23 F6
Old Forge La. ME9 .... 79 F3
Old Forge Way. DA14 .... 24 B4
Old Garden The. TN13 .... 83 D4
Old Gardens Cl. TN2 .... 163 B8
Old Hadlow Rd. TN10 .... 117 F4
Old Ham La. ME17 .... 111 A4
Old Hill. Chislehurst BR7 .... 37 A8
Old Hill. Orpington BR6 .... 51 E4
Old Homesdale Rd. BR2 .... 36 C5
Old House La. TN3 .... 147 D4
Old House Rd. ME9 .... 64 E4
Old Kent Rd. TN12 .... 136 A6
Old La. TN15 .... 86 C4
Old Lain. ME17 .... 110 F6
Old London Rd.
Badgers Mount TN14 .... 53 A1
Old London Rd. Tonbridge TN10 117 C3
Old London Rd. Wrotham TN15 .. 71 F4
Old Loose Hill. ME15 .... 106 F4
Old Maidstone Rd. BR8 & DA14 .. 24 F1
Old Manor Dr. DA12 .... 30 C7
Old Manor Way. Bexley DA7 ...... 8 D5
Old Manor Way.
Chislehurst BR7 & SE9 .... 22 F3
Old Mill Cl. DA4 .... 40 E1
Old Mill La. ME20 .... 76 C3
Old Mill Rd. Silver Hill ME17 .... 93 F1
Old Mill Rd. Woolwich SE18 ...... 6 D8
Old Oast Bsns Ctr The. ME20 .. 76 A1

Old Orch. TN11 .... 115 A3
Old Orch The. ME8 .... 64 A8
Old Orchard La. ME19 .... 74 D1
Old Otford Rd. TN14 .... 69 B1
Old Park Rd. SE2 .... 3 A1
Old Parsonage Ct. ME19 .... 89 C7
Old Pattens La. ME1 .... 47 D2
Old Perry St. Chislehurst BR7 .. 23 E1
Old Perry St. Northfleet DA11 .. 29 E6
Old Polhill. TN14 .... 68 D4
Old Rd. Chatham ME4 .... 47 F4
Old Rd. Crayford DA1 & DA7 ...... 8 D3
Old Rd. East Peckham TN12 .... 120 A6
Old Rd. Wateringbury ME18 .... 104 C7
Old Rd E. DA12 .... 30 D7
Old Rd W. DA11 & DA12 .... 30 B7
Old Regent Dr. TN17 .... 181 E4
Old Riding School The. TN3 .... 161 B2
Old School Cl. ME17 .... 111 D4
Old School Ct. Chattenden ME3 .. 33 F4
Old School Ct. Egerton TN27 .. 127 F3
Old School House The. TN8 .... 112 C1
Old School La. ME19 .... 73 F4
Old Soar Rd. TN15 .... 87 C1
Old Station Rd. TN5 .... 174 E6
Old Tannery Cl. TN30 .... 182 F7
Old Terry's Lodge Rd. TN15 .... 71 A4
Old Timber Top Cotts The.
TN13 .... 84 C4
Old Tovil Rd. ME15 .... 92 A2
Old Trafford Cl. ME16 .... 91 B6
Old Tramyard. SE18 .... 2 E2
Old Tree La. ME17 .... 107 D3
Old Wardsdown. TN5 .... 177 B3
Old Watling St. Cuxton ME2 .... 46 B8
Old Watling St. Gravesend DA13 30 A3
Old Wlk The. TN14 .... 69 C2
Old Yews The. DA3 .... 43 B6
Oldborough Manor Com Coll.
ME15 .... 107 B6
Oldbury Cl. Oldbury TN15 .... 86 B5
Oldbury Cl. Orpington BR5 .... 38 D5
Oldbury Cotts. TN15 .... 86 B6
Oldbury La. TN15 .... 86 B6
Oldchurch Ct. 3 ME16 .... 91 E3
Oldfield Cl. Bromley BR1 .... 36 F5
Oldfield Cl. Gillingham ME8 ...... 63 D8
Oldfield Cl. Maidstone ME15 .... 92 E1
Oldfield Rd. Bexley DA7 .... 7 E5
Oldfield Rd. Bromley BR1 .... 36 F5
Oleander Cl. BR6 .... 51 D5
Olive Rd. DA1 .... 26 D7
Oliver Cl. Chatham ME4 .... 48 B2
Oliver Cl. West Thurrock RM16 .. 11 B7
Oliver Cres. DA4 .... 40 F2
Oliver Ct. SE18 .... 2 C2
Oliver Gdns. E6 .... 1 E8
Oliver Rd. Staplehurst TN12 .... 139 E4
Oliver Rd. Swanley BR8 .... 39 D6
Oliver Rd. West Thurrock RM16 .. 11 A7
Oliver Twist Cl. ME1 .... 47 B4
Olivers Cotts. ME14 .... 93 C4
Olivers Mill. DA3 .... 56 E8
Olivine Cl. ME5 .... 77 A8
Olliffe Cl. ME5 .... 61 F2
Olron Cres. DA6 .... 7 E2
Olven Rd. SE18 .... 6 C8
Olyffe Ave. DA16 .... 7 A5
Onslow Cres. BR7 .... 37 B8
Onslow Dr. DA14 .... 24 D6
Onslow Rd. ME1 .... 47 D3
Opal Cl. E16 .... 1 D7
Opal Rd. ME5 .... 62 B2
Openshaw Rd. SE2 .... 3 B2
Orache Dr. ME14 .... 92 E5
Orange Court La. BR6 .... 51 A2
Orange Terr. ME1 .... 47 D5
Orangery La. SE9 .... 5 F2
Orbit Cl. ME5 .... 77 A8
Orbital One. DA1 .... 27 B6
Orchard Ave. Aylesford ME20 .... 75 E1
Orchard Ave. Dartford DA1 .... 26 B7
Orchard Ave. Erith DA17 .... 7 F8
Orchard Ave. Gravesend DA11 .. 30 B3
Orchard Ave. Rochester ME2 .... 32 F1
Orchard Bank. ME17 .... 108 B1
Orchard Bsns Ctr.
Maidstone ME16 .... 91 C8
Orchard Bsns Ctr.
Paddock Wood TN12 .... 136 A8
Orchard Bsns Ctr.
Royal Tunbridge Wells TN4 .. 149 D8
Orchard Bsns Ctr.
Tonbridge TN9 .... 117 E1
Orchard Cl. Bexley DA7 .... 7 E6
Orchard Cl. Coxheath ME17 .... 106 C3
Orchard Cl. Edenbridge TN8 .... 112 B2
Orchard Cl. Horsmonden TN12 .. 152 F6
Orchard Cl. Langley Heath ME17 108 E4
Orchard Cl. New Barn DA3 .... 43 B7
Orchard Cl.
Royal Tunbridge Wells TN1 .. 149 D6
Orchard Cl. Sevenoaks TN14 .... 84 C7
Orchard Cotts. ME15 .... 106 A8
Orchard Cres. TN2 .... 153 A6
Orchard Ct. TN17 .... 180 D6
Orchard Dr. Edenbridge TN8 .. 112 B2
Orchard Dr.
Meopham Station DA13 .... 43 F4
Orchard Dr. Newington ME9 ...... 65 A5
Orchard Dr. Tonbridge TN10 .... 117 E5
Orchard Glade. TN27 .... 141 E5
Orchard Gn. BR6 .... 51 E8
Orchard Gr. Larkfield ME20 ...... 75 B2
Orchard Gr. Orpington BR6 ...... 37 F1
Orchard Gr.
Royal Tunbridge Wells TN1 .. 149 B5
Orchard Hill. DA1 .... 8 E2

Orchard House. DA8 .... 8 F6
Orchard Ind Est. ME15 .... 107 F3
Orchard Pl. St Paul's Cray BR5 .. 38 C6
Orchard Pl. 2 Maidstone ME16 .. 91 E3
Orchard Pl. Sundridge TN14 .... 82 D3
Orchard Rd. Bexley DA16 .... 7 B4
Orchard Rd. Bromley BR1 .... 36 C8
Orchard Rd. East Peckham TN12 120 A6
Orchard Rd. Erith DA17 .... 4 A2
Orchard Rd. Maidstone ME14 .. 92 E4
Orchard Rd. Northfleet DA11 .... 29 C6
Orchard Rd. Orpington BR6 ...... 51 B5
Orchard Rd. Otford TN14 .... 68 F3
Orchard Rd. Pratt's Bottom BR6 .. 52 C1
Orchard Rd. Sevenoaks TN13 .... 83 E5
Orchard Rd. Sidcup DA14 .... 23 E4
Orchard Rd. St Michaels TN30 .. 173 A3
Orchard Rd. Swanscombe DA10 .. 11 E2
Orchard Rise. TN3 .... 161 B7
Orchard Rise E. DA15 .... 6 F2
Orchard Rise W. DA15 .... 6 E2
Orchard St. Dartford DA1 .... 9 E1
Orchard St. Gillingham ME8 ...... 63 E8
Orchard St. Maidstone ME15 .... 92 A3
Orchard Terr. DA9 .... 10 E2
Orchard The. Maidstone ME14 .. 93 B4
Orchard The. Sevenoaks TN13 .. 83 E6
Orchard The. Swanley BR8 .... 39 D7
Orchard View. TN30 .... 183 C8
Orchard Villas. ME14 .... 122 A4
Orchard Way.
Horsmonden TN12 .... 153 A6
Orchard Way. Kemsing TN15 .... 70 A2
Orchard Way. Snodland ME6 .... 74 F7
Orchard Way. Turnden TN17 .... 169 B4
Orchard Way. Wilmington DA2 .. 26 D5
Orchardlea. DA13 .... 28 F3
Orchards Sh Ctr The. DA1 .... 9 E1
Orchid Cl. 1 Newham E16 .... 1 E8
Orchid Cl. Rochester ME2 .... 46 C6
Orchidhurst. TN2 .... 149 D7
Ordnance Rd. Gravesend DA12 .. 13 C1
Ordnance Rd. Woolwich SE18 .... 6 A8
Ordnance St. ME4 .... 47 E3
Ordnance Terr. ME4 .... 47 E4
Oregon Sq. BR6 .... 37 D1
Oriental Rd. E16 .... 1 D5
Oriole Way. Larkfield ME20 ...... 74 F2
Oriole Way. Woolwich SE28 .... 3 B6
Orion Rd. ME1 .... 61 C7
Orissa Rd. SE18 .... 2 E1
Orlestone Gdns. BR6 .... 52 E5
Orlick Rd. DA12 .... 31 B7
Ormesby Cl. SE28 .... 3 D6
Ormiston Rd. SE10 .... 1 A1
Ormond Ave. BR6 .... 51 C8
Ormsby Gn. ME8 .... 63 E3
Ormsby Point. 6 SE18 .... 2 B2
Orpines The. ME8 .... 104 F7
Orpington By-Pass Rd. TN14 .. 53 A2
Orpington Coll. BR6 .... 38 A1
Orpington Hospl. BR6 .... 51 F6
Orpington Rd. BR7 .... 37 E6
Orpington Sta. BR6 .... 51 E8
Orpington Trad Est. BR5 .... 38 C5
Orwell Cl. Lunsford ME5 .... 74 F3
Orwell Cl. Rainham RM9 .... 4 D8
Orwell House. 6 ME15 .... 107 E8
Osberton Rd. SE9 .... 5 A2
Osborne Rd. Dartford DA1 .... 7 F8
Osborne Rd. Gillingham ME7 .... 48 C5
Osbourne Rd. DA2 .... 10 B1
Osgood Ave. BR6 .... 51 F5
Osgood Gdns. 1 BR6 .... 51 F5
Osmers Hill. TN5 .... 174 F7
Osmunda Ct. TN2 .... 149 C4
Osney House. 4 SE2 .... 3 D4
Osney Way. DA12 .... 30 F6
Osprey Ave. ME5 & ME7 .... 48 E2
Osprey Cl. E6 .... 1 E8
Osprey Wlk. ME20 .... 74 F1
Ospringe Ct. SE9 .... 6 D1
Osterberg Rd. DA1 .... 9 F3
Osterley Cl. BR5 .... 38 A8
Ostlers Cl. 2 ME6 .... 75 A8
Otford Cl. Bromley BR1 .... 37 A6
Otford Cl. Sidcup DA15 .... 8 B1
Otford Court (St Michael's Sch).
TN14 .... 69 E4
Otford Cty Prim Sch. TN14 ...... 69 B3
Otford La. TN14 .... 68 B6
Otford Rd. TN14 .... 84 B7
Otford Sta. TN14 .... 69 C3
Otham La. ME15 .... 93 C2
Otham St. Maidstone ME15 ...... 93 C2
Otham St. Otham ME15 .... 108 B7
Otley Rd. E16 .... 1 C7
Otlinge Cl. BR5 .... 38 D5
Ottawa Rd. RM18 .... 13 A5
Otterbourne Pl. ME15 .... 92 E1
Otterden Cl. BR6 .... 51 E6
Otterham Quay La. ME8 .... 64 B8
Otteridge Rd. ME14 .... 93 A3
Ottershaw House. BR5 .... 38 B8
Otway St. ME4 .... 48 A3
Otway Terr. 1 ME4 .... 48 A3
Our Lady of Grace RC Jun Mix Sch.
SE5 .... 5 B8
Our Lady of Hartley RC Prim Sch.
DA3 .... 42 F4
Our Lady of the Rosary
RC Prim Sch. DA3 .... 43 B6
Our Lady's RC Prim Sch. DA1 .... 9 D1
Oval The. New Barn DA3 .... 43 C6
Oval The. Sidcup DA15 .... 24 A8
Ovenden Rd. Chevening TN14 .. 82 E5
Ovenden Rd. Sundridge TN14 .. 82 D6
Over Minnis. DA3 .... 56 F7

Overcliffe. DA11 .... 13 A1
Overcourt Cl. DA15 .... 7 B1
Overdale. TN14 .... 99 B2
Overmead. Eltham SE9 .... 23 D8
Overmead. Swanley BR8 .... 39 E4
Overton Rd. SE2 .... 3 D3
Overy St. DA1 .... 9 E1
Owen Cl. East Malling ME19 .... 89 F8
Owen Cl. Woolwich SE28 .... 3 C5
Owenite St. SE2 .... 3 B2
Owens Way. ME7 .... 49 A6
Owletts. DA12 .... 44 F6
Ox La. TN30 .... 173 B2
Ox Lea. TN3 .... 148 A3
Oxenden Wood Rd. BR6 .... 52 C4
Oxenhill Rd. TN14 .... 69 E2
Oxenhoath Rd. TN11 .... 102 D4
Oxfield. TN8 .... 112 D3
Oxford Cl. DA12 .... 30 F6
Oxford Mews. DA5 .... 25 A7
Oxford Rd. Maidstone ME15 .... 107 D8
Oxford Rd. Sidcup DA14 .... 24 B3
Oxford St. ME6 .... 75 A8
Oxhawth Cres. BR2 .... 37 B3
Oxleas. E6 .... 2 B7
Oxleas Cl. DA16 .... 6 D5
Oxley Shaw La. ME19 & ME20 .. 74 E2
Oyster Catchers Cl. E16 .... 1 B7
Ozolins Way. E16 .... 1 A7

Pacific Rd. E16 .... 1 A7
Packer Pl. ME5 .... 62 A8
Packham Rd. DA11 .... 29 F5
Packhorse Rd. TN13 .... 83 C4
Packmores Rd. SE9 .... 6 E2
Pad's Hill. ME15 .... 92 A4
Paddlesworth Rd. ME6 .... 59 D1
Paddock Cl. Fordcombe TN3 .... 147 B5
Paddock Cl. Greenwich SE3 .... 5 A5
Paddock Cl. Orpington BR6 ...... 51 B6
Paddock Cl. Platt TN15 .... 87 C6
Paddock Cl. South Darenth DA4 .. 41 C8
Paddock Rd. DA6 .... 7 E2
Paddock Rd. Chatham ME4 ...... 47 F4
Paddock The. Hadlow TN11 .... 102 E1
Paddock The. Pembury TN2 .... 150 C6
Paddock The. Vigo Village DA13 .. 72 F7
Paddock The. Westerham TN16 .. 81 C1
Paddock Way. BR7 .... 23 D1
Paddock Wood Cty Prim Sch.
TN12 .... 136 A6
Paddock Wood Sta. TN12 .... 136 A7
Paddocks Cl. BR5 .... 52 D8
Paddocks The. Cowden TN8 .... 145 B7
Paddocks The.
East Peckham TN12 .... 119 E6
Paddocks The. Sevenoaks TN13 .. 84 D3
Padsole La. ME15 .... 92 A4
Padstow Manor. ME7 .... 48 C6
Page Cl. DA2 .... 28 C5
Page Cres. DA8 .... 8 F7
Page Heath La. BR1 .... 36 D6
Page Heath Villas. BR1 .... 36 D6
Pageant Cl. RM18 .... 13 C6
Pageburst Rd. TN12 .... 139 B3
Paget Gdns. BR7 .... 37 B8
Paget Rise. SE18 .... 6 A7
Paget St. ME7 .... 48 A5
Paget Terr. SE18 .... 6 A7
Pagitt St. ME4 .... 47 E3
Paiges Farm Cl. TN14 .... 99 C2
Painters Ash La. DA11 .... 29 D5
Palace Ave. ME15 .... 92 A4
Palace Ct. Chatham ME5 .... 48 D2
Palace Ct. Eltham SE9 .... 5 F1
Palace Gr. BR1 .... 36 B8
Palace Ind Est. ME15 .... 107 F4
Palace Rd. Bromley BR1 .... 36 B8
Palace Rd. Hill Park TN16 .... 81 A6
Palace View. Bromley BR1 .... 36 B6
Palace View. Lewisham SE12 .... 22 A6
Palace Wood Cty Inf Sch. ME16 91 C6
Palace Wood Cty Jun Sch.
ME16 .... 91 C6
Palewell Cl. BR5 .... 38 B7
Pallant Way. BR6 .... 51 A7
Pallet Way. SE18 .... 5 E6
Palm Ave. DA14 .... 24 D2
Palmar Cres. DA7 .... 8 A5
Palmar Rd. Bexley DA7 .... 8 A5
Palmar Rd. Maidstone ME16 .... 91 D6
Palmarsh Cl. BR5 .... 38 D5
Palmeira Rd. DA16 .... 7 D4
Palmer Ave. DA12 .... 30 C7
Palmers Brook. TN11 .... 102 F2
Palmers Green La. TN12 .... 136 D1
Palmers Orch. TN14 .... 68 F8
Palmerston Cres. SE18 .... 6 C8
Palmerston Rd. Chatham ME4 .. 47 F1
Palmerston Rd. Grays RM16 .... 11 D8
Palmerston Rd. Orpington BR6 .. 51 C5
Panbro House. SE18 .... 5 F6
Panfield Rd. SE28 .... 3 A3
Pankhurst Rd. ME3 .... 34 D6
Pannell Rd. ME3 .... 21 A6
Panter's. BR8 .... 25 F1
Pantiles The. Bromley BR1 ...... 36 E6
Pantiles The. Erith DA7 .... 7 F7
Pantiles The. 17
Royal Tunbridge Wells TN2 .. 149 A2
Panton Cl. ME5 .... 62 C4
Pantyles The. TN14 .... 98 B5
Papillons Wlk. SE3 .... 5 A4
Papion Gr. ME5 .... 61 E2

Parade The. Crayford DA1 .... 8 F2
Parade The. Gravesend DA12 .... 30 D6
Parade The. Kemsing TN14 .... 69 C2
Parade The.
Meopham Station DA13 .... 44 A2
Parade The. Staplehurst TN12 .. 139 F3
Parade The. Swanscombe DA10 .. 11 F2
Paradise Cotts. ME9 .... 64 E5
Paradise Pl. 13 SE7 .... 1 E2
Paragon Cl. E16 .... 1 A7
Paragon The. SE3 .... 5 A5
Parham Rd. ME4 .... 47 F2
Parish CE Prim Sch. BR1 .... 22 A1
Parish Gate Dr. DA15 .... 6 E1
Parish Wharf. 6 SE18 & SE7 ...... 1 E2
Park App. DA16 .... 7 B3
Park Ave. Bromley BR1 .... 22 A2
Park Ave. Edenbridge TN8 .... 112 B2
Park Ave. Gillingham ME7 .... 48 D3
Park Ave. Gravesend DA12 .... 30 C7
Park Ave. Hildenborough TN11 .. 116 F5
Park Ave. Loose ME17 .... 106 E2
Park Ave. Maidstone ME14 .... 92 B6
Park Ave. Northfleet DA11 .... 29 E7
Park Ave.
Orpington,Goddington BR6 .... 52 B7
Park Ave.
Orpington,Locksbottom BR6 .. 51 A8
Park Ave. West Thurrock RM16 .. 11 B8
Park Barn Rd. ME17 .... 109 C5
Park Corner Rd. DA13 .... 28 F4
Park Cotts. 8 TN18 .... 179 A2
Park Cres. Chatham ME4 .... 61 F8
Park Cres. Erith DA8 .... 8 D8
Park Crescent Rd. DA8 .... 8 D8
Park Dr. Longfield DA3 .... 42 E6
Park Dr. Woolwich SE7 .... 5 E8
Park Farm Houses. ME19 .... 90 B8
Park Farm Rd. Bromley BR1 ...... 36 D8
Park Farm Rd. Ryarsh ME19 .... 73 F6
Park Gdns. DA8 .... 4 D2
Park Gr. Bexley DA7 .... 8 C3
Park Gr. Bromley BR1 .... 36 B8
Park Hill. Bromley BR1 .... 36 F5
Park Hill. Meopham Station DA13 43 F5
Park Hill Rd. TN14 .... 69 E2
Park House. Maidstone ME14 .. 92 B6
Park House. Sevenoaks TN13 .... 84 C5
Park House. Sidcup DA14 .... 24 A3
Park House Gdns. TN4 .... 133 A2
Park La. Cock Street ME17 ...... 107 D2
Park La. Gill's Green TN18 ...... 178 D7
Park La. Godden Green TN15 .... 85 A4
Park La. Kemsing TN15 .... 70 A1
Park La. Maidstone ME14 .... 91 F7
Park La. Sevenoaks TN13 .... 84 C3
Park La. Swanley Village BR8 .... 40 C7
Park Manor. ME7 .... 48 B5
Park Mead. DA15 .... 7 B1
Park Mews. ME7 .... 23 B2
Park Pl. Gravesend DA12 .... 30 C8
Park Pl. Sevenoaks TN13 .... 83 D4
Park Rd. Addington ME19 .... 73 C3
Park Rd. Bromley BR1 .... 36 B8
Park Rd. Chislehurst BR7 .... 23 B2
Park Rd. Dartford DA1 .... 27 A8
Park Rd. Dunk's Green TN11 .... 102 C5
Park Rd. Gravesend DA11 .... 30 B7
Park Rd. Leybourne ME19 .... 74 D3
Park Rd. Marden Thorn TN12 .. 139 A4
Park Rd. Mereworth ME18 ...... 103 F5
Park Rd. Orpington BR5 .... 38 C4
Park Rd. Royal Tunbridge Wells,
Southborough TN4 .... 133 A2
Park Rd. Royal Tunbridge Wells,
St John's TN4 .... 149 B5
Park Rd. Swanley BR8 .... 39 F5
Park Rd. Swanscombe DA10 ...... 11 E1
Park Road Ind Est. BR8 .... 39 F6
Park St. TN2 .... 149 C3
Park Terr. Sundridge TN14 .... 82 D3
Park Terr. Swanscombe DA9 ...... 11 B2
Park The. DA14 .... 24 A3
Park View. TN15 .... 57 C2
Park View Cl. TN8 .... 112 B2
Park View Ct. ME15 .... 92 E1
Park View Rd. Bexley DA16 .... 7 C4
Park View Rd. Eltham SE9 .... 23 B6
Park Villas. TN11 .... 102 F1
Park Wallis. DA11 .... 12 B2
Park Way. Coxheath ME17 ...... 106 D3
Park Way. Joyden's Wood DA5 .. 25 E5
Park Way. Maidstone ME15 ...... 92 B1
Park Way Cty Prim Sch. ME15 .. 92 B1
Park Wood Gn. ME8 .... 63 D5
Park Wood La. TN12 .... 140 C1
Park Wood Par. ME15 .... 107 F5
Park Wood Trad Est. ME15 ...... 107 F4
Parkdale Rd. SE18 .... 2 E1
Parker Ave. RM18 .... 13 C6
Parker Cl. Gillingham ME8 .... 63 E5
Parker Cl. Newham E16 .... 1 E5
Parker House. 4 SE18 .... 2 B1
Parker Rd. RM17 .... 11 F8
Parker St. E16 .... 1 E5
Parker's Cnr. ME3 .... 19 C8
Parkfield. Hartley DA3 .... 42 F5
Parkfield. Wilderness TN15 ...... 84 F4
Parkfield Rd. ME8 .... 49 F1
Parkfield Way. BR2 .... 36 F4
Parkfields. ME2 .... 46 C7
Parkgate Cotts. BR6 .... 53 C6
Parkgate Rd. BR6 .... 53 C6
Parkhill Rd. Sidcup DA15 .... 23 E5

Parkhill Rd. Sidcup DA5 ... 24 F8
Parkhurst Gdns. [2] DA5 ... 25 A8
Parkhurst Rd. DA5 ... 25 A8
Parkland Cl. TN13 ... 99 D6
Parklands. TN4 ... 148 E8
Parkside. Cliffe Woods ME3 ... 33 B7
Parkside. Halstead TN14 ... 67 F6
Parkside. Sidcup DA14 ... 24 B6
Parkside Ave. Bromley BR1 ... 36 E5
Parkside Ave. Crayford DA1 & DA7 ... 8 E5
Parkside Ave. Tilbury RM18 ... 13 B5
Parkside Cross. DA7 ... 8 E5
Parkside Ct. TN30 ... 182 F7
Parkside Lodge. DA17 ... 4 C1
Parkside Rd. DA17 ... 4 C2
Parkview Ct. DA11 ... 30 A6
Parkway. Erith DA18 ... 3 E3
Parkway. Tonbridge TN10 ... 117 D5
Parkway Prim Sch. DA18 ... 3 E3
Parkwood Cl. TN1 ... 149 C6
Parkwood Hall Sch. BR8 ... 40 B6
Parkwood Rd. DA17 ... 24 F8
Paroma Rd. DA17 ... 4 A3
Parr Ave. ME7 ... 48 D6
Parrock Ave. DA12 ... 30 C7
Parrock Rd. DA12 ... 30 C7
Parrock St. DA11 ... 30 B8
Parrock The. DA12 ... 30 C7
Parrs Head Mews. ME1 ... 47 C6
Parry Ave. E6 ... 1 F7
Parry Pl. SE18 ... 2 B2
Parsonage Cl. TN4 ... 148 B5
Parsonage La. Cold Harbour ME9 ... 65 F8
Parsonage La. Lamberhurst TN3 166 B6
Parsonage La. Rochester ME1 ... 47 C8
Parsonage La. Sidcup DA14 ... 24 F4
Parsonage La.
  Sutton at Hone DA4 ... 27 B2
Parsonage Manorway.
  DA8 & DA17 ... 8 A8
Parsonage Rd. Rusthall TN4 ... 148 B5
Parsonage Rd.
  West Thurrock RM16 ... 11 C8
Parsons La. Heath Side DA2 ... 26 B5
Parsons La. Stansted TN15 ... 56 E1
Partridge Ave. ME20 ... 74 F3
Partridge Cl. [1] E16 ... 1 D8
Partridge Dr. BR6 ... 51 C7
Partridge Gn. SE9 ... 23 A5
Partridge Rd. DA14 ... 23 E4
Partridge Sq. [3] E6 ... 1 E8
Pasley Rd. ME7 ... 48 A7
Pasley Rd E. ME7 ... 48 B7
Pasley Rd W. ME4 ... 48 A7
Passey Pl. SE9 ... 5 F1
Passfield House. SE18 ... 2 D2
Passfield Path. [13] SE28 ... 3 B6
Paston Cres. SE12 ... 22 B8
Patch The. TN13 ... 83 E5
Patience Cotts. TN14 ... 99 B2
Patricia Ct. Bexley SE2 ... 7 B7
Patricia Ct. Chislehurst BR7 ... 37 D8
Patrixbourne Ave. ME8 ... 49 C2
Pattenden Gdns. TN12 ... 120 A4
Pattenden La. TN12 ... 138 C7
Pattens Gdns. ME4 ... 47 E2
Pattens La. ME4 ... 47 E1
Pattens Pl. ME1 ... 47 D2
Patterdale Rd. DA2 ... 27 D7
Patterson Ct. DA1 ... 10 A2
Pattison Point. [14] E16 ... 1 A8
Pattison St. SE18 ... 2 C1
Paulinus Cl. BR5 ... 38 C6
Pavement The. TN30 ... 173 B3
Pavilion Gdns. TN13 ... 84 C3
Pavilion La. ME14 ... 104 A8
Pavilion The. [5] TN9 ... 117 B1
Paxton Rd. BR1 ... 22 A1
Payne's La. ME15 ... 107 F5
Paynes Cotts. ME15 ... 121 D7
Peace Cotts. ME15 ... 68 D1
Peace St. SE18 ... 6 A8
Peach Croft. DA11 ... 29 E4
Peacock Mews. [7] ME16 ... 91 E4
Peacock St. DA12 ... 30 C8
Pear Tree Ave. ME20 ... 75 D1
Pear Tree Cl. Bexley DA2 ... 8 D6
Pear Tree Cl. Cranbrook TN17 . 169 D3
Pear Tree Cl. Swanley BR8 ... 39 D7
Pear Tree La. Gillingham ME7 ... 62 E7
Pear Tree La. Maidstone ME15 . 107 B6
Pear Tree Pl. ME3 ... 32 B3
Pear Tree Row. ME17 ... 108 B5
Pear Tree Wlk. ME9 ... 65 A5
Pearesword Rd. ME8 ... 8 F6
Pearl Cl. E6 ... 2 A7
Pearse Pl. TN3 ... 166 B5
Pearson Way. ME1 ... 26 F6
Pearson's Green Rd. TN12 ... 136 D3
Pearson's Green Rd. TN12 ... 136 D5
Peartree Cotts. ME8 ... 64 B8
Peartree La. ME2 ... 32 A2
Pease Hill. TN15 ... 56 F4
Peasley La. TN17 ... 167 D6
Peat Way. ME3 ... 20 E6
Peatfield Cl. DA15 ... 23 E5
Peckham Cl. ME2 ... 47 C8
Peckham Rd. TN12 ... 119 F6
Peckham House. [6] BR5 ... 38 D1
Peel Rd. BR6 ... 51 C5
Peel St. ME1 ... 47 C5
Peel Yates House. [13] SE7 ... 1 E2
Peens La. ME17 ... 123 C7
Pegasus Ct. DA12 ... 30 C5

Peggoty Cl. ME3 ... 32 B3
Pegley Gdns. SE12 ... 22 A6
Pegwell St. SE18 ... 6 E7
Pelham Cotts. DA5 ... 25 B7
Pelham Prim Sch. DA7 ... 8 A4
Pelham Rd. Bexley DA7 ... 8 A4
Pelham Rd. Gravesend DA11 ... 30 A8
Pelham Rd S. DA11 ... 29 F7
Pelham Terr. DA11 ... 29 F8
Pelican Cl. ME2 ... 46 C6
Pelican Ct. ME18 ... 104 E7
Pell Cl. TN5 ... 175 A6
Pellipar Gdns. SE18 ... 1 F1
Pellipar Rd. SE18 ... 1 F1
Pells La. TN15 ... 71 A7
Pemberton Gdns. BR8 ... 39 E7
Pemberton Sq. ME2 ... 47 C8
Pemble Cl. TN12 ... 135 A7
Pembroke. ME4 ... 48 B8
Pembroke Cl. DA8 ... 4 D2
Pembroke Ct. ME4 ... 48 A4
Pembroke Gdns. ME8 ... 63 E4
Pembroke Pl. DA4 ... 41 B8
Pembroke Rd. Bromley BR1 ... 36 D7
Pembroke Rd. Coxheath ME17 . 106 C3
Pembroke Rd. Erith DA8 ... 4 D2
Pembroke Rd. Newham E6 ... 1 F8
Pembroke Rd. Sevenoaks TN13 .. 84 B2
Pembroke Rd. Tonbridge TN9 .. 117 A1
Pembury Cl. TN2 ... 150 D7
Pembury Cres. DA14 ... 24 E6
Pembury Cty Prim Sch. TN2 .. 150 D8
Pembury Gdns. ME16 ... 91 D3
Pembury Gr. TN9 ... 133 C8
Pembury Grange. TN2 ... 150 A6
Pembury Hall Rd. TN11 & TN2 . 134 C3
Pembury Hospl. TN2 ... 150 B7
Pembury Rd. Erith DA7 ... 7 E8
Pembury Rd. Pembury TN11 ... 134 A2
Pembury Rd.
  Royal Tunbridge Wells TN2 .. 149 E4
Pembury Rd.
  Tonbridge TN11 & TN9 ... 133 D7
Pembury Walks. TN11 & TN2 .. 134 C2
Pembury Way. ME8 ... 49 C2
Pen Way. TN10 ... 117 C5
Pencroft Dr. DA1 ... 26 C8
Penda Rd. DA8 ... 8 B7
Pendennis Rd. Orpington BR6 .. 52 C8
Pendennis Rd. Sevenoaks TN13 . 84 B4
Penderel Mews. TN30 ... 183 B8
Pendlebury House. SE16 ... 5 E6
Pendragon Rd. BR1 & SE12 ... 22 A5
Pendragon Sec Sch. BR1 ... 22 A5
Pendrell St. SE18 ... 6 D8
Pendrill Pl. TN5 ... 174 F5
Penenden. DA3 ... 56 F8
Penenden Ct. ME14 ... 92 B7
Penenden Heath Rd. ME14 ... 92 C7
Penenden St. ME14 ... 92 A6
Penfold Cl. Chatham ME5 ... 62 B7
Penfold Cl. Park Wood ME15 .. 107 E5
Penfold Hill. ME17 ... 109 B8
Penfold House. [14] SE18 ... 6 B8
Penfold Way. ME15 ... 106 F6
Penfolds Cl. TN10 ... 117 C5
Penford Gdns. SE9 ... 5 D4
Pengarth Rd. DA5 ... 7 D1
Penguin Cl. ME2 ... 46 D6
Penhall Rd. SE7 ... 1 D2
Penhill Rd. DA5 ... 24 C8
Penhurst Cl. ME14 ... 92 F5
Penlee Cl. TN8 ... 112 C2
Penmon Rd. SE2 ... 3 A3
Penn Gdns. BR7 ... 37 B7
Penn La. DA5 ... 7 E1
Penn Yd. TN2 ... 150 C6
Pennant Rd. ME1 ... 61 C7
Penney Cl. DA1 ... 26 D8
Pennine Way. Erith DA7 ... 8 E6
Pennine Way. Maidstone ME15 . 93 A1
Pennine Way. Northfleet DA11 .. 29 E5
Pennine Wlk. TN2 ... 149 D5
Pennington Manor. [1] TN4 .. 132 F2
Pennington Pl. TN4 ... 133 B1
Pennington Rd. TN4 ... 133 A2
Pennington Way. SE12 ... 22 B6
Pennyfields. TN17 ... 169 D4
Pennyroyal Ave. E6 ... 2 A7
Penpool La. DA16 ... 7 B4
Penryn Manor. ME7 ... 48 C6
Penshurst Ave. DA15 ... 7 A1
Penshurst CE Prim Sch. TN11 131 A4
Penshurst Cl. Gillingham ME8 .. 49 E2
Penshurst Cl. New Barn DA3 ... 43 D7
Penshurst Cl.
  West Kingsdown TN15 ... 55 E4
Penshurst Enterprise Ctr.
  TN11 ... 131 C4
Penshurst Place. TN11 ... 131 B4
Penshurst Rd. Bexley DA7 ... 7 F6
Penshurst Rd. Penshurst TN11 . 131 C8
Penshurst Rd.
  Poundsbridge TN11 & TN3 .. 147 E8
Penshurst Rd.
  Printstile TN11 & TN3 & TN4 . 131 E3
Penshurst Sta. TN11 ... 114 F1
Penshurst Vinyard. TN11 ... 130 F2
Penshurst Way. BR5 ... 38 C5
Penstocks The. ME16 ... 91 D2
Penton House. [3] SE2 ... 3 D4
Penventon Ct. [3] RM18 ... 13 A5
Pepingstraw Cl. ME19 ... 88 D7
Pepper Cl. E6 ... 2 A7
Pepper Hill. DA11 ... 29 C5
Pepy's Way. ME2 ... 46 F8
Pepys Cl. [5] Dartford DA1 ... 10 A3

Pepys Cl. Northfleet DA11 ... 29 D5
Pepys Cl. Tilbury RM18 ... 13 C6
Pepys Cres. E16 ... 1 A5
Pepys Rise. E16 ... 37 F1
Percival Rd. BR6 ... 51 B8
Percy Rd. DA7 ... 7 E5
Percy St. [8] RM17 ... 12 C8
Peregrine Ct. DA16 ... 6 F6
Peregrine Dr. ME18 ... 89 A2
Peridot St. E6 ... 1 E8
Perimeter Rd. ME20 ... 75 C3
Periton St. SE9 ... 5 D3
Perkins Cl. DA9 ... 10 F2
Perpins Rd. SE9 ... 6 E1
Perran Cl. DA3 ... 42 F5
Perry Gr. DA1 ... 10 A3
Perry Hall Cl. BR6 ... 38 A2
Perry Hall Prim Sch. BR6 ... 37 F3
Perry Hall Rd. BR6 ... 38 A2
Perry St. Chatham ME4 ... 47 E3
Perry St. Chislehurst BR7 ... 23 E2
Perry St. Crayford DA1 ... 8 E4
Perry St. Maidstone ME14 ... 91 F6
Perry St. Northfleet DA11 ... 29 F7
Perry Street Gdns. BR7 ... 23 E2
Perryfield St. ME14 ... 91 F6
Perrys La. BR6 & TN14 ... 67 C6
Perth House. [4] RM18 ... 13 A5
Pescot Ave. DA3 ... 43 B6
Pested Bars Rd. ME17 ... 107 D5
Peter St. [5] DA11 ... 30 B8
Peterborough Gdns. ME2 ... 46 C6
Peters Cl. DA16 ... 6 E5
Petersfield. TN2 ... 150 E7
Petersfield Dr. DA13 ... 57 F1
Petersham Dr. BR5 ... 38 A6
Petersham Gdns. BR5 ... 37 F7
Peterstone Rd. SE2 ... 3 B4
Petham Court Cotts. BR8 ... 39 F4
Petham Gn. ME8 ... 49 C2
Petrie House. [3] SE18 ... 6 A8
Pett St. SE7 ... 1 E2
Petten Cl. BR5 ... 38 D1
Petten Gr. BR5 ... 38 D1
Petteridge La. TN12 ... 151 F7
Pettits Row. TN12 ... 137 D8
Pettman Cres. SE18 & SE28 ... 2 D3
Petts Wood Rd. BR5 ... 37 D4
Petts Wood Sta. BR5 ... 37 C4
Petworth Rd. DA6 ... 8 A2
Peverel. E6 ... 2 A7
Peverel Dr. ME14 ... 93 A5
Peverel Gn. ME8 ... 63 D4
Peveril Ct. [3] DA2 ... 10 B1
Pheasant Cl. E16 ... 1 B7
Pheasant La. ME15 ... 107 B8
Pheasant Rd. ME4 ... 48 C2
Phelps Cl. TN15 ... 55 E4
Philipot Almshouse. SE9 ... 5 F1
Philipot Path. SE9 ... 5 F1
Philippa Gdns. SE9 ... 5 D2
Phillip Ave. BR8 ... 39 D5
Phillips Cl. DA1 ... 9 B1
Phillips Ct. ME8 ... 49 B2
Philpots Cl. TN11 ... 115 E6
Philpott's Cross. TN18 ... 178 E2
Phineas Pett Road Rd. SE9 ... 5 E4
Phipps House. [1] SE7 ... 1 B1
Phoenix Cotts. ME18 ... 104 D6
Phoenix Dr. Keston Mark BR2 .. 50 D7
Phoenix Dr. Wateringbury ME18 104 E7
Phoenix Ind Est. ME2 ... 47 D7
Phoenix Pk. ME15 ... 107 F4
Phoenix Pl. DA1 ... 26 D8
Phoenix Rd. ME5 ... 62 B2
Phoenix Yard Cotts. ME18 ... 89 F1
Picardy Manorway. DA17 ... 4 B3
Picardy Rd. DA17 ... 4 A2
Picardy Sch (Beeches Site).
  DA17 ... 4 B2
Picardy St. DA17 ... 4 A3
Piccadilly The. [6] ME4 ... 48 B3
Pickering Ct. [8] DA2 ... 10 B1
Pickering House. [4] SE18 ... 2 A2
Pickering St. ME15 ... 107 B6
Pickford Cl. DA7 ... 7 E5
Pickford La. DA7 ... 7 E5
Pickford Rd. DA7 ... 7 E4
Pickhill Oast. TN30 ... 183 B4
Pickhurst La. BR2 ... 36 A1
Pickle's Way. ME3 ... 16 A6
Pickmoss La. TN14 ... 69 A3
Pickwick Cres. ME1 ... 47 C3
Pickwick Ct. SE9 ... 22 F7
Pickwick Gdns. DA11 ... 29 D5
Pickwick House. DA11 ... 29 D5
Pickwick Way. BR7 ... 23 C2
Piedmont Rd. SE18 ... 2 D1
Pier Approach Rd. ME7 ... 48 D7
Pier Par. [3] E16 ... 2 A5
Pier Pl. DA11 ... 34 A3
Pier Rd. Erith DA8 ... 4 E8
Pier Rd. Gillingham ME7 ... 48 E7
Pier Rd. Newham E16 ... 2 A4
Pier Rd. Northfleet DA11 ... 12 F1
Pier Rd. Swanscombe DA9 ... 11 B3
Pier Rd Ind Est. ME7 ... 48 D7
Pier Way. SE18 ... 2 D3
Pierce Mill La. TN11 ... 119 C6
Piermont Pl. BR1 ... 36 E7
Pigdown La. TN8 ... 129 D4
Piggott's Cross. TN8 ... 113 D7
Pigsdean Rd. DA13 ... 45 B2
Pike Cl. BR1 ... 22 B3
Pikefields. ME8 ... 49 C2

Pikefish La. TN12 ... 120 F2
Pikey La. ME19 ... 89 E5
Pilgrim's Way Cotts. TN15 ... 70 A2
Pilgrims Ct. Dartford DA1 ... 10 A2
Pilgrims Ct. Greenwich SE3 ... 5 A6
Pilgrims Lakes. ME17 ... 110 E6
Pilgrims' Rd. DA10 ... 11 E3
Pilgrims View. Sandling ME14 .. 77 B6
Pilgrims View. Swanscombe DA9 11 C3
Pilgrims Way. Boxley ME14 ... 77 E3
Pilgrims Way.
  Broad Street ME14 & ME17 ... 94 C6
Pilgrims Way. Cuxton ME2 ... 46 C3
Pilgrims Way. Dartford DA1 ... 27 B8
Pilgrims Way. Detling ME14 ... 78 B1
Pilgrims Way. Eccles ME20 ... 76 B6
Pilgrims Way.
  Hollingbourne ME17 ... 94 C3
Pilgrims' Way.
  Kemsing TN15 & TN14 ... 70 C3
Pilgrims Way. Lenham ME17 .. 111 B7
Pilgrims Way.
  Twitton TN13 & TN14 ... 68 E3
Pilgrims Way.
  Upper Halling ME2 & DA13 ... 59 D3
Pilgrims Way. Upper Halling ME2 59 D3
Pilgrims Way. Vigo Village TN15 . 73 B2
Pilgrims Way. Wouldham ME1 .. 60 E5
Pilgrims Way. Wrotham TN15 .. 72 A3
Pilgrims Way. Wrotham TN15 .. 72 C4
Pilgrims Way E. TN14 ... 69 D3
Pilgrims Way W. Otford TN14 .. 68 F3
Pilgrims Way W. Twitton TN13 . 68 D7
Pilkington Rd. BR6 ... 51 C8
Pillar Box La. TN11 ... 102 D5
Pillar Box Rd. TN15 ... 85 E5
Pilot Rd. ME1 ... 61 C8
Pilots Pl. DA12 ... 13 C1
Pimp's Court Cotts. ME15 ... 106 E6
Pimp's Court Farm Ctr. ME15 106 E6
Pimpernel Cl. ME14 ... 93 B4
Pimpernel Way. ME5 ... 61 E4
Pinchbeck Rd. BR6 ... 51 F4
Pincott Rd. DA6 ... 8 A3
Pincroft Wood. DA3 ... 43 C6
Pine Ave. DA12 ... 30 D7
Pine Cl. Larkfield ME20 ... 75 A2
Pine Cl. Swanley BR8 ... 39 F5
Pine Cotts. ME14 ... 91 E8
Pine Glade. BR6 ... 50 F6
Pine Gr. Edenbridge TN8 ... 112 B2
Pine Gr. Gillingham ME7 ... 63 A5
Pine Gr. Maidstone ME14 ... 92 B6
Pine House. [3] ME5 ... 61 F5
Pine Lodge. ME16 ... 91 C3
Pine Rd. ME2 ... 46 F6
Pine Rd. TN10 ... 117 B6
Pine Rise. DA13 ... 44 A3
Pine Tree La. TN15 ... 86 A2
Pine View. TN15 ... 87 C7
Pinecrest Gdns. BR6 ... 51 B6
Pinecroft. DA16 ... 7 A7
Pinehurst. Chislehurst BR7 ... 23 B2
Pinehurst.
  Sevenoaks TN14 & TN15 ... 84 E6
Pinehurst Wlk. [4] BR6 ... 37 D1
Pineneedle La. TN13 ... 84 B4
Pines Rd. BR1 ... 36 E7
Pinesfield La. ME19 ... 73 B6
Pinewood. BR7 ... 23 A2
Pinewood Ave. Sevenoaks TN13 . 84 D6
Pinewood Ave. Sidcup DA15 .. 23 E7
Pinewood Cl. Orpington BR6 .. 37 D1
Pinewood Cl.
  Paddock Wood TN12 ... 135 F6
Pinewood Ct. TN4 ... 133 A1
Pinewood Dr. Chatham ME14 .. 77 D8
Pinewood Dr. Orpington BR6 .. 51 E5
Pinewood Gdns. TN4 ... 133 A1
Pinewood Rd. Bromley BR2 ... 36 A5
Pinewood Rd. Erith SE2 ... 7 D8
Pinewood Rd.
  Royal Tunbridge Wells TN2 .. 149 D5
Pinkham. TN12 ... 120 A5
Pinkham Gdns. TN12 ... 120 A6
Pinks Hill. BR8 ... 39 E4
Pinnacle Hill. DA7 ... 8 B3
Pinnacle Hill N. DA7 ... 8 B3
Pinnell Rd. SE9 ... 5 D3
Pinnock La. TN12 ... 139 E1
Pinnock's Ave. DA11 ... 30 B7
Pintail Cl. Grain ME3 ... 21 B6
Pintail Cl. Newham E6 ... 1 E8
Pintails The. ME4 ... 34 B1
Pinto Way. SE3 ... 5 B3
Pinton Hill. TN5 ... 176 B3
Pioneer Way. BR8 ... 39 E6
Piper's Green Rd. TN16 ... 97 B7
Pipers Cl. TN5 ... 175 A4
Pipers La. TN16 ... 97 A8
Pippenhall. SE9 ... 6 B1
Pippin Cl. ME17 ... 106 B2
Pippin Croft. ME7 ... 63 A6
Pippin Rd. TN12 ... 119 F6
Pippin Way. ME18 ... 89 A2
Pippins The. DA13 ... 44 A3
Pirbright Cl. ME5 ... 62 D2
Pirie St. E16 ... 1 B5
Pirrip Cl. DA12 ... 30 F6
Pit La. TN8 ... 112 C4
Pitfield. DA3 ... 42 F5
Pitfield Cres. SE28 ... 3 A5
Pitfield Dr. DA13 ... 57 F7
Pitt Cl. ME17 ... 109 A2
Pitt Rd. Langley Heath ME17 .. 109 A2
Pitt Rd. Maidstone ME16 ... 91 B1
Pitt Rd. Orpington BR6 ... 51 C6

Pittlesden. TN30 ... 183 A7
Pittlesden Pl. [1] TN30 ... 183 A7
Pittsmead Ave. BR2 ... 36 A2
Pittswood Cotts. TN11 ... 118 A8
Pix's La. TN17 ... 182 A3
Pixot Hill. TN12 ... 136 B2
Pizien Well Rd. ME18 ... 104 E3
Place Farm Ave. BR5 & BR6 ... 37 D1
Place La. ME2 ... 64 C4
Plain Rd. TN12 ... 138 C4
Plain The. TN17 ... 167 E8
Plains Ave. ME15 ... 92 C1
Plaistow Gr. BR1 ... 22 B1
Plaistow La. BR1 ... 36 C8
Plaistow Sq. ME14 ... 92 C6
Plane Ave. DA11 ... 29 D8
Plane Tree House. SE7 ... 1 D1
Plane Wlk. TN10 ... 117 C1
Plantagenet House. SE18 ... 1 F3
Plantation Dr. BR5 ... 38 D1
Plantation La. ME14 ... 93 A3
Plantation Rd. Erith DA8 ... 9 A6
Plantation Rd. Gillingham ME7 . 49 A6
Plantation Rd. Hextable BR8 ... 26 A2
Plantation The. SE3 ... 5 A5
Plat The. TN8 ... 112 D1
Platt CE Prim Sch. TN15 ... 87 C7
Platt Comm. TN15 ... 87 C7
Platt House La. TN15 ... 72 C6
Platt Ind Est. TN15 ... 87 C8
Platt The. Frant TN3 ... 163 B1
Platt The. Sutton Valence ME17 124 E7
Platt's Heath Cty Prim Sch.
  ME17 ... 110 F3
Platters The. ME8 ... 63 C7
Plaxdale Green Rd. TN15 ... 71 D7
Plaxtol Cl. BR1 ... 36 C8
Plaxtol Cty Prim Sch. TN15 .. 101 E7
Plaxtol La. TN15 ... 101 D8
Plaxtol Rd. DA8 ... 8 A7
Playstool Cl. ME9 ... 65 B6
Playstool Rd. ME9 ... 65 A6
Pleasance Rd. BR5 ... 38 B6
Pleasant Row. [2] ME4 ... 48 A6
Pleasant View. DA8 ... 4 E1
Pleasant View Pl. BR6 ... 51 C5
Pleasaunce Ct. SE9 ... 5 F3
Pleasure House Rd. ME17 ... 125 A8
Plewis House. ME7 ... 48 E7
Plomley Cl. ME8 ... 63 D4
Plough Cotts. ME17 ... 108 E2
Plough Hill. TN15 ... 86 F4
Plough Wents Rd. ME17 ... 108 B2
Plough Wlk. TN8 ... 112 C4
Ploughmans Way. Chatham ME5 62 A1
Ploughmans Way.
  Gillingham ME8 ... 63 E6
Plover Cl. Chatham ME5 ... 62 D1
Plover Cl. Marlpit Hill TN8 ... 112 C3
Plover Rd. ME20 ... 74 F2
Plowenders Cl. ME19 ... 73 D2
Pluckley Cl. ME8 ... 49 C3
Pluckley Rd. TN27 ... 143 D2
Plug La. TN15 ... 58 D5
Plum La. SE18 ... 6 C7
Plum Tree Cotts. TN18 ... 184 E8
Plum Tree Rd. ME9 ... 79 B8
Plumcroft Prim Sch. SE18 ... 6 C8
Plumley Feather Cotts. TN3 .. 160 B3
Plummer La. TN30 ... 182 F6
Plummers Croft. TN15 ... 83 E6
Plumpton Wlk. [9] ME15 ... 107 F6
Plumstead Common Rd. SE18 .. 6 A8
Plumstead High St. SE18 & SE2 . 2 E2
Plumstead Manor Sch. SE18 ... 6 C8
Plumstead Rd. SE18 & SE28 ... 2 C2
Plumstead Sta. SE18 ... 2 D2
Plumtree Gr. ME7 ... 63 A4
Plumtree Rd.
  Plumtree Green TN27 ... 125 A1
Plumtree Rd.
  Plumtree Green TN27 ... 140 F7
Plumtrees. ME16 ... 91 A2
Plymouth Dr. TN13 & TN15 ... 84 C3
Plymouth Pk. TN15 ... 84 C3
Plymouth Rd. Bromley BR1 ... 36 B8
Plymouth Rd. Newham E16 ... 1 A8
Plympton Cl. [8] DA17 ... 3 E3
Plymstock Rd. DA16 ... 7 C7
Poachers Cl. ME5 ... 62 C5
Pococks Bank. TN8 ... 113 C3
Podkin Wood. ME5 ... 76 F8
Pointer Cl. SE28 ... 3 D7
Pointer Sch The. SE3 ... 5 A7
Pointers Ash Cty Prim Sch.
  DA11 ... 29 D5
Pokes Cott. TN17 ... 166 F2
Polebrook Rd. SE3 ... 5 C4
Polesden Rd. TN2 ... 149 D2
Polhill. TN14 ... 68 C4
Polhill Dr. ME5 ... 61 F2
Police Station Rd. ME19 ... 89 C8
Pollard Cl. E16 ... 1 A6
Pollard Ct. ME7 ... 48 C5
Pollard Wlk. DA14 ... 24 C2
Polley Cl. TN2 ... 150 D7
Pollhaugh. DA4 ... 54 E7
Pollyhough. DA4 ... 54 E7
Polperro Cl. BR6 ... 37 F3
Polthorne Gr. SE18 ... 2 D2
Polytechnic St. SE18 ... 2 A2
Pond Cl. SE3 ... 5 A5
Pond Farm Rd. Hucking ME9 ... 79 D1
Pond Farm Rd. Oad Street ME9 . 65 F1
Pond La. TN15 ... 85 E2
Pond Path. BR7 ... 23 B2
Pondfield La. DA12 ... 31 E1
Pondfield Rd. BR6 ... 51 B7

Pondwood Rise. BR6 .... 37 E2
Pontefract Rd. BR1 .... 22 A3
Pontoise Cl. TN13 .... 83 F5
Pook La. TN27 .... 158 D3
Poona Rd. TN1 & TN2 .... 149 B2
Pootings Rd. TN8 .... 112 E7
Pope Dr. TN12 .... 139 E4
Pope House La. TN30 .... 173 B4
Pope Rd. BR2 .... 36 D4
Pope St. ME16 .... 91 C2
Pope Street Ct. SE9 .... 22 F7
Poplar Ave. Gravesend DA12 .... 30 C4
Poplar Ave. Orpington BR6 .... 51 B8
Poplar Cl. ME3 .... 34 E3
Poplar Field. TN30 .... 189 D4
Poplar Gr. ME16 .... 91 C5
Poplar Mount. DA17 .... 4 C2
Poplar Pl. SE28 .... 3 C6
Poplar Rd. Rochester ME2 .... 46 E5
Poplar Rd. Wittersham TN30 ... 189 D4
Poplar Wlk. DA13 .... 44 B3
Poplars Cl. DA3 .... 43 C6
Poplicans Rd. ME2 .... 46 B3
Poppy Cl. ME7 .... 48 E5
Popular Cl. ME2 .... 46 F5
Porchester Cl. Hartley DA3 .... 42 F5
Porchester Cl. Maidstone ME15 107 A6
Porchfield Cl. DA12 .... 30 C6
Porcupine Cl. SE9 .... 22 E6
Porrington Cl. BR7 .... 37 A8
Port Ave. DA9 .... 11 B1
Port Cl. Chatham ME5 .... 62 B3
Port Cl. Maidstone ME14 .... 93 A5
Port Hill. BR6 .... 67 B7
Port Rise. ME4 .... 47 F3
Port Victoria Rd. ME3 .... 21 C4
Porter Cl. RM16 .... 11 C8
Porter Rd. E6 .... 1 F7
Porters Cl. TN12 .... 151 F6
Porters Wlk. ME17 .... 108 E4
Porters Wood. TN12 .... 151 E6
Porteus Ct. DA1 .... 26 D6
Porthkerry Ave. DA16 .... 7 A3
Portland Ave. Gravesend DA12 ... 30 B6
Portland Ave. Sidcup DA15 .... 7 A1
Portland Cres. SE9 .... 22 E6
Portland Pl. 1 ME6 .... 75 A8
Portland Rd. Bromley BR1 .... 22 C3
Portland Rd. Chislehurst SE9 .... 22 E6
Portland Rd. Gillingham ME7 .... 48 E6
Portland Rd. Gravesend DA11 ... 30 B7
Portland Rd. Northfleet DA11 ... 12 D1
Portland Rd. Wouldham ME1 ... 60 C4
Portland St. ME4 .... 48 B2
Portman Cl. Bexley DA7 .... 7 E4
Portman Pk. Maypole DA5 .... 25 E7
Portman Pl. TN10 & TN9 ...... 117 C3
Portobello Par. TN15 .... 56 A2
Portsdown Cl. ME16 .... 91 B2
Portsea Rd. RM18 .... 13 C6
Portsmans Cotts. ME19 .... 89 B5
Portsmouth Cl. ME2 .... 46 D6
Portway Gdns. SE18 .... 5 D7
Portway Rd. ME3 .... 33 B7
Post Barn Rd. ME4 .... 47 F2
Post Office Rd. 12 TN18 ...... 178 F2
Postern La. TN9 .... 117 E1
Postley Commercial Ctr. ME15 92 A2
Postley Rd. ME15 .... 92 A1
Postmill Dr. ME15 .... 91 F1
Potash La. TN15 .... 87 C6
Potter's La. TN18 .... 179 A6
Pottery Rd. Coldblow DA5 .... 25 C6
Pottery Rd. Hoo St Werburgh ME3 34 D5
Potyn House. ME1 .... 47 C4
Poulters Wood. BR2 .... 50 D5
Pound Bank Cl. TN15 .... 55 F2
Pound Cl. BR6 .... 51 D8
Pound Court Dr. BR6 .... 51 D8
Pound Green Ct. 4 DA5 .... 25 A8
Pound House. TN11 .... 118 E8
Pound La. Knockholt Pound TN14 67 D4
Pound La. Sevenoaks TN13 ...... 84 C3
Pound Park Rd. SE7 .... 1 D2
Pound Pl. SE9 .... 6 A1
Pound Rd. TN12 .... 119 F6
Poundfield Rd. TN18 .... 186 B5
Poundsbridge Hill. TN11 & TN3 147 D7
Pounsley Rd. TN13 .... 83 E6
Pout Rd. ME6 .... 74 F7
Poverest Prim Sch. BR5 .... 38 A4
Poverest Rd. BR5 .... 38 A4
Povey Ave. ME2 .... 33 C2
Powder Mill La. Dartford DA1 ... 26 F6
Powder Mill La. Leigh TN11 ... 116 B1
Powder Mill La.
  Powder Mills TN11 .... 116 E2
Powder Mill La.
  Royal Tunbridge Wells TN4 ...... 149 B8
Powdermill Cl. TN4 .... 149 C8
Powell Cl. ME20 .... 76 A3
Power Ind Est. DA8 .... 9 A6
Powerscroft Rd. DA14 .... 24 C2
Powis St. SE18 .... 2 A3
Powlett Rd. ME2 .... 33 C1
Powster Rd. BR1 .... 22 A3
Powys Cl. DA7 .... 7 D8
Poynder Rd. RM18 .... 13 A7
Poynings Cl. BR6 .... 52 C8
Poyntell Cres. BR7 .... 37 D8
Poyntell Rd. TN12 .... 139 F4
Pragnell Rd. SE12 .... 22 B6
Prall's La. TN12 .... 135 E2
Pratling St. ME20 .... 76 C4
Pratt's Bottom Prim Sch. TN14 67 C8
Premier Par. ME20 .... 75 E1
Prentiss Ct. SE7 .... 1 D2
Prescott Ave. BR5 .... 37 B3

Presentation House. 9 DA11 .. 30 B8
Prestbury Sq. SE9 .... 22 F4
Prestley Dr. TN10 .... 117 E7
Preston Ave. ME7 .... 48 E1
Preston Ct. DA14 .... 23 F4
Preston Dr. ME16 .... 7 D6
Preston Hall Hospl. ME20 ...... 75 F1
Preston House. 1 SE18 .... 2 A2
Preston Rd. Northfleet DA11 ... 29 E7
Preston Rd. Tonbridge TN9 ... 117 A1
Prestons Rd. BR2 .... 50 A8
Pretoria House. 4 Erith DA8 ...... 8 E7
Pretoria House. 8
  Park Wood ME15 .... 107 E5
Pretoria Rd. Chatham ME4 ...... 47 F2
Pretoria Rd. Gillingham ME7 ... 48 D3
Prettymans La. TN8 .... 112 F4
Pridmore Rd. ME6 .... 74 F8
Priest's Wlk. DA12 .... 31 A6
Priestfield Rd. ME7 .... 48 E5
Priestfield Stad (Gillingham FC).
  ME7 .... 48 E5
Priestfields. ME1 .... 47 B3
Priestlands Park Rd. DA15 ...... 23 F5
Priestley Dr. Lunsford ME20 ... 74 F4
Priestley Dr. Tonbridge TN10 ... 117 E7
Priestwood Rd. DA13 .... 58 C5
Primrose Ave. ME8 .... 63 B5
Primrose Cl. ME1 .... 61 E7
Primrose Dr. ME20 .... 75 D1
Primrose Rd. ME2 .... 59 E5
Primrose Terr. DA12 .... 30 C7
Prince Arthur Rd. ME7 .... 48 B6
Prince Charles Ave.
  Chatham ME5 .... 62 B4
Prince Charles Ave.
  South Darenth DA4 .... 41 D7
Prince Charles House. DA4 ... 41 D7
Prince Consort Dr. BR7 .... 37 D8
Prince Henry Rd. SE7 .... 5 D7
Prince Imperial Rd.
  Chislehurst BR7 .... 23 B1
Prince Imperial Rd.
  Woolwich SE18 .... 5 F6
Prince John Rd. SE9 .... 5 E2
Prince Of Wales Rd.
  Greenwich SE3 .... 5 A6
Prince Of Wales Rd. Newham E16 1 C7
Prince Regent La. E16 .... 1 C7
Prince Regent Sta. E16 .... 1 C6
Prince Rupert Rd. SE9 .... 5 F3
Prince's Plain. BR2 .... 36 E1
Prince's Plain Prim Sch. BR2 .. 36 E2
Prince's St. Rochester ME1 ...... 47 C4
Prince's St.
  Royal Tunbridge Wells TN2 ... 149 C3
Princes Ave. Chatham ME5 ...... 62 B5
Princes Ave. Dartford DA2 ...... 27 B7
Princes Ave. Orpington BR5 ... 37 E4
Princes Cl. DA14 .... 24 D5
Princes Rd. Dartford DA1 ...... 26 B7
Princes Rd. Dartford DA1 ...... 26 D7
Princes Rd.
  Dartford,Fleet-Down DA1 & DA2 .. 27 C7
Princes Rd. Gravesend DA12 ... 30 C5
Princes Rd. Hextable BR8 ...... 26 A2
Princes St. Bexley DA7 .... 7 F4
Princes St. Gravesend DA11 ... 13 B1
Princes St. Maidstone ME14 ... 92 A5
Princes View. DA1 .... 27 A7
Princes Way. ME14 .... 78 A1
Princess Christian's Hospl.
  TN11 .... 100 E2
Princess Margaret Rd. RM18 .. 14 D7
Princess Mary Ave. ME7 ...... 48 B7
Princess Par. BR6 .... 51 A7
Prinys Dr. ME8 .... 63 C4
Priolo Rd. SE7 .... 1 C1
Prior's Way. TN8 .... 145 A6
Priorsdean Cl. ME16 .... 90 E1
Priorsford Ave. BR5 .... 38 B5
Priory Ave. BR5 .... 37 D3
Priory Cl. Bromley BR1 & BR7 .. 36 F8
Priory Cl. Dartford DA1 .... 9 D2
Priory Cl. East Farleigh ME15 .. 106 B8
Priory Ct. 3 Dartford DA1 ...... 9 D1
Priory Ctr The. DA1 .... 26 E8
Priory Dr. SE2 .... 3 D1
Priory Fields. DA4 .... 54 F8
Priory Gate. 4 ME14 .... 92 A5
Priory Gdns. DA1 .... 9 D2
Priory Gr. Aylesford ME20 ...... 75 D1
Priory Gr. Tonbridge TN9 ...... 133 B8
Priory Hill. DA1 .... 9 D1
Priory House. 3 SE7 .... 5 C8
Priory La. DA4 .... 40 F1
Priory Leas. SE9 .... 22 E7
Priory Mews. DA2 .... 27 C8
Priory Pl. DA1 .... 9 D1
Priory Rd. Dartford DA1 .... 9 D1
Priory Rd. Dartford DA1 .... 9 D2
Priory Rd. Gillingham ME8 ...... 49 A2
Priory Rd. Maidstone ME15 ... 92 A3
Priory Rd. Rochester ME2 ...... 47 A6
Priory Rd. Tonbridge TN9 ...... 133 C8
Priory Sch The. BR5 .... 38 C1
Priory St. TN9 .... 133 B8
Priory Way. TN30 .... 183 C7
Priory Wlk. TN9 .... 133 B8
Pristling La. TN12 .... 155 B8
Progress Est The. ME15 ...... 108 A4
Prospect Ave. ME2 .... 47 B8
Prospect Cl. DA17 .... 4 A2
Prospect Cotts.
  Pratt's Bottom BR6 .... 52 C2
Prospect Cotts. The Down TN3 . 166 A3

Prospect Gr. DA12 .... 30 D8
Prospect Pk. TN4 .... 132 F1
Prospect Pl. Bromley BR2 ...... 36 B6
Prospect Pl. Collier Street TN12 121 C2
Prospect Pl. Dartford DA1 ...... 9 E1
Prospect Pl. Gravesend DA11 .. 30 D8
Prospect Pl. Grays RM17 ...... 12 B8
Prospect Pl. Maidstone ME16 .. 91 A2
Prospect Rd.Royal Tunbridge Wells
  TN1 & TN2 .... 149 C3
Prospect Rd.Royal Tunbridge Wells,
  Southborough TN4 .... 132 F1
Prospect Rd. Sevenoaks TN13 ... 84 C4
Prospect Row. Chatham ME4 .. 48 A3
Prospect Row. Gillingham ME4 .. 48 A6
Prospect Vale. SE18 & SE7 ...... 1 E2
Prospero Way. ME14 .... 92 E5
Provender Way. ME14 .... 92 E5
Providence Chapel. TN12 ...... 138 C6
Providence Cotts.
  Groombridge TN3 .... 161 C7
Providence Cotts. Higham ME2 . 32 B2
Providence La. ME1 .... 47 C5
Providence Pl. TN27 .... 141 A7
Providence St. DA9 .... 11 A2
Prudhoe Ct. 13 DA2 .... 10 B1
Pudding La. Maidstone ME14 ... 91 F4
Pudding La. Seal TN15 .... 84 F6
Pudding Rd. ME8 .... 63 F8
Puddingcake La. TN17 .... 182 C5
Puddledock La.
  Hextable BR8 & DA2 .... 25 F2
Puddledock La.
  Toy's Hill TN16 & TN8 .... 97 A3
Puffin Rd. ME3 .... 21 B5
Pullington Cotts. TN17 .... 180 E6
Pullman Pl. SE9 .... 5 E2
Pump Cl. ME9 .... 74 D1
Pump La. Gillingham ME8 ...... 49 D2
Pump La. Gillingham ME7 & ME8 . 49 D3
Punch Croft. DA3 .... 56 E7
Purbeck Rd. ME4 .... 47 E2
Purcell Ave. ME10 .... 117 F6
Purfleet By-Pass. RM16 ...... 10 D8
Purland Rd. SE28 & SE18 ...... 2 F4
Purneys Rd. SE9 .... 5 D3
Purrett Rd. SE18 .... 2 F1
Purser Way. ME7 .... 48 C7
Putlands L Ctr. TN12 .... 136 A5
Puttenden Rd. TN11 .... 101 F3
Pym Orch. TN16 .... 82 C3
Pynham Cl. SE2 .... 3 C1
Pyrus Cl. ME5 .... 77 A8

Quadrant The. DA7 .... 7 D7
Quaggy Wlk. SE3 .... 5 A3
Quaker Cl. TN13 .... 84 D4
Quaker Dr. TN17 .... 169 D6
Quaker La. TN17 .... 169 D6
Quaker's Hall La. TN13 .... 84 C5
Quakers Cl. DA3 .... 42 E6
Quantock Rd. DA1 .... 8 E5
Quarries The. ME17 .... 107 C4
Quarry Cotts. TN5 .... 174 D7
Quarry Hill. TN15 .... 84 D4
Quarry Hill Par. 1 TN9 .... 133 B8
Quarry Hill Rd.
  Borough Green TN15 .... 86 F6
Quarry Hill Rd. Tonbridge TN9 . 133 B8
Quarry Rd. ME15 .... 92 A2
Quarry Rise. TN9 .... 133 A7
Quarry Sq. ME14 .... 92 A5
Quarry Way. ME10 .... 10 F8
Quarry Wood Ind Est. ME20 ... 90 E8
Quay La. DA9 .... 11 B3
Quay Rd. TN1 .... 149 B5
Quayside. ME4 .... 48 B8
Quebec Ave. TN16 .... 81 D1
Quebec Cotts. 6 TN16 .... 81 D1
Quebec Rd. RM18 .... 13 A5
Quebec Sq. 5 TN16 .... 81 D1
Queen Anne Ave. BR2 .... 36 A6
Queen Anne Gate. DA7 .... 7 D4
Queen Anne Rd. ME14 .... 92 B4
Queen Borough Gdns. BR7 ...... 23 D2
Queen Elizabeth Military Hospl The.
  SE7 .... 5 E7
Queen Elizabeth Pl. RM18 ...... 13 A3
Queen Elizabeth Sq. ME15 ... 107 D6
Queen Mary's Hospl. DA14 ...... 24 A2
Queen Mother Ct The. ME1 ... 47 B4
Queen St. Bexley DA7 .... 7 F4
Queen St. Chatham ME4 ...... 48 A4
Queen St. Erith DA8 .... 8 E8
Queen St. Gravesend DA11 ... 13 B1
Queen St. Queen St TN12 ...... 136 D7
Queen St. Rochester ME1 ...... 47 C4
Queen St. Sandhurst TN18 ...... 186 B5
Queen's Ave. Maidstone ME16 . 91 D5
Queen's Ave. Snodland ME6 ... 75 A8
Queen's Dr. TN4 .... 149 B6
Queen's Farm Rd. DA12 ...... 31 E7
Queen's Gdns. TN4 .... 149 B6
Queen's Mews. 12 TN18 ...... 179 A2
Queen's Pas. BR7 .... 23 B2
Queen's Rd. Bexley DA16 ...... 7 B5
Queen's Rd. Bromley BR1 ...... 36 A7
Queen's Rd. Chatham ME5 ...... 48 D1
Queen's Rd. Chislehurst BR7 ... 23 B2
Queen's Rd. Gillingham ME7 ... 48 C4
Queen's Rd. Hawkhurst TN18 ... 179 A2
Queen's Rd. Maidstone ME16 . 91 C4
Queen's Rd.
  Royal Tunbridge Wells TN4 ...... 149 B6
Queen's Rd. Snodland ME6 ...... 75 A8
Queendown Ave. ME8 .... 63 D5
Queens Cotts. TN5 .... 174 E6
Queens Ct. Edenbridge TN8 ... 112 D1

Queens Ct. 11 Hawkhurst TN18 . 179 A2
Queens Gate Gdns. BR7 ...... 37 C8
Queens Gdns. DA1 & DA2 ...... 27 B7
Queens Rd. Erith DA8 .... 8 E8
Queens Rd. Gravesend DA12 ... 30 C5
Queens Way. ME14 .... 78 A1
Queenscroft Rd. SE9 .... 5 D1
Queensland House. 2 E16 ...... 2 A5
Queensway.
  Allhallows-on-Sea ME3 .... 19 D9
Queensway. Hayes BR2 & BR4 ... 50 A6
Queensway. Orpington BR5 ...... 37 C3
Queenswood Rd. Kit's Coty ME20 76 D7
Queenswood Rd. Sidcup DA15 ... 6 F1
Quern The. ME15 .... 91 E1
Quernmore Cl. BR1 .... 22 A2
Quernmore Rd. BR1 .... 22 A2
Quested Way. ME17 .... 110 C6
Quickrells Ave. ME3 .... 16 B5
Quickthorn Cres. ME5 .... 61 E5
Quiet Nook. BR2 .... 50 D7
Quilter Gdns. BR5 .... 38 C1
Quilter Rd. BR5 .... 38 D1
Quilter St. SE18 .... 2 F1
Quincewood Gdns. TN10 ...... 117 B7
Quinion Cl. ME5 .... 77 A8
Quinnell St. ME8 .... 49 E1
Quixote Cres. ME2 .... 33 B1

Rabbits Rd. DA4 .... 41 E7
Rablus Pl. DA4 .... 40 F3
Racefield Cl. DA12 .... 31 E1
Radfield Way. SE9 .... 23 D8
Radland Rd. E16 .... 1 A7
Radleigh Gdns. ME4 .... 47 E1
Radley House. 15 SE2 .... 3 D4
Radnor Ave. DA16 .... 7 B2
Radnor Cl. BR7 .... 23 E2
Radnor Cres. SE18 .... 7 A7
Raeburn Ave. DA1 .... 9 B2
Raeburn Cl. TN10 .... 117 E6
Raeburn Pl. DA10 .... 11 E2
Raeburn Rd. DA15 .... 6 E1
Rafford Way. BR1 .... 36 B6
Raggatt Pl. ME15 .... 92 B2
Ragge Way. TN15 .... 84 F7
Raggleswood. BR7 .... 37 A8
Raglan Cl. SE12 .... 5 A2
Raglan Prim Sch. BR2 .... 36 D5
Raglan Rd. Bromley BR2 ...... 36 C5
Raglan Rd. Erith DA17 .... 3 F2
Raglan Rd. Woolwich SE18 ...... 2 C1
Ragstone Ct. ME19 .... 90 C8
Ragstone Rd. ME15 .... 93 A2
Railway App. TN9 .... 133 B8
Railway Cotts. Cowden TN8 ... 145 D8
Railway Cotts. Hartley TN17 ... 168 E2
Railway Cotts. Marden TN12 ... 138 D6
Railway Pl. Erith DA17 .... 4 A1
Railway Pl. 18 Gravesend DA11 . 13 B1
Railway Sidings The. DA13 ...... 44 B4
Railway St. Chatham ME4 ...... 47 F4
Railway St. Gillingham ME7 ... 48 D6
Railway St. Northfleet DA11 ... 12 A2
Railway Terr. TN16 .... 81 D1
Rainham Cl. Eltham SE9 ...... 23 E6
Rainham Cl. Maidstone ME15 .. 92 A1
Rainham Mark Gram Sch. ME8 49 D2
Rainham Rd. Mees & ME7 ...... 48 E8
Rainham Sch for Girls. ME8 ... 63 C8
Rainham Sh Ctr. ME8 .... 63 F8
Rainham St. ME8 .... 49 F1
Rainton Rd. SE7 .... 1 A1
Raleigh Cl. Chatham ME5 ...... 62 B4
Raleigh Cl. Erith DA8 .... 8 F8
Raleigh Mews. 6 BR6 .... 51 F5
Ramac Ind Est. SE7 .... 1 B1
Ramac Way. SE7 .... 1 B1
Ramillies Cl. ME5 .... 62 A6
Ramillies Rd. DA15 .... 7 B1
Rammell Mews. TN17 .... 169 D4
Rampion Cl. ME14 .... 92 E5
Ramsden Cl. TN17 .... 180 F4
Ramsden Prim Sch. BR5 ...... 38 C2
Ramsden Rd. Erith DA8 .... 8 D7
Ramsden Rd.
  Orpington BR5 & BR6 .... 38 B1
Ramslye Rd. TN2 & TN4 ...... 162 E8
Ramus Wood Ave. BR6 ...... 51 E5
Rance House. 12 SE7 .... 1 E2
Rancliffe Gdns. SE9 .... 5 E3
Randall Cl. DA8 .... 8 C8
Randall Hill Rd. TN15 .... 71 F3
Randall Rd. ME4 .... 47 E1
Randall St. ME14 .... 91 F6
Randalls Row. ME15 .... 106 F5
Randle's La. BR6 & TN14 ...... 67 D5
Randolph App. E16 .... 1 C7
Randolph Cl. DA7 .... 8 C4
Randolph Cotts. ME2 .... 33 B1
Randolph Rd. Gillingham ME7 ... 48 C5
Randolph Rd. Keston Mark BR2 . 36 F1
Ranelagh Gdns. DA11 .... 29 F8
Range Rd. DA12 .... 30 E8
Rangefield Rd. BR1 .... 22 A3
Rangeworth Pl. DA15 .... 23 F5
Rankine Rd. TN1 .... 149 D7
Ranleigh Gdns. DA7 .... 7 F7
Ranmore Path. BR5 .... 38 A5
Ranscombe Cl. ME2 .... 46 C6
Ranscombe Farm Cotts. ME2 .. 46 C4
Ransom Rd. 1 SE7 .... 1 C1
Ranters La. TN17 .... 167 C7
Ranters Oak. TN17 .... 181 B4
Ranworth Cl. DA7 & DA8 ...... 8 F7
Raphael Ave. RM18 .... 13 B7
Raphael Ct. TN11 .... 116 E7
Raphael Rd. DA12 .... 30 C8

Rare Farm Animals Pk. TN11 . 100 C2
Rashleigh Way. DA4 .... 41 C5
Ratcliffe Cl. SE12 .... 22 A8
Ratcliffe Highway.
  Hoo St Werburgh ME3 .... 34 C7
Ratcliffe Highway.
  St Mary Hoo ME3 .... 18 D5
Rathmore Rd. Gravesend DA11 .. 30 B8
Rathmore Rd. Greenwich SE7 ... 1 B1
Raven Cl. ME20 .... 75 A1
Ravens Dane Cl. ME15 .... 93 A1
Ravens Knowle. ME1 .... 60 D4
Ravens Way. SE12 & SE3 ...... 5 A2
Ravens Wood Sch for Boys.
  BR2 .... 50 D7
Ravensbourne Coll of Design &
  Communication. BR7 .... 22 F3
Ravensbourne Ct. 23 BR5 ...... 38 D1
Ravensbourne Rd.
  Bromley BR1 & BR2 .... 36 A6
Ravensbourne Rd. Crayford DA1 . 9 A4
Ravensbourne Sch. BR2 ...... 36 B4
Ravensbury Rd. BR5 .... 38 A5
Ravenscourt Rd. BR5 .... 38 B7
Ravenscroft Rd. 5 E16 .... 1 A8
Ravenscroft Cres. SE9 .... 22 F5
Ravenscroft Rd. E16 .... 1 A8
Ravenshill. BR7 .... 37 B8
Ravensquay Bsns Ctr. BR5 ...... 38 B4
Ravenswood. DA5 .... 24 E7
Ravenswood Ave. Rochester ME1 33 B1
Ravenswood Ave. Royal Tunbridge Wells
  TN1 & TN2 .... 149 D6
Ravensworth Rd. SE9 .... 23 A5
Ravine Gr. SE18 .... 6 E8
Rawdon Rd. ME15 .... 92 A3
Rawlings Cl. 3 BR6 .... 51 F5
Rawsthorne Cl. E16 .... 1 F5
Rayfield Cl. BR2 .... 36 E3
Rayford Cl. DA1 .... 9 C2
Rayleas Cl. SE18 .... 6 B6
Raymer Rd. ME14 .... 92 B8
Raymere Gdns. SE18 .... 6 E7
Raymond Postgate Ct. 5 SE28 .. 3 B6
Raynehurst Cty Prim Sch. DA12 30 F5
Rayners Ct. DA11 .... 12 B1
Raynham Villas. TN12 .... 122 A4
Rays Hill. DA12 .... 41 C4
Read Way. DA12 .... 30 E3
Reader's Bridge Rd.
  TN27 & TN30 .... 172 E4
Readscroft Rd. ME8 .... 63 D5
Rebecca Ct. DA14 .... 24 B4
Recreation Ave. ME6 .... 75 A8
Recreation Cl. ME14 .... 92 B6
Recreation Ground Rd. TN30 . 183 B7
Rectory Bsns Ctr. DA14 ...... 24 B4
Rectory Cl. Crayford DA1 ...... 8 E3
Rectory Cl. Sidcup DA14 ...... 24 B4
Rectory Cl. Snodland ME6 ...... 75 A8
Rectory Cl. Wouldham ME1 ... 60 C5
Rectory Dr. TN4 .... 132 D3
Rectory Field Cres. SE7 ...... 5 C7
Rectory Fields. TN17 .... 169 D5
Rectory Grange. ME1 .... 47 C2
Rectory La. Brasted TN16 ...... 82 C3
Rectory La. Harrietsham ME17 .. 110 E5
Rectory La. Ightham TN15 ...... 86 C5
Rectory La. Maidstone ME16 ... 91 A1
Rectory La. Sevenoaks TN13 ... 84 C1
Rectory La. Sutton Valence ME17 124 C6
Rectory La. Sutton Valence ME17 124 F7
Rectory La N. ME19 .... 74 E2
Rectory La S. ME19 .... 74 E1
Rectory Meadow. DA13 ...... 29 A2
Rectory Paddock Sch &
  Research Unit. BR5 .... 38 C7
Rectory Park Rd. TN12 ...... 153 A2
Rectory Pl. SE18 .... 2 A2
Rectory Rd. Cliffe ME3 ...... 16 A3
Rectory Rd. 3 Grays RM17 ... 12 D8
Rectory Rd. Keston BR2 ...... 50 D3
Rectory Rd. Low Street RM18 ... 13 D8
Rectory Rd. Ridley TN15 ...... 57 C5
Rectory Rd. Swanscombe DA10 .. 28 E8
Rectory Rd. Tonbridge TN9 ... 133 B7
Reculver Wlk. Maidstone ME15 107 F6
Reculver Wlk. Maidstone ME15 107 F7
Red Barracks Rd. 4 SE18 ...... 1 F2
Red Cedars Rd. BR6 .... 37 E2
Red Hill. Chislehurst BR7 ...... 23 B3
Red Hill. Red Hill ME18 ...... 89 F1
Red Hill Prim Sch. BR7 ...... 23 B3
Red House Gdns. ME18 ...... 104 C7
Red House La. DA6 .... 7 E3
Red Lion Cl. BR5 .... 38 C3
Red Lion La. SE18 .... 6 A6
Red Lion Pl. SE18 .... 6 A6
Red Lodge Cres. DA5 .... 25 E5
Red Lodge Rd. DA5 .... 25 D5
Red Oak. TN18 .... 184 E8
Red Oak Cl. BR6 .... 51 B8
Red Oast Cotts. TN5 .... 177 C3
Red Robin Cotts. ME9 .... 65 B6
Redbank. ME19 .... 74 E2
Redbridge Cl. ME5 .... 62 C4
Redcliffe La. ME14 .... 92 B7
Reddy Rd. DA8 .... 8 F8
Rede Court Rd. ME2 .... 46 E8
Rede Wood Rd. ME16 .... 90 F3
Redgate Dr. BR2 .... 50 B8
Redhill Rd. TN15 .... 56 F6
Redhill Wood. DA3 .... 57 A7

Redland Shaw. ME4 .... 47 E1
Redlands Rd. TN13 .... 83 F3
Redleaf Cl. Erith DA17 .... 8 A8
Redleaf Cl.
　Royal Tunbridge Wells TN2 ..... 149 D6
Redmans La. BR6 & TN14 ...... 53 E4
Redpoll Way. SE2 .... 3 D3
Redpoll Wlk. TN12 .... 136 A5
Redruth Manor. ME7 .... 48 C6
Redsells Cl. ME15 .... 93 A1
Redstart Cl. E6 .... 1 E8
Redvers Rd. ME4 .... 48 A2
Redwall La. ME15 & ME17 .... 122 C6
Redwall La. TN15 .... 86 B4
Redwing. ME20 .... 75 A2
Redwing Path. SE28 .... 2 D4
Redwing Rd. ME5 .... 62 B7
Redwings La. TN2 .... 134 C2
Redwood Cl. Chatham ME5 ..... 62 B7
Redwood Cl. Sidcup DA15 ..... 24 A7
Redwood Cl. DA1 .... 10 A1
Redwood Pk. TN11 & TN12 ... 135 A5
Reed Ave. BR6 .... 51 E7
Reed Cl. Eltham SE12 .... 5 A2
Reed Cl. Newham E16 .... 1 A8
Reed Court Cotts. TN12 .... 122 A5
Reed St. ME3 .... 16 B6
Reedham Cres. ME3 .... 33 C7
Reeds Cotts. TN17 .... 170 A4
Reeds La. TN11 .... 101 E5
Reeves Cl. TN12 .... 139 E4
Reeves Cres. BR8 .... 39 D6
Reeves Ct. TN3 .... 147 B5
Reeves Rd. SE18 .... 6 B8
Reeves Terr. TN5 .... 176 E1
Reform Rd. ME4 .... 48 B2
Regency Cl. Gillingham ME8 .... 63 C3
Regency Cl.
　West Kingsdown TN15 .... 55 E4
Regency Hall. **19** TN2 .... 149 A2
Regency Way. DA7 .... 7 E4
Regent Dr. ME15 .... 107 A8
Regent Pl. TN2 .... 149 D3
Regent Rd. ME7 .... 48 C4
Regent Sq. DA17 .... 4 B2
Regent St. TN17 .... 181 E4
Regent's Pl. SE3 .... 5 A5
Regents Ct. **2** DA11 .... 13 B1
Regents Dr. BR2 .... 50 D5
Regina Ct. TN4 .... 148 F4
Reginald Ave. ME2 .... 46 C3
Reginald Rd. ME16 .... 91 E3
Reidhaven Rd. SE18 .... 2 E2
Reigate Rd. BR1 & SE12 .... 22 A5
Reinden Gr. ME15 .... 92 F1
Rembrandt Cl. TN10 .... 117 E6
Rembrandt Dr. DA11 .... 29 E5
Remington Rd. E6 .... 1 E7
Rendlebury House. **17** SE18 .. 1 F2
Renfrew Cl. E6 .... 2 A6
Rennets Cl. SE9 .... 6 E2
Rennets Wood Rd. SE9 .... 6 D2
Renown Rd. ME5 .... 62 C2
Renshaw Cl. **7** DA17 .... 7 F8
Renton Dr. BR5 .... 38 D2
Repository Rd. SE18 & SE7 ...... 1 F1
Repton Rd. BR6 .... 52 A6
Repton Way. ME5 .... 61 F4
Resolution Cl. ME5 .... 62 A6
Resolution Wlk. SE18 .... 1 F3
Restharrow Rd. ME14 .... 92 E4
Restons Cres. SE9 .... 6 E1
Retreat The. Grays RM17 .... 12 B8
Retreat The. Orpington BR6 .... 52 B4
Revell Rise. SE18 .... 6 F8
Revenge Rd. ME5 .... 77 C8
Reventlow Rd. SE9 .... 23 C7
Reynard Cl. BR1 .... 37 A6
Reynolds Cl. TN10 .... 117 E6
Reynolds Fields. ME3 .... 32 C6
Reynolds La. TN4 .... 148 F6
Reynolds Pl. SE3 .... 5 B7
Rhode St. ME4 .... 48 A4
Rhodes House. ME5 .... 48 C2
Rhodewood Ave. DA13 .... 58 A2
Rhododendron Ave. DA13 ...... 58 A2
Ribblesdale Rd. DA2 .... 27 C7
Ribston Cl. BR2 .... 36 F1
Ribston Gdns. TN12 .... 135 F7
Ricardo Path. **5** SE28 .... 3 C5
Rich Ind Est. DA1 .... 8 F2
Richard Cl. SE18 .... 1 E2
Richard St. Chatham ME4 .... 47 F4
Richard St. Rochester ME1 ..... 47 C3
Richard's Cl. TN11 .... 114 F2
Richardson Cl. DA9 .... 11 A2
Richardson Rd. TN4 .... 149 A5
Richborough Cl. BR5 .... 38 D5
Richborough Drive. ME2 .... 33 A1
Richings House. BR5 .... 38 A8
Richmer Rd. DA8 .... 9 A7
Richmond Cl. Chatham ME5 ... 62 B4
Richmond Cl. Upper Upton ME2 .. 33 F1
Richmond Cty Inf Sch. ME7 .... 48 C6
Richmond Pl. SE18 .... 2 C2
Richmond Rd. Gillingham ME7 .. 48 C7
Richmond Rd. **1** Grays RM17 .. 12 C8
Richmond Way. ME15 .... 107 A8
Richmount Gdns. SE3 .... 5 A4
Rickyard Path. SE9 .... 5 E8
Riddlesdale Ave. TN4 .... 149 A6
Riddons Rd. SE12 .... 22 C4
Rideout St. SE18 .... 1 F2
Rider Cl. DA15 .... 6 E1
Ridge Ave. DA1 .... 8 F1

Ridge La. DA13 .... 58 A2
Ridge Meadow Cty Prim Sch.
　ME5 .... 61 F6
Ridge The. Groombridge TN3 .. 161 A6
Ridge The. Orpington BR6 ...... 51 D8
Ridge The. Sidcup DA5 .... 24 F8
Ridge Way. Crayford DA1 .... 8 F1
Ridge Way. Marlpit Hill TN8 ... 112 D4
Ridgebrook Rd. SE3 & SE9 ...... 5 D4
Ridgecroft Cl. DA5 .... 25 C7
Ridgelands. TN3 .... 132 C4
Ridgeway. Hayes BR2 .... 50 A8
Ridgeway. Hurst Green TN19 .. 184 A3
Ridgeway. Lane End DA2 .... 27 E3
Ridgeway. Pembury TN2 .... 150 D7
Ridgeway. The Moor TN18 .... 184 E8
Ridgeway Ave. DA12 .... 30 B5
Ridgeway Bglws. DA12 .... 31 F1
Ridgeway Cres. Orpington BR6 .. 51 E7
Ridgeway Cres. Tonbridge TN10 117 D4
Ridgeway Crescent Gdns. BR6 .. 51 E7
Ridgeway Dr. BR1 .... 22 B4
Ridgeway E. DA15 .... 6 F2
Ridgeway The. Chatham ME4 ... 61 E7
Ridgeway The. Gillingham ME7 .. 48 C7
Ridgeway The.
　Shorne Ridgeway DA12 .... 31 E1
Ridgeway The. Tonbridge TN10 117 D4
Ridgeway W. DA15 .... 6 E2
Ridgewood. DA3 .... 43 C7
Ridgway. ME16 .... 91 B2
Ridgwell Rd. E16 .... 1 C8
Riding La. TN11 .... 100 D2
Riding Pk. TN11 .... 116 D7
Ridings The.
　Paddock Wood TN12 .... 136 A7
Ridings The.
　Royal Tunbridge Wells TN2 ... 149 C6
Ridley Rd. Bexley DA16 .... 7 B6
Ridley Rd. Bromley BR2 .... 36 A6
Ridley Rd. Rochester ME1 ...... 47 C4
Riefield Rd. SE9 .... 6 C2
Riggs Way. TN15 .... 71 F3
Ring Cl. RR1 .... 22 B1
Ringden Ave. TN12 .... 135 F5
Ringer's Rd. BR1 .... 36 A6
Ringle Gn. TN18 .... 186 C5
Ringlestone Cres. ME14 .... 91 F8
Ringlestone Rd. ME17 .... 95 D4
Ringmer Way. BR1 .... 36 F4
Rings Hill. TN11 .... 116 B4
Ringshall Rd. BR5 & BR7 .... 38 A6
Ringwood Ave. BR6 .... 52 C1
Ringwood Cl. ME8 .... 63 D8
Ringwood Rd. ME15 .... 107 C8
Ripley Cl. BR1 .... 36 F4
Ripley Rd. Erith DA17 .... 4 A2
Ripley Rd. Newham E16 .... 1 C7
Ripon Cl. ME8 .... 49 D3
Ripon Rd. SE18 .... 6 B8
Rippersley Rd. DA16 .... 7 A6
Risden La. TN18 .... 185 D7
Rise The. Crayford DA1 .... 8 F3
Rise The. Gillingham ME7 ...... 63 A3
Rise The. Gravesend DA12 ...... 30 E4
Rise The. Rochester ME1 .... 47 D3
Rise The. Sevenoaks TN13 ...... 99 C7
Rise The. Sidcup DA5 .... 24 C8
Risedale Rd. DA7 .... 8 C4
Riseden Rd. TN5 .... 174 C1
Ritch Rd. ME6 .... 74 E8
Ritter St. SE18 .... 6 A8
River Cl. ME15 .... 106 A7
River Cotts. BR5 .... 38 C7
River Ct. TN13 .... 83 E5
River Dr. ME2 .... 46 E7
River Lawn Rd. TN9 .... 117 B1
River Park View. BR6 .... 38 B2
River Rd. IG11 .... 3 A8
River St. **3** ME4 .... 48 A6
River View. **7** Dartford DA1 ... 10 A3
River View. Gillingham ME8 .... 49 D3
River View. Maidstone ME15 ... 91 F2
River Way. ME20 .... 75 B4
River Wlk. TN9 .... 117 B1
Riverdale Est. TN9 .... 133 D8
Riverdale Rd. Erith DA8 .... 4 C1
Riverdale Rd. Sidcup DA5 .... 7 F1
Riverdale Rd. Woolwich SE18 .... 2 F1
Riverhead Cl. ME16 .... 91 D6
Riverhead Cty Inf Sch. TN13 .... 83 F5
Riverhill. TN13 & TN15 .... 99 E4
Riverhill Cotts. TN15 .... 99 E5
Riverhill House Gdns. TN15 .... 99 E5
Rivers Wlk. ME17 .... 111 C5
Riversdale. DA11 .... 29 E5
Riverside. Edenbridge TN8 .... 112 C1
Riverside. Eynsford DA4 .... 54 D8
Riverside. Greenwich SE7 .... 1 B3
Riverside Cl. BR5 .... 38 C7
Riverside Cotts. TN14 .... 53 F1
Riverside Ct. **2** BR5 .... 38 C4
Riverside Ind Est. DA1 .... 9 E2
Riverside North Rd. ME4 .... 34 B2
Riverside Rd. DA14 .... 24 E6
Riverside Sch. DA1 .... 3 E4
Riverside Way. DA1 .... 9 E2
Riverside West Rd. ME4 .... 34 A2
Riverston Sch. SE12 .... 5 A2
Riverview Cty Inf Sch. DA12 ... 30 E4
Riverview Cty Jun Sch. DA12 ... 30 E4
Riverview Hts. SE18 .... 6 B7
Riverview Rd. ME9 .... 11 A2
Riverwood La. BR7 .... 37 D8

Rixon House. SE18 .... 6 B8
Roach St. ME2 .... 47 A7
Roan Ct. ME2 .... 46 F8
Robert Napier Sch The. ME7 ... 48 E3
Robert St. Newham E16 .... 2 B5
Robert St. Woolwich SE18 .... 2 D2
Roberton Dr. BR1 .... 36 C8
Roberts Cl. Eltham SE9 .... 23 D7
Roberts Cl. **8** Orpington BR5 .. 38 C4
Roberts House. SE18 .... 6 B8
Roberts Orchard Rd. ME16 ..... 90 F3
Roberts Rd. Erith DA17 .... 4 A1
Roberts Rd. Gillingham ME8 .... 63 E8
Roberts Rd. Snodland ME6 ..... 74 F8
Robertson House. SE18 .... 5 F6
Robin Cres. E16 .... 1 D8
Robin Hill Dr. BR7 .... 22 E2
Robin Hood Gn. BR5 .... 38 A4
Robin Hood La. Bexley DA6 ...... 7 E2
Robin Hood La. Chatham ME5 .. 61 F3
Robin Hood Lane (Lower). ME5 61 F2
Robin Hood Lane (Upper). ME5 61 E1
Robin House. **5** ME16 .... 91 E4
Robin Way. BR5 .... 38 B6
Robina Cl. DA6 .... 7 D3
Robina Ct. BR8 .... 40 A5
Robinia Ave. DA11 .... 29 D8
Robins Ave. ME17 .... 111 C5
Robins Cl. ME17 .... 111 C4
Robins Ct. Lewisham SE12 ...... 22 C5
Robins Ct. Maidstone ME14 .... 92 B7
Robins Gr. BR4 .... 50 A7
Robinwood Dr. DA15 .... 84 F8
Robson Cl. E6 .... 1 E7
Robson Dr. Aylesford ME20 .... 75 D2
Robson Dr. Hoo St Werburgh ME3 34 D6
Robyns Croft. **6** DA11 .... 29 E5
Robyns Way. Edenbridge TN8 .. 128 D8
Robyns Way. Sevenoaks TN13 .. 83 F5
Rocfort Rd. ME6 .... 75 A8
Rochdale Rd.
　Royal Tunbridge Wells TN1 ... 149 C6
Rochdale Rd. Woolwich SE2 ..... 3 B2
Rochester Airport. ME1 & ME5 .. 61 C6
Rochester Ave. Bromley BR1 .... 36 A6
Rochester Ave. Rochester ME1 .. 47 C4
Rochester Cath. ME1 .... 47 C6
Rochester Cl. **1** DA16 .... 7 B1
Rochester Cres. ME3 .... 34 D6
Rochester Ct. ME2 .... 47 E8
Rochester Dr. DA5 .... 8 A1
Rochester Gram Sch for Girls The.
　ME1 .... 47 C2
Rochester House. **1** ME15 .. 107 D7
Rochester Rd. Burham ME1 ..... 60 E2
Rochester Rd. Chalk DA12 ...... 31 B6
Rochester Rd. Chatham ME5 ... 61 C4
Rochester Rd. Dartford DA1 .... 27 A8
Rochester Rd.
　Pratling Street ME20 .... 76 B4
Rochester Rd. Rochester ME2 .. 46 D4
Rochester Rd. Tonbridge TN10 117 D4
Rochester Rd. Wouldham ME1 .. 60 C7
Rochester St. ME4 .... 47 E3
Rochester Sta. ME1 .... 47 D5
Rochester Way. Dartford DA1 .. 25 F8
Rochester Way. Eltham SE9 ...... 6 B4
Rochester Way.
　Eltham,Kidbrooke SE3 & SE9 ... 5 D4
Rock Ave. ME7 .... 48 C3
Rock Cotts. TN3 .... 163 B1
Rock Farm Cotts. ME18 .... 104 C6
Rock Hill. BR6 .... 53 B4
Rock Hill Rd. TN27 .... 127 E2
Rock Rd. Borough Green TN15 .. 86 F7
Rock Rd. Maidstone ME14 ...... 92 A6
Rock Villa Rd. TN1 .... 149 A4
Rockdale. TN13 .... 84 B2
Rockdale Rd. TN13 .... 84 C2
Rockliffe Manor Prim Sch. SE18 .. 6 F8
Rockmount Rd. SE18 & SE2 ...... 2 F1
Rocks Cl. ME19 .... 90 A6
Rocks Hill. TN17 .... 156 A4
Rocks Rd The. ME19 .... 90 B6
Rocky Hill. ME16 .... 91 E4
Rocky Hill Terr. **2** ME16 ...... 91 E4
Roding Rd. E6 .... 2 B8
Rodmell Rd. TN1 .... 149 A2
Rodney Ave. TN10 .... 117 E4
Rodney Gdns. BR4 .... 50 A6
Rodway Rd. BR1 .... 36 B8
Roebourne Way. E16 .... 2 A4
Roebuck Rd. ME1 .... 47 C5
Roedean Cl. BR6 .... 52 B6
Roedean Rd. TN1 & TN2 ...... 149 A1
Roehampton Cl. DA12 .... 30 E8
Roehampton Dr. BR7 .... 23 C2
Roethorne Gdns. TN30 .... 183 B8
Roffen Rd. ME1 .... 47 C2
Rogers Ct. BR8 .... 40 A5
Rogers Rough Rd. TN17 .... 167 B2
Rogers Wood La. TN15 .... 56 B6
Rogersmead. TN30 .... 183 A7
Rogley Hill. TN27 .... 171 B6
Rogues Hill. TN11 .... 131 C3
Rokesby Cl. DA16 .... 6 D5
Rolinsden Way. BR2 .... 50 D6
Rollesby Way. SE28 .... 3 C1
Rolleston Ave. BR5 .... 37 B3
Rolleston Cl. BR5 .... 37 B2
Rollo Rd. BR8 .... 25 F1

Rolvenden Sta. TN30 .... 182 D6
Roman Cl. ME5 .... 61 D1
Roman Hts. ME4 .... 92 C6
Roman Rd. Edenbridge TN8 .. 128 D5
Roman Rd. Northfleet DA11 .... 29 C5
Roman Rd. Snodland ME6 ...... 74 F8
Roman Sq. SE28 .... 3 A5
Roman Villa Rd. DA2 & DA4 .... 27 D7
Roman Way. Crayford DA1 .... 8 E2
Roman Way. Rochester ME2 .... 46 F4
Romany Ct. ME5 .... 48 D1
Romany Rd. ME8 .... 49 C2
Romany Rise. BR5 .... 37 C1
Romden Dr.
　Haffenden Quarter TN27 ..... 159 B8
Romden Rd. Romden TN27 .... 143 D1
Romero Sq. SE9 .... 5 C3
Romford Rd. TN2 & TN12 ..... 150 F7
Romney Cl. ME14 .... 93 A3
Romney Dr. BR1 .... 22 D1
Romney Gdns. DA7 .... 7 F6
Romney Pl. ME15 .... 92 A4
Romney Rd. Chatham ME5 ..... 62 B5
Romney Rd. Northfleet DA11 ... 29 C5
Romney Rd. Woolwich SE18 ..... 2 C3
Romney Way. TN10 .... 117 E5
Romsey Cl. Orpington BR6 ..... 51 C6
Romsey Cl. Rochester ME2 .... 46 E3
Ronald House. SE9 .... 5 C3
Ronalds Rd. BR1 .... 36 A8
Ronaldstone Rd. DA15 .... 6 E1
Ronfearn Ave. BR5 .... 38 D4
Ronver Rd. SE12 .... 22 A7
Rook La. ME9 .... 65 F6
Rookdean. TN13 .... 83 C5
Rookery Cres. ME3 .... 16 B6
Rookery Ct. RM16 .... 11 A8
Rookery Dr. BR7 .... 37 A8
Rookery Gdns. BR5 .... 38 C4
Rookery Hill. ME6 .... 74 F8
Rookery La. BR2 .... 36 D3
Rookery Rd. BR6 .... 51 A1
Rookery The. RM16 .... 11 A8
Rookery View. **4** ME17 .... 12 D8
Rookesley Rd. BR5 .... 38 D2
Rookley Cl. TN2 .... 149 D2
Rooks Hill. TN15 .... 100 D6
Roopers. TN3 .... 148 A7
Roosevelt Ave. ME5 .... 62 A8
Rope Wlk. ME4 .... 47 F5
Rope Wlk The. TN18 .... 186 B5
Rope Yard Rails. SE18 .... 2 B3
Ropemakers Ct. ME4 .... 48 A1
Roper Cl. ME8 .... 63 C3
Roper St. **1** SE9 .... 6 A1
Roper's Gate. TN2 .... 148 E1
Roper's Green La. ME3 .... 18 B2
Roper's La. ME3 .... 34 F8
Ropery Bsns Est. SE7 .... 1 C2
Ropewalk. TN17 .... 169 C5
Rose Ave. DA12 .... 30 E7
Rose Bruford Coll The. DA15 ... 24 B7
Rose Ct. ME17 .... 106 D1
Rose Dale. BR6 .... 51 B8
Rose Hill Sch. TN4 .... 148 E5
Rose St. Northfleet DA11 .... 12 B1
Rose St. Rochester ME1 .... 47 D3
Rose St. Tonbridge TN9 .... 133 C8
Rose Terr. ME19 .... 88 D7
Rose Villas. BR6 .... 52 C2
Rose Way. SE12 .... 5 A2
Rose Yd. ME14 .... 92 A4
Roseacre Gdns. ME14 .... 93 A4
Roseacre Jun Sch. ME14 .... 93 A4
Roseacre La. ME14 .... 93 A4
Roseacre Rd. DA16 .... 7 B4
Rosebank Wlk. **14** SE7 .... 1 E2
Roseberry Gdns. Dartford DA1 .. 26 C8
Roseberry Gdns. Orpington BR6 .. 51 E7
Rosebery Ave. DA15 .... 23 E8
Rosebery Rd. Chatham ME4 .... 47 E2
Rosebery Rd. Gillingham ME7 .. 48 D7
Rosebery Rd. Grays RM17 ...... 11 B8
Rosecroft Cl. BR5 .... 38 C3
Rosedale Cl. Dartford DA2 ..... 27 B8
Rosedale Cl. Woolwich SE2 ...... 3 B3
Rosedene Cl. DA1 .... 26 C8
Rosefield. TN13 .... 84 A3
Rosegarth. DA13 .... 43 E8
Rosehill Wlk. TN1 .... 149 A3
Roseholme. ME16 .... 91 D2
Roselare Cl. TN16 .... 81 D1
Roseleigh Ave. ME16 .... 91 C5
Rosemary Cl. **4** ME5 .... 61 F4
Rosemary La. Hodsoll Street TN15 57 D2
Rosemary La. Stonecrouch TN5 177 A5
Rosemary La.
　Swift's Green TN27 .... 142 F5
Rosemary Rd. Bexley DA16 ...... 6 F6
Rosemary Rd. East Malling ME19 74 F1
Rosemary Rd. Maidstone ME15 .. 93 A3
Rosemount Cl. ME15 .... 106 F4
Rosemount Dr. BR1 .... 36 F5
Rosenheath Cl. BR6 .... 52 C3
Rosetta Prim Sch. E16 .... 1 B8
Roseveare Rd. SE12 .... 22 C4
Rosewood. DA2 .... 25 E4
Rosewood Cl. DA14 .... 24 C5
Rosewood Ct. BR1 .... 36 D8
Rosherville CE Prim Sch. DA11 12 E1
Rosherville Way. DA11 .... 12 E1
Roslin Way. BR1 .... 22 A3
Ross Ct. **9** ME7 .... 22 F1
Ross House. SE18 .... 5 E6
Ross Rd. DA1 .... 9 A1
Ross St. ME1 .... 47 D4
Ross Way. SE9 .... 5 E4
Rossdale. TN2 .... 149 D5

Rosse Mews. SE3 .... 5 B6
Rossell Rd. RM18 .... 12 F5
Rosslair Cl. DA6 .... 8 B2
Rosslyn Gn. ME16 .... 91 B5
Rother Ct. **24** BR5 .... 38 D1
Rother House. **5** ME15 ...... 107 D8
Rother Rd. TN10 .... 117 C5
Rother Vale. ME5 .... 62 C3
Rothermere Cl. TN17 .... 180 A3
Rothesay Ct. SE12 .... 22 B5
Rothley Cl. TN30 .... 183 B8
Rouge La. DA11 .... 30 B7
Roughetts Rd. ME19 .... 73 F3
Roughway La. TN11 .... 102 C2
Round Ash Way. DA3 .... 42 E3
Round Green Cotts. TN17 ..... 154 F4
Round St. DA12 & DA13 .... 44 D5
Roundel Way. TN12 .... 138 D5
Roundhay. ME19 .... 74 E1
Roundhill Rd. TN2 .... 149 D1
Roundlyn Gdns. BR5 .... 38 B5
Roundtable Rd. BR1 .... 22 A5
Roundwell. ME14 .... 93 D3
Roundwood. BR7 .... 37 B7
Routh St. E6 .... 1 F8
Rover Rd. ME5 .... 62 B2
Row The. DA3 .... 56 F8
Rowan Cl. Aylesford ME20 ...... 75 E1
Rowan Cl. Longfield DA3 .... 42 D7
Rowan Cl. Meopham Station DA13 44 B3
Rowan Cl. Putlands TN12 ..... 135 F5
Rowan Cres. 26 C7
Rowan House. **4** Chatham ME5 61 F5
Rowan House. Sidcup DA14 .... 23 B5
Rowan Lea. ME5 .... 48 B1
Rowan Rd. Bexley DA7 .... 7 E4
Rowan Rd. Swanley BR8 .... 39 D6
Rowan Shaw. TN10 .... 117 D6
Rowan Tree Rd. TN2 .... 148 E1
Rowan Wlk. Chatham ME4 ..... 47 E3
Rowan Wlk. Keston Mark BR2 .. 50 F7
Rowanwood Ave. DA15 .... 24 A7
Rowbrocke Cl. ME8 .... 63 D3
Rowdow La. TN14 .... 69 E5
Rowe Pl. ME20 .... 75 F6
Rowfield. **6** TN8 .... 112 D3
Rowhill Cotts. DA2 .... 25 E2
Rowhill Rd. DA2 .... 26 A3
Rowhill Sch. DA2 .... 26 C4
Rowland Ave. ME7 .... 48 E2
Rowland Cl. ME5 .... 48 E1
Rowlatt Cl. DA2 .... 26 A5
Rowlatt Rd. DA2 .... 26 C5
Rowley Ave. DA15 .... 24 B8
Rowley Hill. TN2 .... 134 D1
Rowntree Path. **1** SE28 .... 3 B5
Rowton Rd. SE18 .... 6 C7
Rowzill Rd. BR8 .... 25 F2
Royal Albert Sta. 1 E6
Royal Albert Way.
　Newham,Custom House E16 .... 1 E6
Royal Albert Way.
　Newham,Cyprus E6 .... 2 A6
Royal Ave. TN2 .... 133 D8
Royal Blackheath Golf Course.
　SE9 .... 23 A8
Royal Chase. TN4 & TN1 ...... 148 F4
Royal Cres. TN2 .... 22 F7
Royal Docks Rd. E6 .... 2 B7
Royal Eagle Cl. ME2 .... 47 E7
Royal Engineers' Rd. ME14 ..... 91 F7
Royal Oak Rd. DA6 .... 8 A3
Royal Par. BR7 .... 23 C1
Royal Park Prim Sch. DA14 .... 24 E5
Royal Parade Mews. BR7 .... 23 C1
Royal Pier Rd. DA11 .... 13 C1
Royal Rd. Hawley DA2 .... 27 A3
Royal Rd. Newham E16 .... 1 D7
Royal Rd. Sidcup DA14 .... 24 D5
Royal Sovereign Ave. ME7 ...... 48 B7
Royal Star Arc. **5** ME14 ...... 91 F4
Royal Tunbridge Wells Bsns Pk.
　TN2 .... 133 D1
Royal Victoria Place Sh Ctr.
　TN2 .... 149 B4
Royal Victoria Sta. E16 .... 1 A6
Royal West Kent Ave. TN10 ... 117 D4
Roydene Rd. SE18 .... 2 E1
Roydon Hall. TN12 .... 103 F4
Roydon Hall Rd. TN12 .... 103 F4
Royston Rd. Crayford DA1 .... 8 F1
Royston Rd. Maidstone ME15 .. 93 A3
Roystons Cl. ME8 .... 49 F2
Royton Ave. ME17 .... 111 D5
Ruck La. TN12 .... 152 E3
Ruckinge Way. ME8 .... 49 C3
Ruddstreet Cl. SE18 .... 2 C2
Rudge Cl. ME5 .... 62 D2
Rudland Rd. DA7 .... 8 B4
Ruegg House. **5** SE18 .... 6 A8
Ruffet Ct. TN2 .... 148 E1
Ruffets Wood. DA12 .... 30 C2
Rugby Cl. ME5 .... 61 F4
Rumania Wlk. DA12 .... 30 F5
Rumbold Rd. SE9 .... 23 C6
Rumptead La. ME17 & ME 9 ... 79 D4
Rumstead Rd. ME9 .... 79 E4
Rumwood Ct. ME17 .... 108 B5
Runciman Cl. BR6 .... 52 C1
Runham La. ME17 .... 110 E3
Running Horse Rndbt The.
　ME20 .... 76 E1
Runnymede Ct. DA2 .... 27 C7
Rural Vale. DA11 .... 29 E8
Ruscombe Cl. TN4 .... 132 F2
Rush Cl. ME5 .... 62 A3
Rushbrook Rd. SE9 .... 23 C6
Rushdean Rd. ME2 .... 46 D5
Rushlane Cl. SE2 .... 3 D3

Rushet Rd. BR5 .... 38 A7
Rushetts. TN3 .... 147 F4
Rushetts Rd. TN15 .... 55 E3
Rushford Cl. TN27 .... 141 D5
Rushgrove St. SE18 .... 1 F2
Rushley Cl. BR2 .... 50 E6
Rushlye Cl. TN3 .... 163 F5
Rushmead Dr. ME15 .... 107 A7
Rushmere. TN15 .... 86 D7
Rushmore Cl. BR1 .... 36 E6
Rushmore Hill. BR6 & TN14 .. 67 D6
Rushymead. TN15 .... 70 A1
Ruskin Ave. DA16 .... 7 A5
Ruskin Cl. ME19 .... 89 F8
Ruskin Ct. SE9 .... 5 F1
Ruskin Dr. Bexley DA16 .... 7 A4
Ruskin Dr. Orpington BR6 ...... 51 E7
Ruskin Gr. Bexley DA16 .... 7 A5
Ruskin Gr. Dartford DA1 .... 10 A2
Ruskin Rd. DA17 .... 4 A2
Ruskin Wlk. BR2 .... 36 F3
Rusland Ave. ME8 .... 51 D7
Russell Cl. Bexley DA7 .... 8 A3
Russell Cl. Crayford DA1 .... 9 A3
Russell Cl. Greenwich SE7 .... 5 C7
Russell Ct. ME4 .... 48 B3
Russell House Sch. TN14 .... 69 C3
Russell Pl. ME4 .... 41 A8
Russell Rd. Gravesend DA12 ... 13 D1
Russell Rd. Kit's Coty ME20 ..... 76 D7
Russell Rd. Newham E16 .... 1 B7
Russell Rd. Tilbury RM18 .... 12 F6
Russell Sq. DA3 .... 42 D6
Russell Terr. ME4 .... 41 C5
Russells Ave. ME8 .... 64 A8
Russet Cl. ME2 .... 46 E8
Russet House. RM17 .... 12 C7
Russet Way. ME18 .... 88 F2
Russets The. Maidstone ME16 .. 91 B5
Russets The.
  Meopham Station DA13 .... 44 A3
Russett Cl. Ditton ME20 .... 90 E8
Russett Cl. Orpington BR6 ...... 52 B5
Russett Rd. TN12 .... 119 F6
Russett Way. BR8 .... 39 D8
Rusthall Grange. TN4 .... 148 D4
Rusthall High St. TN4 .... 148 C4
Rusthall Pk. TN4 .... 148 D4
Rusthall Rd. TN4 .... 148 D4
Rustwick. TN4 .... 148 E5
Ruth House. ME16 .... 91 E5
Rutherford Way. TN10 .... 117 D7
Rutherglen Rd. SE2 .... 7 A8
Ruthin Rd. SE3 .... 5 A8
Rutland Ave. DA15 .... 24 A8
Rutland Cl. Dartford DA1 .... 26 D8
Rutland Cl. Sidcup DA5 .... 24 D7
Rutland Ct. Chislehurst BR7 .... 37 A8
Rutland Ct. Sidcup BR7 .... 23 C6
Rutland Gate. DA17 .... 4 B1
Rutland House. SE18 .... 1 F2
Rutland Pl. ME8 .... 63 C3
Rutland Way. Maidstone ME15 . 107 E8
Rutland Way. Orpington BR5 .... 38 C3
Ruxley Cl. ME4 .... 24 E2
Ruxley Cnr. DA14 .... 24 E2
Ruxley Corner Ind Est. DA14 ... 24 D2
Ruxley Golf Course. BR5 .... 38 D8
Ruxley Manor Prim Sch. SE9 ... 23 A4
Ruxton Cl. BR8 .... 39 E6
Ruxton Ct. BR8 .... 39 E6
Ryan Cl. SE9 .... 5 C3
Ryan Dr. ME15 .... 93 A2
Ryarsh Cres. BR6 .... 51 E6
Ryarsh Cty Prim Sch. ME19 ... 74 A4
Ryarsh La. ME19 .... 74 B1
Ryarsh Rd. ME19 .... 74 B5
Rycaut Cl. ME8 .... 63 D3
Rycroft La. TN14 .... 98 E5
Rydal Cl. TN4 .... 148 E5
Rydal Dr. Bexley DA7 .... 8 A6
Rydal Dr.
  Royal Tunbridge Wells TN4 .. 148 E5
Ryde Cl. ME5 .... 62 B8
Rydens House. SE9 .... 22 C5
Ryder Cl. BR1 .... 22 B3
Ryders. TN3 .... 148 A3
Rydons Cl. SE9 .... 5 E4
Rye Cl. DA5 .... 8 B1
Rye Cres. BR5 .... 38 D1
Rye Field. BR5 .... 38 D1
Rye La. Otford TN14 .... 69 A2
Rye La. Sevenoaks
  TN13 & TN14 .... 83 F7
Rye Rd. TN18 .... 179 B1
Rye Wood Cotts. TN13 .... 83 F7
Ryecourt Cl. ME16 .... 91 E3
Ryecroft. DA12 .... 30 E3
Ryecroft Rd. Orpington BR5 .... 37 D3
Ryecroft Rd. Otford TN14 .... 69 A3
Ryedale Ct. TN13 .... 83 E6
Ryegrass Cl. ME5 .... 62 C6
Ryelands Cres. SE12 .... 5 C1
Rymers Cl. TN1 .... 149 D7
Rymill St. E16 .... 2 A1
Rysted La. TN16 .... 81 D1

Sabre Ct. ME7 .... 49 A1
Sackville Ave. BR2 .... 36 A1
Sackville Cl. TN13 .... 84 B5
Sackville Rd. DA1 .... 26 E6
Sackville Sch. TN3 .... 148 A5
Sacred Heart Sch. TN5 .... 174 D5
Saddington Cl. DA12 .... 30 D4
Saddler's Pk. DA4 .... 54 D7
Saddlers Cl. ME14 .... 92 E5
Sadlers Cl. ME5 .... 61 D2

Saffron Way. ME5 .... 61 F5
Sage Cl. E6 .... 1 F8
Saigasso Cl. E16 .... 1 D7
Sailfield Cl. ME4 .... 47 F7
Sailmakers Ct. ME4 .... 48 B2
SS Peter & Paul RC Prim Sch.
  BR5 .... 37 E7
St Aidan's Way. DA12 .... 30 E5
St Alban's Cl. DA12 .... 30 D5
St Alban's Gdns. DA12 .... 30 D5
St Alban's Rd. DA1 .... 9 F1
St Alban's Rd Cty Sch. DA1 ...... 9 F1
St Albans Cl. ME7 .... 48 E7
St Albans Rd. ME2 .... 46 C6
St Alfege Rd. SE7 .... 5 D8
St Andrew Rd. ME7 .... 48 D7
St Andrew's Cl. ME16 .... 91 A2
St Andrew's Ct. BR8 .... 39 E6
St Andrew's Rd.
  Gravesend DA11 .... 30 B8
St Andrew's Rd. Maidstone ME16 91 A3
St Andrew's Rd. Tilbury RM18 .. 12 E5
St Andrews Cl. TN12 .... 136 A6
St Andrews Ct.
  Gravesend DA11 .... 13 B1
St Andrews Ct.
  Royal Tunbridge Wells TN4 .. 133 A1
St Andrews Dr. BR5 & BR6 ..... 38 B2
St Andrews Mews. SE3 .... 5 A7
St Andrews Park Rd. TN4 ..... 133 A1
St Andrews Rd.
  Paddock Wood TN12 .... 136 A6
St Andrews Rd. Sidcup DA14 ... 24 D5
St Ann's Green La. TN12 ...... 138 F8
St Anne Ct. ME16 .... 91 E4
St Anselm's RC Prim Sch. DA1 . 10 A2
St Anthony's Ct. BR6 .... 51 B8
St Aubyns Cl. BR6 .... 51 F7
St Aubyns Gdns. BR6 .... 51 F8
St Audrey Ave. DA7 .... 8 A5
St Augustine of Canterbury
  RC Prim Sch. ME8 .... 63 D3
St Augustine's Ave. BR1 & BR2 . 36 E4
St Augustine's Jun Sch. DA17 ... 3 F2
St Augustine's RC Prim Sch.
  TN4 .... 149 A7
St Augustine's Rd. DA17 .... 3 F2
St Barnabas CE Prim Sch.
  TN1 .... 149 B5
St Barnabas Cl. Gillingham ME7 . 48 D3
St Barnabas Cl. Maidstone ME16 91 C8
St Barnabas' Cl.
  Royal Tunbridge Wells TN1 ... 149 B5
St Bartholomew's Hospl. ME1 . 47 E4
St Bartholomew's La. ME1 ..... 47 E4
St Bartholomew's Terr. ME1 ... 47 E4
St Bartholomews RC Prim Sch.
  BR8 .... 39 E6
St Benedict Rd. ME6 .... 74 E8
St Benedict's Ave. DA12 .... 30 E6
St Benedicts RC Prim Sch. ME5 62 C2
St Benets Cl. TN30 .... 183 B8
St Benets Way. TN30 .... 183 B8
St Benjamins Dr. ME8 .... 52 C2
St Bernards Rd. TN10 .... 117 C6
St Blaise Ave. BR1 .... 36 B7
St Botolph Rd. DA11 .... 29 D5
St Botolph's Ave. TN13 .... 84 A3
St Botolph's CE Prim Sch.
  DA11 .... 29 D8
St Botolph's Rd. TN13 .... 84 B3
St Brelade's St. TN8 .... 112 A3
St Brides Cl. DA18 .... 3 D4
St Catherine's Hospl. ME1 ..... 47 D4
St Catherine's Sch for Girls.
  DA6 .... 8 B2
St Chad's Dr. DA12 .... 30 E5
St Chad's Rd. RM18 .... 13 A7
St Chad's Sch. RM18 .... 13 A6
St Christopher's (Trng Coll,
  Dr Barnado's Home). TN2 ... 149 D4
St Clement's Ave. ME16 .... 11 B8
St Clement's House. ME1 ...... 47 D5
St Clement's Rd. RM16 .... 11 C7
St Clements Cl. DA11 .... 29 F5
St Clements Ct. RM17 .... 11 F8
St Clere Hill Rd. TN15 .... 70 F7
St Columba's Cl. DA12 .... 30 E5
St Columba's RC Boys Sch. DA6 8 B2
St David's Bridge. TN17 ...... 169 D4
St David's Cres. DA12 .... 30 E5
St David's Rd. Allhallows ME3 .. 19 D8
St David's Rd. Hextable BR8 ... 25 F1
St David's Rd.
  Royal Tunbridge Wells TN4 .. 149 B6
St Domingo House. SE18 .... 1 F3
St Dunstan's Dr. DA12 .... 30 E5
St Edith's Rd. TN15 .... 70 A2
St Edmund's Cotts. TN15 .... 56 A2
St Edmund's Ct. TN15 .... 56 A2
St Edmunds Cl. DA18 .... 3 D4
St Edmunds Rd. DA1 .... 10 A3
St Faith's La. ME14 .... 93 B4
St Faith's St. ME14 .... 91 F4
St Fidelis RC Sch. DA8 .... 8 C8
St Fidelis' Rd. DA8 .... 4 D1
St Francis Ave. DA12 .... 30 E4
St Francis Cl. BR6 .... 37 E3
St Francis RC Prim Sch. ME14 . 92 B7
St Francis' Rd. Erith DA8 .... 4 D2
St Francis Rd. Harvel DA13 .... 58 B3
St Francis Sch. ME14 .... 92 B7
St George's Bickley CE Prim Sch.
  BR1 .... 36 B7
St George's CE Prim Sch. TN15 71 F3
St George's CE Sch. DA11 ...... 30 A6
St George's Cres. DA12 .... 30 D4

St George's Ct. TN15 .... 71 F3
St George's Ctr. DA11 .... 13 B1
St George's Pk. TN2 .... 162 F8
St George's Rd. Gillingham ME7 . 48 C6
St George's Rd. Sevenoaks TN13 84 B5
St George's Rd. Sidcup DA14 ... 24 D2
St George's Sq. ME16 .... 91 E3
St Georges Mews. TN9 .... 133 B8
St Georges Rd. Bromley BR1 ... 36 F6
St Georges Rd. Orpington BR5 . 37 D3
St Georges Rd. Swanley BR8 ... 39 F5
St Georges Rd W. BR1 .... 36 E7
St Georges Sq. DA3 .... 42 E6
St German's Pl. SE3 .... 5 A6
St Giles Cl. BR6 .... 51 D5
St Gregory's Catholic Comp Sch.
  TN4 .... 149 A7
St Gregory's Cres. DA12 .... 30 E6
St Gregory's Ct. DA12 .... 30 E6
St Helens Cl. Erith ME3 .... 16 B5
St Helens La. ME15 .... 105 E3
St Helier's Cl. ME16 .... 91 B2
St Hilary's Sch. TN13 .... 84 B5
St Hilda's Way. DA12 .... 30 E5
St Hildas. TN15 .... 101 F8
St James' CE Aided Inf Sch.
  TN2 .... 149 C4
St James' CE Jun Sch. TN2 ... 149 C4
St James' CE (VA) Sch. ME14 .. 21 B6
St James Cl. East Malling ME19 . 89 F8
St James Cl. Grain ME3 .... 21 B6
St James Cl. SE3 .... 5 B6
St James' Cty Inf Sch. ME19 ... 89 F8
St James La. DA2 & DA9 .... 27 E8
St James Oaks. DA11 .... 30 A8
St James' Pk. TN1 & TN2 ..... 149 C5
St James Pl. DA1 .... 9 D1
St James RC Prim Sch. BR5 ... 37 B4
St James Rd. Grain ME3 .... 21 B5
St James' Rd. Gravesend DA11 . 13 A1
St James Rd. Sevenoaks TN13 .. 84 B5
St James's Cl. SE18 .... 2 C1
St James's Rd. Royal Tunbridge Wells
  TN1 & TN2 .... 149 C5
St James Sq. DA3 .... 42 E6
St James Way. DA14 .... 24 E3
St James's Ave. DA11 .... 30 A8
St James's Cl. SE18 .... 2 C1
St James's St. TN1 .... 149 B4
St James's Rd. Gravesend DA11 . 13 A1
St James's Rd. Sevenoaks TN13 . 84 B5
St James's St. TN1 .... 149 B4
St Joachim's RC Sch. E16 .... 1 C7
St John Fisher Catholic Comp Sch.
  ME4 .... 47 E3
St John Fisher Catholic Sch
  (Lower Sch). ME4 .... 47 F2
St John Fisher RC Prim Sch.
  DA18 .... 3 E3
St John's CE Inf Sch. ME4 ..... 47 E3
St John's CE Prim Sch.
  Royal Tunbridge Wells TN4 .. 149 A5
St John's CE Prim Sch.
  Sevenoaks TN13 .... 84 D4
St John's CE (VA) Prim Sch.
  ME16 .... 92 E4
St John's Cl. ME3 .... 32 C4
St John's Ct. TN13 .... 84 C5
St John's Hill. TN13 & TN14 ... 84 C5
St John's La. DA3 .... 42 F3
St John's Par. DA14 .... 24 B4
St John's Pk. Greenwich SE3 .... 5 A7
St John's Pk.
  Royal Tunbridge Wells TN4 .. 149 A8
St John's RC Prim Sch. DA12 .. 30 E7
St John's RC Sch. DA12 .... 30 D7
St John's Rd. Bexley DA16 .... 7 B4
St John's Rd. Dartford DA2 .... 27 C8
St John's Rd. Erith DA8 .... 4 D1
St John's Rd. Gillingham ME7 .. 48 C3
St John's Rd. Gravesend DA12 .. 30 D8
St John's Rd. Higham ME3 ..... 32 C4
St John's Rd. Newham E16 .... 1 A7
St John's Rd.
  Orpington BR5 & BR6 .... 37 E3
St John's Rd. Royal Tunbridge Wells
  TN1 & TN4 .... 149 A6
St John's Rd. Sevenoaks TN13 .. 84 C5
St John's Rd. Sidcup DA14 ..... 24 B4
St John's Terr. SE18 .... 6 D8
St Johns CE Prim Sch. TN4 ... 149 B7
St Johns Rd. ME3 .... 34 D6
St Johns Way. ME1 .... 47 A2
St Joseph's RC Prim Sch.
  Bromley BR1 .... 22 B1
St Joseph's RC Prim Sch.
  Crayford DA1 .... 8 E3
St Joseph's RC Prim Sch.
  Northfleet DA11 .... 29 D8
St Josephs Cl. BR6 .... 51 F6
St Justin Cl. BR5 .... 38 D6
St Katherine's Cty Prim Sch.
  ME6 .... 74 F7
St Katherine's La. ME6 .... 74 F7
St Katherines Rd. DA18 .... 3 D4
St Keverne Rd. BR7 & SE9 ..... 22 E4
St Kilda Rd. BR6 .... 37 F1
St Laurence Ave. ME16 .... 91 C8
St Laurence Cl. BR5 .... 38 D6
St Lawrence Ave. TN4 .... 132 D3
St Leonards Ave. ME4 .... 47 F2
St Leonards Cl. ME19 .... 89 B7
St Leonards Cl. BR8 .... 7 A4
St Leonards Rd. ME16 .... 91 C8
St Leonards Rise. BR6 .... 51 E6
St Luke's Ave. ME14 .... 92 A5
St Luke's CE Inf Sch. TN4 .... 149 C7
St Luke's Rd. Maidstone ME14 . 92 B5

St Luke's Rd.
  Royal Tunbridge Wells TN4 .. 149 B6
St Luke's Way. ME3 .... 19 D8
St Lukes Cl. Lane End DA2 ..... 27 E8
St Lukes Cl. Swanley BR8 ...... 39 D7
St Margaret Clitherow
  RC Prim Sch. Tonbridge TN10 117 B6
St Margaret Clitherow
  RC Prim Sch. Woolwich SE28 .. 3 B5
St Margaret's at Troy Town
  CE Prim Sch. ME1 .... 47 C4
St Margaret's Banks. ME1 ..... 47 D5
St Margaret's CE Inf Sch. ME8 . 63 E8
St Margaret's CE Jun Sch. ME8 63 E8
St Margaret's CE Prim Sch. SE18 22 C1
St Margaret's Cres. DA12 ...... 30 E5
St Margaret's Ct. ME23 .... 17 E3
St Margaret's Gr. SE18 .... 6 C8
St Margaret's Mews. ME1 ..... 47 C5
St Margaret's Rd.
  Northfleet DA11 .... 29 E7
St Margaret's Rd.
  St Margarets DA2 & DA4 ...... 27 E2
St Margaret's Sch. ME1 .... 47 C5
St Margaret's Terr. SE18 .... 2 C1
St Margarets Ave. DA15 .... 23 D5
St Margarets Cl. Maidstone ME16 91 B2
St Margarets Cl. Orpington BR6 . 52 B6
St Margarets Dr. ME8 .... 63 C5
St Margarets Villas. TN12 .... 137 D8
St Mark's Ave. DA11 .... 29 F8
St Mark's CE Prim Sch.
  Bromley BR2 .... 36 A6
St Mark's Rd.
  Royal Tunbridge Wells TN4 .. 162 F7
St Marks CE Inf Sch. ME20 .... 75 F6
St Marks Cl. ME20 .... 75 F6
St Marks House. ME7 .... 48 C5
St Marks Ind Est. E16 .... 1 D5
St Martin's Cl. ME14 .... 78 A1
St Martin's Dr. DA4 .... 54 D7
St Martin's Rd. DA1 .... 9 F1
St Martins Cl. Erith DA18 .... 3 D4
St Martins Cl. Newington ME9 . 65 C7
St Martins Meadow. TN16 ..... 82 C1
St Mary Cray Prim Sch. BR5 ... 38 C3
St Mary Cray Sta. BR5 .... 38 B5
St Mary St. SE18 .... 2 A2
St Mary & St Joseph's Sch.
  DA14 .... 24 A3
St Mary's. ME3 .... 18 D5
St Mary's Abbey. ME19 .... 89 C8
St Mary's CE (VA) Prim Sch.
  BR8 .... 39 F4
St Mary's Church Rd. TN14 .... 82 F2
St Mary's Cl. Gravesend DA12 .. 30 D6
St Mary's Cl. Grays RM17 ..... 12 D8
St Mary's Cl. Laddingford ME18 120 E4
St Mary's Cl. Platt TN15 .... 87 C7
St Mary's Cl. Ticehurst TN5 ... 176 D1
St Mary's Cl. St Paul's Cray BR5 . 38 C7
St Mary's Cty Prim Sch. ME2 ... 47 B7
St Mary's Dr. TN13 .... 83 E4
St Mary's Gdns. ME7 .... 48 B7
St Mary's La. Speldhurst TN3 . 148 A8
St Mary's La. Ticehurst TN5 ... 176 D1
St Mary's Pl. Eltham SE9 .... 6 A1
St Mary's Pl. Newington ME9 .. 65 C7
St Mary's RC Prim Sch.
  Eltham SE9 .... 6 A2
St Mary's RC Prim Sch.
  Gillingham ME7 .... 48 D6
St Mary's Rd. Coldblow DA5 ... 25 C7
St Mary's Rd. Gillingham ME7 .. 48 C6
St Mary's Rd. Rochester ME2 .. 47 B7
St Mary's Rd.
  St Mary's Island ME4 .... 34 A2
St Mary's Rd. Stone DA9 ...... 10 E2
St Mary's Rd. Swanley BR8 .... 39 E5
St Mary's Rd. Tonbridge TN9 .. 133 B7
St Mary's View. ME7 .... 65 C7
St Mary's Wlk. ME1 .... 60 F1
St Marys Cl. SE7 .... 5 D7
St Marys Rd. TN15 .... 72 A2
St Marys Way. DA3 .... 42 E6
St Matthew's CE (VC) Inf Sch.
  ME1 .... 47 C4
St Matthew's Cl. ME9 .... 65 C7
St Matthew's Way. ME3 .... 19 D8
St Matthews Dr. Bromley BR1 .. 36 F6
St Matthews Dr. Rochester ME1 47 A2
St Merryn Cl. SE18 .... 6 D7
St Michael's CE Inf Sch. ME16 . 91 E3
St Michael's CE Jun Sch. ME16 91 E3
St Michael's CE Prim Sch.
  TN30 .... 173 A3
St Michael's Cl. Chatham ME1 .. 47 A2
St Michael's Cl. Erith DA18 ...... 3 D4
St Michael's Ct. ME2 .... 47 B7
St Michael's Cty Prim Sch.
  TN7 .... 160 B5
St Michael's East Wickham
  CE GM Prim Sch. DA16 .... 7 C6
St Michael's RC Prim Sch. ME4 47 F3
St Michael's Rd. Bexley DA16 ... 7 B4
St Michael's Rd. Maidstone ME16 91 D2
St Michael's Rd.
  Royal Tunbridge Wells TN4 .. 149 B7
St Michael's Rise. DA16 .... 7 B6
St Michaels Terr. TN30 .... 173 B3
St Michaels Cl. Newham E16 .... 1 D8

St Michaels Cl.
  Pratling Street ME14 & ME20 .. 76 C3
St Michaels Ct. TN11 .... 116 E7
St Michaels Dr. TN14 .... 69 E3
St Mildred's Cl. TN30 .... 183 A7
St Mildreds Rd. SE12 .... 22 A8
St Nicholas CE Inf Sch. ME2 ... 47 A7
St Nicholas Cl. SE18 .... 2 F1
St Nicholas Dr. TN13 .... 84 C1
St Nicholas Gdns. ME2 .... 46 F8
St Nicholas La. BR7 .... 36 E8
St Olave's Sch. BR6 .... 52 B7
St Olaves Prep Sch. SE9 .... 23 B6
St Patrick's Gdns. DA12 .... 30 D5
St Patrick's RC Prim Sch. SE18 . 2 D2
St Paul's CE Prim Sch. BR8 .... 40 B8
St Paul's Cl. Greenwich SE7 .... 1 D1
St Paul's Cl. Rochester ME2 .... 47 A5
St Paul's Cl. Swanscombe DA10 . 28 E8
St Paul's Cray Rd. BR7 .... 37 D8
St Paul's Ct. TN4 .... 148 C4
St Paul's RC Sec Sch. SE2 .... 7 A8
St Paul's Rd. DA8 .... 8 C7
St Paul's Sq. BR2 .... 36 A7
St Paul's St. TN4 .... 148 C4
St Paul's Wood Hill. BR5 & BR7 . 37 F7
St Paulinus' CE Prim Sch. DA1 .. 8 E3
St Paulinus Ct. DA1 .... 8 E3
St Pauls CE Inf Sch. TN4 ..... 148 B4
St Pauls CE Jun Sch. TN4 ..... 148 B4
St Pauls Cl. TN10 .... 117 D5
St Pauls Cray CE Prim Sch.
  BR5 .... 38 D6
St Pauls Cty Inf Sch. ME14 .... 92 A7
St Peter Chanel RC Prim Sch.
  DA14 .... 24 C3
St Peter St. ME1 .... 47 D4
St Peter's Bridge. ME16 .... 91 F4
St Peter's CE Prim Sch.
  Aylesford ME20 .... 76 A3
St Peter's CE Prim Sch.
  Royal Tunbridge Wells TN2 .. 149 C3
St Peter's Cl. DA10 .... 28 F8
St Peter's Cty Inf Sch. ME1 .... 47 C3
St Peter's Path. ME1 .... 47 D5
St Peter's RC Prim Sch. SE18 ... 2 B2
St Peter's St. TN2 .... 149 C3
St Peters Cl. Chislehurst BR7 .. 23 D1
St Peters Cl. Ditton ME19 ..... 75 B1
St Peters Pl. ME20 .... 75 F6
St Peters Rd. ME19 .... 75 B1
St Peters Row. TN3 .... 147 A5
St Peters St. ME1 .... 91 F4
St Philip's Ave. ME15 .... 92 B2
St Philip's CE Prim Sch. ME15 . 92 A3
St Philips Ct. TN1 .... 149 D6
St Philomena's Prim Sch. BR5 . 38 C2
St Quentin Rd. DA16 .... 6 F4
St Ronan's Cl. ME15 .... 107 C7
St Ronan's Sch. TN18 .... 179 D2
St Saviours Rd. ME15 .... 107 D6
St Simon Stock RC Sch. ME14 . 91 C4
St Stephen's CE Inf Sch. ME15 91 E2
St Stephen's Cl. ME9 .... 65 C7
St Stephen's Cty Prim Sch.
  TN9 .... 133 B8
St Stephen's RC Prim Sch. DA16 7 A5
St Stephen's Sq. ME15 .... 91 E2
St Stephen's St. TN9 .... 133 B8
St Stephens Ct. TN1 .... 149 B5
St Thomas Cl. DA5 .... 25 A8
St Thomas Rd. DA11 .... 30 B7
St Thomas More RC Prim Sch.
  Bexley DA7 .... 7 F5
St Thomas More RC Prim Sch.
  Eltham SE9 .... 5 E4
St Thomas More RC Sec Sch.
  SE9 .... 6 A1
St Thomas More Roman Catholic
  Prim Sch. ME5 .... 62 A5
St Thomas of Canterbury
  Cath Prim Sch. ME8 .... 49 B2
St Thomas RC Prim Sch. TN13 84 B2
St Thomas Rd. Erith DA17 ...... 4 C4
St Thomas Rd. Newham E16 .... 1 A7
St Thomas Rd. Northfleet DA11 . 29 E6
St Thomas's Almshouses. DA11 30 B7
St Thomas's Ave. DA11 .... 30 B7
St Thomas's CE Prim Sch.
  TN3 .... 161 C6
St Thomas's Pl. RM17 .... 12 C8
St Thomas-a-Becket RC Prim Sch.
  SE2 .... 3 A3
St Timothy's Mews. BR1 ...... 36 B8
St Vincents Ave. DA1 .... 10 A2
St Vincents La. TN30 .... 183 A7
St Vincents RC Prim Sch. SE9 . 22 E4
St Vincents Rd. DA1 .... 10 A1
St Welcume's Way. ME17 .... 110 E6
St Werburgh Cres. ME3 .... 34 D5
St Werburgh Sch. ME3 .... 34 D5
St William of Perth RC Prim Sch.
  ME1 .... 47 B2
St William's Way. ME1 .... 47 D2
St Williams Hospl. ME1 .... 47 D2
Saints Hill. TN11 .... 147 A8
Sala House. SE3 .... 5 B3
Salamons Way. RM13 .... 4 E7
Salcote Rd. DA12 .... 30 E3
Salem Pl. DA11 .... 29 D8
Salem St. ME15 .... 92 A3
Salisbury Ave. Gillingham ME8 . 63 D8
Salisbury Ave. Swanley BR8 .... 40 A5

Salisbury Cl. TN10 .... 117 D5
Salisbury House. **5** ME15 ...... 107 D7
Salisbury Mews. BR2 .... 36 E4
Salisbury Rd. Bromley BR2 ...... 36 E4
Salisbury Rd. Chatham ME4 ...... 48 A3
Salisbury Rd. Dartford DA2 ...... 27 C7
Salisbury Rd. Gravesend DA11 ... 29 F7
Salisbury Rd. **2** Grays RM17 ... 12 C8
Salisbury Rd. Kit's Coty ME20 ... 76 D7
Salisbury Rd. Langton Green TN3 147 C1
Salisbury Rd. Maidstone ME14 ... 92 A6
Salisbury Rd.
  Royal Tunbridge Wells TN4 ... 149 C8
Salisbury Rd. Sidcup DA5 .... 25 A7
Salisbury Rd. Tonbridge TN10 .. 117 D4
Salix Rd. RM17 .... 12 D8
Sallows Shaw. DA13 .... 44 C4
Sally Port. ME7 .... 48 A6
Sally Port Gdns. ME7 .... 48 B6
Salmon Rd. DA17 .... 4 A1
Salomons Rd. Newham E13 ...... 1 C8
Salomons Rd. Rusthall TN4 ..... 148 C4
Salt La. ME3 .... 15 F4
Salt's Ave. ME15 .... 106 F3
Saltash Rd. DA16 .... 7 C6
Salter's Cross. ME18 .... 105 A1
Saltford Cl. DA8 .... 4 E1
Saltings Rd. ME6 .... 75 A7
Saltley Cl. E6 .... 1 E7
Salts La. ME15 .... 107 A4
Saltwood Cl. BR6 .... 52 C6
Saltwood Rd. ME15 .... 91 F1
Sam Bartram Cl. SE7 .... 1 C1
Samara Cl. ME5 .... 62 A1
Samphire Cl. ME14 .... 92 E4
Samphire Ct. RM17 .... 12 E8
Sampson Cl. DA17 .... 3 D3
Samson House. SE18 .... 2 C2
Samuel Cl. SE18 .... 1 E2
Samuel Palmer Ct. BR6 .... 38 A2
Samuel St. SE18 .... 1 F2
Sanctuary Cl. DA1 .... 9 D1
Sanctuary Rd. ME8 .... 49 A3
Sanctuary The. DA5 .... 7 D1
Sand La. TN17 .... 156 F4
Sand Rd. TN3 .... 166 A4
Sandalwood House. DA15 .... 23 F5
Sandbach Pl. SE18 .... 2 C1
Sandbanks Hill. DA2 .... 28 B2
Sandbourne Dr. ME14 .... 76 F1
Sandby Gn. SE9 .... 5 E4
Sandcliff Rd. DA8 .... 4 D1
Sanderling Ct. SE28 .... 3 C6
Sanderson Way. TN9 .... 117 E1
Sandersons Ave. TN14 .... 53 B1
Sanderstead Rd. BR5 .... 38 B3
Sandfield Rd. TN11 .... 147 A7
Sandford Rd. Bexley DA2 & DA6 ... 7 F4
Sandford Rd. Bromley BR2 ...... 36 A5
Sandgate Ct. ME8 .... 63 F4
Sandgate Rd. DA16 .... 7 C7
Sandham Point. **10** SE18 ...... 2 B2
Sandhill La. ME3 .... 32 D6
Sandhurst Ave. TN2 .... 150 E6
Sandhurst Cl. Gillingham ME8 .. 49 C3
Sandhurst Cl.
  Royal Tunbridge Wells TN1 .. 149 C6
Sandhurst Cl.
  Sandhurst Cross TN18 .... 186 A4
Sandhurst Cross. TN18 .... 140 F1
Sandhurst Cty Prim Sch. TN18 186 C5
Sandhurst House. TN2 .... 149 D5
Sandhurst La. TN17 .... 181 B2
Sandhurst Pk. TN1 .... 149 C6
Sandhurst Rd. Sidcup DA5 ...... 7 D2
Sandhurst Rd. Orpington BR6 ... 52 A6
Sandhurst Rd. Royal Tunbridge Wells
  TN1 & TN2 & TN4 .... 149 D6
Sandhurst Rd. Sidcup DA15 ..... 24 A5
Sandhurst Rd. Tilbury RM18 ..... 13 C5
Sandilands. TN13 .... 83 D5
Sandling Cty Prim Sch. ME14 ... 92 B8
Sandling La. ME14 .... 92 A8
Sandling Rd. Maidstone ME14 ... 91 F6
Sandling Rd.
  Maidstone,Ringlestone ME14 .. 91 F7
Sandling Rise. SE9 .... 23 A5
Sandown Cl. TN2 .... 149 F6
Sandown Court Com Coll.
  TN2 .... 149 F5
Sandown Dr. ME8 .... 63 D7
Sandown Gr. TN2 .... 149 F6
Sandown Pk. TN2 .... 149 F6
Sandown Rd. Gravesend DA12 ... 30 C2
Sandown Rd. New Town ME19 ... 89 B8
Sandpiper Rd. ME5 .... 62 D2
Sandpiper Way. BR5 .... 38 D6
Sandpipers The. DA12 .... 30 D6
Sandpit Pl. SE7 .... 1 E1
Sandpit Rd. DA1 .... 9 C3
Sandringham Dr. DA16 .... 6 E5
Sandringham House. ME1 .... 47 B4
Sandringham Rd. Bromley BR1 ... 22 A3
Sandringham Rd. Gillingham ME8 63 E3
Sandrock House. TN2 .... 149 D4
Sandrock Rd. TN2 .... 149 C4
Sandrock Villas. TN18 .... 178 F3
Sandstone Rd. SE12 .... 22 B6
Sandstone Rise. ME14 .... 77 C8
Sandtoft Rd. SE7 .... 5 B5
Sandway Path. **6** BR5 .... 38 C5
Sandway Rd. Orpington BR5 ..... 38 C5
Sandway Rd. Sandway ME17 ... 110 F4
Sandy Bank Rd. DA12 .... 30 B7
Sandy Bury. BR6 .... 51 D7

Sandy Dell. ME7 .... 63 A3
Sandy Hill Ave. SE18 .... 2 B1
Sandy Hill La. SE18 .... 2 B2
Sandy Hill Rd. SE18 .... 2 B1
Sandy La. Bean DA13 & DA2 ... 28 D5
Sandy La. Ightham Common TN15 86 B3
Sandy La.
  Maidstone,Harbourland ME14 .. 92 C8
Sandy La.
  Maidstone,Penenden Heath ME14 92 C7
Sandy La.
  Maidstone,Ware Street ME14 ... 93 B5
Sandy La. New Town ME19 ...... 74 A1
Sandy La. Orpington BR6 .... 38 A2
Sandy La. Sevenoaks TN13 ...... 84 C4
Sandy La. Snodland ME6 .... 74 E6
Sandy La. St Paul's Cray BR5 ... 38 D8
Sandy La. Tenterden TN30 ..... 183 B7
Sandy La. Tilbury RM17 .... 13 B8
Sandy La. West Thurrock RM16 .. 11 B8
Sandy La. Westerham TN16 ..... 81 D2
Sandy La. Wrotham Heath TN15 .. 72 F1
Sandy Mount. ME14 .... 93 B5
Sandy Ridge.
  Borough Green TN15 .... 87 A7
Sandy Ridge. Chislehurst BR7 ... 23 A2
Sandycroft. SE2 .... 7 A8
Sandycroft Rd. ME2 .... 32 F1
Santana House. SE18 .... 6 B7
Santer House. TN18 .... 184 E8
Sapho Pk. DA12 .... 30 F4
Saphora Cl. BR6 .... 51 D5
Sapphire Cl. E6 .... 2 A7
Sara House. **1** DA8 .... 8 E7
Sara Pk. DA12 .... 30 E4
Sara Turnbull House. **2** SE18 ... 1 F2
Saracen Cl. ME7 .... 49 A1
Saracen Fields. ME5 & ME14 ... 77 C8
Sark Wlk. E16 .... 1 B7
Sarsen Hts. ME5 .... 61 F1
Sarsens Cl. DA12 .... 44 F6
Sassoon Cl. ME20 .... 75 A4
Satanita Cl. E16 .... 1 D7
Saunder's Cross. TN14 .... 53 B2
Saunders Cl. DA11 .... 29 E6
Saunders Rd.
  Royal Tunbridge Wells TN4 ... 148 E1
Saunders Rd. Woolwich SE18 ... 2 F1
Saunders St. ME7 .... 48 C6
Saunders Way. Dartford DA1 ... 26 F6
Saunders Way. Woolwich SE28 ... 3 B6
Savage Gdns. E6 .... 1 F7
Savage Rd. ME5 .... 62 B3
Savill House. E16 .... 1 E5
Saville Rd. E16 .... 1 E5
Savoy Rd. DA1 .... 9 D2
Sawyers Ct. ME4 .... 48 B2
Saxby Wood. TN11 .... 115 F1
Saxbys Rd. TN16 .... 85 D5
Saxon Cl. Kings Hill ME18 ...... 88 F2
Saxon Cl. Northfleet DA11 ...... 29 C5
Saxon Cl. Otford TN14 .... 68 F2
Saxon Cl. Rochester ME2 .... 32 F1
Saxon Pl. DA4 .... 41 C4
Saxon Rd. Bromley BR1 .... 22 A1
Saxon Rd. Hawley DA2 .... 26 E4
Saxon Wlk. DA14 .... 24 C2
Saxons Dr. ME14 .... 92 B7
Saxton St. ME7 .... 48 C5
Saxville Rd. BR5 .... 38 B6
Sayer Cl. DA9 .... 11 A2
Sayers La. **4** TN30 .... 183 A7
Sayes Court Rd. BR5 .... 38 B5
Scabharbour Rd. TN11 & TN14 .. 99 C1
Scadbury Park Nature Reserve.
  BR7 .... 23 F2
Scads Hill Cl. BR5 & BR6 .... 37 F3
Scarborough La. ME1 .... 60 D2
Scarlet Cl. BR5 .... 38 B5
Scarlett Cl. ME5 .... 62 C5
Scarsbrook Rd. SE3 .... 5 D4
Schofield Wlk. SE3 .... 5 A7
Scholars Rise. ME2 .... 46 D7
Scholey Cl. ME2 .... 60 B4
School App. TN15 .... 86 F7
School Ave. ME7 .... 48 E4
School Cl. DA13 .... 44 A7
School Cotts. Crockenhill BR8 ... 39 D2
School Cotts. Sidcup DA14 ..... 24 C3
School Cres. DA1 .... 8 F3
School Field. TN8 .... 112 C4
School Hill. TN3 .... 166 B6
School House La. TN12 .... 153 E7
School La. Bean DA2 .... 28 C5
School La. Bexley DA16 .... 7 B4
School La. Borden ME9 .... 65 F4
School La. Hadlow TN11 .... 118 E8
School La. Hextable BR8 .... 26 B1
School La. Higham ME3 .... 32 C5
School La.
  Horton Kirby DA3 & DA4 ...... 41 E4
School La. Knockmill TN15 ...... 70 F8
School La. Maidstone ME15 ..... 92 E1
School La. Newington ME9 ...... 65 B7
School La. Platt's Heath ME17 .. 110 F2
School La. Plaxtol TN11 & TN15 . 101 E6
School La. Seal TN15 .... 84 F6
School La. Sutton Valence ME17 124 E7
School La. Trottiscliffe ME19 ... 73 A5
School La. Vigo Village DA13 ... 58 A2
School La. Wouldham ME1 .... 60 D5
School La.
  Horton Kirby DA3 & DA4 ...... 41 E4
School Rd. Chislehurst BR7 ...... 23 C1
School Rd. Gravesend DA12 ..... 30 C5
School Rise. TN2 .... 148 F1
School Terr. **6** TN18 .... 178 F2
School Villas. SE18 .... 104 C3
Schoolfield Rd. RM16 .... 11 A8
Schooner Ct. DA9 .... 10 C3

Scilla Ct. **10** RM17 .... 12 D8
Scimitar Cl. ME7 .... 49 A1
Scords La. TN16 .... 97 C4
Scotby Ave. ME5 .... 62 B4
Scotland La. Cobham DA12 ...... 44 F6
Scotland La. Cobham DA12 ...... 45 A8
Scotney Castle. TN3 .... 166 D3
Scotney House. ME2 .... 33 C1
Scotsdale Cl. BR5 & BR7 .... 37 E5
Scotsdale Rd. SE12 .... 22 B8
Scott Ave. ME8 .... 64 A8
Scott Cl. ME19 & ME20 .... 90 C8
Scott Cres. DA8 .... 8 F6
Scott House. **4** DA17 .... 3 F1
Scott Rd. Gravesend DA12 ...... 30 D3
Scott Rd. Tonbridge TN9 .... 132 F8
Scott St. ME4 .... 47 F3
Scott Wilkie Prim Sch. E16 ...... 1 C7
Scott's Terr. ME4 .... 47 F3
Scottswood Ave. ME4 .... 47 F2
Scotts Park Prim Sch. BR1 ...... 36 C8
Scotts Rd. BR1 .... 22 A1
Scotts Way.
  Royal Tunbridge Wells TN2 ... 162 E8
Scotts Way. Sevenoaks TN13 ... 83 E5
Scoulding Rd. E16 .... 1 A7
Scragged Oak Rd. Detling ME14 78 C5
Scragged Oak Rd. Hucking ME14 79 C1
Scratchers La. TN15 .... 55 E7
Scratton Fields. DA12 .... 44 D4
Scrubbs La. ME16 .... 91 D4
Scudders Hill. DA3 .... 42 C3
Seabrook Rd. TN11 .... 117 A3
Seabrooke Rise. RM17 .... 12 B8
Seacourt Rd. SE2 .... 3 D4
Seaford Ct. ME1 .... 47 B5
Seagull Rd. ME2 .... 46 D6
Seal CE Prim Sch. TN15 .... 84 F7
Seal Dr. TN15 .... 84 F6
Seal Hollow Rd. TN13 & TN15 ... 84 D4
Seal Rd. TN13 & TN14 & TN15 ... 84 C6
Seal St Lawrence CE Prim Sch.
  TN15 .... 85 A3
Sealand Ct. ME1 .... 47 B5
Seamew Ct. ME2 .... 46 C7
Seaton Rd. Bexley DA16 .... 7 C7
Seaton Rd. Dartford DA1 .... 26 A8
Seaton Rd. Gillingham ME8 ..... 48 E3
Seaview. ME3 .... 21 B5
Seaview Rd. ME7 .... 48 C4
Second Ave. Chatham ME4 & ME5 48 C1
Second Ave. Gillingham ME8 .... 48 E3
Second Ave. West Thurrock RM16 11 A8
Secretan Rd. ME1 .... 47 B1
Sedcombe Cl. DA14 .... 24 C4
Sedge Cres. ME5 .... 61 E4
Sedgebrook Rd. SE3 .... 5 D4
Sedgemere Rd. SE2 .... 3 C3
Sedley. DA13 .... 29 A2
Sedley Cl. Aylesford ME20 .... 75 F2
Sedley Cl. Cliffe Woods ME3 .... 33 C7
Sedley Cl. Gillingham ME8 ...... 63 C3
Sedley's CE Fst Sch. DA13 ...... 29 A3
Sefton Cl. BR5 .... 37 F5
Sefton Rd. BR5 .... 37 F5
Sejant House. **4** RM17 .... 12 B8
Selah Dr. BR8 .... 39 C8
Selborne Ave. DA5 .... 24 E7
Selborne Rd. DA14 .... 24 B4
Selbourne Cl. DA3 .... 43 D6
Selbourne Rd. ME7 .... 48 D7
Selbourne Wlk. ME15 .... 107 F6
Selby Cl. Chislehurst BR7 .... 23 A2
Selby Cl. **13** Newham E16 ...... 1 E8
Selby Rd. Newham E13 .... 1 B8
Selby Rd. Park Wood ME15 .... 107 F4
Selkirk Dr. DA8 .... 8 E6
Sellbourne Pk. TN3 .... 163 C4
Sellinge Gn. ME8 .... 49 C3
Sellwood Ct. DA1 .... 27 B7
Selsey Cres. DA16 .... 7 D6
Selstead Cl. ME8 .... 49 C2
Selwyn Cres. DA16 .... 7 B3
Selwyn Pl. **1** BR5 .... 38 B6
Selwyn Rd. RM18 .... 12 F5
Semple Gdns. ME4 .... 47 E3
Senacre La. ME15 .... 107 E6
Senacre Sq. ME15 .... 107 F7
Senacre Tech Coll. ME15 ...... 107 D6
Senacre Wood Cty Prim Sch.
  ME15 .... 107 F7
Senator Wlk. SE28 .... 2 D3
Sencler House. SE2 .... 7 D8
Senlac Pl. TN1 .... 161 C7
Senlac Rd. SE12 .... 22 B7
Sennen Wlk. SE9 .... 22 E5
Sennocke Ct. TN13 .... 84 B2
Sequoia Gdns. BR6 .... 37 F2
Sermon Dr. BR8 .... 39 C6
Serpentine Ct. TN13 .... 84 D5
Serpentine Rd. TN13 & TN15 ... 84 D4
Serviden Dr. BR1 .... 36 D8
Setford Rd. ME5 .... 62 C6
Settington Ave. ME5 .... 48 C1
Seven Acres. Crockenhill BR8 ... 39 D3
Seven Acres.
  New Ash Green DA3 .... 56 E7
Seven Mile La.
  Herne Pound ME18 .... 88 A3
Seven Mile La.
  Mereworth ME18 & TN12 ..... 103 E3
Seven Mile La.
  Wrotham Heath TN15 .... 87 F7
Seven Wents. TN15 .... 86 A4
Sevenoaks By-Pass.
  TN13 & TN14 .... 98 F7
Sevenoaks Cty Prim Sch. TN13 84 B5

Sevenoaks Hospl.
  Sevenoaks TN13 .... 84 B2
Sevenoaks Hospl.
  Sevenoaks,St John's TN13 ..... 84 C6
Sevenoaks Prep Sch. TN15 ..... 85 A1
Sevenoaks Rd.
  Borough Green TN15 .... 86 F7
Sevenoaks Rd.
  Ightham Common TN15 .... 86 B4
Sevenoaks Rd. Orpington BR6 .. 51 F6
Sevenoaks Rd. Otford TN14 .... 69 B3
Sevenoaks Rd.
  Pratt's Bottom BR6 & TN14 ... 52 C2
Sevenoaks Sch. TN15 .... 84 C1
Sevenoaks Sta. TN13 .... 84 A3
Sevenoaks Way. BR5 .... 38 C7
Sevenoaks Wildfowl Reserve.
  TN14 .... 84 A7
Severn Cl. TN10 .... 117 C5
Severn Rd. ME5 .... 62 C5
Sevington Pk. ME15 .... 106 F6
Sewell Rd. SE28 .... 3 B4
Sextant Pk. ME2 .... 47 E6
Sexton Rd. RM18 .... 12 F6
Seymour Dr. BR2 .... 36 F1
Seymour Rd. **1** Chatham ME4 .. 48 B3
Seymour Rd. Moor Street ME8 .. 64 C8
Seymour Rd. Northfleet DA11 ... 29 F6
Seymour Rd. Tilbury RM18 ..... 12 F6
Seymour St. SE18 .... 2 C3
Seymour Wlk. DA10 .... 28 E8
Shacklands Rd. TN14 .... 53 D1
Shackleton Cl. ME5 .... 62 B6
Shades The. ME2 .... 46 C7
Shaftesbury Cl. ME19 .... 74 F1
Shaftesbury Ct. **3** SE28 .... 3 C5
Shaftesbury Dr. ME16 .... 91 C4
Shaftesbury La. DA1 .... 10 B3
Shaftesbury Rd. TN4 .... 149 A5
Shaftsbury Ct. E6 .... 2 A7
Shakespeare Ave. RM18 .... 13 B6
Shakespeare Farm Rd. ME3 ..... 18 F7
Shakespeare Rd. **1** TN11 ...... 3 F1
Shakespeare Rd. Bexley DA7 .... 7 E6
Shakespeare Rd. Dartford DA1 ... 10 B3
Shakespeare Rd. Gillingham ME7 48 C3
Shakespeare Rd. Tonbridge TN9 132 F8
Shalder House. ME7 .... 48 D7
Shalford Cl. BR6 .... 51 C6
Shallons Rd. SE9 .... 23 B4
Shambles The. TN13 .... 84 C2
Shamel Bsns Ctr. ME2 .... 47 C7
Shamley Rd. ME5 .... 62 D2
Shamrock Rd. DA12 .... 30 F8
Shandon Cl. TN2 .... 149 C6
Shanklin Cl. ME5 .... 62 C8
Shannon Cres. BR6 .... 38 A2
Sharfleet Dr. ME2 .... 46 B7
Sharland Rd. DA12 .... 30 C6
Sharman Ct. DA14 .... 24 A4
Sharnal La. ME6 .... 60 B8
Sharnal St. ME3 .... 18 A2
Sharnbrooke Cl. DA16 .... 7 C4
Sharon Cres. ME5 .... 61 F4
Sharp Way. DA1 .... 9 F4
Sharp's Field. TN27 .... 141 E5
Sharsted Way. Gillingham ME7 .. 63 A3
Sharsted Way. Maidstone ME14 . 93 B5
Shaw Cl. Cliffe Woods ME3 ..... 33 B8
Shaw Cl. Woolwich SE28 .... 3 B5
Shaw Cres. ME18 .... 13 B6
Shaw House. **6** Erith DA17 ...... 3 F1
Shaw House. **5** Newham E16 ... 2 A5
Shaw The. TN2 .... 149 C2
Shawbrooke Rd. SE9 .... 5 D3
Shawcroft Sch. BR5 .... 38 E4
Shawfield Pk. BR1 .... 36 D7
Shaws Way. ME1 .... 47 C3
Shawstead Rd. ME7 & ME7 ..... 62 D5
Sheafe Dr. TN17 .... 169 C5
Sheal's Cres. ME15 .... 92 A2
Sheals Ct. ME15 .... 92 A2
Shearers Ct. ME14 .... 92 E4
Shears Green Ct. DA11 .... 30 A6
Shears Green Cty Inf Sch.
  DA11 .... 29 F5
Shears Green Cty Jun Sch.
  DA11 .... 29 F5
Shearwater. Maidstone ME16 ... 91 B5
Shearwater. New Barn DA3 ...... 43 B6
Shearwater Cl. ME2 .... 46 C7
Sherwood Cres. DA1 .... 9 A4
Sheen Rd. BR5 .... 37 F5
Sheepcote La. BR5 & BR8 .... 38 E4
Sheephurst La. TN12 .... 137 E5
Sheerness Harbour Est. ME12 .. 21 F3
Sheerwater Rd. E16 .... 1 D8
Sheet Hill. TN15 .... 86 D2
Sheffield Rd. **4** TN4 .... 132 F2
Sheilings The. TN15 .... 84 F7
Shelbury Cl. DA14 .... 24 A5
Shelden Dr. ME8 .... 63 F8
Sheldon Bsns Ctr. ME2 .... 47 D8
Sheldon Cl. SE12 .... 5 B2
Sheldon Rd. DA7 .... 7 F6
Sheldon Way. ME20 .... 75 F6
Sheldrake Cl. E16 .... 1 F5
Shell Cl. BR2 .... 36 E3
Shellbank La. DA2 .... 28 B4
Shelldrake Cl. ME3 .... 21 B5
Shelley Cl. BR6 .... 51 E7
Shelley Dr. DA16 .... 6 E6
Shelley Pl. RM18 .... 13 B6
Shelley Rd. ME16 .... 91 C2
Shelleys La. TN14 .... 67 A3
Shelton Cl. TN10 .... 117 C5
Shenden Cl. TN13 .... 99 C7
Shenden Way. TN13 & TN15 ... 99 C7

Shenfield House. SE18 .... 5 D7
Shenley Gr. ME14 .... 76 F2
Shenley Rd. DA1 .... 27 A8
Shenstone Sch. DA1 .... 8 D2
Shepherd St. DA11 .... 29 D8
Shepherds Cl. BR6 .... 51 F7
Shepherds Gate. ME7 .... 62 F5
Shepherds Gate Dr. ME14 ...... 92 E6
Shepherds Gn. BR7 .... 23 D1
Shepherds La. DA1 .... 26 B8
Shepherds Leas. SE9 .... 6 D3
Shepherds Way.
  Langley Heath ME17 .... 108 E4
Shepherds Way.
  Lower Stoke ME3 .... 19 C4
Shepherds Wlk. TN2 .... 149 D4
Shepherdsgrove La. RH19 ...... 144 A4
Shepperton Cl. ME5 .... 62 C4
Shepperton Rd. BR5 .... 37 C3
Sheppey Cl. DA8 .... 9 B7
Sheppey Rd. ME15 .... 107 A7
Sheppy Pl. DA11 .... 30 B8
Shepway Cl. ME15 .... 107 C8
Shepway Cty Inf Sch. ME15 ... 107 E8
Shepway Cty Jun Sch. ME15 .. 107 E8
Sherard Rd. SE9 .... 5 E2
Sheraton Ct. ME5 .... 61 F1
Sherborne Rd. BR5 .... 37 F4
Sherbourne Cl.
  Royal Tunbridge Wells TN2 ... 149 D2
Sherbourne Cl.
  West Kingsdown TN15 .... 55 E4
Sherbourne Dr. ME16 .... 91 B2
Sherbrooke Cl. DA7 .... 8 A3
Sherenden La. TN12 .... 154 D8
Sherenden Pk. TN11 .... 119 A5
Sherenden Rd. TN11 .... 134 D7
Sherfield Rd. RM17 .... 12 B8
Sheridan Cl. Chatham ME5 ...... 62 C7
Sheridan Cl. Maidstone ME14 ... 91 E8
Sheridan Cl. Swanley BR8 .... 39 F6
Sheridan Cres. BR7 .... 37 B7
Sheridan Ct. DA1 .... 10 A3
Sheridan Rd. Bexley DA7 .... 7 E4
Sheridan Rd. Erith DA17 .... 4 A2
Sheriff Dr. ME5 .... 62 A2
Sherington Prim Sch. SE7 .... 5 B8
Sherington Rd. SE7 .... 5 B8
Sherlies Ave. BR6 .... 51 E8
Sherman Cl. ME7 .... 49 B1
Sherman Rd. BR1 .... 36 A8
Shernden La. TN8 .... 128 C4
Shernold Sch. ME16 .... 91 D5
Shernolds. ME15 .... 107 B7
Sherway Cl. TN27 .... 141 E5
Sherway Rd. TN27 .... 142 D6
Sherwin Knight Cty Prim Sch.
  ME2 .... 46 E5
Sherwood Ave. ME5 .... 62 A2
Sherwood Cl. DA5 .... 7 C1
Sherwood House. Chatham ME5 62 A3
Sherwood House. Erith DA8 ...... 8 E8
Sherwood Park Ave. DA15 .... 7 B1
Sherwood Park Cty Prim Sch.
  TN2 .... 149 D6
Sherwood Rd. Bexley DA16 ...... 6 E4
Sherwood Rd.
  Royal Tunbridge Wells TN2 ... 149 D5
Sherwood Way. TN2 .... 149 D6
Shieldhall St. SE2 .... 3 C2
Shillingheld Cl. ME14 .... 92 F5
Shinecroft. TN14 .... 69 A3
Shingle Barn La. ME15 .... 105 C3
Shinglewell Rd. DA8 .... 8 A7
Ship La. Chatham ME1 .... 47 E4
Ship La. Sutton at Hone BR8 ... 40 E8
Shipbourne Cty Prim Sch.
  TN11 .... 101 C4
Shipbourne Rd.
  Shipbourne TN11 & TN10 .... 101 D2
Shipbourne Rd. Tonbridge TN10 117 C5
Shipley Ct. ME14 .... 92 E6
Shipley Hills Rd. Meopham DA13 43 E1
Shipman Rd. E16 .... 1 C7
Shipwrights Ave. ME4 .... 48 B2
Shire Ct.
  Farthing Street BR6 & BR2 ... 51 C3
Shire La. Orpington BR6 .... 51 E5
Shirebrook Rd. SE3 .... 5 D4
Shirehall Rd. DA2 .... 26 E4
Shires The. TN2 .... 136 A7
Shirley Ave. Chatham ME5 ...... 61 D5
Shirley Ave. Sidcup DA5 .... 24 D7
Shirley Cl. Chalk DA12 .... 31 B6
Shirley Cl. Dartford DA1 .... 9 C3
Shirley Gdns. TN4 .... 148 C5
Shirley Gr. TN4 .... 148 C5
Shirley House Dr. SE7 .... 5 C7
Shirley Rd. DA15 .... 23 E5
Shirley Way. ME15 .... 93 A3
Sholden Gdns. BR5 .... 38 C4
Sholden Rd. ME2 .... 33 C1
Shooters Hill. SE18 .... 6 A6
Shooters Hill Golf Course. SE18 6 C6
Shooters Hill Rd.
  SE18 & SE3 & SE9 .... 5 D6
Shore The. Northfleet DA11 ..... 12 C2
Shore The. Northfleet DA11 ..... 12 F1
Shoreham Cl. DA5 .... 7 C1
Shoreham Cty Prim Sch. TN14 68 F8
Shoreham House. TN14 .... 69 A8
Shoreham La.
  Badgers Mount TN14 .... 68 A7
Shoreham La. Maypole BR6 ..... 53 A3
Shoreham La. Sevenoaks TN13 .. 83 F4
Shoreham La. St Michaels TN30 173 A3
Shoreham Pl. TN14 .... 69 A7

Shoreham Rd. Otford TN14 .... 69 B5
Shoreham Rd. St Paul's Cray BR5 38 B7
Shoreham Sta. TN14 .... 69 B8
Shoreham Way. BR2 .... 36 A3
Shoreham Wlk. ME15 .... 107 F7
Shorehill La. ME15 .... 69 F4
Shoreland Ct. ME1 .... 47 B5
Shorne CE Prim Sch. DA12 .. 31 E3
Shorne Cl. Orpington BR5 .... 38 D5
Shorne Cl. 3 Sidcup DA15 .... 7 B1
Shorne Ifield Rd. DA12 .... 31 C2
Shorne Wood (Ctry Pk). DA12 . 31 C1
Shornefield Cl. BR1 .... 37 A6
Short La. Brenchley TN12 .... 152 A6
Short La. Gillingham ME7 .... 49 A6
Short St. 3 ME4 .... 48 B3
Shortlands Cl. DA17 .... 3 F3
Shortlands Gn. ME15 .... 107 F5
Shorts Way. ME1 .... 47 A3
Shortway. SE9 .... 5 E4
Shottenden Rd. ME7 .... 48 D7
Shottery Cl. SE9 .... 22 E5
Showfields Rd. TN2 .... 148 F1
Shrapnel Cl. SE18 .... 5 E7
Shrapnel Rd. SE9 .... 5 F4
Shrewsbury La. SE18 .... 6 B6
Shroffold Rd. BR1 .... 22 A5
Shropshire Terr. 3 ME15 .... 107 E7
Shrubbery Rd. Gravesend DA12 . 30 C7
Shrubbery Rd.
  South Darenth DA4 .... 41 D8
Shrubcote. TN30 .... 183 C7
Shrublands Ct.
  Royal Tunbridge Wells TN2 . 149 C4
Shrublands Ct. 1
  Tonbridge TN9 .... 117 C2
Shrubsall Cl. SE9 .... 22 E7
Shrubsole Dr. ME14 .... 76 F3
Shurlock Ave. BR8 .... 39 D7
Shurlock Dr. BR6 .... 51 C6
Shuttle Cl. Biddenden TN27 .. 158 A2
Shuttle Cl. Sidcup DA15 .... 23 F8
Shuttle Rd. DA1 .... 9 A4
Shuttlemead. DA5 .... 24 F8
Sibley Cl. DA6 .... 7 E2
Sibthorpe Rd. SE12 .... 22 C8
Sidcup By Pass Rd. Sidcup DA14 23 F3
Sidcup By Pass Rd.
  St Paul's Cray BR5 & BR7 .. 24 B1
Sidcup Hill. DA14 .... 24 B3
Sidcup Hill Gdns. DA14 .... 24 C3
Sidcup Hill Prim Sch. DA14 .... 24 B3
Sidcup Pl. DA14 .... 24 A3
Sidcup Rd. Eltham SE12 & SE9 .. 22 D7
Sidcup Rd. Eltham SE9 .... 22 E7
Sidcup Rd. Eltham BR7 & SE9 .. 23 B6
Sidcup Rd. DA14 & DA15 .... 24 A6
Sidewood Rd. SE9 .... 23 D7
Sidmouth Cl. DA1 .... 27 B7
Sidmouth Rd. Bexley DA16 .... 7 C7
Sidmouth Rd. Orpington BR5 .. 38 B5
Sidney Cl. TN2 .... 162 F8
Sidney Gdns. TN14 .... 69 C2
Sidney House. SE18 .... 5 F6
Sidney Rd. Gillingham ME7 .. 48 C7
Sidney Rd. Rochester ME1 .. 47 A2
Sidney St. ME6 .... 91 C2
Siebert Rd. SE3 & SE7 .... 5 A8
Siedle House. 9 SE18 .... 6 A8
Siemens Rd. SE18 .... 1 D3
Silchester Ct. ME14 .... 92 C7
Silecroft Rd. DA7 .... 8 A6
Silk Cl. SE12 .... 5 A1
Silver Bank. ME5 .... 62 A6
Silver Birch Ave. DA13 .... 57 F1
Silver Birch Cl. DA2 .... 25 E4
Silver Birches. ME5 .... 62 A3
Silver Cl. TN9 .... 133 B6
Silver Hill. Chatham ME4 .... 47 F3
Silver Hill. Rochester ME1 .... 46 F2
Silver Hill. Silver Hill TN19 .. 184 B1
Silver Hill. Tenterden TN30 .... 173 B1
Silver Hill Gdns. ME4 .... 47 F3
Silver Rd. DA12 .... 30 E6
Silver Spring Cl. DA8 .... 8 B8
Silver St. ME9 .... 80 F5
Silver Tree. ME5 .... 62 B1
Silverdale. Hartley DA3 .... 42 F5
Silverdale. Maidstone ME16 .. 91 A2
Silverdale Dr. Chislehurst SE9 22 E6
Silverdale Dr. Gillingham ME8 .. 63 F7
Silverdale La. TN4 .... 149 B6
Silverdale Rd. Bexley DA7 .... 8 B5
Silverdale Rd. Orpington BR5 .. 37 C5
Silverdale Rd.
  Royal Tunbridge Wells TN4 149 B6
Silverdale Rd. St Paul's Cray BR5 38 A6
Silverden Cotts. TN18 .... 185 F4
Silverhurst Dr. TN10 .... 117 C7
Silverland St. E16 .... 1 F5
Silverlocke Rd. RM17 .... 12 D8
Silverspot Cl. ME8 .... 63 F7
Silversted La. TN16 .... 81 D6
Silverstone Ct. 6 BR1 .... 36 C7
Silvertown By-Pass. E16 .... 1 D5
Silvertown Sta. E16 .... 1 E5
Silvertown Way. E16 .... 1 A5
Silverweed Rd. ME5 .... 61 F4
Silwood Cl. TN2 .... 149 E7
Simmonds Ct. ME14 .... 148 B4
Simmonds Dr. DA3 .... 43 A4
Simmons La. ME15 .... 108 B6
Simmons Rd. SE18 .... 2 B1
Simnel Rd. SE12 .... 22 B8
Simon Ct. 5 SE28 .... 3 A5
Simone Cl. BR1 .... 36 D8
Simpson Rd. ME6 .... 75 A6
Simpson's Cotts. BR2 .... 50 C7

Simpson's Rd. BR2 .... 36 A6
Sinclair Cl. ME8 .... 63 E5
Sinclair Way. DA2 .... 27 D4
Singapore Dr. ME7 .... 48 B5
Single St. BR6 & TN16 .... 66 B4
Single's Cross. TN14 .... 67 D4
Single's Cross La. TN14 .... 67 C5
Singlewell Cty Prim Sch. DA12 30 E2
Singlewell Rd. DA11 .... 30 B4
Sinkertweazel. TN17 .... 169 E2
Sir David's Pk. TN4 .... 132 E1
Sir Evelyn Rd. ME1 .... 47 B1
Sir John Hawkins Way. ME4 .. 47 F4
Sir Joseph Williamson's
  Mathematical Sch. ME1 .... 47 C1
Sir Martin Bowes House. 15
  SE18 .... 2 A2
Sir Thomas Longley Rd. ME2 .. 47 E6
Sirdar Strand. DA12 .... 30 F3
Siskin Gdns. TN12 .... 136 A5
Siskin Wlk. ME20 .... 74 F2
Sissinghurst Castle. TN17 .... 156 D1
Sissinghurst Cty Prim Sch.
  TN17 .... 170 B8
Sissinghurst Dr. ME16 .... 91 B4
Sissinghurst Rd.
  Biddenden TN27 & TN17 .... 157 C2
Sissinghurst Rd.
  Sissinghurst TN17 .... 170 D8
Sittingbourne Rd.
  Maidstone,Detling ME14 .... 92 B8
Sittingbourne Rd.
  Maidstone,Penenden Heath ME14 92 B6
Siward Rd. BR2 .... 36 C6
Six Bells La. TN13 .... 84 C1
Six Fields Path. TN30 .... 183 A7
Skeet Hill La. BR5 & BR6 .... 52 E8
Skeffington St. SE18 .... 2 C3
Skeynes Rd. TN8 .... 112 B1
Skibbs La. BR5 & BR6 .... 52 E7
Skinner Gdns. SE17 .... 170 A4
Skinner St. Chatham ME4 .... 47 F3
Skinner St. Gillingham ME7 .. 48 C5
Skinner St. Gillingham ME7 .. 48 C6
Skinner Street Cty Prim Sch.
  ME7 .... 48 C6
Skinner's Way. ME17 .... 108 E4
Skinners Cl. ME20 .... 76 A6
Skinners La. TN8 .... 112 D2
Skinners' Sch The. TN4 .... 149 A6
Skippers Cl. DA9 .... 11 B2
Skua Cl. ME2 .... 46 C7
Skye Cl. ME15 .... 107 A7
Slade Cl. ME5 .... 62 B2
Slade Cty Prim Sch. TN9 .... 117 B2
Slade Gdns. DA8 .... 8 F6
Slade Green Inf Sch. DA8 .... 9 A7
Slade Green Jun Sch. DA8 .... 9 A7
Slade Green Rd. DA8 .... 9 A6
Slade Green Sta. DA8 .... 9 A6
Slade The. The Down TN3 .... 166 A3
Slade The. Tonbridge TN9 .... 117 B2
Slade The. Woolwich SE18 .... 6 E1
Sladebrook Rd. SE3 .... 5 D4
Sladedale Rd. SE18 .... 2 E1
Slades Dr. BR7 .... 23 C4
Slaney Rd. TN12 .... 139 F4
Slaters. TN18 .... 113 F2
Slatin Rd. ME2 .... 47 B8
Sleeches Cross. TN3 .... 163 B2
Sleepers Stile Rd. TN5 .... 165 B1
Slicketts Hill. ME4 .... 48 A4
Slip Mill Rd. TN18 .... 178 E2
Slip Rd. ME4 .... 48 A8
Slip The. TN16 .... 81 C1
Slipway Rd. ME12 .... 21 F3
Sloane Gdns. BR6 .... 51 C7
Sloane Sq. DA3 .... 42 E6
Slocum Cl. SE28 .... 3 C6
Small Bridge Cotts. TN17 .... 153 B2
Small Bridge Rd. TN12 & TN17 153 B2
Small Grains. DA3 .... 56 B7
Small Hythe Rd. TN30 .... 183 C3
Small Profits. ME18 .... 105 A4
Smallhythe Rd. TN30 .... 183 A6
Smarden Bsns Est. TN27 .... 158 D7
Smarden Cl. 7 DA17 .... 4 A1
Smarden Cty Prim Sch. TN27 143 A1
Smarden Gr. SE9 .... 22 F4
Smarden Rd. East End TN27 .. 142 B4
Smarden Rd. Standen TN27 .. 158 B6
Smarts Cotts. ME14 .... 93 C4
Smarts Hill. TN11 .... 131 A1
Smarts Rd. DA12 .... 30 C6
Smith Rd. ME5 .... 62 B3
Smith St. ME7 .... 47 A6
Smith's Hill. ME15 .... 105 C5
Smithers Cl. TN11 .... 102 E1
Smithers Ct. TN12 .... 120 A7
Smithers La. TN12 .... 120 A7
Smithfield Rd. ME3 .... 21 C5
Smithies Rd. SE2 .... 3 B2
Smiths La. TN8 .... 96 C2
Smithy Field. 7 TN8 .... 112 D3
Smugglers Mews. TN18 .... 179 A1
Smugglers Wharf. DA9 .... 11 B2
Smythe Cl. TN14 .... 132 E3
Smythe Rd. DA4 .... 41 A8
Snag La. TN14 .... 66 D7
Snape View. TN5 .... 174 F4
Snelling Ave. DA11 .... 29 F6
Snipe Cl. Erith DA8 .... 9 B7
Snipe Ct. Pembury TN2 .... 150 E8
Snipe Ct. TN12 .... 46 C7
Snoad La. TN12 .... 155 A8
Snodhurst Ave. ME5 .... 61 E5
Snodland CE Prim Sch. ME6 .. 74 F8
Snodland Rd. ME19 .... 74 D7

Snodland Sta. ME6 .... 75 B8
Snodlands Cl. BR6 .... 51 A1
Snoll Hatch Rd. TN12 .... 119 F5
Snow House. ME7 .... 48 E7
Snowdon Ave. ME14 .... 92 B5
Snowdon Cl. ME5 .... 62 B7
Snughorne La. TN27 .... 158 D8
Sole Fields. TN13 .... 99 C8
Sole St. DA12 & DA13 .... 44 D4
Sole Street Sta. DA13 .... 44 D4
Solefield Prep Sch. TN13 .... 99 C8
Solefields Rd. TN13 .... 99 C8
Solent Gdns. ME5 .... 62 B8
Soleoak Dr. TN13 .... 99 C8
Solomon Rd. Gillingham ME8 .. 49 F1
Solomon Rd. Gillingham ME8 .. 64 A8
Solomons Rd. ME4 .... 47 F4
Somerden Rd. BR5 .... 38 D2
Somerfield Cl. ME16 .... 91 D5
Somerfield Hospl The. ME16 .. 91 C5
Somerfield La. ME16 .... 91 D4
Somerfield Rd. ME16 .... 91 D4
Somerhill Ave. DA15 .... 24 B8
Somerhill Rd. Bexley DA15 .. 7 B5
Somerhill Rd. Tonbridge TN9 133 D8
Somerlea Ct. DA16 .... 6 F3
Somerset Cl. ME5 .... 62 B8
Somerset Rd. Dartford DA1 .. 26 B8
Somerset Rd. Maidstone ME15 .107 C8
Somerset Rd. Orpington BR6 .. 38 A2
Somerset Rd.
  Royal Tunbridge Wells TN4 149 A6
Somerset Villas. TN3 .... 161 C7
Somersham Rd. DA7 .... 7 E5
Somertrees Ave. SE12 .... 22 B6
Somerville Gdns. TN4 .... 148 F4
Somerville Rd. DA1 .... 9 F1
Somner Wlk. ME15 .... 107 F4
Soper's La. TN18 .... 178 D4
Sophia Rd. E16 .... 1 B7
Sophurst La. TN12 .... 151 C5
Sopurst Wood. TN12 .... 151 D5
Sorrel Cl. SE28 .... 3 A5
Sorrel Ct. 7 RM17 .... 12 D8
Sorrel Gdns. E6 .... 1 E8
Sorrell Cl. 4 TN8 .... 112 D3
Sorrell Rd. ME5 .... 61 F4
Sorrell Way. DA11 .... 29 E4
Sortmill Rd. ME6 .... 75 B7
Sounds Lodge. BR8 .... 39 C3
South Ash Rd. TN15 .... 56 E4
South Ave. ME8 .... 49 B2
South Aylesford Ret Pk. ME20 . 90 E8
South Bank. Cliffe Woods ME3 .. 16 B2
South Bank. Stapleburst TN12 .. 139 E2
South Bank.
  Sutton Valence ME17 .... 124 E7
South Bank. Westerham TN16 .. 81 D1
South Borough Cty Prim Sch.
  ME15 .... 92 A2
South Bush La. ME8 .... 64 B6
South Cl. DA6 .... 7 D3
South Cres. ME17 .... 106 C4
South Eastern Rd. ME2 .... 47 C7
South Frith. ME4 .... 133 A6
South Glade. DA5 .... 24 F7
South Gr. TN1 .... 149 A2
South Green La. ME9 .... 79 F6
South Hall Cl. DA4 .... 40 F2
South Hill. BR7 .... 22 F2
South Hill Rd. DA12 .... 30 C7
South Kent Ave. DA11 .... 12 C1
South La. ME17 .... 124 E6
South Molton Rd. E16 .... 1 A7
South Park Bsns Village. ME15 92 A1
South Park Rd. ME15 .... 92 C1
South Pondside Rd. ME4 .... 48 A8
South Rd. Erith DA8 .... 8 F7
South Rd. Gillingham ME7 .. 48 A7
South Rd. Gillingham ME4 .. 48 B7
South Rd. Marden TN12 .... 138 E5
South Rise Jun & Inf Sch. SE18 2 D1
South Row. Greenwich SE3 .. 5 A5
South Row. Weller's Town TN8 130 D5
South Side Three Rd. ME4 .. 48 C8
South St. Bromley BR1 .... 36 A7
South St. Gravesend DA11 .. 30 B8
South St. Maidstone ME16 .. 90 E1
South St. Meopham Green DA13 . 57 F7
South Street Rd. ME9 .... 79 C7
South Terr. DA4 .... 40 F2
South View. BR1 .... 36 C7
South View Ave. RM18 .... 13 A6
South View Cl. DA5 .... 7 F1
South View Rd.
  Royal Tunbridge Wells TN4 .. 149 B8
South View Rd.
  Turner's Green TN5 .... 174 F6
South View Rd.
  West Thurrock RM16 .... 11 C8
South View Rd. Wilmington DA2 26 D5
South Wharf Rd. RM17 .... 11 F8
Southborough CE Prim Schs.
  TN4 .... 148 F8
Southborough Ct. TN4 .... 133 A2
Southborough La. BR1 & BR2 .. 36 E4
Southborough Prim Sch. BR2 . 37 A4
Southborough Rd. BR1 & BR2 .. 36 E5
Southbourne. BR2 .... 36 A2
Southbourne Gdns. SE12 .... 5 B2
Southbourne Gr. ME5 .... 62 C1
Southcroft Ave. DA16 .... 6 E4
Southcroft Rd. BR6 .... 51 E7
Southdene. TN14 .... 67 F6
Southend Cl. SE9 .... 6 B1
Southend Cres. SE9 .... 6 B1

Southern Pl. BR8 .... 39 D5
Southernden Rd. TN27 .... 126 E1
Southey Way. 1 ME20 .... 74 F4
Southey Wlk. RM18 .... 13 B6
Southfield Rd.
  Royal Tunbridge Wells TN4 . 149 A6
Southfield Rd. Speldhurst TN3 . 148 A7
Southfield Rd. St Paul's Cray BR7 38 A6
Southfield Shaw. DA13 .... 58 B1
Southfields. Rochester ME1 .. 47 A7
Southfields. Turner's Green TN5 174 F6
Southfields Rd. TN15 .... 55 F2
Southfields Sch. DA12 .... 30 C3
Southfields Way. TN4 .... 149 B8
Southfleet Ave. DA3 .... 43 B7
Southfleet Rd. Bean DA2 .... 28 C4
Southfleet Rd. 7
  Northfleet DA11 .... 29 F7
Southfleet Rd. Orpington BR6 . 51 E6
Southfleet Rd. Swanscombe DA10 29 A7
Southgate. TN4 .... 148 F3
Southgate Rd. TN30 .... 183 C7
Southill Rd. Chatham ME4 .... 47 F3
Southill Rd. Chislehurst BR7 .. 22 F1
Southlake Prim Sch. SE2 .... 3 D4
Southland Rd. SE18 .... 6 F7
Southlands Ave. BR6 .... 51 E5
Southlands Gr. BR1 .... 36 E6
Southlands Rd. BR1 & BR2 .. 36 D5
Southlees La. ME9 .... 79 F3
Southold Rise. SE9 .... 22 F5
Southover. BR1 .... 22 A3
Southport Rd. SE18 .... 2 D2
Southspring. SE9 .... 23 D8
Southview Cl. BR8 .... 40 A5
Southwark Pl. BR1 .... 36 F6
Southwark Rd. ME2 .... 46 D6
Southway. ME2 .... 36 A2
Southways. ME17 .... 124 E7
Southwell Rd. ME2 .... 46 D6
Southwold Rd. DA16 .... 8 B1
Southwood. ME16 .... 90 F2
Southwood Ave. TN4 .... 149 A6
Southwood Cl. BR1 .... 36 F5
Southwood House. SE18 .... 23 B6
Southwood Rd. Eltham SE9 .. 23 B6
Southwood Rd. Rusthall TN4 . 148 B5
Southwood Rd. Woolwich SE18 . 3 B5
Sovereign Bvd. Gillingham ME7 . 48 F2
Sovereign Bvd.
  Gillingham,Twydall ME8 .... 49 A2
Sovereign Cl. Bromley BR2 .. 36 F4
Sovereign Ct. Sutton at Hone DA4 41 B8
Sovereign House. SE18 .... 1 F3
Sovereign Way. TN9 .... 117 C1
Sovereigns The. ME16 .... 91 D4
Sovereigns Way. TN12 .... 138 C6
Sowerby Cl. SE9 .... 5 F2
Spa Golf Course. TN4 .... 148 E3
Spa Ind Est. TN2 .... 149 E8
Spade La. ME8 & ME9 .... 64 C6
Sparepenny La. DA4 .... 40 E1
Sparkeswood Ave. TN17 .... 181 F3
Sparkeswood Cl. TN17 .... 181 F3
Sparrow Dr. BR5 .... 37 D1
Sparrow's Farm L Ctr. SE9 .. 23 C8
Sparrows Green Rd. TN5 .... 174 F5
Sparrows La. SE9 .... 23 C7
Spearhead Rd. ME14 .... 91 F7
Spearman St. 8 SE18 .... 6 A8
Spectrum Bsns Ctr. ME2 .... 47 E8
Spectrum Bsns Est. ME15 .. 107 F4
Speedgate Hill. DA3 .... 56 A8
Speedwell Ave. ME5 .... 61 F4
Speedwell Cl. Gillingham ME7 . 48 E5
Speedwell Cl. Maidstone ME14 . 92 E5
Speedwell Cl. 5
  Marlpit Hill TN8 .... 112 D3
Speedwell Ct. RM17 .... 12 C7
Spekehill. SE9 .... 22 F5
Spekes Rd. ME7 .... 63 B6
Speldhurst CE Prim Sch. TN3 148 A7
Speldhurst Cl. BR2 .... 36 A3
Speldhurst Hill. TN3 .... 148 B8
Speldhurst Rd.
  Langton Green TN3 .... 147 F4
Speldhurst Rd. Royal Tunbridge Wells
  TN3 & TN4 .... 148 E8
Spelmonden Rd. TN12 & TN12 . 152 F2
Spencer Cl. Chatham ME5 .. 62 A5
Spencer Cl. Orpington BR6 .. 51 F8
Spencer Ct. 5 BR6 .... 51 C5
Spencer Flats. ME5 .... 62 B8
Spencer Mews. 6 TN1 .... 149 A2
Spencer St. DA11 .... 30 A8
Spencer Way. ME15 .... 107 E7
Spencer Wlk. RM18 .... 13 B5
Spencer's Mews. 4 TN1 .. 149 B4
Spenlow Dr. ME5 .... 77 A8
Spenny La. TN12 .... 137 B7
Speranza St. SE18 .... 2 F1
Speyside. TN10 .... 117 B5
Spielman Rd. DA1 .... 9 F3
Spiers The. ME7 .... 49 C5
Spillway The. ME15 .... 91 D2
Spindle Glade. ME14 .... 92 C5
Spindle House. 8 DA15 .... 24 A5
Spindles. ME1 .... 13 A7
Spindlewood Cl. ME5 .... 62 B3
Spinel Cl. SE18 .... 2 F1
Spinnaker Ct. 3 ME1 .... 47 C1
Spinnens Acre Cty Jun Sch.
  ME5 .... 62 C1
Spinners Cl. TN27 .... 158 A2
Spinners Wents. TN15 .... 102 D8
Spinney Oak. BR1 .... 36 E7
Spinney The. Chatham ME5 .. 62 A1
Spinney The. Maidstone ME15 . 92 B2

Spinney The. Sidcup DA14 .... 24 E3
Spinney The. Swanley BR8 .. 39 E7
Spinney The. Tonbridge TN9 . 133 A7
Spinney Way. TN14 .... 66 D8
Spinneys The. BR1 .... 36 F7
Spire Cl. DA12 .... 30 B7
Spires The. Dartford DA1 .... 26 D6
Spires The. Maidstone ME16 . 91 B4
Spires The. Rochester ME2 .. 46 D5
Spital St. DA1 .... 9 D1
Spitfire Cl. ME5 .... 62 B6
Spitfire Rd. ME19 .... 88 F3
Spode La. TN8 .... 145 A7
Sponden La. Field Green TN18 . 185 F8
Sponden La. Sandhurst TN18 .. 186 A7
Spongs La. TN17 .... 156 A1
Sportsfield. ME14 .... 92 B5
Sportsmans Cotts. ME19 .... 89 A5
Spot La. ME15 .... 93 A2
Spout La. Brenchley TN12 .... 152 C5
Spout La. Crockham Hill TN8 .. 96 C1
Spray Hill. TN3 .... 166 B4
Spray St. SE18 .... 2 B2
Sprig The. ME14 .... 93 A4
Spring Cross. DA3 .... 57 A7
Spring Gdns. Orpington BR6 .. 52 B4
Spring Gdns. Rusthall TN4 .. 148 B4
Spring Gr. DA12 .... 30 B7
Spring Head Rd. TN15 .... 69 F2
Spring Hill. TN11 & TN3 .... 147 A7
Spring La. Bidborough TN4 .. 132 D3
Spring La. Oldbury TN15 .... 86 B5
Spring Lodge. 3 ME5 .... 38 C4
Spring Shaw Rd. BR5 .... 38 A8
Spring Vale. Bexley DA7 .... 8 B3
Spring Vale. Dartford DA1 .... 26 D8
Spring Vale. Maidstone ME16 . 91 E4
Spring Vale. Swanscombe DA9 . 11 C1
Spring Vale Cl. BR8 .... 39 F8
Spring Vale N. DA1 .... 26 D8
Spring Vale S. DA1 .... 26 D8
Springcroft. DA3 .... 43 A4
Springdale Cotts. ME3 .... 33 A3
Springett Almshouses. TN18 . 184 E8
Springett Way. ME17 .... 106 D3
Springfield Ave.
  St Michaels TN30 .... 173 C2
Springfield Ave. Swanley BR8 . 39 F5
Springfield Cotts. TN12 .... 152 F5
Springfield Gdns. BR1 .... 36 F5
Springfield Ind Est. TN18 .... 178 F3
Springfield Rd.
  Bexley,Bexleyheath DA7 .... 8 B3
Springfield Rd.
  Bexley,Welling DA16 .... 7 B4
Springfield Rd. Bromley BR1 .. 36 F5
Springfield Rd. Edenbridge TN8 112 B1
Springfield Rd. Gillingham ME7 . 48 E6
Springfield Rd.
  Groombridge TN3 .... 161 C7
Springfield Rd. Lunsford ME20 . 74 F4
Springfield Rd.
  Royal Tunbridge Wells TN4 . 132 F1
Springfield Way. BR5 .... 38 C6
Springfield Wlk. 3 BR6 .... 37 D1
Springfields. TN5 .... 176 E1
Springhead. TN2 .... 149 D5
Springhead Ent Pk. DA11 .... 29 C7
Springhead Rd. Erith DA8 .... 8 F8
Springhead Rd. Northfleet DA11 29 C7
Springrove Cotts. TN12 .... 138 B5
Springshaw Ct. TN13 .... 83 D4
Springvale. ME8 .... 63 C6
Springvale Ct. Chisleburst SE12 . 5 A3
Springvale Ct. Northfleet DA11 29 C6
Springview Apartments. TN1 149 D6
Springwater Cl. SE18 .... 6 A6
Springwell Rd. TN9 .... 133 B8
Springwood Cl. ME16 .... 91 A3
Springwood Rd. ME16 .... 91 A3
Spruce Cl. ME20 .... 75 B2
Sprucedale Cl. BR8 .... 39 E7
Spur Rd. BR6 .... 52 A8
Spurgeons Cotts. ME17 .... 106 E2
Spurrell Ave. DA2 & DA5 .... 25 D4
Spurway. ME14 .... 93 A4
Square Hill. ME15 .... 92 B4
Square Hill Rd. ME14 & ME15 .. 92 B4
Square The. Cowden TN8 .... 145 B6
Square The. Hadlow TN11 .. 118 E8
Square The. Hunton ME15 .. 121 D7
Square The. Leigh TN11 .... 115 F1
Square The. Lenham ME17 .. 111 D5
Square The. Swanley BR8 .... 39 D6
Square The. Wadhurst TN5 .. 175 A4
Squerryes Court. TN16 .... 96 C7
Squerryes Mede. TN16 .... 96 C7
Squires Cl. ME2 .... 46 B7
Squires Field. BR8 .... 39 F8
Squires House. 3 SE18 .... 2 A2
Squires Way. DA2 .... 25 D4
Squires Wood Dr. BR7 .... 22 C7
Squirrel Cl. TN2 .... 149 E5
Stable Cl. ME5 .... 62 A5
Stabledene Way. TN2 .... 150 D6
Stables End. BR6 .... 51 C7
Stace Cl. TN30 .... 183 C8
Stacey Cl. DA12 .... 30 E3
Staceys St. ME14 .... 91 F5
Stack La. DA3 .... 42 F4
Stack Rd. DA4 .... 41 D5

Stacklands Cl. TN15 .... 55 E4
Stadium Rd. SE18 & SE7 .... 5 F8
Stadium Way. DA1 .... 8 E2
Staffa Rd. ME15 .... 107 A7
Stafford Cl. DA9 .... 10 F2
Stafford Rd.
Royal Tunbridge Wells TN2 .. 149 E4
Stafford Rd. Sidcup DA14 ..... 23 E4
Stafford Rd. Tonbridge TN9 .. 117 B2
Stafford St. ME7 .... 48 C5
Stafford Way. TN13 .... 99 C8
Stag Rd. Chatham ME5 .... 62 B5
Stag Rd.
Royal Tunbridge Wells TN2 .. 149 D8
Stainer House. SE9 .... 5 C3
Stainer Rd. TN10 .... 117 F6
Staines Wlk. DA14 .... 24 C2
Stainmore Cl. BR7 .... 37 D8
Stair Rd. TN14 .... 117 F4
Stairfoot La. TN13 .... 83 C5
Stake La. ME2 .... 60 A6
Staleys Rd. TN15 .... 86 F7
Stalham Ct. ME7 .... 63 B4
Stalin Ave. ME5 .... 62 B8
Stalisfield Pl. BR6 .... 51 A1
Stampers The. ME15 .... 91 D2
Stan La. ME18 .... 103 A7
Stanam Rd. TN2 .... 150 E6
Stanbridge Rd. TN8 .... 112 B2
Stanbrook Cl. Northfleet DA11 .. 29 F8
Stanbrook Rd. Woolwich SE2 .... 3 B4
Standard Ind Est. E16 .... 1 F4
Standard Rd. Bexley DA6 .... 7 E3
Standard Rd. Erith DA17 .... 4 A2
Standard Rd. Farthing Street BR6 51 A1
Standen Cl. ME8 .... 63 E4
Standen Cl.
Iden Green TN17 & TN18 ...... 180 D2
Standen St.
Royal Tunbridge Wells TN4 .. 149 A5
Standings Cross. TN12 .... 135 E1
Standish House. SE3 .... 5 B3
Stane Way. SE18 .... 5 E7
Stanford Dr. ME16 .... 91 C3
Stanford La. TN11 & TN12 .... 103 C3
Stanford Way. ME2 .... 46 C2
Stangate Rd. Birling ME19 ..... 74 B8
Stangate Rd. Rochester ME2 ... 46 C7
Stangrove Rd. TN8 .... 112 C1
Stanham Pl. DA1 .... 9 A3
Stanham Rd. DA1 .... 9 C2
Stanhill Cotts. DA2 .... 25 D2
Stanhope Ave. BR2 .... 36 A1
Stanhope Cl. ME14 .... 91 E7
Stanhope Rd. Bexley DA7 .... 7 E5
Stanhope Rd. Rochester ME2 ... 47 A7
Stanhope Rd.
Royal Tunbridge Wells TN1 .. 149 C5
Stanhope Rd. Sidcup DA15 .... 24 A4
Stanhope Rd. Swanscombe DA10 11 F1
Stanhope Way. TN13 .... 83 D5
Stanley Cl. Staplehurst TN12 .. 139 E4
Stanley Cl. Stone DA9 .... 10 E2
Stanley Cotts. DA2 .... 27 E3
Stanley Cres. TN12 .... 30 D3
Stanley Rd. Bromley BR2 .... 36 C5
Stanley Rd. Chatham ME5 ..... 62 C6
Stanley Rd. Gillingham ME7 ... 48 C6
Stanley Rd. Grays RM17 .... 12 B8
Stanley Rd. Marden TN12 .... 138 D5
Stanley Rd. Orpington BR6 .... 37 F1
Stanley Rd.
Royal Tunbridge Wells TN1 .. 149 B5
Stanley Rd. Sidcup DA14 ...... 24 A5
Stanley Rd. Swanscombe DA10 .. 11 F1
Stanley Way. BR5 .... 38 B4
Stanmore Rd. DA17 .... 4 C2
Stansfeld Rd. E6 .... 1 D7
Stansted CE Prim Sch. TN15 ... 56 F1
Stansted Cres. ME16 .... 91 D7
Stansted Cres. DA7 .... 24 D7
Stansted Hill. TN15 .... 57 A1
Stansted La. TN15 .... 56 C1
Stanton Cl. BR5 .... 38 C2
Stanton Ct. **5** DA15 .... 24 A5
Staple Cl. DA5 .... 25 D5
Staple Dr. TN12 .... 139 F4
Stapleford Ct. TN13 .... 83 F4
Staplehurst Cty Prim Sch.
TN12 .... 139 E3
Staplehurst House. BR5 .... 38 C4
Staplehurst Rd. Bogden TN12 .. 123 C2
Staplehurst Rd. Gillingham ME8 . 49 B3
Staplehurst Rd.
Sinkhurst Green TN12 & TN17 .. 140 D1
Staplehurst Sta. TN12 .... 139 E5
Staplers Ct. ME14 .... 92 B8
Stapleton Rd. Erith DA7 .... 8 A7
Stapleton Rd. Orpington BR6 .. 51 F7
Stapley Rd. DA17 .... 4 A1
Star Bsns Ctr. RM9 .... 4 D8
Star Cl. Crayford DA1 .... 8 E2
Star Hill. Rochester ME1 ...... 47 D5
Star Hill Rd. TN14 .... 68 A2
Star La. Gillingham ME7 .... 63 A7
Star La. St Paul's Cray BR5 ... 38 E5
Star Mill Ct. ME5 .... 48 D2
Star Mill La. ME5 .... 48 D2
Starboard Ave. DA9 .... 11 B1
Starling Cl. DA3 .... 43 B6
Starnes Ct. **5** ME14 .... 92 A5
Starr Cotts. TN12 .... 121 C2
Starts Cl. BR6 .... 51 A7
Starts Hill Ave. BR6 .... 51 B6
Starts Hill Rd. BR6 .... 51 B6

Starvecrow Cl. TN11 .... 117 D8
State Farm Ave. BR6 .... 51 C6
Station App.
Bexley,Barnehurst DA7 .... 8 C5
Station App.
Bexley,Bexleyheath DA7 .... 7 E5
Station App. Bexley,Welling DA16 . 7 A5
Station App. Chislehurst BR7 ... 37 A7
Station App.
Chislehurst,Elmstead BR7 .... 22 E2
Station App. Dartford DA1 .... 9 E1
Station App. Edenbridge TN8 .. 112 C2
Station App. Grays RM17 ...... 12 A8
Station App. Greenwich SE3 .... 5 B4
Station App. Halling ME2 ...... 60 A5
Station App. Hayes BR2 .... 36 A1
Station App. Maidstone ME16 .. 91 F3
Station App. Orpington BR6 ... 51 F8
Station App.
Orpington,Chelsfield BR6 ..... 52 B5
Station App.
Paddock Wood TN12 .... 136 A7
Station App. St Paul's Cray BR5 .. 38 B5
Station App. Staplehurst TN12 .. 139 E5
Station App. Swanley BR8 ...... 39 E5
Station Approach Rd. RM18 ... 13 A3
Station Cotts. Gill's Green TN18 178 F5
Station Cotts. Horsmonden TN12153 B5
Station Cres. SE3 .... 1 A1
Station Ct. TN15 .... 86 F7
Station Hill.
Chiddingstone Causeway TN11 .. 114 F1
Station Hill.
Chiddingstone Causeway TN11 .. 131 A8
Station Hill. Hayes BR2 .... 50 A8
Station Rd. Aylesford ME20 ... 75 E2
Station Rd. Betsham DA13 .... 29 A4
Station Rd. Bexley DA7 .... 7 E4
Station Rd. Borough Green TN15 . 86 F7
Station Rd. Brasted TN16 ..... 82 B4
Station Rd. Bromley BR1 ...... 36 A8
Station Rd. Cliffe ME3 .... 16 B3
Station Rd. Crayford DA1 .... 8 F1
Station Rd. Cuxton ME2 ...... 46 C2
Station Rd. East Farleigh ME15 106 A7
Station Rd. East Tilbury RM18 .. 14 B7
Station Rd. Edenbridge TN8 .. 112 C2
Station Rd. Erith DA17 .... 4 A3
Station Rd. Eynsford DA4 ..... 54 D7
Station Rd. Gillingham ME8 ... 49 F1
Station Rd. Goudhurst TN17 .. 167 C2
Station Rd. Groombridge TN3 .. 161 C7
Station Rd. Halstead TN14 .... 67 F8
Station Rd. Harrietsham ME17 . 110 D6
Station Rd. Headcorn TN27 .. 141 D5
Station Rd. Hurst Green TN19 . 184 A3
Station Rd. Longfield DA3 .... 42 E6
Station Rd. Maidstone ME14 .. 91 F5
Station Rd.
Meopham Station DA13 .... 44 A4
Station Rd.
Nettlestead Green ME18 ..... 104 C1
Station Rd. Newington ME9 .... 65 B6
Station Rd. Northfleet DA11 ... 12 B1
Station Rd. Northiam TN31 .. 187 C1
Station Rd. Orpington BR6 .... 51 F8
Station Rd. Otford TN14 ...... 69 C3
Station Rd. Paddock Wood TN12 135 F7
Station Rd. Rochester ME2 .... 47 C7
Station Rd. Rockrobin TN5 ... 174 C6
Station Rd. Sevenoaks TN13 ... 83 E7
Station Rd. Shoreham TN14 ... 69 A7
Station Rd. Sidcup DA14 & DA15 . 24 A5
Station Rd. St Paul's Cray BR5 . 38 C5
Station Rd. Staplehurst TN12 .. 139 F5
Station Rd. Sutton at Hone DA4 . 41 B7
Station Rd. Swanley BR8 ...... 39 E5
Station Rd. Swanscombe DA9 .. 11 A2
Station Rd. Tenterden TN30 .. 183 A7
Station Rd. Withyham TN7 .... 160 B5
Station Rd N. DA17 .... 4 B3
Station Sq. BR5 .... 37 C4
Station St. E16 .... 2 B5
Steadman Cl. ME3 .... 32 C6
Stede Hill. ME17 .... 95 F3
Stedman Cl. DA5 .... 25 E5
Steele Rd. DA9 .... 11 A2
Steele St. ME2 .... 47 A8
Steele's La. DA13 .... 58 A6
Steep Cl. BR6 .... 51 F4
Steerforth Cl. ME1 .... 47 C2
Steers Pl. TN11 .... 102 E2
Stella Cl. TN12 .... 138 D5
Stelling Rd. DA8 .... 8 D7
Stephen Cl. BR6 .... 51 F7
Stephen Rd. DA7 .... 8 C4
Stephen's Rd. TN4 .... 149 B6
Stephenson Ave. RM18 .... 13 A6
Stephenson House. SE2 .... 3 D1
Stepneyford La. TN17 .... 181 C7
Steps Hill Rd. ME9 .... 79 D6
Sterling Ave. ME16 .... 91 C5
Sterling House. SE3 .... 5 B3
Sterndale Rd. DA1 .... 26 F8
Stevanne Ct. **1** DA17 .... 4 A1
Stevedale Rd. DA16 .... 7 C5
Stevens Cl. Joyden's Wood DA5 . 25 D4
Stevens Cl. Lane End DA2 ..... 27 E3
Stevens Cl. Maidstone ME15 ... 91 F3
Stevens Cl. Snodland ME6 ..... 75 A8
Stevens Rd. ME20 .... 75 F6
Stevenson Cl. DA8 .... 9 B7
Stevenson Way. ME20 .... 74 F4
Stewart Cl. BR7 .... 23 B4
Stewart House. ME3 .... 34 F6
Stewart Rd. TN4 .... 149 C7
Steyning Gr. SE9 .... 22 F4
Steynton Ave. DA5 .... 24 D6

Stickens La. ME19 .... 89 E7
Stickfast La. TN27 .... 125 D3
Stickland Rd. **2** DA17 .... 4 A2
Stilebridge La.
Underling Green TN12 .... 122 E3
Stilebridge La.
Underling Green ME17 .... 123 A5
Stiles Cl. Bromley BR2 .... 36 F3
Stiles Cl. Erith DA8 .... 4 B1
Still La. TN4 .... 132 F2
Stirling Cl. Gillingham ME8 ... 63 E4
Stirling Cl. Rochester ME1 .... 47 A3
Stirling Dr. BR6 .... 52 B5
Stirling House. **5** SE18 .... 2 B1
Stisted Way. TN27 .... 127 F3
Stock La. DA2 .... 26 C4
Stockbury Dr. ME16 .... 91 C7
Stockbury House. **7** BR5 ..... 38 D1
Stockenbury. TN12 .... 119 F6
Stockett La. ME15 .... 106 D6
Stockfield. **1** TN8 .... 112 D3
Stockland Green Rd. TN3 .... 148 B8
Stocks Green Cty Prim Sch.
TN11 .... 116 C5
Stocks Green Rd. TN11 .... 116 C5
Stocks Rd. TN30 .... 189 F3
Stockton Cl. ME14 .... 92 B8
Stockwell Cl. BR1 .... 36 B7
Stofield Gdns. SE9 .... 22 D5
Stoke Cty Prim Sch. ME3 .... 19 C5
Stoke Rd. Allhallows ME3 ..... 19 C5
Stoke Rd. Hoo St Werburgh ME3 . 34 F6
Stoke Rd. Kingsnorth ME3 .... 35 C8
Stoke Rd. Stoke ME3 .... 18 E1
Stone CE Prim Sch. DA2 ...... 27 E8
Stone Cotts. TN3 .... 165 F4
Stone Court La. TN2 .... 150 E8
Stone Cross Rd. TN5 .... 175 A4
Stone Crossing Halt. DA9 .... 10 E2
Stone Ct. DA8 .... 4 F1
Stone Hill Rd. TN27 .... 127 F2
Stone House Hospl. DA2 ..... 10 C1
Stone Lodge Farm Park. DA2 . 10 D1
Stone Pit La. TN18 .... 186 E5
Stone Place Rd. DA9 .... 10 E2
Stone Rd. BR2 .... 36 A5
Stone Row. IN3 .... 147 B5
Stone Row Cotts. TN3 .... 147 D1
Stone St. Cranbrook TN17 ... 169 D5
Stone St. Gravesend DA11 ... 13 B1
Stone St.
Royal Tunbridge Wells TN1 .. 149 B4
Stone Street Rd. TN15 .... 85 C2
Stone Wood. DA2 .... 28 C5
Stoneacre Cl. ME8 .... 63 D5
Stoneacre La. ME15 .... 108 B7
Stoneacre (NT). ME15 .... 108 B7
Stonebridge Green Rd. TN27 . 127 F4
Stonebridge Rd. DA11 .... 12 B2
Stonechat Sq. **6** E6 .... 1 E8
Stonecroft. DA13 .... 73 A8
Stonecroft Rd. DA8 .... 8 C7
Stonecross Lea. ME5 .... 48 C1
Stonefield Cl. DA7 .... 8 A4
Stonefield Way. SE7 .... 5 D7
Stonegate Cl. BR5 .... 38 C6
Stonegate Rd. TN5 .... 175 C1
Stonehorse La. ME3 .... 33 A2
Stonehouse Cnr. RM16 .... 10 E8
Stonehouse La.
Pratt's Bottom BR6 & TN14 ... 52 E1
Stonehouse La. Purfleet RM16 .. 10 E8
Stonehouse Rd. BR6 .... 52 D1
Stoneings La. TN14 .... 81 F8
Stoneness Rd. RM16 .... 11 C7
Stones Cross Rd. BR8 .... 39 C4
Stonestile Rd. TN27 .... 141 A7
Stonewall. E6 .... 2 A8
Stonewall Park Rd. TN3 ..... 147 F3
Stonewood Rd. DA8 .... 4 E1
Stoney Alley. SE18 .... 6 A5
Stoney Bank. ME7 .... 48 F1
Stony Cnr. DA3 .... 43 E6
Stony La. ME5 .... 61 C5
Stonyfield. TN8 .... 112 D3
Stopford Rd. ME7 .... 48 D4
Store Rd. E16 .... 2 A4
Storehouse Wharf. ME12 ..... 21 F3
Storey Prim Sch. E16 .... 2 B5
Storey St. E16 .... 2 A4
Stornaway Strand. DA12 ..... 30 F4
Stour Cl. Keston BR2 .... 50 C6
Stour Cl. Rochester ME2 ...... 46 F7
Stour Cl. Tonbridge TN10 ... 117 B5
Stour Ct. **22** BR5 .... 38 D1
Stour House. **4** ME15 ...... 107 D8
Stour Rd. DA1 .... 9 A4
Stowe Rd. BR6 .... 52 B6
Stowting Rd. BR6 .... 51 E6
Strait Rd. E6 .... 1 F6
Strand Approach Rd. ME7 .... 48 E7
Strand Cl. DA13 .... 44 A3
Strandfield Cl. SE18 .... 2 E1
Stratfield House. SE12 .... 22 A6
Stratford Ave. ME8 .... 63 D8
Stratford House Ave. BR1 ... 36 E6
Stratford La. ME8 .... 63 F8
Stratford Rd. ME19 .... 89 A8
Stratford St. TN1 .... 149 C5
Strathaven Rd. SE12 .... 5 B1
Stratheden Par. SE3 .... 5 A7
Stratheden Rd. SE3 .... 5 A7
Stratton Cl. DA7 .... 7 E4
Stratton Rd. DA7 .... 7 E4
Stratton Terr. TN9 .... 96 C8
Straw Mill Hill. ME15 .... 91 E1
Strawberry Cl. TN2 .... 162 E7
Strawberry Fields. BR8 .... 39 E7

Strawberry Vale. TN9 .... 117 C1
Stream La. TN18 .... 185 A7
Stream Lane Cotts. TN18 ... 185 A7
Stream Pit La. TN18 .... 186 B6
Stream Side. TN10 .... 117 D6
Stream The. ME19 .... 75 C1
Stream Way. DA17 .... 8 A8
Streamdale. SE2 .... 7 B8
Streamside. ME19 .... 75 B1
Streamside Cl. BR2 .... 36 A5
Streatfield. TN8 .... 112 D1
Street End Rd. ME5 .... 48 B1
Street Farm Cotts. ME3 ...... 34 F6
Street The. Ash TN15 .... 56 E5
Street The. Benenden TN17 .. 180 D6
Street The. Boxley ME14 ..... 77 C3
Street The. Bredhurst ME7 ... 63 B1
Street The. Cobham DA12 .... 44 F6
Street The. Detling ME14 ..... 78 A1
Street The. Egerton TN27 ... 127 F3
Street The. Fenn Street ME3 . 18 A3
Street The. Hartlip ME9 ...... 64 D5
Street The. High Halstow ME23 . 17 E3
Street The. Horton Kirby DA4 . 41 C5
Street The. Ightham TN15 .... 86 D6
Street The. Maidstone ME14 . 93 C4
Street The. Meopham DA13 ... 44 A1
Street The. Mereworth ME18 . 103 D8
Street The. Plaxtol TN15 .... 101 F7
Street The. Ryarsh ME19 ..... 73 F4
Street The. Shorne DA12 ..... 31 E3
Street The. Silver Street ME9 . 80 F5
Street The. Sissinghurst TN17 . 170 B8
Street The. Teston ME18 .... 105 A7
Street The. Trottiscliffe ME19 . 73 A5
Street The. Ulcombe ME17 .. 125 F7
Street The. Upper Halling ME2 . 59 E5
Street The. Wittersham ME9 . 189 D3
Street The. Wormshill ME9 .. 95 F7
Streetfield. ME17 .... 125 F7
Streetfield Mews. SE3 .... 5 A4
Streetfield Rd. ME8 .... 49 F1
Strettitt Gdns. TN12 .... 119 F5
Strickland Ave. DA1 .... 9 F4
Strickland Way. **4** BR6 ...... 51 F6
Strongbow Cres. SE9 .... 5 F2
Strongbow Rd. SE9 .... 5 F2
Strood Sta. ME2 .... 47 C7
Strover St. ME7 .... 48 C7
Strumer Cl. ME18 .... 89 A2
Struttons Ave. DA11 .... 29 F6
Stuart Ave. BR2 .... 36 A1
Stuart Cl. Hextable BR8 ...... 26 A1
Stuart Cl. Maidstone ME14 ... 92 C6
Stuart Cl.
Royal Tunbridge Wells TN2 .. 162 F8
Stuart Evans Cl. DA16 .... 7 C4
Stuart Mantle Way. DA8 .... 8 E7
Stuart Rd. Bexley DA16 .... 7 B6
Stuart Rd. Gillingham ME7 .... 48 D3
Stuart Rd. Gravesend DA11 ... 13 A1
Stubbs Hill. BR6 & TN14 ..... 67 C6
Stubbygrove Cotts. TN3 ..... 163 E4
Studland Cl. DA15 .... 23 F5
Studley Cres. DA3 .... 43 C7
Studley Ct. DA14 .... 24 B3
Stumble Hill. TN11 .... 101 C5
Sturdee Ave. ME7 .... 48 E4
Sturdee Cotts. ME3 .... 35 A6
Sturges Field. BR7 .... 23 D2
Sturla Rd. ME4 .... 48 A3
Sturry Way. ME8 .... 49 C2
Styants Bottom Rd. TN15 .... 85 F5
Style Cl. ME8 .... 63 E4
Styles Cl. TN8 .... 113 B5
Styles Cotts. TN8 .... 113 B5
Sudbury. E6 .... 2 A7
Sudbury Cres. BR1 .... 22 A3
Suffolk Ave. ME8 .... 49 F1
Suffolk Rd. Dartford DA1 ...... 9 E1
Suffolk Rd. Gravesend DA12 .. 13 D1
Suffolk Rd. Maidstone ME15 .. 107 D8
Suffolk Rd. Sidcup DA14 ..... 24 C2
Suffolk Way. TN13 & TN15 ... 84 C2
Sullivan Ave. E16 .... 1 D8
Sullivan Cl. DA1 .... 26 C8
Sullivan Rd. Tilbury RM18 .... 13 A6
Sullivan Rd. Tonbridge TN10 . 117 C5
Sultan Rd. ME5 .... 62 C2
Summer Cl. TN30 .... 173 C1
Summer Hill. BR7 .... 37 A7
Summerfield. **6** Bromley BR1 . 36 B8
Summerfield. Winchet Hill TN17 154 B6
Summerfield St. SE12 .... 22 A8
Summerhill. TN27 .... 141 A6
Summerhill Ave. TN4 .... 132 F1
Summerhill Cl. BR6 .... 51 E7
Summerhill Rd. Bogden TN12 . 123 C1
Summerhill Rd. Dartford DA1 . 26 D8
Summerhouse Dr. DA2 & DA5 . 25 D4
Summerlands Lodge. BR6 ..... 51 A6
Summerton Way. SE28 .... 3 D7
Summervale Rd. TN2 & TN4 .. 148 E1
Sumner Cl. Orpington BR6 ... 51 C6
Sumner Cl. Rolvenden TN17 . 181 F3
Sun Ct. DA8 .... 8 F5
Sun Hill. DA3 .... 56 A8
Sun La. Gravesend DA12 ...... 30 C6
Sun La. Greenwich SE3 .... 5 B7
Sun Rd. DA10 .... 11 F1
Sun Terr. ME5 .... 62 B4
Sunburst Cl. TN12 .... 138 D5
Sunbury St. SE18 .... 1 F3
Sunderland Cl. ME1 .... 47 A3
Sunderland Dr. ME8 .... 64 A8
Sunderland House. **2** ME7 .. 48 C7
Sundew Cl. **8** RM17 .... 12 D8
Sundorne Rd. SE7 .... 1 C1

Sundridge Ave. Bexley DA16 .... 6 D4
Sundridge Ave.
Bromley BR1 & BR7 .... 22 C1
Sundridge & Brasted CE Prim Sch.
TN14 .... 82 C2
Sundridge Cl. DA1 .... 10 A1
Sundridge Dr. ME5 .... 62 A1
Sundridge Hill. Cuxton ME2 .. 46 C3
Sundridge Hill. Knockholt TN14 . 67 C1
Sundridge Hospl. TN14 .... 97 E8
Sundridge La. TN14 .... 67 C2
Sundridge Park Golf Course.
BR1 .... 22 C2
Sundridge Park Sta. BR1 ..... 22 B1
Sundridge Rd. TN14 .... 83 B8
Sunfields Pl. SE3 .... 5 B7
Sunhill Ct. TN2 .... 150 C6
Sunland Ave. DA6 .... 7 E3
Sunningdale Cl. ME8 .... 63 D6
Sunningdale Ct. ME15 .... 92 B4
Sunningdale Dr. ME8 .... 63 D6
Sunningdale Rd. BR1 & BR2 .. 36 E4
Sunninghill. DA11 .... 29 E6
Sunnybank. TN5 & TN19 .... 177 E3
Sunnydale. BR6 .... 51 A8
Sunnydale Rd. SE12 .... 5 B1
Sunnyfield Rd. BR5 & BR7 ... 38 A6
Sunnymead Ave. ME7 .... 48 E5
Sunnyside. TN8 .... 112 B3
Sunnyside Rd. TN4 .... 148 C4
Sunray Ave. BR2 .... 36 F3
Sunrise Ind Pre-Prep Sch.
ME17 .... 108 D4
Sunset Cl. DA8 .... 9 B7
Sunset Rd. SE28 .... 3 A5
Superabbey Est. ME20 .... 76 B2
Superior Dr. **4** BR6 .... 51 F4
Surlingham Cl. SE28 .... 3 D6
Surrenden Rd. TN12 .... 139 E3
Surrey Cl. TN2 .... 162 F8
Surrey Rd. ME15 .... 107 D8
Susan Rd. SE3 .... 5 B5
Susan Wood. BR7 .... 37 A8
Sussex Cl. TN2 .... 149 C1
Sussex Dr. ME5 .... 62 A4
Sussex Mews. **16** TN2 ...... 149 A2
Sussex Rd. Dartford DA1 ..... 27 A8
Sussex Rd. Erith DA8 .... 8 B7
Sussex Rd. Maidstone ME15 .. 107 D8
Sussex Rd. Orpington BR5 ... 38 C3
Sussex Rd. Sidcup DA14 ...... 24 B3
Sussex Rd. Tonbridge TN9 .. 133 A8
Sussex Road Cty Prim Sch.
TN9 .... 133 A8
Sutcliffe Rd. Bexley DA16 ..... 7 C5
Sutcliffe Rd. Woolwich SE18 ... 6 E8
Sutherland Ave. Bexley DA16 . 6 E3
Sutherland Ave. Orpington BR5 . 37 F4
Sutherland Cl. DA12 .... 31 B6
Sutherland Gdns. ME8 .... 63 E6
Sutherland House. SE18 .... 5 F6
Sutherland Rd. Erith DA17 ..... 4 A3
Sutherland Rd. Royal Tunbridge Wells
TN1 & TN2 .... 149 B3
Sutlej Rd. SE7 .... 5 C7
Sutton at Hone CE Prim Sch.
DA4 .... 27 A1
Sutton Cl. ME8 .... 64 A8
Sutton Ct. TN12 .... 138 C5
Sutton Forge. TN12 .... 138 D5
Sutton Rd. Langley ME17 .... 108 C5
Sutton Rd. Maidstone ME15 .. 107 D6
Sutton St. ME14 .... 93 D4
Sutton Valence Cty Prim Sch.
ME17 .... 124 E7
Sutton Valence Sch. ME17 .. 124 C7
Swadelands Cl. ME17 .... 111 C5
Swadelands Sch. ME17 ...... 111 C5
Swaffield Rd. TN13 .... 84 C5
Swain Cl. ME2 .... 46 F8
Swain Rd. Gillingham ME8 ... 63 B6
Swain Rd. St Michaels TN30 . 173 D3
Swaisland Rd. DA1 .... 9 B1
Swaislands Dr. DA1 .... 8 F2
Swale House. **1** ME15 ...... 107 E7
Swale Rd. Crayford DA1 .... 9 A3
Swale Rd. Rochester ME2 .... 46 C7
Swaledale Rd. DA2 .... 27 C7
Swallow Cl. Erith DA7 .... 8 E6
Swallow Cl. Stone DA9 .... 10 F2
Swallow Cl. **3** SE12 .... 22 A8
Swallow Dr. TN2 .... 149 F6
Swallow House. **4** ME16 .... 91 E4
Swallow Rd. ME20 .... 74 F2
Swallow Rise. ME5 .... 62 A5
Swallow St. E6 .... 1 E8
Swallowfield Rd. SE7 .... 1 B1
Swallowlands. **2** DA11 ...... 29 E5
Swan Apartments. **10** ME15 . 107 E5
Swan App. E6 .... 1 E8
Swan Bsns Pk. DA1 .... 9 C3
Swan Cl. BR5 .... 38 A6
Swan Cotts. TN30 .... 189 D4
Swan La. Brandfold TN17 .... 153 F3
Swan La. Dartford DA1 .... 25 F8
Swan La. Marlpit Hill TN8 ... 112 C4
Swan Rd. SE18 .... 1 D3
Swan Ridge. TN8 .... 112 D4
Swan St. West Malling ME19 . 89 C8
Swan St. Wittersham TN30 .. 189 C3
Swanbridge Rd. DA7 .... 8 B6
Swanland Dr. TN9 .... 132 F7
Swanley Ctr. BR8 .... 39 E6
Swanley La. BR8 .... 39 F6
Swanley Rd. DA16 .... 7 C6
Swanley Sch. BR8 .... 39 E6
Swanley Sta. BR8 .... 39 D5

Swanley Village Rd. BR8 .... 40 B8
Swanmead Way. TN9 .... 117 D2
Swanscombe Bsns Ctr. DA10 ... 11 E2
Swanscombe Cty Inf Sch. DA10 28 F8
Swanscombe House. **1** BR5 .. 38 B7
Swanscombe St. DA10 .... 11 F1
Swanscombe Sta. DA10 .... 11 F2
Swanton Rd. Erith DA8 .... 8 B7
Swanton Rd. Swanton ME18 .. 103 A8
Swanzy Rd. TN14 .... 84 C7
Sward Rd. BR5 .... 38 A3
Swattenden La. TN17 .... 169 B1
Swaylands Rd. DA17 .... 8 A8
Sweeps Hill Cl. TN2 .... 150 D7
Sweeps La. BR5 .... 38 D5
Sweetings La. TN3 & TN5 .... 165 D1
Sweets La. ME19 .... 90 A4
Swetenham Wlk. SE18 .... 2 C1
Sweyn Pl. SE3 .... 5 A5
Sweyne Cty Prim Jun Sch The.
DA10 .... 28 F8
Sweyne Rd. DA10 .... 11 E1
Swift Cl. ME20 .... 75 A2
Swift Cres. ME5 .... 62 C6
Swift House. **6** ME16 .... 91 E4
Swift's Ct. TN15 .... 85 A6
Swifts View. TN17 .... 169 D6
Swiller's La. DA12 .... 31 E3
Swinburne Gdns. RM18 .... 13 B5
Swingate Ave. ME3 .... 16 B6
Swingate Cl. ME5 .... 62 B2
Swingate Cty Inf Sch. ME5 ... 62 C1
Swingate La. SE18 .... 6 E7
Swinton Ave. ME3 .... 33 F5
Swires Shaw. BR2 .... 50 D6
Swithland Gdns. SE9 .... 23 A4
Sycamore Ct. DA8 .... 4 D1
Sycamore Ave. DA15 .... 6 F1
Sycamore Cl. Eltham SE9 .... 22 E6
Sycamore Cl. Gravesend DA12 ... 30 D8
Sycamore Cl. Tilbury RM18 .... 13 A5
Sycamore Cotts. TN2 .... 150 C6
Sycamore Cres. ME16 .... 91 C5
Sycamore Ct. DA2 .... 27 E8
Sycamore Dr. Aylesford ME20 ... 75 E1
Sycamore Dr. Swanley BR8 ...... 39 E7
Sycamore Gdns. TN12 .... 135 F5
Sycamore Lodge. BR6 .... 52 A8
Sycamore Rd. Dartford DA1 .... 26 D7
Sycamore Rd. Rochester ME2 ... 46 B5
Sychem La. TN11 & TN12 ...... 135 A6
Sychem Pl. TN12 .... 135 A7
Sydney Rd. Bexley DA6 .... 7 D3
Sydney Rd. Chatham ME4 .... 48 A3
Sydney Rd. Erith SE2 .... 3 D3
Sydney Rd. Sidcup DA14 .... 23 E4
Sydney Rd. Tilbury RM18 .... 13 A5
Sydney St. SE18 .... 2 C3
Sydney Terr. TN18 .... 178 F3
Sylewood Cl. ME1 .... 61 B8
Sylvan Glade. ME5 .... 77 A8
Sylvan Rd. ME8 .... 63 C8
Sylvan Wlk. BR1 .... 36 F6
Sylvester Ave. BR7 .... 22 F2
Sylvestre Cl. ME2 .... 60 A4
Sylvestres. TN13 .... 83 E6
Symons Ave. ME4 .... 48 A2
Symons La. ME18 .... 120 F6
Symons Rd. ME3 .... 16 A4
Symons Ave. ME4 .... 48 A2
Syon Lodge. **9** SE12 .... 22 A8
Syringa Ct. **9** RM17 .... 12 D8

Tabor Ct. TN12 .... 153 A6
Tadburn Gn. ME5 .... 62 B4
Taddington Wood La. ME5 ... 61 E2
Tadley Ct. ME7 .... 48 F6
Tail Race The. ME15 .... 91 E2
Tainter Cl. TN11 .... 102 E1
Talbot Pk. TN2 .... 149 D5
Talbot Rd. Maidstone ME16 .. 91 C6
Talbot Rd. The Moor TN18 .. 184 F8
Tall Trees Cl. TN12 .... 109 D2
Tallents Cl. DA4 .... 27 B1
Tallis Cl. E16 .... 1 B7
Tallis Gr. SE7 .... 5 B8
Tamar Ct. ME2 .... 46 F7
Tamar House. **4** ME15 .... 107 E8
Tamar Rd. TN10 .... 117 B5
Tamar St. SE7 .... 1 E3
Tamarind Cl. ME7 .... 63 A4
Tamesis Strand. DA12 .... 30 E3
Tan Yard La. DA5 .... 25 A8
Tandridge Dr. BR5 & BR6 ...... 37 D1
Tandridge Pl. **2** BR6 .... 37 D1
Tangier La. TN8 .... 163 B6
Tangleberry Cl. BR1 .... 36 F5
Tanglewood Cl. ME8 .... 63 C6
Tanglewood Cl. BR5 .... 38 C6
Tangmere Cl. ME7 .... 48 F5
Tanker Hill. ME8 .... 63 D6
Tanners Mead. TN8 .... 112 C1
Tannery Rd. TN9 .... 117 C1
Tansy Cl. E6 .... 2 A7
Tanyard. Rolvenden TN17 .... 181 E4
Tanyard. Sandhurst TN18 ... 186 B5
Tanyard Cotts. DA12 .... 31 E1
Tanyard Hill. DA12 .... 31 E2
Tanyard La. TN4 .... 132 F1
Tanyard The. TN17 .... 169 D4
Tapsell's La. TN5 .... 174 D5
Tarbutts. TN17 .... 169 D4
Target Bsns Ctr. ME15 ...... 107 F4
Tarling Cl. DA14 .... 24 B5
Tarnwood Pk. SE9 .... 22 F7
Tasker Cl. ME15 .... 93 B3
Tasman Wlk. E16 .... 1 D7
Tasmania House. RM18 .... 13 A6

Tate Rd. E16 .... 1 F5
Tates. TN18 .... 179 A1
Tates Orch. DA3 .... 42 F3
Tatler Cl. ME5 .... 62 D2
Tatsfield Cl. ME8 .... 49 A2
Tatsfield La. TN16 .... 81 A6
Tattersall Cl. SE9 .... 5 E2
Tattlebury La. TN17 .... 153 F1
Tattlebury Rd. TN27 .... 141 C8
Taunton Cl. DA3 .... 8 D5
Taunton Cl. Maidstone ME15 .. 107 F6
Taunton Rd. DA11 .... 12 A2
Taunton Vale. DA12 .... 30 D5
Tavern Cl. TN15 .... 86 F7
Tavern Cotts. TN15 .... 85 A3
Taverners Rd. ME8 .... 63 E7
Tavistock Cl. Gillingham ME8 .. 63 E7
Tavistock Rd. Bexley DA16 ... 7 C6
Tavistock Rd. **2** Bromley BR2 .. 36 A5
Tavy Bridge. SE2 .... 3 C4
Tawney Rd. SE28 .... 3 B6
Tay Cl. ME5 .... 62 B5
Taylor Cl. **3** BR6 .... 51 F6
Taylor Rd. ME6 .... 74 F8
Taylor St. TN4 .... 149 A8
Taylor's Bldgs. SE18 .... 2 B2
Taylor's La. Lower Higham ME3 .. 32 B5
Taylor's La. Rochester ME2 ... 47 B7
Taylors Cl. DA14 .... 23 F4
Taylors La. SE15 .... 72 F6
Tea Garden La. TN3 & TN4 .. 148 C2
Teal Cl. Grain ME3 .... 21 B5
Teal Cl. Newham E16 .... 1 D8
Teapot La. ME20 .... 75 E1
Teasaucer Hill. ME15 .... 106 F8
Teasel Cl. ME14 .... 92 F4
Teasel Rd. ME5 .... 61 F4
Teasels. TN27 .... 158 A1
Tebbs Way. TN15 .... 86 C3
Ted Williams Ct. **6** SE18 ... 1 F2
Tedder Ave. ME5 .... 62 A7
Tedder Rd. TN4 .... 149 B7
Tees House. **9** ME15 .... 107 E8
Teesdale Rd. DA2 .... 27 C7
Teeswater Cl. SE2 .... 3 D3
Teignmouth Rd. DA16 .... 7 C5
Telegraph Hill. ME3 .... 32 C3
Telemann Sq. SE3 .... 5 B4
Telford House. **2** Erith DA17 ... 4 A3
Telford House.
Maidstone ME14 .... 92 A6
Telford Rd. BR7 .... 23 D6
Tellson Ave. SE18 .... 5 E6
Telscombe Cl. BR6 .... 51 E8
Telston La. TN13 & TN14 ...... 68 F2
Tempest Rd. ME19 .... 88 F3
Templar Dr. Gravesend DA11 .. 30 D3
Templar Dr. Gravesend DA11 .. 30 D3
Templars Ct. **11** TN8 .... 112 D3
Temple Cl. SE18 .... 2 C3
Temple Gdns. ME2 .... 47 A6
Temple Hill. DA1 .... 9 F2
Temple Hill Cty Prim Inf Sch.
DA1 .... 10 A2
Temple Hill Cty Prim Jun Sch.
DA1 .... 10 A2
Temple Hill Sq. DA1 .... 9 F2
Temple Sch. ME2 .... 33 B2
Temple Way. ME19 .... 74 F1
Templemore. DA14 .... 24 B3
Tenby Rd. DA16 .... 7 D6
Tenney House. RM17 .... 12 B7
Tennyson Ave. ME3 .... 33 B7
Tennyson Cl. DA16 .... 6 F6
Tennyson House. **2** DA17 ... 3 F1
Tennyson Rd. Dartford DA1 .. 10 A2
Tennyson Rd. Gillingham ME7 .. 48 C3
Tennyson Wlk. Northfleet DA11 .. 29 D5
Tennyson Wlk. Tilbury RM18 .. 13 B5
Tensing Ave. TN15 .... 29 E5
Tenterden CE Jun Sch. TN30 . 183 B7
Tenterden Cl. SE9 .... 22 F4
Tenterden Cty Inf Sch. TN30 183 B7
Tenterden Rd. Biddenden TN27 172 B7
Tenterden Rd. Chatham ME5 ... 62 B5
Tenterden Rd. Parkgate TN27 .. 171 F7
Tenterden Rd. Strood TN17 .. 182 A5
Tenterden Town Sta. TN30 ... 183 A8
Tenzing Ct. SE9 .... 22 E6
Terence Cl. Chatham ME4 ...... 48 A2
Terence Cl. Gravesend DA12 ... 30 F6
Terence Cl. **6** DA17 .... 7 F8
Terminus Rd. ME16 .... 91 A2
Tern Cres. ME2 .... 46 C6
Terrace Rd. ME16 .... 91 E3
Terrace St. DA11 .... 13 B1
Terrace The. Chatham ME4 ... 47 F7
Terrace The. **2** Gravesend DA11 13 B1
Terrace The. Gravesend DA11 .. 13 C1
Terrace The. Rochester ME1 ... 47 C5
Terrace The. Sevenoaks TN13 .. 83 D5
Terraces The. DA2 .... 27 C8
Terry Wlk. ME20 .... 74 E2
Terry's Lodge Rd. TN15 ...... 71 C6
Teston House. ME18 .... 105 A7
Teston La. ME15 & ME18 ..... 105 C7
Teston Rd. Kings Hill ME19 .... 89 A7
Teston Rd. Offham TN15 & ME19 . 88 C7
Teston Rd. Red Hill ME19 ...... 89 E2
Teston Rd.
St Leonard's Street ME19 .. 89 A6
Tetty Way. BR1 & BR2 .... 36 A7
Teviot Cl. DA16 .... 7 B6
Tewson Rd. SE18 .... 2 E1
Teynham Gn. Gillingham ME8 .. 49 A4
Teynham Gn. Hayes BR2 .... 36 A4
Teynham House. SE9 .... 6 D1

Thackeray Ave. RM18 .... 13 B6
Thackeray Rd. ME20 .... 74 F3
Thames Ave. High Halstow ME23 17 E4
Thames Barrier Visitor Ctr. SE18 1 D3
Thames Gate. DA1 .... 10 A3
Thames House. **3** ME15 .... 107 D8
Thames Rd. Crayford DA1 .... 9 A4
Thames Rd. Grays RM17 .... 12 B7
Thames Rd. Newham E16 ...... 1 D5
Thames Rd. Tonbridge TN10 .. 117 C5
Thames Road Ind Est. E16 .... 1 D4
Thames Terr. ME1 .... 16 B6
Thames View. ME3 .... 33 C7
Thames View Cotts. ME3 ...... 32 D3
Thames View Cty Inf Sch. ME8 49 D2
Thames View Cty Prim Sch (Jun).
ME8 .... 49 D2
Thames Way. Gravesend DA11 .. 13 A1
Thames Way. Northfleet DA11 .. 29 E7
Thamesbank Pl. SE28 .... 3 C7
Thameside Ind Est. E16 ...... 1 D4
Thamesmere Dr. SE28 .... 3 A6
Thamesview Sch. DA12 .... 30 F5
Thanet Dr. BR2 .... 50 D7
Thanet House. **2** DA11 ...... 29 F7
Thanet Rd. Erith DA8 .... 8 E7
Thanet Rd. Sidcup DA5 .... 25 A8
Thanington Ct. SE9 .... 6 E1
Thatch Barn Rd. TN27 ...... 141 D6
Thatcher Ct. DA1 .... 26 D8
Thatcher Rd. TN12 .... 139 E4
Thatchers La. ME3 .... 16 B5
Thatchers The. ME16 .... 91 B5
Thaxted Rd. SE9 .... 23 C6
Theatre Sq. **5** TN30 .... 183 A7
Thelma Cl. DA2 .... 30 F3
Thelma Gdns. SE18 .... 5 E6
Theobalds. TN18 .... 178 F2
Theobalds Cl. TN15 .... 70 A1
Theodore Cl. TN2 .... 149 E7
Theodore Pl. ME7 .... 48 C5
Thicketts. TN13 .... 84 C4
Third Ave. Chatham ME4 & ME5 .. 48 C1
Third Ave. Gillingham ME7 ... 48 F4
Third Ave. West Thurrock RM16 .. 11 A8
Third St. TN3 .... 147 F3
Thirlmere Cl. Gillingham ME7 .. 49 A5
Thirlmere Cl. Rochester ME2 .. 33 C1
Thirlmere Rd. Bexley DA7 ...... 8 C6
Thirlmere Rd.
Royal Tunbridge Wells TN4 .. 148 E5
Thirza Rd. DA1 .... 9 F1
Thistle Ct. DA1 .... 27 B7
Thistle Rd. DA12 .... 30 B8
Thistlebank. ME16 .... 62 A3
Thistlebrook. SE2 .... 3 C4
Thistledown. DA2 .... 30 D2
Thistledown. Maidstone ME14 .. 92 F4
Thistledown Cl. ME7 .... 63 A4
Thistlemead. BR7 .... 37 B7
Thomas Aveling Sch The. ME1 61 C8
Thomas Cotts. DA13 .... 29 B1
Thomas Dinwiddy Rd. SE12 ... 22 B6
Thomas Dr. DA12 .... 30 D6
Thomas St. Rochester ME1 .... 47 C3
Thomas St.
Royal Tunbridge Wells TN4 .. 149 A5
Thomas Tallis Sch. SE3 ...... 5 B4
Thomas Wyatt Way. TN15 .... 71 F3
Thompson Cl. ME8 .... 64 A8
Thomson Cl. ME6 .... 60 A1
Thong La. Basted TN15 .... 86 F5
Thong La. Thong DA12 .... 31 A2
Thorn Cl. Bromley BR2 .... 37 A3
Thorn Cl. Chatham ME5 .... 61 D1
Thorn Rd. TN12 .... 138 E4
Thorn's Meadow. TN16 .... 82 C4
Thorndale Cl. ME5 .... 61 D4
Thornden Cl. TN17 .... 188 A8
Thornden La. TN17 .... 182 A1
Thorndike Cl. ME4 .... 61 F8
Thorndon Cl. BR5 .... 37 F7
Thorndon Rd. BR5 .... 37 F7
Thorndyke Way. TN15 .... 71 F3
Thorne Cl. Erith DA8 .... 8 B8
Thorne Cl. Newham E16 ...... 1 A7
Thornet Wood Rd. BR1 .... 37 A6
Thorney Croft Cl. ME17 .... 109 D2
Thornfield Gdns. TN2 .... 149 F5
Thornham Rd. ME8 .... 49 C3
Thornhill Ave. SE18 .... 6 E7
Thornhill Pl. ME14 .... 92 A6
Thornton Rd. Bromley BR1 .... 22 A3
Thornton Rd. Erith DA17 ...... 4 B2
Thorntree Inf Sch. SE7 .... 1 B1
Thorntree Rd. SE7 .... 1 D1
Thorold Rd. ME4 .... 48 B3
Thorpe Ave. TN10 .... 117 C5
Thorpe Cl. BR6 .... 51 E8
Thorpe Wlk. ME8 .... 63 D3
Thorpe Works. TN4 .... 148 F8
Thrale Way. ME8 .... 63 E4
Three Corners. DA7 .... 8 B5
Three Elm La. TN10 & TN11 .. 118 D5
Three Gates Rd. DA3 .... 42 A2
Three Oaks La. TN5 .... 174 D7
Thresher Fold. TN8 .... 130 A6
Threshers Dr. TN14 .... 92 E5
Thrift The. DA2 .... 28 C5
Throckmorten Rd. E16 ...... 1 B7
Throwley Way. TN4 .... 23 C3
Thrush Cl. ME5 .... 62 B7
Thunderer Rd. RM9 .... 3 F8
Thurnham CE Inf Sch. ME14 .. 93 A4
Thurnham House. **5** BR5 ... 38 D1

Thurnham La. ME14 .... 93 C6
Thurrock Bsns Ctr. RM16 ...... 10 E7
Thurrock Ent Ctr. RM17 ...... 12 A8
Thurrock Park Way. RM17 .... 12 D7
Thursland Rd. DA14 .... 24 E3
Thursley Rd. SE9 .... 22 F5
Thurston Dr. ME2 .... 46 D7
Thurstone Ct. ME14 .... 91 F6
Thwaite Cl. DA8 .... 8 C8
Thyer Cl. BR6 .... 51 C6
Tibbs Court La. TN12 .... 152 A7
Ticehurst Cl. BR5 .... 24 A1
Tichborne Cl. ME16 .... 91 C6
Tickford Cl. SE2 .... 3 C4
Tidal Basin Rd. E16 .... 1 A6
Tidebrook Cl. **4** BR5 .... 38 C5
Tideway The. ME1 .... 61 C8
Tidford Rd. DA16 .... 6 F5
Tiger La. BR2 .... 36 B5
Tilbrook Rd. SE3 & SE9 ...... 5 D4
Tilbury Cl. BR5 .... 38 B7
Tilbury Gdns. RM18 .... 13 A3
Tilbury Manor Cty Jun Sch.
RM18 .... 13 B7
Tilbury Town Sta. RM18 ...... 12 F5
Tilden Cl. TN26 .... 173 D7
Tilden Gill Rd. TN30 .... 183 C7
Tilden La. TN12 .... 122 C3
Tilden Rd. TN27 .... 125 E2
Tile Farm Rd. BR6 .... 51 D7
Tile Fields. ME17 .... 94 D2
Tile Kiln La. Coldblow DA5 .... 25 C6
Tile Kiln La.
Joyden's Wood DA2 & DA5 .. 25 F5
Tilebarn Cnr. TN10 .... 117 A4
Tilehurst Point. **2** SE2 ...... 3 C4
Tilghman Way. ME4 .... 60 B1
Till Ave. DA4 .... 40 F2
Tillingbourne Gn. BR5 .... 38 A5
Tilmans Mead. DA4 .... 41 A2
Tilsden La. TN17 .... 169 E3
Tilt Yard App. SE9 .... 5 F1
Tilton Rd. TN15 .... 86 F7
Timber Bank. DA13 .... 72 F8
Timber Cl. BR7 .... 37 A7
Timber Tops. ME14 .... 77 D8
Timberbank. ME5 .... 62 A6
Timbercroft. SE18 .... 6 C6
Timbercroft La. SE18 .... 6 E7
Timothy Cl. DA6 .... 7 E3
Timothy House. DA18 .... 3 E4
Tinker Pot La. TN15 .... 70 D6
Tinkerpot Rise. TN15 .... 70 C5
Tinkers La. TN5 .... 176 E3
Tintagel Gdns. ME2 .... 46 F7
Tintagel Manor. ME7 .... 48 C6
Tintagel Rd. BR5 .... 38 C1
Tintern Rd. ME16 .... 91 D7
Tippens Cl. TN17 .... 169 D4
Titan Rd. RM17 .... 12 B8
Titchfield Cl. **5** ME15 .... 107 F6
Titchfield Rd. ME15 .... 107 F6
Tithe Yd. ME17 .... 111 D5
Titmuss Ave. SE28 .... 3 B6
Tivoli Gdns. Gravesend DA11 .. 30 B7
Tivoli Gdns. **11** Woolwich SE7 .. 1 E2
Tobruk Way. ME5 .... 61 F6
Toby Gdns. TN11 .... 118 E8
Toddington Cres. ME5 ...... 61 D1
Tolcairn Ct. **2** DA17 ...... 4 A1
Tolgate Ct. ME14 .... 47 B7
Tolgate Way. ME14 .... 76 E4
Tolhurst Rd. TN12 .... 135 A7
Tollgate Pl. TN27 .... 141 E5
Tollgate Rd. Dartford DA2 ... 27 D8
Tollgate Rd. Newham E6 ...... 1 E8
Tolsey Mead. TN15 .... 87 A8
Tom Coombs Cl. SE9 .... 5 E3
Tom Cribb Rd. SE18 & SE28 ... 2 D3
Tom Joyce Cl. ME6 .... 74 F7
Tomlin Cl. Snodland ME6 ...... 75 A8
Tomlin St. Staplehurst TN12 .. 139 E4
Tonbridge By-Pass.
Stocks Green TN11 & TN9 & TN4 &
TN14 & TN15 .... 116 D3
Tonbridge By-Pass.
Tonbridge TN11 & TN4 ...... 133 C2
Tonbridge Chambers. **3** TN9 133 B8
Tonbridge Cottage Hospl.
TN11 .... 133 C6
Tonbridge Ct. ME16 .... 91 D3
Tonbridge Gram Sch for Girls.
TN9 .... 133 C7
Tonbridge House. ME2 .... 33 C1
Tonbridge Rd.
Hadlow TN10 & TN11 ...... 118 C7
Tonbridge Rd.
Hildenborough TN11 ...... 116 E5
Tonbridge Rd.
Ightham Common TN15 ...... 86 C3
Tonbridge Rd.
Little Mill TN11 & TN12 .... 119 D4
Tonbridge Rd. Maidstone ME16 .. 90 E1
Tonbridge Rd. Royal Tunbridge Wells
TN2 & TN11 .... 150 A7
Tonbridge Rd.
Sevenoaks TN13 & TN15 .... 99 D7
Tonbridge Rd.
Wateringbury ME18 ...... 104 C8
Tonbridge Sch. TN10 .... 117 B3
Tonbridge Sta. TN9 .... 117 B1
Tong La. TN12 .... 152 B2
Tong Rd. TN12 .... 152 A4
Tongswood Dr. TN18 .... 179 C1
Tooley St. DA11 .... 29 D8
Top Dartford Rd. BR8 .... 26 A2
Topcliffe Dr. BR6 .... 51 D6

Topley St. SE9 .... 5 D3
Tor Rd. DA16 .... 7 C6
Torbay Rd. TN12 .... 120 B5
Tormount Rd. SE18 .... 6 E8
Toronto Rd. Gillingham ME7 .. 48 E4
Toronto Rd. Tilbury RM18 ... 13 A5
Torrens Wlk. DA12 .... 30 E3
Torrington Cl. ME18 .... 103 D8
Torver Way. BR6 .... 51 D7
Totnes Rd. DA16 .... 7 C7
Tovil Gn. ME15 .... 91 E2
Tovil Green Bsns Pk. ME15 .. 91 E1
Tovil Hill. ME15 .... 91 E2
Tovil Rd. ME15 .... 91 F2
Tower Cl. Gravesend DA12 .... 30 E3
Tower Cl. Orpington BR6 ...... 51 F7
Tower Croft. DA4 .... 54 E8
Tower Gdns. ME14 .... 93 B4
Tower Hill. ME19 .... 88 D7
Tower Ind Est. TN15 .... 71 D5
Tower La. ME14 .... 93 B4
Tower Rd. Bexley DA7 .... 8 A3
Tower Rd. Dartford DA1 ...... 9 C1
Tower Rd. Erith DA17 .... 4 C2
Tower Rd. Orpington BR6 .... 51 F7
Tower View. ME19 .... 89 B5
Towers Wood. DA4 .... 41 B8
Town Acres. TN10 & TN9 .... 117 C4
Town Hill. Lamberhurst TN3 .. 166 A4
Town Hill. West Malling ME19 .. 74 C1
Town Hill Cl. ME19 .... 74 C1
Town Lock House. **3** TN9 .. 117 C2
Town Meadow. TN17 .... 169 D4
Town Pier. **4** DA11 .... 13 B1
Town Rd. ME3 .... 33 A6
Town Sq. DA8 .... 8 E8
Town Station Cotts. TN8 .... 112 D1
Towncourt Cres. BR5 .... 37 D5
Towncourt La. BR5 .... 37 D2
Townfield Cnr. DA12 .... 30 D7
Townland Cl. TN27 .... 158 A2
Townlands Rd. TN5 .... 174 F4
Townley Gram Sch for Girls.
DA5 .... 7 F1
Townley Rd. DA6 .... 7 F2
Townsend Rd. Snodland ME6 .. 74 F8
Townsend Rd. Woolwich SE18 .. 2 B3
Townshead Cl. DA14 .... 24 C2
Townshend House. **18** SE18 ... 1 F2
Townshend Rd. BR7 .... 23 B3
Toy's Hill. TN16 & TN8 ...... 97 C3
Toynbec Cl. BR7 .... 23 B4
Tracies The. ME9 .... 65 C6
Trader Rd. E6 .... 2 B7
Tradescant Dr. DA13 .... 44 B3
Trafalgar Rd. Dartford DA1 ... 26 E6
Trafalgar Rd. Gravesend DA11 .. 30 A8
Trafalgar Rd. Wouldham ME1 .. 60 C4
Trafalgar St. ME7 .... 48 C5
Tranquil Rise. DA8 .... 4 E1
Transfesa Rd. TN12 .... 136 A7
Transmere Cl. BR5 .... 37 C3
Transmere Rd. BR5 .... 37 C3
Transom House. **2** ME1 .... 47 C1
Trapfield Cl. ME14 .... 93 C4
Trapfield La. ME14 .... 93 C4
Trapham Rd. ME16 .... 91 D5
Travers Gdns. ME9 .... 80 F5
Travertine Rd. ME5 .... 62 B1
Trebble Rd. DA10 .... 11 E1
Trebilco Cl. TN1 .... 149 D7
Tredegar Rd. DA2 .... 26 A5
Tredwell Cl. BR2 .... 36 E5
Tree La. TN15 .... 101 E5
Tree Rd. E16 .... 1 C7
Treetops. Gravesend DA12 .... 30 B4
Treetops. Tonbridge TN9 .... 133 B7
Treetops Cl. SE2 .... 3 E1
Treewall Gdns. BR1 .... 22 B4
Trefoil House. Erith DA18 .... 3 E4
Trefoil House. Grays RM17 ... 12 B7
Trelawn Cres. ME5 .... 62 B2
Trellyn Cl. ME16 .... 90 F2
Trench Rd. TN10 .... 117 C6
Trent House. **2** ME15 ...... 107 E7
Trent Rd. ME5 .... 62 B5
Trentham Dr. BR5 .... 38 B5
Trenton Cl. ME16 .... 91 B7
Trevale Rd. ME1 .... 47 B1
Trevelyan Cl. DA1 .... 9 F3
Trevereux Hill. RH8 .... 96 A3
Trevino Dr. ME2 .... 61 F2
Trevithick Dr. DA1 .... 9 F3
Trevor Cl. BR2 .... 36 A2
Trevor Dr. ME16 .... 91 C5
Trewin Cl. ME20 .... 75 D2
Trewsbury House. **2** SE2 .... 3 D4
Triangle Ct. E16 .... 1 C8
Trident Cl. ME2 .... 47 D7
Trinity Cl. Keston Mark BR2 .. 36 E1
Trinity Cl.
Royal Tunbridge Wells TN2 .. 149 D4
Trinity Ct. Aylesford ME20 ... 76 A3
Trinity Ct. Dartford DA1 ...... 27 B7
Trinity Ct. Eltham SE9 ...... 6 B1
Trinity Pl. DA1 .... 7 F3
Trinity Rd. Gillingham ME7 ... 48 C6
Trinity Rd. Gravesend DA12 ... 30 C8
Trinity Sch, Belvedere. DA17 .. 4 C1
Trinity St. **12** E16 .... 1 A8
Tristan Gdns. TN4 .... 148 D4
Triumph Rd. E6 .... 2 A7
Trivett Cl. DA9 .... 11 A2
Trolling Down Hill. DA2 ...... 27 C6
Troodos Hill. ME14 .... 91 F8

Trosley Ave. DA11 .... 30 B6
Trosley Ctry Pk. ME19 .... 73 A7
Trosley Rd. DA17 .... 8 A8
Trottiscliffe CE Prim Sch.
ME19 .... 73 A5
Trottiscliffe Rd. ME19 .... 73 D3
Trotts La. TN16 .... 96 C8
Trotwood Cl. ME5 .... 77 A8
Troughton Rd. SE7 .... 1 B1
Troutbeck House. ME19 .... 75 C1
Troy Ct. 5 SE18 .... 2 B2
Troys Mead. ME17 .... 94 D2
Trubridge Rd. ME3 .... 34 E5
Truro Cl. ME18 .... 49 D3
Truro Rd. DA12 .... 30 D5
Truro Wlk. TN10 .... 117 C5
Trusedale Rd. E6 .... 1 F7
Trycewell La. TN15 .... 86 D6
Tuam Rd. SE18 .... 6 D8
Tubbenden Cl. BR6 .... 51 E7
Tubbenden Dr. BR6 .... 51 E6
Tubbenden Inf & Jun Sch. BR6 51 D6
Tubbenden La. BR6 .... 51 E7
Tubbenden La S. BR6 .... 51 D5
Tubs Hill. TN13 .... 84 B3
Tubs Hill Par. TN13 .... 84 A3
Tudeley La. Tonbridge TN9 .... 133 D7
Tudeley La. Tudeley TN11 & TN9 134 B8
Tudor Ave. ME14 .... 92 B6
Tudor Cl. Bromley BR7 .... 36 F8
Tudor Cl. Dartford DA1 .... 9 B1
Tudor Cl. Northfleet DA11 .... 29 E7
Tudor Cres. TN14 .... 69 D3
Tudor Ct. Crockenhill BR8 .... 39 C2
Tudor Ct. R Tunbridge Wells TN2 148 E1
Tudor Ct. Sidcup DA14 .... 24 A5
Tudor Dr. TN14 .... 69 C3
Tudor Gr. Chattenden ME3 .... 33 F4
Tudor Gr. Gillingham ME8 .... 63 F8
Tudor Par. SE9 .... 5 E6
Tudor Way. BR5 .... 37 D3
Tudor Wlk. ME5 .... 7 E1
Tudway Rd. SE3 & SE9 .... 5 C3
Tufa Cl. ME5 .... 62 B1
Tuff Cotts. ME3 .... 19 C3
Tuffield House. 9 SE18 .... 2 A2
Tufnail Rd. ME5 .... 9 F1
Tufton Rd. ME8 .... 49 F1
Tufton St. ME14 .... 92 A4
Tugboat St. SE28 .... 2 E4
Tugmutton Cl. BR6 .... 51 B6
Tulip Cl. 5 E6 .... 1 F8
Tulip Tree Cl. TN9 .... 133 B8
Tumblefield Est. TN15 .... 71 F8
Tumblefield Rd. TN15 .... 71 E7
Tumblers Hill. ME17 .... 124 F7
Tunbridge Wells Golf Club.
TN4 .... 148 E3
Tunbridge Wells
Gram Sch for Boys. TN4 .... 149 A7
Tunbridge Wells
Gram Sch for Girls. TN4 .... 149 A6
Tunbridge Wells Ind Hospl The.
TN3 .... 147 B3
Tunbury Ave. Chatham ME5 .... 61 F1
Tunbury Ave. Chatham ME5 .... 61 F2
Tunbury Ave S. ME5 .... 61 F1
Tunbury Cty Prim Sch. ME5 .... 61 F1
Tunnan Leys. E6 .... 2 A7
Tunnel Ave. SE10 .... 1 A1
Tunnel Est. RM16 .... 10 F8
Tunnel Rd. TN1 .... 149 B4
Tunstall Cl. BR6 .... 51 E6
Tunstock Way. DA17 .... 3 E3
Tupman Cl. ME1 .... 47 B4
Turgis Cl. ME17 .... 108 E4
Turks Hall Pl. ME2 .... 59 E5
Turley Cotts. TN3 .... 148 A8
Turnberry Way. BR6 .... 37 D1
Turnbull Cl. DA2 .... 27 E8
Turnden Rd. TN17 .... 169 A3
Turner Ave. TN17 .... 169 D3
Turner Ct. DA1 .... 9 C2
Turner House. DA12 .... 30 C6
Turner Rd. Bean DA2 .... 28 B5
Turner Rd. Tonbridge TN10 .... 117 E5
Turner St. ME3 .... 16 B5
Turners Ave. TN30 .... 183 B8
Turners Gdns. TN13 .... 99 C7
Turners Green La. TN5 .... 174 F6
Turners Green Rd. TN5 .... 174 F6
Turnpike Ct. DA6 .... 7 D3
Turnpike Dr. BR6 .... 52 D2
Turnpike La. RM18 .... 13 D8
Turnstone. DA13 .... 43 A7
Turnstone Rd. ME5 .... 62 C1
Turnstones The. DA12 .... 30 D6
Turpin La. DA8 .... 9 A8
Turpington Cl. BR2 .... 36 E2
Turpington La. BR2 .... 36 E3
Turton House. 5 SE18 .... 6 B8
Tuscan Dr. ME5 .... 62 C1
Tuscan Rd. SE18 .... 2 D1
Tutsham Way. TN12 .... 135 F6
Tuxford Rd. TN4 .... 148 B5
Tweed Rd. TN10 .... 117 C5
Tweedy Rd. BR1 .... 36 A8
Twigg Cl. DA8 .... 8 E7
Twisden Rd. ME19 .... 89 F8
Twiss House. 6 SE18 .... 2 B1
Twistleton Ct. DA1 .... 9 D1
Twitton La. TN14 .... 68 E3
Twitton Meadows. TN14 .... 68 E3
Two Gates Hill. ME3 .... 32 F5
Twydall Cty Inf Sch. ME8 .... 49 B2

Twydall Cty Prim Jun Sch. ME8 49 B2
Twydall Gn. ME8 .... 49 B3
Twydall La. ME8 .... 49 B2
Twyford Ct. ME14 .... 92 D6
Twyford Rd. TN11 .... 102 E1
Twysden Cotts. TN18 .... 186 A4
Tydeman Rd. ME15 .... 92 F2
Tye La. ME7 .... 51 C5
Tyeshurst Cl. SE2 .... 3 E1
Tyland La. ME14 .... 76 F3
Tyler Cl. ME19 .... 89 F8
Tyler Dr. ME8 .... 63 E4
Tyler Gr. DA1 .... 9 F3
Tylers Green Rd. BR8 .... 39 C2
Tylney Rd. BR1 .... 36 D7
Tyndall Rd. DA16 .... 6 F4
Tyne Cl. ME5 .... 62 C5
Tyne House. 10 ME15 .... 107 E7
Tyne Rd. TN10 .... 117 B5
Tynedale Cl. DA2 .... 27 D7
Tynemouth Cl. E6 .... 2 B7
Typhoon Rd. ME19 .... 88 F3
Tyron Way. DA14 .... 23 F3
Tyrrell Ave. DA16 .... 7 B2
Tyrrells Hall Cl. RM17 .... 12 D8

Uckfield La. TN8 .... 129 D4
Ufton Cl. ME15 .... 92 E1
Ulcombe CE Prim Sch. ME17 . 125 F6
Ulcombe Hill. ME17 .... 109 F1
Ulcombe Rd. Headcorn TN27 ... 141 C6
Ulcombe Rd.
Langley Heath ME17 .... 108 G3
Underdown Ave. ME4 .... 47 F1
Underhill Jun Sch. ME17 .... 124 C7
Underlyn Ind Est. TN12 .... 122 F2
Underlyn La. TN12 .... 122 D1
Underriver House Rd.
TN11 & TN15 .... 100 D5
Underwood. ME19 .... 88 D7
Underwood Cl. ME15 .... 91 F2
Underwood The. SE9 .... 22 F6
Unicorn Wlk. DA9 .... 10 F2
Unicumes La. ME16 .... 91 C2
Union Pk. ME15 .... 107 F4
Union Rd. BR2 .... 36 D4
Union Sq. 11 TN2 .... 149 A2
Union St. Chatham ME4 .... 48 A3
Union St. Maidstone ME14 .... 92 A5
Union St. Rochester ME1 .... 47 C5
Union St. Union Street TN5 ... 177 B3
Unity Way. SE18 .... 1 D3
Univ of Greenwich. SE18 .... 2 A2
Univ of Greenwich
Avery Hill Campus. SE9 ...... 6 C1
Univ of Greenwich Avery Hill
Campus Southwood Site. SE9 23 D8
Univ of Greenwich
(Dartford Campus). DA1 ..... 26 C6
Univ of Greenwich
(Riverside House Annexe).
SE18 .... 2 A3
Univ of Greenwich
(Southwold Site). SE9 .... 6 C2
University Gdns. DA5 .... 24 F8
University Pl. DA8 .... 8 C7
University Way. DA1 .... 9 E4
Unwin Cl. ME20 .... 76 A3
Upbury Manor High Sch. ME7 . 48 B4
Upbury Way. ME4 .... 48 A4
Upchat Rd. ME2 & ME3 .... 33 F3
Updale Rd. DA14 .... 23 F4
Upland Inf Sch. DA7 .... 7 F4
Upland Jun Sch. DA7 .... 7 F4
Upland Rd. DA7 .... 7 F4
Uplands Cl. Rochester ME2 .... 46 D6
Uplands Cl. Sevenoaks TN13 .... 83 F4
Uplands Com Coll. TN5 .... 175 A4
Uplands Rd. BR6 .... 38 B1
Uplands Way. TN13 .... 83 F4
Upnor Castle. ME2 .... 33 F2
Upnor Rd. Rochester ME2 .... 47 D8
Upnor Rd. Upper Upton ME2 ... 33 E2
Upper Abbey Rd. DA17 .... 4 A2
Upper Austin Lodge Rd. DA4 ... 54 D4
Upper Ave. DA13 .... 43 E8
Upper Barn Hill. ME15 .... 105 E3
Upper Britton Pl. ME7 .... 48 B5
Upper Bush Rd. ME2 .... 45 F2
Upper Church Hill. DA9 .... 10 E2
Upper Cumberland Wlk. TN1 . 149 B1
Upper Dunstan Rd. TN4 .... 149 B6
Upper East Rd. ME4 .... 48 B8
Upper Fant Rd. ME16 .... 91 D2
Upper Green La. TN11 .... 101 C5
Upper Green Rd. TN11 .... 101 D5
Upper Grosvenor Rd.
TN1 & TN4 .... 149 B6
Upper Grove Rd. DA17 .... 7 F8
Upper Haysden La. TN4 & TN9 132 E6
Upper Holly Hill Rd. DA17 .... 4 B1
Upper Hunton Hill. ME15 .... 106 A3
Upper Luton Rd. ME4 & ME5 ... 48 C2
Upper Mill. ME18 .... 104 D8
Upper Nellington. TN3 .... 148 B4
Upper Park Rd. Bromley BR1 ... 36 C8
Upper Park Rd. Erith DA17 .... 4 B2
Upper Platts. TN5 .... 176 F1
Upper Profit. TN3 .... 148 A3
Upper Rd. ME15 .... 92 B2
Upper Sheridan Rd. DA17 .... 4 A2
Upper Spring La. TN15 .... 86 B5
Upper St. Hollingbourne ME17 .. 94 E3
Upper St. Leeds ME17 .... 108 F5
Upper St. Rusthall TN4 .... 148 D4
Upper Stephens. TN3 .... 148 A3
Upper Stone St. ME15 .... 92 A3
Upper Street N. DA3 .... 56 F8

Upper Street S. DA3 .... 56 F8
Upper Wickham La. DA16 .... 7 B6
Upperton Rd. DA14 .... 23 F3
Upton Cl. DA5 .... 7 F1
Upton Day Hospl. DA6 .... 7 E3
Upton Prim Sch. DA6 .... 7 F2
Upton Quarry. TN3 .... 147 F3
Upton Rd. Bexley DA6 .... 7 E2
Upton Rd. Woolwich SE18 .... 6 C8
Upton Rd S. DA5 .... 7 F1
Upton Villas. 4 DA6 .... 7 E3
Uptons. TN27 .... 141 C6
Upwood Rd. SE12 .... 5 A1
Uridge Cres. TN10 .... 117 C4
Uridge Rd. TN10 .... 117 C4
Urquhart Cl. ME5 .... 62 A5
Ursula Lodge. DA14 .... 24 B3
Usborne Cl. TN12 .... 139 E3

Vale Ave. Royal Tunbridge Wells,
Mount Sion TN1 .... 149 A3
Vale Ave. Royal Tunbridge Wells,
Southborough TN4 .... 132 F1
Vale Cl. BR6 .... 51 A6
Vale Cotts. ME9 .... 80 A8
Vale Cl. TN4 .... 133 A2
Vale Dr. ME5 .... 61 E6
Vale Rd. Bromley BR1 & BR7 ... 37 A7
Vale Rd. Dartford DA1 .... 26 B7
Vale Rd. Hawkhurst TN18 .... 178 F3
Vale Rd. Loose ME15 .... 106 A4
Vale Rd. Northfleet DA11 .... 29 E7
Vale Rd. Royal Tunbridge Wells,
Mount Sion TN1 .... 149 A3
Vale Rd. Royal Tunbridge Wells,
Southborough TN4 .... 132 F1
Vale Rd. Tonbridge TN9 .... 117 D1
Vale Rd. Tonbridge TN9 .... 133 C8
Vale Rise. TN9 .... 133 E8
Valence House. ME15 .... 107 C7
Valence Rd. DA8 .... 8 D7
Valence Sch. TN16 .... 81 F1
Valence View. TN17 .... * ... 156 E7
Valentine Ave. DA5 .... 24 E7
Valentine Cl. ME7 .... 49 A1
Valentine Rd. ME15 .... 107 E7
Valerian Cl. ME5 .... 61 E4
Valiant House. 5 SE7 .... 1 C1
Valiant Rd. ME5 .... 62 C2
Valiant Way. E6 .... 1 F8
Valley (Charlton Athletic FC) The.
SE7 .... 1 C1
Valley Cl. DA1 .... 8 F1
Valley Dr.
Gravesend,Riverview Park DA12 .. 30 D4
Valley Dr.
Gravesend,Singlewell DA12 .... 30 E1
Valley Dr. Maidstone ME15 .... 106 F6
Valley Dr. Sevenoaks TN13 .... 84 B1
Valley Forge Cl. TN10 .... 117 F4
Valley Gdns. DA9 .... 11 B1
Valley Gr. SE7 .... 1 C1
Valley L Ctr. SE9 .... 23 C8
Valley La. DA13 .... 58 B2
Valley Rd. Crayford DA1 .... 8 F1
Valley Rd. Erith DA8 .... 4 D2
Valley Rd. Fawkham Green DA3 .. 42 C2
Valley Rd. Gillingham ME7 .... 48 E4
Valley Rd. Rusthall TN4 .... 148 D4
Valley Rd. St Paul's Cray BR5 ... 38 B8
Valley Rise. ME5 .... 61 F1
Valley The. ME17 .... 106 D3
Valley View.
Royal Tunbridge Wells TN4 ... 133 A2
Valley View. Swanscombe DA9 .. 11 B1
Valley View Rd. ME1 .... 47 B1
Valley View Terr. DA4 .... 40 F1
Valleyside. SE7 .... 1 D1
Valliers Wood Rd. DA15 .... 23 E7
Vambery Rd. SE18 .... 6 C8
Vanbrugh Pk. SE3 .... 5 A7
Vanbrugh Cl. 2 Newham E16 ... 1 D8
Vanbrugh Rd. Orpington BR6 ... 37 E1
Vancouver Dr. ME8 .... 49 C1
Vandome Cl. E16 .... 1 B7
Vandyke Cross. SE9 .... 5 E2
Vanessa Cl. DA17 .... 4 A1
Vanessa Way. DA5 .... 25 D5
Vanessa Wlk. DA12 .... 30 F3
Vange Cottage Mews. ME1 .... 47 B4
Vanity La. ME17 .... 106 D1
Vanoc Gdns. BR1 .... 22 A4
Vanquisher Wlk. DA12 .... 30 F5
Varley Rd. E16 .... 1 B7
Varnes St. ME20 .... 75 F6
Vaughan Ave. TN10 .... 117 E6
Vaughan Rd. DA16 .... 6 F5
Vauxhall Cl. DA11 .... 29 E8
Vauxhall Cres. ME6 .... 75 A6
Vauxhall Gdns. TN9 .... 133 C7
Vauxhall La.
Bidborough TN11 & TN4 .... 133 B4
Vauxhall La.
Tonbridge TN11 & TN9 .... 133 D6
Vauxhall Pl. DA1 .... 26 E8
Veitchil Barn. BR8 .... 39 F8
Veles Rd. ME6 .... 74 F8
Venmead Ct. 4 DA17 .... 4 A2
Venners Cl. DA7 .... 8 E5
Ventnor Cl. ME5 .... 62 C8
Venture Cl. DA5 .... 24 E8
Venture Ct. 5 SE12 .... 22 A8
Venus Wlk. SE18 .... 1 F3
Verdun Rd. SE18 & SE2 .... 7 A8
Vermont Rd. TN4 .... 148 C4
Vernham Rd. SE18 .... 6 C8
Vernon Cl. St Paul's Cray BR5 ... 38 B6
Vernon Cl. West Kingsdown TN15 55 F2

Vernon Rd.
Royal Tunbridge Wells TN1 ... 149 C6
Vernon Rd. Swanscombe DA10 .. 11 F1
Veroan Rd. DA7 .... 7 E5
Verona Gdns. DA12 .... 30 E4
Verona House. DA8 .... 8 F7
Vert House. RM17 .... 12 C7
Vesper Ct. TN27 .... 143 A1
Vestry Cotts. DA3 .... 43 C5
Vestry Rd. TN14 .... 84 C8
Via Romana. DA12 .... 31 B7
Viaduct Terr. DA4 .... 41 C7
Vicarage Ave. SE3 .... 5 A7
Vicarage Cl. Aylesford ME20 .... 75 F3
Vicarage Cl. Erith DA8 .... 8 C8
Vicarage Cl. Halling ME2 .... 60 A5
Vicarage Cl. Stoke ME3 .... 19 A3
Vicarage Ct. Chalk DA12 .... 31 A7
Vicarage Ct. Newington ME9 ... 65 B7
Vicarage Dr. DA11 .... 12 C1
Vicarage Hill. TN16 .... 81 D1
Vicarage La. Chalk DA12 .... 31 A6
Vicarage La. East Farleigh ME15 106 B6
Vicarage La.
Hoo St Werburgh ME3 .... 34 E4
Vicarage La. Sevenoaks TN13 ... 83 D8
Vicarage Pk. SE18 .... 2 C1
Vicarage Rd. Coldblow DA5 .... 25 B7
Vicarage Rd. Gillingham ME7 ... 48 C5
Vicarage Rd. Halling ME2 .... 59 F5
Vicarage Rd. Rochester ME2 ... 47 B8
Vicarage Rd.
Royal Tunbridge Wells TN4 ... 132 F2
Vicarage Rd. Woolwich SE18 ... 2 C1
Vicarage Rd. Yalding ME18 .... 105 A1
Vicarage Row. ME3 .... 32 C4
Vicarage Sq. RM17 .... 12 B8
Vicarage Way. TN19 .... 184 A3
Vicary Way. ME16 .... 91 D5
Vickers Rd. DA8 .... 4 D1
Victor Mills Cotts. BR8 .... 25 A1
Victoria Ave. 3 DA11 .... 30 B8
Victoria Bsns Ctr. DA11 .... 7 B5
Victoria Cl. Chatham ME5 .... 61 D2
Victoria Cl. Edenbridge TN8 ... 128 C8
Victoria Cotts. Cranbrook TN17 169 D5
Victoria Cotts. Edenbridge TN8 . 128 C8
Victoria Ct. 6 ME15 .... 91 E3
Victoria Dock Rd. E16 .... 1 B6
Victoria Dr. Kings Hill ME18 .... 88 F1
Victoria Dr. South Darenth DA4 .. 41 D7
Victoria Hill Rd. BR8 .... 40 A8
Victoria Ind Pk. DA1 .... 9 E2
Victoria Rd. Bexley DA6 .... 8 A3
Victoria Rd. Bromley BR2 .... 36 D4
Victoria Rd. Chatham,Luton ME4 . 48 B2
Victoria Rd.
Chatham,Walderslade ME5 .... 61 E3
Victoria Rd. Chislehurst BR7 .... 23 A3
Victoria Rd. Dartford DA1 .... 9 E2
Victoria Rd. Edenbridge TN8 ... 128 C8
Victoria Rd. Erith DA8 .... 8 E8
Victoria Rd. Golden Green TN11 118 F6
Victoria Rd. Gravesend DA11 ... 29 F7
Victoria Rd.
Royal Tunbridge Wells TN1 ... 149 B4
Victoria Rd. Royal Tunbridge Wells,
Modest Corner TN4 .... 132 C1
Victoria Rd. Sevenoaks TN13 ... 83 B2
Victoria Rd. Sidcup DA15 .... 24 A5
Victoria St. Eccles ME20 .... 75 F6
Victoria St. Erith DA8 .... 3 F1
Victoria St. Gillingham ME7 .... 48 D6
Victoria St. Maidstone ME16 ... 91 E3
Victoria St. Rochester ME2 .... 47 B7
Victoria St.
Rochester,Troy Town ME1 .... 47 D5
Victoria Terr. ME7 .... 47 A2
Victoria Way. SE7 .... 1 B1
Victoria Wharf. DA1 .... 9 E2
Victory Ctr. TN14 .... 99 C2
Victory Pk. ME7 .... 47 E7
Vidal Manor. ME7 .... 48 C5
Vidgeon Ave. ME3 .... 34 D6
View Rd. ME3 .... 33 B7
View The. SE2 .... 3 E1
Viewfield Rd. DA5 .... 24 C7
Viewland Rd. SE18 .... 2 F1
Viewlands Ave. TN16 .... 81 F7
Viewpoint Ct. DA3 .... 42 F5
Vigilant Way. DA12 .... 30 F3
Vigo Cty Prim Sch. DA13 .... 73 A8
Vigo Rd. TN15 .... 72 C7
Viking Gdns. E6 .... 1 E8
Viking House. 3 SE7 .... 1 E2
Viking Rd. DA11 .... 29 E7
Viking Way. Erith DA8 & DA17 ... 4 C3
Viking Way.
West Kingsdown TN15 .... 55 E5
Villa Cl. DA12 .... 31 B6
Villa Ct. DA1 .... 26 E6
Villa Rd. ME3 .... 32 B3
Villacourt Rd. SE18 & SE2 ...... 7 A8
Village Green Rd. DA1 .... 9 A3
Village The. SE7 .... 5 D8
Villas Rd. SE18 .... 2 C2
Vincent Cl. Bromley BR2 .... 36 B5
Vincent Cl. Sidcup DA15 .... 23 E7
Vincent Rd. Kit's Coty ME20 ... 76 C7
Vincent Rd. Woolwich SE18 ... 2 F2
Vincent St. 13 E16 .... 1 A8
Vine Ave. TN13 .... 84 B3
Vine Court Rd. TN13 .... 84 C4
Vine Lodge Ct. TN13 .... 84 C3
Vine Rd. BR6 .... 51 F4
Vine The. TN13 .... 84 C4
Vine Wlk. TN12 .... 139 E3

Vineries The. ME7 .... 48 E5
Vines La. Rochester ME1 .... 47 C5
Vines La. Watt's Cross TN11 .... 100 C1
Viney's Gdns. TN30 .... 173 C1
Vineyard La. TN5 .... 176 C2
Vinson Cl. BR6 .... 38 A1
Vinters Rd. ME14 .... 92 A4
Vinters Sch for Boys. ME14 .... 92 C4
Vintners Way. ME14 .... 92 A4
Viola Ave. SE2 .... 3 B1
Violet Cl. ME5 .... 77 A8
VIP Trad Est. SE7 .... 1 C2
Virginia Rd. ME7 .... 48 C7
Virginia Wlk. DA12 .... 30 E2
Viscount Dr. E6 .... 1 F8
Vista The. SE9 .... 22 E8
Vixen Cl. ME5 .... 62 C6
Voce Rd. SE18 .... 6 D7
Volante Way. DA12 .... 30 E4
Vulcan Cl. ME5 .... 62 B7
Vyne The. DA7 .... 8 B4
Vyvyan Cotts. TN17 .... 180 C3
Vyvyon House. SE18 .... 6 A6

Wadard Terr. BR8 .... 40 C4
Wade Ave. BR5 .... 38 D2
Wade Rd. E16 .... 1 C7
Wadeville Cl. DA17 .... 4 A1
Wadhurst Bsns Pk. TN5 .... 174 B7
Wadhurst CE Prim Sch. TN5 ... 174 F5
Wadhurst Par. TN5 .... 174 F4
Wadhurst Sta. TN5 .... 174 C6
Wadlands Rd. ME3 .... 16 B5
Waghorn Rd. ME6 .... 75 A8
Waghorn St. ME4 .... 48 B3
Wagon La. TN12 .... 120 C1
Wagoners Ct. ME14 .... 92 E1
Waid Cl. DA1 .... 9 F1
Wainscott Cty Prim Sch. ME2 .. 33 D2
Wainscott Rd. ME2 .... 33 D2
Wainscott Wlk. ME2 .... 33 D3
Waite Davies Rd. 6 SE12 .... 22 A8
Wake Rd. ME1 .... 61 C8
Wakefield Cl. ME2 .... 46 D6
Wakefield Rd. DA9 .... 11 C2
Wakehurst Cl. ME17 .... 106 B3
Wakeleys Cotts. ME8 .... 64 B8
Wakerly Cl. E6 .... 1 F7
Waldair Ct. E16 .... 2 D4
Waldeck Rd. DA1 .... 10 A1
Waldegrave Rd. BR1 .... 36 F5
Walden Ave. BR7 .... 22 F4
Walden Cl. DA17 .... 3 F1
Walden Rd. BR7 .... 22 F2
Waldenhurst Rd. BR5 .... 38 D2
Waldens Cl. BR5 .... 38 D2
Waldens Rd. BR5 .... 38 E3
Waldens The. ME17 .... 109 E2
Walderslade Cty Prim Sch. ME5 62 A3
Walderslade Girls Sch. ME5 .... 61 F5
Walderslade Rd. ME5 .... 61 F6
Walderslade Woods.
Chatham ME5 .... 61 E3
Walderslade Woods.
Chatham ME5 & ME14 .... 77 B8
Waldo Ind Est. BR1 .... 36 D6
Waldo Rd. BR1 .... 36 D6
Waldrist Way. DA18 .... 3 F4
Waldron Dr. ME15 .... 106 F6
Walk The. ME17 .... 109 E2
Walken Rd. BR7 .... 23 A3
Walker Cl. Crayford DA1 .... 8 F4
Walker Cl. Woolwich SE18 .... 2 C2
Walkhurst Cotts. TN17 .... 180 F7
Walkhurst Rd. TN17 .... 180 F7
Walkley Rd. DA1 .... 9 B2
Walks The. TN3 .... 161 C8
Wall Cl. ME3 .... 34 C4
Wallace Cl.
Royal Tunbridge Wells TN2 ... 163 A8
Wallace Gdns. DA10 .... 11 E1
Wallace Rd. ME1 .... 61 E8
Wallace Terr. TN15 .... 56 E4
Waller Hill. TN17 .... 156 B5
Wallers. TN3 .... 148 A3
Wallhouse Rd. DA8 .... 9 C7
Wallis Ave. ME15 .... 107 E5
Wallis Cl. DA2 .... 25 F5
Wallis Field. TN3 .... 161 B6
Walmer Cl. BR6 .... 51 D6
Walmer Ct. 3 ME14 .... 92 A5
Walmer House. ME2 .... 33 C1
Walmer Terr. SE18 .... 2 D2
Walmers Ave. ME3 .... 32 A4
Walnut Cl. Chatham ME5 .... 62 B8
Walnut Cl. Paddock Wood TN12 . 136 A6
Walnut Cl. Yalding ME18 .... 104 F1
Walnut Hill Rd. DA3 & DA13 ... 43 E6
Walnut Tree Ave. Dartford DA1 . 26 E6
Walnut Tree Ave.
Loose Hill ME15 .... 107 A5
Walnut Tree Cl. BR7 .... 37 C8
Walnut Tree Cl. ME20 .... 75 B1
Walnut Tree Cl. ME15 .... 107 A5
Walnut Tree Rd. DA8 .... 4 E1
Walnut Tree Way. DA13 .... 44 B3
Walnut Way.
R Tunbridge Wells TN2 & TN4 ... 113 D1
Walnut Way. Swanley BR8 .... 39 D7
Walnuts Rd. BR6 .... 38 B1
Walnuts The. BR6 .... 38 A1
Walpole Cl. ME19 .... 74 F1
Walpole Pl. 3 SE18 .... 2 B2
Walsall Rd. ME2 .... 36 D4
Walsham Cl. SE28 .... 3 D6
Walsham Rd. ME5 .... 61 F1
Walshaw House. 2 ME14 .... 92 A6

Walsingham Cl. ME8 .... 63 D3
Walsingham House. **3** ME14 ... 92 A6
Walsingham Pk. BR7 .... 37 D7
Walsingham Rd. BR5 .... 38 B8
Walter Burke Ave. ME1 .... 60 C5
Walter's Farm Rd. TN9 .... 117 C1
Walters Green Rd. TN11 & TN3 146 F6
Walters Rd. ME3 .... 34 E6
Walters Yd. BR1 .... 36 A7
Waltham Cl. Dartford DA1 .... 9 A1
Waltham Cl. Orpington BR5 ...... 38 D1
Waltham Rd. ME8 .... 49 C3
Walthamstow Hall. TN13 .... 84 C4
Walthamstow Hall Jun Sch.
TN13 .... 84 C4
Walton Rd. Sidcup DA14 .... 24 C5
Walton Rd. Tonbridge TN10 ... 117 F6
Walwyn Ave. BR1 .... 36 D6
Wanden La. TN27 .... 143 C8
Wansbury Way. BR8 .... 40 A5
Wanstead Cl. BR1 .... 36 C7
Wanstead Rd. BR1 .... 36 C7
Wansunt Rd. DA5 .... 25 C7
Warblers Cl. ME2 .... 47 A7
Ward Cl. Durgates TN5 .... 174 E5
Ward Cl. Erith DA8 .... 8 D8
Ward's La. TN5 .... 175 E4
Warde's. ME18 .... 104 F2
Warden Cl. ME16 .... 91 C4
Warden Mill Cl. ME18 .... 104 E7
Warden Rd. ME1 .... 47 C2
Wardens Field Cl. **2** BR6 .... 51 F4
Wardona Ct. DA10 .... 11 F1
Wardwell La. ME9 .... 65 C8
Ware St. ME14 .... 93 A5
Warepoint Dr. SE28 .... 2 D4
Warham Rd. TN14 .... 69 B3
Waring Cl. BR6 .... 51 F4
Waring Dr. BR6 .... 52 A4
Waring Rd. DA14 .... 24 C2
Warland Rd.
West Kingsdown TN15 .... 55 F2
Warland Rd. Woolwich SE18 ...... 6 E7
Warmlake. ME17 .... 108 F1
Warmlake Est. ME17 .... 108 E1
Warmlake Rd. ME17 .... 108 C1
Warne Pl. **4** DA15 .... 7 B1
Warner St. ME4 .... 47 F3
Warnett Cl. ME4 .... 60 A1
Warnford Gdns. ME15 .... 107 A8
Warnford Rd. BR6 .... 51 F5
Warren Ave. BR6 .... 52 A4
Warren Cl. DA6 .... 8 A2
Warren Cotts. TN11 .... 131 A3
Warren Ct. TN15 .... 84 C3
Warren Dr. BR6 .... 52 B5
Warren Farm La. TN3 .... 162 B4
Warren Gdns. BR6 .... 52 A5
Warren La. Hartlip ME9 .... 64 C3
Warren La. Woolwich SE18 .... 2 B3
Warren Rd. Bexley DA6 .... 8 A2
Warren Rd. Dartford DA1 .... 26 E5
Warren Rd. Hayes BR2 .... 50 A8
Warren Rd.
Kit's Coty ME5 & ME20 .... 76 D7
Warren Rd.
Lower Bush DA12 & DA13 ..... 45 D3
Warren Rd. Orpington BR6 ...... 52 C5
Warren Rd. Sidcup DA14 .... 24 C5
Warren Rd. Southfleet DA13 .... 29 B3
Warren Ridge. TN3 .... 163 C3
Warren Road Prim Sch. BR6 ... 51 F6
Warren The. Gravesend DA12 .. 30 D4
Warren The. Penshurst TN11 . 131 A4
Warren The. Ticehurst TN5 ... 176 E1
Warren View. DA12 .... 31 E2
Warren Wlk. **1** SE7 .... 5 C8
Warren Wood Cl. BR2 .... 50 A8
Warren Wood Cty Prim Sch.
ME1 .... 61 C8
Warren Wood Rd. ME1 .... 61 C7
Warrens The. DA3 .... 42 F3
Warrington Rd. TN12 .... 136 A6
Warrior Ave. DA12 .... 30 C4
Warspite Rd. SE18 & SE7 .... 1 E3
Warwall. E6 .... 2 B7
Warwick Cl. Orpington BR6 ..... 52 A7
Warwick Cl. Sidcup DA5 .... 24 F8
Warwick Cres. ME1 .... 46 F2
Warwick Gdns. DA13 .... 58 A8
Warwick Pk. TN1 & TN2 .... 149 B1
Warwick Pl. Maidstone ME15 ... 91 E3
Warwick Pl. Northfleet DA11 ... 12 B2
Warwick Rd. Bexley DA16 .... 7 C4
Warwick Rd. **4**
Royal Tunbridge Wells TN1 .. 149 A2
Warwick Rd. Sidcup DA14 ...... 24 B3
Warwick Terr. SE18 .... 6 D8
Washneys Rd. BR6 & TN14 ..... 67 B6
Washwell La. TN5 .... 174 F3
Wassall La. TN17 .... 187 E7
Wat Tyler Way. ME15 .... 92 A4
Watchgate. DA2 .... 27 E3
Water La. Four Wents TN18 ... 179 B4
Water La. Harrietsham ME17 .. 110 B5
Water La.
Headcorn TN17 & TN27 ...... 141 A4
Water La. Kingswood ME17 ... 109 F3
Water La. **4** Maidstone ME15 .. 92 A4
Water La.
Maidstone,Bearsted ME14 .... 93 E6
Water La. Shoreham TN14 ...... 68 F6
Water La. Sidcup DA14 .... 24 F6
Water La. West Malling ME19 .. 89 C8
Water Mill Way. DA4 .... 41 B7
Water Slippe. TN11 .... 102 D1

Watercress Cl. TN14 .... 84 C7
Watercress Dr. TN14 .... 84 C7
Watercroft Rd. TN14 .... 52 F1
Waterdale Rd. SE2 .... 7 A8
Waterdales. DA11 .... 29 D7
Waterdown Rd. TN4 .... 148 E1
Waterfield. TN2 .... 163 A7
Waterfield Cl. Erith DA17 .... 4 A3
Waterfield Cl. Woolwich SE28 ... 3 B5
Waterfield Sch. SE28 .... 3 A5
Waterfrets Cotts. TN3 .... 147 F5
Watergate House. **5** SE18 .... 2 A2
Watergale Ind Pk. RM16 .... 10 F8
Waterhead Cl. DA8 .... 8 E7
Waterhouse Cl. E16 .... 1 D8
Wateringbury CE Prim Sch.
ME18 .... 104 E6
Wateringbury Cl. BR5 .... 38 B7
Wateringbury Rd. ME19 .... 89 F3
Wateringbury Sta. ME18 .... 104 E6
Waterlakes. TN8 .... 128 C8
Waterloo Pl. Cranbrook TN17 . 169 D5
Waterloo Pl. Tonbridge TN9 .. 133 B8
Waterloo Rd. Cranbrook TN17 . 169 D6
Waterloo Rd. Gillingham ME7 . 48 C5
Waterloo St. **1** Gravesend DA12 30 C8
Waterloo St. Maidstone ME15 . 92 A3
Waterlow Rd. Maidstone ME14 . 92 A6
Waterlow Rd. Vigo Village DA13 . 72 F7
Waterman's La. TN12 .... 136 B3
Watermeadow Cl. ME7 .... 62 F6
Watermill Cl. Maidstone ME16 . 91 B5
Watermill Cl. Rochester ME2 ... 47 C8
Waters Cotts. TN5 .... 175 A4
Waters Edge. ME15 .... 91 F2
Waters Pl. ME7 .... 63 A6
Waterside. DA1 .... 8 F2
Waterside Ct. ME20 .... 74 E2
Waterside La. ME7 .... 48 D7
Waterside Mews. ME18 .... 104 D6
Watermeet Way. SE28 .... 3 D7
Waterton Ave. DA12 .... 30 E8
Watery La. Heaverham TN15 ... 85 D7
Watery La. Sidcup DA14 .... 24 B2
Watford Rd. E16 .... 1 A8
Watkins Cl. TN12 .... 139 E5
Watling Ave. ME5 .... 48 C2
Watling House. **10** SE18 .... 6 A8
Watling St. Bexley DA6 & DA7 ... 8 C3
Watling St. Chatham ME5 & ME7 . 48 D2
Watling St. Dartford DA1 & DA2 . 27 C8
Watling St. Gillingham ME5 & ME7 48 D2
Watling St. Gravesend DA11 .... 30 B3
Watling St. Gravesend DA11 .... 30 C2
Watling St.
Northfleet DA11 & DA13 .... 29 C5
Watling St. Rochester ME2 ...... 46 D7
Watson Ave. ME5 .... 61 D5
Watson Cl. RM16 .... 11 A6
Watt's Cross Rd. TN11 .... 116 B6
Watt's La. BR7 .... 37 C8
Watts' Ave. ME1 .... 47 C4
Watts Cl. Snodland ME6 .... 75 B8
Watts Cl. Wadhurst TN5 .... 174 F4
Watts' St. ME4 .... 47 E3
Wavell Dr. DA15 .... 6 E1
Waveney House. **7** ME15 ...... 107 E8
Waveney Rd. TN10 .... 117 B5
Waverley Cl. Bromley BR2 ...... 36 D4
Waverley Cl. Chatham ME5 ..... 62 D2
Waverley Cl. Coxheath ME17 .. 106 C3
Waverley Cres. SE18 .... 2 D1
Waverley Dr. TN2 .... 149 F6
Waverley Gdns. E6 .... 1 E8
Waverley Rd. SE18 .... 2 D1
Wayfield Cty Prim Sch. ME5 ... 62 A7
Wayfield Link. SE9 .... 6 D1
Wayfield Rd. ME5 .... 62 A7
Waylands. BR8 .... 39 F5
Waylands Cl. TN14 .... 67 E4
Wayne Cl. BR6 .... 51 F7
Wayne Ct. ME2 .... 33 D2
Wayside. TN30 .... 173 B2
Wayside Ave. TN30 .... 173 B3
Wayside Dr. TN8 .... 112 D3
Wayside Flats. TN30 .... 173 B2
Wayside Gr. BR7 & SE9 .... 22 F4
Wayville Rd. DA1 .... 27 B8
Weald Cl. Istead Rise DA13 ..... 29 E1
Weald Cl. Keston Mark BR2 .... 50 E8
Weald Cl. Maidstone ME15 .... 107 C6
Weald Cl. Sevenoaks Weald TN14 99 C2
Weald Ct. TN11 .... 116 D6
Weald Cty Prim Sch. TN14 ..... 99 B2
Weald of Kent
Gram Sch for Girls The. TN9 133 C7
Weald Rd. TN13 .... 99 B7
Weald The. BR7 .... 22 F2
Weald View. Castle Hill TN12 . 136 E1
Weald View. Frittenden TN17 . 156 E6
Weald View. Turner's Green TN5 174 F6
Weald View Rd. TN9 .... 133 B7
Wealden Ave. TN30 .... 173 B1
Wealden Cl. TN11 .... 116 E5
Wealden Cl. **5** ME4 .... 48 B3
Wealden Pl. TN13 .... 84 D6
Wealden Way. ME20 .... 90 E7
Wealdon View. TN17 .... 167 E8
Weardale Ave. DA2 .... 27 C7
Weare Rd. TN4 .... 149 C8
Weatherly Cl. ME1 .... 47 C4
Weathersfield Cl. SE9 .... 5 F1
Weaver Cl. E6 .... 2 B7
Weaver's Orch. DA13 .... 29 A2
Weavering Cl. ME2 .... 33 B2
Weavering St. ME14 .... 92 E3
Weavers Cotts. ME14 .... 92 E3
Weavers Cl. Gravesend DA11 ... 30 A7

Weavers Cl. Staplehurst TN12 . 139 F4
Weavers Cotts. TN17 .... 167 E8
Weavers La. TN14 .... 84 C6
Weavers The. Biddenden TN27 . 158 A1
Weavers The. Maidstone ME16 . 91 B5
Webb Cl. ME3 .... 34 D6
Webb Ct. **6** SE28 .... 3 B6
Webb's Meadow. TN15 .... 84 C2
Webber Cl. DA8 .... 9 B7
Webster Rd. ME8 .... 49 F1
Wedgewood Cl. ME16 .... 91 B5
Wedgewood Ct. DA5 .... 24 F8
Wedgewood Dr. ME5 .... 62 A7
Weeds Wood Rd. ME5 .... 61 F4
Week St. ME14 .... 92 A4
Weeks La. TN27 .... 158 A5
Weigall Rd. SE12 & SE3 .... 5 A3
Weinhouse Cl. TN8 .... 112 D3
Weir Rd. DA5 .... 25 B8
Weird Wood. DA3 .... 43 C6
Welbeck Ave. Bromley BR1 ...... 22 B4
Welbeck Ave.
Royal Tunbridge Wells TN4 .. 149 C8
Welbeck Ave. Sidcup DA15 ...... 24 A7
Welcombe Ct. ME8 .... 63 D8
Weld Cl. ME12 .... 139 F4
Well Cl. TN11 .... 115 F1
Well Field. DA3 .... 42 F5
Well Hall Par. SE9 .... 5 F3
Well Hall Rd. Eltham SE9 .... 5 F2
Well Hall Rd. Eltham SE18 & SE9 . 5 F5
Well Hill. BR6 .... 53 B5
Well Hill La. BR6 .... 53 B4
Well Penn Rd. ME3 .... 16 C3
Well Rd. Maidstone ME14 .... 92 A5
Well Rd. Otford TN14 .... 69 C3
Well St. Loose ME15 & ME17 .. 106 E4
Well St. Well Street ME19 .... 89 E6
Wellan Cl. DA16 .... 7 B2
Welland House. **8** ME15 .... 107 E8
Welland Rd. TN10 .... 117 B4
Wellands Cl. BR1 .... 36 F7
Wellbrook Rd. BR6 .... 51 A6
Wellcome Ave. DA1 .... 9 E3
Weller Ave. ME1 .... 47 D2
Weller Pl. BR6 .... 66 A8
Weller Rd. TN4 .... 148 C4
Wellers Ct. TN16 .... 96 C8
Wellesley Cl. **8** SE7 .... 1 C1
Welling High Sch. DA16 .... 7 B4
Welling Sch. DA16 .... 7 B6
Welling Sta. DA16 .... 7 A5
Welling Way. DA16 .... 6 D4
Wellingfield Ct. **1** DA16 .... 7 A4
Wellington Ave. Woolwich SE18 . 2 C3
Wellington Cotts.
Gill's Green TN18 .... 178 E4
Wellington Cotts.
Meopham DA13 .... 58 A7
Wellington Gdns. SE7 .... 1 C1
Wellington House. **6** ME15 ... 107 E5
Wellington Par. DA15 .... 7 A2
Wellington Pl.
Sparrow's Green TN5 .... 174 F5
Wellington Rd. Bexley DA5 .... 7 D2
Wellington Rd. Bromley BR2 .... 36 C5
Wellington Rd. Dartford DA1 ..... 9 C1
Wellington Rd. Erith DA17 .... 3 F1
Wellington Rd. Gillingham ME7 . 48 C4
Wellington Rd. Orpington BR5 .. 38 C3
Wellington Rd. Tilbury RM18 ... 13 A5
Wellington St. Gravesend DA12 . 30 C8
Wellington St. Woolwich SE18 ... 2 A2
Wellington Way. ME19 .... 88 F3
Wellingtonia Way. TN8 .... 112 C2
Wellmeade Dr. TN13 .... 99 B8
Wells Cl.
Royal Tunbridge Wells TN1 .. 149 A3
Wells Cl. Tenterden TN30 ...... 183 B8
Wells Cl. Tonbridge TN10 & TN9 117 D4
Wells Cotts. ME18 .... 104 C2
Wells House. BR1 .... 22 B3
Wells Rd. Bromley BR1 .... 36 F7
Wells Rd. Rochester ME2 .... 46 D5
Wellsmoor Gdns. BR1 .... 37 A6
Welton Cl. TN9 .... 132 F7
Welton Rd. SE18 .... 6 E7
Wemmick Cl. ME1 .... 61 D7
Wendover Cl. ME2 .... 60 B5
Wendover Ct. BR2 .... 36 B6
Wendover Rd. Bromley BR1 & BR2 36 B6
Wendover Rd. Eltham SE9 .... 5 D4
Wendover Way. Bexley DA16 ..... 7 A3
Wendover Way. Orpington BR6 . 38 A3
Wensley Cl. SE9 .... 5 F1
Wents Wood. ME14 .... 92 F5
Wentworth Cl. Gravesend DA11 . 30 A3
Wentworth Cl. Hayes BR2 .... 50 A8
Wentworth Cl. Orpington BR6 .. 51 C5
Wentworth Cty Prim Sch. DA1 . 26 A8
Wentworth Dr. Cliffe Woods ME3 . 33 B8
Wentworth Dr. Dartford DA1 ..... 9 A1
Wentworth Dr. Gillingham ME8 . 63 E7
Wenvoe Ave. DA7 .... 8 B3
Wernbrook St. SE18 .... 6 C8
Wesley Ave. E16 .... 1 A5
Wesley Cl. Maidstone ME16 ..... 90 F3
Wesley Cl. St Paul's Cray BR5 .. 38 C6
Wessex Dr. DA8 .... 8 E6
West App. BR5 .... 37 C4
West Borough Cty Prim Sch.
ME16 .... 91 B3
West Brow. ME7 .... 48 B4
West Common Rd. BR2 .... 50 B7
West Crescent Rd. DA11 .... 13 C1
West Cross. TN30 .... 182 F7

West Cross Gdns. TN30 .... 182 F7
West Dr. Chartway Street ME1 . 125 B7
West Dr. Chatham ME5 .... 61 D5
West End. Brasted TN16 .... 82 B2
West End. Kemsing TN15 .... 70 A2
West End. Marden TN12 .... 138 C5
West Hallowes. SE9 .... 22 E7
West Heath Cl. DA1 .... 8 F1
West Heath La. TN13 .... 99 B7
West Heath Rd. Crayford DA1 .... 8 F1
West Heath Rd. Erith SE2 .... 7 D8
West Heath Sch. TN13 .... 99 B6
West High Sch for Boys. DA1 .. 26 D8
West High Sch for Girls. DA1 .. 26 D8
West Hill. DA1 .... 9 D1
West Hill Cty Prim Inf Sch. DA1 . 9 C1
West Hill Cty Prim Jun Sch. DA1 9 C1
West Hill Dr. DA1 .... 9 C1
West Hill Hospl. DA1 .... 9 D1
West Hill Rise. DA1 .... 9 D1
West Holme. DA8 .... 8 C6
West Kent Ave. DA11 .... 12 C1
West Kent Coll. TN9 .... 133 A7
West Kent Coll of FE. TN4 .... 149 A7
West Kingsdown CE Jun Sch.
TN15 .... 56 A2
West Kingsdown Cty Inf Sch.
TN15 .... 56 A2
West Kingsdown Ind Est. TN15 55 F2
West La. ME3 .... 21 A6
West Lodge Sch. DA14 .... 24 A5
West Malling CE Prim Sch.
ME19 .... 89 B8
West Malling Ind Pk. ME19 ..... 73 C2
West Malling Sta. ME19 .... 89 D8
West Mill. DA11 .... 12 F1
West Mill Rd. ME20 .... 75 C4
West Park Ave. TN4 .... 132 F1
West Park Rd. ME15 .... 92 B2
West Pk. SE9 .... 22 E7
West Rd. Gillingham ME4 .... 48 A7
West Rd. Goudhurst TN17 .... 167 E8
West Shaw. DA3 .... 42 D7
West St. Bexley DA7 .... 7 F4
West St. Bromley BR1 .... 36 A7
West St. Erith DA8 .... 4 E1
West St. Gillingham ME7 .... 48 D6
West St. Gravesend DA11 .... 13 B1
West St. Grays RM17 .... 12 A8
West St. Harrietsham ME17 ... 110 C6
West St. Hunton ME15 .... 121 D7
West St. Rochester ME2 .... 33 B1
West St. West Malling ME19 .... 89 B8
West St. Woodside Green ME17 . 111 E8
West St. Wrotham TN15 .... 71 F3
West Terr. DA15 .... 23 E7
West Thurrock Cty Prim Sch.
RM16 .... 11 A8
West Thurrock Way. RM16 ..... 11 B8
West View Hospl. TN30 .... 182 E6
West View. Crockenhill BR8 .... 39 D3
West View. Dartford DA1 .... 9 F1
West View. Swanley BR8 .... 40 A5
West Way. BR5 .... 37 D4
West Wlk. ME16 .... 91 B3
West Wood Rd. ME9 .... 79 B8
West Woodside. DA5 .... 24 E7
Westbere House. BR5 .... 38 C4
Westbourne Rd. DA7 .... 7 E7
Westbrook Ct. SE3 .... 5 A7
Westbrook Dr. BR5 .... 38 D1
Westbrook Rd. SE3 .... 5 B6
Westbrook Terr. TN2 .... 149 D1
Westbrooke Cl. ME4 .... 48 A2
Westbrooke Cres. DA16 .... 7 C4
Westbrooke Rd. Bexley DA16 .... 7 C4
Westbrooke Rd. Sidcup DA15 .. 23 D6
Westbrooke Sch. DA16 .... 7 D4
Westbury Rd. BR1 .... 36 D8
Westbury Terr. TN16 .... 96 C8
Westcombe Hill. SE3 & SE10 ..... 5 A8
Westcombe Park Sta. SE3 .... 1 A1
Westcott Ave. DA11 .... 30 A5
Westcott Cl. BR1 .... 36 D6
Westcourt Cty Prim Sch. DA12 30 E6
Westdale Rd. SE18 .... 6 B8
Westdean Ave. SE12 .... 22 C7
Wested Farm Cotts. BR8 .... 39 F2
Wested La. Swanley BR8 .... 40 A3
Wested La. Swanley BR8 .... 40 A4
Westerdale Rd. **3** SE10 .... 1 A1
Westergate Rd. Erith SE2 .... 7 E8
Westergate Rd. Rochester ME2 . 32 F1
Westerham Cl. ME8 .... 49 B3
Westerham Dr. DA15 .... 7 B1
Westerham Hill. TN16 .... 81 B5
Westerham Rd. Brasted TN16 ... 82 A2
Westerham Rd. Keston BR2 .... 50 D4
Westerham Rd.
Sevenoaks TN13 & TN14 ..... 83 C4
Westerham Rd. Westerham TN16 96 A8
Westerhill Rd. ME17 .... 106 C1
Westerland. BR7 .... 23 C2
Western Ave. **7** TN18 .... 178 F2
Western Cross Cl. DA9 .... 11 C1
Western Gateway. E16 .... 1 B6
Western Rd. Borough Green ME19 88 F7
Western Rd. Hawkhurst TN18 . 178 F2
Western Rd. Maidstone ME16 ... 91 C2
Western Rd.
Royal Tunbridge Wells TN1 .. 149 C5
Western Rd. Royal Tunbridge Wells,
Southborough TN4 .... 133 A1
Western Rd. Turner's Green TN5 174 F6
Western Way. SE28 .... 2 E4
Westfield. New Ash Green DA3 . 56 F6

Westfield. **1** Orpington BR6 ..... 51 C5
Westfield. Sevenoaks TN13 ..... 84 C5
Westfield Bsns Ctr. ME2 .... 47 C7
Westfield Cl. DA12 .... 30 C2
Westfield Cotts. Cudham TN14 . 66 D3
Westfield Cotts.
West Kingsdown TN15 .... 55 F4
Westfield House. TN30 .... 182 F7
Westfield Rd. DA7 .... 8 C4
Westfield Sole Rd. ME14 .... 77 D8
Westfield St. SE18 .... 1 D3
Westfield Terr. TN17 .... 168 F1
Westgate Ct. SE12 .... 22 A7
Westgate Cty Prim Sch. DA1 ... 26 D8
Westgate Rd. DA1 .... 9 D1
Westharold. BR8 .... 39 D6
Westhill Cl. DA11 .... 30 B7
Westholme. BR6 .... 37 F2
Westhorne Ave. SE12 & SE9 ..... 5 C2
Westhurst Dr. BR7 .... 23 B3
Westleigh Dr. BR1 .... 36 E8
Westmarsh Cl. ME15 .... 107 F7
Westmead. ME20 .... 75 C4
Westminster Ind Est. E16 .... 1 D3
Westmoor St. SE7 .... 1 D3
Westmoreland Ave. DA16 .... 6 E3
Westmoreland Pl. **5** BR1 .... 36 A6
Westmorland Cl. ME15 .... 107 E7
Westmorland Gn. ME15 .... 107 E7
Westmorland Rd. Bromley BR2 . 36 A5
Westmorland Rd.
Maidstone ME15 .... 107 E7
Westmount Ave. ME4 .... 47 F3
Westmount Rd. SE9 .... 6 A3
Weston Ave. RM16 .... 10 F8
Weston Rd. ME2 .... 47 A8
Westport Rd. E13 .... 1 B8
Westree Rd. ME16 .... 91 E3
Westrise. TN9 .... 133 A7
Westway. Beckenham ME17 ... 106 C3
Westways. Pembury TN2 .... 150 D7
Westways. Marlpit Hill TN8 .... 112 C2
Westwell Cl. BR5 .... 38 D1
Westwell Ct. TN30 .... 182 F7
Westwell House. TN30 .... 182 F7
Westwood Cl. BR1 .... 36 D6
Westwood Inf Sch. DA16 .... 6 E3
Westwood La. DA16 .... 6 F4
Westwood Rd.
East Peckham TN12 .... 119 E6
Westwood Rd. Maidstone ME15 107 A7
Westwood Rd. Newham E16 ...... 1 B5
Westwood Rd. Rusthall TN4 .. 148 C5
Westwood Rd. Westwood DA13 . 28 E2
Westwood Tech Coll. DA16 .... 6 E3
Westwood Way. TN13 .... 83 F5
Wetheral Dr. ME5 .... 62 B4
Wey Cl. ME5 .... 62 C5
Weybridge Cl. ME5 .... 62 C4
Weyhill Cl. ME14 .... 92 C6
Weyman Rd. SE3 & SE7 .... 5 C6
Weymouth Cl. E6 .... 2 B7
Wharf La. ME3 .... 16 B6
Wharf Rd. Gillingham ME7 .... 48 C7
Wharf Rd. Gravesend DA12 ...... 13 E1
Wharf Rd. Grays RM17 .... 11 F8
Wharf Rd. Maidstone ME15 ..... 91 E2
Wharfedale Rd. DA2 .... 26 C7
Wharncliffe. DA9 .... 11 B1
Wharton Rd. BR1 .... 36 B8
Whatman Cl. ME14 .... 92 C6
Wheatcroft Gr. ME8 .... 63 F7
Wheatear Way. ME5 .... 62 B7
Wheatfield. ME19 .... 74 E1
Wheatfield Cl. TN17 .... 169 C5
Wheatfield Dr. TN17 .... 169 C5
Wheatfield Lea. TN17 .... 169 C5
Wheatfield Way. TN10 .... 117 C5
Wheatfields. Chatham ME5 ..... 62 D2
Wheatfields. Maidstone ME14 . 92 D4
Wheatfields. Newham E6 .... 2 B7
Wheatley Cl. DA9 .... 11 A2
Wheatley Terrace Rd. DA8 .... 8 F8
Wheatsheaf Cl. ME15 .... 107 B8
Wheatsheaf Hill. Ide Hill TN14 . 97 F4
Wheatsheaf Hill. Maypole TN14 . 52 F2
Wheelbarrow Park Est. TN12 . 138 B7
Wheeler St. Headcorn TN27 ... 141 E5
Wheeler St. Maidstone ME14 ... 92 A5
Wheeler's La. ME17 .... 122 E7
Wheelers The. ME8 .... 63 B6
Whenman Ave. DA5 .... 25 C5
Whernside Cl. SE28 .... 3 C6
Whetsted Rd.
Five Oak Green TN12 .... 135 C8
Whetsted Rd. Whetsted TN12 . 119 C3
Whetstone Rd. SE3 .... 5 D6
Whiffen's Ave. ME4 .... 47 F5
Whiffen's Ave W. ME4 .... 47 F5
Whimbrel Cl. SE28 .... 3 C6
Whimbrel Gn. ME20 .... 74 F2
Whimbrel Wlk. ME5 .... 62 C1
Whinchat Rd. SE18 & SE28 .... 2 D3
Whinfell Way. DA12 .... 30 F4
Whinyates Rd. SE9 .... 5 E4
Whippendell Cl. BR5 .... 38 B8
Whippendell Way. BR5 .... 38 B7
Whistler Rd. TN10 .... 117 D6
Whitby Cl. DA9 .... 11 A2

Whitby Rd. SE18 .... 1 F2
Whitchurch Cl. ME16 .... 91 E4
Whitcombe Cl. ME5 .... 62 C3
White Ave. DA11 .... 29 F5
White Bear Pas. 3 TN1 & TN4 149 A2
White Cottage Rd. TN10 .... 117 D6
White Hart Cl. TN13 .... 99 C7
White Hart Par. TN13 .... 83 E5
White Hart Rd. Orpington BR6 .. 38 A2
White Hart Rd. Woolwich SE18 .. 2 E2
White Hart Wood. TN13 .... 99 C6
White Hill Rd. ME14 .... 63 D1
White Horse Hill. BR7 & SE9 .... 23 A4
White Horse La.
  Otham Hole ME15 .... 108 A6
White Horse Rd. DA13 .... 58 E1
White House La. TN14 .... 98 F5
White House Rd. TN14 .... 98 F5
White Lodge. TN1 .... 149 C4
White Lodge Cl. TN13 .... 84 B4
White Oak Cl. 10 TN9 .... 133 B8
White Oak Cty Inf Sch. BR8 .... 39 E7
White Oak Cty Prim Sch. BR8 .. 39 E7
White Oak Gdns. DA15 .... 23 F8
White Oak Sq. 3 BR8 .... 39 E6
White Post. Four Elms TN8 ...... 113 A6
White Post Cnr. TN11 .... 101 F5
White Post Hill. DA4 .... 41 A2
White Post La. DA13 .... 44 B5
White Rd. ME4 .... 48 A2
White Rock Ct. ME16 .... 91 E3
White Rock Pl. 5 ME16 .... 91 E3
White's La. TN18 .... 179 B2
White's Meadow. BR1 .... 37 A5
Whitebeam Ave. BR2 .... 37 A3
Whitebeam Dr. ME17 .... 106 B3
Whitebine Gdns. TN12 .... 120 A6
Whitebread La. TN31 .... 187 D1
Whitecroft. RR8 .... 39 E7
Whitefield Cl. BR5 .... 38 C6
Whitefield Rd. TN4 .... 149 A6
Whitefriars. TN13 .... 99 A8
Whitegate Cl. TN4 .... 149 A8
Whitegates Ave. TN15 .... 55 E4
Whitegates La. TN5 .... 174 D8
Whitehall Dr. ME17 .... 109 D3
Whitehall La. Erith DA8 .... 8 F5
Whitehall La. Grays RM17 ...... 12 C8
Whitehall Rd. Broad Street ME14 94 A4
Whitehall Rd. Bromley BR2 .... 36 D5
Whitehaven Cl. BR2 .... 36 A5
Whitehead Cl. DA2 .... 26 C5
Whiteheads La. ME14 .... 93 B4
Whitehill. TN15 .... 72 B3
Whitehill Cty Inf Sch. DA12 .... 30 C5
Whitehill Cty Jun Sch. DA12 .... 30 C5
Whitehill La. DA12 .... 30 D5
Whitehill Par. DA12 .... 30 C5
Whitehill Rd. Crayford DA1 .... 9 A2
Whitehill Rd. Gravesend DA12 .. 30 C6
Whitehill Rd.
  Longfield,Whitehill DA13 ...... 42 D8
Whitehill Rd. Meopham DA13 .. 58 B7
Whitehorse Hill. ME4 .... 48 B3
Whitehouse Cl. ME3 .... 34 E4
Whitehouse Cres. ME1 .... 76 A8
Whitelake Rd. TN10 .... 117 C7
Whiteleaves Rise. ME2 .... 46 B3
Whitelimes. TN18 .... 178 D8
Whiteoak Ct. 1 BR8 .... 39 E6
Whitepost La.
  Culverstone Green DA13 ...... 57 F2
Whitepost La. Vigo Village DA13 .. 73 A8
Whites Cl. DA9 .... 11 C1
Whitewall Ctr. ME2 .... 47 D8
Whitewall Rd. ME2 .... 47 D7
Whitewall Way. ME2 .... 47 D7
Whitewebbs Way. BR5 .... 37 F8
Whitfield Rd. DA7 .... 7 F7
Whitings Way. E6 .... 2 A8
Whitmore St. ME16 .... 91 D2
Whittaker St. ME4 .... 48 A4
Whitworth Rd. SE18 .... 6 A7
Whybourne Crest. TN2 .... 149 D1
Whyman Ave. ME4 .... 48 A1
Wichling Cl. BR5 .... 38 D1
Wicken House. ME16 .... 91 E4
Wickenden Rd. TN13 .... 84 C5
Wickens Pl. ME19 .... 89 C8
Wickets The. TN14 .... 99 C2
Wickham Cl. ME9 .... 65 B6
Wickham Common Prim Sch.
  BR4 .... 50 A6
Wickham Ct. DA16 .... 6 E5
Wickham Field. TN14 .... 68 F3
Wickham Gdns. TN4 .... 148 D5
Wickham La. SE2 & SE18 .... 7 A8
Wickham Pl. ME17 .... 111 D5
Wickham St. Bexley DA16 ...... 7 A6
Wickham St. Rochester ME1 .... 47 D3
Wickhams Way. DA3 .... 42 F4
Wickhurst Rd. TN14 .... 98 F3
Wicks Cl. SE12 .... 22 D4
Wicksteed Cl. DA5 .... 25 D5
Widbury Cl. TN3 .... 147 F2
Widecombe Rd. SE9 .... 22 E5
Widgeon Cl. E16 .... 1 B7
Widgeon Path. SE28 .... 2 D3
Widgeon Rd. ME2 .... 46 D6
Widmore Lodge Rd. BR1 .. 36 D7
Widmore Rd. BR1 .... 36 C7
Wierton Hill. ME17 .... 123 D7
Wierton La. ME17 .... 107 E1

Wierton Rd. ME17 .... 123 E8
Wigmore Rd. Gillingham ME8 .. 63 B4
Wigmore Rd. Gillingham ME8 .. 63 B5
Wilberforce Ct. 2 SE28 .... 3 C5
Wilberforce Rd. ME17 .... 106 D3
Wilberforce Way. DA12 .... 30 D3
Wilde Cl. RM18 .... 13 C5
Wilde Rd. DA8 .... 8 B7
Wilderness Rd. BR7 .... 23 B1
Wilderness Sch for Boys The.
  TN15 .... 84 E6
Wildernesse Ave. TN15 .... 84 E5
Wildernesse Golf Course. TN15 85 A4
Wildernesse Mount. TN13 ...... 84 D5
Wildfell Cl. ME14 .... 77 C8
Wildman Cl. ME8 .... 63 D3
Wildwood Cl. Kingswood ME17 . 109 E2
Wildwood Cl. 1 Lewisham SE12 12 A8
Wildwood Glade. ME7 .... 63 B4
Wilford House. 3 SE18 .... 2 B1
Wilfred St. 20 DA11 .... 13 B1
Wilkinson Cl. Dartford DA1 .... 9 F3
Wilkinson Cl. 1 Dartford DA1 .. 10 A3
Wilkinson Rd. E16 .... 1 C7
Wilks Ave. DA1 .... 26 F6
Will Adams Ct. ME7 .... 48 C6
Will Adams Way. ME7 .... 48 F1
Will Crooks Gdns. SE9 .... 5 D3
Will Thorne Pav The. E16 ...... 1 E7
Willenhall Rd. SE18 .... 2 B1
Willersley Ave. Orpington BR6 .. 51 D7
Willersley Ave. Sidcup DA15 .. 23 F7
Willersley Cl. DA15 .... 23 F7
Willesley Gdns. TN17 .... 169 D6
Willett Cl. BR5 .... 37 E3
Willett Way. BR5 & BR6 .... 37 E3
Willetts Cotts. TN3 .... 146 C4
Willetts La. TN3 .... 146 C4
William Baker House. ME20 .... 90 F8
William Barefoot Dr. SE9 ...... 23 A5
William House. 4 DA11 .... 30 B8
William Judge Cl. TN30 .... 183 D7
William Luck Cl. TN12 .... 119 E6
William Rd. ME2 .... 46 C2
William Smith House. 10 DA17 .. 4 A3
William St. Gravesend DA11 .... 30 B8
William St. Grays RM17 .... 12 C8
William St.
  Royal Tunbridge Wells TN4 .. 149 A5
Willington Gn. ME15 .... 107 E7
Willington St. ME15 .... 92 F2
Willis House. ME1 .... 47 C4
Willis Rd. DA8 .... 4 D2
Willoughby Way. SE7 .... 1 B2
Willow Ave. Hoo St Werburgh
  ME3 .... 34 E3
Willow Ave. Sidcup DA15 ...... 7 A1
Willow Ave. Swanley BR8 ...... 39 F5
Willow Cl. Bromley BR2 .... 36 F4
Willow Cl. Orpington BR5 ...... 38 B2
Willow Cl. Sidcup DA5 .... 7 F1
Willow Cres.
  Five Oak Green TN12 .... 135 B7
Willow Cres. Staplehurst TN12 . 139 F5
Willow Gr. BR7 .... 23 B2
Willow House. 2 ME5 .... 61 F5
Willow La. TN12 .... 136 E6
Willow Lea. TN10 .... 117 C7
Willow Pk. TN14 .... 68 F2
Willow Rd. Dartford DA1 .... 26 C7
Willow Rd. Erith DA8 .... 9 A6
Willow Rd. Larkfield ME20 .... 74 F3
Willow Rd. Rochester ME2 .... 46 E6
Willow Rise. ME15 .... 92 F1
Willow Terr. DA4 .... 54 E8
Willow Tree Ct. DA14 .... 23 F3
Willow Tree Rd. TN2 .... 148 F1
Willow Tree Wlk. BR1 .... 36 B8
Willow Vale. BR7 .... 23 B2
Willow Way. ME15 .... 92 B3
Willow Wents. ME1 .... 88 D1
Willow Wlk.
  Culverstone Green DA13 ...... 57 F3
Willow Wlk. Orpington BR6 .... 51 B7
Willow Wlk.
  Royal Tunbridge Wells TN2 .. 149 E8
Willow Wood Rd. DA13 .... 57 F2
Willowbank Dr. ME23 .... 17 E4
Willowby Gdns. ME8 .... 63 E4
Willowmead. ME20 .... 74 E2
Willows The. Gillingham ME8 .. 49 E2
Willows The. Grays RM17 ...... 12 D8
Willows The. Newington ME9 .. 65 B6
Willowside. ME6 .... 60 A1
Willrose Cres. SE2 .... 3 B1
Willys Cotts. TN8 .... 96 C2
Wilman Rd. TN4 .... 149 B7
Wilmar Way. TN15 .... 84 F7
Wilmecote Cl. ME8 .... 63 D8
Wilmington Ave. BR6 .... 52 C8
Wilmington Court Rd. DA2 .. 26 A6
Wilmington Gram Sch for Boys.
  DA2 .... 26 B5
Wilmington Hall Sch. DA2 .... 26 B5
Wilmington Prim Sch. DA2 .... 26 B5
Wilmington Way. ME8 .... 49 B2
Wilmot Rd. DA1 .... 9 B2
Wilmount St. SE18 .... 2 B1
Wilson Ave. ME1 .... 47 B4
Wilson Cl. Hildenborough TN11 . 116 E5
Wilson Cl. Maidstone ME15 .... 107 E7
Wilson House. 2 SE7 .... 5 C8
Wilson Rd. TN10 .... 117 E5
Wilsons La. ME15 .... 106 A5
Wilsons Way. DA13 .... 57 F3
Wilton Dr. ME19 .... 90 B8
Wilton Rd. SE2 .... 3 C2
Wiltshire Cl. Chatham ME5 .... 62 C8

Wiltshire Cl. Dartford DA2 .... 27 D8
Wiltshire Rd. BR6 .... 38 A2
Wiltshire Way. Maidstone ME15 107 E8
Wiltshire Way.
  Royal Tunbridge Wells TN1 .. 149 D7
Wimborne. DA14 .... 24 A4
Wimborne Ave. BR5 & BR7 .... 37 F6
Wimbourne Dr. ME8 .... 63 D6
Wimpole Cl. BR2 .... 36 C5
Winch Cl. TN17 .... 169 D3
Winch's Garth. TN12 .... 139 F5
Winchcomb Gdns. SE9 .... 5 D4
Winchelsea Ave. DA7 .... 7 F7
Winchelsea Rd. ME5 .... 62 B5
Winchester Ave. ME5 .... 61 F4
Winchester Cl. 11 E6 .... 1 F7
Winchester Cres. DA12 .... 30 D5
Winchester Gr. TN13 .... 84 B4
Winchester House.
  Greenwich SE18 .... 5 D7
Winchester House. 4
  Maidstone ME15 .... 107 D7
Winchester Pl. 7 ME14 .... 92 A5
Winchester Rd. Bexley DA16 .. 7 D5
Winchester Rd.
  Hawkhurst TN18 .... 179 A2
Winchester Rd. Orpington BR6 . 52 C6
Winchester Rd. Tonbridge TN10 117 C5
Winchester Way. ME8 .... 64 A8
Wincliff Rd. TN9 .... 133 B8
Wincrofts Dr. SE9 .... 6 D3
Windermere Cl. Dartford DA1 .. 26 B7
Windermere Cl. Orpington BR6 . 51 B7
Windermere Dr. ME8 .... 63 D7
Windermere Rd. DA7 .... 8 C5
Windhover Way. DA12 .... 30 E4
Windmill Cl. ME2 .... 33 B1
Windmill Cotts. Lower Stoke ME3 19 C5
Windmill Cotts.
  Wilsley Green TN17 .... 169 D6
Windmill Ct.
  Boughton Monchelsea ME17 . 107 B3
Windmill Ct.
  Royal Tunbridge Wells TN2 .. 149 C3
Windmill Dr. BR2 .... 50 C5
Windmill Hill. Hill Top TN12 .. 136 B1
Windmill Hill. Platt TN15 ...... 87 D7
Windmill Hill. Pye Corner ME17 126 B7
Windmill Hts. ME14 .... 93 B4
Windmill La. Cousley Wood TN5 175 C8
Windmill La. Durgates TN5 .... 174 E4
Windmill La.
  Wrotham Heath TN15 .... 87 E8
Windmill La E. ME19 .... 89 C6
Windmill La W. ME19 .... 89 A6
Windmill Pk. TN15 .... 87 E7
Windmill Rd. Gillingham ME7 .. 48 C4
Windmill Rd. Sevenoaks TN13 . 99 B6
Windmill Rd.
  Sevenoaks Weald TN14 ...... 99 B2
Windmill Row. ME17 .... 108 D2
Windmill St. Gravesend DA11 .. 30 B7
Windmill St. Rochester ME2 .... 33 B1
Windmill St.
  Royal Tunbridge Wells TN2 .. 149 C3
Windrush Prim Sch. SE28 ...... 3 B5
Windsor Ave. ME4 .... 47 F2
Windsor Cl. Chislehurst BR7 .... 23 B3
Windsor Cl. Maidstone ME14 .. 92 B6
Windsor Ct. BR1 .... 36 E6
Windsor Dr. Dartford DA1 ...... 9 A1
Windsor Dr. Orpington BR6 .... 52 A4
Windsor Rd. Bexley DA6 .... 7 E3
Windsor Rd. Gillingham ME7 .. 48 D5
Windsor Rd. Gravesend DA12 .. 30 B4
Windward Rd. ME1 .... 47 C1
Windy Ridge. BR1 .... 36 E8
Windyridge. ME7 .... 48 E1
Winfield La. TN15 .... 86 E3
Wingate Rd. DA14 .... 24 C2
Wingfield Prim Sch. SE3 ...... 5 B4
Wingfield Rd. DA11 .... 30 B8
Wingham Cl. Gillingham ME8 .. 49 C3
Wingham Cl. Maidstone ME15 . 107 F7
Wingrove Dr. Maidstone ME15 . 92 E5
Wingrove Dr. Rochester ME2 .. 47 C8
Winifred Rd. Dartford DA1 ...... 9 B2
Winifred Rd. Erith DA8 .... 4 E1
Winifred Rd. Maidstone ME15 .. 92 F3
Winn Common Rd. SE18 .... 6 E8
Winn Rd. SE12 & SE9 .... 22 B7
Winnipeg Dr. 3 BR6 .... 51 F4
Winser Rd. TN17 .... 182 A1
Winsor Prim Sch. E6 .... 2 A7
Winsor Terr. E6 .... 2 A8
Winston Cl. DA9 .... 10 F1
Winston Cl. 7 BR1 .... 36 B8
Winston Dr. ME2 .... 33 D2
Winston Rd. ME2 .... 46 D5
Winstone Scott Ave. TN3 ...... 147 E4
Winterborne Ave. BR6 .... 51 D7
Winterfield La. ME19 .... 89 E8
Wintergreen Cl. 7 E6 .... 1 E8
Winters Croft. DA12 .... 30 D2
Winton Cl. BR8 .... 39 E5
Winton Rd. BR6 .... 51 B6
Wirral Wood Cl. BR7 .... 23 A2
Wirrals The. ME5 .... 62 A4
Wise's La. TN15 .... 56 E2
Wiseacre. TN3 .... 166 A3
Wishart Rd. SE3 .... 5 D5
Wisley Rd. BR5 .... 24 B1
Wistaria Cl. BR6 .... 51 B8
Wisteria Gdns. BR8 .... 39 D7
Witches La. TN13 .... 83 D4
Witham Way. ME2 .... 46 F7
Withens Cl. BR5 .... 38 C5

Witherston Way. SE9 .... 23 A5
Withyham Rd. TN3 .... 161 A6
Wittersham CE (VA) Prim Sch.
  TN30 .... 189 D2
Wittersham Cl. ME5 .... 62 B5
Wittersham House. 2 BR5 ...... 38 D1
Wittersham Rd.
  Potman's Heath TN17 & TN30 . 188 D4
Wittersham Rd.
  Wittersham TN30 .... 189 C5
Wittersham Road Sta. TN17 .. 188 D6
Wixom House. SE9 .... 5 C3
Woburn Ct. 1 DA6 .... 7 F2
Wodehouse Rd. ME20 .... 74 F4
Woldham Pl. BR2 .... 36 C5
Woldham Rd. BR2 .... 36 C5
Wolds Dr. BR6 .... 51 A6
Wolfe Cl. BR2 .... 36 A3
Wolfe Cres. SE7 .... 1 D1
Wolfe Rd. ME16 .... 91 B2
Wollaston Cl. ME8 .... 63 D3
Wolseley Rd. ME4 .... 149 C2
Wolsey Ct. SE9 .... 5 F1
Wolsey Mews. BR6 .... 51 F5
Wolsley Cl. DA1 .... 8 E2
Wolvercote Rd. SE2 .... 3 D4
Wombwell Gdns. DA11 .... 29 E6
Wood Cl. Ditton ME20 .... 90 E8
Wood Cl. Joyden's Wood DA5 .. 25 E5
Wood Dr. Chislehurst BR7 ...... 22 E2
Wood Dr. Sevenoaks TN13 .... 83 F1
Wood La. East End TN17 ...... 171 C3
Wood La. Lane End DA2 .... 27 F4
Wood Lodge Gdns. BR1 .... 22 C1
Wood Lodge Grange. TN13 .... 84 C5
Wood Point. 10 E16 .... 1 A8
Wood Ride. BR5 .... 37 E5
Wood St. Cuxton ME2 .... 46 B2
Wood St. Gillingham ME7 ...... 48 A6
Wood St. 6 Grays RM17 ...... 12 C8
Wood St. Newham E16 .... 1 B6
Wood St.
  Royal Tunbridge Wells TN1 .. 149 B4
Wood St. Swanley Village BR8 .. 40 D8
Wood View Cl. TN15 .... 55 E3
Wood Way. BR6 .... 51 A8
Woodberry Gr. DA5 .... 25 D5
Woodbridge Dr. ME15 .... 91 F1
Woodbrook Rd. SE2 .... 7 B8
Woodbury Cl. TN4 .... 149 A5
Woodbury La. TN30 .... 183 A7
Woodbury Park Gdns. TN4 .... 149 B5
Woodbury Park Rd. TN4 ...... 149 B5
Woodbury Rd. Chatham ME5 .. 61 F1
Woodbury Rd. Hawkhurst TN18 179 A2
Woodchurch Cl. Chatham ME5 . 62 B5
Woodchurch Cl. Sidcup DA14 .. 23 D5
Woodchurch Cres. ME8 .... 49 C2
Woodchurch Cl. 1 BR5 .... 38 C4
Woodchurch Dr. BR1 .... 22 D1
Woodchurch House. ME8 ...... 49 C2
Woodchurch Rd. TN30 .... 183 D8
Woodclyffe Dr. BR7 .... 37 A7
Woodcock La.
  Grafty Green ME17 .... 126 E5
Woodcock La. Iden Green TN17 180 E3
Woodcocks. E16 .... 1 D8
Woodcote Dr. BR6 .... 37 D2
Woodcote Wlk. DA15 .... 24 A7
Woodcroft. SE9 .... 22 F5
Woodcut. ME14 .... 92 A8
Woodfall Dr. DA1 .... 8 F3
Woodfalls Ind Est. ME18 .... 120 D6
Woodfield Ave.
  Hildenborough TN11 .... 116 E5
Woodfield Rd. TN9 .... 133 B8
Woodfield Way. ME3 .... 33 E4
Woodfields. TN13 .... 83 D4
Woodford House. 13 SE18 ...... 6 B8
Woodford Rd. ME16 .... 91 B2
Woodgate La. ME7 .... 65 C2
Woodgate Rd. ME19 .... 73 D4
Woodgate Way. TN9 .... 133 E7
Woodgers Gr. BR8 .... 39 F7
Woodget Cl. E6 .... 1 E7
Woodhatch Cl. E6 .... 1 E8
Woodhayes. BR7 .... 23 B2
Woodhead Dr. BR6 .... 51 F7
Woodhill. SE18 & SE7 .... 1 E2
Woodhill Pk. TN2 .... 150 C6
Woodhill Prim Sch. SE18 ...... 1 E2
Woodhurst. ME5 .... 61 D4
Woodhurst Ave. BR5 .... 37 C3
Woodhurst Cl. ME2 .... 46 B2
Woodhurst Rd. SE2 .... 3 A2
Woodington Cl. SE9 .... 6 A1
Woodknoll Dr. BR7 .... 36 F8
Woodland Ave. DA3 .... 42 F5
Woodland Cl. New Barn DA3 .. 43 C6
Woodland Cl. New Town ME19 . 89 A8
Woodland Cl.
  Royal Tunbridge Wells TN4 .. 149 C2
Woodland Dr. TN8 .... 112 D3
Woodland Rd. TN4 .... 149 C2
Woodland Rise. TN15 .... 84 E4
Woodland Terr. SE7 .... 1 E2
Woodland View. TN30 .... 189 E4
Woodland Way.
  Bidborough TN4 .... 132 D3
Woodland Way. Erith SE2 ...... 3 D2
Woodland Way. Maidstone ME14 92 B7
Woodland Way. Orpington BR5 . 37 C4
Woodlands.
  Swanscombe DA9 .... 11 A3
Woodlands. Chatham ME5 ...... 62 A2
Woodlands. Coxheath ME17 .... 106 B3

Woodlands. Paddock Wood TN12 135 F7
Woodlands. Romford TN2 ...... 150 F7
Woodlands.
  Royal Tunbridge Wells TN4 .. 133 A2
Woodlands. Swanley BR8 ...... 39 E6
Woodlands. Wilsley Green TN17 169 D6
Woodlands Ave. Sidcup DA15 .. 23 E7
Woodlands Ave. Snodland ME6 . 74 F8
Woodlands Cl. Bromley BR1 .... 36 F7
Woodlands Cl. Maidstone ME14 . 92 B7
Woodlands Cl. Swanley BR8 .... 39 F7
Woodlands Cl. Teston ME18 .. 105 B8
Woodlands Cty Jun Sch. TN10 117 C6
Woodlands Cty Prim Sch. ME7 48 F4
Woodlands High Sch. ME7 .... 48 F4
Woodlands La. DA12 .... 31 E3
Woodlands Manor Golf Course.
  TN15 .... 70 C6
Woodlands Pk. DA5 .... 25 D4
Woodlands Rd. Bexley DA7 .... 7 E4
Woodlands Rd. Bromley BR1 .. 36 F7
Woodlands Rd. Ditton ME20 .. 90 D8
Woodlands Rd. Gillingham ME7 . 48 F4
Woodlands Rd. Orpington BR6 . 52 A4
Woodlands Rd. Tonbridge TN9 . 133 A7
Woodlands Rise. BR8 .... 39 F7
Woodlands Terr. BR8 .... 39 B3
Woodlands The. BR6 .... 52 B4
Woodlands View. TN14 .... 53 A1
Woodlea. ME20 .... 74 F2
Woodleas. ME16 .... 90 F2
Woodley Rd. BR6 .... 52 C8
Woodman Par. 4 E16 .... 2 A5
Woodman St. E16 .... 2 A5
Woodmere. SE9 .... 22 F7
Woodmount. BR8 .... 39 D2
Woodpecker Cl. 2 TN8 .... 112 D3
Woodpecker Glade. ME8 .... 63 D6
Woodpecker Rd. Larkfield ME20 74 F1
Woodpecker Rd. Woolwich SE28 . 3 C6
Woodrow. SE18 .... 1 F2
Woods Green Cotts. TN5 ...... 174 F7
Woodsgate Way. TN2 .... 150 B6
Woodside. Gillingham ME8 .... 63 C6
Woodside. Orpington BR6 ...... 52 B5
Woodside. Vigo Village DA13 .. 72 F8
Woodside Ave. BR7 .... 23 C3
Woodside Cl. Crayford DA1 & DA7 8 D3
Woodside Cl. Pembury TN2 .. 150 E6
Woodside Cres. DA15 .... 23 E5
Woodside Dr. DA2 .... 25 E4
Woodside Gn. ME3 .... 33 B3
Woodside La. DA5 .... 7 D1
Woodside Rd. Bromley BR1 .... 36 E4
Woodside Rd. Crayford DA7 .. 8 D3
Woodside Rd. Maidstone ME15 107 C7
Woodside Rd. Pembury TN2 .. 150 E6
Woodside Rd. Rusthall TN4 .. 148 D4
Woodside Rd. Sevenoaks TN13 . 84 B4
Woodside Rd. Sidcup DA15 .... 23 E5
Woodside Rd. Sundridge TN14 . 82 E3
Woodside Rd. Tonbridge TN9 .. 133 B7
Woodside Sch. DA7 .... 8 D3
Woodstock Cl. DA5 .... 24 F7
Woodstock Cl. SE12 .... 5 A1
Woodstock Rd. ME2 .... 47 A4
Woodvale Ct. BR1 .... 36 B7
Woodview Cl. BR6 .... 51 C8
Woodview Cres. TN11 .... 116 F5
Woodview Cty Prim Sch. DA3 . 43 A6
Woodview Rd. BR8 .... 39 D7
Woodview Rise. ME2 .... 32 F1
Woodville. SE3 .... 5 B6
Woodville Cl. SE12 .... 5 A2
Woodville Gr. 2 DA16 .... 7 A4
Woodville Pl. DA11 .... 30 B8
Woodville Rd. ME15 .... 92 A2
Woodville St. 16 SE7 .... 1 E2
Woodward Terr. DA9 .... 10 E1
Woodyates Rd. Lewisham SE12 . 5 A1
Woodyates Rd. Lewisham SE12 . 22 B8
Woolacombe Rd. SE3 .... 5 C5
Woolaston Cl. ME15 .... 91 F1
Wooldeys Rd. ME8 .... 49 F2
Woolf Cl. SE28 .... 3 B5
Woolf Wlk. RM18 .... 13 C5
Woollett Cl. DA1 .... 9 A3
Woollett St. ME14 .... 92 A5
Woolley Cl. TN4 .... 132 F1
Woolley Rd. Maidstone ME15 .. 107 F7
Woolley Rd.
  Royal Tunbridge Wells TN4 .. 132 F1
Woolpack Cnr. TN27 .... 172 A7
Woolwich Arsenal Sta. SE18 .. 2 B2
Woolwich Church St. SE18 & SE7 1 E3
Woolwich Cl. ME5 .... 62 A7
Woolwich Coll. SE18 .... 2 D2
Woolwich Coll (Charlton). SE7 . 1 D2
Woolwich Comm. Woolwich SE18 2 B2
Woolwich Comm. Woolwich SE18 6 A8
Woolwich Dockyard Ind Est.
  SE18 .... 1 E3
Woolwich Dockyard Sta. SE18 . 1 F2
Woolwich High St. SE18 .... 2 A3
Woolwich Manor Way.
  Newham,Beckton E6 .... 2 A7
Woolwich Manor Way.
  Newham,North Woolwich E16 . 2 B5
Woolwich Manorway. E16 ...... 2 B4
Woolwich Poly Sch.
  Woolwich SE18 .... 2 B1
Woolwich Poly Sch .
  Woolwich SE18 .... 2 B1
Woolwich Rd. Bexley DA7 ...... 8 A4
Woolwich Rd. Erith SE2 .... 3 E1
Woolwich Rd.
  Greenwich SE10 & SE7 ...... 1 C2
Wootton Gn. ME8 .... 49 D3

Wootton House. SE9 .... 6 D1
Wopsle Cl. ME1 .... 61 D7
Worcester Ave. ME18 & ME19 .... 89 A2
Worcester Cl. Istead Rise DA13 .. 29 F1
Worcester Cl. Rochester ME2 ..... 46 E8
Worcester Cl. Swanscombe DA9 . 11 B3
Worcester Rd. ME15 .... 107 D7
Wordsworth Cl. Chatham ME5 .... 62 C7
Wordsworth Cl. Tilbury RM18 .... 13 C5
Wordsworth House. 16 SE18 .... 6 A8
Wordsworth Rd. Bexley DA16 .... 6 E6
Wordsworth Rd.
   Maidstone ME14 .... 92 B7
Wordsworth Way.
   Dartford DA1 .... 10 A3
Wordsworth Way.
   Lunsford ME20 .... 75 A4
Workhouse La. ME15 .... 106 C4
Workhouse Rd.
   Chartway Street ME17 .... 125 A4
Workhouse Rd. Ryarsh ME19 ..... 73 F4
Worlds End La. BR6 .... 52 B3
Wormdale Hill. ME9 .... 65 B3
Wormdale Rd. ME9 .... 65 B4
Worsenden. TN27 .... 157 E1
Worships Hill. TN13 .... 83 E4
Worth Cl. BR6 .... 51 E6
Wotton Cl. ME15 .... 107 E5
Wotton Gn. BR5 .... 38 C5
Wouldham CE Prim Sch. ME1 . 60 C5
Wouldham Rd. Grays RM16 .... 11 E8
Wouldham Rd.
   Rochester ME1 .... 46 E1
Wouldham Terr. 8 BR5 .... 38 B6
Wrangleden Cl. ME15 .... 107 E5
Wrangleden Rd. ME15 .... 107 E5
Wrangling La. DA13 .... 58 F3
Wratham Road Cty Prim Sch.
   DA11 .... 30 B8
Wrekin Rd. SE18 .... 6 C7

Wren Cl. Larkfield ME20 .... 74 F1
Wren Cl. St Paul's Cray BR5 .... 38 D6
Wren Ind Est. ME15 .... 107 F4
Wren Path. SE28 .... 2 D4
Wren Rd. DA14 .... 24 C5
Wren Way. ME5 .... 62 B6
Wren Wlk. RM18 .... 13 B7
Wrens Croft. DA11 .... 29 E4
Wrens Rd. ME9 .... 80 F6
Wricklemarsh Rd.
   Greenwich SE3 .... 5 B6
Wricklemarsh Rd.
   Greenwich SE3 .... 5 D6
Wright Cl. Gillingham ME8 .... 49 C2
Wright Cl. Swanscombe DA10 ...... 11 D1
Wrights Cl. TN30 .... 183 A8
Wrot & Hill Ct. DA4 .... 41 B8
Wrotham Hill Rd. TN15 .... 72 A6
Wrotham Rd. Bexley DA16 .... 7 C6
Wrotham Rd.
   Borough Green TN15 .... 87 A8
Wrotham Rd.
   Culverstone Green DA13 .... 57 E2
Wrotham Rd.
   Gravesend DA11 & DA13 .... 30 A4
Wrotham Rd.
   Meopham Station DA13 .... 44 A3
Wrotham Sch. TN15 .... 72 A1
Wrotham Water La. ME19 .... 72 E5
Wrotham Water Rd. TN15 .... 72 E4
Wrottesley Rd. SE18 .... 6 C8
Wroxham Rd. SE28 .... 3 D6
Wulfred Way. TN15 .... 70 B1
Wyatt Cl. TN15 .... 86 F7
Wyatt House. 2 ME2 .... 47 A7
Wyatt Pl. ME2 .... 47 A7
Wyatt Rd. DA1 .... 8 F4
Wyatt St. ME14 .... 92 A4
Wyborne Prim Sch. SE9 .... 23 B7
Wybourne Rise. TN2 .... 163 B8

Wybournes La. ME23 .... 17 C3
Wycliffe Cl. DA16 .... 6 F6
Wycliffe House. 5 DA11 .... 29 F7
Wycliffe Row. DA11 .... 29 F7
Wycombe Ct. SE3 .... 5 A7
Wydeville Manor Rd. SE12 .... 22 B4
Wye Cl. BR6 .... 37 F2
Wye Rd. Borough Green TN15 .... 87 A8
Wye Rd. Gravesend DA12 .... 30 D6
Wye Rd. Tonbridge TN10 .... 117 C5
Wyfold House. 10 SE2 .... 3 D4
Wyke Manor Rd. ME14 .... 92 A4
Wykeham Cl. DA12 .... 30 E2
Wykeham Cotts. ME17 .... 106 F2
Wykeham Gr. ME17 .... 109 A7
Wykeham St. ME2 .... 47 B8
Wyles Rd. ME4 .... 47 E2
Wyles St. ME7 .... 48 C7
Wylie House. ME3 .... 33 B6
Wylie Rd. ME3 .... 34 D6
Wyncham Ave. DA15 .... 23 E7
Wyncroft Cl. BR1 .... 36 F6
Wyndam Rd. ME4 .... 47 E2
Wyndcliff Rd. SE3 & SE7 .... 5 B8
Wyndham Ave. TN11 .... 115 F1
Wyndham Cl. Leigh TN11 .... 115 F1
Wyndham Cl. Orpington BR6 ...... 37 C1
Wynford Gr. BR5 .... 38 B6
Wynford Pl. DA17 .... 8 A8
Wynford Way. SE9 .... 22 F5
Wynn's Ave. DA15 .... 7 A2
Wytchlings The. ME17 .... 109 D2
Wythens Wlk. SE9 .... 6 B1
Wytherling Cl. ME14 .... 92 F5
Wythes Cl. BR1 .... 36 F7
Wythes Rd. E16 .... 1 E5
Wythfield Rd. SE9 .... 5 F1
Wyvern Cl. Dartford DA1 .... 26 C8
Wyvern Cl. Orpington BR6 .... 52 B7
Wyvern Cl. Snodland ME6 .... 75 A7

Wyvern House. 3 RM17 .... 12 B8
Wyvill Cl. ME8 .... 63 E5

Yalding Cl. Orpington BR5 .... 38 D5
Yalding Cl. Rochester ME2 .... 33 B1
Yalding Hill. ME18 .... 105 A3
Yalding Prim Sch. ME18 .... 105 A1
Yalding Sta. ME18 .... 104 D1
Yantlet Dr. ME2 .... 46 C7
Yardley Cl. TN9 .... 117 D3
Yardley Park Rd. TN9 .... 117 D3
Yarnton Way. DA17 & DA18 .... 3 E4
Yarrow Cres. E6 .... 1 E8
Yarrow Ct. ME14 .... 92 F5
Yarrow Rd. ME5 .... 61 F4
Yateley St. SE18 & SE7 .... 1 D3
Yaugher La. ME9 .... 64 C3
Yelsted La. Chatham ME14 .... 77 D7
Yelsted La. Yelsted ME9 .... 64 A1
Yelsted Rd. ME9 .... 79 A7
Yeoman Ct. ME14 .... 93 B3
Yeoman Dr. ME7 .... 48 F1
Yeoman Gdns. TN12 .... 135 F6
Yeoman La. ME14 .... 93 B4
Yeoman Way. ME15 .... 93 A2
Yeoman's Meadows. TN13 .... 84 A1
Yeovil Cl. BR6 .... 51 E8
Yester Dr. BR7 .... 22 E1
Yester Pk. BR7 .... 22 F2
Yester Rd. BR7 .... 22 F1
Yew Rd. ME3 .... 34 E3
Yew Tree Cl. Aylesford ME20 ...... 75 E1
Yew Tree Cl. Bexley DA16 .... 7 A6
Yew Tree Cl. Chatham ME5 .... 62 D1
Yew Tree Cl. New Barn DA3 .... 43 D7
Yew Tree Cl. Sevenoaks TN13 ..... 83 D4
Yew Tree Cotts.
   Groombridge TN3 .... 161 F8
Yew Tree Cotts. Halstead TN14 . 67 F7
Yew Tree Cotts. Sandling ME14 . 76 F1

Yew Tree Green Rd. TN12 .... 137 A1
Yew Tree Pl. ME7 .... 63 B1
Yew Tree Rd. TN4 .... 149 B8
Yews The. DA12 .... 30 D7
Yewtree Ind Est. ME20 .... 75 D2
Yolande Gdns. SE9 .... 5 E2
Yopps Gn. TN15 .... 86 E1
York Ave. Chatham ME5 .... 61 F3
York Ave. Gillingham ME7 .... 48 C4
York Ave. Sidcup DA15 .... 23 F6
York Cl. E6 .... 1 F7
York Hill. ME4 .... 48 C2
York Par. TN10 .... 117 C6
York Pl. RM17 .... 12 A8
York Rd. Dartford DA1 .... 26 F8
York Rd. Gravesend DA12 .... 30 C5
York Rd. Maidstone ME15 .... 92 C2
York Rd. Northfleet DA11 .... 29 D8
York Rd. Rochester ME1 .... 47 C3
York Rd.
   Royal Tunbridge Wells TN1 ... 149 A4
York Rd. Tonbridge TN10 .... 117 D5
York Rise. BR6 .... 51 E8
York Road Cty Jun Sch. DA1 .... 26 F8
York Terr. DA8 .... 8 C6
Yorkland Ave. DA16 .... 6 F3
Youens Pl. ME3 .... 32 B3
Young Rd. E16 .... 1 C7

Zambra Way. TN15 .... 84 F7
Zangwill Rd. SE18 & SE3 .... 5 D6
Zealand House. 4 SE7 .... 1 E2
Zelah Rd. BR5 .... 38 C2
Zetland Ave. ME7 .... 48 E2
Zion Pl. DA11 .... 30 B8
Zion St. TN15 .... 84 F6

STREET ATLASES ORDER FORM

The Street Atlases are available from all good bookshops or by mail order direct from the publisher. Orders can be made in the following ways. **By phone** Ring our special Credit Card Hotline on **01933 443863** during office hours (9am to 5pm) or leave a message on the answering machine, quoting your full credit card number plus expiry date and your full name and address. **By post or fax** Fill out the order form below (you may photocopy it) and post it to: **Philip's Direct, 27 Sanders Road, Wellingborough, Northants NN8 4NL** or fax it to: **01933 443849**. Before placing an order by post, by fax or on the answering machine, please telephone to check availability and prices.

COLOUR LOCAL ATLASES

	PAPERBACK	
	Quantity @ £3.50 each	£ Total
CANNOCK, LICHFIELD, RUGELEY	☐ 0 540 07625 2	➤ ☐
DERBY AND BELPER	☐ 0 540 07608 2	➤ ☐
NORTHWICH, WINSFORD, MIDDLEWICH	☐ 0 540 07589 2	➤ ☐
PEAK DISTRICT TOWNS	☐ 0 540 07609 0	➤ ☐
STAFFORD, STONE, UTTOXETER	☐ 0 540 07626 0	➤ ☐
WARRINGTON, WIDNES, RUNCORN	☐ 0 540 07588 4	➤ ☐

COLOUR REGIONAL ATLASES

	HARDBACK	SPIRAL	POCKET	
	Quantity @ £10.99 each	Quantity @ £8.99 each	Quantity @ £5.99 each	£ Total
BERKSHIRE	☐ 0 540 06170 0	☐ 0 540 06172 7	☐ 0 540 06173 5	➤ ☐
	Quantity @ £10.99 each	Quantity @ £8.99 each	Quantity @ £4.99 each	£ Total
MERSEYSIDE	☐ 0 540 06480 7	☐ 0 540 06481 5	☐ 0 540 06482 3	➤ ☐
	Quantity @ £12.99 each	Quantity @ £9.99 each	Quantity @ £4.99 each	£ Total
DURHAM	☐ 0 540 06365 7	☐ 0 540 06366 5	☐ 0 540 06367 3	➤ ☐
HERTFORDSHIRE	☐ 0 540 06174 3	☐ 0 540 06175 1	☐ 0 540 06176 X	➤ ☐
EAST KENT	☐ 0 540 07483 7	☐ 0 540 07276 1	☐ 0 540 07287 7	➤ ☐
WEST KENT	☐ 0 540 07366 0	☐ 0 540 07367 9	☐ 0 540 07369 5	➤ ☐
EAST SUSSEX	☐ 0 540 07306 7	☐ 0 540 07307 5	☐ 0 540 07312 1	➤ ☐
WEST SUSSEX	☐ 0 540 07319 9	☐ 0 540 07323 7	☐ 0 540 07327 X	➤ ☐
SOUTH YORKSHIRE	☐ 0 540 06330 4	☐ 0 540 06331 2	☐ 0 540 06332 0	➤ ☐
SURREY	☐ 0 540 06435 1	☐ 0 540 06436 X	☐ 0 540 06438 6	➤ ☐
	Quantity @ £12.99 each	Quantity @ £9.99 each	Quantity @ £5.50 each	£ Total
GREATER MANCHESTER	☐ 0 540 06485 8	☐ 0 540 06486 6	☐ 0 540 06487 4	➤ ☐
TYNE AND WEAR	☐ 0 540 06370 3	☐ 0 540 06371 1	☐ 0 540 06372 X	➤ ☐
	Quantity @ £12.99 each	Quantity @ £9.99 each	Quantity @ £5.99 each	£ Total
BIRMINGHAM & WEST MIDLANDS	☐ 0 540 07603 1	☐ 0 540 07604 X	☐ 0 540 07605 8	➤ ☐
BUCKINGHAMSHIRE	☐ 0 540 07466 7	☐ 0 540 07467 5	☐ 0 540 07468 3	➤ ☐

COLOUR REGIONAL ATLASES

	HARDBACK	SPIRAL	POCKET	£ Total
	Quantity @ £12.99 each	Quantity @ £9.99 each	Quantity @ £5.99 each	
CHESHIRE	0 540 07507 8	0 540 07508 6	0 540 07509 4	➤
DERBYSHIRE	0 540 07531 0	0 540 07532 9	0 540 07533 7	➤
SOUTH HAMPSHIRE	0 540 07476 4	0 540 07477 2	0 540 07478 0	➤
NORTH HAMPSHIRE	0 540 07471 3	0 540 07472 1	0 540 07473 X	➤
OXFORDSHIRE	0 540 07512 4	0 540 07513 2	0 540 07514 0	➤
WARWICKSHIRE	0 540 07560 4	0 540 07561 2	0 540 07562 0	➤
WEST YORKSHIRE	0 540 06329 0	0 540 06327 4	0 540 06328 2	➤
	Quantity @ £14.99 each	Quantity @ £9.99 each	Quantity @ £5.99 each	£ Total
LANCASHIRE	0 540 06440 8	0 540 06441 6	0 540 06443 2	➤
NOTTINGHAMSHIRE	0 540 07541 8	0 540 075426 6	0 540 07543 4	➤
STAFFORDSHIRE	0 540 07549 3	0 540 07550 7	0 540 07551 5	➤

BLACK AND WHITE REGIONAL ATLASES

	HARDBACK	SOFTBACK	POCKET	£ Total
	Quantity @ £11.99 each	Quantity @ £8.99 each	Quantity @ £3.99 each	
BRISTOL AND AVON	0 540 06140 9	0 540 06141 7	0 540 06142 5	➤
	Quantity @ £12.99 each	Quantity @ £9.99 each	Quantity @ £4.99 each	£ Total
CARDIFF, SWANSEA & GLAMORGAN	0 540 06186 7	0 540 06187 5	0 540 06207 3	➤
EDINBURGH & East Central Scotland	—	0 540 06181 6	0 540 06182 4	➤
EAST ESSEX	0 540 05848 3	0 540 05866 1	0 540 05850 5	➤
WEST ESSEX	0 540 05849 1	0 540 05867 X	0 540 05851 3	➤
	Quantity @ £12.99 each	Quantity @ £9.99 each	Quantity @ £5.99 each	£ Total
GLASGOW & West Central Scotland	0 540 06183 2	0 540 06184 0	0 540 06185 9	➤

Post to: Philip's Direct,
27 Sanders Road, Wellingborough,
Northants NN8 4NL

◆ Free postage and packing

◆ All available titles will normally be dispatched within 5 working days of receipt of order but please allow up to 28 days for delivery

☐ Please tick this box if you do not wish your name to be used by other carefully selected organisations that may wish to send you information about other products and services

Registered Office: Michelin House, 81 Fulham Road, London SW3 6RB

Registered in England number: 3597451

I enclose a cheque / postal order, for a **total** of ☐
made payable to *Octopus Publishing Group Ltd*, or please debit my

☐ Access ☐ American Express ☐ Visa ☐ Diners

account by ☐

Account no
☐☐☐☐ ☐☐☐☐ ☐☐☐☐ ☐☐☐☐

Expiry date ☐☐ ☐☐

Signature..

Name...

Address...

....

....POSTCODE

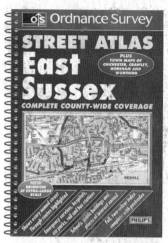

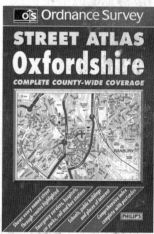

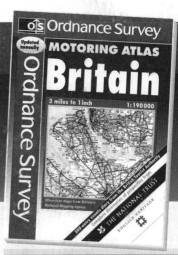

Ordnance Survey

MOTORING ATLAS
Britain

Updated annually

The best-selling *OS Motoring Atlas Britain* uses unrivalled and up-to-date mapping from the Ordnance Survey digital database. The exceptionally clear mapping is at a large scale of 3 miles to 1 inch (Orkney/Shetland Islands at 5 miles to 1 inch).

A special feature of the atlas is its wealth of tourist and leisure information. It contains comprehensive directories, including descriptions and location details, of the properties of the National Trust in England and Wales, the National Trust for Scotland, English Heritage and Historic Scotland. There is also a useful diary of British Tourist Authority Events listing more than 300 days out around Britain during the year.

Available from all good bookshops or direct from the publisher:
Tel: 01933 443863

The atlas includes:

- 112 pages of fully updated mapping
- 45 city and town plans
- 8 extra-detailed city approach maps
- route-planning maps
- restricted motorway junctions
- local radio information
- distances chart
- county boundaries map
- multi-language legend